Argufying

Argufying

Essays on Literature and Culture

William Empson

Edited with an Introduction by
JOHN HAFFENDEN

University of Iowa Press

Iowa City

University of Iowa Press, Iowa City
Copyright © 1987 by the Estate of Sir William Empson
Introduction and notes © 1987 by John Haffenden
All rights reserved
Printed in Great Britain
First edition, 1987

International Standard Book Numbers 0–87745–198–2 cloth,
0–87745–199–0 paper
Library of Congress Catalog Card Number 87–82164

Contents

Introduction

'The practice of making a book out of old magazine articles might seem scraping the barrel rather,' William Empson observed in one of his most lively and responsive reviews, 'Still the Strange Necessity' (number 11 below). But, he went on, 'it seems sensible enough.' He had been proposing to compile various collections of his own essays at least since 1958, when he told his publisher Ian Parsons at Chatto & Windus that his next book would include 'essays on Donne Milton Fielding Joyce and a few extras, aiming at the general point that the neo-Christian movement has greatly upset the natural and traditional way of reading such authors; so that there has to be a certain air of challenge about the book'. In 1973 he reported to Parsons that 'there are various essays that need collecting, and some could well be added to the Clark Lectures volume' (never published as such); and then again, in October 1975, 'if I keep it up [I] will finish "Elizabethan Plays" within a year at least.... I don't want to bring out the rag-bag before the consecutive one or they would say I was gaga.'

In the event, after publishing *Milton's God* in 1961, he concentrated on three specific volumes – *Using Biography, Essays on Shakespeare* and a book of Renaissance essays (as well as an extended study of Marlowe's *Doctor Faustus*). Yet at his death in April 1984 he had finished only the first, which was published by Chatto & Windus later that year; the other two volumes have since been assembled from his working papers and are being published by Cambridge University Press. The present volume therefore constitutes what Empson might have considered his rag-bag, though it should be said that it has been put together without any knowledge of the contents he himself would have favoured. A number of the shorter essays and reviews he might have regarded as parerga not worth resurrecting, but substantial items – including 'The Verbal Analysis', 'Rhythm and Imagery in English Poetry', 'The Hammer's Ring', 'The Cult of Unnaturalism' and 'Literary Criticism and the Christian Revival' – require a place in any permanent collection of his critical writings. Likewise, the full spectrum of his career cannot be appreciated without perhaps the majority of his occasional pieces: this collection therefore includes general essays on language and meaning, rhythm and rhyme, and articles on poetry, fiction and epic, including interpretations of Rochester, Wordsworth, Yeats, Auden, Joyce, Kafka, Woolf and Orwell. A reluctant metacritic, Empson nonetheless tackled the follies of his fellows with tremendous vigour, and gave them a thorough drubbing on various issues of principle such as 'the cluster of Imagist beliefs' and the supposed Fallacy of Intentionalism. Previously unpublished pieces include essays and talks on Buddhism, ethics, the Christian God and Gray's Cat. The majority of the essays in this collection date from the post-war years; and like *Using Biography* they cohere in terms of Empson's own prescription: 'I propose to say that Eng. Lit. Crit. has been getting onto a wrong tack, and try to explain what and why, and of course the more examples of that the better.'

Although he saw no book of his own through the press after 1961, the present collection alone – even if it surfaced without any evidence of the three canonical volumes – shows that he never ceased writing and was endlessly fertile and productive. To the public eye (and to some extent to his own), it may have seemed that he had dropped out of the limelight of controversy into occasional journalism; but his habits of work and his output remained as continuous as they were wide-ranging. The one problem, as he told Ian Parsons in 1958, was that 'I have always worked slowly and would still do so if I didn't have to mess about being a Professor, but I hope you don't regard me as already dead.' His extended apologia – which stands as fair warning to any literary critic, whether hack or professor – figures in a letter from the following year:

literary criticism . . . has become a much more powerful and interesting tool since about 1900, and many of the able literary young want to go in for it. They can I think certainly do it quite as well while employed as dons, though they must be warned against insisting they must be Professors, a capacity in which they are liable to get heavy extra chores. Bonamy Dobrée warned me like that when I was looking for a job after leaving Communist China . . . I do not regret the way it fell. But at least a literary critic can become a university lecturer without feeling that he is wasting his talent, and indeed is likely to improve it that way. . . . I do not know how a literary critic could be in such close contact with the existing audience reaction anywhere else; he certainly won't do it by writing journalism in obedience to the hunch of an editor. . . . You must remember that, if a young critic makes the great renunciation, saying 'It is beneath me to read all these horrid essays,' the next thing he will have to do is turn out a lot of shockingly coarse hackwork, which really is beneath him and will remain permanently in print to shame his later years. A university job does at least mean that you are free to print in a decently considered manner . . . [1]

Empson stated it as 'a general truth about the pleasant and economical habit of reprinting old articles that the author had better say each time how far his opinion had changed now' (number 11); furthermore, the critics of the critic should always be answered, as a point of honour: 'In the learned world, a man loses his standing if he refuses to answer a plain refutation' (number 26). He himself was stubborn in his opinions and pugnacious in answering back; in fact, he could be downright rude to both friend and foe – for reasons set out at the very beginning of his career, in the long and hitherto unpublished trial piece 'Obscurity and Annotation' (number 2), written at the same time as *Seven Types of Ambiguity*:

if you attack a view in any detail that proves you to have some sympathy with it; there is already a conflict in you which mirrors the conflict in which you take part; that is why you understand it sufficiently to take part in it. Only because you can foresee and enter into the opposing arguments can you answer them; only because it is interesting to you do you engage in argument about it.

For personally I am attracted by the notion of a hearty indifference to one's own and other people's feelings, when a fragment of the truth is in question...

The proposition might have been a prophecy: his readers have always insisted that he had much to answer for, not the least that his 'ingenious' interpretations showed inspired insight, along with a dubiously applicable methodology, but no real theory of literary analysis. He became highly skilled at operating the 'machinery' but produced few critical judgements. While the results showed considerable discernment in Empson himself, his critics alleged, more frequently his methods induced a form of delinquency both in their author and in his epigoni among the so-called 'New Critics'.

His career has popularly been reckoned to fall into roughly two halves, the first ending with *The Structure of Complex Words* (1951), the second appearing to foresake semantic interests in favour of chastising the aberrant morality of what Empson himself styled the 'Neo-Christian' school of critics. Even Empson felt that after writing three books covering the subject of literary ambiguity – *Seven Types of Ambiguity* (1930), *Some Versions of Pastoral* (1935) and *The Structure of Complex Words* – he had shifted ground from linguistics to ethics. 'There is in my later work what may look like a failure, I now see,' he wrote to Roger Sale,

in my practically giving up Ambiguity as a method of exegesis. I had better have explained myself there. Reviewers were telling me, as soon as *Ambiguity* came out, that not all poetry was ambiguous, and I could see that the method worked best where the authors had had some impulse or need for the process; but, as it had become my line, I went on slogging at it for two more books. Then I thought I had given a rounded view of the subject, and unless challenged to debate had no need to go on about it.[2]

If it is now widely agreed that his taxonomy (or hierarchy, if it is one) of the seven types of ambiguity did not actually provide a permanently workable system of classification, at the time of its first publication the book provoked most outrage with the very suggestion – and indeed the demonstration – that poetic effects could be analysed through their diction, that a poem is a compound of analysable meaning. As the *Times Literary Supplement* protested on 18 December 1930, 'a poem is a poem not least by virtue of its power to ward off these vagaries of the intellect. It is to some degree an incantation.' To put it bluntly, he had the nerve to show that poetry should add up to sense: it consisted of words with meaning, not just approximate sensations and sounds. But the first affront gave way to two pertinent objections. First, his analytical mode seemed to bypass any judgements of value, and he had anyway been too prodigal in his associative and sometimes impressionistic interpretations. Second, he too often worried the parts without reference to the whole; local effects of word and phrase did duty for the total context. In sum, he displayed all possible meanings but with scant regard to relevance. As Elder Olson later expressed the problem, Empson constantly confounded 'potential with actual meaning'; and in any case what he took to be 'the definitive property of poetry, ambiguity ... [was] not a poetic principle; it [was] the rationalisation of an opinion ... Empson's hypothesis ... neither implies the data nor is implied by them.'[3]

With all its apparently undisciplined enthusiasm, *Seven Types of Ambiguity* does indeed locate ambiguity more as critical performance than as poetic principle; despite its numerical organisation, it offers less a methodology than Empson's own methodised brilliance. While he never retracted his opinion that ambiguity was inherent in all good poetry, the question as to whether it is in fact a necessary property must remain in question.[4] His claim about ambiguity most likely falls into the category of what E. D. Hirsch Jr has termed 'broad genre theory'; it is a 'value-preference'.[5] But what Empson did manage with consummate success was to scrutinise innumerable cases where it had a significant presence and fundamental effect. 'The class of readers I addressed in *Ambiguity* were those interested in this subject, explaining how an agreed effect was obtained,' he explained in 1971.[6] Not prescribing but explicating. Yet if Empson believed that he was simply teasing out the parts of a radical though obscure machine, many reviewers charged him with drowning in his own incontinence. In their judgement, he multiplied extravagant possibilities to the point of utter redundancy. By 1937, it might have appeared, he had momentarily chosen to take refuge in *l'esprit de l'escalier*, when he remarked that 'some kinds of error are best avoided if you just jump at the thing' (number 6); but by the 1950s he had assuredly resumed his characteristic combativeness in defending his position: 'if [a] poem was good, and if I could go at it the way I wanted to,' he wrote in 'Still the Strange Necessity' (number 11), 'nothing in the poem would be irrelevant by the time the critic had finished explaining. I still think this a proper objective.'

He always deprecated the importance of proclaiming a theory, a code of critical practice. In 1936 he wrote in 'Teaching the Meaning in Poetry' (number 5), 'it is hard to feel that an adequate theory of literary criticism, if obtained, would be much more than a device for stopping inadequate theories from getting in your way' – a point he exactly reiterated in 1950, in his credal essay 'The Verbal Analysis' (number 7): 'a critic ought to trust his own nose, like the hunting dog, and if he lets any kind of theory or principle distract him from that, he is not doing his work.' A professional critic who refuses to legislate on ways and means, let alone ends, might well slip up on analytical rigour and so fall foul of irresponsible amateurishness; and several readers charged Empson accordingly. Yet on two matters he remained staunch. While other critics may choose to make value judgements, he felt in no way obliged to do so: 'to assess the value of the poem as a whole is not the primary purpose of [my] kind of criticism, or at any rate ought only to emerge from the analysis as a whole' (number 7).[7] Second, on the crucial issue of ambiguity, he regarded it as axiomatic that 'Good poetry is usually written from a background of conflict.'[8] Poetry is by definition a complex and condensed mode of utterance, a kind which requires the poet to have comprehended alternative and probably conflicting forms of expression, attitude or ideology. How else does one explain (he asked in the preface to the second edition of *Seven Types of Ambiguity*, 1947) the cause of the presence in all good poetry of 'so straddling a commotion and so broad a calm'?[9] If a poem is answerable to intelligence, it does not comprise merely emotive gestures and suggestive sounds, it speaks a grammar of inevitably plural meaning.

Just as many reviewers had felt vexed by Empson's practice of distilling the complex meanings of poetry – his way of generating what he considered 'the possible alternative reactions' to be derived from 'the full intention' of a poem[10] – so many were equally disconcerted when in *Some Versions of Pastoral* he discussed full texts in terms not only of psychology but also of social relationships. In good poetry, he later stipulated, 'there is always an appeal to a background of human experience which is all the more present when it cannot be named.'[11] Good poetry always excites puzzlement, even when the author may not quite have intended it. Empson's progression from types of ambiguity to versions of pastoral was thus far less the radical shift that contemporary readers suspected, more a natural development – for the pastoral mode of 'putting the complex into the simple' is like the heroic, he stressed, in assuming or preaching 'a proper or beautiful relation between rich and poor'.[12] In postulating such a harmony, in conveying the impression that society is integrated, the pastoral convention in fact operates just like ambiguity against 'a background of conflict'. Dilys Powell correctly observed: 'Pastoral, as [Empson] understands it, while preserving the balance of sympathy between, let us say, peasant and aristocrat, is able, by its detachment, both to criticise and ennoble.'[13] In such terms, the convention functions as a critique – a mode of scepticism, independence of judgement and even subversion – as much as it balances the conflicts within society. Desmond Hawkins pinpointed the argument when he remarked that Empson 'treats a text, not as a unanimous resolution, but as ... a harmony of conflicting impulses. And his critical purpose is to recreate the initial terms of the conflict.'[14] Where poetry is inevitably complex and ambiguous in meaning because it externalises the conflict of the individual, pastoral likewise embraces the 'commotion' of social opposition within the 'calm' of its form. Society thus requires the pastoral hero at once to embody and to purge it of its own dissenting impulses. Both insider and outsider, he is the necessary and welcome token sacrifice, and thus paradoxically the very model of a 'unifying social force'. So it is that in 'Mrs Dalloway as a Political Satire' (number 75), Empson perceives Septimus Warren Smith as a further example of the pastoral hero, 'the sacrificial hero' – the 'Christ and scapegoat' – whose tragedy 'reconciles' Mrs Dalloway to the world. The effect, he concludes, 'is to make Mrs Dalloway seem more real and deeply rooted...' Contrary to popular opinion, there is a straight line between that early 'pastoral' insight and the anti-Christian views that Empson expressed in the post-war years: the continuum can be seen, for example, in the context of his writing about Dylan Thomas in 1963: 'The idea that any man can become Christ, who is a universal, was a major sixteenth-century heresy and has been kept up among the poets' (number 59). As in his discussion of poetic ambiguity, Empson sees the poet as just such an insider-outsider whose work serves to bridge and balance mental, social and ideological conflicts.

Pastoral is an indirect form which strikes to the heart of social tensions, a literary model of how society reconciles itself to itself. If in that sense *Some Versions of Pastoral* examines the One and the Many, *The Structure of Complex Words* pursues the same microcosmic–macrocosmic enquiry on the level of individual words. Empson's theory that 'key words' incorporate 'compact doctrines' leads him essentially to a process of undeceiving. The supposedly 'emotive' use of language in literature must be brought to account in a public and cognitive way, for words invariably assert propositions or arguments even as they conceal them by appealing to common understanding. Apparently simple words such as 'wit', 'sense', 'honest' and 'all', he works to demonstrate, include within themselves various senses, attitudes and (crucially) assertions. Empson regarded his 'attempt to codify some basic facts about language' – how words accumulate strata of senses and implications, and how imaginative literature exploits those layered suggestions – as an essentially linguistic pursuit.[15] He set out to describe what he called 'the primitive mental operations'[16] by which the current suggestions of words behave as encapsulated thoughts or (sometimes dubiously) compact doctrines; to find the 'logical structure' at work in the process. Most notably, as he later wrote in 'Professor Lewis on Linguistics' (number 16), 'Readers need to be warned that a writer often means by a word something other than what their own background leads them to expect; a working understanding of the historical process of change of meaning, by giving this awareness, may be enough.' Whether or not readers can actually apply Empson's difficult analytical machinery for themselves, that process of 'unpacking' or atomising words is again essentially a development of his examination of ambiguity and pastoral: it insists that the commotion and conflict – 'the complexity of meaning in poetry' – is always available to rational analysis. 'Roughly,' he wrote in summing up his first three books, 'the moral is that a developing society decides practical questions more by the way it interprets words it thinks obvious and traditional than by its official statements of current dogma.'[17]

Empson's long training in the complexities of linguistic interpretation made him a peculiarly appropriate choice for the BBC 'propaganda machine' during the war, when he worked as Chinese Editor (alongside the Indian Editor, his friend George Orwell). But even before that, a happy chance brought together his critical interests and his professional career. During the 1930s, while working on *Pastoral* and *Complex Words*, he taught first in Japan and then in China, where he often expounded C. K. Ogden's system of Basic English (numbers 26–29): 'it was sometimes the only thing that gave me a feeling I was of any use,' he wrote about the experience of teaching English letters in Japan (number 28). Indeed, he discovered, the system was instructive for both his pupils and himself: 'For myself at least it has become a fixed process on reading something deeply true to see if it is still good sense in Basic ... turning the poetry into Basic is a help, because it makes you put the right questions' (see for example 'Basic English and Wordsworth', number 29).

Basic began not as a teaching tool, he advised his audience during a talk on 'Basic and Communication' (*c.* 1939), but as an investigation into 'the root ideas needed for any language, or any clear thought. Dr Richards's book *Basic Rules of Reason* was made as a paper for the Aristotelian Society, a society of philosophers, and he made it in Basic because that seemed to him the only hope of getting the ideas of philosophers in order, or making a connection between the opinions of different philosophers'

(Empson Papers). He points to the coincidence of his own theoretical and practical procedures later in the same piece, when he argues that Basic naturally develops intellectual clarity and critical sensibility:

Basic is not specially simple English; it keeps back the 'exceptions', the words with tricks that are of no value, but it makes necessary (if anything) more attention to 'grammar', to the general principles of word order and structure in English, than the language commonly used in talking; and to get a thing said fully in Basic may be a training in thought.... The limited word-list is not only the quickest way to give a man a working knowledge of English, of the sort that will be of most use; it is the best way to give him good taste, later on, in writing English or reading English books.

Empson took a firm, though not unequivocal, stand in favour of Basic as probably the best medium for giving foreign learners a working access to the English language, and he could be waspishly witty in defending it. When a correspondent complained to the *Japan Chronicle*, for example, that the system was unsymbolic, artificial, not an introduction to literary English and not suited to the Japanese, he retorted: 'No one denies that Basic is simple; it is as compact as a bomb; at worst it is only a part of English you have to learn anyway; and it is a valuable, as well as a convenient, thing to learn first.' Personally he feared 'the despair of waste and the squalor of misunderstanding', so that one should welcome a system that dispelled irrationalism and incomprehension. 'That it is not suited to the Japanese I can believe; it is not suited to our mortal nature; it is a logical and analytical system which may prove too sharp a mental discipline, by itself, for people to use. But surely it would be a more cheerful first step in English than learning 20,000 words bang off.'[18]

Isolated in China in the late 1930s, he felt encouraged to know that the faith he placed in Basic was no mere fancy. He remembered with gratitude that even T. S. Eliot had once highlighted, at least, the virtues of the system, when he replied to Ezra Pound's review of his *After Strange Gods*: 'If Mr Pound would rewrite paragraph 9 in Basic English, avoiding phrases like "when religion was real", and "vital phenomena", it might possibly turn out to be a statement which I could accept.'[19] Empson learned too, however, that a blind allegiance to the limited word-list of Basic could well invite some absurd periphrases or artificial locutions: in 1939, for example, he reported to I. A. Richards that his Chinese colleague George Yeh 'is trying to do a textbook using and acknowledging Basic methods. But he says he must have (for instance) "big" and "wife", not the great cat and the woman I am married to. I have tried to be loyal about Basic for a number of years now, but on those details I think he is simply right. He is certainly not plotting against Basic, anyway.'[20] Evidently Empson judged that he had to include the last sentence in order to reassure his mentor that there was no serious evidence of disloyalty among the teachers of Basic, for Richards spent years of his life in dedicating himself to the cause. But C. K. Ogden, the originator of the system, undid his own devices when he came to promote it in a manner that too readily suggested imperialistic designs; as Empson ruefully remembered in a late tribute to Richards, 'it was a fatal mistake for Ogden to keep on boosting the scheme as an international language' (number 26).

Throughout the 1930s Empson knew that his work with Basic English intimately informed and linked his critical writings from *Ambiguity* to *Complex Words*. In a draft talk on the use of Basic in teaching criticism (dating from 1939, and probably written as part of a series he broadcast on Radio WRUL in Boston when he needed to make money for the onward journey home from China), he set out his joint terms of reference, while offering a partial answer to those reviewers who had accused him of abnegating the critic's putative responsibility to make judgements of value:

I got interested as an undergraduate in the verbal analysis of literary effects. This is only a part of literary criticism, because the interest is the quasi-scientific one of showing how a literary effect is produced. It does not in itself give a judgement of value. It assumes an agreement, among those who seem most likely to know, as to what effect a given bit of writing produces, and goes on to argue that this can only have been produced by a curious but demonstrable process of interlocking and interacting structures of meaning. You may later get judgements of value from this line of approach, but it does not start with them. The fundamental idea in this sort of criticism is that the human mind (as a fact of psychology) does not naturally assume *one* structure of grammar in a sentence, or *one* sense to each word, or even one structure of implication within the single word, from the relations between that word's possible senses. In the casual use of language which goes straight ahead, and also in the literary reading which tastes the possibilities, the human mind has *more* grasp of the structure of the possible meanings than it has when trying to weigh the sense of the words carefully.... But the full logical analysis of what seems a casual literary experience is not merely not single; it is often so complicated that it seems tedious and very improbable. Now if you accept this rather paradoxical theory, and I convinced myself that it worked, then the whole question of criticism looks rather different. All criticism since Aristotle has assumed that some understanding, of how a bit of literature works on you, makes you appreciate it better. But on this view there is a good deal to understand. So, before Basic English had been published, I was already trying in a blind way to work out a handy machine for analysis, and ready to believe in this one. [Empson Papers]

The key to his cross-breeding of Basic English and complex words follows in this passage: 'one purpose in choosing the list was to be free from words with confused double meanings and added emotional claims. Or rather, because these two may come to the same thing, from words with the sort of associated meanings which imply a special attitude or doctrine.'

II

So often when Empson speaks of ambiguity or complexity of meaning in poetry, he invokes considerations of 'associated meanings' or the claims of doctrine: that intimate connection distinguishes his aims from those of the strict grammarian or linguistician. Geoffrey Strickland, in 'The Criticism of William Empson', asserted that his 'theory of ambiguity and complexity is largely technical. It is concerned with analysis rather than with judgement.'[21] But to suggest that evaluation is the only alternative to technical analysis is to overlook the rich territory in between. Empson himself sniffed at the very idea of laying down 'rules for critics';[22] he travelled at will all the way from technique to interpretation. Still, at every stage, he was baited for his supposed trespasses; and he felt honour-bound to answer every challenge, acknowledging that his opponents often made strong cases. 'Controversy demands imagination,' he foresaw as early as 1931; 'you must try to understand your opponent's position, so that you can select the things worth talking about; so that you can find the root of his errors, or of your disagreement with him' (number 22).

In addition to the accusation that he offered no judgements of value in his early work – which he answered with the not altogether satisfactory assurance that he would hardly have bothered to examine his examples unless he had believed them to be good poetry – critics have most commonly levelled against him the charge that in *Ambiguity* in particular he flourished all too many 'possible alternative reactions' (his own words).[23] The critically promiscuous juvenile (he was twenty-four when he wrote the book) scored some hits but many misses: he paid too little attention to questions of authorial aim and literary and historical relevance. According to R. G. Cox in a review of the second edition, for example, 'His characteristic fault, the lack of control by any overriding sense of relevance, comes out interestingly in his very first example, the note on "Bare ruined choirs, where late the sweet birds sang" [Shakespeare, Sonnet 73].'[24] Empson conceded in a BBC broadcast, 'Literary Opinion', on 20 October 1954,

The argument which seems to me strongest, in these literary critics who say that Empson is absurd, is that they say the overall effect of a piece of writing, the general intention of the author, is what decides what you make of a particular line. The critic mustn't pick on one line and get astonishingly irrelevant meanings out of it, because that isn't what anybody does if he is reading properly. Yes, but I never denied that; and I have been able to argue back, three or four times, never leaving out a serious attack, that I *was* considering the whole background, all the time, and that was why I thought the extra meanings fitted in. The three main cases have been a line in a Shakespeare sonnet, and a poem by George Herbert, and a poem by Gerard Manley Hopkins ... I know I made mistakes, but you can't laugh the whole method off; it can still stand up even when the fashion changes.

F. W. Bateson (in an article assuming Matthew Arnold's title 'The Function of Criticism at the Present Time' and in correspondence arising out of it) borrowed the accusation that Edmund Wilson had first levelled against T. S. Eliot's criticism – that it was 'fundamentally non-historical' – in order to tax Empson for showing a 'defective contextual sense' when he invented 'the by now almost notorious list of reasons, ten in all' for linking Shakespeare's boughs (in Sonnet 73) with ruined monasteries. 'The real critical error is more fundamental,' Bateson claimed. 'It is simply that the line on which Empson expatiates is not a separate sentence or even a separate subordinate clause. It is a verbal fragment that is, strictly speaking, *unintelligible* when lifted like this out of its syntactic context.' Empson's response was in that instance not very convincing, his final comment brave though perhaps a little bruised: 'The intention of this passage, which came early in my old *Ambiguity*, before the real problems began, was just to show what putting in some background is like: in Shakespeare's time, the ruins of monasteries must have been a prominent feature, so that *any* contemporary reader would easily think of this meaning for the line – it isn't a question of the peculiar mind of Shakespeare. I don't think it need have startled people into either kisses or kicks to have me offer this placid example of a bit of background.'[25] In other cases he returned with a far more aggressive defence, in particular on Herbert's 'The Sacrifice' (numbers 32–33) and Hopkins's 'The Windhover' (number 44).

The most damaging charge, which is almost always based on the youthful excesses of *Seven Types of Ambiguity*, gave him issue in the form of the so-called New Criticism (John Crowe Ransom must take responsibility for settling the paternity case in his book *The New Criticism*, 1941) and its succeeding 'schools' – all of which Empson fiercely resented and disclaimed. Even in 1986 Professor John Carey recycled in the *Sunday Times* a commonplace misrepresentation with this casual report of *Seven Types of Ambiguity* (unqualified by any consideration of Empson's later position):

Essentially what this book showed was that if you were ingenious enough you could find alternative meanings which no one, least of all the poet, had suspected before. Consequently you could rewrite the whole canon of literature an almost infinite number of times. There was no longer any question of looking for a final or 'authorial' meaning – the critic's job was to extract those meanings that would appeal to his public ...

One aspect of this approach is that the author ceases to matter, since literature is no longer regarded as the expression of a personality. For Empson this was an advantage.[26]

The truth is that Empson felt appalled at what he termed those 'bother-headed theoretical critics' (number 11) who dismissed authorial intentions and despised historicism, which is the certain reason why he took such pains to patch in the 'background' to some of the key analyses on which critics challenged *Ambiguity* (though it does seem likely that at the time of writing the book he had been short of deep historical knowledge); and thereafter he always attempted to recover or reconstruct a tenable interpretation of intention, to plot both the circumstances and the most probable aims of a literary work. He wrote in 1979,

Carey, in his Inaugural Lecture on becoming a Professor [in 1976], announced a rigorous policy; there must be no more paraphrase, no more reading in or spelling out, because all such tampering with a text was the work of vandals. I came in for some of the rough stuff myself, and thought he could have found stronger examples in what I wrote fifty years ago, though I would never have intentionally gone beyond the intention of an author, either in his consciousness or his unconsciousness. But it struck me that the programme as he announced it was actually incompatible with teaching, let alone his own style of written criticism; it became a question whether he would achieve a Houdini-like reappearance. [number 35][27]

Three years on, he felt genuinely pleased to find that Carey was in fact 'deeply in sympathy with the author, knowing what he often wants to do ... it is a welcome advance on [his] Inaugural'.

W. K. Wimsatt Jr and Monroe C. Beardsley ordained in 1946 that 'the design or intention of the author is neither available nor desirable as a standard for judging the success of a work of literary art'; and 'Intention is design or plan in the author's mind ... to insist on the designing intellect as a *cause* of a poem is not to grant the design or intention as a *standard* by which the critic is to judge the worth of the poet's performance.' They go on to say that 'Judging a poem is like judging a pudding or a machine ... A poem can *be* only through its *meaning* – since its medium is words – yet it *is*, simply *is*, in the sense that we have no excuse for enquiring what part is intended or meant ... [the poem] is detached from the author at birth and goes about the world beyond his power to intend about it or control it.' The poem is a linguistic *product* – a product that we can judge only on its own terms – with the result that any attempt to make sense of the product by asking about the plans of the producer is locked out of the factory. Although Wimsatt and Beardsley seem at first glance to be concerned with evaluation, their strictures apply just as much to the actual interpretation of meaning. 'There is a difference between internal and external evidence for the meaning of a poem,' they point out in part IV of their essay. The intrinsic meaning of a poem (which is what they value) 'is discovered through [its] semantics and syntax', whereas external evidence is 'private or idiosyncratic; not a part of the work as a linguistic fact: it consists of revelations (in journals, for example, or letters or reported conversations) about how or why the poet wrote the poem – to what lady, while sitting on what lawn, or at the death of what friend or brother'.[28] Such dicta were the orthodoxy of the New Criticism. As a reaction against the long dominance of the Romantic tradition of (as critics now say) 'privileging' the author, the notions of organic form and semantic autonomy were quite understandable and even salutary. And yet, as another writer has argued, the 'idea of a work of literature as "a linguistic fact" or an "integrated symbol" is comparable to the notions of "a concept" in philosophy or "behaviour" in psychology in being the manifestation of an irresistible demand for discrete, coherent and enduring objects of investigation'.[29]

Empson writes in his review of Wimsatt's book *The Verbal Icon* (1954):

Mr Wimsatt's drive against what he calls the Fallacy of Intentionalism ... seems almost a behaviourist position ... Estimating other people's intentions is one of the things we do all the time without knowing how we are doing it, just as we don't play catch by the theory of dynamics. Consider the law, which ... recognises amply that one can judge a man's intention, and ought to judge him by it. Only in the criticism of imaginative literature, a thing delicately concerned with human intimacy, are we told that we must give up all idea of knowing his intention ...

To say that you won't be bothered with anything but the words on the page (and that you are within your rights, because the author didn't *intend* you to have any more) strikes me as petulant. [number 11]

Elsewhere (in a letter) he argued further,

I feel strongly about Intentionalism, but in a psychological not a theoretical way. Maybe, as an intention is only known as it is shown, all references to intentions can in theory be avoided. The same is true of forces, in dynamics, which never come into the equations – one might say, they live in the equals sign, where the cause meets the effect. But all the same nobody could learn dynamics without learning the rules about forces, and using them all the time. This, by the way, is not 'like' empathy but the same fact of our natures. Still, I couldn't really agree that other people's intentions are meant to be bypassed in this way; it seems to me that the chief function of imaginative literature is to make you realise that other people are very various, many of them quite different from you, with different 'systems of value' as well; but the effect of almost any orthodoxy is to hide this, and pretend that everybody *ought* to be like Homer or Dr Leavis.[30]

The New Critical concept of semantic autonomy did not disallow the idea of an axis of communication between writer and reader. All it insisted was that the reader has access only to the thing communicated – the work of verbal art as achieved – and not to the prior person or viewpoint of the writer; that any extrinsic information about his or her disposition, ideology and literary endeavours is by definition external to the coded product of literature. Yet as Empson counterattacks in 'Still the Strange Necessity': 'in the teasing work of scholarship a man must all the time be trying to imagine another man's mind; as soon as that stops, he is off the rails.'

Empson's tutor I. A. Richards, in *Principles of Literary Criticism* (1924), clearly felt chary of assessing literature by the criterion of intrinsic value, simply because 'The separation of poetic experience from its place in life and its ulterior worths involves a definite lopsidedness, narrowness and incompleteness in those who preach it sincerely.' As a case in point, he argued, it would appear to be what he calls 'mental timidity' to take a purely aesthetic approach to Christ's Sermon on the Mount. Furthermore, certain works of art – including the Psalms, Dante's *Divine Comedy*, and Swift's *A Modest Proposal* – have obviously *ulterior* motives, so that 'consideration of the ulterior ends involved is inevitable to the reader.'[31] Terry Eagleton, in his lively and otherwise helpfully informed *Literary Theory: An Introduction*, has written that 'I. A. Richards had naively assumed that the poem was no more than a transparent medium through which we could observe the poet's psychological processes: reading was just a matter of recreating in our own mind the mental condition of the author.'[32] But that account of Richards's position is fallacious, because in fact Richards had argued that 'communication defined as strict transference of or participation in identical experiences does not occur.'[33] Richards had not been innocent of the fact that a verbal communication is itself an intervention: to cast an experience into linguistic form is a mediation, not a direct transmission. Moreover, he was quick to point out – just like Wimsatt and Beardsley over twenty years later – 'what concerns criticism is not the avowed or unavowed motives of the artist'; and he considered it unprofitable to try to examine the psychology of the poet – much of which, he wrote, 'is, of course, unconscious'.[34] Empson gave his response to Richards's deterrent view in a questionnaire dating from 1976: 'The deep intention may often be a thing the author himself is doubtful about, but this is no reason for forbidding us to recognise the more superficial layers.'[35]

T. S. Eliot's famous stand on the 'impersonality' of the poet (in 'Tradition and the Individual Talent', 1917) has become a kind of canon law of criticism; and certainly from the point of view of literary history his posture can be seen as vindicating the Symbolist heritage to which his early work belonged. As Roland Barthes has more recently written, 'Mallarmé was doubtless the first to see and to foresee in its full extent the necessity to substitute language itself for the person who until then had been supposed to be its owner. For him, for us too, it is language which speaks, not the author; to write is, through a prerequisite impersonality . . . to reach that point where only language acts, "performs", and not "me".[36]

Empson considered that the Symbolist movement invited nothing but irrationalism in both poet and critic, who satisfied their abrogation of intelligence with 'these apparently ineffable verbal communications' (number 19); and he leagued Symbolism together with Imagism as 'determinedly anti-intellectual' and telling us 'that we ought to try to be very stupid' (number 17). Symbolist poetry, he alleges searingly in 'Argufying in Poetry' (number 18), 'is the poetry of the hamstrung, the people who have cut the strings in their legs'. Throughout the essays on criticism that I have included in the section 'Literary Interpretation: The Language Machine', he takes issue with what is essentially the modernist programme of poetry as percept, the portrayal of states of feeling with sensuous particularity. He sees the arch-theorist T. E. Hulme as the villain in the case, for Hulme had dubiously proclaimed that 'Thought is prior to language and consists in the simultaneous presentation to the mind of two images.'[37] Empson took that claim as a vile shibboleth: he refers to it crossly a number of times in these essays. 'The positive fundamental quality of verse ... the very essence of an intuitive language,' Hulme also pronounced, is 'accurate description': that is, precision of image.[38] Likewise, the logic of Archibald MacLeish's dictum that 'A poem should not mean / But be' (the last verset of his poem 'Ars Poetica'), which Wimsatt and Beardsley happily endorse in 'The Intentional Fallacy', is anti-rationalist: it accords with the Imagist tenet 'No ideas but in things,' which is itself an anti-intellectual blow against what Ezra Pound and his associates took to be the moribund self-indulgence of Romantic subjectivity. On those terms, the poem is jealously guarded against the excrescences of 'meaning' which the poet might otherwise have considered himself to be proposing. Put simply, the argument is that to realise an emotion in images is to have interpreted that emotion, without the interposition of the poet's ego; the poet is the agent of his vision, not the active proponent. Images are a self-sufficient mediation to which the deliberate consciousness of the author would be an irrelevance. Empson argues back in 'Rhythm and Imagery in English Poetry' (number 17):

Non-visualisers are often intellectuals, and I am sure it does intellectuals good to have their noses rubbed in their sensual corruption; I agree that it's disgusting not to have images; but all the same even people who do have images don't use them for thinking ... The first thing to get clear, I think, is that this Imagist account of the human mind (which often sounds to be making it angelic) makes it totally subhuman, sub-canine for that matter, the mind of a black-beetle.

We know that Ezra Pound supplied Eliot with Hulme's ideas; we know too that Eliot read Hulme's posthumous *Speculations* when it came out (misleadingly edited by Herbert Read) in 1924,[39] and that the book must therefore have underwritten Eliot's continual stress on the visual imagery of Dante. Against Hulme's delimited doctrine, which is still current in some poetic circles – as in Craig Raine's adopted view that 'Description is revelation'[40] – Empson believed that the best poetry (in particular his favourite metaphysical poetry) handles philosophical and ontological problems, being interested in far more than the process of mind – the apotheosis of the individual sensorium – and striving beyond egoism to articulate ideas and statements of meaning: ideas interpreted and evaluated with logical coherence. 'It is a misfortune,' he felt, 'that the whole literary tradition of Symbolism has grown up so completely divorced from the tradition of fair public debate' (number 17). As far as he was concerned, imagery is not an end in itself but has the office of serving a larger structure. His view of poetry is not just reactionary, but it is radical: it has a proven pedigree. As early as 1927, when he started to publish his own poems, he laid down this conviction: 'It is a fallacy that men of great abilities can produce what Mr Eliot calls a "synthesis" simply by explaining their mental habits; they must do it by producing a work of art.'[41]

Empson much later wrote about *The Waste Land*: 'The poem is inherently a mystery; I would never have believed that the Symbolist programme could be made to work at all, if it had not scored a few resounding triumphs, such as this. Many people, when the poem was new, felt greatly affected by it without understanding why; and even if you decide that the effect was an accident you cannot help wanting to know how it happened.'[42] Well-disposed contemporary critics had been quick to apply to Eliot's poetry the vocabulary of his own running commentary as supplied by his critical prose, as well as to distil the sources and influences of the mode that Eliot brought to fruition in England. In *Axel's Castle* (1931), for instance, Edmund Wilson happily placed Eliot in the tradition of French Symbolist poetry, pointing out that 'The Symbolist movement ... finally succeeded in throwing overboard completely the clarity and logic of the French classical tradition. ... To intimate things rather than state them plainly was thus one of the primary aims of the Symbolists.' With specific reference to *The Waste Land*, Wilson observed that Eliot 'succeeds in conveying his meaning, in communicating his emotion, in spite of all his learned or mysterious allusions, and whether we understand them or not'.[43] The status of Eliot's 'learned or mysterious allusions' certainly bothered Wimsatt and Beardsley in 'The Intentional Fallacy'. One classic reason for alluding to works of the past had clearly been to borrow some of their 'prestige and authority', on the understanding that readers would apprehend the models and complete the circuit of communication (as Linda Hutcheon has argued in an authoritative study of parody).[44] The practice, in other words, had been intentional. Wimsatt and Beardsley, taking their cue from F. O. Matthiessen's *The Achievement of T. S. Eliot* (1935), declare that it really does not matter if we have no intellectual understanding of Eliot, for his allusions work through their 'suggestive power'.[45] (In a chapter on Eliot's poetry appended in 1926 to *Principles of Literary Criticism*, I. A. Richards had similarly wriggled away from aim and meaning by talking about 'emotional symbolism' and 'the music of ideas'.)[46] In a rather evasive argument, Wimsatt and Beardsley discount Eliot's annotations to *The Waste Land* as an illegitimate sort of explanatory intervention; they say that 'whereas notes tend to seem to justify themselves as external indexes to the author's *intention*, yet they ought to be judged like any other parts of a composition (verbal arrangement special to a particular context), and when so judged their reality as parts of the poem, or their imaginative integration with the rest of the poem, may come into question.'[47] They propose a problem, so to speak, simply because they feel obliged to take the poem as what formalist critics call a 'phenomenally existent event' and not as a 'verbally constructed historical event'.

Empson had anticipated the problem as early as 1930, in the hitherto unpublished 'Obscurity and Annotation' (number 2), where he persuasively judges that it is valid for criticism to heed almost every possible extrinsic resource, including authorial statements of intention and explication. Elsewhere he argued that Wimsatt and Beardsley's suspicions about Eliot's notes to *The Waste Land*

seem rather indefinite, and can surely not be offered as a proof that it would be better without notes. It is quite true, as is hardly recognised enough by the placid remarks of the essay, that Eliot could shake the literary world by the mere force of the poem *before* it was tolerably understood; that this can happen is one of the basic surprising truths about poetry; but you can't argue from there that to understand *The Waste Land* a bit better makes it any weaker. Nor do I find the final joke, to the effect that it is no use asking such a poet what he meant, though of course it has a broad truth, any serious ground for imposing a New Rule that a critic 'ought' not to ask him. As J. B. S. Haldane remarked some while ago, arguing against some other line of purism, 'I find geometry sufficiently difficult to justify my using any method which I find will work.'

The argument that it is romantic to bother about what the poet intended, and therefore must be wicked, only seems to me fatuously poky.[48]

'I was much struck by the young lady who found it suspicious that I tried to explain my poems, after being warned not to by W. K. Wimsatt,' Empson observed in a letter to Christopher Ricks. 'It will be interesting to see what the Anti-Intentionalists make of the problem of editing, which I don't know that they have considered before (but maybe Bateson was doing that).'[49] Traditionally, editorial and textual critics have found it necessary to set absolute store by the author's intentions; any theory of

copy-text – where a work may survive in various versions, draft manu-
scripts, memorial reconstructions, or in different published states – has
tried to reconstruct the author's intentions (or even 'final intentions'). Editors seek to establish a legitimate or 'authoritative' state of the text, not a
degraded version. 'The most obvious breakdown of [the New Critical] position, I think, though it is healthy within limits,' Empson commented in
another letter, 'is when you try to decide about Hamlet or Falstaff, and find
that one of the major subjects being discussed is just what words the author
did want to have on the page. It is all right drawing the curtains and making
the evening cosy, but you want to feel you can get out again if need arise.'[50]
More recently, Jerome McGann, in *A Critique of Modern Textual Criticism* (1983), has argued that 'A hypnotic fascination with the isolated
author has served to foster an overdetermined concept of authorship,' and
that

all literary works undergo transformations in their production – involving the
translation of an initially psychological phenomenon (the 'creative process') into a
social one (the literary work) ... As soon as an author utters or writes down his
work, even for the first time, a mediation has to some degree come between or
'interfered with' the original, unmediated 'text'.[51]

In short, no author could at any time be freely creative or 'autonomous':
every author is subject to the social and linguistic codes and constraints of
his or her culture. Although Ezra Pound's treatment of *The Waste Land*
may seem to be an extreme case, it is not unlike what happens to every literary work when it becomes public property, when it ceases to be a 'personal
possession' and gains authority as what McGann calls 'a social nexus'.[52]
All the same, K. K. Ruthven still makes Empson's point in a sprightly chapter on Intentionalism in his good book *Critical Assumptions:* 'Literary
scholarship – especially textual scholarship – is heavily committed to intentionalism, and regards the correction of corrupt texts as an essential step
towards the recovery of authorial intentions and therefore of literary meaning.'[53]
    Professor Alastair Fowler (in an essay entitled 'Intention Floreat') pro-
poses that we should respect an author's awareness of meaning, at least at
the first level of enquiry:

unless one ignores the nature of literary transmission and communication links in
general, one must acknowledge the privileged status of the particular set of words
intended by the author ... The lexical string expresses, in fact, the writer's gram-
matic and semantic intention; and in turn it binds the recipient to understand one
specific communication, in contrast to numerous others ... Respect for the text of
the author seems to constitute *de facto* recognition of the privileged status of his
intention ...

The reason for insisting on intention is that without it the work disappears altogether.[54]

The argument endorses the view that intention cannot be simplistically regarded as a 'single entity' (as anti-intentionalists need to believe it) – merely an originating or prescriptive idea – but that 'Intention means different things at different stages of composition.' Fowler is equally correct to point out that 'intention' must be seen to have numerous aspects and phases: practical, generic, semantic and also unconscious (all of which are blandly overlooked in F. R. Leavis's remark that 'intentions are nothing in art except as realised').[55] The inescapable paradox is that, if you deny any critical reference to an author's conscious intentions, you are left with nothing but to infer unconscious intentions – which are still *intentions*. As K. K. Ruthven adroitly puts it, 'For as long as we can go on saying that certain meanings are "unintentional", it will not be possible for us to dispense entirely with purposeful intentions, however troublesome they may prove to formalist critics. We all hope to be understood as having said what we intended to say . . .'[56] Empson commented on Wimsatt and Beardsley's edicts against the critical consideration of both conscious and unconscious aims:

What one can sometimes say, I think, is that the poet was inspired and meant more than he knew, and that the later reader can recognise in his working the growth of ideas which though also working in his contemporary public, and therefore accepted when they accepted his poem, were then obscure or even forbidden. Milton seems the main interesting possible case; Shakespeare isn't 'interesting' in this sense because he wouldn't have been upset if you had told him. But in any case the mind of the author, both conscious and unconscious, has to continue being an accepted topic for the critic; it can't be swept off the table just because the room looks a bit untidy.[57]

The New Critical insistence upon the semantic autonomy of the text, treating the literary object as a self-enclosed or organic system of signs – an approach which Empson dubbed the 'print-centred or tea-tasting outlook'[58] – had a number of pitfalls. Not the least was the doubly ironic consequence that in practice the New Criticism, far from establishing any unified meaning in a work of literature, found itself multiplying ambiguities and ironies. Paul de Man points this out in his essay 'Form and Intent in the American New Criticism'. But, as a deconstructionist, de Man has capitalised on the logic of that position: he postulates what he calls 'the intentional structure of literary form' – a form which is 'never anything but a process on its way to completion'. His theory amounts to making absolute claims for what the jargon now calls 'valorising' the reader, for he explains that the literary form 'is constituted in the mind of the interpreter as the

work discloses itself in response to his questioning. But this dialogue between work and interpreter is endless.'[59]

The concept of 'the death of the author' has been enshrined for recent
critical ideologues in Roland Barthes's essay with that title dating from
1968 (*Image–Music–Text*, 1977), which proclaims 'the essentially verbal
condition of literature':

> Linguistically [Barthes asserts], the author is never more than the instance writing,
> just as *I* is nothing other than the instance saying *I*: language knows a 'subject', not
> a 'person' ... the text is henceforth made and read in such a way that at all its levels
> the author is absent ... every text is eternally written *here and now*. ...
>   Once the Author is removed, the claim to decipher a text becomes quite futile. To
> give a text an Author is to impose a limit on that text, to furnish it with a final signi-
> fied, to close the writing ... writing ceaselessly posits meaning ceaselessly to evapo-
> rate it, carrying out a systematic exemption of meaning.

Barthes's heady rhetoric ends with a claim to liberate the reader along with
the text: 'the birth of the reader must be at the cost of the death of the
Author.'[60] The argument is anti-historicist, and also leaves out of account
the many modes of writing which involve definite signals from author to
reader. Irony, for instance, requires the reader to recognise a statement and
also whatever else is (intentionally) implied by that statement. Likewise,
numerous modern examples of metafiction employ irony, allusion and
parody in sophisticated and supremely self-conscious ways – ways which
serve to reinstate the position of what canting critics now style an 'enunciating encoder' or at least an 'implied author'. As Linda Hutcheon has commented, 'it is part of the particular strategy of both parody and irony that
their acts of communication cannot be considered completed unless the
precise encoding *intention* is realised in the recognition of the receiver' [my
stress].[61] In any event, the 'author' in some sense returns, even if one is
obliged to put the thing back to front and say that the author is only
'implied' by the text.

But is it still necessary for us to undergo the analytical contortions of pretending to 'imply' an author, even when we might otherwise – in many
cases – accept the fact that an actual, historical author is addressing us? The
problem again goes back to Wimsatt and Beardsley, whose axioms included the proposition that every poem is *of course* dramatic: 'We ought to
impute the thoughts and attitudes of the poem immediately to the dramatic
speaker, and if to the author at all, only by an act of biographical
inference.'[62] Such a gospel demeans any notion of sincerity in a poet; in
fact, it ordains the opposite and puts the reader at two removes from the
author. Poetic statements – pseudo-statements, fictive statements – are not
really statements at all; they are *representations* of the verbal acts they
might otherwise seem to resemble. John Reichert has satirically summed up

this consensus among recent critical theorists: 'In their eyes the poet could hardly be thought to mean what he says, because he is not saying, and the reader does not take him to be saying. Indeed he is not writing either, at least in that special sense where writing something *is* saying something and implies assertion.' Instead of such nonsense, Reichert proposes, we should recognise a genre of affirmative poems which includes 'all those poems which we read as real speech acts performed by their authors – real, that is, as opposed to pretend or fictional', and with 'statements seriously meant':

the presence of this genre is corroborated by the way critics talk about poems when they are not burdened by the unnecessary precautions imposed by a rigid theory ... It is at times very interesting to learn that a certain person or poet was just posing. But it would not be interesting at all if it were always true of everyone.[63]

Empson provided a perfect example in the poetry of Rochester (number 36): 'He is a test case, I think, against some recent critics who have said that one ought to ignore biography because a poem ought to stand by itself – if one didn't believe Rochester, his poems couldn't come off properly.'

In sum, Empson thought the theory of the Intentional Fallacy simply 'self-blinding'; and he said about Intentionalism:

I must not make extravagant claims for a process which all persons not insane are using in all their social experience; I have only to say that the effect of renouncing it (in the unique case of the most delicate and intimate formulations of intention) produces dirty nonsense all the time, with a sort of tireless unconscious inventiveness for new kinds of nonsense.[64]

Like Alastair Fowler, he felt determined to acknowledge the privileged status of an author's intentions – *not* so that those intentions should be taken as prescriptive or pre-emptive, but because good authorship means a good critical mind operating *in* the writing (as T. S. Eliot among many other writers has recognised). Moreover, as E. D. Hirsch Jr has properly observed, 'no logical necessity compels us to banish an author in order to analyse his text.'[65]

III

'The modern classroom demands that the children need only read the words on the page before them,' Empson wrote in a letter (*c.* 1973), 'and must never be expected to have any general information or knowledge of life (except of course the raw mass of prejudice which Teacher has to cater for): so I do feel mildly cheerful when I can speak as from outside this airless place.'[66] If 'bother-headed theoretical critics' confirmed him in his disinclination to venture a theory of criticism, the open air of human

contextualism persuaded him never to underestimate a writer's intelligence
– that any author would naturally question and probably dissent from prevailing cultural doctrines. 'Contradiction is a powerful literary weapon,' he
had insisted even in *Seven Types of Ambiguity* (p. 197); and in the preface
to the second edition (1947): 'When Mr James Smith objected to my dealing with "conflicts supposed to have ranged within the author", I think he
was overplaying his hand very seriously; he was striking at the roots of
criticism, not at me.'[67] To strike at the roots of criticism was to deny that
the critic could achieve a valid interpretation: it denied him access to the
full social and ideological context of the poetry.

As Empson interprets it, good poetry never makes glib syntheses but
struggles to cope with the claims and counterclaims of the poet's culture; it
certainly does not solve the struggle by the grace of irony or paradox, which
would mean saving faith and thought. By definition, the best authors
always reserve their independence of judgement and outwit subservience;
art is at odds with orthodoxy. 'A society is always in development, and an
artist has a function in it like that of the designer of fashions,' he wrote
about Coleridge (number 40) – taking his cue from Herbert Read's
account, in *The True Voice of Feeling* (1953), of the claims of the Romantic
artist, which Empson thought no novelty but a permanent condition of the
creative mind. 'The paradox of the artist is thus the opposite of the Christian one; he must say ruthlessly what he himself likes or wants, and only by
this selfishness can he help his fellows.' The paradox accords with the
Benthamite ethic that he learned first from I. A. Richards, and which I shall
discuss later. This abiding concern with rational resistance bridges the
apparent gap between his supposedly exclusive and unjudging interests in
the early books – first with technical analysis, then with linguistics – and
the openly ethical declarations of *Milton's God* and its related later essays.
In *Some Versions of Pastoral* he had argued that 'the artist never is at one
with any public';[68] and Richard Sleight found the key to Empson's subtext
in *The Structure of Complex Words* when he wrote: 'Complex words and
key-words incline to represent the unofficial view.'[69]

Hugh Kenner once highlighted what he called the 'picaresque zest'[70] of
Ambiguity; and more than twenty years later (in 1974) Empson himself
tended to agree, though with firmly redeeming qualifications:

The term Ambiguity was a bad choice so far as it suggested that the author was
being artful and tricky – he need only be conscious of the process, I suppose,
enough to make him try for a different form of words if he has lit on a damaging
ambiguity. Perhaps I liked the word because I was myself gleefully engaged in
regarding the result of imagination as trick-work. But I think a willing reader soon
got to ignore this harmful suggestion, which I certainly didn't want in serious
cases.[71]

Certainly the two most serious cases had been his climactic analyses of Hopkins's 'The Windhover' and George Herbert's 'The Sacrifice', where he argued that the authors had felt obliged to confront rather than to accommodate themselves to the comforting but insidious paradoxes of Christian doctrine. In other words, *Seven Types of Ambiguity* was already gathering the storm that broke out in *Milton's God*. Stylistically and in many of its terms of reference, the book at once succeeded in changing the outlook of criticism and suffered because of its youthful extravagances. In substance, it not only purveyed a new mode of submitting imaginative literature to the test of the discursive reason, it had also culminated – artfully and gleefully – with two analyses that outraged Christian doctrine and history. While critics eventually caught up with Empson's heterodoxy, contemporary reviewers had generally found themselves too stunned by his whole approach to poetry to seize on his transgressiveness. But this is not to find fault with the perception of those readers who first winced or wondered at the new criticism. At the time of writing, not even Empson himself fully appreciated the import of his inflammatory insights, especially when (as he later came to think) they had been distractingly infected by the equally new and ravishing model of Freudian analysis. He recalled in 1947 (clearly with an eye on his own short career as a poet) that in recent years 'the effort of writing a good bit of verse has in almost every case been carried through almost as a clinical thing: it was done to save the man's sanity. Exceedingly good verse has been written under these conditions in earlier centuries as well as our own, but only to externalise the conflict of an individual.'[72] As Empson interpreted their poems, Hopkins and Herbert had – in just such a manner – externalised in their poetry the sense of conflict between the call of Christ and the resistant call of human intelligence. Even though he had partly couched his original analysis of 'The Sacrifice' in Freudian terms, he insisted in after years, his interpretation of the contradictions balanced within the poem was still absolutely correct. Readers should not neglect the true meaning just because the critic had overindulged himself in the way that he chose to explicate it. George Herbert had faced up to a genuine 'mental conflict', not a peculiar problem of a psychological order. 'I can claim,' Empson wrote in 1947, 'that my last example of the last type of ambiguity was not concerned with neurotic disunion but with a fully public theological poem.'[73] Still later, in 1963, he reiterated in 'Herbert's Quaintness' (number 33):

I put 'The Sacrifice' last of the examples in my book, to stand for the most extreme kind of ambiguity, because it presents Jesus as at the same time forgiving his torturers and condemning them to eternal torture. It strikes me now that my attitude was what I have come to call 'neo-Christian'; happy to find such an extravagant speci-

men, I slapped the author on the back and egged him on to be even nastier....
Clearer now about what the light illuminates, I am keen to stumble away from it.

What Herbert confronted in his poetry, Empson insists, was the fundamental opposition between the demands of the Christian God and the birthright
of humanity, the responsibility to exercise individual judgement. Those
imperatives are traditionally incompatible, and the conflict in poets who
felt compelled to tackle the subject stems from the effort not to dissolve but
to encompass its intolerable stresses. 'It was in the air of Herbert's time that
the paradoxes of Christianity were a moral embarrassment,' he commented. 'The basic need of Metaphysical Wit, though seldom its conscious purpose, was to keep these new qualms at bay.'
    In terms of Empson's critical career as a whole, therefore, his few early
pages on 'The Sacrifice' are a cardinal text; dating from 1930, they seeded
the catechising writings of his later years, most notably *Milton's God*. Yet
again, however, at the time when he wrote about 'The Sacrifice' his analysis
seemed far less perfidious than accepted good sense. By Empson's reckon-
ing, the damage was done to 'traditional' critical readings such as his own
by the reactionary forces of the Christian religion, with T. S. Eliot as its literary high priest. In 1932 Eliot made the unsupported assertion, 'Donne
was, I insist, no sceptic';[74] and in due order Allen Tate (among many other
critics) bowed to the new wisdom. In 1611, John Donne balefully discerned
in 'The First Anniversarie' that the 'new Philosophy calls all in doubt'; but
following Eliot's lead in 1932 Tate chose to observe in his review of *A Garland for John Donne* (the volume in which Eliot's reactionary essay
appeared) that Donne's interest in the new cosmologists, Copernicus and
Kepler, took the straightforward form of

an anxiety about the physical limits of consciousness and the bearing of that
question on the scholastic conception of body and soul, which Donne presents in
the terminology of St Thomas. Donne knew nothing of a scientific age, or of the
later open conflict between the two world views, science and religion.[75]

Given the compelling evidence that Professor Marjorie Nicolson presently
marshalled in 'The "New Astronomy" and English Imagination' (1935),[76]
Empson felt justified in scorning what he termed Tate's 'elegant muffle-
ment'. Christian critics celebrate the Creator, yet they deny that a
seventeenth-century poet could have felt staggered by the soul-provoking
news about the true disposition of the cosmos He created. Empson obviously enjoyed pointing up the ironically heretical implications of Tate's
false position:

Well come now, this bit of hush-up naturally excites an impulse to hush-up this
awful bit of hush-up too, as it happened to be a frightful gaffe our old pal made.

Donne invented this conflict at the same time as the Roman Inquisition, but apart from the high terrible example of Donne it has been rare among English poets; it is a gross slander to pretend that they all despise the works of their Creator and the discoveries of the divine plan achieved during their lifetime.[77]

Reviewing his career in the early 1970s, when he felt the time had come 'to bring out editions of old essays which often need rewriting, and in general to round things off after retirement', Empson wrote in response to Roger Sale's essay 'The Achievement of William Empson' (in *Modern Heroism*, Berkeley and Los Angeles: University of California Press, 1973):

Complex Words was written before I had been confronted with the new orthodoxy in the Eng Lit profession; no doubt I was reading enough of it to learn, but I quite failed to realise how much we disagreed – it did not happen till I got to Sheffield, some time after the book was out. I really did not write that book, as you say, in an effort to toe the academic line. (A 'desperate struggle', you suggest later on.) I wanted to offer a coherent linguistic theory about ambiguity, with examples that could be followed up again and again to demonstrate its truth. Most of the literary examples had occurred to me before, and I had unfinished articles about them ready, but luckily they turned out to suit this other purpose. It would be no use to have lots of bright ideas, staving off boredom, because I needed to show that the same ideas worked out consistently over a large field.... There was a sturdy attempt to carry out an argument, so that I had a logical reason for the order of the illustrations, even in *Ambiguity* and *Pastoral*, and I can't feel that they are Symbolist poems either. I did, I can't deny, feel it was rather fun to work up some particularly loathsome bit of Christian torture-worship, as the bang at the end of a chapter; but I think I explained that these were cases of particularly advanced logical and emotional disorder. It did not mean that I was slavering to engage in these tortures myself, and thought they were the prettiest fancy in my bag. If there is any insincerity about the change in Empson, it comes in the first two books, where I did not explain that I thought the Father who was satisfied by the Crucifixion disgusting; but really, everyone I knew thought that already, and accepted reserve about it as mere politeness. The topic did not seem to crop up in *Complex Words*.... What next confronted me was the appalling mass of misreading which has now become established in Eng Lit and makes a variety of authors quite unreadable for the young who accept their teachers. This misreading is always of a pietistic character, but otherwise just whatever will serve.[78]

He acquired massive publicity for his views on the wickedness of the Christian religion when he published *Milton's God* in 1961, with his thesis essentially following in the footsteps of Voltaire, Samuel Butler, Gibbon, Buckle and J. M. Robertson. The crux of his argument he left in no doubt at all, though subsequent critical misapprehensions forced him to repeat it again and again, as in this letter from 1967: 'Shelley found it plain that, the more he reverenced the Son who endured, the more he must execrate the Father who was satisfied by his pain.'[79] The snag in his approach, which certainly gave some reviewers the opportunity to crab the book, lay in the very fact

that he confronted the Christian God through a work of literary imagination, on the perilous assumption that Milton's version of God could be
identified with the 'truth' of the Gospel. While C. S. Lewis, in *A Preface to
Paradise Lost* (1942), had convincingly demonstrated the orthodoxy of
Milton's theology, other critics found poem and doctrine incommensurable
and objected to Empson's evident equation. The book thus contrived to run
up against an unforeseeable but perhaps unsurmountable irony: that, as
one notice deftly put it, 'Empson's every insult to God should prove a compliment to Milton.'[80] By arguing that Christianity was radically incoherent
and morally ugly, he praised Milton's integrity in outstaring the embarrass-
ments of the myth in poetry that was all the more brilliant because unblink-
ing. John Bayley discriminated the central irony of Empson's approach
when he observed, 'Unlike most critics, Lewis and Empson make a stead-
fast claim for Milton's complete moral coherence.'[81] The 'obstacles to
grasping' the power of the poem, Empson wrote later, 'come from the basic
fallacies of the Christian religion, or indeed the whole previous cult of
human sacrifice. But Milton's treatment of the subject has to be
approached through his language.'[82] And again: 'I am such an old academic that I agree with Blake and Shelley ... I think the main points which
have been found bad about *Paradise Lost* are precisely what made it so
good, because they amount to a profound analysis of what is fundamentally wrong with the Christian God.'

A defender of the faith, F. N. Lees, who had earlier taxed Empson over
Hopkins's 'The Windhover' (see number 44), argued that 'many readers
... would recognise a failure in the story-telling enterprise' – which is to
say that the myth is simply unavailable for treatment as epic drama – and
so left himself short of argument, protesting only that 'Professor Empson is
wrong about Christianity...'[83] The anonymous reviewer for the *Times
Literary Supplement* likewise laughed the matter off as an impossible paradox: 'Once the critic strays from his text in order to exploit the many theoretical absurdities of an epic which has an omniscient character in it, there
can be no end to the anti-Christian fun and games.'[84] But fun and games
were not the point for Empson: it was a matter of true life and death, as he
told the *TLS* the next week: 'I deny that a poem is a private self-subsisting
world.'[85] From deep inside the Christian camp, Helen Gardner delivered a
persuasive piece of special pleading that is worth quoting at some length:

the book has a radical flaw in its refusal to recognise that theology, like philosophy,
has a history, and that Milton's highly individual emphasis on certain doctrines
makes it impossible to equate his God with the Christian God.... [Milton] accepted by and large the form of the doctrine of the Atonement current in his day and
presented it in a crude form. But I do not believe this doctrine meant much to him
imaginatively or religiously. The interest of *Paradise Lost* does not lie here but in

the doctrines that Milton lived by and to which he gave memorable expression: the doctrine of Creation, the doctrine of Providence, and the belief that the root of all goodness is freedom. Milton's passionate belief in God as Creator and Ruler, and in the freedom of the will, allied to his noble confidence in reason as the master faculty of the human mind, produces a God seen almost wholly in terms of Power and Will, who argues his case at the bar of human reason. This Being seems to have little relation to the 'Father' of Christ's discourses, and to have been created without reference to the fundamental Christian belief that the supreme revelation of the nature of the Deity is to be found in the life and death of Christ.[86]

Yet whatever discriminations apologists may make between religious absolutes and the evolution of Christian doctrine, it can hardly be disputed that Empson had in fact been intently concerned with 'the life and death of Christ' in relation to 'the nature of the Deity'. Professor Graham Hough seized the nub of Empson's matter: 'The Son who suffers on the Cross is not the victim of a Father who can only be satisfied by blood; he is identical with the Father ... Whatever he came to believe later Milton seems to have been an orthodox Trinitarian at the time he wrote *Paradise Lost*. But Empson ... brushes off the consubstantiality of the Son with the Father as a mere form of words ...'[87] *Mere form of words*: few critics would dare argue that Empson was innocent of verbal complexities; and as to the doctrine of the Trinity, Empson saw it as an article of evasion, so to speak, a sophistical formulation surely devised to overcome a morally ugly alternative.[88]

S. G. F. Brandon, in *The Judgment of the Dead* (1967) – which Empson reviewed some six years after publishing *Milton's God* (number 115) – provided an objective assessment of the meaning and implications of Christ's ministry in terms that in no way shirk the issues that goaded Empson. Starting out from the eschatological tradition of Jewish apocalyptic belief that the Messiah would reward his faithful servants with everlasting bliss and damn his enemies to eternal torment, Brandon observes, Catholic Christianity presently emerged as 'a salvation-religion centred on a saviour-god'. Notwithstanding the increasing stress that the historical Church laid on a wholesome soteriology, however, 'Christ appears [in the liturgy] in two different, and logically contradictory roles, namely, as the Saviour and the Judge of mankind.'

We are naturally shocked [Brandon goes on] at the readiness with which earlier generations of Christians believed that the larger part of mankind would ultimately be doomed to hell. Their attitude, however, was logical; for Christian eschatology taught that faith in Christ was essential to salvation ... The dilemma of modern Christian theology is that of shedding the mythology of an ancient eschatology and its rigorist exclusiveness which involves contemplating the eternal damnation of most of mankind, while maintaining faith in Christ as the unique Saviour of men.

His conclusion is therefore inescapable, though it is difficult to judge whether he is implying an argument for more rigour or deep regret: 'because belief in judgement after death, with its eternal consequences of Heaven or Hell, constitute[s] the "teeth" or ultimate authentication of the Christian ethic, that belief has now become practically even more necessary than it was before'. In any event, he adds a footnote that presses home the terrible irony that this religion of merciful redemption somehow requires the sanction of everlasting punishment: 'Ideally, of course, the Christian moral code should be practised for love of God, and not for the hope of gaining Heaven or escaping Hell. Nevertheless, the validity of that code depends logically upon an ultimate distinction, made by God, between the just and the unjust.'[89]

By referring such observations back to the central argument of *Milton's God*, it is possible to see that Empson had reached an unerringly logical and devastating conclusion, as he framed it in 'Herbert's Quaintness' (number 33):

The doctrine of the Trinity is necessary, or the Father appears too evil in his 'satis-faction' at the crucifixion of his Son. But to present Jesus as one with the Father only turns him into a hypocrite; when he prays for his enemies to be forgiven, he knows under his other title he will take revenge.

Kenneth Burke commented on Empson, 'by his stress upon "torture" rather than the sacrificial principle in general, he picturesquely deflects attention from the central relationship between religion and the social order.'[90] The adverb 'picturesquely' is of course a sarcastic euphemism: Burke also called him 'rabid', as did other critics who considered him 'vitriolic' in his fixation on the horrid meaning of what Burke terms 'the sacrificial principle in general' – a sentimental locution if ever there was one. If some readers put him down for the funny farm, however, Empson clearly saw no other way than nagging and slanging to drive home his point. Graham Hough remarked that when Empson 'presents the early Christians as gloating over human sacrifice in a world otherwise civilised enough to have grown out of it, he ought to take a rest from the Rationalist Press classics and re-read Suetonius';[91] but, as E. M. W. Tillyard agreed in private correspondence with Empson, any appeal to Suetonius must pale beside the evidence of Tertullian.[92]

Empson may be faulted for inappropriately levelling his rational human-ism at a transcendent and, in his terms, tyrannical deity – a God who not only held all the cards (gods will be theocratic) but also maliciously stacked them against mankind; perhaps more so for trying to deconstruct the Chris-tian God by way of Milton's imagination. But his critical approach fol-lowed from principle: 'A man who believes in Hell can't help relating the prospect of it to his feelings about life in general,' he wrote in a letter to Frank Kermode.[93] That conviction explains exactly why he became so intent in the last thirty years of his career on rescuing literature from Christian readings. In *Ambiguity* he had addressed 'the class of readers' who agreed with him about 'certain effects' in poetry; not perceiving himself as a polemicist, he had simply practised the close reading of literature in terms of what he considered 'depth psychology'. In his later years he resolved to reconstruct any and every kind of literary student – the mass of misreaders – for 'the intentions of the authors [they read],' he insisted in another letter, 'were very unlikely to be so nasty as those of your many-legged neo-Christian torture-worshippers'.[94]

The customary critical verdict on the post-war Empson is that he became exclusively obsessed with exploding the myths of Christianity, in toppling God: he had become bitterly negative, even virulently destructive in his views, determined only to lam into both the intrinsic wickedness and the wicked effects of worshipping the Christian God. And so, sadly, ends the story. But any such delimiting interpretation of his later career makes a grave mistake. On the strongest natural and moral grounds he felt sickened by the practice of cruelty or sadism: appalled at the notion of the Father in Heaven being 'well pleased' with witnessing the mortal sufferings of Christ (see 'The Satisfaction of the Father', number 116). He had also studied the ethics of what he called 'the other half of Christian theology, let alone the other half of the old world – India and China and their satellites' (number 100). All his researches convinced him that none of mankind's religious or social customs should be taken as absolute, only as relative. He hoped to demolish the Christian God, it is true, but he attacked only one version of godhead and thought it a sickening symptom of the very habit of mind he opposed that all too many critics interpreted his anti-Christianity as a blind attack on the One God. 'To say I hate God seems to me an example of pretending that Christianity is the only religion,' he protested in a letter; 'I hate Moloch, the god who was satisfied by crucifying his son.'[95] A number of readers therefore see only the one facet of Empson, the supposed bigot who assailed Christianity. The side they neglect, which is in fact the concomitant and equally important aspect of his revisionary campaign, is the Empson who laboured to recover a positively hopeful and humane view of ethics and literary interpretation. Milton's God, he had argued, 'cannot be the metaphysical God of Aquinas ... he has such a bad character'; and his postulate for a far better version of godhead is assuredly set out in *Milton's God*, just as it is intimated in this later letter:

The rebel angels ... grant that a personal creator is conceivable, but such a being must satisfy the conditions of Aquinas, which include absolute omnipotence. (He must be built into the structure of the universe, as no creator can be.) ... The poem sets out to explain why the world is bursting with sin and misery, and the only reason it can find is that God is tirelessly spiteful. He therefore cannot be the metaphysical God of Aquinas, and the heroic rebels were right on the essential point.[96]

The conception of a divinity somehow 'built into the structure of the universe' figures throughout his later writings, as his constructive alternative to the Christian God. It is a secularised version of godhead, following the pantheistic paradigm; and he was pleased to find it in evidence in many authors – including Yeats (numbers 46–7)[97] and Dylan Thomas (numbers 56–61); as an aspect of the early poetry of Kathleen Raine (number 66); and even in Tennyson's 'Tithonus'.[98] 'Dylan Thomas's religion is pantheistic and absorbs the Godhead into the world,' he declared in 1947 (number 56). He had good reason for believing so, for in an early letter Thomas had delightedly cited a passage in Donne's *Devotions* 'where he describes man as earth of the earth'. T. S. Eliot's unacknowledged literary curates would of course pooh-pooh the ignorant fancy that Donne (if not Thomas) could have been signalling something pantheist, Empson acknowledged in 1965:

That would be 'provincial' no doubt, as Eliot called the beliefs of Yeats, so that they too become invisible. I do not mean to say that Dylan Thomas's philosophising, apart from its expression, is very recondite; he could have found most of it in Shelley, and probably did; but the indoctrinated modern reader is unwilling to find it anywhere. [number 60]

If Empson trod on rocky ground in suspecting Milton's Trinitarianism, he almost certainly stumbled over his argument that even Milton might have been pointing to the same happy prospect – a fortunate future when God would 'dissolve into the landscape'. At least in this instance, his eagerness to repudiate the Christian God led him to too partial a reading of the textual evidence. In respect of Christianity he overlooked the principle that in general he practised religiously, and for which he praised Arthur Waley in these terms: 'A large capacity to accept the assumptions of any worldview, without assuming any merit for our own, is the basic virtue of Waley's mind' (number 73). But as far as he was concerned Christianity was beyond tolerance. Looking for a redeeming feature in the way *Paradise Lost* depicts its God, he persuaded himself that Milton foresaw that God should abdicate his station. The passage in question is the Father's speech to the Son, ending

> Then thou thy regal sceptre shalt lay by,
> For regal sceptre then no more shall need,
> God shall be all in all

(III. 339–41)

– which is in fact difficult to construe as anything other than a versification of St Paul's First Epistle to the Corinthians (xv. 28): 'When all things shall be subdued unto him, then shall the Son also himself be subject unto him that put all things under him, that God may be all in all.' Empson once wrote, 'The standard literary training treats history pretty rough, but I don't'; yet here it seems likely that he chose to read into Milton's language a prospective dispensation on the order of Shelley's 'one Spirit' – at the expense of the more obvious theological gloss. Edward L. Hirsh offered Empson the sideways compliment that his 'incredibly simplified view of Christian history and thought and his frank reliance on a totally secular humanism whose ethical prophet is Bentham together give *Milton's God* a certain clarity and honesty'; but, his review went on, severely though with some justice:

Unhindered by a knowledge of seventeenth-century or other Christian theology and biblical exegesis, he is able to conclude that Milton worked recalcitrantly, although necessarily, with the God of Moses, but left Him much better than he found Him and anticipated the day when He would abdicate His throne to become Spinoza's God of total immanence.[99]

It does indeed seem far-fetched for Empson to have conceived the idea that the Christian God might consign his status to that of an invisible, albeit material, soul; or even that, as Dr W. R. Matthews (Dean of St Paul's) put it, 'Milton could consciously abandon the dogma of the immutability of God.'[100] Only by divesting Milton's lines of their allusion could he have drawn such a happy lesson.

Be that interpretative mishap as it may, Empson's belief that Christianity should die of its own destructive element went hand in hand with his genuine desire for a more generous scheme of life and death – not with scoffing at any possible religious values. It entailed too his conviction that Christianity had exercised a withering effect upon literary interpretation, insultingly reducing to pious paradox all too many productions of complex mental struggle – whether metaphysical poetry (number 35), Coleridge's the 'Ancient Mariner' (number 40), or Yeats's *Byzantium* poems – and so robbing them of the largest part of their human and poetic value. 'The Neo-Christian method of literary criticism leads to large and unpleasant misinterpretations,' he alleged. In place of the self-serving personal theocracy of Christianity, therefore, he advanced his interest in a religious scheme with a longer and more beneficent history – a scheme in which man humbly perceives himself as being at the service of the cosmos. Interestingly enough, this benign and unbigoted conception figures in Empson's thinking as early as 1935, in 'The Use of Poetry': 'all thoughtful egotists come to disbelieve in the individual. The event, not the person, is alone and unique and includes

the universe in itself' (number 62). As against the common critical view that
Empson's examination of religion was a post-war departure from his early
work on semantics and society, his central concern with ethical values is
likewise adumbrated in *Some Versions of Pastoral*, as the *TLS* review perceived in 1935: '[Pastoral] is, in fact, though he does not say this explicitly,
a form of the religious idea – a means of pitting the ideal creatively against
the real.'[101] It was actually in Japan at the very beginning of the 1930s that
he first felt drawn to a quasi-Buddhist faith in a Spirit of Nature, even then
opposing it to the Christian God who purported to resolve the contradiction of being both loving redeemer and triumphant torturer.

The problem for the critical reception of Empson has been that he invariably intimated his positive proposals so much less prominently (in occasional reviews and letters) in comparison with his overt vilification of the
Christian God that readers could be forgiven for seeing him as exclusively
negativistic. Only by reading the present fuller collection of his essays and
occasional writings is it possible to appreciate just how strongly the plus
counterbalances the minus. In the letters included under 'Resurrection'
(number 113), for example, he writes: 'I did not say [the Father] was bad
because he created the world, and I think that idea a disgusting one ... The
world is equally good whether made by a personal God or not.' Likewise, in
response to S. G. F. Brandon's account of the tortuous teachings of Church
history cited above, he observes in 'Heaven and Hell' (number 115), 'The
difference between right and wrong does not depend upon an arbitrary decision by a divine tyrant,' while posing as a corollary this fundamental
question: 'Why is it always taken for granted that the belief in life after
death (always a very strained thing) actually produced better behaviour?' –
for his study of Buddhism had alerted him to the redeeming fact that 'the
Chinese mind habitually winced away from the belief that there had to be a
personal lawgiver before the laws of Nature, at all their levels, could exist,
with at their summit the Natural Law of man' (number 107).

The Western world frequently takes the conception of a 'Divine Ground'
as eccentric because absurdly unconventional, Empson knew; it seems little
more than a fad imported from beyond its narrow cultural ken. But he
found authoritative grounds for believing that such a faith threaded prehistory, the Renaissance and the Romantic movement. 'The Active Universe',
dating from 1963, provides sound historical evidence for that belief, along
with his personal testimony and a philosophical and ecological aspiration
that is as relevant today as it was in the beginning:

The doctrine that Nature is a spirit peopled by spirits was a return to the science of
the Renaissance, which made real discoveries by using it ...
    The assertions about Nature were thus partly an allegory about human affairs,
but they become trivial if viewed as that only. We are nowadays inclined to resist

them as being too rosy, not realising that the rosy side of them was intended as a defiance to the torture-worship inherent in Christianity.... It looks as though the race of man needs a feeling of being accepted by the universe, such as is immensely conveyed by Shelley, if it is to live with mental health or perhaps survive at all in the world presented by modern science. [number 41]

From the early 1950s to the end, he consistently pursued this point – that mankind should seek not for transcendence but for conciliation with the universe. The proposition is continuous with the underlying message of *Some Versions of Pastoral*, that (as Guy Hunter discerned in a contemporary review) 'the simple man in touch with Nature somehow knows everything.' Hunter went on pertinently: 'This book, to use the terminology of Dr Richards's *Science and Poetry* (which is very relevant here) is the Scientific View criticising the Magical View.'[102] Some twenty years later Empson recovered ancient wisdom as the best available answer to the modern crisis.

[The Chinese] insisted on an organic approach to Nature, and this (whether or not 'scientific humanism' is a suitable term) will be found the only philosophy tolerable to man in the world he is discovering. ['The Wisdom of the East', number 107]

Just over twenty years later again, in 1976, he observed about *The Epic of Gilgamesh* (number 89) that 'The desire to find some kind of relation between civilised man and wild Nature ... lies at the heart of the whole story...' And there again, he discovered, Western readers need to be ticked off for glossing an alien and – as far as he was concerned – superior ethos by the nasty measure of Christian ethics: 'An obstinate determination may be observed among commentators on the epic to make the gods act on moral grounds, so that the sufferings of men are punishments for their sins... This mean-minded line of moralising runs through the schools of English Literature like a plague...'

In place of the Christian quest for a personal immortality vouchsafed by an 'all-executive Father', Empson thus advocated a longer-standing and more selfless tradition in which the individual is accommodated to an infinite impersonality – the 'world-spirit'. While 'neo-Christian' critics may often annex literature to an illiberal orthodoxy, however, Empson was not always innocent of the temptation to read into a text his own kind of 'moral freedom'. An incidental but telling example – telling because it illustrates his urgent desire to liberate literature from the bonds of Christian convention – is a private dispute that he undertook with Alan Rudrum in 1973 over the meaning of Henry Vaughan's poem 'The Water-fall', which I quote in part:

> Why should frail flesh doubt any more
> That what God takes, he'll not restore?
> ...

> What sublime truths, and wholesome themes,
> Lodge in thy mystical, deep streams!
> Such as dull man can never find
> Unless that Spirit lead his mind,
> Which first upon thy face did move,
> And hatched all with his quickening love.
> As this loud stream's incessant fall
> In streaming rings restagnates all,
> Which reach by course the bank, and then
> Are no more seen, just so pass men.
> O my invisible estate,
> My glorious liberty, still late!
> Thou are the channel my soul seeks,
> Not this with cataracts and creeks.

The contretemps arose when Professor Rudrum (who was then editing the *Complete Poems* for Penguin) happened to mention to Empson the curious case of the word 'restagnates', for which the *Oxford English Dictionary* cites this instance as the first known example. Rudrum authoritatively interprets the poem as a metaphorical depiction of 'the processes of life which lead inevitably to death',[103] but Empson's detailing of likely logical senses for 'restagnates' led him to offer this unconventional and grander reading, which is in harmony with his re-appropriating purposes in general:

The poem of course uses the water-cycle of the planet as a kind of proof of human immortality; we need not fear 'that what God takes, he'll not restore'. But Vaughan was sticking his neck out here, because this analogy, that the soul returns to its source as the raindrops to the sea, had always been used for a heretical opinion, that the individual is reabsorbed into the Absolute, as in Hinduism or the perennial 'advanced thought' of Europe (see Norman Cohn, *The Pursuit of the Millennium*). Marlowe at the end of *Faustus* makes the hero try to escape hell with it. Maybe Donne, who was clearly interested in the Radical Reformers but very leery of them, avoided the belief on this ground. (It implies Reincarnation but no permanent self.)

However, there is no sign that Vaughan feels any tension about it, as a heresy. He seems to regard it as the minimum belief in immortality, such as we might expect Nature to teach us, not entailing the rejection of a more ambitious addition; this I should expect was usual among hermeticists. And so he would not feel any need for a deep ambiguity about the matter, as in suggesting that a man's experience after death may be stagnation.[104]

IV

The reading public 'is less easily frightened than bored', Empson observed in 1955 (number 15). Notwithstanding the fact that he occasionally over-stepped the mark, Empson's mission to rescue literature from what he called the 'Unnaturalists' (see number 117) otherwise showed consistent in-tegrity, generosity and courage. The finest authors, he argued, should always be given credit for having engaged in a rational struggle with real issues of conscience. It is demeaning for putatively 'Christian' critics to arrogate the complex conflicts and the independence of mind at work in any poetry to the pietistic paradoxes of their religious views. 'The jeers of the orthodox at the religious sentiments of the free-thinkers have long seemed to me the kind of bad propaganda that comes from bad feelings,' he justly commented in 1952 (number 8); and three years later, in 'Still the Strange Necessity' (number 11): 'The idea that a piece of writing which ex-cited moral resistance might be a discovery in morals, a means of learning what was wrong with the existing system ... has often happened.'

Just as it is essential to meet scientific developments with moral self-revaluation (as he believed Donne must have done) – since anything less would mean a blind determination to preserve cultural fictions in the face of facts which could well gainsay them – so it seemed to Empson that some modes of behaviour can convey truths which are neglected only because they appear to infringe religious or social customs. Convention outlaws them simply because they cannot be countenanced within the terms of its own provisionality. At any rate, the crimes of one age are always in the pro-cess of becoming part of the acknowledged ordinariness of another, as history shows us – quite apart from the consideration that other cultures have regarded as altogether natural and traditional some acts which have been forbidden in the West (and vice versa). At a time when homosexual practices, for instance, were liable to criminal prosecution, W. H. Auden believed in his homosexuality as a moral good – even after he had joined the Christian Church. 'Because it is through you that God has chosen to show me my beatitude,' he wrote to his lover on Christmas Day, 1941 – with what once would have sounded like blasphemy but now like the highest love – 'As this morning I think of the Godhead, I think of you.'[105]

For a man who is unable to accept the moral ideas of his society, Empson had argued in the early 1930s ('Alice in Wonderland: The Child as Swain', *Some Versions of Pastoral*), to base his dissent on intellectual dishonesty is 'to short-circuit it'. Oscar Wilde and his associates, for example, must be seen as what Empson calls 'slavish': 'By their very hints that they deserved notice as sinners they pretended to accept all the moral ideas of society, because they wanted to succeed in it, and yet society only took them seriously because they were connected with an intellectual movement which refused to accept some of those ideas.'[106] *Épater le bourgeois*: that was not Empson's aim at all, merely to reckon with the fact that one of the

supreme values of literary endeavour – like the act of scientific discovery –
is 'precisely that of stepping outside preconceptions' (to use a phrase he
employed in a review dating from 1930).[107] As he reminded his readers in
1963, 'the highest event in ethics' is 'the moral discovery, which gets a man
called a traitor by his own society' (number 55).

In the early essay 'Death and Its Desires' (1933), he points out:

There is a very nice postage-stamp collection of perversions in Romantic poetry by
Mario Praz called *The Romantic Agony*, but it is prevented from being anything
more important, I think, by its reproving tone. Also he is convinced that the
appearance of perversions in literature is something peculiar to nineteenth-century
romanticism, an idea which ... is in any case untrue. The critic who takes a Freudian point of view is in the opposite difficulty: there is so much perversion at the
back of the normal, and so much oddity about the position of the artist in particular, that there seems no way of deciding what version of a perversion is to be
admired. [number 95]

Empson did not draw the conclusion that whatever is, is natural and therefore good. The fact that unorthodoxy, in life as in art, can still be moral and
in certain circumstances acceptable is the paradoxical truth to be understood. 'One rough principle can be invoked to avoid portentousness,' he
argued (re-invoking a kind of Humean critical consensus):

work known to be good by the critics influenced by a fairly long series of changing
fashions is not going to be spoilt by being explained. The combination of Freudian
understanding and puritan sentiments is liable to be a paralysing one... To say
that the 'Ode to a Nightingale' involves death wishes and the 'Ode on Melancholy'
masochism, or that Shakespeare uses the language of love about the pleasures of
fighting, is to point out what was always on the surface; a psychoanalysis of the
authors would not show why generations of various readers have found these versions of these perversions noble and sensible.

Another of the early essays, 'The Ideal of the Good' (number 96), surveys
the ethical schemes which man has proposed to himself as providing ultimate satisfaction. It begins by disputing La Rochefoucauld's assertion (in
the *Maximes*) that human actions are inevitably selfish: 'a noble mind
never wishes to make claims that its acts are truly generous, but is concerned to see all the possible sources of satisfaction in a given situation,'
Empson comments.

A more scientific theory was provided by the Marquis de Sade, whose disciple Swinburne gives evidence about the effects of the theory when put into action as literature. This theory treats the lust to inflict pain on others as fundamental, as the idea
in terms of which a complex affair should be analysed and understood. Swinburne
cannot set out to describe passion felt between even ordinary lovers ... without
dragging in the tortures that they inflict on each other:

> By the lips intertwisted and bitten
> Till the foam has a savour of blood
>
> ['Dolores', ll. 115–16]

is the centre of his invocation of the Queen of Passion. Of course it is not the perversion as such which one cocks one's eye at. If they both liked it (and many couples do like a reasonable amount of biting) they are only giving each other a nice time. The question is rather what they think radically nice; whatever the means, what is the end.

After next discussing the moral implications both of Darwinian evolutionism (much misunderstood as a theory advocating that struggle and survival are themselves the only good: 'There is a large background of wilfulness, obviously, to the moral theories derived from the biology') and of Freudian theory – from which he deduces that Freudian 'healing' is concerned only with the disappointingly negative work of effecting 'release from torment', not with providing a new ideal of the good – Empson draws on to consider the practicality of theories of value when one comes to the question of sleep. 'To get to sleep you must ... in some moderate degree have reached a state of permanent satisfaction.'

'How do Swinburne's biters get to sleep?' he asks simply:

No doubt if they both enjoyed it they can go to sleep not only satisfied but proud; feeling 'My word, I've given this girl a good time – she's almost bitten to rags' and so forth. The fundamental pleasure to which they sink back, in such an arrangement, is a feeling of pride in their own generosity ...

Bearing in mind that he loved Swinburne's poetry while deploring sadism,[108] Empson exercises fundamental common sense to resolve an apparent contradiction:

Much fuss has been made about the idea that the primitive instincts of sex are fundamentally brutal ... the desire to please is not a brutal thing. Pure sadism, in the sense of only wanting the partner to suffer, is not an outbreak of the primitive but a very specialised form of disease. It should not therefore, it seems to me, be regarded as a fundamental thing in terms of which you interpret a more complex situation ... I am not pretending that the mental disease of pure sadism does not occur; I am arguing that it needs to be analysed into other terms and not treated as fundamental.

His proper discrimination between the infliction of pain where it might give welcome satisfaction and the exercise of sadistic feelings (a mental disease) provides an important index of his sense of relative value. His procedure is not simply to dismiss sadism as an unthinkable perversion but open-mindedly to allow for and analyse different standards of conduct.

His straightforwardly modest conclusion to the question of what mankind really does want and value is that we cannot separate 'the good in

action' from 'the absolute good in peace' – for both are inextricably necessary in the final analysis. 'It seems to me that they have a more practical connection than they appear to do, and that the ideal which stands up to both
criteria is the humble but not irreligious absolute good of affection and
good humour on a basis of adequate mutual respect.'

'Really heroic love is superior to social convention,' Empson wrote in
1935.[109] His determination to challenge orthodoxy drew him so far as to
commend as positively good certain activities which society traditionally
regards as outrageous. For example, early in the 1950s – and certainly
before the flower children took to acting out William Blake's book – he
praised the virtue of a kind of 'free love' on the ground that it expressed a
noble selflessness. He found his occasion for articulating such an apparently 'advanced' theory in reviewing the poetry of Rochester (number 36):

> his attitude to [pleasure] has a heartwarming generosity. Humanly speaking, his ob-
> scenity is the most moral thing about him, indeed the chief thing that appears
> obscene is that he will have no nonsense about jealousy at all. The excuse for leav-
> ing his mistress ... rises ... into a splendidly gay picture of universal kindness,
> which really does treat her as a goddess ... He praises pleasure as a philosopher,
> whose serious opinion is that it makes people kind to each other. There is enough
> truth in this, especially after wars of religion, to have a startling moral weight.

The philosophical model he had in mind was a Benthamite utilitarianism.
But he was never so irresponsible as to champion an unfelt and glib libertinism: he would certainly have searched his own conscience before deciding
that simple logic alone would serve to derive such an example of 'practical
kindness' from an otherwise theoretical position. Still, he could validly
argue, Christianity has no monopoly on morality, which is as various as the
world is wide. 'Some Christians have claimed that their religion invented
benevolence, which is absurd,' he wrote in 1952; 'but it is not insane like
this Neotheory, that a Christian has to reprobate benevolence as a form of
libidinousness' (number 8).

He extended the same argument to his consideration of James Joyce's
purposes in writing *Ulysses* (numbers 83–85), which he saw as featuring an
'unacceptable ideal'. The apparent paradox of Empson's phrase makes
sense in terms of his full analysis of the true story of the novel, according to
which the character Bloom endeavours to negotiate an ultimately happy
Eternal Triangle – a *ménage à trois* with Stephen and Molly. In one of his
uncollected trial essays on Joyce, Empson pointed to the critically indisput-
able fact that 'the notes written by Joyce to advise himself how to write the
play *Exiles* ... show that he regarded the Consenting Triangle as an exalted and progressive ideal.'[110] Knowingly running the risk of scandalising
narrow-minded readers, Empson associated himself with Joyce's putative

opinion in interpreting such a sexual triangle as a worthy object – as being practicable and proper between mutually respecting partners, not as unconscionable. Christian legalism and social custom may reprehend it, but that does not make it fundamentally wrong – especially when the arrangement may serve 'the good in action and the absolute good in peace'. Wittgenstein wrote in 1921, 'What we cannot speak about we must pass over in silence,' but of course he was referring to pure conjecture rather than moral prohibition; he also wrote: 'What is thinkable is possible too.'[111] Empson represents his interpretation of *Ulysses* as a form of moral idealism, not perverse inclination; and as such it stands in the respectable tradition of utopianism. Plato's *Republic*, the origin of that tradition, ventured the morally progressive view that citizens of the state should go shares with each other in wives. Wives ought to be held in common (*koina*), Socrates argues, for the sake of the amity and unity of the association, and to remove temptations to selfishness and to rivalry between individuals. Aristotle, in his *Politics*, found Plato's idealism wanting in the face of his own partial scepticism, but he could scarcely impugn Plato's motive – only the apparent naivety of his nobility of mind.

Empson's more extended discussion of Joyce's intentions in writing *Ulysses* ('The Ultimate Novel', in *Using Biography*) argues that Joyce most likely 'thought the happy triangle a noble ideal, and tried to arrange one'; that for Bloom to offer Stephen his wife shows a generous confidence in its being 'a good action'; and that Joyce's evident impatience with moralistic fussing about adultery clearly means that he intended to recommend 'an advanced or permissive attitude to sex' – all of which matches the Platonic ideal and is far from advocating shocking libertinism. The aim is 'something homely and practical', Empson points out; and he cites in support of his argument the fact that Shakespeare's sonnets, the most notable literary *exempla*, 'report the only happy triangle in literature'. 'Why then does the book make a secret of it?' Empson pertinently asks. 'Because the procedure which it regards as an innocent act of charity is heavily penalised by the law.'[112]

While Hugh Kenner among other critics regards this interpretation of the novel as an improper allegation (as he knew),[113] Empson considered his exposition of its secret story in no way a slander on Joyce; rather, it was entirely to his credit; 'he would believe the practice to be quite usual, though treated with absurd secrecy...' Empson was concerned with rescuing, not damaging, Joyce's reputation; and he thought it 'a high-minded thing' for him to present 'a current problem' – 'a blow for freedom'.[114] The Consenting Triangle is therefore to be seen as generous and innocuous.

'No wonder critics find the book sordid and gloomy,' he observed, 'if the hopeful and high-minded side of it must at all cost be ignored' (number 85);

and in a letter of 9 March 1970 to Darcy O'Brien, a Joyce scholar who contested his reading, he elaborated upon the invigorating unconventionality of his ironic idealism:

the whole elaborate structure of the book, let alone the special psychology given to each of the three main characters, becomes pointless unless it [is] allowed to concentrate and interpret itself, as by a sudden revelation, upon making this great hope seem evidently possible even if hallucinatingly so, a 'complete solution'. Joyce was still near enough to the imagining of this great happiness to make a good book out of it, even though a sad one. ... I can have no patience with the pretence that this kind of happiness does not often occur, is not genuine, must be some nasty madness. Even less can I agree that Joyce expresses despair with life on earth and therefore a self-abandonment to the priests of the loathsome Christian torture-monster.[115]

As if by reflex, the letter (like so many of his writings from the 1950s onwards) links his insistence upon critical generosity with his need to defy any narrow – and specifically Christian – creed of life and value. 'I am afraid that nothing can purge Christianity of the Father who was satisfied by the Crucifixion,' he states in 'The Cult of Unnaturalism' (number 117); 'an impersonal Divine Ground, as in Aldous Huxley's *Perennial Philosophy*, is the only Supreme Being who can be worshipped without moral shame.' And in the same piece he makes this countercharge against anyone who might accuse him of taking improper licence in his revaluations: 'The books which ought to be banned for obscenity are those which pander to sadism, but what can you expect from a state religion whose symbol is a torture?'

V

'In the year when I. A. Richards was tutoring me [at Magdalene College],' Empson recalled in 1966,

some of my friends at Cambridge (especially James Smith, who wrote well in the early volumes of *Scrutiny*) thought that his 'scientism' was philosophically very absurd, and I could usually, after my weekly hour with Richards, go and tell them some particularly absurd thing he had said. They of course were following T. S. Eliot, early members of the neo-Christian movement. I really was much influenced by Richards, but I thought it proper to learn from both sides, and would probably have said that I was on the side opposed to him. I am not sure when I decided that he had been quite right. In 1939, after being robbed in Chicago on my way from China to England, I was kindly given work writing radio scripts in favour of Basic English for Richards on the station WRUL [Boston], so that I could pay the boat fare and repay the very generous loan of Auden, made when repayment seemed impossible. Chatting in a script about why the word LIFE, among others, was not in the Basic 850, I said the word was liable to rhetorical misuse, and offered some mild examples. I was surprised when Richards came back very indignant, and distinctly Welsh as he becomes at such times, saying that this kind of stuff must be stopped at once. The stench of an ill-cured saintly relic was what I had preferred, very disgustingly, to Nature. I thought he was quite right to be firm about it, and felt rather surprised that I was still copying out fallacies at random from the death-worshippers. This moment perhaps, ten years later, was when I positively chose the side of 'scientism', though it wasn't till I began teaching in a Christian country that I realised the active harm done by the religion.[116]

The burden of his talk on 'LIFE' can be given in the following extracts:

For about ten years after the end of 'War I' there was a great time for the religion of life. LIFE, the brightest persons would say, is good. Respect for LIFE is our religion ... But it is seriously a strange thing that this form of words 'LIFE is good, LIFE is our religion' seemed to these able and expert writers even to have any sense. The ideals of good and bad are very wide ones. Pain is a bad thing even to the smallest bit of living jelly. But still good and bad even in their widest use have no sense at all if not used about living beings. If then I say 'LIFE is good,' in the only simple sense of my words it is like saying 'All colours are white.' That is, any person able to get the sense of the statement is conscious before reading it that it is untrue ... In what possible way might they have been giving a narrow base sense to the word LIFE?

It is soon clear in reading them that the good sort of LIFE is natural. And it is quite clear after a short walk round the word 'natural' that this is true in all sorts of ways, deeply true, and at the same time full of tricks and dangers ... Now I have to go on saying all the time that the judging of persons in these books is probably quite right. It is not foolish talk at all. It comes from a great amount of knowledge, though maybe about a narrow group of persons. But at the same time it is some sort of religion. And in making a religion it is necessary to give some sort of sense to your key words ... When you are looking at these writers from a Basic point of view, that is, looking at the sense of their key words, what is true about them seems so bad that it is not possible. And maybe it is not. They are in fact writing about political questions all the time that they say they are writing about LIFE, and saying that LIFE is good. But if that is true, still they are putting their political ideas in an unnecessarily mixed form ...

It is no pleasure to be saying all this. What made me get started on this bit of writing was simply the news of the death of Laurence Housman, at last. And 'at last' here has this sense – he had been keeping himself living and working for the last ten years by being interested and strong and by having no fear, and that was what seemed to him his religion of LIFE ... So it seems probable that there is after all some sense in this form of words. But I am not able to see any sense in it that would not be so strange and complex that it would make a very bad working religion. [Empson Papers]

In a scribbled note to Empson, Richards in fact put three glosses on what he would have regarded as the deplorable senses of the word 'life' which made Laurence Housman's 'sort of view (and religion) possible'. Empson must have taken the first two as crucial enough to check his dallying with a dangerously religious sense of the word:

1. *Life* as the process of the coming into being of a God.
2. *Life* as the highest form of organisation (i.e. dependence within a system of one part of it on another). 'Highest' because the parts are more dependent and in more ways. And so the system is more *one*. Life makes *units* out of less connected bits. [Empson Papers]

Any full account of Empson's critical career should really begin and end with I. A. Richards, for his career constitutes in many ways a fifty-year debate, and sometimes indeed a dispute, with his mentor. Commentators on the couple often seem to assume that the lines of influence all run in one direction, from Richards to Empson, but it should be said that in all his writings after 1930 Richards is constantly responding to Empson's published and private views, and attempting to adjust his own position by definition against Empson's. Richards had argued in *Science and Poetry* (1926), for example, that 'thought is not the prime factor' in poetry. 'Misunderstanding and under-estimation of poetry are mainly due to over-insistence on the thought in separation from the rest ... It is never what a poems *says* which matters, but what it *is*.'[117] The latter assertion is a variant of Archibald MacLeish's 'poeticised' dictum that 'A poem should not mean / But be', which (as I have already discussed) Empson deplored for its bland irrationalism. Much of Empson's early criticism worked to heal the rupture Richards seemed to have introduced between sense and emotion. In literature, Empson wrote elsewhere, 'the medium is close to the discursive reason, and to cut them apart is unnatural.'[118] Making shifts between moral philosophy and the psychology both of creativity and of reader-response, the terminology of Richards's first writings truly begged as many questions as it asserted answers: it varied even in its own references. In *The Structure of Complex Words* Empson observed, for example, 'The trouble I think is that Professor Richards conceives the Sense of the word in a given use as something single, however "elaborate", and therefore thinks that anything beyond that Sense has got to be explained in terms of feelings, and feelings of course are Emotions, or Tones. But much of what appears to us as a "feeling" (as is obvious in the case of a complex metaphor) will in fact be quite an elaborate structure of related meanings. The mere fact that we can talk straight ahead and get the grammar in order shows that we must be doing a lot more rational planning about the process of talk than we have to notice in detail' (pp. 56–57). Richards commented on the fly-leaf of his own copy of Empson's book: 'Disagreements with IAR? e.g. pp. 56–57. These seem, in the theoretic chapters (1 & 2) to be well worth study. My feeling is that W. E. is almost always right in dissenting from what he takes I. A. R. to be saying, but nearly invariably wrong about that. In many instances, the two seem to be trying to say much the same thing in different ways. In others, some chance phrase of mine leads him to suppose in me a view I would violently disown...'[119] Empson can scarcely be blamed for some of his misunderstandings.[120] Richards had been 'slightly wrong' in making a distinction between the affective and the referential modes of language, Empson later explained in an indulgently understated letter, and he himself had 'intended to restore the unity ... What Richards and I both recognised was that analysis must be able [to] say when language is used dishonestly, as when a demagogue attempts to cheat his hearers by exploiting the emotive uses of words so as to prevent them from following up the referential uses.'[121] In any event, Richards's unstable early rhetoric had been a tremendous irritant to the younger Empson; as Christopher Norris has observed in a fine recent essay, *The Structure of Complex Words* was assuredly his 'full-scale rejoinder to Richards on the topic of language, poetry and truth'.[122]

But the full story of Empson's reciprocal relationship with Richards must be told in another place. Notwithstanding, the point of departure for several of the pieces in the present volume is Richards's so-called 'Theory of Value'. Empson's endless responsiveness to the theory links the final chapter of *Seven Types of Ambiguity* and 'A Doctrine of Aesthetics' (1949), for example, as well as 'Death and Its Desires' (1933) and 'Literary Criticism and the Christian Revival' (1966). 'Nothing less than our whole sense of man's history and destiny is involved in our final decision as to value,' Richards wrote in *Principles of Literary Criticism* (1924) – a claim which Empson implicitly heeded throughout his career. 'To set up as a critic is to set up as a judge of values ... For the arts are an appraisal of existence,' he added in a ringing challenge.[123] His theory of value concerned itself centrally with what he called 'the effort to attain maximum satisfaction through coherent systematisation' – 'the systematisation of impulses'.[124] Positive impulses he termed 'appetencies', and anything which worked to satisfy such impulses must be regarded as good or valuable. The full and ordered life necessarily maximised its varied satisfactions and minimised suppression and sacrifice. Given such a goal, the individual's accession to a life replete with self-realisation and self-knowledge, poetry must take up the role of religion for the modern world. Poetry's intrinsic, vital and self-justifying function is to engender 'the best life ... that in which as much as possible of our possible personality is engaged'.[125] In short, poetry fulfils itself in creating mental and moral health. In *The Foundations of Aesthetics* (1922; written in collaboration with C. K. Ogden and James Wood), Richards had taken the term 'synaesthesis' to stand for the state of equilibrium and harmony thus engendered, for 'A complete systematisation must take the form of such an adjustment as will preserve free play to every impulse, with entire avoidance of frustration.' Equilibrium 'brings into play all our faculties ... Through no other experience can the full richness and complexity of our environment be realised. The ultimate value of equilibrium is that it is better to be fully than partially alive.'[126]

Despite the evident frailties of his rhetoric in such writings, Richards more or less retained the theory of impulses in his later criticism. At the first, Empson seemed staunch in his loyalty, claiming without further exploration in 1930 that Richards had 'produced a workable theory of aesthetic value' (number 22). But he actually registered misgivings from an early stage, and by 1937 reserved judgement in characterising it as 'a police theory [which] helps you to stop the narrower theories from obstructing your practice' (number 24). Then by 1950, in 'The Verbal Analysis' (number 7), he seemed momentarily to surrender his faith to scepticism:

I do not deny that it may be a splendid thing to have a grand synthesis of human experience, a single coherent Theory of Value which could be applied to all works of art and presumably to all human situations; but it seems hardly reasonable to grumble, in the present state of affairs, that nobody has provided one; and if it did exist it would clearly be a philosophical synthesis rather than a literary one.

Yet earlier in the same piece he proposed his own practice of the 'depth analysis' of poetry as 'probably the best way out of this limiting critical impasse' – the impasse created by

the idea that poetry is good in proportion as it is complicated, or simply hard to construe; it seems quite a common delusion, and always shocks me when expressed. And yet I suppose it is very near my own position; in any case it joins on to I. A. Richards's Theory of Value as the satisfaction of more impulses rather than less, and T. S. Eliot's struggle to find a poetic idiom adequate to the complexity of modern life.

Among the many problems posed by Richards's epistemology is the precise meaning of the term 'impulse'. Is the concept psychological or philosophical? Has it to do with poetic creativity or reception theory? 'The impulse theory provides no real explanation of the genesis or nature of attitudes,' Jerome P. Schiller has lamented. 'It simply assures us that Richards believed them to be central to the reading of poetry.'[127] Empson proposed to put his own qualms directly to Richards in 1933 (in an undated draft version of the letter included under 'Death and Its Desires', number 95): 'I don't understand whether an impulse is defined as physiological or not. If it is I don't understand what its satisfaction is.' More recently again, John Needham has pointed out the grave deficiency of the general Theory of Value when it is applied to poetry:

Richards himself seems to be implicitly aware of the difficulty, because when he is presenting his general theory of value he talks straightforwardly of the 'satisfaction of appetencies', but when he is applying it to poetry he uses, not 'satisfaction', but words like 'balancing', 'reconciliation', 'adjustment', 'resolution', and so on ... 'Impulse', as he defines it, is a useful term for Richards because it enables him, albeit unjustifiably, to slide from stimulus to response and back again as the needs of the moment dictate; but it brings him into intolerable difficulties. As his insights into the complexity of poetic *language* develop, he has to re-formulate the general theory of complexity in terms of a creative account of the mind, rather than a stimulus-response account.[128]

Richards did indeed appear to believe (at least initially) that literary criticism was merely an auxiliary mode of psychology. Such a presupposition would go far to explain his own neglect of close critical analyses in his writings. (It assuredly incited Empson to make good the neglect in his own precise attention to language and meaning in poetry.) In *Practical Criticism* in particular, as Needham rightly regrets, 'the doctrine of equilibrium inhibits a fruitful development of Richards's work on poetic language.'[129]

According to the Theory of Value, poetry – which Richards later exalted as 'the supreme organ of the mind's self-ordering growth'[130] – can literally 'save' us: it will replace religion by relegating any magical view of the world and enthroning a fundamental secularism. Richards arrived at this doctrine by way of a distinction already mentioned – between the language employed for enunciating true beliefs (essentially, scientific verities) and the language of poetry, which comprises 'pseudo-statements'. Pseudo-statements are 'not necessarily false', he explained, but 'merely a form of words whose scientific truth or falsity is irrelevant to the purpose in hand'.[131] Thus his argument runs:

Countless pseudo-statements – about God, about the universe, about human nature, the relations of mind to mind, about the soul, its rank and destiny – pseudo-statements which are pivotal points in the organisation of the mind, vital to its well-being, have suddenly become, for sincere, honest and informed minds, impossible to believe as for centuries they have been believed ...

This is the contemporary situation. The remedy ... is to cut our pseudo-statements free from that kind of belief which is appropriate to verified statements. So released they will be changed, of course, but they can still be the main instruments by which we order our attitudes to one another and to the world.[132]

In short, belief in God (for example) is far less actual than figural. T. S. Eliot deprecated this secular salvationism as a boss shot; it seemed to him hardly more than a revival of Matthew Arnold's views on literature and dogma – 'it is like saying that the wallpaper will save us when the walls have crumbled.' But strangely enough, even though that sharp simile might appear to dismiss Richards's aberration, Eliot conceded earlier in the same review of *Science and Poetry* that the theory is probably quite true. Nevertheless it is only one aspect; it is a psychological theory of value, but we must also have a moral theory of value. The two are incompatible, but both must be held, and that is just the problem. If I believe, as I do believe, that the chief distinction of man is to glorify God and enjoy Him for ever, Mr Richards's theory of value is inadequate: my advantage is that I can believe my own and his too, whereas he is limited to his own.[133]

Not surprisingly, Empson felt baffled by Eliot's claim that he could readily accommodate both his own faith in the transcendent truths of his religion and a doctrine of value which to all intents and purposes profaned it.

Empson accordingly sought to strengthen the foundations of the doctrine, to stop the holes in Richards's rhetoric of assertion (and hence in his theory), and he believed he could best do so by challenging it. If it makes any sort of claim to universal validity, he felt, Richards's argument for a humanistic standard of valuation – which amounted to an argument for irreligion – must be capable of accounting for other cultures and religions. When Richards judged that traditional beliefs about God and destiny should properly be levelled to the status of pseudo-statements, for example, he had clearly fixed his sights on the Christian conception of Heaven. Empson publicly, though sympathetically, put in question the effectively wholesale anti-religiosity of that judgement by way of the wider angle of his first Appendix to *The Structure of Complex Words*. '"Theories of Value" is a brilliant essay,' Empson's bibliographer Frank Day has rightly suggested, 'broad in understanding and eloquent in expression. It is one of the best things Empson has written and deserves to be more widely discussed, especially by those interested in Stanley Fish's notion of interpretive communities. Unless one insists that a value system has to be externally grounded – as I suppose [Hugh] Kenner does – ... then Empson's rational appeal to community should be esteemed for its avoidance of egoism. If it's ultimately judged to be a sleight-of-hand trick in logic, then it's at least as convincing a magic show as any other under the big tent.'[134]

Since he was in Japan from 1931 to 1934 when he first started working towards 'Theories of Value', Empson found it both convenient and fascinating to submit Richards's theory to the best local test, the Buddhist religion. He argues that the construction nowadays put upon the concept of Nirvana – that it stands for 'a re-absorption into the Absolute' (exactly the same alternative to the Christian concept of godhead for which he argued from the 1950s onwards) –

brings [Buddhism] into line with a mystical strain within all the great religions, one which has usually been at loggerheads with the offer of Heaven; and there I think we find the great historical antagonist of anything like the Richards Theory of Value – that is, of any self-fulfilment theory. It is opposed to any such theory not because it is pessimistic but because it does not believe in the individual. I cannot pretend that I have any capacity to act as a go-between in this quarrel. ... if the Theory of Value merely recommends the satisfaction of the human creature, whatever makes it really satisfied, Professor Richards need not be as secure against the religions as he intended to be. What satisfied the most impulses might turn out to be the same as what was to the glory of God or even as what tended to Nirvana.[135]

There is ultimately 'something of a notional Buddhism lurking in Empson's strenuously rational humanism', Harold Beaver has observed in a notable essay.[136] Indeed; and one of the aspects of Buddhism that he particularly favoured – as 'Death and Its Desires' (number 95) makes clear in its preliminary expatiation on the arguments of 'Theories of Value' – was what he called its 'rationalising escape from the fear of death [which] is carried so far that there is much less sense of tragedy and of the fascination of a sacrificial death than in Christianity with its certainly immortal individuals'. If any culture necessarily values the purposes of life by its estimate of the meaning of death, one certain attraction of Buddhism is that it seemed to resolve the paradox of at once doubting immortality and planning for a better life on earth. Buddhist art, it seemed to Empson, expressed just such 'a fundamental contradiction between death and a completely satisfying life'. Even in his 1939 radio broadcast on 'Life' he felt bound to bring up Buddhism as paradoxically the most heartening rival to Christianity – and it is noticeable that on this topic his tone heightens with enthusiasm, and his rhythm seems even to mime the 'Fire Sermon' itself:[137]

This is the teaching that went across all the east of Asia and by only touching a country made it strong. It seemed beautiful, it seemed safe, it seemed a new way of living and a good one and it gave fruit to millions of men. And this is what it said, and it said, 'Death, there is no other possible good thing but death,' and it said that very clearly. The facts about the behaviour of men are very much stranger than they seem to us. And so it is important to say ... that almost all the effects of the Fire Sermon were good effects. For example, hundreds of thousands of men have been burned while still living in the name of Jesus, and probably no man has been so burned in the name of Buddha. But the Buddha said things that gave much more reason for burning, much more hate of common living, much more poison, if you are looking at the simple words, than the words of Christ. But in fact they did no damage. As a question of history, where these words came they did good.

(Because of that extraordinary and indeed amazing paradox, Empson appropriately brings into play in 'Death and Its Desires' the analogous psychological dimension of Freud's proposition in *Beyond the Pleasure Principle* (1920) that *'the end of all life is death'* – a formulation which Freud based on the natural observation that organic life can be seen ironically to desire its own demise: that is, it actually aims at self-extinction.)[138]

What particularly exercised Empson about Richards's Theory of Value was that its best case appeared to hinge on a delicate semantic distinction between 'balance' (or 'equilibrium') and 'deadlock' – as here in *Principles of Literary Criticism*: 'The equilibrium of opposed impulses, which we suspect to be the ground-plan of the most valuable aesthetic responses, brings into play far more of our personality than is possible in experiences of a more defined emotion ... what happens is the exact opposite of a deadlock, for compared to the experience of great poetry every other state of mind is one of bafflement.'[139] Clearly, Empson took the cue for his own conflict theory of poetry from that very concept of an 'equilibrium of opposed impulses'; but he felt vexed that Richards's language appeared to polarise satisfaction and frustration, pleasure and pain, in a way that was linquistically beguiling but scarcely tenable in fact. 'It looks, however, as if there is one chink through which a Buddhist conclusion might creep into the arguments of Professor Richards; his rather mysterious distinction between a deadlock (which is bad) and a balance (which is good),' he wrote in 'Theories of Value'[140] (just as he had written in his late revaluation of *The Foundations of Aesthetics*, number 25). As he phrased his objection in the draft version of his letter of 2 April 1933 – again with reference to the alternative perspective offered by Buddhism –

pain (I understand) is not an essential opposite of pleasure but a separate biological invention. The Buddhist position seems to be that pain is a result as well as cause of pleasure, that pleasure is essentially misleading because it is a creator of desire that eventually leads to pain. But this is mere assertion made convincing by seeming to invoke the removal-of-stimulus idea only (and backed up by transmigration): clearly some people escape from this life (supposing it is their only one) without getting much pain out of their pleasures. (Fatuous these terms are: the air as I write is full of pain and despair from a Russian prostitute being very slowly turned out of the bar – everybody having to collect the money and ornaments she has flung all over the floor, so that she is tremendously in command of the situation.) But if pain is quite separate from pleasure it seems even less likely that the satisfaction and frustration of an impulse are (other things being equal) of equal and opposite value, which is (apparently) needed for your theory.

Even though the Theory of Value was in no sense hedonistic, Richards put it forward in the language of behaviourist psychology and hence made value an essentially unconscious gain. Empson's rational humanism prohibited a state of unknowing; as far as he was concerned, any theory of value must afford a sense of deliberate responsibility – it must strike a fully conscious balance between 'charity and a sense of social values' – for the final criterion is 'more nearly a political one'. By way of obvious logical example, he suggests,

[Behaviourists] would say that having an appetite for dinner, feeling sure you will get it, and getting it, is of negative value (or null as a limit): because a need has been unsatisfied and then merely satisfied after an interval. Obviously there is positive pleasure at both stages. It seems to me that there is positive pleasure in appetite because the creature is (a) conscious (b) capable of knowledge ...

And so follows the crux of his argument – it informs all his writings on poetic and human value, as well as his onslaught against Christianity – 'it is the intellectuality of the creature that turns a state of need into a state of pleasure.'

Empson thus became intent on turning what he regarded as Richards's theory of an essentially passive (because behaviouristic) acquisition of value into a statement of conscious apprehension. 'It seems clear that consciousness is somehow involved in value, because if there was no consciousness we would at any rate feel there was no value,' he declares in the letter of 2 April 1933 (number 95). Nonetheless, although he worried Richards's Theory of Value only in order to make it in every sense more purposeful, he continually endorsed Richards's secular morality – the morality he derived from Jeremy Bentham's concept of the individual as a 'trustee for the community'. Richards's theory of the fullest satisfaction of positive impulses (or 'appetencies') essentially constituted a reprise of Bentham's proposition that some kind of 'moral arithmetic' can determine the value of the pleasurable and the good, which is in itself socially serviceable. He expressed it in this form in *Principles of Literary Criticism:*

the only reason which can be given for not satisfying a desire is that more important desires will thereby be thwarted. Thus morals become purely prudential, and ethical codes merely the expression of the most general scheme of expediency to which an individual or race has attained. ... Particularly is this so with regard to those satisfactions which require humane, sympathetic and friendly relations between individuals. The charge of egoism, or selfishness, can be brought against a naturalistic or utilitarian morality such as this only by overlooking the importance of these satisfactions in any well-balanced life.[141]

Continually seeking to apply such a Helvetian principle in his own life and writings, Empson reaffirmed in 'The Hammer's Ring' (number 26), his 1973 testimonial to Richards, 'The idea of making a calculation to secure the greatest happiness for the greatest number is inherently absurd, but it seems the only picture we can offer.' Among the best reasons for supporting this 'Calculable Value' theory, he believed, is the necessity both to avoid arrogantly self-confirming critical judgements (what Matthew Arnold called the fallacy of the 'personal estimate') – 'the only alternatives to Bentham are arty and smarty moralising; giving unreasoned importance either to a whim of one's own or to the whim of a social clique' – and to appreciate different world-views without cultural prepossession:

The main purpose of reading imaginative literature is to grasp a wide variety of experience, imagining people with codes and customs very unlike our own; and it cannot be done except in a Benthamite manner, that is, by thinking, 'How would such a code or custom work out?'

Thus Kenneth Burke's accusation against Empson that *Milton's God* 'deflects attention from the central relationship between religion and the social order' could hardly be farther from the mark, because Empson's high concern with social morality (evident even in his work of the 1930s, especially in *Some Versions of Pastoral*) led him to repudiate a religion which in his judgement served only to damage a decent sense of life and literature. The Christian God offered man a casuistical contract; whereas for Empson, as Frank Day correctly observed, 'the bedrock of systems of value is human rationality.'[142]

But if putatively Christian critics offended authorial integrity by bleeding works of literature of their rational conflicts and moral resistances, perhaps the worst charge that can be made against Empson is that he too indulged a *parti pris* – making his critical findings a function of his own moral expectations. Where the New Criticism virtually hypostatised the concepts of semantic autonomy and intrinsic value, he insisted upon authorial rationality and critical common sense. If he could not be disinterested, however, he endeavoured always to resist reductivism, whether Christian or New Critical – the constrictions of doctrinaire morality or tidy theory. 'Mr Empson, perhaps, will never elaborate a critical, political or metaphysical system,' Michael Roberts percipiently forecast in 1936.[143] Instinct told him that to enunciate any theory was to impose illogical and unnecessary limits on critical and ethical enquiry. Iconoclastic but never anarchistic, he stood out for the dignity of social order and the prerogative of individual human reason. If he also eschewed the call to proclaim a critical creed, however, reserving to his own practice all the rights of pragmatism, still it can be seen from the bulk of his work that he avows at least an implicit theory of the creative imagination itself. By definition, he judged, the best literature is rationally protestant, often dissentient and rebellious, the expression not of neurosis but of real mental conflict, and it externalises the specific case in a publicly accountable form. Empson's theory (if it is one) thus works to emancipate the human mind from all dogma and to make literature continuous with all human experience.

Various claims and attempts have been made to trace a line of descent from Richards and Empson directly to the New Critics and thence to the recent school of deconstructionists. Professor Carey has commented, 'The vogue for "deconstruction" in the 1970s – regarded at the time as dazzlingly new and French – was basically a rerun of Empson's ideas' (the putative 'ideas' of *Seven Types of Ambiguity*, that is to say); and even Empson's bibliographer, who has weighed both primary and secondary sources, appears to acquiesce in the notion that 'the ingenuity he displayed in jumping at short texts made him, perhaps, a proto-deconstructionist and, at least, a major influence on the New Criticism. This much is hardly disputed by anyone.'[144] If the pyrotechnics of *Ambiguity* gave Empson any cause for regret, however, it would surely have been because commentators took the improvident genius of that book as sufficient in itself to have him sire what he regarded as the pretentious rigour of those very schools of criticism. The New Critics constantly made efforts to call him to order – especially when it seemed to them that he was behaving like the sow eating her own farrow – although he had distinguished his own practice from their doctrines at the earliest possible stage (both his actual criticism and his expressed opinions from the early 1930s onwards prove as much). Cleanth Brooks, in a review of *The Structure of Complex Words*, complained that Empson's 'confusion' and 'inconsistencies' made him 'the incorrigible amateur': Empson explored everything from author-psychology to reader-response and historicism – evidently in a manner that put proper formalist criteria in jeopardy.[145] Empson's reply was impatiently dismissive of the 'artificial elegance' of the New Critical creed: 'What is really being felt by Mr Cleanth Brooks is that a literary critic must behave like a psychologist or whatnot; he must pretend he doesn't know what is ordinary knowledge till he has proved it by his direct analysis of the text before him.'[146]

Were it necessary to make choice of forebear, a stronger case could be made for affiliating the more recent 'readers' to I. A. Richards than to Empson. Ronald Shusterman has in fact argued the case for discerning some real affinities between Richards's seminal theories and both 'reader-response' and 'deconstructive' criticism – largely because the variousness of Richards's terminological formulations and his 'picture of language' unluckily beg continual re-interpretation. 'It is true that the early Richards was vague about what "reconciliation" meant,' Shusterman writes, for example. 'But in his later work he clearly had in mind not a *resolution* of conflict but an *awareness* of it.'[147] Richards's principles can thus be found to coincide with the interpretative scepticism of the deconstructionists (although they themselves have often argued against any likely link with him).

Such kinships as may be found between formalist theories and the 'inde-terminacies' that delight the deconstructionists have been explored in an article with the apt title 'New Criticism and Deconstructive Criticism, Or What's New?', by Shuli Barzilai and Morton W. Bloomfield, who rightly argue among other things that 'whereas the New Critic uses close analysis to try and arrive at definitive thematic statements which are presumably present within the formal structures of the poem itself . . . the deconstructor resorts to close analysis to subvert the self-authenticating status of texts and to disclose the deconstructive situation, the enigmas and undecidables that destabilise meaning and open up the text to semantic dispersal and the free-play of significations or, in a word, to "dissemination".' Except for the fact that Barzilai and Bloomfield seem to accept Paul de Man's identification of Empson as a formalist critic, their presentation is in general helpful, making some good discriminations between the methodological similarities of New Criticism and deconstruction and the divergence of their aims and methods – though their final word is (self-admittedly) lame after the spry substance of the body of the article: 'Deconstruction as exegesis has indeed learned and borrowed from the wisdom which preceded it.'[148] Christopher Norris, who has done well to divine points of likeness and unlikeness between Empson and deconstructionism, has intelligently concluded that it is 'impossible to claim Empson for either side in the current debate about literary theory'.[149]

On principle and in practice, Empson himself deplored 'the literary mystagoguery of France and the United States' (number 19). But it would be patronising for any critic to suggest that he was simply taking refuge in a kind of self-defensive British bluffness when he described certain critical writings as 'a very foreign language, the high guff of US Eng Lit which can only be breathed by angels' (number 46). He was simply not given to speaking from ignorant prejudice; on trips to America, for example, he met and talked with some prime exponents of deconstruction (who had won a kind of freedom, he believed, 'at the ghastly cost ... of denying that there are any authors at all'), and he personally liked at least one of them – even while pitying him for being 'Yaled for life'.[150]

Jacques Derrida had emerged as a significant theoretical force outside France as early as 1967, with the publication of *Of Grammatology, Writing and Difference*, and *Speech and Phenomena*; and just four years later Christopher Norris naturally thought it reasonable – having regard to the close interpretative practice that Derrida undertook in his early works – to encourage Empson to read them. Empson responded with such impatient distaste that he managed to conflate Norris and Derrida in a choice slip; but, more seriously, his impatience was justifiably informed by his own long years of linguistic analysis:

I feel very bad not to have answered you for so long, and not to have read those horrible Frenchmen you posted to me. I did go through the first one, in translation, Jacques Nerrida, and nosed about in several others, but they seem to me so very disgusting, in a simple moral or social way, that I cannot stomach them. Nerrida does express the idea that, just as people were talking a grammar before grammarians arose, so there are other unnoticed regularities in human language and probably in other human systems. This is what I meant by the book title *The Structure of Complex Words*, and it was not an out-of-the-way idea, indeed I may have got it from someone else, but of course it is no use unless you try to present an actual grammar, an actual grammar of the means by which a speaker makes his choice while using the language correctly. This I attempted to supply, and I do not notice that the French ever even try.

They use enormously fussy language, always pretending to be plumbing the very depths, and never putting your toe into the water. Please tell me I am wrong...[151]

Similarly, while he early disassociated himself from the limiting formalistic criteria of organic form and intrinsic value, for example, and had no truck with notions such as textual discontinuity, so he also knew that his own criticism was concerned to establish meaning and at no time to rest content with 'indeterminacy' or 'undecidability'. Even when he first inscribed ambiguity as his analytical preference, he made no suggestion that 'unreadability' could ever be a happy outcome. Derrida's pronouncement that 'il n'y a pas de hors-texte' would have appalled him; and indeed when Empson spoke of 'this limiting critical impasse' – the impasse that regrettably stems from 'the idea that poetry is good in proportion as it is complicated' (number 7) – he resolved simply to analyse the poetry ever more deeply and to determine the meaning in it. Empson's sense of ambiguity could never stand for the very different impasse of *aporia* in which deconstructionists rejoice.

All told, what he said in his broadcast 'Literary Opinion' on 20 October 1954 could well serve to represent his opinion both of the New Criticism and of the theoretical fashions that have emerged in more recent years:

There was a tremendous thing said by the poet A. E. Housman, in the preface to an edition of a Latin author: he said that the German professor A when he read the German professor B, must have felt like Sin when she brought forth Death. Now I am willing to confess I have sometimes felt like this when reading modern literary criticism, but not at all often. People aren't such fools as all that; the thing settles itself.

In the post-war years he came more and more to believe that 'the whole of "Eng Lit" as a University subject needs to return to the Benthamite position' (number 26), very much for the reason that the liberation of the author cannot be achieved unless the critic is made equally free – and vice versa. In 1949, in 'A Doctrine of Aesthetics' (number 25), he observed, 'Perhaps the real test of an aesthetic theory, at any rate while so little is known about the matter, is how far it frees the individual to use his own taste and judgement; it must be judged in practice rather than abstract truth' – so reaffirming the principle he had avouched at the outset of his career: 'the crucial judgement lies with taste,' he insisted in 1939, for example; 'it is hard to feel that an adequate theory of literary criticism, if obtained, would be much more than a device for stopping inadequate theories from getting in your way' (number 5). He reiterated the sentiment in 1961, in 'Rhythm and Imagery in English Poetry' (number 17): 'It is not even clear that you want a theory, because its findings must always be subject to the judgement of taste.' Yet to the end of his life he applauded Richards's Theory of Value, even while remaining doubtful that it had really and permanently defined the good effects of an aesthetic experience. Critics who ignore it, he felt, inevitably offend against the fundamental Benthamite spirit of capacious generosity. 'It was a fatal step, I always think,' he wrote in a letter of 1959,

when Leavis began attacking Richards's Theory of Value, which however hard to express properly is an essential plank in his platform; Leavis has never shown any philosophical grasp of mind, and took for granted that he could strut about on the rest of the platform without ever falling through the hole. The effect has been to turn his intensely moral line of criticism into a quaintly snobbish one, full of the airs and graces of an elite concerned to win social prestige, though this is much opposed to his real background and sympathies.[152]

Studying a literature, he stressed in the same letter, 'is frivolous unless related to judgements of value, experience of life, some kind of trying out [of] the different kinds of attitude or world-view so as to decide which are good ones'. It was exactly the same fine conviction he had voiced twenty-five years earlier, in 1934, while still finding his way as critic and teacher. In 'Teaching Literature' (number 4) he stipulated that the benefits a student gains from literature are – in addition to pleasure – 'fullness or breadth of emotional life, independence of mind and a sense of proportion'.

'I well know that the night cometh when no man can work, and that I had much better be getting my affairs in order,' Empson wrote to his publisher on 4 November 1972 – just over a year after his retirement from Sheffield University but some twelve years before he died. It has been a mixed pleasure for me to assemble this volume – especially when I think that Empson might have baulked at some of its contents and told me (in no uncertain terms) to leave well alone – and I am grateful for all the help and advice I have received. First and foremost, as in editing *The Royal Beasts*, I must thank Lady (Hetta) Empson for her continual encouragement and confidence. Dr David Jones made a preliminary sifting of the papers that Empson left stockpiled in his den: I am indebted to him for saving me that first headache, and for his cheer on my visits to Hampstead. The British Academy kindly awarded me a research grant so that I could spend more days going through the still unsorted cartons of the Empson Papers in their new home at the Houghton Library, Harvard University; and I appreciated the assistance of the librarian Rodney G. Dennis and his staff, who did much to ease my frantic efforts. For their valuable help in various capacities I am grateful also to Professor Arthur Efron, Professor Terence Hawkes,

Professor Yukio Irie, Professor Kim Jong-Gil, Dr Michael Leslie, Dr Richard Luckett (Magdalene College, Cambridge), Dr Christopher Norris, Professor Christopher Ricks and Professor Alan Rudrum. At Chatto & Windus, Andrew Motion has been both friend and fellow enthusiast; and Allegra Huston has calmly urged the book to the line and saved it from many slips on my part: those that remain are still my fault. This introduction might have been indefinitely delayed but for the help of my kind hostess Basia, who quartered and cornered me – well away from telephones, memos and minutes – with a typewriter in Spain.

Notes

1 Letter to Boris Ford, 28 April 1959 (copy in Empson Papers).

2 Undated letter (*c.* 1973) to Roger Sale (copy in Empson Papers).

3 Elder Olson, 'William Empson, Contemporary Criticism and Poetic Diction', *Modern Philology*, 47: 4 (May 1950), pp. 227, 233–34.

4 'What claim do I make for the sort of ambiguity I consider here,' he wrote in the preface to the second edition (1947), 'and is all good poetry supposed to be ambiguous?

'I think that it is; but I am ready to believe that the methods I was developing would often be irrelevant to the demonstration' (*Seven Types of Ambiguity*, London: Hogarth Press, 1984, p. xv).

5 E. D. Hirsch Jr, *The Aims of Interpretation*, Chicago & London: University of Chicago Press, 1976, pp. 116, 122.

6 WE, letter to 'Mr Sha' (? 'Jha'), 20 June 1971 (copy in Empson Papers).

7 Cf. E. D. Hirsch Jr's justifiable claim that 'the goal of a definitive, literary evaluation of literature is actually a mirage masked by a tautology. The ideal of a privileged "literary mode" of evaluation is rendered hopeless by the impossibility of deducing genuinely privileged, literary criteria of evaluation. I make this statement categorically, because an analysis of the various types of evaluative principles which have evolved in the history of criticism reveals that such criteria have never been successfully formulated, and, in the nature of the case, never could be' (*The Aims of Interpretation*, p. 114).

8 *Seven Types of Ambiguity*, p. xiii.

9 Ibid., p. xv.

10 Ibid., p. x.

11 Ibid., p. xv.

12 *Some Versions of Pastoral*, London: Hogarth Press, 1986, p. 196.

13 Dilys Powell, 'Elusive "Pastoral"', *Sunday Times*, 9 February 1936.

14 Desmond Hawkins, 'Illuminated Texts', *The Spectator*, 15 November 1935.

15 Letter to 'Mr Sha', as note 6 above.

16 Undated (*c.* 1953) draft letter to the editor of *Mind* (copy in Empson Papers).

17 Quoted in Stanley J. Kunitz (ed.), *Twentieth-Century Authors: A Bibliographical Dictionary of Modern Literature, first supplement*, New York: H. W. Wilson, 1955, p. 308.

18 'The Learning of English' (letter to the editor), *Japan Chronicle*, 25 November 1931, p. 5.

19 T. S. Eliot, 'Mr Eliot's Virginian Lectures' (letter to the editor), *New English Weekly*, IV: 22 (15 March 1934), p. 528.

20 Letter to I. A. Richards, n.d. (copy in Empson Papers).

21 Geoffrey Strickland, 'The Criticism of William Empson', *Mandrake*, II (Winter 1954–55), pp. 322–23.

22 'Answers to Comments', *Essays in Criticism*, 3: 2, 1953, p. 120.

23 *Seven Types of Ambiguity*, p. x.

24 R. G. Cox, *Scrutiny*, Spring 1948.

25 F. W. Bateson, 'The Function of Criticism at the Present Time', *Essays in Criticism*, vol. 3, pp. 8–9; WE's 'Answers to Comments', pp. 114–20; and a final exchange, '"Bare Ruined Choirs"', pp. 357–63. Despite dutifully baiting Empson on Shakespeare, Bateson still considered him 'the best living lit. critic' (Bateson, letter to Empson, 24 January 1953; Empson Papers).

26 John Carey, 'Burnt-Out Case', *Sunday Times*, 30 November 1986, p. 53. Carey also remarked that Empson 'always seems to have been happier with ideas than people: even in his friendships, traces of repulsion appear. For example, he knew and liked George Orwell, and worked with him at the BBC during the war. But after Orwell's death Empson recorded among his most vivid impressions of his friend that Orwell "stank". A sickening odour, he alleged, accompanied him everywhere, possibly emanating from his "rotting lungs".' Carey's imputations should be judged in the full context of Empson's 'Orwell at the BBC' (number 88): '"The working classes smell" was one of [Orwell's] famous debunking pronouncements ... and this was a settled enough assumption in his mind to make him feel that only tramps and other down-and-outs were genuinely working-class. It was a serious weakness in his political judgement ... and it clearly resulted from deep internal revulsions. ... Bodily disgust, or rather a fear that a good man may at any moment be driven into some evil action by an unbearable amount of it, is deeply embedded in his best writing...'

27 In his inaugural lecture, 'The Critic as Vandal', John Carey had stated: 'We take it as an axiom that paraphrase inevitably alters meaning. To reword is to destroy.' As one of his specific (and well-chosen) examples of criticism that separates form and content by paraphrasing a poem, he cited Empson's discussion of George Herbert's 'Affliction' (from chapter VI of *Seven Types of Ambiguity*), commenting: 'Empson wants to deter his readers from the way of understanding the line that will probably have occurred to them, and accordingly he reduces it to a comic paraphrase so that they will feel ashamed of thinking the line meant that, and be readier to believe Empson's less likely alternative' ('The Critic as Vandal – 1', *New Statesman*, 6 August 1976, p. 178). Empson produced a fighting defence including the following remarks: 'The poem outlines the life of Herbert, saying he had desired the ruling-class career which was open to him but had also felt God was calling him to religion; yet now, having obeyed the call, he feels that God no longer wants him. He is plucky about being jilted in this way, and plans to take up some other line of life:

> Well, I will change the service, and go seek
> Some other master out.
> Ah, my dear God, though I be clean forgot,
> Let me not love thee, if I love thee not.

'Clearly there is an interval before the final couplet, while he finds that he cannot bring himself to go. The last line may express total self-abandonment: "I will love you however badly you treat me," and then "let me not love thee" has to become, very oddly, a kind of swearing – he invokes the worst penalty he can think of. "Damn me if I don't stick to the parsonage," I am blamed [by Carey] for writing down, but it does bring out the queer logic of syntax of this version. Another version would follow more naturally from the lines just before, by making a practical appeal: "Stop calling me if I have no real vocation. Do not make me love you in desire if I am incapable of loving you in achievement." There is no conflict between the two meanings; he hardly knows which he can afford to say; but unless he means both there is no reason for giving the final line its peculiar form, that of a paradox or riddle. Very likely I phrased the alternatives clumsily, but that is a minor matter. As to the main point, if a man calls me a cheat for saying it I think he is practically deranged' (*New Statesman*, 13 August 1976, p. 208). See also Empson's fierce and maybe unforgiving '"There Is No Penance Due to Ignorance"' (a review of *John Donne: Life, Mind and Art*, by John Carey), *New York Review of Books*, XXVIII: 19 (3 December 1981), pp. 42–50.

28 W. K. Wimsatt, Jr and Monroe C. Beardsley, 'The International Fallacy', in The *Verbal Icon: Studies in the Meaning of Poetry*, Louisville: University of Kentucky Press, 1954, pp. 3–5, 10.

29 Frank Cioffi, in David Newton-De Molina (ed.), *On Literary Intention*, Edinburgh: Edinburgh University Press, 1976, p. 73.

30 Letter to Philip Hobsbaum, n.d. (copy in Empson Papers).

31 I. A. Richards, *Principles of Literary Criticism* (1924), London: Routledge & Kegan Paul, 1967, pp. 58, 60.

32 Terry Eagleton, *Literary Theory: An Introduction*, Oxford: Basil Blackwell, 1983, p. 47.

33 I. A. Richards, *Principles of Literary Criticism*, p. 135.

34 Ibid., p. 20.

35 Answers to a questionnaire on criticism, *Agenda*, 14: 3, Autumn 1976, p. 24.

36 Roland Barthes, 'The Death of the Author', *Image–Music–Text*, London: Fontana, 1977, p. 143.

37 T. E. Hulme, quoted in Herbert Read, *The True Voice of Feeling: Studies in English Romantic Poetry*, London: Faber & Faber, 1953, p. 109; also in Michael Roberts, *T. E. Hulme*, London: Faber & Faber, 1938, p. 281.

38 T. E. Hulme, *Speculations* (ed. Herbert Read), London: Kegan Paul, 1924, pp. 133, 135.

39 See 'T. E. Hulme's *Speculations*' (number 9), 'Jam Theory and Imagism' (number 9), 'Rhythm and Imagery in English Poetry' (number 17), and 'Argufying in Poetry' (number 18), for Empson's views on Hulme. For an excellent account both of the curious development of Hulme's theories and of critical misapprehensions, see Michael Levenson, *A Genealogy of Modernism: A Study of English Literary Doctrine 1908–1922*, Cambridge: Cambridge University Press, 1984. See also I. A. Richards, 'The Command of Metaphor', lecture VI of *The Philosophy of Rhetoric*, Oxford: OUP, 1936; and Graham Hough's firmly-argued *Image and Experience: Studies in a Literary Revolution*, London: Gerald Duckworth, 1960.

40 See, for example, Craig Raine, 'So Kisse Good Turtles' (a review of *John Donne: Language and Style*, by A. C. Partridge), *New Statesman*, 16 March 1979, pp. 368–69: 'In metaphor, Donne outstrips Dryden and Browning, as they are more than a match for his argufying verse ... And if Pope Eliot defended Donne's difficulty, we ought to realise that he was also defending himself against the charge of obscurity. Eliot's obscurity is radically different in kind from that of Donne, whose only real follower in recent times has been William Empson.'

41 *Granta*, 18 November 1927, p. 123.

42 'My God, man, there's bears on it', *Using Biography*, London: Chatto & Windus, 1984, p. 190.

43 Edmund Wilson, *Axel's Castle: A Study in the Imaginative Literature of 1870–1930*, London: Collins Fontana, 1961, pp. 20, 23, 94.

44 Linda Hutcheon, *A Theory of Parody: The Teachings of Twentieth-Century Art Forms*, London: Methuen, 1985, p. 88.

45 Wimsatt, *The Verbal Icon*, p. 15.

46 I. A. Richards, 'The Poetry of T. S. Eliot', *Principles of Literary Criticism*, pp. 231–35.

47 Wimsatt, *The Verbal Icon*, p. 16.

48 Letter to John Wain, n.d. (copy in Empson Papers).

49 Letter to Christopher Ricks, 21 November 1969 (Christopher Ricks).

50 Unpublished draft letter, n.d. (copy in Empson Papers), to the editor of the *Kenyon Review* – in response to Cleanth Brooks, 'Hits and Misses' (a review of *The Structure of Complex Words*), *Kenyon Review*, Fall 1952, pp. 669–78. Elsewhere, in another letter, Empson also wrote: 'It is true of course that a decision about an author's intention can easily be made

wrongly, so that when it is relied upon the evidence needs to be surveyed in breadth, also that it is only a step towards a decision about the merits of some piece of his writing. But I think it is sometimes an essential one ... A producer [of *King Lear*, for example] has to make some kind of decision, and one which feels certainly not what the author meant, because totally unhistorical, reduces the play to a kind of burlesque (whether solemn or not). Professor Kot of *Shakespeare Our Contemporary* has that effect, it seems clear from his book. However, I would not feel so cross with an interpretation which was historically possible, however much I felt it to misinterpret the author; maybe because it would have a chance of reaching a partial truth.

'I have been mulling over two familiar cruxes lately, *The Phoenix and the Turtle* and the Byzantium poems. Both are commonly misread nowadays in a manner which makes them disgusting, so as to gratify the Christian craving to gloat over tortures inflicted for punishment; and I think that reading them like this is a direct result of the doctrine that you mustn't attend to the author's intention. The effect is that the critic can smear the same fashionable nastiness over every author he considers; that is why it is so popular among herd-critics. In both cases there is a good deal of evidence from the setting, the circumstances under which the poem came to be written, as well as from the rest of the author's work; and it is totally ignored by the current pious torture-embroidery. Both are charming, playful, expectant of good ... I realise that this is not a logically necessary part of the doctrine, but I expect it is why the doctrine is championed so enthusiastically.' For myself, Empson concludes, he favours 'the old custom of placing a poem in its milieu, and remembering the circumstances in which it was written. This does seem a basic need; having some grasp of the mind of the author is more of a luxury, though I don't believe you can have real criticism without it' (letter to Philip Hobsbaum, 24 March 1966; copy in Empson Papers).

　　51　Jerome J. McGann, *A Critique of Modern Textual Criticism*, Chicago & London: University of Chicago Press, 1983, pp. 122, 62, 102.

　　52　Ibid., p. 48.

　　53　K. K. Ruthven, *Critical Assumptions*, Cambridge: Cambridge University Press, 1979, p. 140.

　　54　Alastair Fowler, 'Intention Floreat', in David Newton-De Molina (ed.), *On Literary Intention*, pp. 248–50.

　　55　Fowler, 'Intention Floreat', p. 244; F. R. Leavis, 'Henry James and the function of criticism', *Scrutiny*, 15 (1947–48), p. 99.

　　56　Ruthven, *Critical Assumptions*, p. 139.

　　57　Letter to John Wain, n.d. (copy in Empson Papers).

　　58　Letter to Philip Hobsbaum, 2 August 1969 (copy in Empson Papers).

　　59　Paul de Man, 'Form and Intent in the American New Criticism', *Blindness and Insight: Essays in the Rhetoric of Contemporary Criticism*, second edn., revised, London: Methuen, 1983, pp. 27, 31–32.

　　60　Roland Barthes, 'The Death of the Author', *Image–Music–Text*, pp. 144–45, 147–48.

　　61　Hutcheon, *A Theory of Parody*, p. 93.

　　62　Wimsatt, *The Verbal Icon*, p. 5.

　　63　John Reichert, 'Do Poets Ever Mean What They Say?' *New Literary History*, XIII: 1, Autumn 1981 (53–68), pp. 55, 58, 62–63.

　　64　Letter to Philip Hobsbaum, 2 August 1969 (copy in Empson Papers).

　　65　E. D. Hirsch Jr, in Newton-De Molina (ed.), *On Literary Intention*, p. 88. On a loose sheet of notes Empson sometime noted, without comment but surely in dumbfounded disbelief, that Hirsch considered him an 'anti-intentionalist'. It is in fact remarkable that in his writings Hirsch mentions Empson only to disparage him – as when he seeks to rescue the idea of 'textual meaning' from the fallacy that it means 'textual achievement' (the text pure and simple), and mistakenly remarks that Empson's early phrase 'a piece of language' is 'typical of the critical school Empson founded' (*Validity in Interpretation*, New Haven & London: Yale University Press, 1967, p. 224) – though Empson would have endorsed the majority of Hirsch's arguments.

66 Letter to Roger Sale, n.d. (copy in Empson Papers).

67 *Seven Types of Ambiguity*, p. xiii.

68 *Some Versions of Pastoral*, p. 14.

69 Richard Sleight, 'Mr. Empson's Complex Words', *Essays in Criticism*, II, 1952, p. 325.

70 Hugh Kenner, 'Alice in Empsonland', *Hudson Review*, I, Spring 1952, p. 138.

71 Letter to 'Mr Miller', 19 November 1974 (copy in Empson Papers).

72 *Seven Types of Ambiguity*, p. ix.

73 *Seven Types of Ambiguity*, p. viii.

74 T. S. Eliot, 'Donne in Our Time', in Theodore Spencer (ed.), *A Garland for John Donne*, Oxford: Oxford University Press, 1931, pp. 11–12.

75 Allen Tate, 'A Note on Donne', *Selected Essays 1928–1955*, Cleveland & New York: Meridian Books, 1955, p. 238.

76 In *Ignatius his Conclave* (1611), 'Donne was smiling over a "new astronomy" that did not yet matter to him,' Marjorie Nicolson wrote. 'Within a year he began to understand its implications more fully. Early in 1610 occurred the death of Elizabeth Drury, daughter of Sir Robert Drury, who was to be Donne's patron. At the time of the young girl's death, Donne wrote his *Funerall Elegie*, conventional enough in its references. For the anniversary of the death in 1611 he composed *The First Anniversarie*. Barely a year had passed, yet Donne who had laughed in *Ignatius* had come to realise that "new Philosophy" might indeed call all in doubt ... I shall continue to believe that the discoveries of the new astronomy, coinciding with a troubled period in his own personal life and in his age, proved the straw that broke the back of his youthful scepticism and led John Donne "from the mistresse of my youth, Poesy, to the wife of mine age, Divinity"' (Marjorie Nicolson, 'The "New Astronomy" and English Imagination' (1935), collected in *Science and Imagination*, Ithaca, New York: Cornell University Press, 1956, pp. 51, 57).

In 1974 Empson wrote, 'It was not a new idea in 1935 that the love poetry of Donne claims a defiant independence for the pair of lovers, especially by setting them to colonise some planet made habitable by Copernicus. A campaign to exterminate the idea was then in progress, using very little reasoned argument, and its success has naturally made the poems seem pretty trivial to a later generation' (*Some Versions of Pastoral*).

77 Letter to 'Mr Shankar', n.d. (copy in Empson Papers).

78 Letter to Roger Sale, n.d. (copy in Empson Papers). In another undated letter, to John Wain, he wrote similarly: 'It wasn't till I had started teaching Eng Lit in England that I realised how much misreading of the older poetry is caused by pious otherworldliness, easily regarded as a historical duty. I did not believe the religion before, but I accepted the religiosity of Eng Lit so far as I could, till 1943 or so. Maybe the modern religion has been cured of doing great harm, but the bogus-historical misreading is still active, and that is directly my business (copy in Empson Papers).

79 Letter to *New Statesman*, 31 March 1967, p. 437.

80 John N. Morris, 'Empson's Milton', *Sewanee Review*, Autumn 1962, p. 676.

81 John Bayley, '... The Ways of Man to Man', *The Spectator*, 30 July 1965.

82 Letter to 'Mr Sha' (? 'Jha'), 20 June 1971 (copy in Empson Papers). Cf. Harold Beaver: '[Empson] is at heart a generous critic, on the lookout for "decent feelings", temperamentally averse to ironic or aesthetic closures, persuaded that an author's intention (be he Milton or Joyce) "is inherently likely to be the best possible, the richest or most humanly responsive, construction we can place upon his work". So interpretation in *Milton's God*, as Stanley Fish remarked, "developed in the space *between* the explorations of verbal texture rather than as a result of them"' ('Tilting at Windbags', *New Statesman*, 11 August 1978, pp. 185–86).

83 F. N. Lees, 'Empson Contra Gentiles', *The Tablet*, 29 September 1961.

84 Anon, 'God and Mr Empson', *Times Literary Supplement*, 29 September 1961.

85 Letter to the *Times Literary Supplement*, 6 October 1961.

86 Helen Gardner, 'Empson's Milton, *Listener*, 5 October 1961.

87 Graham Hough, 'Mr Empson on Milton's God', BBC Third Programme broadcast, 21 October 1961.

88 Empson wrote in an undated letter of John Wain: 'When I said that one can't discuss whether a man believes in the Trinity, I gave the reason: that it is a set of verbal contradictions (in Athanasius at least), so that he can only inure his mind to accepting them' (copy in Empson Papers).

89 S. G. F. Brandon, *The Judgment of the Dead*, London: Weidenfeld & Nicolson, 1967, pp. 104, 108, 98, 134–35, 196.

90 Kenneth Burke, 'Invective Against the Father', *The Nation*, 16 June 1962, p. 541.

91 Graham Hough, 'Mr Empson on Milton's God'.

92 E. M. W. Tillyard, letter to WE, 27 October 1961 (Empson Papers). Among the many Miltonists Empson took to task, in fact, Tillyard considered himself well reproved by *Milton's God*: the book had 'thrilled' him, he told Empson, largely because its thesis embodied a forceful *a priori* case – it fulfilled the Bradleyan principle that the best way to comprehend Wordsworth's strangenesses was not by circumvention but by the approach direct. He also favoured Empson's coinage 'neo-Christian', and feared certain writers who manifested the tendency (though somehow not T. S. Eliot).

93 Letter to Frank Kermode, 27 March 1961 (copy in Empson Papers).

94 Letter to 'Mr Montague', n.d. (copy in Empson Papers).

95 Undated and unpublished draft letter to the editor of the *Hudson Review* (in response to Roger Sale's article 'The Achievement of William Empson', *Hudson Review*, 19, Autumn 1966, pp. 369–90). See also WE's published letter, *Hudson Review*, 20, 1967, pp. 434–38.

96 Letter to the editors, *PMLA*, January 1978, p. 118.

97 In a letter about his article 'The Variants for the Byzantium Poem' (see *Using Biography*, London: Chatto & Windus, 1984, pp. 163–86), Empson wrote to Professor Kim Jong-Gil on 23 April 1965: 'It is not offensive in Asia, being concerned to say that Christian critics fail to understand what the Byzantium poems were about because Yeats genuinely did think like a Buddhist or Hindu...' (Kim Jong-Gil).

98 In 1972 Empson contributed to a BBC broadcast, 'Tennyson: Eighty Years On', produced by Hallam Tennyson: see 'Empson on Tennyson', *The Tennyson Research Bulletin*, IV: 3, November 1984, pp. 107–09. 'I wrote a piece about Mouldy Wedding Cake for Hallam Tennyson,' he reported in a letter to Christopher Ricks on 27 August 1972, 'and he wouldn't believe that Tithonus was kept back for twenty years before printing, till he had searched through your edition. He thought it a rude insinuation to suppose that the poet thought the wish for Nirvana a bit rakish and unChristian. But I don't know why else he would hold it back, do you? – except simply as saying the opposite of "In Memoriam", which might I suppose be commented on' (Christopher Ricks).

99 Edward L. Hirsh, untitled reivew, *America*, 28 April 1962.

100 *Daily Telegraph*, 20 October 1961.

101 Anon, 'Pastoral and Proletarian', *Times Literary Supplement*, 30 November 1935.

102 Guy Hunter, 'Science and Magic', *London Mercury*, February 1936.

103 See Alan Rudrum (ed.), Henry Vaughan, *The Complete Poems*, Harmondsworth, Middlesex: Penguin, 1976, p. 639.

104 Letter to Alan Rudrum, n.d. (Alan Rudrum).

105 W. H. Auden, quoted in Dorothy J. Farnan, *Auden in Love*, London: Faber & Faber, 1985, p. 66.

106 *Some Versions of Pastoral*, p. 284.

107 Empson reiterated that conviction in an unfinished piece (incorporated with slight revisions in *Milton's God*, p. 261): 'The peculiar moral impudence of the neo-Christian literary critic comes from believing that his God is the only source of goodness; whereas the central function of imaginative literature is to make you realise that other people are often acting on moral convictions different from yours. Also it has been thought, from Aeschylus to Ibsen, that a literary work may raise a moral problem, and partly alter the judgement of those who ap-

preciate it by making them see the case as a whole. I was rather startled to realise that Professor W. K. Wimsatt, in his essay "Poetry and Morals" (*The Verbal Icon*, 1954), rejects the whole conception as romantic, and presumes that he already knows all moral truth from a better source than the records of human experience. One would expect that this left you with only a rather marginal interest in literature...'

In 'Hunt the Symbol' (*Times Literary Supplement*, 23 April 1964), he wrote: 'As to the moralising which these religious critics [of Shakespeare] naturally insert as part of their programme, I have a different objection: I think their morals are bad. Just as there isn't only one "religion", but a lot of religions, so there are many different ethical beliefs and a man who is simply in favour of "religion and morality" is pretty sure to include bad ones.'

108 When asked exactly what he admired in Swinburne, Empson responded in a letter to the *Times Literary Supplement* (20 February 1969): 'I meant the sadistic or masochistic passages in the first *Poems and Ballads* as what are frightfully good poetry though morally most undesirable...

'No doubt positive virtues in Swinburne, such as readiness to take a dare, are part of what the reader admires; and I do not expect that the verses do actual harm. I was devoted to them as a schoolboy, when I was being beaten rather too often; and it was quite clear to me that this literary taste did nothing to make one enjoy being beaten. (Can the poet really have been removed from Eton because he proved that he did? What a triumph that would be!) But I cannot help regarding sadism very glumly, as the only perversion really deserving the name, and it seems important to get clear that one can appreciate the poetry without sharing the mental disease ... our current orthodoxy has succeeded in blinding itself to quite large areas of English poetry.

'Marking students does seem necessary, but marking the authors studied, as is done now with such immense self-satisfaction, feels to me odd.'

In 'Statements in Words' (1937) Empson observed that while Swinburne assuredly presents sadism in his 'very fine' poem 'The Leper', 'the sadism is adequately absorbed and dramatised into a story where both characters are humane, and indeed behave better than they think; Swinburne nowhere else (that I have read him) succeeds in imagining two people' (*The Structure of Complex Words*, p. 78).

109 'The Beggar's Opera: Mock-Pastoral as the Cult of Independence', *Some Versions of Pastoral*, p. 197.

110 'The Theme of *Ulysses*', *Twentieth-Century Studies*, November 1969, p. 40. Cf. Richard Ellmann, *Four Dubliners*, London: Hamish Hamilton, 1987.

111 Ludwig Wittgenstein, *Tractatus Logico-Philosophicus* (trans. D. F. Pears & B. F. McGuinness), London: Routledge & Kegan Paul, 1961, pp. 74, 11.

112 'The Ultimate Novel', *Using Biography*, pp. 223, 246, 248, 252–53.

113 'His intention was thus the opposite one to that ascribed to him in the earlier books by Kenner, which supposed him to bemoan the entire European development of thought since the Middle Ages' (ibid., p. 254). Empson's remarks are partly explained in an undated letter to Roger Sale (c. 1973): 'I don't believe, and never have believed, that a social and literary "dissociation of sensibility" ever occurred; I don't even believe that everything is getting worse and worse ... Eliot merely threw the idea out in passing when young, and is not responsible for its proliferation since. Evidently this split is believed to have occurred soon after the Reformation, so the belief is best explained as R.C. propaganda. I think a great deal of progress has gone on since then, pretty steadily' (copy in Empson Papers).

114 'The Ultimate Novel', *Using Biography*, pp. 224, 254.

115 Letter to Darcy O'Brien, 9 March 1970 (copy in Empson Papers). Empson entered into correspondence with O'Brien after the appearance (alongside his own 'The Theme of *Ulysses*') of an article by O'Brien, 'Joyce and Sexuality', *Twentieth Century Studies*, November 1969, pp. 32–38.

116 Comment on James Jensen's article, 'The Construction of *Seven Types of Ambiguity*', *Modern Language Quarterly*, XXVII, 1966, p. 257.

117 I. A. Richards, *Science and Poetry* (1926), reprinted as *Poetries and Sciences*, London: Routledge & Kegan Paul, 1970, pp. 32–33.

118 Answers to a questionnaire on criticism, *Agenda*, 14: 3 (Autumn 1976), p. 24.

119 Richards's copy of *The Structure of Complex Words* is in the Old Library, Magdalene College, Cambridge.

120 See W. H. N. Hotopf, *Language, Thought and Comprehension: A Case Study of the Writings of I. A. Richards*, London: Routledge & Kegan Paul, 1965, esp. pp. 169–76. For a decent short account of Richards's critical career, see John Paul Russo, 'I. A. Richards in Retrospect', *Critical Inquiry*, vol. 8, Summer 1982, pp. 743–60.

121 Letter to Philip Hobsbaum, 2 August 1969 (copy in Empson Papers).

122 Christopher Norris, 'The Importance of Empson (II): The Criticism', *Essays in Criticism*, XXXV: 1, January 1985 (25–44), p. 32. See also his finely studied *William Empson and the Philosophy of Literary Criticism*, London: Athlone Press, 1978.

123 I. A. Richards, *Principles of Literary Criticism* (1924); reset edition, London: Routledge & Kegan Paul, 1967, pp. 230, 46.

124 Ibid., pp. 42, 38.

125 Ibid., p. 229.

126 C. K. Ogden, I. A. Richards, James Wood, *The Foundations of Aesthetics*, London: Allen & Unwin, 1922, pp. 75, 91. E. D. Hirsch Jr is not alone in his significant misrepresentation: 'Psychologically, the most beneficial literature, in Richards's view, is the kind that harmonises a large number of different and conflicting psychic impulses. Thus, a formal or purely literary criterion of excellence, according to the kind proposed by Coleridge, is altogether concordant with Richards's psychological criterion. Literature that is formally rich and complex, and brings into unity a great many opposite and discordant elements achieves excellence both as literature and as therapy. Since the two kinds of criteria coincide, the psychological values of literature can be accommodated to literary categories' (*The Aims of Interpretation*, p. 125).

127 Jerome P. Schiller, *I. A. Richards' Theory of Literature*, New Haven & London: Yale University Press, 1969, p. 67.

128 John Needham, *The Completest Mode: I. A. Richards and the Continuity of English Literary Criticism*, Edinburgh: Edinburgh University Press, 1982, p. 35.

129 Ibid., p. 49.

130 I. A. Richards, *Speculative Instruments*, London: Routledge & Kegan Paul, 1955, p. 9.

131 I. A. Richards, *Poetries and Sciences*, p. 60 footnote.

132 I. A. Richards, *Poetries and Sciences*, pp. 60–61.

133 T. S. Eliot, 'Literature, Science, and Dogma', *Dial*, LXXXII: 3 (March 1927) pp. 243, 241.

134 Frank Day, *Sir William Empson: An Annotated Bibliography*, New York: Garland, 1984, pp. xxix–xxx.

135 *The Structure of Complex Words*, pp. 424–25.

136 Harold Beaver, 'Tilting at Windbags' (a review of *William Empson and the Philosophy of Literary Criticism*, by Christopher Norris), *New Statesman*, 11 August 1979, p. 186.

137 Empson wrote in a published letter: 'Basic gives a natural English for careful plain statement, but that is not always the natural way to talk ... But ... Basic itself is a dignified and rational means of expression, quickly learned and at once widely understood' ('Basic English', *The Spectator*, 2 August 1935, p. 191).

138 See *Beyond the Pleasure Principle*, in James Strachey (ed.), *The Standard Edition of the Complete Psychological Works of Sigmund Freud*, London: Hogarth Press (1953–74), vol. 18.

139 I. A. Richards, *Principles of Literary Criticism*, pp. 197–98.

140 *The Structure of Complex Words*, p. 425.

141 I. A. Richards, *Principles of Literary Criticism*, pp. 36, 40.

142 Frank Day, *Sir William Empson: An Annotated Bibliography*, p. xxix.

143 Michael Roberts, untitled rev. of *Some Versions of Pastoral*, in *Criterion*, January 1936, p. 345.

144 John Carey, 'Burnt-Out Case', *Sunday Times*, 30 November 1986, p. 53; Frank Day, *Sir William Empson: An Annotated Bibliography*, p. xvii.

145 Cleanth Brooks, 'Hits and Misses', *Kenyon Review*, Fall 1952, p. 676.

146 Letter to the editor of *Kenyon Review*, n.d. (*c.* January 1953; Empson Papers).

147 Ronald Shusterman, 'Blindness and Anxiety: I. A. Richards and some current trends of criticism', *Études Anglaises*, XXXIX: 4 (October–December 1986), pp. 419–20.

148 Shuli Barzilai and Morton W. Bloomfield, 'New Criticism and Deconstructive Criticism, Or What's New?', *New Literary History*, 18: 1 (Autumn 1986), pp. 154, 167.

149 Christopher Norris, 'The Importance of Empson (II): The Criticism', p. 41. See also Terry Eagleton, 'The Critic as Clown', *Against the Grain: Essays 1975–1985*, London: Verso, 1986, pp. 149–65.

150 Letter to Christopher Ricks, 25 April 1981 (Christopher Ricks).

151 Letter to Christopher Norris, 7 October 1971 (Christopher Norris).

152 Letter to Mark Roberts, 8 February 1959 (copy in Empson Papers).

A Note on the Text

The majority of the essays and articles in this volume are reprinted from their first periodical appearances. In general, I did not think it behoved me to make significant editorial interventions, apart from correcting infrequent misspellings and normalising or supplying some points of punctuation for the sake of syntactic clarity. Other silent emendations have been of a usual copy-editing order.

Hitherto unpublished essays are mostly taken from Empson's own typescript drafts. Exceptions to that rule include the pieces on Byron (number 42) and T. S. Eliot's 'Marina' (number 49) – which are taken from uncomplicated holograph copy – and the draft essay I have entitled 'Death and Its Desires' (number 95). While the bulk of the last piece follows Empson's own clear order, I found other autograph passages in a less finished state and with some pages obviously missing; rather than try to construct a synthetic version of the essay, I have elected simply to append such fragments to the main draft, in discretely numbered passages which do not pretend to stand for any sequence Empson may have had in mind. 'Teaching Literature' (number 4) first appeared in a Japanese translation, but I have fortunately been able to find Empson's original and so reproduce it here.

The arrangement of the Contents into six sections aims to distinguish the thematic coherence of Empson's interests and the interrelationships of the essays. It seemed to me sensible to group together his writings on I. A. Richards, for example, and to separate them from his essays on literary theory and on specific authors. Even though such an organisation can not (and should not) prevent thematic overlapping from one section to another, each section still basically follows the chronological order of composition. Departures from that sequence occur only in order to bring together for the reader's convenience essays on related subjects – most notably in the Poetry sections (III and IV), where I hoped it would be helpful to juxtapose Empson's pieces on such figures as Yeats, Eliot, Auden and Dylan Thomas.

In editing both published and previously unpublished essays, I have been mindful of Empson's comment, in a letter to the *New Statesman* (5 June

1955), that 'the bits of my prose which Mr Vallins blamed in *Good English* had been written with particular care, chiefly to avoid misunderstanding in the reader, and ... I thought the complaints against them wrong-headed.' Similarly, Empson is famous for being able to quote vast amounts of poetry from memory, and equally famous for misquoting in his published works. In 1951, for example, his publisher reported 900 cases of incorrect quotation in the typescript of *The Structure of Complex Words*; that is, 80 per cent of all the quotations in the book needed to be corrected before publication. Empson's 'sins' in that respect have been well known since 1930, though reviewers seem to need to rediscover them from age to age. In 1966, Roger Sale complained, for instance, 'He mispunctuates [T. S. Eliot's] "Whispers of Immortality" so as to give the poem a reading not available to readers of the correct version'; and in general, it seemed to him, Empson manifested an 'almost incredible penchant to be lax about details' ('The Achievement of William Empson', *Hudson Review*, 19, Autumn 1966). Empson's reply is worth quoting at length:

I am very bad at correcting proofs of my own writing, always seeing what I meant to write and considering whether it should be improved, and in my first book I foolishly imitated Hazlitt in what seemed a civilised practice, making incidental quotations as I remembered them, which was sufficient for the purpose. The effect of the combination was that a close study of an odd bit of punctuation in a poem would sometimes appear with the punctuation wrong, and nearby there were evidently careless quotations. My paragraph would make nonsense until the punctuation was put right, and I struggled to do this as soon as possible, but my opponents were already saying that I had cheated; I had misquoted the text in order to make it fit my interpretation, they said, and they have continued to do so. Now, in dealing with a long poem, I can see, one might be tempted to fudge a detail to fit an overall interpretation; but here I was dealing almost entirely with short lyrics. I was keen on explaining why they were so beautiful, and of course I was not interested in faking the text; almost any other form of our mortal frailty would then have tempted me more. And what I had written about the text did not apply to the erroneous version which had got printed. For years I have sometimes looked up the facts about these accusations, and they would always seem to me such obvious lies that I need not refute them. It has cured me of feeling any great reverence for textual scholars. [*Hudson Review*, 20, Winter 1967–68]

It does not seem possible, even if it were desirable, for an editor to associate himself fully with that response (especially not with the last sentence); but perhaps one can take some sort of cover in Empson's sentiments. In any event, I have attempted to check the majority of the quotations in this volume, though I cannot claim to have been comprehensive (some of them I just could not locate). I can only hope against hope not to have introduced additional misquotations, and more importantly not to have damaged any of Empson's interpretations and their supportive evidence.

Unless otherwise stated, references to *Seven Types of Ambiguity*, *Some Versions of Pastoral* and *The Structure of Complex Words* are to the standard editions published by the Hogarth Press.

Readers interested in pursuing Empson's further writings on Yeats, T. S. Eliot and Joyce should go to the extended essays on those authors included in *Using Biography* (Chatto & Windus, 1984). Empson's recapitulations of several of the 'argufyings' in the present volume (including his quarrels about 'The Windhover', *Ulysses, 1984* and *Waiting for Godot*) feature in the final chapter of *Milton's God* (1961) — a book which now needs to be read, with the author's 'Final Reflections', in the paperback edition published by Cambridge University Press in 1981. 'The Ancient Mariner' (number 40) is Empson's first big shot at writing on Coleridge: he substantially developed the piece in order for it to stand as the 100-page 'Introduction' to *Coleridge's Verse: A Selection*, edited by Empson and David Pirie (London: Faber & Faber, 1972). The length of his augmented essay alone made it regrettably too long to be included in the present single-volume miscellany, but it does in any case need to be studied alongside the text of the 'Rime' as reconstituted (with Empson's advice) by Dr Pirie. Although that Faber volume is now out of print, I am hopeful that it will soon be republished elsewhere. Both Empson's 'The Ancient Mariner' and his Introduction to *Coleridge's Verse* should be read in conjunction with Jerome G. McGann's brilliantly challenging chapter 'The Ancient Mariner: The Meaning of the Meanings', in *The Beauty of Inflections: Literary Investigations in Historical Method and Theory* (Oxford: Clarendon Press, 1985) — though I believe that Empson's argument for Coleridge's original intentions still holds up strikingly well against Professor McGann's insistence that the 'Rime' is 'Coleridge's imitation of a culturally redacted literary work' which deliberately follows the paradigm of the Higher Critical analytic. 'In the case of a poem like the "Rime", hermeneutics is criticism's grand illusion,' McGann writes. His observation seems to suggest that Coleridge gave the poem a knowingly deconstructive turn and so allowed for all possible re-readings — except for the fact that 'it was equally committed, by its own hermeneutic ideology, to a ... determinative, *a priori* ideology.' By making the poem 'assume into itself its own critical tradition', McGann concludes (in an agile argument that looks quite like a version of having it both ways), 'Coleridge successfully sustained his theistic and Christian views ... Though its meaning is not so extensive or open as the meaning of a *symboliste* poem, the "Rime" relaxes the allegorical urgency of its materials just enough to permit "personal" interpretations that will yet not violate the poem's essentially Christian structure of concepts and values.' Empson would have had an answer to that one.

I
Literary Interpretation:
The Language Machine

Curds and Whey

Granta, 11 May 1928

George Rylands, *Words and Poetry*

The Robert Graves school of criticism is only impressive when the analysis it employs becomes so elaborate as to score a rhetorical triumph; when each word in the line is given four or five meanings, four or five reasons for sounding right and suggesting the right things. Dazzled by the difficulty of holding it in your mind at once, you feel this at any rate is complicated enough, as many factors as these could make up a result apparently magical and incalculable. Mr Rylands, however, is seldom bringing off the trick with sufficient concentration; there is a great deal of pleasing information scattered about (the Shakespeare end of the book is evidently to be preferred) but too diffusely to make much impression, and the remarks on the associations of the moon in poetry, for instance, a promising subject for this method, are rich in quotation rather than explanation. And surely Mr Rylands did not really mean that the best poetry was always simple.

There is a charming introduction by Lytton Strachey, about Poetry being written with words, but it is a tiresome dogma; he would at once see through something a trifle more sophisticated, and there seems to be nobody who is teased when it is brought forward. In fact, all the bad poetry of the moment is written with words; I believe myself poetry is written with the sort of joke you find in hymns.

Obscurity and Annotation[1]

c. 1930

Poetry at present is in a difficult position. All the recent good poetry is obscure, and more recent good poetry is more obscure, and becoming more so; both because there are many more things for poetry to refer to and because of the nature of those things. They centre round surrealism and psychology; that is, they are an attempt to deal rationally with the irrational regions of the mind. This means that you have got to put irrational processes of thought in your poem, and assume the reader will know enough about the matter to understand them, on the principles you have both been taught. One would not think this was a very solemn matter, but the consequences are far reaching.

Whether that is an adequate explanation or not, most people will agree that poetry seems, by some inner necessity, to be becoming more difficult to read. This may seem a portentous and unanswerable notion, like the belief that childbirth is becoming more difficult with every generation; but in fact it seems no more than a matter (no doubt involving some give and take on both sides) which can be settled by private treaty between writer and reader. Poets, on the face of it, have either got to be easier or to write their own notes; readers have either got to take more trouble over reading or cease to regard notes as pretentious and a sign of bad poetry. And yet, though some agreement is no doubt possible, one finds on examination, as in most such cases of rival interests, that there are many aspects of the matter to be borne in mind. It is the object of this essay to bring some of them forward.

I wish, then, to mention four main sorts of occasion on which a poem is obscure, and to consider the arguments for and against notes to clear up such an obscurity.

In the first and simplest case, where no problems might seem to be involved, the poet has used an obscure, perhaps technical, word, or has chosen to leave a main verb which might be mistaken for a participle, or would like the reader to know that he is repeating in the ninth book a line that came in the first, or was thinking, when he wrote what he did, of a passage in Virgil. Now it seems to me, as indeed to most people, that there are many examples of this simplest type of obscurity where it is both entirely innocuous to write, and positively impertinent not to write, the note which would save further trouble. But difficulties arise when you consider which these cases may be. For one thing, people are annoyed; they regard it as a sign of unnecessary pedantry, as a reproach to them for not being better informed, or as an unwarranted insult to them if they are informed already. Further there is a notion, widely prevalent, and certainly in some degree reasonable, that any note confesses that the poet has failed; that 'the first business of a singer is to sing,' and that you can't be listening to a song if you are perpetually grubbing about in the notes at the end of the book.

Certainly some notes may be pedantic, and some impertinent, but the idea that all are likely to be (that one should look harshly on them at first sight) is unwise at all times, and particularly unwise just now. For it seems important that both parties should try to be tolerant on the matter; there is a genuine crux about notes giving information because the notion of general knowledge has changed. In the eighteenth century culture was unified; every educated person knew about Virgil; you could fairly, without causing offence, introduce a reference to Virgil without explaining it, so as to imply 'well, if you don't know that, you had better go and find out at once.' But nowadays there is no (or only a very bare) field of knowledge that an educated person is sure to know about; by an educated person I mean merely a person who would appreciate the poem if he could understand the references. You may know a lot about the classics, and a lot about psychology and anthropology, and yet not know some quite simple term in physiology. I do not mean simply that anyone may have a gap in his general knowledge; I mean that there is now no normal field of general knowledge, no hierarchy even of pieces of knowledge some of which it is less discreditable not to know than others. When Mr Eliot writes notes to *The Waste Land* so as to imply 'well, if you haven't read such and such a play by Middleton, you had better go and do it at once' – the schoolmaster's tone is an anachronism, it belongs to a time when knowledge could be treated as a unified field. An odd reference does not even show that the writer is learned on a subject; it may merely be a piece of information that had stuck in his head, and become useful as a metaphor. Everybody's reading is miscellaneous and scrappy, like his.

In these circumstances it really ought to be possible to write simple, goodhumoured, illuminating and long notes to one's own poems without annoying the reader. I quite see that no one has yet written notes to his own poems without looking a fool, but as knowledge becomes increasingly various it will eventually have to be done. Nor is this an arrogant act;

people tend to be offended if a word is explained in the notes which they happen to know, but this is simply a mistake on their part. They merely happen to know it; nothing that anyone is likely to explain in notes is now a thing that every cultured man ought to know. And on the other hand not to explain a term which competent readers of the poem may have to go and look up *is* an arrogant act; it assumes that the line is worth their taking the trouble to go and find a dictionary. Much of the present day distaste for modern poetry arises simply from this change in the relation of the cultured public to general knowledge; no one is to be blamed for it, and it could be got over sensibly enough if the poets were sufficiently sure of themselves to adopt the right tone, and if the public would take a sufficiently historical point of view not to be easily offended. As for the view that notes are liable to be boring: after all, you needn't [read] them if you don't choose to.

Of course the notes ought merely to give information, as to grammar, purpose, and meanings of words, and the mode of action of tropes. (All these are proper.) One must not try to put some more into the poem through the notes, like Mr Eliot on *Shantih* – 'I suspect you are not being as impressed as you ought to be by the depths of meaning to be found in this word.' I have been talking as if this situation was a matter of the Future, and belonging to an unprecedented situation in which the human mind was only now discovering itself. But of course it is true of any poetry in which thought is sufficiently active; Shakespeare wants all the notes he now has, and could have written most of them himself if he would have taken the trouble. It is true one must have a great deal of sympathy for people who don't take the trouble, but there comes a time when the reader has a right to demand that they should. To leave your poetry to be annotated by someone else, with much greater trouble than it would have cost you, is again an impertinence under the disguise of modesty.

And it seems also to be true that people demand a certain undress of a book or an author; they do not like it to keep them strung up to a high level of difficulty or exultation, when they are sure the author is not like that all the time. A whole new book of poetry without prose seems to them rather like a seduction without conversation; it becomes almost indecently portentous, which one feels sure it wouldn't be if it was talked about sensibly. What's more, there is a fairly large public for critical writing; much larger than for good modern poetry. There seems to be no doubt that poetry published with long discursive notes, taking the tone of ordinary critical writing, would be much nearer the concentration they are prepared to swallow. But such notes must be general critical remarks arising from a point, and claiming to be detached from it.

Indeed, I think a poet may reasonably, now as in some previous generations, feel a little impatient of the cult of general knowledge; it gives one rather a shock, for instance, in a cinema, when all prices of seats (showing animation for the first time) break out into a roar of satisfied and scornful laughter, because the low character uses a word in the phonetic and historically correct way. The glutton for general knowledge is not necessarily the person whose sensibility a poet wishes to affect, or feels sympathy with, and yet even for such a poet it is hard to avoid making obscure references. I believe it is true to say that most research workers in the sciences have not a wide general knowledge, they are too seriously and completely satisfied by the knowledge they need and the knowledge they have themselves given to the world. Now it is no sort of use for the poet to claim that these people are too low and stupid for him to mind about them, or that they do not care about what is happening to contemporary sensibility, or that they would necessarily be bad judges if they had the evidence before them; people who have acquired many branches of knowledge are often people who have not been satisfied by any, and it is precisely the people who genuinely understand some one branch of knowledge who would profit by a single poem, a single effort of the sensibility, which united it to many others.

I feel no doubt, myself, that once you regard poetry as a medium which is entitled to deal with a variety of matters, then the side in favour of notes is much the more sympathetic of the two. But even in this, the simplest, case there are weighty arguments on the other side.

As for hard words, people can use the dictionary for themselves if they want to, and where there is a difference of opinion as to whether it is more impertinent to send a reader to the dictionary or to tell what he already knows, a writer may be forgiven if he chooses the less laborious alternative. As for the latent quotation from another writer or another part of the poem, it is not interesting for a reader to know this as a separate piece of information; he will find it out for himself, at the only moment when it can be useful to him; that is, when he reads one of the poems without having forgotten the other. But these may seem flimsy arguments such as imply their own answer; the important argument (applying chiefly to difficult grammar, or complex movements of thought) concerns the general mode of action of poetry.

A thing seems more interesting when you have worked it out for yourself; you know more about it, and you have the fondness of a proprietor. Furthermore, you have in any case to discover the poet's feeling; how or why he thought as he did; the thing is not a puzzle but a process, it is not your immediate object to get to the other end; and a note may be like those charmingly courteous motorists who offer you a lift when you are only going for a walk (even so, of course, it need not excite hatred or contempt).

But certainly the note may be more annoying than the motorist, because not only is a poetical device more interesting when you have found it for

yourself, it is actually different. You can refuse the lift, but the note may
have finally interrupted the process of understanding a thing without it,
and if you are told the last part first you have been given the thing in the
wrong order (at any rate, not in the order intended by the poem); it may be
like taking a Seidlitz powder backwards.

This argument assumes that the process of understanding some lines of
poetry is an essential part of their value, and the natural reply is like that
about what the landscape gardener called the element of surprise in a vista;
'Pray what do you call it when you walk round the garden for a second
time?' Thus stated, the objection illustrates its own answer; there is undoubtedly something akin to surprise when you come again upon the vista,
and the most natural suggestion would be that it was a memory of your previous surprise, or an imagination (if you are walking in the other direction
when you first come to the spot) of what the surprise would have been if
you had experienced it. Having thus referred the element of process to the
original experience, we can consider its nature in the case of poetry.

In first reading a passage of poetry, such as requires attention, there are
likely to be a series of stages where, knowing it in part, you judged it as
what you understood; these stages in understanding the passage are likely
to remain in your mind as part of its tone. On this view, there will be little
harm in a note if you read it only after you have thoroughly accepted the
poem without it; a re-reading with the notes may then take you into it further. One would at least deduce from this the usual practice of collecting
notes at the end of the book, except indeed in the case of scholar's texts, an
edition of Shakespeare, say, when the reader is assumed to have read the
play already. One might also deduce that the notes should not be published
with the first edition; the collected edition, for instance, would be a suitable
occasion, and the writer himself would then be better able to regard his
work objectively. Some poets and writers of programme music adopt a
teasing variant of this plan.

Strauss used to mystify his hearers at first; tell them he proposed not to
give them the clue to his literary scheme, then give one clue after another to
his personal friends, till at last sufficient information was gathered to
reconstruct the story he had worked upon. Gibbon, too, published the
notes as the last volume of his history.

This argument, based on the mode of action of the imagination, is certainly not a generally reliable one; the powers of the imagination are great
enough to refute an argument based on any limited view of their nature,
and a poem is more like a garden than a Seidlitz powder. In whatever order
you come to understand a structure, you can in some degree imagine what
it would have been like to have come by another route. All one can say is
that the work of imagining this cannot be done for you by any system of

notes, and a very elaborate system of notes may actually make it harder. A test case is provided by Mr John Livingston Lowes's *The Road to Xanadu* [London: Constable, 1927], which sets out the historical material from which Coleridge distilled 'Kubla Khan' and the 'Ancient Mariner'. It is a very large book, and the sources are of very great variety; even when you know them all it is hard to hold them in your mind and re-distil them into the poems. Now one can hardly doubt that, if Coleridge had published, at the same time as the poems, a complete account of their sources (from what travel-book he had taken the epithets; what legend was in his mind to suggest the incidents; for what personal reasons they had appealed to him) their merits would have been as easily or as generally recognised as they were. The stress would have been different; we would be asked to admire the erudition, the interest, the grasp of mind, in the poems, rather than their poetical qualities as such. Of course they would be no less good in themselves, but it would have been harder, when they were novelties, to see their peculiar merits. For the business of finding the materials, the operation of distilling them, are not here the most important points; the main thing about them is the resulting order of Coleridge's sensibility. Indeed, the notes here (this is not so true of the Khan as of the Mariner) hardly affect the poem as a separate organism; they do not obviously fall in the province either of the critic or of the biographer; they simply make an extremely interesting and satisfying book on their own. The fusion of materials here is unusually perfect; most poems gain far more definitely from a knowledge of their sources; and if you say this shows their imperfection the reply is that one does not read a poem for being 'perfect', but for conveying something, a sensibility, a mode of experience, which cannot be conveyed in any other way. Certainly the mode of statement is connected more intimately in a poem than anywhere else with the thing stated, but even though they be conceived as one, that is only to say that, given an inadequate statement of something worth stating, the inadequacy must be only apparent since the thing has been stated; the conditions admit that it is known. That all good poems do not need notes cannot be stated as a deduction from some theory; being capable of being tested, it can at best only be an empirical generalisation. The essential point, I think, is that after reading *The Road to Xanadu* you have to make the same effort of selection from the material as was made by the poet, in order to get back to feeling about them as he did in the poem.

People would have realised the complexity of the material but not how effectively it was applied, how little irrelevant detail entered into the final result; even how little necessary the notes were to it. And it would have been harder for them to see that a new thing had been made out of the materials; that there was something in the poem which was not by any care to be discovered in its sources. That the materials are complex is not interesting unless they are well used, in the result, and to insist on the materials is to put less stress on the result. Many people would have been frightened off, many would have been irritated, and the unity of effect would have been destroyed.

But if the notes as to sources are unnecessary to the 'Ancient Mariner', that is not to say they were irrelevant to *The Waste Land*. The Romantic Revival was interested in far away, richly coloured, strange things as such, not as exciting a historical sense and reminding you of a way of feeling or judging. The references in *The Waste Land* remind you of whole elements of your own mind, which everyone now uses in coming to decisions; when Coleridge packs into the same verse a detail from Polar voyages and a detail from *Purchas's Pilgrims* in the tropics, we are meant to think of both of them as far and strange; to think of them, indeed, as we would have done if we had met them in the original, though our sense of their romance would have been weaker, because not so much heightened by their setting. It is in such cases as this that it is not necessary to know the actual source, though it may be reassuring to know that there is one. When a citation or memory of some other writer carries with it a historical sense, some criticism of him and an interest in its original setting, then it is necessary to know the source if one is not to miss much of the original effect.

Here, then, a reasonable argument against notes would be that all citation of this sort is wrong, perhaps because always ill-digested; that it asks the reader to think about the sources and listen to what is implied about them; that it is criticism and not poetry. But the distinction here is only as to the degree of consciousness of the variety of elements referred to; no one objects to a *general* effect such as excites the historical sense; and now that the historical sense is coming to occupy so large a part of the ordinary cultivated mind it seems a natural material to use very frequently in poetry. And though, very often, the note could be avoided by longer and more explanatory writing in the poem; though it is true that poetry should not be criticism, should include its material dissolved into itself; yet it is precisely this which is aimed at by the compactness which is likely to require notes. It is better to be brief in the actual poem, rather than explain your reference, even though that involves a note, because then when the reader had read the note and understood the collocation he will, *in future*, read it directly as poetry and not have to read it as criticism; not have to read the note every time because it is part of the text. One great important function of poetry is precisely this; to make the reader connect naturally, with understanding, things which he had not connected before; this is done pre-eminently by a collocation which needs at first to be explained by a note (more usually, needs at first to be worked out and known as a discovery) and afterwards taken for granted and remembered as a feeling, as a handy unit which can be applied in judging. If poetry must use a greater variety of materials, it is almost always better that it should use them in a concentrated way so as to insist that they had been digested into poetry (even if this means that the poetry must have a limited body of readers) than that it should explain itself in the text so as not to be poetry at all. These are arguments used often against notes, but they are stronger arguments against what is a natural consequence of refusing notes, the poem which carries its own annotation.

The argument that *The Road to Xanadu* would have obscured the poems it explains, if published too early, is one that applies to notes in general, not only to notes by the author himself. Most of the earlier arguments apply only to notes by the author himself.

This example from Coleridge may seem an extreme case, like the sources of experience, now perhaps forgotten, from which an illuminating detail was drawn, rather than like the materials which actually make units of the material which the reader must interpret; you might think that the understanding of Coleridge's sources in this case was not an understanding of the same sort of element as must be understood to enjoy poetry. But the act of communication in the arts is so queer that one cannot know it is unlike this; in particular, it involves a great deal of social sense, of knowledge as to what kind of life the author or persons described were leading, which is not overt when the poetry you admire is all of one school but becomes among the most important matters when you admire a wide variety of schools. And even when you admire only one, such elements are concerned, however little important it may be to know about them. A passage of Gurney's about melody may be illuminating here.

A melody

seems like a fusion of strong emotions transfigured into a wholly new experience, whereof if we seek to bring out the separate threads we are hopelessly baulked; for triumph and tenderness, desire and satisfaction, yielding and insistence, may seem to be all there at once, yet without any dubiousness or confusion in the result; or rather elements seem there which we struggle dimly to adumbrate by such words, *thus making the experience seem vague only by our own effort to analyse it*, while really the beauty has the unity and individuality pertaining to clear and definite form. [Edmund Gurney, *The Power of Sound*, London: Smith, Elder & Co, 1880, p. 120; Empson's italics]

The second main case occurs when the author does not himself clearly understand how the effect has been produced. Thus a word may be used typically, as if it were a symbol, and actually take effect as if it were; but the author may not know how it does this, what it is a symbol of, and the reader may (this does not follow, necessarily, but is more often true than one would suppose) need not know about it either, before it can take effect on him in the same way. You might say that there is no difficulty here because the effect by definition cannot be explained, so there is no question as to whether it should be. But there may still be doubt as to whether the poet ought to say clearly that this is not a metaphor, or that he does not understand it; further whether this should be considered creditable; whether it is the business of a poet to have understood his own writings, and whether it would always be possible to have done so.

Now I do not myself believe that any poetical effect is of its own nature permanently inexplicable; this is an act of faith, and in practice only means that I think it worth while to try and explain things. But there is no doubt that there have been excellent poets who could not have explained their own methods, and this not for any lack of intelligence, cultivation, or critical powers; I should take Milton as an example. One might even say, indeed, that the most intimate, valuable, and interesting devices of a period, its peculiar contribution to literature, is likely to be just the one that it is least able to explain; chiefly because, being a novelty, it cannot then be phrased in terms other than its own; partly because it is taken for granted, and not thought a thing that needs explaining, nor indeed could have been done differently. Thus the fact that a poet cannot himself explain an effect is certainly no argument for rejecting it; nor is the fact that a critic of a later age cannot explain an effect any reason for rejecting it; for while it can then be viewed more objectively, it is known less intimately; these two on the face of it about counterbalance each other. Very curious evidence on this last point may be found in Bentley's under-rated notes on Milton, and the answers to him in the ensuing controversy. The fury with which Pope attacked pedants has this real justification, that there was no other way of answering them; the only way of defending Milton's text against Bentley's emendations was to laugh at Bentley; critics who tried to give reasons for what was, then as now, obviously the more beautiful reading gave away point after point, for sheer lack of the necessary critical machinery. I think that nowadays we can explain why Milton was right, but the explanations usually seem long and fanciful; they would only convince men who believed already that the line was beautiful, and only wanted to know why.[2]

On the other hand, poets nowadays understand fairly thoroughly what they are doing, and our critical machinery, I believe, is good enough to deal with most immediate technical problems such as would be required to show the force of a particular word or line. There is no doubt that explanation may be hard, but I think myself that, when a poem is safely written, a poet ought to try to understand his own mental operations, and if he can't understand them there is no harm (though there is little virtue) in his saying so. Of course, in another sense, there is no question that he *must* understand them when he is writing them; that is, he must apprehend them fully, and must know how they will affect a reader who does not come to them with his own assumptions; he must then feel how they work; but that is not to say that he must be able to write a critical defence of them. The power of writing a critical defence one would expect to come later, for one thing because he has too much in his mind at the time of writing to be able to focus all its parts.

But one must insist on the phrase 'when the poem is safely written', because there is often an intervening stage, while he is still willing to alter it, not yet detached or informed enough to understand it critically, but already out of the period when he could apprehend it directly as a solution of the problems that he was dealing with. It is essential to let a thing settle before you start messing it about; the paint must dry before you varnish; apart from that, one must at any time hesitate to emend, from the point of view of the analytical critic, what has at the time seemed satisfying from the point of view of the author. It is easy to do to one's own writings what Bentley tried to do to Milton's, and if the alternative, to satisfy the critic, must be to explain why the original is better, this might well lead to the suppression of most poetry. For even though explanation were possible to you, it might often seem impertinent, and would certainly often seem useless, to give your own writing as complicated an explanation as most good writing deserves. Furthermore, an author himself cannot well do this for himself, because the problems of communication must leave him in doubt. A critic, when public opinion has settled down as to the merits of a poem, can set to work to explain the full complexity of its mode of action, but it is no use for an author to do that, because he does not yet know whether his private fancies get across, how far the poem *has* a mode of action at all. There is usually a process of crystallisation, so to speak, in a poet's attitude to a poem when it is written; for some time he is liable to alter it whenever he reads it, perhaps to alter it back again; then, perhaps simply after it has appeared in print, or (thinking of Shakespeare) after it has been acted or shown to particular people, there comes a time when, partly by a sense that he wants to know how other people are seeing it, partly because the state of mind which produced it has really become alien to him, it becomes an external object, he looks at it as a member of the public, there is no further question of altering the thing; and he can treat it as a datum to reason about, and defend if he chooses. The best plan in most cases, then, on this ground as on the previous one, is that the author should not write notes till the poem has at least appeared in print, probably not till some time has past, till he has written something else, and is bringing out a collected edition.

The notion that it would be absurd for a poet, even if it were possible, to justify a phrase with as complex an argument as many phrases require, must act as an additional argument against the demand for explanation before a critic can take a new poet seriously.

The third case where notes might seem called for occurs when the author, while he knows something which is true about the poem as a matter of biography, does not know whether it is part of the poem as an independent organism, whether it is a useful thing for the reader to know. For a poem arises from some sort of experience, which it transmutes into more general, more complete, more satisfying, more valuable, and perhaps simply different experience. So, the original experience may have very little to do with the final product; and yet the poet may like to remember that it occurred, because to write a poem is an act of self-knowledge which he likes to feel has its basis of fact. Hence an author generally knows things about the imagery or proper names used in the poem which are to him part of its contact with his own life, which gives it its sap; but these may be irrelevant to, or may actually be misleading about, the particular experience conveyed in the poem. They are interesting, if at all, to the biographer, not to the critic. 'A phenomenon I have often noticed,' as Mr Eliot says in one of the strangest of his notes.

Now of course a great deal of biographical information is very useful in understanding a poem, and mere quantity of biographical information is not likely to do much harm. A poem is a very independent organism, and once people have got used to it they are not likely to be disturbed by information about its origins. In a sense, too, it is a compliment to your readers to imply that they are not easily disturbed, for instance, by prosaic associations; that they can afford to be given information of this kind, which they probably ought not to take too seriously. On the other hand, to give such information assumes that people want to know about your biography; it ought to be said casually, as a sort of gossip, when the subject comes up, and not put in the notes very grandiosely. Wordsworth was fond of telling his readers just where he was sitting when he wrote a poem, and whom he had gone for a walk with; it is rather a winning trait, which I suppose no one is irritated by, and no one finds very useful as a source of interpretation.

Still, a difficulty might arise from not knowing whether a piece of information was of this sort, which does not deserve a very orderly note by the author, or whether it is of the first sort and should be explained. The trouble about writing notes to your own poems, especially at an early stage, is that you do not know how much people want to know; what is trivial to them, not to you; what to you, not to them; what is vulgar, abject, or boastful, what brave and searching, what merely a bore, to give a reader at the end of the volume.

The crux of the matter is that writing a poem is an act of much more intimate self-knowledge than writing notes to a poem, and the second may interfere with the first. In particular, poets often describe, so as to diagnose, situations which are then strange to them, but into which they afterwards tumble and even then fail to deal with; not remembering then what they had described, not remembering afterwards from what experience they had first described it. In cases like this, if he had written full notes at first, they would later seem to him surprising and probably wrong. How is a poet to say why, from what experience, he writes as he does, when the experience has not yet happened to him, when it exists only as an attitude to life which will attract such experiences to him? Nor is this a freak case; all elaborate choice involves knowing what you will feel like under very different and quite new circumstances; and a poet as an artist is often anticipating experiences which may never, or only in the most distant future, occur. (That is a fancy of Herbert Spencer's, about musicians.)

The justification of 'poses' follows on from this; it is that you are trying things out to see if they fit. You may easily enough grow out to fill the area afterwards, if you have begun by making an adequate city wall. So much of life – any sustained activity – involves an act of faith, even an act of impertinence, of this kind. Milton, one may suspect, was for most of his life what he was then called, a shallow-pated young puppy; it was only late in life that he justified the claims he had lived by. Not to make such claims is never to justify them. There are often periods in an artist's life, or indeed in anybody else's, when he is merely holding on, hoping that he will tumble into the situations which he already knows how to deal with. One might deduce from this that, however much the biographer may be called in, the notion of 'sincerity', that the impulses concerned must be genuine, can never be applied simply.

The question here (waiving these more fantastic points) is very like that about the notes to the 'Ancient Mariner'; the poem has been extracted from the material, and it is not obviously an advantage to put the material into its neighbourhood, or it may be soaked up again. You may give away the flower of beauty easily enough, but when plucked it may wither; you can give it with the roots and tell the reader to plant it in his own garden, and it may live; but it is a question whether you need give him the weight and inconvenience of the surrounding soil.

The fourth and last case occurs when it could be inconvenient, for biographical reasons, to put the note in at all; at any rate for a large interval of time. The obvious case of this is a sort of extension of the third case, when the note gives information about the poet's private life; a note by Shakespeare, for instance, as to whom the sonnets were written about, even if we could imagine him writing notes, would not have been written. Statements perhaps more useful for criticism, though hardly less personal (statements such as Wordsworth claimed to be making in *The Prelude*), would be as to the motives and experience behind, or psychological principles at work in, *Manfred* and Pope's satires; in each case the idea is absurd, and they are not, after all, similar writers; Wordsworth's own self-revelation, if it comes to that, drew its splendour from the energy of the hypocrisy that soon afterwards overwhelmed him; if people nowadays write poetry which they can afford to analyse, in this fundamental sense, in public, it is because they do not put things they immediately care about, and are in the thick of, into their poems. It would be absurd to expect poets to take up the scientific line of rational curiosity on such points; the convention here, as in the rest of life, must be that you cannot expect people to explain the experiences one most guesses at in them, because, even if they could be sure they were among friends, still by the act of explaining all kinds of stresses would be set up, and the process might turn out, in any degree, unexpectedly painful. Indeed that, in many cases, was precisely why the subject of the poem was interesting, why it was worth while to them to labour at the form in which the sensibility resulting from the experience was conveyed. Such poetry was in part only satisfying because it enabled them to speak through a veil of decency; in part only useful because it enabled them to speak through a veil of ignorance.

An explanation of these biographical cases would certainly have done much towards explaining the poems, and would reasonably have been refused. But one can find less direct cases, where it is a question of explaining the actual imagery of the poem, or the motives and experience behind Pope's satires, of which the same is true. I do not suppose Keats could have explained his very straightforward use of Freudian symbolism, though he must in some sense have known all about it; but certainly if he could have done it would have been very unwise of him to do it.

But I do not know that that is true nowadays; one could claim any amount of sexual symbolism in a poem without exciting much interest, and certainly without exciting much indignation. That may indeed be fairly generally true of the technical devices, as apart from the subjects, of literature; when they are understood and accepted they may safely be used in explanations. It seems to be true that there has been, and ought to be a further, change in public opinion to make this last class smaller than it was. I do not think anyone now has that horror and terror felt by Tennyson and Browning, for prying critics who at once settled upon their corpses.

In any case, even when the note would lie between the third case and the fourth, the notion of dignity is an important one; 'It does not matter what the original event, or the formative impulse, may have been; because I claim to have built them up into something of more permanent value.' It is important, because if a poet knows he is to be challenged on such matters, as a test of his merit as a poet, then this consciousness is bound to interfere with his poetry; if not, you may say, he is not so sensitive as to be a good poet.

But it is possible to turn sharply round at this point, and view a poet very differently; for a poet, particularly of this sort, who is riding the storm rather than recollecting in tranquillity, must have a great deal of the scientist in him; he must have just that toughness, that indifference to the source of the original feeling, that power to stand outside his feelings and generalise, at some distance, from the materials that his feelings present him with, which is necessary for a self-analysis of the kind in question. He must be able to kick down the ladder by which he has climbed the haystack; even to let it dwindle to a needle which it may be hard for him to pick up (so that the fourth may dwindle to the third type of obscurity); and yet again he must have an eye that can find it, and through the eye of that needle he must troop all his camels. Such a poet – to drop all this – must have peculiar powers of explaining his writings, even though to use them must expose him to peculiar dangers, and I suspect that Pope, if such an activity had seemed to him (for some unimaginable reason) worth his while, could have published a very complete analysis of the processes of mind at work, the sources of satisfaction, in his satires.

I appear to have been arguing against some person who thinks that poets ought to explain themselves as completely as possible. I do not know of any body of opinion which thinks that; I discuss it because it is what I would like to think myself. This is generally true; if you attack a view in any detail that proves you to have some sympathy with it; there is already a conflict in you which mirrors the conflict in which you take part; that is why you understand it sufficiently to take part in it. Only because you can foresee and enter into the opposing arguments can you answer them; only because it is interesting to you do you engage in argument about it.

For personally I am attracted by the notion of a hearty indifference to one's own and other people's feelings, when a fragment of the truth is in question; I enjoy the chatty reading of poetry in the chatty explanatory frame of mind which could annotate its own works. But it is useless to pretend that the best poetry is written in this frame of mind, that a completely satisfying life can centre round truth like this. The notion that one ought to be interested in truth, indeed, is connected by Mr Wyndham Lewis, somewhere, with the child who is always asking questions; the only question he wants to ask is 'how do babies come,' and he asks the others because he is not allowed to ask that one. I was saying just now that the glutton for general knowledge is not necessarily the best reader of the poet; but nor can one assume that the glutton for explanations is the best interpreter of a poet.

Evidently it is no use blaspheming at random against the spirit of curiosity, which was one of the causes necessary to raise man from the beasts, whether it was a sexual perversion or no (and it casts a strange light on Neanderthal home life if the human spirit of enquiry was first developed in this way). Furthermore, the particular form of curiosity relevant to this essay, the desire to understand one's surroundings, poems and states of mind, rather than to accept them, is a curiously important part of present-day sensibility. Just as the prevailing notion of the Romantics was 'life in itself is prosaic, so let us think about the occasions where, or when, it may be interesting, and have as interesting feelings as possible,' so now there is a prevailing excitement connected with the sciences, and drawing much of its energy from a sense of the disorder of the world. 'Any minute now we may be blown up or bankrupt,' begins the creed of the age, 'we don't, therefore, stand to lose much by digging up the bulbs to see if they are sprouting. While yet the bombs hold off, and may they hold off for a sufficient number of weeks, let us not live or build but dig into the foundations, let us expose what has been since creation in darkness now for the first time to the light of day.' The merits of this age, to speak less flamboyantly, are among the critics rather than poets, or rather among the poets who are critics than the poets who are distilling their material from life itself. The arguments against notes, against the inquisitive attitude, are, we need to be reminded of the [   ] but it is they which are our chief glory, if we have one; and it is unwise to avoid doing, even for the best reasons, what may turn out to have been the only thing we could do.

Another cause making for the self-explanatory or critical poet, rather than the poet as such, is the gradual extension into ordinary consciousness of the time-scale of the sciences; this seems bound to affect the artist, especially now that the historical sense is becoming so important, and it may be one of the few reasons why the scientist can reasonably be regarded as a danger to the artist. It goes in exactly the opposite direction to the process of thought I have just considered; but that is only because a disturbance in either of two directions (especially when there is a compensation mechanism such as causes oscillation) acts chiefly as a disturbance, and in much the same way.

The last idea was that things are now very unstable, and therefore it is better to try to understand our foundations than to build upon them, because the understanding will survive even if the foundations go wrong. The other idea is that, though we personally or our government may be unstable, human life as a whole is likely to last longer than people had thought. It is no use feeling bored by this irruption of astronomy into literary criticism; the estimated endurance of civilisation has often affected literature before. It seems to be an important part of the seventeenth-century attitude to life that they believed the world was coming to an end quite soon; their sonorousness, their concentration whether on death and the macabre or on the fleeting moment, are continually to be understood in terms of the astronomical belief of the time. If the critic admits that their beliefs affected them, he must admit that our beliefs may affect us.

Most people have been told, and few people have been able to forget entirely, that the astronomers give the earth, as a habitable planet, a probable life of at least a thousand million years; it is not widely believed that the human race will allow or encourage itself to evolve at all rapidly, and we are left to digest the fact that our descendants, very like ourselves, will go steadily on performing their natural functions on this planet for appalling periods of time. Literary critics have been fond of talking about what 'posterity will say' of a particular poet. Posterity is likely to last as long as all vitality has yet lasted since the first jellies. It is not Dante only when he searched hell with the eye of an enquirer, it is terrestrial life, which is no more than halfway upon its road. Now people at present are still able to avoid bearing this in mind, but it is rapidly filtering into the general consciousness, and once it has done so it seems to me bound to affect the arts very greatly, it may be very much for the worse.

An anxiety about the future; a wish to know what, at some undefined date, it will be like; a sense that the future will think us very absurd, and therefore that we must do at once what the future will be doing; these I suppose are the first fruits of the doctrine. But it is difficult to suppose, for instance, that there will be an accumulation of love lyrics, burrowing deeper and deeper, century by century, below the British Museum, unto the last durations. I do not believe that, ten thousand years hence, it will be thought at all absurd to learn Elizabethan English in order to read Shakespeare, but a hundred thousand years hence it seems hard to believe that people will not be otherwise employed. Surely, once you have accepted the time-scale of our current faith, the idea of eternal fame becomes ridiculous, and surely a great deal goes with it; the artist becomes either a man with a hobby or, for however long a day, a journalist; and he can hardly feel, if he is not read now, that he will ever be read later.

On the other hand the idea of scientific truth is given a strong leg-up; any definite piece of knowledge, though of course it must be expected to be included as a small deduction from much larger generalisations, though it may be only included by negatives in the larger generalisation, though it may apparently cease to exist by destroying its own field of application (if enough was known about tapeworms, for instance, the study of tapeworms would cease to be a matter of importance because there would not be any) still has a permanent importance as making part of the body of knowledge. Dr Mackail's view that poetry is 'a continuous substance or energy whose progress is immortal' would seem much more sensible if it were said about the sciences. If you are doing a scientific research the prospects of futurity do not make you ridiculous; it seems to me that this fact is bound to affect the arts in the direction of the sciences, that it will make poets treat poetry as a form of self-knowledge, and so as a branch of knowledge in general.

Phrasing it in this way one escapes the obvious fallacy in the idea of mixing up the sciences and the arts. Such a mixture suggests that the poet must stop doing what he wants to; or write about matters which he is interested in, but which are irrelevant to his sensibility. Of course that would be as little use to the psychologist as to the aesthete. All that can be said is that poets are likely to possess an increasing degree of self-consciousness, in the sense that they will understand both their impulses and the methods involved and further, what may be more important, they will expect their readers, also, to possess an increasing degree of psychological knowledge, of interest in, and power to understand, the impulses and the methods involved. I do not think that a generation accustomed to psychoanalysis could either produce, or be sufficiently impressed by to encourage, a poet like Byron. To the objection that a poet ought not to be expected to psychoanalyse himself in the notes, because if he knows that this will happen it will destroy his poetry, I should reply that in that case his poetry is going to be destroyed anyway.

Certainly this may seem a dismal prospect; a poet writing for psychoanalysts does not cut so dignified a figure as a poet writing for the delight of a reverent posterity. The sense that poetry will be understood in this sense, whether the poet explains it or not, seems to let us in for being awfully good and rather puppyish; the more pathetic virtues are called for. On the other hand, Freud's remark that artists gain success, and the gratification of their desires, by exploiting a fantasy gratification of those desires, is sufficiently true to be an irritation to the artist; and it seems likely that when this process is generally understood by the public works of this kind are likely to become less effective, or to be accepted only when they are frankly admitted, as for instance in the writings of Baron Corvo.

Arguments against analysis tend to broaden to an unreasonable degree of generalisation, and become arguments against understanding anything. 'It is not safe to get to understand anything, because at any moment you may find that true beliefs are making it impossible to act rightly.' And certainly this is quite true; you can never know that a new piece of knowledge may not suddenly make you very unhappy. It is an act of faith which experience, on the whole, makes plausible, that when you are interested you can say 'it will do no harm to examine this; this is a point where I may use reason.' Certainly all new acts are dangerous, but it is not necessarily less dangerous to avoid them. I may be run over if I go into the street, but the roof may fall on me if I stay indoors. Where nothing is known beforehand there is nothing for it but to be hopeful, and where there is no means of deciding between two courses of action it is more cheerful to choose the more active one.

But another sort of objection to notes centres round the word 'esoteric'; 'it is no use explaining to those who do not feel rightly about the matter; indeed it might do harm; and it is no use explaining to those who already feel rightly, because they do not need the explanation.' This is only a statement that there are some matters about which it is no use to write notes, which is no novelty. [Incomplete]

Notes

1 Untitled in manuscript.
2 See Empson's essay 'Milton and Bentley' in *Some Versions of Pastoral*; and J. W. Mackail, *Bentley's Milton*, Proceedings of the British Academy, vol. XI, London: Oxford University Press, 1924.

'Sound and Meaning in English Poetry'[1]

Criterion, X, April 1931

Katherine M. Wilson, *Sound and Meaning in English Poetry*

Miss Wilson, in this stimulating work, has heaped together a great deal of evidence that words are only distinguishable, and speech only intelligible, through the musical functions of the ear; that it is through the tune of a sentence that we must judge its feeling; that the aim of the poet must be to write musically; that the aim of the literary must be to use the methods of the musical critic; that poetry, in fact, is 'like' music. There is a certain honesty about the disorder of her learned and sensitive writing; it acts as a demonstration that the subject has not been cleared up: and it is very useful (especially as her bibliography, in footnotes, is so wide) that the evidence for these alarming opinions should be collected together.

She goes about this with a great air of brisk rationality, and evidently feels that she is clearing things up. But, obviously, so far from explaining anything about poetry, these opinions (which certainly have some degree of truth) open up abyss after abyss of the inexplicable beneath the plainest set of verses. A great deal can be said about why a line of verse is effective, but practically nothing is known about the mode of action of a tune; indeed, 'so impenetrable does the subject seem,' said Dr [Edmund] Gurney, 'as to nourish the suspicion ... that an adequate solution might throw light on many hidden aspects of mind and emotion'; and I believe I am right in saying that no glimmer of this light has yet been thrown. It is not really very illuminating, therefore, to say that verses act in the same way as tunes; no use could be made of the relationship even if we could establish it. And, indeed, the musicians, if they would endure it, have more to gain from the relationship than the poets. For the most striking thing about contemporary music is that it is losing the power of writing melody; one reason for this may be that the modern musician is a highly conscious and cultivated person, such as needs to understand what he is doing if he is to do it well, and while he

88

understands well enough how counterpoint and 'architectonics' work, he does not know how a tune works (why it affects people as it does) at all. I should imagine that this is a case where the artist needs the help of the scientist; people have become strangely dependent on understanding what they are doing; and it seems possible that melody will not revive till it has been explained. Miss Wilson would strongly disagree with this fancy; I mention it only to suggest that melody cannot itself be used to explain poetry.

I called her opinions alarming because they make the critic so helpless; a word which seems obviously wrong on grounds of sense and tone may be just the thing to complete what Miss Wilson, intending no metaphor, calls the tune; you can never know why you feel as you do about a line; and if meaning and music act independently of one another, as is assumed, it is obviously only by a lucky accident that they can both be right. In some degree all this is true, but the critic must want to limit that degree as far as possible; so far as it is true the whole matter is one of luck or magic; poetry is inexplicable, and criticism impossible.

No one denies that the sound of words is important, but there are two main ways in which it may act. It may add to or qualify the meaning, in several ways; by connecting two words together, by implying a rate of movement, by onomatopoeia, or by making a reader interpret the actual movement of the mouth as a gesture. Or it may act on the reader directly, so as not to mean anything, like a tune. Now these two modes of action seem to me as far apart as light and darkness; one of them seems to me intelligible and the other perhaps permanently a mystery. Miss Wilson seems to feel that they are much the same; in her detailed criticism one often does not know which she is thinking of. Her long sound-analysis of the 'Ancient Mariner', for instance, is most delicately observed; but she says almost nothing about *why* the sounds are like that. Again and again she puts down an observation without deducing anything from it, without saying why she thinks it makes part of a right apprehension of the poem. The effect is as if she had begun a sentence and not finished it.

It is the more important to distinguish between these two modes of action because it is hard; because they feel alike. And, further than that, being unconscious of most of what happens to us, we interpret in terms of 'sound' a variety of experiences; people say 'wait a bit, that doesn't sound right,' and then make a purely logical correction; and Robinson Crusoe no less profoundly treats consciousness of the sound of a word as an act of belief in it.

These words were very apt to my case, and made some impression on my thought at the time of reading them, though not so much as they did afterwards; for, as for being delivered, the word had no sound, as I may say, to me; the thing was so remote, so impossible in my apprehension of things.

So one must be suspicious of people who say that poetry is all an observable matter of music; it may be, for instance, that certain rudimentary movements of muscles can be transferred and apprehended as sound; a reader's total apprehension of a passage is felt as something like a sensation, which is made intelligible by attaching it to one of the senses.

But it would be unfair not to repeat some of Miss Wilson's evidence, which is impressive enough; and as, after all, tunes act on people directly, it is very possible that verses may do the same. The essential likeness of speech to music, apart from their common use of rhythm, is that all vowels and most consonants take their character from a sort of chord made up of notes of roughly constant pitch; these appear either as overtones of the note of the voice, or presumably sometimes (as when the word is whispered so as to have no note, or when the note of the voice is higher than the note wanted as its overtone) as separate notes produced in the mouth and throat. A series of words with different vowels, then, does actually contain a series of rather vaguely defined chords. Further, independently of this, the note of the voice changes to give expression; indeed, changes continuously, but not so harshly that it may not give some impression as of a series of notes. And it seems to be true that there is only one, or not many, ways of varying the pitch in a sentence, if you are saying it to convey a particular shade of meaning. One must remember, too, that spoken poetry, or imagined poetry, or the language of strong feeling, tends to give a series of notes more definitely than the language of prose. Thus there are several tunes, or things of the same kind, latent in a line of verse; they don't seem, in the examples given by Miss Wilson, to be at all good tunes, but one need not expect that; what cannot be denied is that they may act on the reader in the same way (whatever that way may be) as a tune does, or another way of the same kind.

Two arguments on the other side deserve notice. Miss Wilson wants song and speech to be intimately connected; she admits that they seem to be controlled from different regions of the brain, but she claims that handwriting and speech are also separate, though handwriting obviously grew from speech, and therefore the argument is a weak one. But the curious thing about the speech centres is precisely that they are themselves a development from the hand-gesture centres; this suggests that the essential thing in the interpretation of speech is not the note but the gesture, the relic of an intelligible symbol. And Sir Charles Paget produces some curious evidence that what we recognise is actually not a sound, but a gesture, which is deduced from what are in fact a variety of sounds. Thus, what the ear recognises, as a musical unit, is a chord; but a vowel is nothing so simple. The pattern of overtones, the shape of the graph of a vowel sound, is entirely different for different pitches of the voice; even the characteristic notes of the vowel vary considerably; the only thing constant for different pitches is the position, the gesture, of mouth and tongue by which it is made. Indeed, some consonants actually have different characteristic notes according to the vowel with which they are associated; it is a fortunate, but surely a most unmusical, delusion which enables us to think they are a definite sound at all. On this evidence, the inventors of language were not drawing on their musical sensibility, and it is not easy to see how written poetry could convey anything definite enough to be like a tune.

Nor is there convincing evidence that a poet needs to be a musician; it may be true that you could tell from a man's poetry that he was not musical, but this would not prove him to be a bad poet. Senator Yeats has remarked that he is tone-deaf; Miss Wilson takes the bull by the horns at this point; quotes one of his less beautiful poems, and remarks that 'it gives the sensation we get from someone singing consistently out of tune.' Now it is quite true that his poems do not read at all like songs; they depend on a delicate and wavering speech-rhythm which does not strike a clear note on single vowels or beat out a plain metre. But surely most people are agreed that, as beauty of sound goes in poetry, Senator Yeats is a poet of very great beauty of sound. This seems to me strong evidence, not that latent music is of no importance in poetry, but that its importance may be very different in the work of different poets; also that there is a great deal more than music in what people speak of as a poem's 'sound'.

Nor do I think that great concentration upon sound is likely to produce good poetry; putting it in the focus of consciousness seems to limit the imagination by limiting what is heard as sound. In any case, there are many other things for a poet to think of at the moment, or at the hour, of composing, and if he has been told to concentrate on what is normally the least conscious part of the whole matter, the other parts are in danger of not getting their due share of attention.

Nor do I think it is likely to produce sensitive criticism; it is no use considering the sound alone, because the sound made is defined, and the sound heard is positively created, by the meaning; Miss Wilson herself sometimes limits her sensibility, isolates the words of a line, and so hears them wrongly. She is shocked to find Donne saying 'So though'; the *th* of "though" damps the tone of *o*, slackens the vibrations, flattens or lowers the pitch, till "though" is out of tune with "so".' I should quote the sentence, but it is twenty lines long ('Obsequies to the Lord Harrington', ll. 111–30). *So* is its turning-point and states the main comparison; *though* only governs four lines, which must be said earnestly, being a compliment, and yet must be kept low, being a minor part of the statement and an argument that goes the wrong way. Hence there is a distinct pause, and a comma, between the two words; it is important to notice them both and say them differently. I agree that *so though*, taken alone, is ugly, but when placed like this its harshness brings out the energy and complexity of the whole argument; no one would notice it as harsh if they were reading the sentence in the right way. This seems to me a good example of how a limited theory may be misleading, because Miss Wilson's powers of observation, in themselves, are extremely delicate; her appreciative criticism, particularly about the Spenserian stanza (p. 156) is beautifully imaginative and precise.

But, of course, to use this argument is to admit Miss Wilson's main thesis; her reason for the fact that *so though* is harsh (which makes it just what Donne wanted) seems true and important; and certainly work on pure sound is a very valuable adjunct to criticism, so long as it is not taken for criticism itself.

Note

1 Untitled in original.

Teaching Literature

Specifically written for Japanese readers, this piece was first published in a translation by Shigehisa Narita in *Literary Art* (Japan), February 1934; text from Empson's original typescript.

A lecturer on literature, especially in a language foreign to those lectured, is often attacked by doubt of the value of the whole process, and needs to have some general ideas about what value it can be to the average student. I shall try to put down such ideas as I have.

It is arguable that all liberal education supported out of taxes is a trick played on the average man for the sake of the exceptional man, that we must go on pretending to think culture worth the while of a lot of people for the sake of the very rare people who do find it worth while, who alone matter, and who could not get it if there was no organisation of it. I shall ignore this view; even if it is true that only these people matter, they depend on the state of the average man; one reason that the many very highly-cultured people in Germany are not safe from Hitler seems to be that culture there is so highbrow.

If the process is not largely useless, the normal student gets from literature pleasure, cheap while he is in reach of libraries, fullness or breadth of emotional life, independence of mind and a sense of proportion. This last involves not the avoidance of emotion (which narrows understanding as much as [?pleasure]) but a power to have strong emotions without forgetting the things he will value at other times, a power to know what his feelings will be under other circumstances so as not to be helplessly surprised by them when they come. It is a by-product of the independence, as are both of the enjoyment.

It is only recently, in England, that discussion of whether the pleasure a particular writer gives has these valuable effects has got loose from the side-issue about whether it promotes chastity. So long as the artist, not thinking chastity of supreme importance, did not dare say so to the moralist he only used the discussion to obscure an already difficult question. We now have a variety of critics attacking many sorts of chaste and idealistic poetry, especially of the late nineteenth century, for being a 'debilitating drug', for being 'an attempt to hide in the warmth of one's own familiar thicket of dream, not to stay out in the wind' (Mr Richards); the charm of this is that it splits the camp of the moralists; a man like Dr Leavis, eager to save his disciples from drugs, is as Puritan as the Censor, and can argue with him on his own ground.

Some very good poetry, for instance the exquisite early poetry of Yeats, is a drug; it gives an extreme pleasure, haunting and sometimes limiting the mind, which is not likely even to give 'breadth of emotional life', much less the other things. But any reading that gives a man pleasure may be valuable to him by giving him the habit of reading, and one would respect anything that put life into the average classroom. I myself as a schoolboy was a slave to the drug of Swinburne, but do not think this has done me permanent harm and cannot even remember a painful disintoxification.

And no rule can be given as to when a poem is a drug. What is a mere drug to one man another may use as a shelter from his immediate environment, behind which more serious things can grow – alcohol itself has this use – or as the direct stimulus of a new way of thinking. Mr Richards in *Science and Poetry* said that De la Mare is a drug-producer *because* he pretends to be admitting the breakdown of the Magical View, the belief that God or Nature is like man and sympathetic to him, and yet secretly assumes and uses it.[1] I think he is a drug-producer, and does do this, but many poets have done it without being drug-producers; number 27 of Housman's *Last Poems* ['The sigh that heaves the grasses'] does exactly this, and is a four-square healthy little poem (only the wind sighs over the dead friend's grave, in the first verse, and does not know if it sighs; only the dew weeps, in the second, and does not weep for the dead man; still it weeps, in the last line, it is firmly personified). For that matter there is no rule for distinguishing otherworldliness from necrophily (e.g. in T. F. Powys) [see 'Death and Its Desires' below], or the mere self-indulgence of indecision from the searching and generalised self-analysis of Catullus' *odi et amo*. No rule, that is, but taste, the free judgement of the whole personality of the reader.

Still it is a real annoyance to be made to *try* to waste your strength on early Yeats when you are ready for stronger meat; indeed is a sufficient explanation of why so many people dislike poetry. The main conclusion relevant to teaching is that a teacher ought to insist on a decent hierarchy of values but not make his students pretend to agree.

The independent mind, the feeling that it is worth while to use one's own reason, that one has a fair chance of seeing the thing for oneself apart from tradition, fashion or caprice, is developed by any process of learning that makes you feel able to understand the things you may have to judge and the world at large. But only a very powerful mind can develop it through a long process of trying to appreciate delicate shades of poetic feeling in a foreign language. There is first a mass of merely submissive memory learning that deals with things like idiom, spelling and pronunciation, where one's own reason is no use, then a hardly less passive if more interesting process of accepting the caprices of the poet and trying to echo his feeling. Most literature students are also made to spend a great deal of time listening to lectures – swallowing what is said as from authority, with no time as in reading to stop and think for themselves; sometimes even in foreign languages, where the mere difficulty of getting the sense occupies the mind; they are then only asked to write from their own judgement as a hectic final test. A worse training for the power of independent judgement could hardly be invented.

This may be an inherent fault of the subject, but various ways can be suggested in which it might be made less serious. All reading of criticism should be connected at once with an independent judgement of the book criticised; the same for lectures (or they may be used as honest but fatuous cramming for an examination, or the student if forced to go should read a book). The student should always write down his own opinion of any book he reads (he needn't keep the criticism; it is used to make him decide something). When you have an opinion of your own, however wrong, some real use may be made of a teacher, because you can argue with him. A Japanese student of literature (e.g.) who proposes afterwards to teach it may make a habit of deciding 'Whatever this stuff may have been in the past, is it important now? Will it be reasonable to ask my audience to worry about it?' And though it is no use specialising *on* literature – he must have wide outside interests if his attitude to it is not to be slavish – he must decide as soon as possible what interests him *in* literature, and not try to get a guidebook knowledge of everything.

It has been argued that the modern system of literary education, obviously so powerful an instrument for smothering independence of mind, was actually designed for that purpose by timid but artful minds hoping to escape political change. If this absurdity is the truth they made a mistake; it should be clear by now that the herd-mind is as easily herded into Communism as Fascism; and it takes considerable independence of mind to keep a country at the same level as its neighbours.

It may be said that a student's opinion is sure to be based on inadequate knowledge, and so a decent modesty will stop him from forming one. But just as you can get nothing from literature without in some degree enjoying it – it is no use treating it as a mere mass of information, because then you don't get the essential information; every reader has to re-make it in his own feelings – so you can only make your feelings real to yourself by recognising them, by forming a 'personal opinion'. If you have had no positive 'reaction' to a book nothing has happened; if you know you thought it ridiculous last year, and why, then you have something to build on and some hope of coming to like it this year. There is always a hideous belief crawling about places of education that you have betrayed yourself if you admit you don't admire a book in the curriculum; this is mere protection for professors.

A lecturer is tempted to put most stress on verse because a concentrated medium is so convenient – one can give short striking examples and find plenty to say about them; besides, as regards English, the best writing in English was done before the ascendancy of prose. But though one can enjoy verse in a foreign language it is peculiarly hard to make an independent judgement of it (apart from the fact that nobody understands English prosody); the student has much more chance to become self-reliant about prose. In any case the Japanese reader does not need to send to the other end of the world for verse of dreamlike, idealistic, poignant lyrical beauty (like the best English nineteenth-century verse); after the trouble of learning to read a foreign literature he may expect something he could not have found at home.

What Japan had really to learn from Europe, the original reason why teachers like myself were imported, was the success of the sciences and of the habit of mind that produced them. The main signs of it in literature are control of logical structure, whose flower is rhetoric, and speed of judgement, whose flower is wit; they are important for poetry, but the source to learn them from is prose.

I should be sorry to write as if it was better to learn chemistry than a foreign literature; most science learning is just memory work too, and to have access to a second living language is a real aid to freedom of judgement and imagination. (What is powerful in one language often seems nonsense in another. Balfour said about one of the German Emperor's pre-war speeches, 'it is only fair to the man to remember he is talking in German.') The question is what book that a student might be interested in would be most useful; I should say that to see the English language really at work one would take e.g. Lord Russell's little book on *The Problems of Philosophy*.

These are strong arguments, I think, for the use of Ogden's Basic as a first stage in learning English, at which you are to stop till you are familiar with it. To get to control those words and their very straightforward grammar does not make you feel frustrated by random tricks, and having done that there is a part of the language in which you are at home, not a passive spectator; this is the essential step towards learning a language. And the parts of the system that may be more difficult than Ogden thinks – e.g. using *it's gone out of my mind* or *memory* for the word 'forget' – are a decent mental training; you have to use the metaphors rationally not just as tricks of the foreign language. It is a very rational instrument; I sometimes find myself turning a sentence into Basic from English in order to decide whether it is nonsense, and I expect one could do that from another language.

The Japanese student is put in a special difficulty in trying to get real use out of the foreign professor because he has very reasonably put most of his effort not into speaking the language but reading its literature. I should like to see this admitted more firmly. Experts on phonetics make out that you have to learn to speak, but, really, ancient Greek has had a considerable effect on Europe, and nobody knows how it was pronounced at all. Elizabethan pronunciation has been partly worked out, so that one or two living Englishmen could understand Shakespeare if they met him; but to say that a Japanese can only approach Shakespeare through the entirely different vowels and rhythms of modern Southern English is absurd.

[2]The English lecturer, if too lazy to learn Japanese, should be expected to write all the remarks he thinks worth attention clearly on the blackboard, while keeping up a flow of talk partly to interest himself, partly to give his students practice in listening; the student should then not be expected to show embarrassment in asking questions afterwards with pen and paper, or in demanding them at a teaparty.

But one cannot set out at the end of an article to show how to stop the Japanese student from feeling embarrassed; if one knew the full answer it would solve many difficulties, both of Japan and of education.

Notes

1 I. A. Richards observed that 'no intimation of the contemporary situation sounds' in De la Mare's poetry. 'He is writing of, and from, a world which knows nothing of these difficulties, a world of pure fantasy for which the distinction between knowledge and feeling has not yet dawned. When in other poems, more reflective, in "The Tryst" for example, Mr De la Mare does seem to be directly facing the indifference of the universe towards "poor mortal longing-ness", a curious thing happens. His utterance, in spite of his words, becomes not at all a recognition of the indifference, but voices instead an impulse to turn away, to forget it, to seek shelter in the warmth of his own familiar thickets of dream, not to stay out in the wind. His rhythm, that indescribable personal note which clings to all his best poetry, is a lulling rhythm, an anodyne, an opiate, it gives sleep and visions, phantasmagoria; but it does not give *vision*, it does not awaken' (*Poetries and Sciences*, London: Routledge & Kegan Paul, 1970, pp. 69–70).

2 Empson deleted one sentence at the beginning of this paragraph of his typescript: 'I suspect too that the Japanese, like the no less insular English, really dislike speaking a foreign language; the absurdly English character Dr Johnson (not at all from our fatuous nineteenth-century pride in being insular, which was not yet invented; and though he had a great command of the language) used to call for pen and paper in dealing with a Frenchman and write down what he had to say.'

Teaching the Meaning in Poetry[1]

Criterion, XV, April 1936

David Daiches, *The Place of Meaning in Poetry*
P. Gurrey, *The Appreciation of Poetry*

Mr Daiches's brief essay is offered as 'an attempt to clear up the contemporary critical confusion' about its subject, but the confusion comes much less into principles than their application. He tells us that meaning is important in poetry, that it must interpret melody and justify emotion, that poetry is different from music, and that it is unwise to write poetry which proves wholly unintelligible. Then there is a jolt when it is apparently assumed that Mr Eliot would reject these truths, owing to the romantic ebullience and wild cult of unreason of that author. It is true that some of the *Waste Land* notes admit to private associations, but that makes one reason why the notes had to be written; the point of such a note is to prevent the reader from worrying and looking deeper. Such a half-apology is obviously quite different to publishing whole poems which make no attempt at communication, and that is what Mr Daiches believes he is attacking. In the same way the following line from Auden's *Orators* is quoted as 'free association', therefore demonstrably bad or rather null. It seems to me plain realism.

> Well?
> As a matter of fact the farm was in Pembrokeshire.
> [Edward Mendelson (ed.), *The English Auden: Poems, Essays and Dramatic Writings* 1927–1939, London: Faber & Faber, 1977, p. 87]

We are told that though the separate lines of the poem have isolated prose meanings they are only connected by Auden's memory or subconsciousness, so cannot make poetry. But if you get the general context, of a man making a shameful confession, this creaking pretence of ease and nervous jerk into irrelevance is no kind of breach with 'meaning', whether with poetry or not; nor is it 'obscure'. It is a piece of horrible photography, and I remember shuddering as I first set eyes on it. But of course if a critic goes on expecting Pembrokeshire to symbolise something he is likely to get irritated. Often indeed when a poem goes on living in your mind, demanding to be re-read, you do not so much penetrate what at first seemed its obscurities as forget about them; they turn out to be irrelevant. The critic therefore cannot come in and demonstrate that a poem is bad because it has no meaning – obviously, in the first place, because he may merely not know the meaning, but he can say it is too hard to know; yet there may be an answer to this too – that he is wrong to expect a meaning at the point he has chosen. Of course there have been puzzling borderline cases in recent poetry; some failures have probably been due to mistaken theory; queer forces have been driving poets into obscurity or into paying a heavy price for clarity; and the critic must be prepared to say firmly in a given case that he judges communication to have failed. But he really cannot do it on a pre-conceived simple theory. It seems fair enough to oppose a platitude to the truths of Mr Daiches, and say that the crucial judgement lies with taste.

The other book, though on the same topic, does not overhang the reader of poetry so much because meant for educators. 'An exact understanding of appreciation can perhaps be attained by noting carefully what it is not,' and the chapters are mainly concerned with telling them *not* to stress unduly technique, imagery, rhythm, emotion, sound ... with examples at the end to show that they do. Even thought must not be overstressed, though mainly because this will make the children bored with the thing, 'and so for them it ceases to be poetry'. No doubt it's good for teachers to be harried, and the only practical advice *is* negative; what is wanted from them is tolerable good taste, power to convey gusto without seeming funny, and room to do it. There seem to be two puzzles, with which Mr Gurrey is not much concerned, centring round compulsion and emotion. He tells you not to stress the things that make an answer in examinations; but you can't help it, and they are liable to be particularly separate here from the real purpose of the teaching. The only tactful thing to do about this is to admit it, and this may give you a chance to treat the genuine part as an occasional holiday, which is heart-warming. (The advantage of dead languages for literary teaching is that by now their questions of taste are fairly settled; you can simply tell people what is the right thing to feel, instead of waiting for them to produce one of the possible reactions and then tampering with it.) Also Mr Gurrey's suspicion of emotions about poetry seems to me too great; the teacher's difficulty is more social than critical. I should not have thought much of an anti-emotive view when I was intoxicated by Swinburne as a schoolboy, but then I had learned to read him from the others, not from a teacher. A class is likely to suspect emotions about poetry of being either unmanly or bogus, and the teacher needs to combat this idea more than sentimentality, though to be sure the two are done in much the same way. He has to show that the feelings possible are of a real and solid kind, and yet treat some of them with a decent detachment as things that need not be aped in a classroom. No doubt he will fail to do this if his theoretical views are grossly wrong, but it is not work into which a theory of appreciation, such as Mr Gurrey's, enters at all directly.

Still, such a theory is more immediately useful to a teacher than to the man Mr Daiches addresses, the appreciator of modern poetry as it comes out; the teacher ought to be stirring up interest in theory and has not as a rule to make new critical decisions. Of course it is an excellent thing for people to discuss their differences of taste, and they need machinery to do it with, but it is hard to feel that an adequate theory of literary criticism, if obtained, would be much more than a device for stopping inadequate theories from getting in your way.

Note

1 Untitled in original.

Explaining Modern Poetry[1]

Criterion, XVI, July 1937

D. G. James, *Scepticism and Poetry*
David Daiches, *New Literary Values*
Dallas Kenmare, *The Future of Poetry*
Martin Gilkes, *Introduction to Modern Poetry*
Bhawani Shankar, *Modern English Poetry*

It must seem a curious thing that there are so many busy little books explaining modern poetry, and apparently finding more readers than the work they explain. Clearly some body of people finds them profitable and agreeable reading, and yet I find it hard to imagine, for myself, supposing I felt baffled altogether by say Auden or Dylan Thomas, either that I should bother to read books denouncing these poets or explaining them by recent history, or that I should like or understand them better if I did. Of course detailed exegesis is another thing; once you like a poet's work you will often find that useful, and anyway you have good reason for starting to read it. But most of these books assume an audience which feels that the stuff is very difficult and often nasty, and yet that in some way there is a duty to worry about it. Mr Daiches leads off with an essay that divides this duty into several heads, a duty to understand the relation of literature to life by studying the unique case where they are now interacting, a duty to make our society healthy by giving it a feeling of reciprocity between author and public, and so on. Now it is a good thing to have some force making people take the trouble to look for tolerable pleasures, but I should fancy the old snob force worked better than this moral one. And as a point of conscience, anyone can think of more pressing duties than reading a new book he dislikes. Nor does it make for particularly good criticism; suddenly a cloud of general reflection, about why these queer men feel the way they do, will swoop down to a small irrelevant point supposed to illustrate a Tendency or an Influence, and then up the mass will soar, back to its billowing. The most alarming statement in Mr Daiches's book is that 'Owen is claimed by some modern poets as an important influence on their poetry'; this he is sure must be untrue, because 'we are not to-day brought suddenly face to face with fundamental values' as Owen was in the war (p. 65). But what a hideous picture this is, of the poets clamouring and jockeying for their Influences. And surely it is a libellous one, be the critics as fussy as they may.

Not that Mr Daiches's criticism is at all bad when he settles down to particular people, though he is best on novelists; he is unfair to Sassoon, through not seeing that political verse satire has to make different points from Owen's. All you want is to remove the portentousness. Mr Kenmare's *Future of Poetry* is a lively indignant work by a Christian poet, rebuking the lack of idealism in present-day critics and poets alike. He believes that the public is still sound, and responds to genuine idealistic work like *The Fountain* by Charles Morgan and *Murder in the Cathedral* by T. S. Eliot. The muddle I think is a theological one; the poets ought to praise the world because God made it good, and yet he says it is illogical to doubt the Christian God merely because of the evil of the world. But it may be the duty of the poet to follow the example of Jeremiah; and surely he throws away his mediating case when he says that Shelley did nothing to help produce the reforms he demanded which have since then been made. And anyway it is not true that recent poetry only bewails the evil of the world. Mr Gilkes's book is a very decent production mainly for students of Birmingham University, and contains one serious piece of exegesis, of a ballad by Auden. Certainly if you were being nagged through an examination course on English Literature it might be a real step to be told Why Auden Writes Like This. It seems to me very doubtful to say that way back in early times all poets wrote like arithmetic, whereas Auden writes like algebra, and it is difficult to say anything for Dryden after you have given the Victorians a monopoly both of Personality and of Beauty of Sound (and that is at least suggested); but still you can guess at a public where the book is useful and not fussy. The Indian book is also for undergraduates (Allahabad) and not so Modern as to reach Mr Eliot except in the introductory essay; it is competent and would be useful; the main human interest in it is a mysterious failure of the tone over Kipling, though what is said is sensible and fair.

Mr James is a different matter. He joins on to the others because he is concerned with the relation of poetry to religion, and this kind of worry is typical. But he is not concerned with recent verse, though recent criticism comes in. Indeed he has a long attack on Dr Richards, fighting for the Imagination against that author, with a late footnote saying that though Dr Richards appears now to agree with him the Doctor must change his position radically before the agreement will count. The main argument is that the work of the poet's Imagination must essentially attempt to form a unified view of the world, and that this is doomed to failure though valuable, because the only unified view is a supernatural one. It is natural then that the great line of English poets is un-Christian, and that the two who became Christian, Shakespeare and Wordsworth, thereby lost their powers. Mr James is himself a Christian. There is a very interesting chapter on the last plays of Shakespeare, as a series of unsatisfactory attempts at Christian symbolism; and another on how near Keats got to Christianity, before the pause before death that surprised him, and in which he wrote nothing. I really think that one sentence is what makes me feel blank about the large thesis of this book. 'The Solitary, indeed, unlike Wordsworth, had known private grief' (p. 150). This has an obscure use for the thesis, because Mr James must keep out of view that Wordsworth had another reason for sterility, not simple Christianity but a smug hiding of the early life that had failed him. Yet granting that it seemed a clear and honest remark, how obscurely anxious for his thesis, how fussy a man must be to write that down. A careful study of these books leads one to agree rather solemnly with what they so often tell us, that to write good criticism is very hard indeed. In fact some kinds of error are best avoided if you just jump at the thing.

Note

1 Untitled in original.

The Verbal Analysis

Kenyon Review, vol. 12, Autumn 1950
A contribution to a symposium entitled 'My Credo'

When I was asked by letter to contribute to the symposium from Peking, my first impulse was to say that I didn't believe in having any Credo; a critic ought to trust his own nose, like the hunting dog, and if he lets any kind of theory or principle distract him from that, he is not doing his work. This does seem to me the deepest truth about the matter; but the bottom, as Mr T. S. Eliot remarked, is a great way down. There is the same position about a moral or ethical theory; however firm your belief in it, and however definite its ruling on a particular case, you still have to see whether your feelings can be brought to accept the results in that case. If they can't, well, you may be wrong, but if it gets too bad, you have to give up the theory. All the same, there is clearly a need for such theories; for one thing, without a tolerable supply of handy generalisations you can't stretch your mind to see all round a particular case. And the theory alters the feelings no less than the feelings alter the theory.

The metaphor to keep in mind, surely, is the standard one of Taste. It has become less obvious in the last generation or two because of a kind of traffic jam in both literature and criticism, one which nobody need be blamed for. We know a good deal more than we did about the human mind, and expect a writer to work from the whole body of his experience, so that references to psychological and sociological and anthropological affairs may very properly be cropping up; and the critic is to expect the same things in earlier writers even if used 'unconsciously'. Also we have only recently begun to try and appreciate all the arts of all periods of all countries, or rather to try and pick out from them representative high-standard cases, fix in our minds the whole range of possible achievement; and meanwhile we have had on our hands the results of the first attempts at universal education ever made. People were bound to look round for some System which would give quick answers and break up some local traffic jam, often very usefully. Going back to the metaphor of Taste, however, any such theory needs to be regarded as a salt or what not which is to be dissolved into the blood; in its crystal form, when it is portable or transferable, it is quite useless for the ultimate purpose; it must be digested, but it may none the less really be needed. What the thing is all *about*, the test of the value of learning these theories, is when a foreign body is masticated and brought up to the taste buds (or palped, if you prefer, by the 'tact' of an exploring fingertip); there is a diffusion across a skin, which needs to hold firm, but there is an otherwise direct action between the foreign body and the living blood (for the finger you would say the living nerves).

It often strikes me that students going through the kind of critical course I think good are liable to get into a mood of excessive anxiety about their own capacity for tasting, and that others (probably the ones with less natural taste to be anxious about) tend to complain fretfully that the machine offered them is not a completely reliable machine, such as would be guaranteed to save them from having to risk tasting anything at all. Of course the second feeling is ridiculous; even with the most self-acting modern machine, some real human being has to check whether it is out of order or broken down. The first is not absurd, and any serious type of training has to be watched for the same danger; it begins to give bad results if it is screwed up to the point of excessive strain, excessive, that is, for the particular people concerned. And of course in any training for literary criticism one needs to get quite clear, what I think usually is clear to those concerned, that they are expected to use their own Taste, and that it would be a very bad sign if they never disagreed with Teacher.

Another trouble that seems to crop up is the idea that poetry is good in proportion as it is complicated, or simply hard to construe; it seems quite a common delusion, and always shocks me when expressed. And yet I suppose it is very near my own position; in any case it joins onto I. A. Richards's Theory of Value as the satisfaction of more impulses rather than less, and T. S. Eliot's struggle to find a poetic idiom adequate to the complexity of modern life. But, without disagreeing with these figures at all, it is necessary to see the point of the reply of Wordsworth:

> The gods approve
> The depth, and not the tumult, of the soul.
>
> ['Laodamia', l. 75]

Indeed 'depth analysis' is probably the best way out of this limiting critical impasse. If you realise the weight of the latent politics in Wordsworth's apparently simple descriptions of Nature, both in the metaphors used and in the intense political experiences he had actually gone through before arriving at them, you are no longer likely to complain (of *The Prelude*, at any rate) that he is only serving up apple-dumplings at his state banquet. It may be, as some critics would object, that this would only mean going off on another side-line (though I do not believe so myself) but it would at least be a reassurance allowing taste to act on the verse without being put off by its absence of surface complexity.

The essential thing is to get the process the right way up. If the reader feels a passage is good, let him by all means direct his attention to considering what the profound complexities are, which his theory leads him to expect there; the trouble is when he presumes it cannot be good if it does not seem complex.

I am thus very little willing to sympathise, in one way or another, with critics who feel objections (or a crusading spirit) against analytical study of literary texts. But I cannot believe they mean to go to the startling lengths they sometimes imply. There is an important distinction to be made here, one that Mr Ransom was pointing out not long ago. It is all very well to say that the learner may learn to use his own taste, and therefore must be simply 'exposed' to the work of art in question; but you have still got to get him exposed to it. As is particularly clear with children from homes where they don't read poetry, but also sometimes true I am afraid of all of us, it is quite possible to be confronted with a work of art and not see what the point of it is, what it is trying to do, how one part of it is supposed to affect another. There is room for a great deal of exposition, in which the business of the critic is simply to show how the machine is meant to work, and therefore to show all its working parts in turn. This is the kind of criticism I am specially interested in, and I think it is often really needed. Anyone who objects to it because it does not try to give a Final Valuation of the work, in relation to all other work, seems to me merely irrelevant. Where I should heartily agree with him would be if he said that, after all this supplying of the reader or the student with the machine, the vital question is whether he can make it go, whether he gets the experience in question; and also, for that matter, whether it leaves him better equipped to do the same thing on another occasion of his own accord.

Going back to the question of Valuation: I do not mean to say, what would be a very foolish thing to say, that criticism has nothing to do with valuation. It has to do with it all the time, because you cannot even say just how some element works without suggesting how well it works. But to assess the value of the poem as a whole is not the primary purpose of this kind of criticism, or at any rate ought only to emerge from the analysis as a whole. There is a tendency to feel that, if the critic is offering a really efficient machine, it ought to be able to say whether marmalade is better than sausages; but even the most expert cook cannot say that; sometimes you want one, sometimes the other. Especially in our own age, the first to make a serious effort to appreciate the whole variety of good literature, this kind of absolutism seems to be comical. In any case, there is no question of the critics providing a Last Judgement about the works of the past; Mr T. S.

Eliot once remarked that a critic could only hope to illuminate the work of a past period from the point of view of his own. The metaphor deserves pondering, because it is not denied that he gives real light such as may clarify the work for a still later generation, but only that he can claim to look from all possible historical or cultural points of view at once. As to the poems of his own generation, surely there can be no doubt that he ought to judge them, after proper mastication, by his own Taste; any theories he may have, based on the experience of the past, are precisely what the new work ought to be testing. Finally I do not deny that it may be a splendid thing to have a grand synthesis of human experience, a single coherent Theory of Value which could be applied to all works of art and presumably to all human situations; but it seems hardly reasonable to grumble, in the present state of affairs, that nobody has provided one; and if it did exist it would clearly be a philosophical synthesis rather than a literary one.

The kind of criticism that most interests me, verbal analysis or whatever one calls it, is concerned to examine what goes on already in the mind of a fit reader; sometimes bringing it up from levels of unconsciousness deep enough to make it look rather surprising, but even so not expected to make much difference to the feelings of the fit reader after he has got over this surprise. Like all theories about the action of the mind, in short, there is a sense in which it does not need to be expounded; if it is true, we are already acting on it all the time. The only *use* of it is when something goes wrong; but this is true of a good deal of knowledge, such as the ordinary car-driver's knowledge of the working of the carburettor. A quite practical problem therefore often arises, as to how much of the analysis needs to be written down; often a very great deal could be written down which though true doesn't need saying (except indeed to forestall a certain type of objector, who likes to tell the critic he was ignorant of what was too obvious to need saying). If you are trying to tell your audience what it is missing, what the Elizabethans for example would feel about a passage whose language has been dulled, it is clear that you need to know your audience as well as your topic. I should think indeed that a profound enough criticism could extract an entire cultural history from a simple lyric, rather like Lancelot Andrewes and his fellow preachers, 'dividing the Word of God,' who were in the habit of extracting all Protestant theology from a single text. A critic obviously does not need to do this kind of thing often, if at all; it is not really a convenient way to teach cultural history. But it is not my fault, or the fault of any other analytical critic, that our equipment threatens to make us become bores; it is wonderful how many ways there are to be a bore, and almost any line of intellectual effort, however true and useful, presents this threat. I do not know that any of us would deny that we had better try to keep to saying what is worth saying.

The business about digging up the Unconscious, at its various levels, has a separate difficulty of exposition. For example Mr Elder Olson, in a recent number of *Modern Philology*,[1] was objecting to a passage I had written long ago (my *Ambiguity*, p. 49) about some remarks of Macbeth:

> If th' Assassination
> Could trammell up the Consequence, and catch
> With his surcease, Success ...

He seemed particularly irritated by the sentence, '*Trammell* was a technical term used about netting birds, hobbling horses in some particular way, hooking up pots, levering, and running trolleys on rails.' This and similar remarks about other words in the speech he called 'a meaningless and taste-less muddle', because these meanings are clearly not all meant to appear. But I do not think I have ever heard anyone use the word *trammell* in ordi-nary life; it still seems to me sensible to go to the dictionary and find what sort of thing it 'meant' to an Elizabethan. These extra meanings are present, not in any deep unconscious, but in the preconscious levels where we handle lexicon and grammar, in our ordinary talk, at the speed we do (surely the various current uses of a word must be in the mind somehow, or how can we pick out the right one so quickly?). These current uses of the word appear to Shakespeare or his audience as a kind of feeling about what you could do with it; and the literary effect here, though simple in its way, is I think very strong. Macbeth is trying to feel that this is only a kind of engin-eering problem; if only he can get the murder done efficiently, he thinks, all this fog will lift and he will be able to see clearly again. Both the mechanical analogy and its underlying complexity still seem to me very direct parts of the speech. You may say, no doubt, that I ought to have indicated how far these meanings were supposed to be 'unconscious', but if I had done that all through it would have made the book much longer without really making it clearer. Mr Olson goes on to argue, from a kind of Aristotelian position I think, that the context of the dramatic character, and the stage reached in the structure of the planned work of art, are both extremely relevant to a lit-erary effect, without being part of the meaning of the words used there. This is merely a question of definition; I should include among what a pass-age 'meant' (to a fit reader) its whole literary effect, from whatever cause, and I claim I was patently considering that here in saying what the words 'meant'. What I would be inclined to claim, after this point of definition had been overcome, is that cases arise where we have forgotten how the whole structure would strike a contemporary, and are doubtful between one theory and another (so far from its always being obvious as Mr Olson appears to assert) and then we can decide between such theories by examining minor word-pointers which at the time merely 'fitted in' and did not seem important.

I hope that this more or less covers the points at issue; but I have not yet approached a passage in the original letter which asked me to discuss the co-operative work of critics, and the social responsibilities which their method of work requires them to assume, as well as the vital philosophy from which it must have proceeded. I do not wish to appear flippant, but cannot at the moment raise the spirits to answer in the high tone which these questions deserve. As to co-operation, I hope I don't refuse it, but I have noticed that, when you give a party, the best thing is not to rush at everybody and try to force them to talk to each other; in a party that goes unexpectedly well (in the way of making disparate groups talk to each other) you often notice that the host has been stuck away in the corner most of the time, talking to some expert about a technical point he is really interested in. As to responsibility, there was an earnest lady in the last war who took the opportunity of an introduction to President Roosevelt to urge upon him the great weight of the responsibility which she trusted he was properly conscious of, and his only reply (with a rudeness quite unusual to him) was an impatient movement of his hand. Obviously it would have made his judgement fatally bad if he worried all the time about his responsibilities. Even in so humble a walk of life as literary criticism, it seems to me, a man might feel the same; the best thing for him to do as a critic is to do his work as best he can, and he has still plenty of responsibilities as a social being. But of course I do not mean to deny that he really has responsibilities as a critic too. It seems clear that critics have been making a steady effort to act on them.

Note

1 Elder Olson, 'William Empson, Contemporary Criticism and Poetic Diction', *Modern Philology*, XLVII: 4 (May 1950), pp. 222–52; one of the most fiercely sustained assaults on Empson's critical approach in *Seven Types of Ambiguity* – which Olson dubbed a 'mechanical method ... capable of all the mindless brutality of a machine' (p. 225).

Monks and Commissars

New Statesman, 13 December 1952

Donald Davie, *Purity of Diction in English Verse*

As I want to attack this book I had best say at the start that it is worth attacking, and contains important truths, and is in line with other influential writers. Mr Davie is right in emphasising that poems of earlier periods which we still admire were praised in their time for chastity and decorum of diction, virtues to which the modern literary critic (though there has never before this century been literary criticism of such breadth and depth) commonly appears blind. A recovery from 'experimental' and 'transitional' work does seem overdue, and many poets seem to be recognising it. The prospect looks a bit flat to old fogeys like me, but that is a familiar historical turn. Mr Davie is right, too, when he breaks an obscure snobbery by praising some hymns by Wesley; not only chaste and decorous in their diction, they are also urbane. He only throws this term in, but it shows, I think, the difficulty of reviving the old terms. He means by 'urbane' (apparently) that Wesley could write concentrated religious verse because he could assume a knowledge of Scripture in his audience; 'urbanity' is being able to assume any form of cultivation in an audience. The mere shift of a term is nothing to grumble about, though surely an eighteenth-century figure who called Wesley urbane would be rather absurd and would not mean that. But I think Mr Davie is under another snobbery when he does not also praise nineteenth-century hymns; for instance, the line

> Glad with Thee to suffer pain

would get a lot of praise from critics if it happened to come in one of Donne's love-poems; but Mr Davie is assuming, apparently, from some political principle, that nineteenth-century writing was Impure, hymns and all. He jeers in passing at a line by Tennyson:

> Tears from the depth of some divine despair
> ['The Princess', IV, l. 22]

as 'an accidental fuzziness' compared to some flat but decent bit of hymn-work, merely because it is not tied to a compact theology.[1] The jeers of the orthodox at the religious sentiments of the free-thinkers have long seemed to me the kind of bad propaganda that comes from bad feelings; their business is to develop such ideas, not try to kill them by boasting that they have the only correct ones. It seems to me stupid not to feel that the Tennyson line is beautiful.

The book has a fine ruthlessness in insisting that purity of diction has a natural connection with purity of character, though stopping at the point: 'It is best to think, therefore, that we condemn Shelley's eroticism (as we do) because it produces a jargon, and not because we dislike it "in itself".' A literary divergence is found in the theoretical programme of Mr Pound (an old leader of the general movement) which of course explains why he went wrong politically, too; Mr Eliot, however, has at last come out just right. I get a strong smell of monks or commissars here. Waiving Mr Pound, who is a deeply charitable man, and his views on Jews, let us consider the yearning Mr Eliot suggesting how to keep the poor tolerably ignorant, out of a genuine public spirit, I don't deny; here is the chastity and decorum of literary style which is so closely related to the moral virtues with the same names; and then cast an eye on the disgustingly self-indulgent Shelley, a man who naturally couldn't write, because he gave away a fortune and lived chiefly on bits of bread and was hag-ridden by the thought of universal welfare. I am inclined to think that the self-indulgent member of this triangle is Mr Davie. He repeatedly claims to offer a moral method of criticism, and even says that he wouldn't bother with his subject except for its moral importance. With ingenuity as well as charity, he finds a kind word for Shelley, that Shelley had an urbane conversational diction for minor poems because he was the only real gentleman among the Romantic poets (Byron hadn't been brought up as one). It suggests to me a Sunday schoolteacher, all the more blankly certain she is right because of her complete non-realisation of what she is saying, who happens to have got round to saying, 'That was a very good lion because it ate so many Christians.' Some Christians have claimed that their religion invented benevolence, which is absurd; but it is not insane like this Neotheory, that a Christian has to reprobate benevolence as a form of libidinousness. I call that getting rattled.

My feeling about Shelley is that he was morally impregnable but had no ear. However, this feeling about sound changes very oddly; one of the Late Victorian pundits, who would reprobate the morals, broke into ecstasy over the sheer beauty of sound of the line:

Fresh spring, and summer, and winter hoar. ['A Lament']

Fresh spring; I would expect this to be used in a bitter satire against the hideousness of English; which has yet a beauty that can only be found by those who love her. Nobody seems to understand these changes of feeling about sound – my own are merely those of my generation – and it seems at least premature to erect a moral theory on the current ones.

As giving a social programme, Mr Davie runs into a contradiction which he hardly recognises. If the urbanity of style possible till the late eighteenth century depended on a class culture and diction which then collapsed, so that the Romantics can't be blamed for losing it, then I can't see how he can ask modern poets to bring it back now. To be sure, I fancy he would be a bit startled by the urbanity of Johnson or Rochester or James I if he met them; the roots of things are not as quiet as he tends to assume; and I daresay some very un-urbane writing just now would be the only way to produce the state of public feeling which he rightly wishes to recommend. But I should think he is probably right, he is making a good spot about what the exam of future life will be, when he recommends Pure Diction to his pupils. I wish I knew how to disentangle the part of this story that is true from the part which could be positively harmful.

Note

1 What Empson terms a 'decent bit of theology' is Charles Wesley's 'Victim divine, Thy grace we claim' (see Davie, *Purity of Diction in English Verse*, London: Chatto & Windus, 1952, pp. 79–80).

Jam Theory and Imagism[1]

The New Statesman and Nation, 21 March 1953

S. J. Kahn, *Science and Aesthetic Judgment*
Herbert Read, *The True Voice of Feeling*

Taine started publishing just over a century ago, thus in a way fixing up the big top of the circus of modern literary criticism, and it is rather startling to be reminded that the thing has been going on in full swing ever since. Both the Germans and the English, of course, had been already coming out with surprising opinions since the final quarter of the eighteenth century, but Taine felt he was equipped to domesticate both of them under the big top of the historical approach. Marx, Darwin, Frazer and Freud had still to bound into the ring, each of them giving yet more startling reasons for believing that the critic ought to know far more about what an author means than the author did, but there was always room for them under the historical approach. It does seem hard to envisage this process as going on for ever; no wonder a number of recent critics, especially in America, have felt that you need to codify literary criticism and tidy it all up.

I feel Mr Kahn is capable of giving a more interesting book than he has done; what he gives (and the title ought to say so) is a conspectus of the statements by Taine about his methods of criticism and his literary views, beginning with his student notebooks and letters, and also of the statements made about him by everybody else. He points out where Taine's views are out of date, but insists at the end of most of the chapters, convincingly I think, that the breadth of mind with which Taine approached a question of principle was masterly and is still needed. It is clearly a valuable as well as an immensely detailed reference book, but I wish he had taken a specific case where opinions differ and shown (if it is true) that all these different theories would actually produce different responses to it.

Sir Herbert Read also carries a great sense of history, but regards himself, very rightly, as an active part of the movement he supports. It is 'the' Romantic position, mainly dated back to a speech by Schelling of which he provides a translation in an appendix. One must respect his firmness, and can hardly deny his main belief, which, as I understand, would have been

accepted by Taine: that the artist should 'create' his own forms, not merely
work within traditional forms, that by expressing himself he should express
the developing society of which he is part, that to do this he needs to insist
on being 'sincere', and that this rather complex truth about the artist and
society was first discovered by the Romantics. He feels we need to grasp it
firmly so as to go forward and do better, whereas Mr Kahn, writing from
Jerusalem University, says in his preface that we need to decide, after studying history, which bits of the past of Europe we can hope to hand down at
all – 'survival itself is involved.' The sturdy anarchism of Sir Herbert,
though heartwarming, does come to seem something like playful.

I keep suspecting I find a twist in his arguments, though I am sure they
don't come from any unconscious bad desire in himself, only from, so to
speak, jollying along his theory. He is concerned to praise what is popular
(low-class) or native (*Beowulf* and all that) or spontaneous (children's
paintings), and to heighten his praise of such art works he tends to make
them out more savage or mindless than they are. I seemed to get a whiff of
the same thing among intellectuals in China at times, when they were praising the recent revival of peasant arts; clearly, if you say 'this coarse stuff is
good because the people like it,' you are in no position to develop it; the
point was rather that surprisingly good traditions had been kept just alive
under difficulties, but needed refurbishing. Sir Herbert thinks of a civilised
man as like a crab, and he thinks of a crab as like a tin of jam, which only
needs the lid taking off; but both ideas are wrong, as the Romantic theory
itself would tell him, indeed as he himself shows when he formulates it. It is
too much for Sir Herbert to say laughingly that the meaning of a poem
doesn't matter (p. 62) and it is actually surprising when one has to deduce
from this that he meant to praise Ezra Pound (p. 134) by saying that the
meaning of the *Cantos* doesn't matter; a view which Pound, to do him
justice, would not hold.

This comes out in all his discussions of metre, where he is in each case
concerned to argue not that there is an 'unconscious' rule, arrived at by
taste, but that there is none; thus, he actually praises Coleridge for being
'free' or even 'sincere' in the peculiar sense that he told a quite unnecessary
lie in his preface advising the reader how to take the metre of 'Christabel'
(p. 27). But I think Coleridge meant something true, and worth looking for.
He said he had written four stresses to each line; when he appears to give
less the reader need only treat dramatically a line which would otherwise
appear flat; the question is what to do when he gives more. I think he treats
two stressed words together as a single stress in English, and I think a
recording machine would actually show them as a continuous peak on the
graph (the idea that consonants don't make much noise is, of course, only
an odd delusion). Also I think many English poets do this, so that Coleridge

had made a useful discovery, though as so often he didn't get it said clearly enough. But anyway, even if this is wrong, I don't think a Romantic need object to it for not being free.

What really happens, in the detail of Sir Herbert's criticism, is that he issues severe laws which any poet must obey if he is to be let go as sincerely free, and then he interprets them as a policeman actually would, trying to carry out the letter of these laws as his duty without seeing any point in them at all. For instance he decides it is eighteenth-century Poetic Diction to say 'O', so any poet who does it must have sold himself to officialdom; and then poor Walt Whitman is given an awful bullying for saying 'O,' whereas I should bet (if you want popular speech from a poet) that Whitman was hearing people around him say 'O' all the time. The same worry goes on about 'inversion' of grammar, as in popular proverbs.

The reason why he wants Coleridge to have believed in the Collective Unconsciousness theory of Jung, I think, is that this highly mystical and refined theory, as often happens, sets you free to act on your primitive Jam theory. How a tradition gets remembered (perhaps by a ruling-class child hearing things from the slaves) is often an interesting sociological question; whether we have actual inborn quirks of thought, vastly older presumably, might be examined; but to say we have all human experience inside us, simply as the jam in our tin, allows us no technique to examine any such question.

Imagism, which is seriously supported by Sir Herbert, seems to me merely a logical deduction from the Jam theory, and therefore wrong. The recent electrical calculating machines, though they needn't be called 'brains', ought to be considered here, because they really are like the human brain, whereas all previous machines have been like other parts of the human body; and they at least give you an impression of what immense equipment we must have even to do what we think elementary. And they don't use 'images' at all; the whole idea of Imagism is a mistake made by philosophers in the seventeenth century. Sir Herbert quotes T. E. Hulme with approval for saying –

Thought is prior to language and consists in the simultaneous presentation to the mind of two images. Language is only a more or less feeble way of doing this.[2]

It is a great misfortune that T. E. Hulme was killed before he learnt better, but Sir Herbert can learn better. A dog couldn't find its way home across a field if it had nothing in its head, at a moment of choice, except a 'simultaneous presentment of two images'. This condition often actually does come to men lost in the desert, and they know themselves that they must either break out of it or perish.

It is also curious to me that the remarks of I. A. Richards in *The Philos-*

ophy of Rhetoric never get even a perfunctory reply from Imagists.[3] Here is
Sir Herbert discussing Coventry Patmore, a poem about 'How full of bonds
and simpleness is God,' and then:

> And all His art
> Is as the babe's that wins his Mother to repeat
> Her little song so sweet!   ['Legem Tuam Dilexi']

Sir Herbert comments: 'What images there are in such a passage are banal
to the point of sentimentality; and what we have, apart from such images, is
merely a sinuous thread of abstractions' [p. 91]. Now a baby gurgling and
therefore getting something it likes done again (not *one* Image but a
sequence) is probably the root of all human thought; I cannot use the
language of fashion which is so natural to Sir Herbert; I am merely glad it
happens often. But if he means by Image the *whole comparison* of the baby
in this sequence to God in his relation to his creatures (and this was the logical point that Richards made), then obviously it is not Banal but too startling; I can't imagine a tribe which acted on this belief and still kept going at
all well. I agree with Sir Herbert's taste here, but I find his way of discussing
the point extremely 'classical' in just the sense of that term that his theory
disapproves. Also, of course, it is rather ludicrous that he has to blame
Michael Roberts for a 'confusing use of the word romanticism' (p. 113)
when Roberts recognises that Hulme considered himself passionately anti-
romantic, whereas Sir Herbert wants to use him as a pillar of Romanticism.

I have felt rather startled, comparing these two books, to realise how
much is still going firmly on in the different booths under the big top, so
confident, so able and busy, so determinedly out of contact with each other.
It does look as if somebody might co-ordinate them a bit more.

Notes

1 Untitled in original.
2 Herbert Read, *The True Voice of Feeling*, London: Faber & Faber, 1953, p. 109. The
aphorism was originally quoted from Hulme by Michael Roberts in *T. E. Hulme*, London:
Faber & Faber, 1938, p. 281.
3 See I. A. Richards's 'The Command of Rhetoric' in *The Philosophy of Rhetoric*,
Oxford: Oxford University Press (1936), rpt. 1965, pp. 127ff.

Words and Techniques

New Statesman, 31 October 1953

George Whalley, *Poetic Process*
W. J. Entwistle, *Aspects of Language*

Mr Whalley draws a radical distinction between the 'prelogical', contemplative, integrative processes on which the arts depend and the technical, logical, analytic processes of scientific thought; the first is the more fundamental and inherently involves judgements of value. This does not seem very controversial. But, as he takes it, he has to confuse his own terms even in trying to define them, because 'poetry constantly strives towards a wholeness in which all technical distinctions interfuse and are obliterated.' Thus in the highest forms of metaphor 'the words say exactly what they mean, refer quite explicitly to what they say, and are in no evident way figurative or allusive' – in fact are not metaphorical. He cites the famous calm at sea:

> No use of lanthorns, and in one place lay
> Feathers and dust; today and yesterday.

The details are 'resonant', he says, and I agree, but what use is the term *metaphor* if it must cover that? It becomes only a cry of praise. In the same way, we find, a rhythm never repeats, no symbolical meaning ever reveals itself completely, a poem though inherently moral is necessarily bad if it expresses a moral, and a myth ought not to tell a story (because 'narrative order is a logical order,' and that is the enemy). As to the highest forms of Imagination, Mr Whalley has a fine quotation from Coleridge: 'the poet wishes to express ... the substitution of a sublime feeling for the unimaginable for a mere image,' and says, 'it is only a convenient device to use the term "image" as if we could, by thinking, detach a single image from its matrix of feeling.' None of it seems at all convenient to me.

He says rather gracefully in the foreword that he went through the book trying to take out his 'note of asperity' against science, but felt he couldn't, because there is so much materialism in North America (he writes from Toronto) which no doubt is invading Europe now. The word *material* has become fascinatingly confused. All that sexiness on the campus, that craving for a shiny motor-car – those states of mind are material; but a printed page by Mr Whalley, when he has got into a real muddle – that's a spiritual thing like a star. My students in Peking, dialectical materialists of course, their eyes shining with idealism and mutual aid, taking their asceticism for granted, would sometimes write down in two consecutive sentences that the Americans were wicked because they were so material and that the Russians were good because they were so material. When I pointed this out, they quite saw it was against the rules but only wanted to know how to express the sentiment correctly. It does not seem to have much to do with science. I cannot see that any of Mr Whalley's views depend on ignoring such knowledge as we have about the little grey cells; indeed to suggest, as his book does, that you can't believe in Value at all unless you ignore them, seems to me a counsel of despair. The mind is a great mystery, even in the beasts, but we need not invent this terrible dichotomy for it. Which is learning to ride a bicycle, contemplative or analytic?

The massive book of the late Professor Entwistle is also affected by the swing away from mechanism, a healthy change no doubt in linguistic theory. He views language as doing on the whole what the speakers want; Plato and Aristotle seem to pluck philosophical rabbits out of the empty linguistic air, but their language had been training to do it for generations. This humane approach, however, makes him treat the more savage languages, by contrast, as practically sub-human, a tendency which might have bad practical effects. I am not competent to review this learned book, but I have read several of the kind, with the eye somehow content to pick up nice bits (as here that the derivation *lucus a non lucendo* was after all correct), and I never understand how the examples are chosen. You may get them from a dozen languages on one point, too many if only definiteness is wanted, too few for a survey, and without even being told whether they are chosen as typical or peculiar examples. A short paragraph here (p. 224) seemed particularly strange. A sentence about the genitive connecting nouns in Semitic (as in the Bible, presumably, but that isn't said). A stern warning that it is hard to distinguish a postposition from a case-suffix. A sad little aside that perhaps there isn't any difference. A philosophical reflection, obviously untrue, that position in space is the fundamental characteristic of nouns. And then the clincher: 'The Bantu system of locations is not highly developed.'

The Bantu use ideophones, which 'are expressive but not intelligible, like a baby's expression *to go bye-bye*' (it seems possible that somebody else understood the baby, though not the professor). 'The 160 ideophones listed by Doke are all sensual; they include such impressions as ... "putting away carefully", "issuing in numbers", "guilty looks".' Now what can possibly be meant by calling such ideas 'sensual', except to express contempt? I take it the words are grammatically peculiar, and in English would be called idiomatic, but there is nothing savage about them. The language of the Australian Arunta, to plunge deeper, is pre-grammatical; he is too dull to invent genders (oddly enough, on a distant page, the genders in French are also called pre-grammatical). He cannot have a future tense because he 'makes no provision for the future' (I would not believe this of a duck-billed platypus). There is an entrancing proof that he has no notion of self: 'An Arunta, when shown his photograph, recognised in it HIMSELF, his brother, and his totemic animal. His life was entirely that of his clan and he had no notion of self.' This is to show that he couldn't have a first personal pronoun. I hope they pinched him to see if he rubbed one of his sibs.

Still the Strange Necessity

Sewanee Review, LXIII: 3, Summer 1955

Edmund Wilson, *The Shores of Light*
R. S. Crane, *The Languages of Criticism and
the Structure of Poetry*
W. K. Wimsatt Jr, *The Verbal Icon*
R. P. Blackmur, *Language as Gesture*

Edmund Wilson comes out best, in this interesting cross-section of American literary criticism; to the eye of a foreigner, at least, and the other books do for once make me feel a bit foreign. Not, of course, that the British critics nowadays don't tend to be fairly sour and dull, in their own way. The directness of Edmund Wilson, the readiness, the mere number of languages he reads – surely that is the kind of thing you want from a critic. He is educated without having to make a fuss about it; nice to see that he printed, a long time ago, in all friendship, that the way Scott Fitzgerald threw the language about was like the man in the Bab Ballads who would diligently play on the zoetrope all day and blow the gay pantechnicon all night. But then, how much you had *better* throw the language about is a practical and recurrent question; indeed, it is perhaps the chief thing that the more solemn critics on this list are really trying to discuss. The practice of making a book out of old magazine articles might seem scraping the barrel rather, but two of the other authors here are doing it as well (Mr Crane is reprinting a lecture course), and it seems sensible enough in all of them. Wilson gets more interest out of it from reprinting his version of any controversy as it happened, back in the twenties and thirties. Interesting to see that in 1925 he thought it basic to Henry James's view of the world that Maggie Verver and her father, in *The Golden Bowl*, were 'unselfish'. This opinion was strongly supported this year in the *Sewanee Review*, whereas at the same time an American critic in the Oxford *Essays In Criticism* was arguing in detail that they are studies of monstrous selfishness incapable of love.[1] It seems to have become a touchstone for the political position of an American critic, and one would like to know what Wilson thinks now; indeed, it is a general truth about the pleasant and economical habit of reprinting old articles that the author had better say each time how far his opinion has changed now. Wilson does that a bit, but if he had done more of it a reviewer would feel there was more to discuss.

Compared to what I had happened to see before of the Chicago Aristotelians, Mr Crane's book struck me as reasonable opinion moderately expressed. If he had maintained that no other kind of criticism could be permitted, that no admission of the workings of the unconscious mind may ever peep out (like the trouser-end from under the sacerdotal robe), that Darwin, Marx, Frazer, and Freud must be totally expunged from the mind of the literary critic, then one could at least have a battle for freedom. But he positively disclaims that in his final summing-up, remarking only that his programme though liable to be dull is the most suitable for teaching at college. It is usual on committee to feel a certain suspicion when a new regulation is proposed with many assurances that it will be used mildly once passed. I can sympathise with Mr Crane if he feels that a great deal too much nonsense is being talked in our subject, and that he needs a convenient smacking weapon for saying so; I might even rather take sides with the don as against the free-lance journalist, which seems to be the main line-up. But I don't think the weapon he proposes would work well for the purpose; surely it would cut out a lot of good stuff, as well as bad – except in the hands of a man who didn't need it anyway.

It seems Chicago attaches great importance to a belief that Aristotle in the *Poetics* was concerned only with 'imitative' poetry, and that he approached this special group empirically; he did not, like some recent and some medieval authors, think that you can talk about poetry in general. I remember in 1937 or so, when Peking University was refugeeing across country without books and giving its lectures from memory, the present Foreign Minister of Formosa [George Yeh] asked me rather shyly whether I remembered what Aristotle *did* mean by imitation; he had been lecturing on it for twenty years but now he hadn't got his notes. I promised him that he couldn't possibly find the answer if he had the biggest library in the world. It is rather unnerving to have Aristotle say that music is imitation too; you think imitation has got to mean something wildly profound to make this fit in. Probably that was not what he intended; he only says '*most* lyre and flute art' (*Poetics* I) and eventually we hear of 'low-class flute players who sway about if they have to imitate discus-throwing' (XXVI). Even so, he need not have meant to imply that there is any good poetry which isn't imitation; he positively asserts, when arguing for the importance of the 'plot', that the poet 'is a poet by virtue of his imitation' (IX). I do not pretend to scholarship, but anybody can find that much out quickly. It is a natural rule that once a term is taken as fundamental for a system it gets unconsciously generalised: you see the same thing when Coleridge rather charmingly explodes against somebody who took a simple view of his fundamental term Imagination; he says that of course it has nothing to do with mere images, as a simpleton might think: 'the poet wishes to express . . . the substitution of a sublime feeling for the unimaginable for a mere image.' It seems clear that you aren't meant just to gulp down one of these slogans.

Where Mr Crane becomes absurd, I think, is in assuming that because *Macbeth* is 'imitative' it can't be 'didactic' as well, and he uses this to sweep away with contempt the remarks of quite a variety of literary critics. No idea must even be entertained that the play was meant to give a warning against civil war, and suchlike; whereas, as a matter of historical fact, of course, the play was a smash hit because it did that so crudely – the remarkable thing is that it could get in so much more. I think this quaint belief in the mind of Mr Crane belongs to the naughty nineties and not to Aristotle at all. I forget who wrote, but I shall never forget the idea, that the Elizabethans took the metaphor of the mirror much more sensibly than we do; we vaguely think of pure thought, perhaps an astronomer with a reflecting telescope; but your only obvious daily use for a mirror is to tidy your hair. This was clearly what was meant by the *Mirror for Magistrates* and 'holding the mirror up to nature' and so forth; so the opposition between the imitative and the didactic collapses. Anyhow, by one of Mr Crane's own historical criteria, the play developed in a tradition of tragedies which gave awful political warnings. But, even if it hadn't, there is no reason to deny that an imaginary experience may affect your later judgements, as may a real one.

But then again, I am not sure whether Mr Crane isn't only using Aristotle as a petty example of the correct general method, so that it couldn't matter what he had meant by imitation. Aristotle is only considering, he says (p. 54), poems 'which happen, when viewed in their concrete wholeness, to be imitations,' and this excludes '*The Divine Comedy, The Faerie Queene*, the "Dunciad", and *The Prelude*'. We might think that this admission relieved us of the entire burden. It is not clear why Mr Crane can remark on p. 140, 'I shall assume, then, without argument,' that *Macbeth* is 'simply an imitative tragic drama based on historical materials.' For that matter, it appears (p. 132) that he believes the same thing about the myth of Oedipus, which I find even more absurd. It is to the credit of Aristotle that he thought so highly of the *Oedipus*, though on his own theory it is merely a hard luck story and presumably quite untragic.[2] There is an effect of sustained metaphysical argument in Mr Crane's lectures which we ought to find attractive; we are right to hope it gets somewhere. But his crucial complaint against verbal analytical criticism seems to be that 'its controlling aim is the differentiation of poetry as poetry from other things.' Now, a man can really try to explain to himself why a poem has the effect on him that it does, and can succeed in getting an answer which feels to him true, and he is interested while he is doing this. If you told him he was only really concerned to know why the poem wasn't a pussycat or a triumvirate you would merely surprise him; it is off the point.

I have long felt uneasy about Mr Ransom's distinction between 'structure' and 'texture', with the texture called 'irrelevant' [see, for example, *The New Criticism*, Norfolk, Conn: New Directions, 1941]; because if the poem was good, and if I could go at it the way I wanted to, nothing in the poem at all would be irrelevant by the time the critic had finished explaining. I still think this a proper objective, but what about the people who can appreciate the poem without this critic? It seems clear that many people can, pretty well, and that he is only sometimes useful. Mr Ransom, I now think, was expressing a permanent truth, because a *feeling* that irrelevancy is allowed is necessary for both author and reader; otherwise the thing feels too fussy, and the real reason for that is that there is not enough freedom to bring into play the unconscious mind. A literary critic must be prepared to say, 'This is good, though I don't know why; not yet anyhow'; indeed his more formative decisions are nearly always like that. So it is off the point here, I think, for Mr Crane to accuse Mr Ransom of 'setting up an abstract arbitrary principle', in order to smuggle in Romanticism (p. 22). The distinction has only local uses, because, though there are always elements in each class, most of them can jump into the other class (if the poem is good) when author or reader redirects his attention; but still, the uses of it are real ones.

Even so, one should not drift away from feeling that Mr Crane is probably right to be irritated by the confusion of high-grade literary criticism. If the neo-Aristotelian is merely saying that a critic ought to hold on to the main point of the work in view, not impute something irrelevant to it, I warmly agree and so presumably would any critic whom the method is used to attack. But there is also a tacit assumption that this basic Form or Plot is easy to find; it is eked out by rather odd turns of language, as when we are told (p. 153) that in a well-made poem everything is made poetic simply by being made to produce a definitely definable effect. This is not only bad English but untrue, because sometimes the feeling given by a poem is very positive though the reason for it is hard to spot. The assumption is also eked out, I think, by making the examples pretty flat. Two opinions of modern critics about the 'Ancient Mariner' are given briefly, in two lists of opinions held up to contempt in different lectures, but Mr Crane never tells us himself what the basic Form of that poem may be. I do not know why he finds it obviously absurd to say that Coleridge was interested in redemption and imagination, and felt a mystery about the healing beauty of the moon. The position is particularly odd, I think, about a Shakespeare play; because here the basic experience, from which (Mr Crane wants to say) the jabber of the critics must never distract us, is not just reading the text but seeing a good production, ideally, one would think, the original Globe production. Somebody has to decide how to put the play on. For example, several recent critics have argued that Ophelia has already been to bed with Hamlet, and the actress could make this idea very obvious; the question is whether she ought to. I think it is badly off the point (it isn't the Aristotelian Form of *Hamlet* or whatever you like to say), but I should be rather afraid I had got hold of the wrong point unless I also thought that the idea can be disproved from the text. I admit that both lines of argument are a bit wire-drawn or something, but they aren't unpractical; you have to have an opinion one way or the other before you can produce the play. I can't see that the Aristotelian approach cuts any knot there whatever. By the way, I gather that Mr Crane's view of 'catharsis' (p. 71) is merely that it is the well-known pleasure of stopping banging your head against a wall.

I have long felt uneasy about Mr Wimsatt's drive against what he calls the Fallacy of Intentionalism; it seems almost a behaviouristic position; and I am not reassured by the photograph he has put on the dustcover of this collection. He looks like a mastodon rising with dripping fangs from a primeval swamp. A generation or two ago he would have made as much effort to look winning and sympathetic, and really, considering what people in our profession undertake to do, that was a more sensible fashion. However, the later essays reprinted here take a more moderate position about Intention than the hard-hitting first one, reprinted from the *Sewanee Review* of 1946 (and, if just a lively paradox, nothing to grumble about, of course). There is a neat bit of legal adjustment on p. 261, to the effect that what the words meant to the author can be regarded as a peculiar part of lexicography, therefore may be studied, and this might give one a lot of freedom. And yet he still seems to feel in an essay of 1953 (p. 56), as he did in his earlier writing (p. 264), that it actually doesn't matter what Shakespeare wanted to mean. It seems clear that a critic needs to wonder what his author wanted to mean, and these slogans take effect from the way they are misunderstood rather than from the qualifications of them.

Among the first things a baby has to learn, and if it can't it's mad, is that other people really exist; if it couldn't feel 'Mum's cross' and so forth before it learned to speak, then it couldn't learn to speak. Estimating other people's intentions is one of the things we do all the time without knowing how we are doing it, just as we don't play catch by the Theory of Dynamics. Consider the Law, which might be expected to reject a popular fallacy; it recognises amply that one can tell a man's intention, and ought to judge him by it. Only in the criticism of imaginative literature, a thing delicately concerned with human intimacy, are we told that we must give up all idea of knowing his intention. Mr Wimsatt includes an article on 'Poetry and Christian Thinking', written seriously as a Christian, and he feels he has to admit that Biblical criticism has been 'implicitly intentionalist' because it has 'dealt with inspiration'. But surely the obvious, as well as the ancient, opinion is that there can indeed be occasions when the author is *hardly* answerable for his intention – when he is inspired. It shows great staying-power, I think, to hold the puzzle so firmly the wrong way up.

To say that you won't be bothered with anything but the words on the page (and that you are within your rights, because the author didn't *intend* you to have any more) strikes me as petulant, like saying 'of course I won't visit him unless he has first-class plumbing.' If you cared enough you would. For one thing, you might want to know whether the author has really had the experience he describes, or is writing 'conventionally'; the poet Rochester, for instance, does not seem impressive unless you decide that he really meant it.[3] I am glad Mr Wimsatt said in that early essay that the history of the maritime empires which Coleridge was drawing upon (and I suppose the discovery that we were nearly destroyed by the earlier land ones) 'has passed and was then passing into the very stuff of our language'. This is much better than pretending you can't know anything (imitating a Logical Positivist in a different field of study). But the sequence of thought in 'Kubla Khan' is not quite as obvious as that; why should we be forbidden to remember that Coleridge only published it after about twenty years, with excuses, and on the encouragement of Byron? He also uses a verse from the famous Donne poem with the compasses – 'Moving of th'earth brings harms and fears,/Men reckon what it did and meant,/But trepidation of the spheres,/Though greater far, is innocent.' He argues strongly that this must mean an earthquake, and that to drag in ideas about Copernicus is irrelevant. Certainly that is the main point; but Donne, unlike his followers, habitually did drag Copernicus into love-poems, making the idea of the inhabited planet a symbol of the lovers' independence from the world. He is quite likely therefore to have felt an insinuation in the argument: 'and also the sudden introduction of the idea that the earth moves, therefore there may be life on other planets out of reach of the Gospel, has affected the Churches like an earthquake'. The issue does seem to me a fundamental one; in the teasing work of scholarship, a man must all the time be trying to imagine another man's mind; as soon as that stops, he is off the rails. One cannot have a sheer theory to *keep* him off them. On the other hand, I easily feel as Mr Wimsatt does; I know *his* Intention all right. He wants a way to discourage guesswork in this field; the only doubt is whether the rule he proposes is likely to work well.

Most of the rest of the book consists of articles on fairly minor points of verbal technique, well done I think but hardly justifying the splendour of the title and the layout. The Concrete Universal seems to me a tiresome paradox, but not one with any potentialities for harm. There are also discussions on general literary topics, and I agree with most of his article on 'Poetry and Morals'; but I became rather startled when I realised that he takes for granted there is only one right code of morals, a thing already known to himself. The idea that a piece of writing which excited moral resistance might be a discovery in morals, a means of learning what was wrong with the existing system, somehow cannot enter his mind; and yet surely this has often happened and provides the only interesting question for his article.

R. P. Blackmur has long seemed to me obviously a good critic, and I am not at all keen to make reservations about this collection of essays, which goes back to 1930. But it has been published at the same time in England, and I ought to report that it has had a pretty bad press here, chiefly on grounds of style. The style indeed is much like Henry James, and Blackmur remarks comfortably (after praising Marianne Moore, p. 285) that it has been 'characteristic in American literature' to write like this, with 'an excessive sophistication of surfaces' which 'contrived to present the conviction of reality best by making it, in most readers' eyes, remote'. I was seeing the old *Dial* when I was a schoolboy in the twenties, and we children were glad to have it, but we already felt as obvious that its prevailing style was like the Transcendental Ladies in *Martin Chuzzlewit*; and so, for that matter, was the later style of Henry James. Sweetly funny in its way, but a patent attempt to cheat; and you must remember that the reason why the Transcendental Ladies were so keen to preen themselves before Martin was that he had the *Beggar's Opera* charm of a foreigner who, as a result of being cheated by an American realtor, was being sent to his death. I do not feel much upset by the style, and am sorry to say disagreeable things; but it is presumably my function here to tell truths of this sort. The British disgust and suspicion for this style has had rather violent things behind it for a century.

Mr Blackmur does I think sometimes use the style to get away with saying too little, for too long, too teasingly. But he has a reason for using the style; he has regularly discussed the recent, or in the case of Emily Dickinson, for instance, the recently fashionable, authors who were most worth discussing and hardest to discuss. As I have not done that myself, I have certainly no business to complain that he regularly expresses a sense of linguistic difficulty, while nearly always reaching a firm critical conclusion, or even that he often suspects that no linguistic analysis could handle the case in view – an idea which I dislike. His record on his collection covering a quarter of a century is greatly to his credit, a matter of coming to the right opinion early (though one would also like to know what he had left out, and whether he had answered the presumable attacks made on his articles).

Perhaps I should explain that I don't mind a certain insolence which he keeps; in fact I like it very much, as long as it isn't expressed in the trick style. To have him rewrite a poem by Hardy so as to make it a bit less bad is entirely convincing; the whole article on Hardy I think is direct and very good. I am less sure about what he calls ad-libbing by Yeats, which he offers to prove by putting in the opposite meaning all along; here is the Ransom theory of irrelevance again. I am sure it *felt* to Yeats like ad-libbing, getting another verse to end with the chorus line; but that isn't why the result is good, and a critic could probably analyse with truth the profundity of the resultant meaning. There is somewhere an insensitiveness in the mandarin when he is sure the opposite would do as well; but also it is somehow fair for Blackmur to talk like that; he has enough nerve to get the proportions right. I think Emily Dickinson was better than he allowed, but it is refreshing to have a major American critic who didn't think it was his duty to boost her (in 1937). His praise and evident affection for Wallace Stevens may well be wise and true; but it chiefly turns on finding profound excuses for his having so little to say, and the foreigner may still feel there is no great need to bother about Wallace Stevens. Indeed the way Blackmur praises him faintly suggests those advertisements in which two comic representatives of a firm say to each other, 'How marvellous you are, Mr Wix.' 'How marvellous you are, Mr Bix,' precisely like characters in Henry James. And yet the style, to do it justice, lets him deflate a reputation firmly without ceasing to be smooth and even warm. I always feel that Hart Crane stands out over the years somehow, and deserves more praise than he has got; but I do not know anything better written on him than the deflating article which Blackmur did in 1935. Blackmur, in any case, feels to me a great deal more humane and less off the point than these bother-headed theoretical critics; even when he is cheating because he has nothing to say *on* the point. But I gather a man has to be a bit unforeign before he can trust Blackmur like that.

Notes

1 Responding to an article, 'The Ververs', by Joseph J. Firebaugh (*Essays in Criticism*, 4: iv, 1954, pp. 400–10), Empson observed: 'I agree with everything in the article about *The Golden Bowl*, except its interpretation of the results. Henry James I think was morally a very confused man, and anyhow it seems impossible to deny that his attitude to sexual passion was confused. Even though his mind insisted (as the article rightly showed) on building up a sickeningly horrible case against both father and daughter Verver, still he was telling himself he was doing what his father would have wanted, that is, showing how the good cool rich Americans can subdue the savagery of the wicked Europeans. Towards the end of the book, far too much

cuddling of dear old Verver by the author is going on for me to believe that James ever admitted to himself what a loathsome picture he was presenting to the outside world. Indeed, if this were not so, the disagreement among critics (which the article admitted with a mild surprise) could never have arisen. No doubt it is hard to say how one arrives at a critical decision when the field is so large; but I have actually come across that kind of puzzle, especially in the reactions of Chinese professors to the Rockefeller Foundation visitors, and the reason *why* I think that James, though he was a wonderful reporter or recorder, did not understand what he was saying is that it is only now beginning to be realised by the American mind. James does not show any sign of thinking himself such a startling moral innovator as he would have to be before telling himself he meant what your critic very properly regards as the only sensible meaning the book could have' ('Yes and No', *Essays in Criticism*, V: i, January 1955, pp. 89–90).

2 Among his loose notes written at about the time of this essay (1955) Empson addressed himself to classical tragedy, particularly the *Agamemnon* of Aeschylus, as a result of reading H. D. F. Kitto's *Form and Meaning in Drama*:

'As Aeschylus actually tells the story, Agamemnon is *compelled, for no fault of his own*, to sacrifice his daughter – "and *necessity* is the word by which Aeschylus describes Agamemnon's submission to the will of Artemis..."

'Now this crime, the sacrifice of Iphigenia, is given by Aeschylus the most extraordinary motive. Instead of tracing it back to the mortal's offence against divinity, or otherwise linking it to the destiny of the house of Atreus, the poet tells us in plain language that Artemis was enraged because eagles, sent by Zeus to be an encouraging portent, happened to devour a hare together with its unborn young; she therefore demanded a "second sacrifice", the death of Iphigenia, in return for the death of the hare and its young. That is what is in the text; and, however crude and inadequate it may appear, in the text it remains, it cannot be removed.

'Surely this is childish incapacity to approach understanding a myth; it always means something else, the only question is what. Kitto is far better here: the objection is to the cruelty of war. Why could he not have deserted with his daughter?

'Would it not have been simpler to portray him as committing the crime as a result of his decision, not under divine compulsion? – only if this had been a simple tale of Crime and Punishment; but it is not. It is a Tragedy of Man's destiny; and that is most moving when the victim is involved against his will (like Agamemnon) or unawares (like Oedipus) in criminal error for which the penalty must be paid. Agamemnon in this Chorus is depicted as a man who has no choice but to kill what is dearest to him – a much likelier and more interesting figure than the weak-willed butcher whom some would apparently prefer to see portrayed.

'– This makes Oedipus nothing but a hard luck story' (Empson Papers).

Furthermore, in an undated letter to Philip Hobsbaum, Empson took the example of the same text to support his argument in favour of Intentionalist enquiries: Kitto starts off, he observed, with 'a sheer paragraph of questions about what the intention of Aeschylus was in the *Agamemnon*, when he wrote things which seem to us confused or absurd. "If he was a competent artist", the argument runs, these details ought all to be useful pointers to us, showing what his theology was or what not. Here, I grant, he is presuming the author is good, but he says later that the plays have to be good enough to explain why they were admired and preserved; having got inside them by this assumption, he is quite prepared to decide that a detail was merely conventional or a bit of theology really confused. Without going to the intention, which I suppose amounts here to testing the coherence of a theory about the first productions of the plays, one could not overcome the historical difficulties in such a case. Euphemisms may be devised, so that one pretends not to be talking about the author's intention, but that is what the mind will be doing really, if what it does is any good' (Empson Papers).

3 See below for Empson's review of V. de S. Pinto (ed.), *Poems by John Wilmot, Earl of Rochester*.

A Theoretical Point

D. David Long and Michael R. Burr (eds.), *John Crowe Ransom: A Tribute from the Community of Letters*, special issue of *Kenyon Collegian*, LXXXX: 7, Supplement, 1964

It was in 1948 that I first met John Crowe Ransom, being kindly allowed to flip over from Peking to the Gambier Summer School, and I was especially keen just then on a programme for explaining all the sources of the beauty of a poem, finding a reason for everything. I was thus disconcerted by his distinction, which kept coming back into the debates, between the 'structure' of a poem and its 'texture', described as logically unrelated to the structure. In fact I suspected that he didn't fully realise what our literary sect was aiming at. One can be more contentedly sectarian while abroad, and it was not till I got back to England that I became struck by the good sense of his position.

I think indeed that some elements may change from structure to texture, or the other way round, according as one realises or ignores 'how they work', though perhaps some are permanently out of reach. But the author while composing needs to feel that he is allowed to be irrelevant, so long as his details are 'in keeping', or the basic reason is that his unconscious mind needs enough freedom to come into play. The critic also must at least be free to say: 'I feel that is good, or in keeping, though I can't see why.' Both must seem to themselves to be choosing without cause, however determinate their world may actually be. A logically unrelated texture is thus always present, and needs recognising, though it may vary on different occasions.

A tone of pawky but fundamental permissiveness underlay, I came to think, the placid firmness with which John Crowe Ransom would regularly come back to this conception; it is a vote for freedom which perhaps derives from Emerson. I was ready to suspect at first that it was too smooth or accepting, but in coming to know him better I had sometimes occasion to observe under his own texture the iron of his structure.

Not a lively present perhaps, but one should make the most of an agreement on these questions, where it does not come very often. I salute the seventy-fifth birthday.

In Eruption

New Statesman, 1 October 1955

Robert Graves, *The Crowning Privilege*

Anybody of literary interests old enough to remember the period between the two wars must realise that we live in a flatter period now, and should feel lucky to have Robert Graves still so wonderfully active, as the lady in Dickens said about Vesuvius. Modern literary criticism was invented by a number of different people, but by Graves as much as any other individual. This book, while throwing in other articles and some poems for good measure, is mainly the text of his recent Clark Lectures at Cambridge, which were reported to be a great personal triumph.

He remarks in the introduction that 'it is doubtful whether lectures intended for delivery to a largely undergraduate audience, and therefore addressed in the first place to the passions, should be published as though they were closely argued critical essays.' No doubt it was an excellent thing for him to bring some life into the benighted old place, but one is bound to ask '*which* passions?' Jealousy and petulance are what get suggested by cold print, rather depressing in so distinguished a man. It was fine when Graves said, 'All the poets testify that my theory is true,' but what he is saying here is pretty close to a hopeless position: 'All the poets are bad because they don't carry out my theory.' Each age of English literature in his survey is presented as a fall from heaven, and yet it is easy to reflect that they can only have been moving from one hell to another. A reasonable man, surely, would be more impressed if Graves proved that he could see the merits of a period in one bit of writing while he could display its fatal demerits in another; on the whole, what has been admired by a sheer generation or two is likely to have some kind of merit. This is the answer to his long-repeated joke that he was blamed at college for liking some writers better than others. I quite agree that students need squibs putting under their chairs; I only feel that the performance would have been better fun if it had conveyed more understanding.

As to the worship of the White Goddess, which is so basic to Graves's position that a critic must discuss it directly, I remember noticing in the twenties, when my mental eyes were peeping open, a rather curious tone about love taken at times by (for instance) Peter Quennell and Edgell Rickword as well as Graves, authors unlike in every other way. They wanted to combat a fashion for male homosexuality among intellectuals, a thing which was becoming tiresome for the boys as well as the girls, and they did this by saying it was sentimental to love other young men (because so reliably agreeable and comforting) whereas any man worth the name would take on a woman (because she would be certain to crucify him after stripping him of all his goods). This has always seemed to me a farcical way to recommend normal life, and if you really had a society in which women were as bad as that I would seriously think a man the more manly for rejecting them. You cannot simply set up a booth offering nothing but blood, toil, tears and sweat; there has to be some other influence, however unreasonable, before the crowd will surge after their leader. This local male revolt against women was chiefly a backwash from their recent liberation – they tended to put their demands too high; but in the mind of Graves, passionately supporting women against injustice, it became part of a universal truth about human life, that men are no good unless they practise Human Sacrifice to a goddess, who is also the Muse.

The scheme has great charms, especially in outfacing the neo-Christians by offering something undoubtedly more savage even than they do, and then tossing it into the lap of our present Majesty. On both halves of that, he is appealing to solid sentiments; but more basically he relies on the belief now chiefly associated with Jung, that each human brain carries inside itself all the past of mankind, and so we will always have to go on committing human sacrifice because it was done in the Stone Age. He has repeatedly argued that the wars which fill history only arose because the prehistoric villages stopped being ruled by women whose lovers were certain of ritual death, and therefore that, unless we return to the practice quickly, the human race is certain to destroy itself. I am willing to believe in the prehistory, but I think the moral we ought to draw is that we should try to avoid repeating its monstrous evils (chiefly due, one would think, to suspicion brooding over the failure of inadequate techniques).

I do not believe that we carry within us a fatal necessity to do again what these people did, but I believe something rather like that; I revere the scholarly attempts to learn what they did, because the knowledge may be needed to *avoid* doing what they did. Now here, instead of being such a philistine as you may think, I can appeal to a splendid literary tradition; the accepted purpose in writing the *Orestes* trilogy, or for that matter *Macbeth*, was to say to the audience, 'Now that you understand this, you won't let it happen again.' To say that you *want* it to happen again does not seem to me the way a sane man would look at the matter, and it actually wasn't the way the authors did. The theory, you understand, is that, because of a Jungian 'racial memory', the human psyche cannot get on without what Robert Graves has frequently called a Bitch Goddess; this would be plausible if we found her regularly harked back to by the appalling items which are always in the newspapers (of both public and private trouble), but I can't see that we do. The poor old human brain may well be hag-ridden by its past somehow, but it is also a wonderfully strongly protected part of the body; and I would guess that the troubles about its construction date from vastly earlier than prehistory. What Robert Graves has done really well by all these books is presumably not what he intended; he has driven home how shockingly nasty the system he recommends must have been.

To return to literary criticism; as I have dog-eared almost every page of the lectures because they are so interesting, it seems a bit mean to give only a flat example from Pope where Graves is obviously wrong; but this would be an untrue report if it did not point out that he can be obviously wrong.

> The huge round stone, resulting with a bound,
> Thunders impetuous down and smokes along the
> ground.[1]

Graves says: 'The false internal rhymes of *round* and *bound* and of *down* and *ground* effectively act as brakes on the stone's merry progress.' No. Every reader feels the violence of the movement, and he could only feel it from the way the stone reacted to its brakes. Halfway down the steep hill it leaps into the air from a small cliff, it then bangs down, still on the hill but scattering dust, then at the meeting of the rock hill with the alluvial plain the stone runs far out still surrounded with dust. Such is the picture; Pope would readily agree that it is a trivial achievement, but he was only showing he could do it in the course of discussing such matters. When Graves argues that he cannot see it, apparently from a moral dislike for Pope, he is exactly echoing a stupidity of Dr Johnson, who once complained (though only in conversation) that Shakespeare failed to describe the fall from Dover Cliff as 'sheer vacuity'. It is a sad thing to have to say about the grand old master, but I suspect that he is often only pretending not to see merits.

May I now prattle about the origin of rhyme, because there I feel like Graves; I share his annoyance that the academic world is becoming too specialised to do large correlations precisely when its labours ought to be making them possible. It is a major question why Europe took to rhyme, whereas classical authors despised it. Graves says the Irish invented it. He produces no evidence that the Irish rhymed of their own accord, but says that rhyme follows from imitating the rhythms of a smith on an anvil, which I neither understood nor believe. The Chinese always rhymed, but the Slav and Mongol bloc between us and them apparently always didn't.

Anybody may learn from the *Encyclopaedia Britannica* that the first known rhymed poems in the Mediterranean area are Latin hymns about the third century AD by authors in the Berber country of North Africa. Well, since the Arabs used rhyme early, and the rather mysterious Berbers whose songs are lost were closer to the Arabs than to Europe, and any hymn-writer for a converted population would try to give them what they already liked, it seems probable that all the rhymes of Europe come from the Berbers. Now, here is a subject where you do need to get outside the ring of experts, each of them saying there isn't enough evidence within his own field; so that a man like Robert Graves might have a useful part to play. But I wouldn't bother much about his contempt for Donne, Milton, Dryden, Pope, Wordsworth, Tennyson, Yeats, Eliot and so forth; I only wish he had sounded a bit more as if he liked poetry when it is good.

Note

1 Homer's Odyssey, ll. 737–38; see Maynard Mack (ed.), *The Odyssey of Homer* (Twickenham Pope, vol. IX), London: Methuen, 1967, for Pope's own commentary on the syllabic difficulties of the Greek, and why he rendered the line 'into the swiftness of an *Alexandrine,* to make it of a more proportionable number of syllables with the *Greek*' (p. 422).

Rhyme

c. 1962

These remarks are concerned to ask a question, not give the answer to it. However a few historical facts need to be recalled if only to show that the question is worth attention.

European classical literature does not use rhyme, or rather does use it occasionally but only as something obviously unpleasant, for example when a character is drunk on the stage (Verrall makes the point about Euripides' Hercules). There is a sudden introduction of rhyme in Latin but not in Greek during the Dark Ages, and from then on it spreads gradually northward. I have neither references nor scholarship here, but the casual remarks on the topic I have met in reading seem very consistent; the use of rhyme was taken over by 'English', German, etc., gradually after the eleventh century, and was regularly first used in the apparently grudging but very impressive form of *bad* rhymes; the idea that a rhyme has to be correct already existed in the south. I do not see how this could be twisted into an argument that the primitive rhyming came from the northern barbarians (otherwise a natural suggestion). In any case the northern barbarians were mostly coming from the nearer east, and on the other hand a lot of Scandinavian influence seems to get into early Russia; the determined absence of rhyme in the Russian ballad tradition seems to me to show that neither Greeks, nor Scandinavians, nor what we call 'Huns' in general, brought it in.

However this attempt to clear away the north at the start has distracted me from the really interesting question. I do not think there is any parallel to this chance of poetic style inside a whole continental tradition; more attention, I think, needs to be given to how it happened; and this suggests the much larger question of which languages use rhyme and why.

The earliest Chinese poetry uses rhyme; I gather from casual inquiry that rhyme only enters Indian poetry with the Moguls; the *Koran* was written in rhyming prose; we all know that the Persians rhymed. Much earlier verse than we commonly realise has been translated from ancient Egyptian and

Babylonian, millennia before Homer, and I wish I knew whether it rhymes. The main points I get from this very inadequate information are two: that there is a curious division across the Eurasian continent, with only the two ends of it rhyming and the western end (even the Arabs) apparently starting later; and that the Arabs (again using a term very loosely) seem to have been earlier than the Europeans.

The *Encyclopaedia Britannica* is very definite under the heading RHYME; the thing was started in the fourth century AD in North Africa for Christian hymns, written in Latin. Surely it is incredible that such a decisive invention should have been made in a rather depressed province, in a language foreign to it, for a liturgical purpose only. The obvious question is who lived there, and were they singing in rhyme already, so I next looked up BERBERS. It appears they are a semi-Arab people, who still sing a good deal, and the reason why we haven't heard of their literature is that the Mohammedan conquest made a much heavier drive against it than against any other. The Berber were induced to suppress all writing in their own language, and to write in future in Arabic only, during the course of their acceptance of the *Koran*. Whether the Berbers even now sing in rhyme seems to me an important point of inquiry. But surely, if they do, and if the *Encyclopaedia* is right, the answer to the historical question lies on the surface; it was the Berbers who gave Europe rhyme, before Islam had started. One should remember, if this conclusion seems improbable, that the Berbers are accepted as the main population of the area at the relevant period; I do not know of any evidence to prove that St Augustine and Origen were not both Berbers, though the successful suppression of the Berbers by Islam has made most authorities think that one was a Roman colonial and the other a negro.

Finally one needs to consider what reasons there may be why one language should prefer the quite odd custom of terminal rhyme (the 'modern bondage' as Milton called it) and another not. A monosyllabic language with no grammar like Chinese clearly needs a good deal of formality in its rules to make poetry different from prose, whereas any language with long inflected words has to accent the words enough to distinguish the roots from the syntax, and a poet can rely on this to give rhythm. Japanese poetry no less than Greek could ignore rhyme for this simple reason, whereas English is enough like Chinese to make unrhymed melodious verse much harder to write than rhymed. On the other hand, a language which rhymes absurdly easily tends to make rhyme seem vulgar; the business of rhyming two ablative plurals in Latin is more than merely easy but a process of putting heavy emphasis on a trivial part of the meaning. The discovery that you could make it *effective* seems to be essentially a popular movement; I do not mean at all that this makes it bad, nor yet for that matter inherently good. But it is a singing process; indeed it nearly takes you back to the older theoretical picture of the dancing throng, as it was called, where each dancer would call out a line and thus they made a 'communal' ballad. Obviously these characters would not feel their delicacy offended if the rhymes were easy; they had a lot of other things to think of quickly. And I have too often made up communal poems with other poets in pubs to be accused of contempt for this process, though I can never be sure it occurs in primitive life. The Chinese of course do rhyme against each other, as a civilised sport. The crucial thing about English, as a language for poetry, is that you cannot rhyme the subject with the verb, because either 'the cat distracts' and 'the nerves swerve' or 'the cats distract' and 'the nerve swerves'; this bit of grammar has been enormously helpful to English poetry by forcing it away from platitude. In any case the English final consonants make rhyme rather difficult in English, unlike Italian and modern Chinese; but then it appears that the first rhyming Chinese (first recorded from perhaps 700 BC) had about as many final consonants as modern English.

All I can think of after this very rough attempt at surveying the conditions for a taste for rhyme is that people sometimes like it because it is easy and sometimes because it is difficult; but that its primitive practical use has been in getting a group of dancers or haulers or devotees to sing together and plug the rhythm. It may well be, as Macaulay said in the preface to his *Lays*, that the Roman ballad poetry had always rhymed, and that Horace sometimes poked his nose into a Roman pub and shrank away without a drink in loathing at the sound of those songs rhyming in two ablative plurals; but I don't myself believe it. I think it is high time somebody did a decent survey of what poetry does rhyme and what doesn't, whether the Chipchakes rhyme, whether the Aztecs used to rhyme, and in fact extract this small piece of information from each one of the experts who know it and don't think it worth telling. It would be foolish to theorise without asking for the knowledge already obtained.

The Calling Trumpets

New Statesman and Nation, 10 December 1955

I. A. Richards, *Speculative Instruments*
John Wain (ed.), *Interpretations*

So far as I have seen (seeing only English and American ones) reviewers of this collection of essays and addresses by Professor Richards have not only found it dull but have felt that he has lost interest; and one might indeed complain that some of the talks are so broad and so 'stimulating' that they suggest nothing definite. He remarks himself at one point, 'It is not easy to let up on the pressure we are under to get something (as we hope) *said* in favour of awareness of the process of *saying*,' and this endeavour might seem wrongheaded. But clearly he may also have been providing what the occasion required, especially a reminder that the very process of 'discussing communication' involves scrutinising itself; to judge the result, one would need to follow the rest of the conference or symposium. He has become concerned with a kind of high-level committee work which can be very valuable though it doesn't look big in a book, and I half wish he could be stung into a boastful essay, describing his successes (let alone his successes at planning crucial rush teaching assignments during the war). At any rate, the old sense of drama is still present; he feels he is handling great affairs. 'We have come to the juncture of the Humanities and the Sciences and all the storm-cones are up,' he says in 'Responsibilities in the Teaching of English'; if one could start 'in the philosophic laboratory' an investigation into 'the general laws of comprehension, which are those of self-ordering and growth' – well, it would take time; but 'these enquiries would be cumulative in effect as no others have been.' 'How to reconcile the possible modes of being? This is no theoretical question but the choice of choices,' he told a Cybernetics Conference, therefore the Faculties of a University should be geared to the faculties of the mind; for that matter 'the world needs a United Studies as it needs a United Government.' One might think that a dangerous excess of organisation is being recommended, but in 'Language and Value' he says 'premature attempts to be scientific in education seem to me as likely to devastate promising segments of mankind as any other peril I have heard of.' Literary critics need not say that a man who writes like this has lost interest. By the way, the only novelty I can see in his theoretical position is on p. 143, that in crucial acts of choice our experience has nothing to do with sensory perception.[1]

The team of practical critics organised by Mr Wain is at the opposite extreme, each of them nose down all the time to the detailed text of a poem printed in full. But they are just as much concerned with education; Mr Wain says in the preface that he wanted 'to get people to be less frightened of literary criticism', to effect a *rapprochement* between the reading public and these experts on reading, who tend to have little influence outside their universities. This indeed, I think, makes them rather uncertain how much needs to be said. Till the English Schools came in it was assumed that the public could read, and the modern worry about exegesis is a recognition of a new situation. The only forerunners who thought it necessary were those (mainly Puritan) preachers who 'divided the Word of God', that is, extracted from any given text, with 'seventeenthly' and so forward, the whole of their theological position. This is not always a good way to teach a subject, and it seems possible that Mr Wain will only frighten the reading public more than ever. But it is less easily frightened than bored; I felt myself that the essays were dull unless I disagreed with them, except of course when they produced a new idea, in the old manner. Still, it does seem to be happening in this field that one is now required to write a full exegesis, on pain of being accused of not knowing what had seemed too obvious to say. The standard of the essays is never badly let down. I suspect there is an unwary reverence for 'history' going on; an idea that, at any given date, everybody in England had the same opinion, *viz.*, the official or fashionable one; but this book does not seem to give startling examples of that delusion.

Mr Gillie, on Pope's 'Unfortunate Lady', says that Pope means that any poet has to face the same martyrdom as the Lady; that is why the poem ends with his death, and the first lines mean that she is inviting him to imitate her suicide. She represents some kind of political ideal (because she had 'ambition' for true love), indeed the essay makes her suggest Yeats's Maud Gonne. But surely the attack on the high-class Arranged Marriage was very familiar to Pope's readers, and would hardly seem a 'challenge' to convention, nor would the condonation of her (imaginary) suicide feel a great strain on one's Christianity. All the same, the essay rightly brings out the explosiveness of the forces that Pope is using.

Mr Wain himself makes a number of good points on Yeats's 'Among School Children', but somehow assumes he has to expound a doctrine of despair, with Work as the only good in life. Yeats need not be made so consistent; he made pessimistic remarks, but did not feel he had to grizzle over them all through a poem. Indeed the final verse, 'Labour is blossoming and dancing where . . .' seems meant to get out of this box, but Mr Wain says it only applies to an unattainable perfect state, and even if we got there we might still not 'escape from the confused relationship of matter and spirit'. I don't see why 'the dancer', in the last line, can only be a houri in Paradise. To do Mr Wain justice, he wins a great struggle over his scholarly conscience, thereby excluding a piece of pessimism from Yeats. 'Honey of generation has betrayed' he makes refer to the labouring mother, whereas Yeats added a learned note saying that it meant whatever had destroyed the baby's recollection of pre-natal freedom. I think Yeats knew very well what his Dublin acquaintances would take 'honey of generation' to mean, and wrote his mystical footnote with a gleaming eye. But anyhow I am not sure why Mr Wain thinks it pessimistic to believe that we are happier before and after this life; to believe that nothing is good but Work seems to me much sadder.

Mr Sleight says about Donne's 'Nocturnal' that the poet is shown 'reintegrating' himself from his sorrow, or (at least, later on), that 'he does not definitely commit himself to the harmony of death nor the dialectic of living.' But the poet does say that his sun will not renew and that he will prepare to rejoin his mistress by death. The subtle analysis of how recovery appears in the metaphors may be true, but Donne was not putting in 'humour' intentionally, and 'tilting at himself taking himself too seriously' about death, a thing he was gloriously unlikely to do. I admired Mr Sleight for feeling sure the word *world* meant something important which he couldn't fathom, because I am sure it meant Copernicus and a separate planet out of reach of the Pope; the frank boggling of a sensitive critic there is evidence that this interpretation is needed.

Mr Dennis Ward, on the Hopkins 'Windhover', says about the final lines —

> and blue-bleak embers, ah my dear,
> Fall, gall themselves, and gash gold-vermilion —

that the embers 'strike their brightest fire . . . when they break from the self-consuming heat of the fire and gash and gall themselves against the outer world'. But it is merely untrue that coals are brighter when separate than when together. The picture is that the top crust of the fire, when its support has burnt away, falls in at a random moment as new fuel for the glowing centre; so the poet's heart, still glowing with the pain of renouncing the world, is brought out of 'hiding' by the accident of seeing the bird's movement. Mr Ward insists that the poem is not 'a weary surrender of the poet to the ascetic demands of the priest', so far from that, 'the Falcon's example has re-animated his failing purpose.' But this anxiety to save Hopkins from an accusation has only landed him in a much worse one; he would be angry to hear that his purpose was failing in the very year of his ordination. Mr Ward admits the double meaning for the verb 'buckle' if it is in the imperative mood, thus not sounding soft; there I agree.

Mr Iain Fletcher, on a religious poem by Lionel Johnson with what seems to be a Pantheist conclusion ('Lonely, unto the Lone I go; Divine, to the Divinity'), merely complains that this is illogical (be that as it may, the idea is prominent in the Romantic poets read by Johnson as well as basic to the religions of Asia). Mr Fletcher also suspects that Johnson wanted to escape Hell by Materialism, the shifty beast, and he recalls that 'Victorian Broad Church Christians were for ever worrying about eternal torment which, they thought, made Christianity immoral.' I think so too, and I am not in the slightest degree impressed by snooty boasts in favour of suffering for other people. The poem is bad because its ideas remain muffled, and that is Mr Fletcher's main point, but his attack on it makes it seem much better.

Mr Lerner writes well on the delicate balance of judgement, so unexpectedly far from flattery, in Marvell's 'Horatian Ode', but he admits being boggled by the last lines, where Cromwell is told to 'keep thy sword erect':

> Besides the force it has to fright
> The Spirits of the shady Night,
> The same arts that did gain
> A Power, must it maintain.

It won't quite do, he says, though it is the only way out, to suppose that Cromwell has bad dreams. 'If this is conscience, why "shady night"? He cannot have painted Cromwell so bad that he has all his values reversed.' This strikes me as too much theology again; the night was always shady, even under the Rule of the Saints. But here again the interest of the essay is in the honesty of the reporting.

Mr W. W. Robson writes well on the Wordsworth 'Resolution and Independence' with the moral 'The awkwardnesses have point; but a point that cannot be brought out if one confines oneself to considering proprieties of diction.' Mr Alvarez brings a grand machine into play on 'The Phoenix and Turtle', though I still think the poem more playful than he does; he had bad luck in just missing the account by Mr Wilson Knight, who has pointed out for the first time that the sexes are the wrong way round. The Turtledove wears the trousers; maybe one of them was Queen Elizabeth after all.[2]

The epilogue by Mr G. S. Fraser, 'On the Interpretation of a Difficult Poem', gives some sensible warnings, especially that even an analytical critic must always be prepared to say, 'This is good, but I don't know why.' He gives what he considers a parody-length analysis of four lines from Denham (the standard bit about the river 'without o'erflowing full') ['Cooper's Hill', l. 193] to show that a great deal can always be said about good verse which doesn't need saying. He then uses a poem by myself called 'The Teasers', in which a metrical invention did not last long enough to make the argument definite (so that a lot of guessing about meaning could go on), to prove that one may need to know 'the cultural context' of an author, 'the kind of influences an author of his class and generation would have come under', but only need to expound it to an audience which does not know it already. The idea of my poem was to go on saying things which applied at once to the high and the low passions, the lusts and the ideals, but other impulses were at work which produced verses I later disliked, and the cut version is inadequate (may I agree with Mr Fraser that I see no point in making 'the flood' mean the act of sex, above all if the poet is supposed to offer it universally). I think Denham and I were fairly chosen by Mr Fraser as test cases, where the reading public is expected to know the kind of thing that is meant without any exegesis; for instance, bringing up Buddhism as rival to Christianity seemed to me sufficiently obvious there.

The English like to assume that they are sensible, therefore don't require abstruse theory, but one can't always gamble on that. The high siren voice of Professor Richards ought to be heard, though I don't know what immediate use can be made of it, above the delicious yelping of the pack.

Note

1 'Empiricists, though they may admit, if pressed, that there is more to experience than its sensory (or perceptual) side, commonly narrow it down to sensory perception when they talk of hypotheses, conceptual schemes, propositions ... being verifiable, corrigible, subject to the control of experience or observation.

'But there is the world of wish, desire, love, hate, hope, fear, and so on, which we experience – not through sensory perception but – in another way and as directly.

'This is the world whose dramatic texture is choice' (I. A. Richards, 'Language and Value', *Speculative Instruments*, London: Routledge & Kegan Paul, 1955, p. 143).

2 See Part II, 'Phoenix and Turtle', in G. Wilson Knight, *The Mutual Flame*, London: Methuen, 1955.

Professor Lewis on Linguistics

Times Literary Supplement, 20 September 1960

C. S. Lewis, *Studies in Words*

This short book traces the main development of only a few English words, in an easy tone, content at times to say that the precise mixture of meaning in some well-known literary use is still uncertain, or more generally that 'the mutual influences between meaning and meaning are as subtle and reciprocal as those between a group of friends'; but it feels somehow weighty, as if the examples are working models of the correct procedure.

The preface says that the book is primarily addressed to students, and that 'if any deeper issues are raised by implication' such was not the author's intention. 'The higher linguistics' have just been disclaimed, too, so perhaps these deeper issues are theological ones; and indeed the chapter on *conscious* and *conscience* (let alone the one on *nature*) holds them just under the surface. Here we feel the ancient flame of the author of *The Allegory of Love*; the ideas which emerged through the words are traced back with a deep curiosity, and it is plainly right to treat Greek and Latin analogues at some length, because the writers, up to Jane Austen at least, are shown to think from the derivation 'knowing with', that is, sharing a secret with another person, though they never mention it when deciding what the words ought to mean, and stubbornly refuse in this case to adopt a Greek word so as to mark a distinction from the Latin ones.

The conviction that a man's own conscience is God's vicegerent and above any human authority is placed as a medieval development, not a Reformation one; not found in the New Testament, nor arising from it, nor leading back to it. After so firm a historical statement one looks for the author's own opinion; and there is a short bracket at the end of the historical survey, when a similar conviction is recorded among

those who claimed (in my opinion rightly) freedom to obey their conscience by maintaining that God does not exist.

The book urges the public to realise how bad it is to 'commit verbicide', to take part in destroying one of these valuable structures by conscripting it into propaganda for a passing controversy. But the treatment is not alarmist, which would amount to being pedantic; it gladly shows how words have sometimes recovered from a dangerous misuse, and at the other extreme grants that our use of *supernatural*, though philosophically shocking to the author, marks a distinction which exists, however wrongly, in the minds of the speakers. One might say the reason why the scope can be limited is that the author does not feel himself to be defending a lost cause. Readers need to be warned that a writer often means by a word something other than what their own background leads them to expect; a working understanding of the historical process of change of meaning, by giving this awareness, may be enough. Thus the important thing is to present the essentials to a large body of students.

The programme should be secure against opposition, all the more when in the hands of a scholar whose use of detail is so continually interesting. Only the underlying tone of anxiety might be felt as excessive. We have many grave things to worry about, but if we look round for a sturdy thing, proved to be able to take knocks, the eye rests with relief upon the English language; a great nuisance to handle, of course, but one need hardly fear that it is in decay. Because of this basic assurance, a literary critic should feel a moderate independence from the decisions of a scholarly linguist, though of course he should admit his need for information, when judging the English literature of the past four centuries. Because the language went on being so rich, requiring, one might think, high peaks of scholarship to interpret any of it, there was an underground development of the meaning before the dates when they can be proved by specific quotation.

Professor Lewis rather often gives a case where he says that the modern reader goes wrong by taking for granted the 'dangerous meaning', that is, the current modern one; and the cases regularly excite doubt in a literary mind. It may be because he tactfully does not choose to remind us of our grosser errors; but still, the firmness of his grasp of the history, till then so very welcome, keeps leading to a doubtful result in the example. Take a word in the most undeniably splendid poem of George Herbert, when the soul cannot endure to accept the divine love –

> I, the unkind, ungrateful? Ah, my dear,
> I cannot look on thee. ['Love (III)']

The modern meaning would be disastrous; the idea of general beneficence from man to God borders on the absurd. Hence, he decides, *unkind* can only mean 'unnatural' here. Border upon the absurd as it may, the 'dangerous' modern meaning here is the overwhelming one, and there are some parallels to justify ascribing it to the first readers of Herbert. They merely had a bit more padding than we have against the shock.

In the masterly chapter on the word *wit*, Professor Lewis rejects the treatment of Pope's 'Essay on Criticism' by Professor Empson ['Wit in the Essay on Criticism', *The Structure of Complex Words*], who had said that every use of *wit* in the poem recalls the then current slang one, which was practically the modern one for a smart joker. Professor Lewis proves that the word was habitually used when Pope wrote to mean the highest powers of the human mind; his quotations are particularly decisive when a man is claiming to translate a classical author literally, and many of Pope's uses here are, so to speak, implied translation. It seems a knock-down case of misreading from the dangerous modern sense of a word. But he goes straight on to give a splendid picture of the nonsense then being talked for polemic by literary critics, each of them saying that *wit* meant the style he had decided to support, as if fighting for possession of a talisman; he is rather severe on them for it, because Dryden at least, when in a more placid mood, would admit he knew better.

Why then is it certain that Pope could not have understood this linguistic situation? He wrote the poem while very young, as a bid for recognition, and it was at once considered very witty, though it is now commonly considered a routine summary of standard classical opinion. Professor Lewis says:

No interpretation of the word *wit* is acceptable unless it can stand up to the couplet:

> Some have at first for wits, then poets passed,
> Turned critics next, and proved plain fools at last.

Clearly the whole rhetorical structure is in ruins unless we can find senses for the key words which provide a continual descent...

so he also provides a special sense for the word *poet*. Pope himself would have been endlessly entertained by this comment; at least, it is very hard to imagine him not being. He was keenly aware that the techniques by which Bentley had thrown so much light upon the ancient languages gave a comical effect when turned upon the homely products of our own language. Also, with his terrible eye for literary anecdote, he would have intended the sequence to be biographical quite as much as rhetorical. He would have polished the couplet to make sure of insinuating that what got the poor young man called a 'wit' was a harmfully confusing question for himself, let alone for later commentators.

Of course, Pope pretends to be using the word in the accepted grand way; for that matter, he was quite capable of writing out as a footnote to a later edition the entire demonstration of Professor Lewis, with all its quotations from contemporary critics; and we would find the joke rather over-laboured. These fighting little epigrams, using the shield as well as the sword, are if anything too conscious of the trickiness of their language; the argument of Professor Lewis cannot prove that they are simple. On the other hand, this rebuttal cannot prove the thesis of Professor Empson. For that, Pope must be supposed to imply:

I have to talk to you in your own language, the language of the world; but I know you have debased it so far that these high matters cannot be discussed in it without some absurdity. Probably you get quite the wrong idea when I call Aristotle a wit.

In such a case there is at least a pretence of not letting the common reader know that he is being insulted, so that evidence either way is inherently hard to get. One might reasonably expect that the child Pope, while putting up a titanic struggle to appear a scholar and a man of the world, was not really at leisure to be supercilious about both of them. Even so, that was how his style worked out; he would come to believe in later life that that was what he had meant; and one might apply to such a case the Platonic formula that his genius had meant more than he knew.

The case of *sense* is different in that it concerns the intentions of a great many people. Professor Lewis, again rebutting Professor Empson [*The Structure of Complex Words*], lays down as a basic fact that 'only the tiny minority who are interested in language' ever even notice that the word is used both for receiving sensations and for broad judgement, therefore he denies that the development of the word was affected by any interaction between its meanings. An English-speaker picks them up at very different levels of learning, therefore without needing to notice what would only seem to him a pun; and both are already standard in the Latin.

This is so; thought about the connection is only likely on occasions where both meanings arise and make a contrast. But Professor Lewis admits at the end of the chapter that the two meanings of 'sensible', for sense and sensibility, 'could not long escape notice'. And we can claim that our present allotment of meanings among this large family of words, after being caught up in both Restoration and Romantic controversy, has worked out in a very intelligent way; suggesting, therefore, that the speakers understood what they were doing. Professor Lewis does show that an interesting and useful treatment can be given without any recognition of interaction, a purely historical one; but, if most of the speakers never reflected on the interactions, they must at least have had remarkable powers of memory. If the matter had turned more upon derivations from Latin, maybe Professor Lewis would not have thought of cutting down the amount of reflection in the speakers; the tidying up of the Elizabethan confusion about the words seems to have been a very home-based affair.

But it may be agreed in any case that theorising about the matter is very little help for the learner. The weight of the book is on the importance of keeping the great language up, and it naturally sweeps aside anything that might be distracting or confusing for that major purpose.

Rhythm and Imagery
in English Poetry

A LECTURE TO THE BRITISH SOCIETY OF AESTHETICS,
3 MAY 1961

British Journal of Aesthetics, 2 January 1962

When I was honoured by being asked to speak here I was doubtful what I could say that would be useful or suitable: I will keep mostly to the subject announced, but I want to begin with some scattered remarks. The field is very large and confused. It is not even clear that you want a theory, because its findings must always be subject to the judgement of taste; I still believe in the Benthamite theory of Ogden and Richards, from the *Foundations of Aesthetics* (1925), but I am not sure what it entails. This is the first century which has tried to appreciate all the art works that ever were, anywhere, and combining this with the first effects of universal education, let alone a variety of revaluations of opinion, was bound to produce a kind of traffic jam. The artist was free to an extent which he often found baffling, and so was the critic. Four major thinkers, Darwin, Marx, Frazer and Freud, gave grounds for the belief that the artist often does not know what he is doing. Darwin, for one reason, because the artist will be exemplifying a stage in an evolutionary trend (one could extract others here), Marx because he will be expressing his society's means of production, Frazer because his mind will be hag-ridden by a group memory of human sacrifice, and Freud because he will be expressing his own unconscious desires; clearly, he had better do what he feels like, and the critic had better say what he likes, he also, in his turn. An interpreter of the artwork cannot set out to bring all this to consciousness, where it does not naturally belong; his main function must be to mediate between the unconsciousness of the artist and the unconsciousness of the public he works for. When I was young I did not mind this, but I find now I have become one of the old buffers who were always made fretful by it. I think that modern art has gone too far, and that aesthetics ought to curb and prune it; and that aesthetics ought to be curbed and pruned too.

Literary critics feel about art writers much as Christians do about

Hindus; they have never had an ideological purge, so they are practically
Ancient Night in person. We literary critics may talk a lot of nonsense, but
we have been scolded out of talking like they do long ago. The catalogue of
a picture exhibition is often very intimidating; a steady iron-hard jet of
absolutely total nonsense, as if under great pressure from a hose, and recalling among human utterances only the speech of Lucky in *Waiting for
Godot*, is what they play upon the spectator to make sure of keeping him
cowed. And I suspect they would often have something to tell us if this stern
convention did not forbid them; I felt it about Mr Roland Penrose, always
an intelligent and well-intentioned man, in the catalogues of the great
Picasso exhibition. In some paintings, I thought, for example, one about
romps at the seaside where a striped balloon appeared to be in flight, the
artist was clearly being jovial about the oddity of the human form; much
like the comic postcards which would be found on display not far from the
bathing beach he was depicting. At other times, it is known that he used his
distortions of the human form to express horror at the cruelty of some political event. Art criticism is naturally vaguer than literary criticism, because
the whole field of mental activity concerned lies much farther away from
the discursive reason; but still, it should be possible to say which of these
Picasso meant. There was one picture which I thought plainly jovial, as
some men had drunk themselves under a table; but the catalogue quoted
Picasso here as saying that a painting is not for the drawing-room, it is a
political act. Here, you see, Penrose had artfully got round the convention
that he is only allowed to talk guff, but this made me feel, ungratefully, that
he could have said more.

The effects of the revolt against reason are, I think, also striking in architecture; all the more because there you really do have trade union rules of
no criticism in public. I think many English architects accept designs for
workers' flats and such-like, believing them to be artistic as well as convenient, and quite without realising that they are grindingly horrible. Horrible because they are meant to be; when they were invented in Germany
they were part of the great surrealist movement of protest against the
machine age and the gathering storm. The Dutch, who have always been
able to get a cosy feeling into domestic architecture, can still manage to get
it into a huge block of workers' flats; but many English architects don't feel
that this is clean-lined or in-the-movement enough for them. They cannot
learn better because they would think it philistine to talk about the matter
in real terms, just as it would be philistine to discuss whether Picasso was
feeling larky or sickened; so they put up, feeling that the work is just pure
and functional and advanced, buildings of a screaming-lunatic horror and
terror. At least, I met a man at a party who had been putting up such things
and this was the best picture of his motives I could extract from him.

I thought I had best begin by expressing some old-buffer prejudices in general, but now I will turn to English Literature, which it is my business to know about, and try to examine the fundamentals, the basic tools; as must be the proper thing for a Society of Aesthetics. I am in favour of rhyme and metre for English poetry, but I realise that there is something queerly accidental about the way they arrived and settled into the traditions of Europe; the founders of the Free Verse movement, a generation or two ago, expected a great gain in energy from introducing radical changes there, and it seems time to ask why that didn't happen.

I must be brief about rhyme because I haven't the information which must be available somewhere; it is hard even to find which peoples rhyme and which don't. We Europeans ought to feel curious about the subject; no other major civilisation had such a total Dark Age, and we emerged no longer quantitative in metre but clutching the divine gift of rhyme, which Greece and Rome had despised and thought suited to Hercules when drunk. If Homer taught the language of the gods to men, who taught us what by this radical change of ear? Professor Robert Graves has stepped gallantly into the very large breach left here by more official pundits, but I cannot understand why hammering on an anvil rhymes, in any sense in which marching or rowing doesn't rhyme, and that seems fundamental to his argument.[1] The Chinese have always rhymed, but the Slavs as well as the Greeks have only taken to it recently; there was a block of non-rhymers in the middle of the land mass. Rhyme is first used by Europeans for Latin hymns, but they were written in North Africa not Europe, as early as the third century A D; and surely a missionary would want to give the congregation what they liked already, rather than start a revolution in poetic technique. I have failed to learn whether the Berbers rhymed, but the Semitic language of the Carthaginians was still not stamped out, and Semites rhyme; I understand that the *Koran* is partly in rhymed prose. Robert Graves thinks we got rhyme from the Irish, not from Carthage, but he seems only to quote repetitions or rough assonances in ancient Irish, and the Irish had in any case an early mastery of Christian techniques. Very little can be understood from all this; it is agreed that most poetry since the Dark Age is the better for rhyme, and that classical poetry would be spoiled by it, but explanations of this seem no longer even to be attempted.

I have just learned, however, one interesting fact about the classical quantitative metres, and am eager to pass it on, though perhaps it is well known. Going back to first principles, a syllable may be louder or softer than the one before, used in a stress metre; also longer or shorter, used in a quantitative metre; and then also the note may be higher or lower on the musical scale. There are thus three dimensions, and even when the rules of scansion use one of them the other two may be needed before the result can be beautiful. Chinese poetry scans by ups and downs, but these movements come within one syllable; the rising and falling-and-rising tones of Mandarin are put in one group of syllables, the level and falling tones in the other group, and patterns are arranged with these two. The poetry is intoned, a process like singing which is a recognised skill. We tend to laugh at Chinese poetry for being meaningless except on paper, but we ourselves don't much expect to be able to follow the words of a song. English itself of course is strongly tonal; only the rise for a question is recognised as part of the meaning, but I believe the Chinese now simply learn English as a tonal language, finding that convenient. Well, then, the accents written on ancient Greek marked a rise and fall of tone, so definite as to make the line like singing. This would tend to reduce interest in the loud–soft contrasts, which we too do not feel to be an inherent part of a melody, whereas long–short contrasts do feel part of it. Loudness does, however, become part of the melody for what was called in Purcell's time his Scotch Snap, where the stressed half of an English disyllabic word is given the shorter note

> And *pity mankind* that will *perish* for gold;

but this charming device does not seem widespread. An emphasis for the meaning, as when hymns put *pp* and *ff* for the same parts of consecutive verses, is evidently not felt as part of the melody. Maybe in Greek there was no prosy way to speak the line, which a man would use if he didn't know it was poetry, as there so definitely is in English; although one might think that only the Garden of Eden could have such an inherently musical language.[2]

Nobody supposes that the Romans had this bird-like tonal quality in their language, and pushing Latin into quantitative metres must have been very artificial. But one should not under-rate bulldog grit; they did make some poetry; and I think the method still works in English, often without being noticed; indeed, it usually takes effect as a source of mysterious romantic beauty. Almost all the English poets of the past had been taught Latin poetry, and the English language makes a quantitative metre always possible, so they are not unlikely to have echoed it. In prose, for that matter, the classical system of rhythm, the *cursus* and so on, was part of the practical training for writing formal English, without anybody bothering about the change to stress-accent.

May I then, to set the pattern, remind you of Tennyson's imitation of Alcaics ['Milton']:

> O mighty-mouthed inventor of harmonies,
> O skilled to sing of time or eternity
>   God-gifted organ voice of England,
>   Milton, a name to resound for ages;

His third verse, I think, is the only other good one:

> Me rather all that bowery loneliness
> The brooks of Eden mazily murmuring
> And bloom profuse and cedar arches
> Charm, as a wanderer out in ocean....

In the following verses A. E. Housman, a Professor of Latin of course, is using the third line of this metre as the last line but one of each verse; and to some extent in all the odd lines of the poem.

> Tell me not here, it needs not saying
> What tune the enchantress plays
> In aftermaths of soft September
> And under branching mays,
> For she and I were long acquainted
> And I knew all her ways....
>
> Possess, as I possessed a season,
> The countries I resign,
> Where over elmy plains the highway
> Would mount the hills and shine,
> And full of shade the pillared forest
> Would murmur and be mine
>
> [*Last Poems*, no. XL]

It is plainly a matter of long–short and not of stress, because *and* in Tennyson and *the* in Housman are erected into long syllables, with aching tenderness, merely by pausing on them. The other verses have for this penultimate line 'And beeches strip in storms for winter', 'And Traveller's Joy beguiles in autumn'. I find that I can't say the lines so as to bring out this rhythm unless I treat them 'lyrically', that is, let my voice go up and down; and I should think quantitative metre always needs this. Homer smote his blooming lyre.

I think the poem is wonderfully beautiful. But a secret gimmick may well be needed in it to overcome our resistances, because the thought must be about the silliest or most self-centred that has ever been expressed about Nature. Housman is offended with the scenery, when he pays a visit to his native place, because it does not remember the great man; this is very rude of it. But he has described it as a lover, so in a way the poem is only consistent to become jealous at the end. Perhaps the sentiment has more truth than one might think (it is natural to reflect, in addressing this Society); many

English painters really are in love with the scenery of England, and nothing else, so they had much better give up their theoretical tiff with Nature and get back to painting it. The last verse of the poem, driving home the moral, is no longer tenderly hesitant and therefore has given up the Alcaic metre.[3]

> For nature, heartless, witless nature,
>   Will neither care nor know
> What stranger's feet may find the meadow
>   And trespass there and go,
> Nor ask amid the dews of morning
>   If they are mine or no.

Granting then that we can use stress and quantity at once, I think we have also a way of using stress which the metrists have refused to recognise. Coleridge remarked in the Preface to 'Christabel' that all the lines were meant to have four stresses, though the number of syllables varied. He was liable to talk rashly, but he seems cool here and I think we should believe him; and yet it is sometimes a strain to keep the stresses on one syllable each:

> ... Thou heardst a low moaning
> And foundst a bright lady, surpassingly fair,
> And didst bring her home with thee in love and in charity
> To shield her and shelter her from the night air. (275)

It is a cantering carthorse, and I think it plainly rolls several syllables together to make one stress. This process was recognised in 1929 by Robert Graves, when he said in *The Future of Poetry*:

In the earlier native prosody the metre was determined by the stress centres of the line and the time-intervals between them. The earlier prosody has never been abandoned by popular poets and is frequently used by poets of culture. Its most familiar use is in nursery rhyme and country ballads:

> Misty, moisty was the morn,
>   Chilly was the weather;
> There I met an old man,
>   Dressed all in leather,
> Dressed all in leather
>   Against the wind and rain.
>
> It was, how do you do? and how do you do?
>   And how do you do? again (etc.)

Though the syllables number most irregularly, nobody can deny that the pieces scan. I write of stress-centres rather than of stresses, because often the stress is not on one syllable but, as in 'how do you do? and how do you do?' spread over two or three.

Graves was recommending flexibility in general, as native to English rhythms, but I think this particular device needs the dignity of being formalised. I am inclined to call it 'jammed stress'; and, once you realise that it is frequent, you feel that a great deal is wrong with our standard account of metre. (Maybe Hopkins has named it already, but I can't make his system, or systems, out.)

Not long ago (August 1960) there was a controversy about metre in the *Times Literary Supplement*, and a metrist asserted as a scientific discovery that there are four degrees of stress in English poetry.[4] I did not understand what had proved that there were no more than four, but I readily believe that this fits the facts much better than the crude Dumdi Dumdi we were taught at school, so that a machine programmed to talk verse on four degrees of stress would sound almost as if it understood it. But this would be a case where the machine isn't interesting because it doesn't use the same method as the mind. In most poetry (not perhaps all good English poetry) there is a tension between the pronunciation demanded by the form and that demanded by the feeling, which may for example be colloquial and down to earth, or dramatic and exalted. Two rival ways of scanning the line are both being used at once, and the less formal, the more colloquial or dramatic, will commonly use a jammed stress. That is why these quarter-stresses are used, if they are really different from a continuous range; the hearer is able to pick up from them what the two rival scansions are and how they balance. I don't understand the thing, but some unconsciously obeyed rule needs to be postulated. It struck me teaching in Japan and China that recognition of a poetic rhythm is a sudden process, though it sometimes only comes after a good deal of patient reading of the author; and I have known students write convincingly that they had discovered one of these beauties of sound, although their own mouths were hardly able to make the noises at all. I had expected to meet a major obstacle there, and was regularly astonished by the confidence and success with which they pronounced about beauty of sound. The human ear, or inner ear, is somehow cleverer than we understand about this matter; we need a theory about what we already do without a theory. It may be said, why then not accept the fact that we use quarter-stresses? Because as they stand they are too unconscious, and the next question is what we use them for. We *think* we are giving five whole stresses to one ten-syllable line, and the unconscious activity needs to grow out of the obvious one. These rhythm-handling centres of the mind are largely autonomous but not at all secret. We know that they are clever at counting ten syllables in a jumble, because the poetry of the French and of Miss Marianne Moore depends on that. They cheerfully accept our rule that there are five stresses in a decasyllable; the only point where they go beyond our expectations is in finding two lots of five

stresses. Considering what goes on in music, especially in syncopation, we
need not be surprised.

The alternative is often there, I think, in very plain and singing lines:

> That time of year thou mayst in me behold
> When yellow leaves, or none, or few do hang
> Upon those boughs that shake against the cold;
> Bare ruined choirs, where late the sweet birds sang.

[Shakespeare, sonnet 73]

The rhythm is steady and sober, but the last line is packed enough to put
strain on it. All the syllables could be stressed except '-ed' and 'the'; and
oddly enough, if you try stressing 'sweet' but not 'birds', and then 'birds'
but not 'sweet', both readings have implications in bad taste. 'Only the
sweeter birds are sweet enough to be like me' with the stress on *sweet*; 'I am
so innocent that I think all birds sweet' with the stress on *birds*. You need
equal stress on both, because of the peculiar way our stress-system handles
the basic logical constants; only equal stress allows of the logic that these
birds are emblematic or typically sweet, so that 'sweet-birds' is practically
their name, like 'black-birds'. These spondees of course are frequent in
English words, and any system of scanning by dumdies has to reckon with
them somehow. The official scansion, with only one of the words stressed,
would turn out here to be a tear-jerking or emotive one. The beginning of
the line illustrates the more usual case, where the jammed stress is the more
emotive of the two alternatives. *Bare* can hardly be said without any stress,
but that could be regarded as thrown in at the start, hardly affecting the
rhythm of the line: when separated like this it feels earnest but prosy. If we
make it emotive, that is, if we make Shakespeare at the age of thirty squeal-
ingly indignant with the stealing clutches of time: 'Why, but I can't be
friends with an exciting young lord, like you; I'm a shambling old man,
with no *teeth*' – then, whether it began as a joke or not, the two syllables
become practically one noise:

BEARRU ined-choirs where-late the sweet-birds sang.

To call the one noise a spondee makes it a foot in quantitative metre, and
we find that reassuring somehow; after all, when all the syllables are
stressed in English the language becomes in effect unstressed. But I don't
think that describes what usually happens. If you record on a graph the
sound of reading a line, two syllables will often make one jagged peak of
noise together. We only fail to realise this because of a secret belief that consonants do not make a noise, only vowels; whereas the consonant R at least
can be used for a loud and sustained noise, as by dogs. One should of course

allow for the feedback of theory upon both poets and readers; any beliefs they hold must be expected to affect the scansion, and as I say I think they are often affected by knowing classical metres. The jammed stress is unconscious for the theoretical part of the mind, but the practice imposes itself and is then not hard to explain away, or explain as something else.

This, at any rate, clears up how to scan the first line of *Paradise Lost*. We must be allowed to stress *Of*, the first syllable, for the meaning: *O Muse, sing of man's disobedience* does not get said for six lines, so the grammar demanding it becomes lost unless *Of* is emphasised. This means that four stresses together have to start the poem; but we are now ready to explain that they are only two jammed stresses:

<u>Of man</u>'s <u>first</u> <u>disobe</u>dience, / and the <u>fruit</u>

Even so, you need not suppose a 'weak stress' at the caesura; the five stresses can be allotted in many ways.

If then the rhythms of English are loose, rich and confused, as one can hardly deny, how far is poetry in English likely to gain from strict metres? And is the language really so very heavily stressed, panting and thudding with emphases inherited from our rough northern forbears? The question has only to be asked to suggest a qualification; the English often feel that some Americans quack on with a terrible monotony and no pause for the opposite number to get in a word. For that matter, I have known American literature students who believed that regular metres if used by literate authors were always meant as a parody of the unsophisticated – the well-known Mock-pastoral. The Free Verse movement began in America, and this might simply be because their language is no longer stressed. Greek lost its tones during some Dark Age, and a similar thing may be happening to English. But it is clearly not true that all American accents are unstressed; perhaps only the Boston accent is. I should guess that Miss Marianne Moore really talks without stress, and only could be scanned by counting syllables, so that she was quite right to make her innovation. It is rather surprising, come to think of it, that American poets have not revived classical metres, as they feel themselves forbidden the standard singing line. Forbidden does seem the word; the *vers libre* movement has meant, for many young poets, a struggle to renounce a pleasure which they feel perfectly capable of. Opinion about William Carlos Williams makes the position clear, I think; English critics don't feel he is a poet at all, but the most unexpected American critics will be found speaking of him with tender reverence; they feel he is a kind of saint. He has renounced all the pleasures of the English language, so that he is completely American; and he only says the dullest things, so he has won the terrible fight to become completely democratic as well. I think that, if they are such gluttons for punishment as all that, they are past help. But then again, I am not sure that we English aren't the ones who are losing the singing line, as apart from renouncing it. Serious poetry written to be set to music would be a striking change in the literary scene, and may be, though we don't know it, already an impossible one.

(After the lecture a young English questioner rebuked me for disrespect to William Carlos Williams, so this attempt to differentiate the two cultures was a failure like so many. He also felt it was rather queer and disagreeable to talk about poetry in this cookery-book way, because unlike the other arts poetry was just a matter of expressing oneself sincerely. This dogma would convince any real poet that he was not a poet, just as Menuhin would have become certain after a few trials that he was not a violinist if he had been brought up to believe that such a man could play well without having to learn. And yet one cannot leave the sincerity dogma there; poets who had acquired high skill have renounced it for the sincerity of free verse. Perhaps this need not always be called renunciation; the delicious social hints and evasive claims-by-mumble of spoken English are a positive intoxicant though externally drab. One may agree that a poet should be enough in contact with the spoken English of his time, and also believe he has always needed to be free enough from it to sing. Taking for granted that mumbling is the only honest mode of speech is I suppose a fog which has thickened steadily for the last fifty years. Still, I don't deny that some English poetry without rhyme or metre has the distinctive feeling they can give, that the words are magically right through satisfying a number of independent conditions; for example, the first version of Auden's 'Spain'.)

Turning now to the subject of Imagery, the second half of my title, I have to say that it is a great delusion. The great word 'Imagination' is from the same root, and there must be some good uses for such words, but it is a misfortune that aestheticians refuse to outgrow a stage of thought which can be recognised as inevitable for primitive man. Or, to make the complaint as small as possible, the people who give 'Images' a high specialised meaning need to be more aware of the delusions caused by the ordinary meaning.

The primitive mind, when asked how the ear does its work, tends to say 'There's a little man in your ear; he listens, and he tells you.' Thus the striking thing about the primitive explanation is that it does not explain anything; the mind feels very rightly that there is room for an explanation here, so then it has to be quieted with a bogus one, as a hungry baby is given a soother. In the same way, when the philosophers asked themselves 'How do we think?' they thought, 'Oh well, we must have copies of everything inside our heads; God and the triangle and tapeworms and everything are laid up in Heaven to start with, but then also laid up inside each man's head.' These are the man's Images. Now this explanation too, you see, has the distinguishing primitive feature of not explaining anything. When you have got all these things inside your head they have still no connections with one another; you are no nearer to starting thinking about them than you were when they were outside your head. The point is made very clear by the modern calculating machines, which really are like brains in the sense that all previous machines have been like other parts of the human body. One of them, out of date now I believe, had a huge column of mercury and worked by the times when a wave in the mercury arrived back; you could feed millions of these rhythms into the one column and it would keep them all going till you wanted to take one out, so the column was the memory of the machine. You could say if you liked that that was where it stored its Images, but if you did you would have got a long way away from what you had meant by Images to start with; what you began by meaning was a sort of picture in your head. People do, of course, get these pictures, some people more than others; but they have so little to do with thinking that it is actually hard to say what they are used for, what function they were evolved to fulfil.

In literary criticism, where people are always talking about images, they have to be assumed to mean visual images; whereas the scientific use of the term includes muscular images. To imagine a movement might well be a preparation for making it; and we know that dogs dream of chasing rabbits because we see them twitch as they lie by the fire. You can imagine riding a bicycle, indeed dream of it, and you need not then be seeing any picture of your own legs. I think it often makes a difference in reading poetry whether you get the muscular image, whereas it seems to be hardly ever important to get a visual image. No doubt 'eyes like almonds' doesn't mean what it should unless you 'see' that the eye is *shaped* like an almond, but there the meaning itself is visual. Keats says in the 'Ode to Autumn':

> And sometimes like a gleaner thou dost keep
> Steady thy laden head across a brook.

This is a very strong piece of muscular imagery, though easily not noticed because of a negative kind. The plank over the drain will be green and slimy in autumn, so that you are liable to fall in even without a weight on your head, and the goddess has to take care not to lose her dignity. At any moment a catastrophe will come; one storm will strip the leaves and turn all this scene to winter – that is the point of the last line 'And gathering swallows twitter in the skies.' Necessarily the poet compares this to his disease; he feels 'it is all so glutted with calm that it feels eternal, and yet really I am racing towards death at the speed of an express train.' The effort of balancing in the calm goddess, the muscular image, is the centre of the poem. I am glad to have one example of an Image being beautiful, but even so it isn't what critics usually mean by the term.

It has been known for at least a century that many people don't have visual images, and think without them, but the literary critics have stubbornly refused to pay any attention. Non-visualisers are often intellectuals, and I am sure it does intellectuals good to have their noses rubbed in their sensual corruption; I agree that it's disgusting not to have images; but all the same even people who do have images don't use them for thinking. This was pointed out by a novelist who was working hard at telling the truth about life with the insights of the most recent philosophy, and nobody I think has yet noticed that he refuted the philosopher he was admiring. Sterne, in *Tristram Shandy*, used Hume on the human mind, rather than safe old Locke as he chose to pretend; after the book had made him famous he became friends with Hume, but neither of them ever realised that it had refuted Hume. The death of the son of Mr Shandy is announced in the novel, and treated with the rather grim coolness of this sentimental author; one of the servant girls, while the death is being talked about, reflects that she will be expected to wear mourning, but she can't be expected to buy a black dress; she will have to be given an old green gown of Mrs Shandy, which she had long waited for, and she will dye it black. She goes on talking and thinking about all this perfectly sensibly, indeed rather artfully; but all the time, Sterne keeps on telling us, she imagines seeing the gown as it is now, green, not black as she is thinking of making it. The simple fact that this is possible is enough to prove that Hume is wrong, when he takes for granted that we can only think by images. The human mind is an enormously elaborate machine, vastly bigger than any artificial one, and it has extra gadgets in careless profusion; we can sometimes learn from diseases, when a bit of the machine goes wrong, what extremely elaborate things have to go on so that we can do what we regard as elementary. Thus there is a disease where a man can't read, though he can see, but with large letters on a blackboard, where he can trace his fingers round the letters, he can switch over to the tactile or muscular centres which sum up a whole shape, and in that way he can make out the letter, A or B. One could not have more direct proof that visual images are not enough for thinking.

It was worth evolving visual images, you can suppose, to try out a movement in your head and imagine its results without having to learn by experience; this would clearly have survival value when the experience itself would kill you. But I don't think there is any kind of thinking which can only be done by visual images. I was once discussing these matters in a splendid hall in Leeds, and after trying to imagine what use imagining could be, by way of showing generosity to the opponent there, I said that images must be the only way to play nineteen simultaneous games of chess blindfold, clearly that can only be done by pictures, probably a photographic memory as it's called; and a man spoke up from the back of the hall and said he had played twelve games of chess at once blindfold and had never had any images at all. I gazed at him as if he was a bug-eyed monster. This was the usual case of falling back upon chatter about images when we don't know how a mind has worked. Certainly what can go on in his mind is a black mystery to me, but then I couldn't play these games of chess with the pictures either. (After the lecture this account was endorsed by scientists in the audience.)

The trouble about Imagism and all its connections, which are still crawling about underfoot in the contemporary jungle and tripping up the innocent reader of poetry, is that it is determinedly anti-intellectual, and tells us that we ought to try to be very stupid. I was having a small controversy some while ago about 'The Garden' by Andrew Marvell, and the opponent said it was inept of me to have said that the word *straight* could mean 'tightly together' as well as 'at once'; because, he said, the poet was writing about the sea, which is big, so the image of being crowded into a small space would be inept.[5]

> Meanwhile the mind, from pleasure less,
> Withdraws into its happiness.
> The mind, that ocean where each kind
> Does straight its own resemblance find;
> Yet it creates, transcending these,
> Far other worlds, and other seas,
> Annihilating all that's made
> To a green thought in a green shade.

The poet is comparing his own mind to the sea, and though the sea is big his head is small. Such would be the position for any poet, but a mystic might feel himself entitled to large claims. Marvell does echo the claims of mystics, but he knows very well that he is being impudent and can only rely upon the humour of a logical analogy. If one of my sons said he needn't hold down a pay packet because he could get as much experience by sitting in Appleton House garden as by learning any skill, I would think it a bit much. Literary critics nowadays I think lose the impact of the poem because they refuse to look at it in this real way. Actually the war had finished in England and gone to Scotland when Marvell was at Appleton House, but he still felt the great estate as an enchanted peace. He had been directed into a very quiet staff job with frightfully useful contacts; and it wasn't his fault, though he knew he ought to be fighting the King. You understand, I am puzzling about what was at the back of his mind when he wrote these few extremely magical poems. There is something about the tone of them, as many critics have felt, which though so deliciously relaxed feels like a challenge. But an Imagist reader is not allowed to understand anything. If the poet says the mind is like the sea, then the Imagist reader must have a picture of the sea, in his head, and he must make a unique kind of muscular effort so as never to think of what is being talked about, the other half of the comparison, at all. The belief that poetry positively ought not to mean anything is still very strong, though mainly held by foreigners I think. I have to meet people in the course of my profession who actually hold these delusions; and are prepared to show me that my poetry too, like all other poetry, is merely a collage of logically unrelated images. I think just the opposite; arguing in verse has always seemed to me a wonderfully poetical thing to do, so I cannot understand the idea that it is prosy to speak up for the human reason. If the modern movement is the revolt against reason I have never been in it at all, so I have not left it merely because I am an old buffer.

Literary critics often talk about Images, or the Imagery of a Shakespeare play, meaning the metaphors in it; and this would only be an unnecessary extra word if they meant nothing else. But probably most people would call 'Hover through the fog and filthy air,' at the beginning of *Macbeth*, part of the imagery of the play. They are right, because the feeling that all the characters are doubtful which side will win and who to trust, so that they are all in a fog, is the atmosphere of the play. It struck me during the Civil War in China how extremely right Shakespeare had been to pick on that. So I kept on writing the lines down in the albums which people would kindly bring me to sign:

> But cruel are the times, when we are traitors
> And do not know, ourselves; when we hold rumour
> From what we fear, yet know not what we fear,
> But float upon a wild and violent sea,
> Each way, and move.

The witches only mean there is a fog, giving flying conditions which they find agreeable; but Shakespeare behind them means, as Dickens did at the start of *Bleak House*, that the characters are in a mental fog too. So that makes the fog part of the Imagery. But even in this atmospheric kind of case you do better if you arrive at seeing the point with both halves of the comparison vivid in your mind; both the Vehicle and the Tenor, as I. A. Richards named them in his *Philosophy of Rhetoric*, the thing which is really meant as well as the thing it is compared to. In fact, when Imagery is known to work well, it works by leading an appeal to experience forward till the rational mind feels it can safely deduce something (usually a very plain fact of life, but not always) from the variety of life and the decisiveness of the immediate judgements upon it which have already been shown in the artwork, taking for granted the experienced sympathy of the reader. I can well believe, on the other hand, that Ezra Pound himself is a very bad judge of Imagery; because he is such a clever man, and has such natural good feelings, that he actually hasn't had to do any conscious thinking for fifty years or so. The way his mind decides for him is rather too much above his own head; he is inspired, and hardly to blame when he is mistaken. What his feelings consider good are homely and practical things, and this has to be recognised as more important for a judgement on him than his views.

It is hard to guess what people who talk about Images mean, but I think most of them expect to mean that they are allowed to think about both halves of the comparison; that is, if young Andrew Marvell says the mind is like the sea, they are allowed to think about a unique mind at a selected date and need not only switch on their standard Image of the eternal sea. But the effect of the word Imagery is that they are very strongly encouraged to attend to the Vehicle and not the Tenor, attend to the decorations only; and a massive line of talk preaches to them that they are more high class and artistic if they do so. The first thing to get clear, I think, is that this Imagist account of the human mind (which often sounds to be making it angelic) makes it totally sub-human, sub-canine for that matter, the mind of a blackbeetle. T. E. Hulme, who had a very lively mind and no doubt would have learned better if he had not been killed in the First World War, said that thought is prior to language and consists in the simultaneous present-ment to the mind of two images.[6] This is not so. A dog could not find its way home across a field if it had nothing more in its head, at a moment of choice, than the simultaneous occurrence of two images. It is fair to sup-pose that the two images here are the cosy inglenook and the raw plain, one of them desired and the other presented by fact; but the dog would need a great deal more in its head than that. There is a sharply horrible answer to this nonsense talked by Hulme; the condition he describes actually occurs among men lost in the desert, and they know themselves that they must break out of it or perish.

What motive then can be found for the theorists who say that this is all the mind can do? The motive is often both generous and politically well-calculated; deserving to win through the confusion of life, and likely enough to do so. The aesthetician wants to recommend some under-privileged group whose art works are being taken up; such as the ballads of the working classes, or the *Beowulf* of our shaggy ancestors, or the carvings of a primitive tribe. Plainly, any city slicker, who wants to snub these worthy people, deserves to be snubbed in his turn; and a convenient way to do this is to say that the intellect is a wicked thing: 'Of course these people are blackbeetles. Aren't we all? That's why they're so nice.' The trouble about this line of talk is that it greatly under-rates the primitive art works, which are almost always found to have strict rules carried out with great care, even if rather loony ones; and it regularly happens, when the tribes-people discover what these sponsors have been saying in their favour, that they become as it is called very ungrateful; and they are quite right of course. However, I must not present this as the only impulse behind the anti-intellectualist movement, a very complicated thing, with some of its motives more respectable than this and some of them less.

Surely, it will be said, the Imagist movement has had some valuable effects, for example, in the study of the 'reiterative imagery' of Shakespeare. I agree that this has increased our understanding of the plays, but I think the pure theory is wrong even there. This became specially clear in the sheep-shearing scene of *The Winter's Tale*, where modern critics of the symbolist school have told us that Perdita was not mature, a grave fault in their system somehow, or more definitely that she was afraid of sexual love, or quite definitely that she is self-pitying (and D. H. Lawrence laid down a rule that any little bird would die with its head under its wing in a frost without ever saying a self-pitying sentence):

> O Proserpina,
> For the flowers now that, frighted, thou letst fall
> From Dis's waggon: Daffodils
> That come before the swallow dares, and take
> The winds of March with beauty; violets dim,
> But sweeter than the lids of Juno's eyes
> And Cytherea's breath; pale primroses
> That die unmarried, ere they can behold
> Bright Phoebus in his strength – a malady
> Most incident to maids ... O, these I lack
> To make you garlands of, and my sweet friend
> To strew him o'er and o'er.

I think that this critical belief comes solely from being too proud to attend to the story. Perdita is behaving with heroic courage, and far more virtue than would be expected in real life. Despairingly in love with Prince Florizel, the supposed peasant girl announces to a casual visitor that she disapproves of princes marrying peasants (she takes for granted that she wouldn't 'breed by him' without his marrying her); and this affects the audience much more than any imagery, because without her farm-bred innocence *breed* would be a shameless word for her to use. She says she will die if her lover abandons her; and in these poetical speeches, while other persons on the stage are supposed to think she is merely acting up to her grand clothes as Queen of the Festival, she is trying to needle her young man into marrying her. Surely it is too ludicrous to have Imagist critics arguing that she is too immature to accept passion, when the meaning of her words, if you attend to the story, is that she will die if she is separated from her lover. Of course her imagery sounds dying; she is using her imagery to fight for the triumph which she achieves, not to betray her own feelings, which many reasons make her want to hide. I think this the greatest nonsense ever talked about dramatic imagery; but of course even here I would agree that recognising the character of the imagery adds to the effect.

Our President, Sir Herbert Read, has long been one of the foremost theorists of the Image, and I want to remark that *The True Voice of Feeling* seems to me much the best exposition of the Romantic doctrine; in fact I always recommend it to students who are thinking about that. And I agree with him that the Romantic doctrine is true, or mostly true. But I don't think its truth depends on the part about the Image. During the last hundred years, the Image has been much mixed up with the Revolt against Reason, a game, I feel, which we can no longer afford to play. There is a belief that Imagery was developed earlier or lies deeper than the rational mind, and helps to protect us from that mind, which is always on the edge of some sordid wickedness. I agree that what is meant here contains important truths, but the expression of it (in D. H. Lawrence, for example) has always depended on very tricky, very intellectual and up-to-the-minute uses of language, by which a highly selected part of the mind is called conscious and wicked and diseased and in short mental, but some other part of the mind, which remains shrouded, is called good. But a great deal of our unconscious thinking, in the preconscious I think it is called, is quite unromantic and straightforward; the staff go loyally on with their routine whether the inspector is passing or not. One is bound to reflect, after one of these tirades: 'Well, the poor old mind may not be worth much, but it's all you've got, anyway.' One may love a fellow creature for all kinds of reasons, such as that it smells nice; the point where the experience becomes serious is when it loves you back, and then the poor old mind has to come into play, one way or another. Exactly which bits of the mind count as mental was, I think, simply a thing D. H. Lawrence habitually cheated about, on the great superlogical and intuitive principle 'Heads I win, tails you lose.' He was often on the right side, in the various quarrels for which he used this trick about the mind; but it is a misfortune that the whole literary tradition of Symbolism has grown up so completely divorced from the tradition of fair public debate. Chatterley, for example, has always been spiritually impotent and you are supposed to know this from a Symbol, that he happened to become wounded in battle. Surely one knows quite well that this is an infantile type of arguing in the author, tirelessly petulant and spiteful, and not unmental in the slightest degree – as artful as a monkey, in fact. Of course Lawrence did not invent it; I am not sure that the first establishing uses of Symbolism weren't the political propaganda of Dickens, though as usual we can't be sure we didn't catch it from the French.

I don't deny that the revolt against reason was often used with success, as was believed at the time, to liberate artists from pedants who tied them down by false arguments to conventional forms. Most of these liberations went on between the two wars, a wonderful time to be alive, when as Wyndham Lewis said the cultural scene was like a great circus with thrills at every turn. 'Oh, it's a wild life in the Near West,' he said, 'between one revelation and another.'[7] The present age is much duller and quieter, in fact it feels to me simply groggy, as if the Atom Bombs have given it a rabbiter on the back of the neck. All the great movements of liberation are still ticking over and emitting their slogans, but the attacks on the rational mind have nearly all been fielded and directed into simple obscurantism. 'You can't avoid being a communist unless you're a Christian, and you know you're frightened of communism, so have a good fright about Hell too. Obviously you can't be a rationalist any more, because the freethinkers have been telling you that for years.' So the residual legatee of all the anti-intellectual movements has been simple old fundamentalism, with a strong flavour of political conformity.

This curious development was described before it had really got started in the horrible book *1984* by George Orwell. If you remember, the story happens in London, and one can't make out whether London is post-communist or post-Christian; the rulers say it is permanently at war with another state in eastern Europe, and daily hate is drummed up on the telly, but the novel gradually lets it emerge that there isn't a pin to choose between them. [See 'Christianity and *1984*' below.] On the whole I find the book tiresomely incredible, which is a comfort as what it prophesies is so very ghastly; but I keep feeling that a bit of the prophecy has already come true. This puts me against all forms of the revolt against reason; I think our only remaining hope lies in getting the poor old mind to do its work just well enough.

Notes

1 See Robert Graves, *The Crowning Privilege*, London: Cassell, 1955; and Empson's review above.

2 A gramophone record of Professor W. H. D. Rouse reading Homer and Pindar was played at the end of the lecture. [Empson]

3 On 30 November 1959 Empson had posed the 'problem' of Housman's use of the Alcaic metre (citing the poem 'Tell me not here, it needs not saying') – 'It is ... I think necessarily a matter not of "stress" but of "length of syllable"' – in a letter to Eric Laughton, Professor of Classics at the University of Sheffield: 'It is a striking metrical effect, unusual in English poetry, and critics seem to agree that there is something odd about his rhythm sometimes (Cyril Connolly called it "decadent" at the time of the funeral) [see footnote 1, p. 420 below]. I wonder if you would agree that this one turns on imputing a long–short Latin rhythm (forcing the English to do it rather surprisingly) instead of a stress rhythm? ... It is a shockingly silly poem: to be offended with the trees when you revisit them because they don't remember you is an almost uniquely self-important way to regard Nature. This I think makes its great beauty all the more surprising; one feels inclined to look for a technical explanation' (Empson Papers).

In a letter of 13 September 1964 to Christopher Ricks, Empson observed that 'the aching thrill for the homosexual [as in Last Poems, no. XL] ... is the really strong point of Housman's poetry' (Christopher Ricks).

4 Page 94 of The Function of Criticism by Yvor Winters (1957) proves that at least four are needed; the chapter is also good on 'spondees' in sixteenth-century English. [Empson]

Terence Hawkes, in a letter to the Times Literary Supplement (1 July 1960, p. 417), defined 'cadence' as an '"intonation-pattern" ... containing one and only one primary stress (however many other degrees of stress there are in it) out of the English range of four stresses ...' Hawkes developed his remarks in a further letter (TLS, 15 July 1960, p. 456), observing among other things that:

'In a four-stress system of analysis, it is a linguistic fact that if any two like stresses occur in conjunction the second will be stronger than the first and, if there are three, the third stronger than the second, and so on ... it can be stated that there is a total of fourteen possible stress matrices for the iambic foot in English, and no more.

'A more exact analysis would also have to take into account the fact of juncture (occurring before, after, and within the iamb) and of the various incidences of the four degrees of pitch and possible pitch-change on each element of the iambic foot.'

On 3 July 1962 Empson wrote to Hawkes, enclosing an offprint of 'Rhythm and Imagery in English Poetry':

'From your recent article on prosody ['The Problems of Prosody', Review of English Studies, III: 2, April 1962, pp. 32–49] I gather we agree more than I had thought from the TLS letters; but I don't think you envisage two different scansions accepted together, which seems to me necessary.

'Enid Hamer's book on metre, thirty years ago [The Metres of English Poetry, London: Methuen, 1930], said that metrists sometimes admit they mean by a "stress" both a louder and a longer syllable – would you admit that this is natural?'

In response to a reply from Terence Hawkes, Empson wrote again on 11 July 1962:

'I think one can have two concurrent rhythms without a jammed stress; jammed stress is merely a special way of forcing a rhythm. I was imagining a complex curve, the graph of the loudness plotted against time, which can be resolved (mathematically by Fourier methods) into a number of regular rhythms of different periods. Now that you make me examine it, this is a false comparison, because there is nothing in the double scansion to correspond to the different periods. But if you are allotting the "five stresses" of a ten-syllable line in two ways at once, the syllables which are stressed by both official and dramatic scansions would take your top stress, those stressed by neither your lowest stress, and one might have a neat arrangement with your remaining two degrees in the middle, that the official stress alone took the lower and the dramatic stress took the higher one. This is a horrible sentence, but perhaps you can make it out. On the other hand, pitch may be somehow used to indicate the two concurrent arrangements. I have no theory about how we do it; I only say that we must do it somehow.

'I don't understand your doubt how one could measure the length of a syllable. If you had the recorded graph of the sound you could presumably measure it with a ruler.

'You don't say whether there is any proof that only four not five degrees of stress exist.

'Interesting that each cadence has only one peak of sonority, which has both top stress and top pitch. I bet you could get an actor to give it bottom pitch with the same effect, except that it made him thrillingly male' (Terence Hawkes).

5 See Empson's essay 'Marvell's Garden' in *Some Versions of Pastoral*.

His replies to various criticisms of his interpretation included the following letter to the *Listener*, 11 October 1956:

'Mr John Holloway, in a talk printed in *The Listener* of 20 September, objected to my having said that "strait" can mean "packed together" as well as "at once" in the grand lines of Marvell:

> The mind, that Ocean where each kind
> Doth strait its own resemblance find.

What ineptitude, he says, it would be for Marvell to say that the mind is like an ocean, and at the same time suggest that it is small. Empson only thinks this because he thinks all complexity is good; whereas he thinks the word "ocean" itself forbids the extra meaning stringently. But the complexity is already there if "strait" only means "at once"; if the kettle goes overboard in the real sea you won't find it at once. The central thought here is that the mind, though very big in one way, is very small in another; Marvell expected this paradox to be perfectly obvious to the reader, as immediate as a joke. One cannot be sure that he intended the double meaning, but it would only heighten the effect of his graceful piece of wit.

'That Mr Holloway cannot see the point at all is surely a curious development in the history of taste; I suspect it comes from "Imagism" – that is, he thinks that, if you are told the mind is like the sea, you ought to make pictures of the sea in your head and forget all about the mind.'

6 According to Hulme. 'Thought is prior to language and consists in the simultaneous presentation of two different images' (quoted in Michael Roberts, *T. E. Hulme*, London: Faber & Faber, 1938, p. 281).

7 Empson is alluding to Wyndham Lewis's *Time and Western Man*, London: Chatto & Windus, 1927.

Argufying in Poetry

Listener, 22 August 1963

I must have had strong feelings about this topic for a considerable time, without recognising them. As a writer of verse myself, I grew up in the height of the vogue for the seventeenth-century poet Donne, and considered that I was imitating him more directly than the others were. We all said we admired him because he was so metaphysical, but I can see now that I really liked him because he argued, whereas the others felt that this side of him needed handling tactfully, because it did not fit the Symbolist theory.

'Argufying' is perhaps a tiresomely playful word, but it makes my thesis more moderate; I do not deny that thoroughly conscientious uses of logic could become a distraction from poetry. Argufying is the kind of arguing we do in ordinary life, usually to get our own way; I do not mean nagging by it, but just a not specially dignified sort of arguing. This has always been one of the things people enjoy in poems; and it can be found in every period of English literature; but the effect of the Symbolist movement is that you are forbidden to do it, with no reason given; except that the anti-intellectual movement, which has been one of the causes of Symbolism, tells you that thinking is sordid or low-class. What I want to say amounts to a revolt against Symbolism.

Good poems have been written which appear to carry out the Symbolist rules; the best poems written in English during this century are Symbolist, and they are very good. But it has gone on long enough; poets now are finding the rules an obstacle, all the more because literary theorists commonly talk as if no other kind of poetry is possible but Symbolist poetry. The main rule is that a poet must never say what he wants to say directly; that would be what is called 'intellectualising' it; he must invent a way of hinting at it by metaphors, which are then called images. I was pleased to see Mr Graham Hough, in a recent book, remark in passing that he could never set out to explain *The Waste Land* to students without feeling 'What a rude way to talk it is!'[1] And what an obstacle, he would surely go on, if a poet is keen to get a message across, as Ezra Pound was for example, to have to bury it according to these arbitrary rules. The doctrine has bad effects on the readers too; for one thing, if they are given a comparison – for example, 'the mind of man is like the sea' – they tend to forget about the mind, especially the particular mind of the person in view (though the author was using the comparison to tell them something about that); they switch on their stock image, their mental picture-postcard of the eternal sea.

I was much struck recently by a young lady I was tutoring who gave the right answer when confronted with a question from an old 'Practical Criticism' paper; that is, a verse was quoted, and she was to spot the date of it, giving her reasons. Sure enough, she found the images showed that this bit was late eighteenth-century; but what the examiners would not have found out was that she had no idea what the verse was saying. It urged you to carry out one of those terrific pieces of landscape gardening, cutting away the side of the hill, digging a lake, planting a forest, to improve the prospect from your country house. She thought the verse was only pictures of scenery, because she never bothered with verbs; to answer questions in the examination you only needed the images. I do not think you could really get through on this plan, but some people think you can. When the examination question says 'Evaluate the following poem,' the student will happily write down, 'Significantly, the images are symbolical.' What they signify, or what they symbolise, he does not say; he considers that if he did he would look low-class and philistine.

But we are more moderate about it in England, as I understand, than either the Americans or the French. The full doctrine says that all poetry consists only of a collage of logically unrelated images, and an American student once tried to prove to me that it was true of my own poetry. This made me realise that I have always considered the theory entirely wrong. It does harm, both in poetry and in prose, chiefly by fostering evasiveness and false suggestions; wherever this tradition comes from, it is completely out of touch with another tradition, that of fair public debate.

It is often said that the French invented Symbolism, and the reason was that the French bourgeois hated and despised the French bourgeois so much that he had to become aesthetically pure. No doubt their feelings did them credit, but we need not keep on saying how logical they were. Or, again, the theory was a weapon for the arts in their great war against the sciences, but there was never much wisdom to be found in that either. Whatever the history, the arguments one hears nowadays to support Symbolism turn on the belief that all thinking is done by images. This was firmly expressed by the Imagist T. E. Hulme, who said shortly before the First World War that thought is prior to language and consists in the simultaneous presentment of two images. [See 'Jam Theory and Imagism' above.]

It is important to realise that this theory was exploded about a century ago. I am not denying that Blake and Joan of Arc and the discoverer of the benzine ring saw visions, but that is different. Also many people do, of course, experience simple images; but some people can undoubtedly think without them, and appreciate poetry too. The belief that we think by images is a typical example of primitive thought. A primitive, if asked how we hear, has been known to say, 'There's a little man in your ear; he listens, and he tells you.' Similarly, when asked how we think, he says, 'You have copies of everything inside your head.' The distinguishing feature of a primitive explanation is that it does not even start to explain; the mind realises that some explanation is needed, but it can be fobbed off, as a hungry baby can with a soother. When you have all these things inside your head there are still no connections between them; you are no nearer thinking about them than when they were outside. Indeed, visual images are so little used that it is hard to see why they were evolved.

I once made a concession while arguing about this, and said that no doubt you needed images to play twelve games of chess at once blindfold, even though you do not need them to read a poem; but a man spoke up at the back of the hall and said he had played twelve games of chess blindfold and never had any images at all. This is a good example of the delusion, because I could not myself have played these games of chess even with the pictures; I just thought that anything I could not imagine must be done by images, as people say of conjuring, 'It's all done by mirrors.' As for T. E. Hulme and his two simultaneous images, a fair case would be a dog finding its way home; the two images are the bleak field before it and the kitchen fireside which it desires. How dogs find their way is a great mystery, but this theory does not take the first step towards explaining it. The condition described by Hulme actually occurs among men lost in the desert, and they know themselves that they must break out of it or perish.

Also, what the literary people mean by an image seems to be nearly always a visual image, a picture in your head, but the psychologists recognise images of all sensations, and also of muscular activity. You can dream of riding a bicycle without having any picture of your legs, and dogs lying by the fire twitch as they dream of chasing rabbits, so the process is an old one. Muscular imagery is the most important kind for reading poetry; at least, it is for the sort of poetry I like. This does not mean being frightfully athletic; when Keats says of the Goddess of Autumn:

> sometimes like a gleaner thou dost keep
> Steady thy laden head across a brook,

we feel in our muscles the effort of balancing, that is, the effort of keeping still, so we realise how precarious the autumn is, in its immense calm, though the deluded bees think it will last for ever; how wisely the swallows in the last line are gathering to emigrate. The muscular image here is the centre of the poem, whereas a visual image is hardly ever essential, I think.

Argufying in poetry is not only mental; it also feels muscular. Saying 'therefore' is like giving the reader a bang on the nose; and though it may be said that 'intellectualised' poetry feels stale and unreal, a bang on the nose does not feel stale and unreal; it is just as fresh the twentieth time as it was the first; that is, if you are granted enough leisure for recovery. The word 'therefore' is no more stale than the word 'dawn', and has just as much imagery about it.

We are now ready to recognise the main fact about Symbolist poetry; it is the poetry of the hamstrung, the people who have cut the strings in their legs. Such a poet cannot go where he wants to; he has to sit and wait like a barnacle and seize on any associations of the kind he wants that happen to drift toward him. This is a distinctive condition, and not pretty; so it is tiresome when a theorist says, 'Ah but all poetry is symbolical; that is in the nature of things; no poet has ever had the use of his legs.' The truth is, it is high time they got the use of their legs back.

I want to give a few examples, and they are bound to show that the distinctions I have drawn are much too simple. Yeats's 'Byzantium', though Symbolist, is magnificently full of muscular images; but I think it is a story, a fascinating bit of science fiction which he annoyingly refused to tell us in enough detail.[2] On the other hand, a trivial argument may still be very good poetry if it sings:

With serving still	this have I won
For my good will	to be undone
And for reward	of all my pain
Disdainfulness	I have again
And for redress	of all my smart
Lo, thus unheard	I do depart
Wherefore all ye	that after shall
By fortune be	as I am, thrall,
Example take	what I have won
Thus for her sake	to be undone.

[Sir Thomas Wyatt]

The famous lute of Wyatt always sounds to me like a banjo; you can hear it twanging. And how right C. S. Lewis was to say: 'How unpleasant it must have been for a woman to have Wyatt in love with her.'[3] I do not want to over-praise the poem. But it is plain that 'Wherefore' comes out not merely with boyish glee but with lyrical grace; the whole movement turns upon it, like the thigh-joint of a ballet dancer. You can get the same effect of song from a much broader line of reflection, as when the young G. S. Fraser, on the troop-ship taking him to Africa, considered why men allow themselves to be conscripted. Here are a couple of verses from his 'Letter to Anne Ridler':

> Or freedom, say, from family love and strife
> And all the female mystery of a room
> That half supports and half imprisons us
> May drive a man from father, mother, wife
> And every soft reminder of the womb.
> Dead Freud in lost Vienna argued thus,
> I hardly know. But Fritz, who's now interned,
> Sober and well-informed like all his race,
> Told me this war might last, say, seven years.
> But right would triumph then, the tide be turned;
> Unless indeed (the night fell on his face)
> Our hopes are just illusions like our fears.

This seems to me magnificent, and plainly not because of imagery; nor is it what would usually be called rhetoric. The seventeenth and eighteenth centuries could both argufy; the eighteenth said that the seventeenth debauched itself with quibbles, and the nineteenth said that the eighteenth was an age of prose, mainly because in their different ways they were both good at rhetoric; I would include that in argufying, but it strikes me as one of the duller kinds. George Fraser here, though surveying mankind like an archangel, is in a pleasant way deliberately off the point; to say on the troop-ship, 'Oh well, the boys were determined to leave home somehow,' would seem flippant if not felt so splendidly. But a last example, a Victorian one, has all the Victorian earnestness; it is Francis Thompson addressing 'The Dead Cardinal at Westminster' – that is, Cardinal Manning lying in state in Westminster Cathedral – on the traditional theme of the status of the artist. 'Do you seriously consider I'm going to Hell?' he asks, 'Because if so it's very unjust.' He is seriously concerned to get an answer and you can feel his elbows coming out as he jabs the argument home: sometimes he puts poetry into it, images and suchlike, and any present-day reader would agree that those parts are much inferior.

In a letter to the Listener *the following week (29 August 1963) William Cookson – who later edited Ezra Pound's* Selected Prose 1909–1965 *(London: Faber & Faber, 1973) – remonstrated against Empson that Symbolism and Imagism are 'totally different things', and quoted Pound's statement* (Gaudier-Brzeska, a Memoir) *that 'Imagism is not Symbolism. The Symbolists dealt in "association" that is, in a sort of allusion, almost of*

allegory. . . . The image, *in our sense, is real because we know it directly.'*
Empson completely misunderstood the difference when he said that an
Imagist poet employs metaphorical hints in order to say what he wants to
say; far from using metaphorical indirection, the Imagist is concerned with
'direct treatment of the object'.

Empson replied with this letter to the Listener *(5 September 1963):*

Mr Cookson says I don't know the difference between Imagism and Symbolism, and I may well be weak on it. I think both theories are very confused, and if my remarks sound confused it is because I meant to show that.
Very likely there is something important to be learned about images, but it
is not present in the usual critical talk about them. My idea about Imagists
is that they were a small group which concentrated upon carrying out with
puritanical rigour an aspect of the general Symbolist theory, around 1912,
and the results were so depressingly poky that even Ezra Pound before long
stopped calling himself one. I am surprised if Mr Cookson means what he
appears to say, that the best poems written in English during this century
are all Imagist not Symbolist.

Surely Yeats, though a friend and pupil of Pound, considered himself
Symbolist not Imagist? *Another emblem there! that stormy white . . .*
['Coole Park and Ballylee, 1931']. Would Mr Cookson say that a swan
literally, without any metaphor, *is* the moral eminence given to human
affairs by an aristocratic system? We expect the poets to tell excellent lies,
but they had better tell more plausible ones. Anyway, this distinction is not
what most critics mean now when they talk about a poem's images. I am
not surprised to learn that Pound, when introducing Imagism from Chicago, insisted that the new revelation was absolutely different from the old
one. Poets would make pronouncements about these Movements in an ex-
pansive tone of voice, like that used when offering one another drinks, and
as a rule they could look after themselves. But when an earnest logical student takes up this line of talk he gets bogged down very rapidly; I have seen
it happen. The theory which set out to praise the wonder of vision acts in
practice as if he had blinded himself.

Notes

1 Empson is paraphrasing Graham Hough's observation, 'To attempt to explain to an
intelligent person who knows nothing about twentieth-century poetry how *The Waste Land*
works is to be overcome with embarrassment at having to justify principles so affected, so perverse, so deliberately removed from the ordinary modes of communication' (*Image and Experience*, London: Gerald Duckworth, 1960, p. 28). The extended argument of Hough's first

chapter, 'Reflections on a Literary Revolution', fully supports Empson in bating the significance of the Imagist 'school' – as in this declaration: 'I should like to commit myself to the view that ... the collocation of images is not a method at all, but the negation of method. In fact, to expose myself completely, I want to say that a poem, internally considered, ought to make the same kind of sense as any other discourse' (p. 25).

2 See Empson's 'Mr Wilson on the Byzantium Poems', *Review of English Studies*, I: 3, July 1960, pp. 51–56; and his more extended discussion, 'The Variants for the Byzantium Poems', in *Using Biography*, London: Chatto & Windus, 1984, pp. 163–86.

3 'Poor Wyatt seems to be always in love with women he dislikes. My sympathy deserts my own sex: I feel how very disagreeable it must be for a woman to have a lover like Wyatt' (C. S. Lewis, *English Literature in the Sixteenth Century excluding drama*, Oxford: Clarendon Press, 1954, p. 229).

An Anatomy of Taste

New Statesman, 2 December 1966

Graham Hough, *An Essay on Criticism*

An Essay on Criticism plainly represents a welcome development, with its numbered paragraphs, as of Spinoza, surveying the foundations of the subject. Cambridge needs this kind of thing, and Professor Hough has the grasp, the breadth of sympathy and of actual reading, the generous acceptances combined with astringent judgement, to be able to do it. I have rested great hopes in him ever since he remarked in print that he never set out to explain *The Waste Land* to his pupils without reflecting 'What a rude way to write it is!' [See note 1, p. 172 above.] But the insight was not recognised as a possible source of further wisdom, and in this book he still seems to me entangled among his different virtues; indeed, it works out as practically a capitulation, though rightly a grudging one, to the literary mystagoguery of France and the United States. But the mind of Professor Hough will go on developing, and the book, owing to its majestic structure, is eminently capable of being revised. A dawn of reason in this field is inherently likely, if only from the necessary swing of fashion, and perhaps the third edition of the book, written after retirement, is likely to be the one reflecting the fullest illumination. I have to make minor complaints about the first edition.

The height and sweep of the generalisations tend to make invisible the quarrels now in progress, so that Professor Hough might be used to support positions he disapproved. Thus the chapter on Interpretation starts by telling us that there are two conceptions of it: (a) revealing the intention of the author, and (b) expounding the latent sense of his work, which he need not have consciously intended; indeed, to think of it may have been impossible for anyone in his time. Quotations are then given to recall that critics of type (b) have always existed. But what was done to the *Song of Solomon* is not being achieved or even attempted by any critic of our time; and the only effect of the extra clause of Professor Hough's generalisation is to insinuate that someone *is* doing it. On the contrary, scholars are always telling us, often while expressing motives of piety, that the dullest meaning of an old text is the only permitted one.

Thus C. S. Lewis maintained that the word 'unkind' in the poem 'Love' by Herbert —

> I, the unkind, ungrateful? Ah, my dear,
> I cannot look on thee.

— means only 'unnatural', because that was the main meaning of the word at the time, and it would have seemed impudent for a man to say he had been unkind to God. But the modern meaning of the word was already a possible special one, and the whole force of the poem came from somehow calling it out. The small-mindedness here was very unlike C. S. Lewis, but he was riding a strong horse and it dragged him that way [see Empson's review of C. S. Lewis's *Studies in Words* above].

It is quite usual now for schools to teach that the Marlowe *Faustus* is simply a Morality Play, so that the author thanks God when the hero goes to Hell. But it seems plain that Marlowe advertised his advanced ideas in pubs, so that the frightened audiences were sure he approved of risking all for knowledge: in fact, that the legend meant to him what it did to Goethe and Spengler, and those who live in the age of the Cobalt Bomb. There is evidence enough in the text, but it is only recognised if you grant the initial probability. (I can never see why it is even considered pious to believe that they were all stupid.) To deny it is like saying that the Savoy Operas contain no satire, because they merely echo 'the accepted opinion of the age': any competent scholar can list references from the contemporary leaders of *The Times* which completely parallel the phrases by W. S. Gilbert now ignorantly supposed to be facetious. Professor Hough would not take part in this blind falsification of history, but his theorising smiles on it benignly.

The book insists from the start that we must get away from realism and naturalism; but these are no longer a temptation. What is needed is for the student to think: 'What *kind* of reality, or natural truth, does the remote convention we have now to consider enshrine?' Unless he does that, he regards the academic subject as admittedly footling except as a means to his own advancement. Professor Hough is very good, though perhaps rather mannered, when he says that the truth of the Bible and of Gibbon's *Decline and Fall* does not matter to a literary reader, but that a novel fails unless it is historically true (because you need to believe in the whole society described). But then he deduces that a novel must not include magical events, this time I think failing to carry the generalisation far enough. Moll Flanders calls in despair for her highwayman husband, the real love of her life, during the day he has left her after the wedding-night at the lonely inn, and he hears her 30 miles away and does return, though at frightful risk; but magic is no use, and they have to wait till the end of the book. The incident proves that they are made for one another — we interpret it in terms of the stubborn magical convictions all around her. The supernatural detail here gives a massive feeling of reality (not of 'romance'), as it often does in *The Tale of Genji*. Still, the parts about the novel seem to me the best of Professor Hough's book, being the least disturbed by Symbolism.

During the chapter on Symbolism, the sun bursts for a moment through the clouds. After pointing out that the French never really had any Symbolist theory, only a determination to express what could not be expressed, Professor Hough tells us that later criticism – and he reports only from the English, not the French – has sometimes succeeded in explaining how these apparently ineffable verbal communications were achieved. Naturally I find this cheerful, as I am listed among those who sometimes did it. But the chapter ends in gloom, reflecting that these explainers may only have created an inferior imitation of the same inexplicable thing.[1] Come now, there are many things we do not have to explain in ordinary practice. A person engaged in the large profession of Eng. Lit. is expected to be able to make the 'magic' of a poem available to many people who could not otherwise have experienced it; if we can agree on ways of doing this, the mystery is no longer particularly oppressive.

Busy thought against thinking, and how to grade the anti-intellectualist intellectual, make the main problems of the later part of the book – with the author (very rightly, of course) always ready to see reason, immensely permissive and concessive. The judge feels obliged to let his own side lose, only allowing himself some witty epigrams against the victors. The Imagist slogan, 'a poem should not mean but be,'[2] is firmly answered: 'It is only by meaning that a poem can be at all.' But this is not followed up. 'Ignorant people who think of Hamlet as real can grasp more about him than the analyst of themes and images': yes indeed, this has become very plain, but no further step is taken to release us from the grip of the Imagists. The most curious of these cracks, I think, is: 'Any graduate student can be taught to recognise a dying god.' It is only passable as an answer to the myth-critics, but the word 'graduate' offers a queer social glimpse. Many students reading for the BA degree at Cambridge, I suppose, are willing to teach at schools, not universities, and they feel confident of winning the needed ticket without pretending to accept the more lunatic theories of their teachers.

However, the book does not continue to be grudging. Towards the end, it glows with an honourable admiration for the Canadian critic Professor Northrop Frye, in which I find it hard to share. Hough admits that the Frye method of classification seems pointless. The classification of comedy is what he most admires, and I think the reason is that Frye here shows a breath of revolutionary sentiment (elsewhere he regards the whole of tradition as an irremovable burden). His five phases of comedy are a sequence in the 'restoration' of a redeemed society (pious, of course, but the basic process is knocking down father). This lets him say, for example, something far less dead than our standard account of Ben Jonson: 'The principle of the Humour is that the literary imitation of ritual bondage is funny.' But, even so, I cannot see that this theory of comedy casts much light (no actual joke is ever considered). And the pious Northrop Frye has also an eerie side. The rebel angels, he was saying in a recent book on Milton,[3] illustrate the error of Ham, who behaved disrespectfully towards the nakedness exhibited by his father Noah when drunk.

Milton, it is presumed here as all along, was following a profound old medieval tradition. But the text of Genesis IX gives us no excuse for supposing that Ham behaved badly when confronted by the exhibition: it only says he went out of the tent and warned his two brothers. They arranged to pull a blanket over father without looking at him, thus proving that they believed even an accidental glimpse sufficient to entail a curse. The descendants of Ham became slaves for ever by this accident, says the Bible, but it gives no excuse for assuming that they became black.[4] The text has long been one of the major pious excuses for negro slavery, and was already very barbaric before being so perverted. To see Frye happily bringing it out, as a thing that Milton would obviously support like all other traditionalists, makes me suspect a basic moral insensitivity. Milton was a courageous defender of freedom: within peculiar limits no doubt, but he was very unlikely to recommend slavery.

Notes

1 'William Empson, by exploiting the concept of ambiguity and multiple meaning, can elucidate the structure of passages that had formerly seemed either to defy analysis or not to require it' (Hough, *An Essay on Criticism*, London: Gerald Duckworth, 1966, p. 136). Hough's concluding remarks include: 'It may be true that poetry presents a system of hidden correspondences that really pervade the universe. It may be true that poetic symbols derive their power from the action of spiritual powers. In that case much recent literary interpretation would be tautologous – repeating in its own terms what has been revealed once and for all; or arid – subjecting to analysis what is only fertile as an unanalysed whole; or pointless – trying to say what cannot be said' (p. 137).

2 From Archibald MacLeish's poem 'Ars Poetica'.

3 Northrop Frye, *Five Essays on Milton's Epics*; reviewed by Empson in the *Listener*, 28 July 1966.

4 Writing to the *New Statesman* (23 December 1966) Henry Adler explained the connection between Ham and black peoples – 'The word Ham comes from "Chem", one of the earliest words for black and, of course, Ham, Shem and Japhet (and such of his sons as Javan) have given their names to the classifications Hamitic, Semitic, Ionian, used anthropologically' – to which Empson commented: 'I ought to have known about the Hebrew for Ham, and am glad to learn; but surely it makes this bit of the Bible even worse.'

The Voice of the Underdog

Journal of General Education, XXVI: 4, Winter 1975, and
New York Review of Books, 12 July 1975

Wayne C. Booth, *A Rhetoric of Irony*

This is a good book. It quotes a number of long examples, arguing from
them in detail 'how we manage to share ironies and why we often do not,'
with mild discouragement for current follies on the subject; and the literary
judgements (as apart from philosophical or historical ones) seem to me
right every time. There is plenty of theoretical discussion, with a five-page
bibliography, and nearly all the names there recur in the index to pages. It
seemed all the more extraordinary that what I had long thought 'irony' to
mean does not get mentioned at all.

The basic situation for this trope, without which it would not have been
invented, involves three people. There is a speaker, 'A', an understanding
hearer, 'B', and a censor who can be outwitted, a stupid tyrant, 'C'. A successful use of the pure form is not very frequent, because people aren't such
fools as you think. However, it is even more satisfactory when 'C', though
he knows what is going on, dare not complain – because the effect would be
a ridiculous confession, or because the only available penalty would appear
so excessive as to make him unpopular. (Pope's 'Epistle to Augustus' is an
example; however stupid the king was, somebody would tell him the
answer, so the pure form could not be achieved.) Or the ironist may be
taking a balanced view, trying to be friends with both sides; but even so one
of them can be picked out as holding the more official or straight-faced
belief, and the literal meaning will support that one. If this condition did
not hold, there would be no impulse to use the form. I warmly agree with
Professor Booth that the term 'irony' gets applied much too loosely, so that
it has become almost useless, and his conception of 'stable irony' is a good
approach to what we need; but it is not nearly so easy to recognise as the
basic situation.

This, although rare, is immediately striking, perhaps because our minds
accept it as archetypal. I heard a case in Seoul in 1933, and (internally)
sprang to attention, clicking my heels together. I had wanted to get close to

the statues visible in the cloisters of a temple, but the gate was locked, so I went to the nearby government offices to ask for a key. I was shown to a door unobtrusively marked in English 'Foreign Office'. Inside there were a rather shamefaced young Englishman and his elderly benign Japanese superior. This was when the Japanese were taking over Manchuria, the beginning of the end for the League of Nations and the Peace Settlement, and there was a good deal of diplomatic activity. The young man said: 'I'm here to put the commas into the True Truth about Manchuria,' and his boss smiled at us in a fatherly way. I had long been hearing, in the English colony at Tokyo, that no Japanese can understand irony (whereas the Chinese, of course, use it all the time), but I had never seen the belief put to the test. Of course you could argue that this Japanese did understand the little attempt at face-saving, and treated it with the contempt it deserved; indeed, perhaps one can never be sure of a success in the basic situation, though a failure may have immediate bad consequences. But I was not misled by any respect for my dashing compatriot (who had only put himself further in the wrong), and I had been working closely with Japanese for the past two years, and I was watching the boss, who had an easy command of English – I am still confident that he accepted the remark as quite innocent. Anyhow, at that stage of my life, when I heard 'irony' mentioned, this quite sharp situation, though unknown to Professor Booth and all his cohort of experts, was what everyone assumed it to be concerned with.

My view would at least allow Professor Booth to reject some borderline cases which he seems to let in for charity. The man who waited through heavy rain all the morning for his day's shooting, and then said 'Do you think it will rain?' was no doubt (as the patient analysis in the book implies) obeying a supposed duty of politeness; but an adequate critical comment would be 'Come off it.' The book ought to give some admitted examples of bad or failed irony, and explain what went wrong. But I grant there are many cases as slight as this in ordinary speech that do not feel bad at all; they treat an ideal politeness as the censor 'C'. An 'ironical tone' means that the speaker is finding politeness too much effort and will use any opportunity for irony that happens to arise. 'Dramatic irony' has only a slender thread of connection with real irony; the author writes down something he knows to be untrue (in the story) for an actor to say, but the character (represented by the actor) is usually not speaking ironically. The history of the word perhaps helps to make us confused; we took it from classical Greek, and in the time of Socrates it meant 'behaving with due modesty in the presence of a superior' (this explains the otherwise baffling quotations from Theophrastus, who flourished in the generation after Aristotle, on p. 139). Of course, modest behaviour was used by Socrates to ironical effect, and Plato seems to have designed more profound ironies in the structure of some of the Dialogues; but the change in the meaning of the word itself was mediated later through the phrase 'Socratic irony'. Having such a notorious past, the poor word has found difficulty in settling down.

It is only misleading, I think, to say that Shakespeare intended irony in the Sonnet beginning 'My mistress' eyes are nothing like the sun.' He claims rather loudly to be telling the flat truth; why must we think he is doing something else? Professor Booth finds him engaged in a literary quarrel, jeering at other poets whose style, or rather whose metaphors, he finds 'unreal' (p. 123). But a fuss of this kind would be unlike him (more like Donne, who did in effect revolt against the style of Spenser, but even he does not seem to have left any parodies); and Shakespeare goes on using these metaphors himself without worry, at any rate in plays. On the other hand, his feelings about this particular woman, as becomes almost gruesomely clear in later sonnets, are painfully mixed. He does not admire or respect her but has an unappeasable craving for her, and her fascination is not to be explained away as merely 'physical'. So *in this case* the exalted language of love-poetry would be unreal, though he will not deny that she is 'rare'. To suppose an irony is a distraction here, because the poet is struggling to make a plain report. On the other hand, the caption on a poster for a Relief Fund (p. 35) 'Ignore the Hungry and they'll go away' (we ought to be told what picture is illustrated) is a plain case of 'implied quotation' – what *they* say, the bad people who won't contribute; and there is no hint of unwilling obedience to a censor, so it is not irony. That is why it feels so flat – surely it would be very ineffective propaganda. The 'Warning to Children' of Robert Graves is a metaphysical poem, giving the children a direct insight into the fascinating or horrifying mystery of the world; it is not even a dramatic irony, as there is no suggestion that the grown-ups understand the world any better than they. Professor Booth extracts an idea that 'the *ironic* Truth' is *amused* as the children 'walk into the eternal trap' (p. 255). The poem does not threaten, and I think this bogeyman insinuation comes up because Professor Booth feels that his own picture of the world has been made to seem inadequate.

His reactions to non-Christian religious implications in literature often feel to me strained. The poem 'Hap' by Thomas Hardy (p. 237) is classed as a 'stable irony', and 'everyone would call the poem ironic, I suppose.' Professor Booth used to feel that the poem was a case of 'whimpering', but does not now. But it is meant to tell a plain truth. Hardy says that he would prefer to believe in God, who must plainly be evil if actual, because then he could defy God, heroically; but he now realises that all his bad luck has come to him by sheer chance, not as the work of an evil intelligence. The poet's 'assertion about the irony of existence' (says Professor Booth) is 'as unquestioned (rhetorically speaking) as if he were preaching a non-ironic message on behalf of belief in Jehovah'. Thus the Professor insinuates, for well-brought-up students I suppose, that any expression of disbelief in Jehovah is always inherently ironic. And yet there is a lot of documentation to prove that Hardy really meant it. This sonnet is very badly written, so badly that it cannot be admired at all, except for a kind of hammered-out sincerity. And I would agree that the feelings of Hardy were painfully mixed, so that he would not help continuing to hate God, and to blame God for all cases of bad luck, even after the relief of learning that God did not exist. When told that many readers thought he believed in his 'Spirit Ironical', a devil who arranges to trip us up, he was piteously eager to rebuff the accusation. By giving the characters in his novels such improbably bad luck, he explained, he was only warning the reader to prepare for bad luck, as lawyers and businessmen are expected to do. So the words of the sonnet are not ironical at all, and when Professor Booth read them as 'whimpering' he was misled by a false expectation.

With the remarks about the introduction to *Tom Jones* (p. 179) we enter a more complex doctrinal field. Squire Allworthy, it says, had lost his beloved wife about five years before the book begins:

This loss, however great, he bore like a man of sense and constancy, though it must be confessed he would often talk a little whimsically on this head; for he sometimes said he looked upon himself as still married, and considered his wife as only gone a little before him, a journey which he should most certainly, sooner or later, take after her; and that he had not the least doubt of meeting her again in a place where he should never part with her more – sentiments for which his sense was arraigned by one part of his neighbours, his religion by a second, and his sincerity by a third.

Calling it whimsical, says Professor Booth, is of course 'a momentary pretence', and the three sorts of neighbour are 'the true butt of the irony'; his only question is how we know it – he explains that there is 'a pattern of inconsistency throughout the passage'. He seems to assume that any decent man holds the belief described as whimsical – that Mom and Pop will meet in heaven is one of the bases of the nuclear marriage; and yet the book itself tells him that a third of the neighbours thought it irreligious. Donne in a sermon says that 'we dispute' about whether we will meet those we love in heaven, and though I am ignorant of the dispute I can see arguments for the unpopular side. Aquinas says that the risen body will have full sexual equipment, but will never use it because the blessed are completely absorbed by the vision of God: evidently the vision is like being under a powerful drug, and the domestic pleasures have little chance if the passions have none. It was the opinion of Plato too that the love of a fellow-creature is only a stepping-stone to the love of God. I agree that Fielding would find this a cold-hearted or mean-minded way to talk, but he had evidently met with it in some clergyman he respected, probably after the death of his own first wife. He is trying to submit to an authority, not covertly revolting against one. He would take a good deal from the State Church, as he thinks the Nonconformists disloyal and low-class, but even if the official theologians are against these meetings in Heaven he feels he can stick to the belief, jovially admitting he is 'whimsical' – and Allworthy can do it too. Maybe this was rather a boss shot, because none of the neighbours actually would call the belief irreligious, but Fielding was not an expert in such things. If you grasp his feeling here, you are prepared for the deep cases of 'double irony' later in the book, as when Tom brings consternation upon Allworthy by forgiving Black George; Fielding is simply not sure himself how far a practical magistrate could allow himself to obey the precepts of Jesus. For most of the book he is confident, especially when he uses irony; but he is aware of extreme cases where he would feel doubtful.

An entire short story by Flannery O'Connor ['Everything That Rises Must Converge'] is quoted (from p. 152), and said to be 'extremely complex, not only in its ironic undercuttings but in its affirmations'. A widowed mother who claims proud memories of the old South is being escorted by bus to her reducing class by her fretful progressive son, Julian, who has just left college and is unemployed. On leaving the bus, she gives a penny to a small black boy who sat next to her and smiled at her, but his black mother throws it back and knocks her down. Julian helps her up and tells her she must learn to live in the modern world; she makes no answer and seems hardly to recognise him, but sets off to walk home. Then she has a stroke and falls down again; he runs for help, but the lights seem to be moving away ahead, and the story ends: 'The tide of darkness seemed to sweep him back to her, postponing from moment to moment his entry into the world of guilt and sorrow.' Professor Booth explains that the accident is a 'gratuitous grace' for the young man, who till then was in mortal sin but through this moment of 'honest nightmare' may become 'genuine'. His 'problematic redemption' is 'presented in a specifically Roman Catholic light,' thus giving one of the 'religious ironies' usual in this author.

There seems no reason to doubt the explanation, but surely even a co-believer may doubt whether the moral follows from the story. The young man *ought* to advise his mother, and I do not see that any of his advice can be called wrong; nor is he to blame for any of the events which got her knocked down. But no doubt he *will* be blamed, for example by his aunt and grandfather; he has failed in an office of trust. Now, the worst thing you can do to a young man prone to imagine himself wronged is give him a real injustice, food for the habit to grow upon. What Julian needs is an unexacting but obviously useful regular job, with human contacts, so that he no longer feels isolated; he is quite high-minded enough already. And, granting that God sent him a long course of suffering merely to do him good, was God quite indifferent to the effects on his mother? Surely, to call the procedure 'grace' is on a par with calling the Furies 'the Kindly Ones', that is, an attempt to avert bad luck, not based on any real conviction that their actions are beneficent. In fact, this God is hard to distinguish from the Spirit Ironical of Thomas Hardy, which Professor Booth felt sure no one could believe in. The technical term 'irony' does not give any help here.

The last chapter is about 'Infinite instabilities', such as the belief that the whole universe is inherently absurd, and I take it that these are presumed to be expressed by irony. Professor Booth writes with an attractive admiration for the work of Samuel Beckett, while finding absurd almost everything that critics find to say in his praise. Beckett seems to express almost total negation, or at least to say that no writing has any value, and yet he does it 'often with great comic power and always with poignancy' (p. 259), indeed with 'a positively bouncy verve' (p. 264). He cannot be giving a courageously truthful picture of his own mental condition; he maintains 'a productive and obviously exhilarating verbal life while cashing checks and resisting the debilitating effects of world fame'. It strikes me that all this, though generously meant, gives a rather debunking impression; and surely the meanings, so far as they are ironical, are something less than exalted. Efforts to express the mystery of the world have usually involved contradictions, but not all contradictions are ironies, and the homely grumbling of the underdog is bound to seem an odd instrument for so high a purpose. By this last chapter the book completes its trajectory, like a rocket; and yet almost at the cost of giving in to the opponents. Besides, when Beckett is writing well in the manner described, I do not get the feeling of irony. I think that the definition of it needs to be narrowed.

Compacted Doctrines

New York Review of Books, 27 October 1977

Raymond Williams, *Keywords: A Vocabulary of Culture and Society*

The book is continually interesting; never more so, from my point of view, than when it is plainly wrong; but it is usually right, I could not deny. More than 100 familiar words, usually with some derivatives and opposites thrown in, are examined for a few pages each, so that it goes at a fair pace. The primary aim is to clear up confusion, so the author describes not only the varieties of meaning in a word but the various controversies in which they get used. Also he recognises that these different meanings within one word are liable to interact, so that they form 'compacted doctrines', as when *native* was taken to imply 'all subjected peoples are biologically inferior'; and he decides that many of our common words regularly tempt us to accept wrong beliefs, usually political ones. He does not say that resistance to them is beyond human power, which would make his book useless, but his introduction offers very little hope from the technique he provides. For example: 'to understand the complexities of the meanings of *class* contributes virtually nothing to the resolution ... of actual class disputes'; 'what can really be contributed is not resolution but perhaps, at times, just that extra edge of consciousness' – meaning perhaps that an enlightened orator might swing votes by understanding the psychology of his audience. It is a dark picture as a whole.

Part of the gloom, I think, comes from a theory which makes our minds feebler than they are – than they have to be, if they are to go through their usual performance with language. The entry on the word *interest* is a good example. Our modern uses of the word, he explains, derive from capitalist procedures, and at first ranged from 'compensation for loss' to 'investment with a right or share'. In medieval times, usury was forbidden, but compensation was allowed, so there could be a gradual development of capitalist practices; *interest* in the modern financial sense had arrived by the end of the sixteenth century. But the 'subjective' use, for curiosity or attention, is not clear before the nineteenth century:

The question of whether this sense of an object generating such *interest* is related to the active sense of *interest* – of money generating money... It seems probable that this now central word for attention, attraction and concern is saturated with the experience of a society based upon money relationships.

So the poor word is like an old prayer-book which had been clutched by Mary Queen of Scots at her beheading and is still saturated with her blood; it is accursed. But there is no evidence for this linguistic phenomenon. We would often *like* an influence from past uses to survive in a word, when it plainly doesn't. Jane Austen was relentless in making phrases for her ladies such as 'found herself obliged to be attached' (to a barely rich enough man); she would be bound to use the pun on *interest*, if it had not felt too remote. A young man of the period who was so interested in poetry that he neglected his city interests would not regard this thought as the material for an epigram, only as a slight ugliness to be avoided by rephrasing. A pun of this sort can only impose a doctrine upon us if both meanings arise naturally in one context, with a standard interpretation, perhaps: 'Everyone knows, in such a case, that the more sordid procedure is the correct one.' The book needed to give an example of it.

This is not to deny that a novelist may think about the word in his own person. Thus Bob Duport, in *The Kindly Ones* (by Anthony Powell, part of a long series), says there is sure to be a way:

If I'd been in South America, I'd have sweated it out there. Might in any case ... I've always been interested in British Guiana aluminium. That might offer something.

Two novels later, we hear that he got caught by the war, and had rather a good one as some kind of army administrator, though it has 'quieted him down'. Almost at the end of the whole series, he turns up in a bath chair at a picture exhibition; he has been collecting late Victorian seascapes for years, making practically a corner in them, and is selling the lot now that the prices are at their peak. No doubt it will see him through his last years. The author may be murmuring: 'Aren't businessmen extraordinary! He really was interested, both times'; but the 'keyword' has only been used once, with no weight on it, at the start of the sequence, and clearly has no effect on the mind of Duport. Probably it makes an intentional dramatic irony, but there is no need for the reader to notice it.

A curious remark in a bracket comes in the middle of the entry on *interest*:

(Disinterested is still used, with what are intended to be positive implications, to express a personal habit not only of 'unbiased' but of 'undogmatic' concern. It is also being used, increasingly often, to mean simply not interested, and this gives substantial offence to those to whom the former sense is still important.)

'Those' are the bosses, a reader may be sure, who have thought up another method here for deceiving the workers with their tainted words. But why *still*, and where does *dogma* come from? Surely, at any date, in a football match, you want a ref who hasn't been nobbled by either side? To imply that only the bosses could want such a thing is an insult to the proles, such as they too often get from their supposed champions. And, the more you feel horrified by even a remote thought of a percentage, the more you need assuring that it is absent. I grant that the ref should not be too bored to pay attention, but an appearance of decent coolness is expected of him. It is not a very good or necessary word, but this furtive explosion against it suggests trouble within.

The word *common* is viewed with grave distaste, all the more because it has good uses such as 'the common weal' or 'the common good':

> It is difficult to date the derogatory sense of *common*. In feudal society the attribution was systematic ... the clear derogatory use seems to increase from the early nineteenth century ... People, sometimes the same people, say 'it's *common* to eat ice-cream in the street' ... but also 'it's *common* to speak of the need for a *common* effort' (which may indeed be difficult to get if many of the people needed to make it are seen as *common*).

The second invented sentence must be supposed to mean 'there is frequent mention of the need for cooperation,' but one has to guess because nobody would say it; we automatically avoid puns that feel pointless. And what bad effect is the sentence supposed to have? Conceivably it might insinuate 'the workers are disloyal,' but this is not one of the regular tricks of the word; I expect it never occurs. To prove that it occurs would take more than a sentence invented for the purpose. And then, the word *common* is used, says the author, 'to mean *vulgar, unrefined* and eventually *low-class*,' but he does not treat these words as bad; they are not, in the same way, suasive. A medieval word meaning serfs is innocent; but, after the serfs have been officially liberated, if a word insinuates that they are not much better off, it is malignant.

I think there really is a trick about *common* for 'low-class'. The usage is assumed to be itself low-class, so that the better-class person saying it is having fun, talking in inverted commas. For example, Maugham in a long article full of praise for Arnold Bennett says he was always very common, though Maugham himself was not at all inclined to daff the demands of gentility aside. Probably he meant that Bennett stuck to the Midland pronunciations of his boyhood, whereas most men who have risen so early adapt their language to their company – and similar points which Maugham could find amusingly stubborn.[1] And then there is a splendid cry in *More Work for the Undertaker* by Margery Allingham, where Clarrie says:

'Dear, dear, sweet old girl. Have a lick, just a lick of common,' and he means 'have the common sense of the common people, to whom you belong' (the situation is too rich to explain briefly). Of course all snob words can be put to bad use, but this one has an unusual beneficent side.

The worst of the political entries, I think, is the one on *educated*. 'There is a strong class sense' about the term, says the book, and:

the level indicated by *educated* has been continually adjusted to leave the majority of people who have received an education below it. . . . It remains remarkable that after nearly a century of universal education in Britain the majority of the population should in this use be seen as *uneducated* or *half-educated*, but whether *educated people* think of this with self-congratulation or self-reproach, or with impatience at the silliness of the usage, is for them to say.

There was a young man reported from America as suing his school because it hadn't taught him to read in five years, and in England the Education Department keeps trying to destroy the old grammar schools, because they actually teach, thus wickedly destroying the indestructible *equality* of the children. This entry implies that we must accept anything whatever that a government imposes upon our children; if the government calls it education, never mind if the child knows less than he would have picked up if left on the streets. It is totalitarian; quite unconsciously, of course.

Many of the entries are not political, and they show great breadth of mind, especially in showing that a controversial word contains both sides of the controversy in itself. *Determine* is used for determinism, the doctrine that we have no free will, but the Calvinists who believed it were particularly 'determined' men, always getting their own way. The meaning of *reform* ranges from 'restore' to 'transform', and so does any debate about how to do it. The entries on *realism* and *representative*, showing how the same range of meaning has developed in their political and artistic uses, are particularly curious, and it does seem reasonable here to ask whether there is some fundamental cause:

In the sense of the *typical*, which then stand *for* ('as' or 'in place of') others or other things, in either context, there is probably a deep common cultural assumption.

But probably the mind has to work like that, so that any culture would make the same deep assumption. As far as 'imagery' goes, the Japanese have the same fallacies as the Europeans.

There is a fine long entry for *subjective*, a real hatchet job, and here for once the author dimly recognises that the word might be abandoned. But no *subject* and *object* are 'inevitable words', he says, and so their derivatives also have to be used; but these 'need to be thought through – in the language rather than within any particular school – every time we wish seriously to use them'. Long ago I decided I would never write down *subjective* except as a quotation, and later I found myself recommending the procedure to foreign students, who need it more obviously than others. Whenever confronted with a difficulty about a word, the learner should decide whether to reject it or promote it to his own list. Intake is always much larger than output, even with native speakers of the language; and 'forming a style' begins with selecting a vocabulary. I am afraid the book is liable to be rejected merely because it seems to impose such a portentous burden on a writer; but if reading it is regarded as a shopping spree the whole enterprise becomes more agreeable.

The entry for *materialism* drives home that this doctrine does not entail selfishness, and I warmly agree so far; but surely it might *seem* to recommend low-minded behaviour, if interpreted coarsely or stupidly? As an account of utilitarianism, the novel *Hard Times* is absurdly unjust, but there actually were people like Gradgrind. And most of the bad words in this book, that get blamed for making undemocratic insinuations, could put up a similar claim to have been misunderstood. The case is perhaps not a pressing one, as the accusation of materialism is less severe than it was; but it shows that the general method of the book is very lopsided. I had a large composition class in communist Peking, soon after the liberation, and tried to set essay subjects which were politically neutral, but the ruling interest could not be kept out, and students would often write down (well, three times, as I remember):

The Americans are very wicked because they are so material, and the Russians are very good because they are so material.

It was not my business to interfere with their propaganda, but I had to say that this was not correct English prose. 'How *do* you say it in English, then?' they answered, unconcerned; and I gave, of course, a rough historical background to the conflict over the word, but what they expected me to do was to turn the sentence into a rousing slogan. I doubt if even Raymond Williams could have done that.

The longest entry in the book, almost seven pages, is for *structural*, and here my sympathy breaks down altogether; the theories he is describing seem to me terrible waffle. What he needs to consider is the structure relating two meanings in any one of his chosen words, so that they imply or insinuate a sentence: 'A is B.' Under what conditions are they able to impose a belief that the speaker would otherwise resist?[2] As he never considers that, he is free to choose any interpretation that suits his own line of propaganda.

Note

1 See W. Somerset Maugham, 'Arnold Bennett', *Life and Letters*, VI, June 1931, p. 416; and *The Vagrant Mood* (London, 1952).

2 See Empson's 'Statements in Words' and 'A is B', in *The Structure of Complex Words* (1951), third edition, London: Chatto & Windus, 1977.

II

I. A. Richards and Basic English

I. A. Richards and
Practical Criticism

1930–31

In February 1930 the Oxford periodical Farrago ran an article entitled
'The New Criticism' (pp. 22–34) by John Sparrow, who had been at Win-
chester with Empson. Sparrow derided I. A. Richards's Practical Criticism:
A Study of Literary Judgement (1929) as the product of 'a school of criticism both wrong-headed and harmful . . . mistaken on fundamental points,
seeking to explain the intellectual in terms of the physical and the beautiful
as the expedient, and finding in psychology a solution for the problems of
criticism . . .' Critics such as Richards, he asserted, 'are unable to define the
values which they . . . try to explain away', and are 'reluctant to regard
literature simply as matter for enjoyment . . .' The so-called 'protocols' in
the volume are no more than 'the untutored reactions of a set of students to
certain poems which have been set before them'; thus their criticisms are by
definition abhorrent – 'tedious rubbish' – simply because they lack any 'discrimination and experience'. Beauty, Sparrow alleged, 'is realised immediately'; it is certainly not (as Richards would have it) something 'having
properties such that it arouses, under suitable conditions, tendencies to self-
completion in the mind' – for 'what, after all, is self-completion?' Sparrow
asked, 'And how are we to discover what creates tendencies towards it?'
Richards's attempts to explain the matter are altogether fruitless, as when
we are told that 'to be sincere is to act, feel and [?or] think in accordance
with "one's true nature".'

'But when we ask [Sparrow goes on] for the meaning of "in accordance
with one's true nature", a phrase . . . crucial in the definition, we are told
that "to define it more exactly would perhaps be tedious and . . . needless".' Readers who are uncertain of their judgements and choose to act on
Mr Richards's advice 'will find it unnecessary to enter libraries, but will sit
comfortably at home, with fingers pressed firmly upon the eyeballs, arousing in their inner natures tendencies to complete their true selves.'

It is easy to see where this sort of criticism will lead . . . we shall be encouraged

193

... to study the reactions of schoolboys, infants, idiots; and finally Mr Richards will read poems good, bad, or indifferent, to cats and dogs, and then present us with a volume faithfully recording their responses.

Empson's answer to Sparrow's diatribe appeared first in Oxford Outlook *(X, May 1930), under the Catullan title 'O Miselle Passer!' ('O poor little Sparrow!'):*

I was delighted to see Mr Sparrow attacking Mr Richards in *Farrago*; much was to be expected from so fundamental a quarrel. But some degree of imaginative sympathy is necessary if criticism is to be profitable. And the stocks here, perhaps, are too different for their union to be fertile. Still, it is nice to be allowed to write about Mr Richards in Oxford, even when the purpose can only be to reduce misconceptions, and the hope be so faint. (It is curious to remember that people think of Oxford and Cambridge as a unit; how strange that I should feel like an envoy between two worlds.)

The root divergence seems to be that Mr Sparrow thinks the meaning of a poem, and its mode of action, ought not to be analysed too deeply, nor ought the poet or his reader to be analysed too deeply. Evidently this is a matter of degree; you have at least got to construe poetry, not merely snuff it up; Mr Sparrow admits that analysis is in some degree possible and at least useful if not necessary. One may say in general that those who judge in literary matters by 'intuition' always assume a legacy of analysis, and complain when it is carried further. This is not in itself unreasonable; one must judge how far a thing needs to be explained both by what seems most agreeable to one's own habits and by what, independently of them, seems most effective; there is little ground here either for me to argue or for Mr Sparrow to be so confident. But he might have paid some attention to the reason Mr Richards himself gave for thinking further analysis urgent: that, as this is the first generation which has tried on a large scale to enjoy simultaneously the literature of a great many generations, of a great many views of life, we need, more than previous generations, an intellectual background for our appreciation. (Certainly appreciation, that is, pleasure, is the object in view, but appreciation is not therefore amoral as Mr Sparrow seems to think: it is the purpose and index of morality: it is the difference between civilisation and barbarism.)

Certainly, too, the protocols, as criticism, were bad; it is just because they are bad that the process of analysis needs to be carried further than Mr Sparrow wishes. I quite see that they give no pleasure to the appreciative critic, who needs to protect a private sensitivity. They are tedious and sometimes facetious; they display to the bitter end what it would be more merciful to hide; I confess I could not attend the original lectures because I found them embarrassing for that reason. But this is not a thing I am proud of; nor ought Mr Sparrow to be; one has been trained to regard literature far too much as a social competition. The interpretation of the protocols is an administrative matter, and a certain rational humility is required if one is to make use of them. It is no use simply saying they are bad; the point of collecting them (among other things) was to show that, in the present bewildered state of the poetical *public* (and it is all very well for Mr Sparrow to be too proud to mind about the public, but if you are a poet, the poetical public is what you are writing for) some form of intelligible process of interpretation is urgently needed, if only to give people confidence. They achieve this aim, with a violence which may be sufficient to convince those who could supply the need. Mr Sparrow gets out of it by saying that the boys were very ignorant, but one of the boys he quotes as particularly (may I say) boyish, was an English don of indubitable taste and learning, and middle age. Either Mr Sparrow himself has made a howler here, or the protocols were not bad merely because the boys had no experience.

As for Mr Richards's particular recipe for being 'sincere', I am very willing to believe that it does not work for everyone, and that Mr Sparrow finds it unnecessary. But his objection to it is that it would produce a nineteenth-century mode of judgement, and that (with all humility) I may say I know to be wrong. For I agree with Mr Sparrow in his tastes; I too prefer Pope to Shelley, in this daring modern way. But I do not read Pope with a sense that it is delightful to escape, just for a moment (in a coy, playful fashion – not, of course, meaning any harm) from one's own good intentions and kind heart; I think it is precisely a serious mode of approach, viewing life as a whole, which makes the 'Rape of the Lock' seem brave and civilised and Shelley hysterical and a child.

> But since, alas, frail beauty must decay,
> Curled or uncurled, since locks will turn to grey.
> Since, painted, or not painted, all shall fade,
> And she who scorns a man must die a maid,
> What then remains, but well our power to use,
> And keep good humour still, whate'er we lose?

It is alarming to hear Mr Sparrow say that one cannot *afford* to sit by the fire and think about death before reading lines like these; it almost makes one believe he reads them with the vulgarity of Mr Strachey, who thought it very clever of the little fellow to be so rude. In the nineties, I quite see, it was urgent for an aesthete not to think about death, because the only 'serious' view of life that he could fall back on was wicked nonsense; but nowadays, really, one is safer. To start at the mere shadow of virtue is a hypochondria in Mr Sparrow. And it is hard, by the way, to see how Mr Sparrow recon-

ciles this solemn cult of triviality with his repeated accusation against Mr
Richards, that he is not interested in 'values'. The most obvious claim of Mr
Richards upon public attention is that he has produced a workable theory
of aesthetic value, I hope it is only some misunderstanding as to what Mr
Sparrow means by the word which leads me to this bald and verifiable contradiction of him. One must feel the same, for instance, about his treatment
of this quotation: 'to be sincere is to act, feel, and (? or) think in accordance
with one's true nature.' Now both *and* and *or*, here, might mean a variety
of things, and Mr Sparrow's correction is very puzzling. Can he really think
it impossible to feel and think at the same time? Obviously the idea of organic coherence, of *and* rather than *or* in this passage, is the whole crux of
that difficult and easily vulgarised notion of sincerity.

Indeed (though it is impossible to deal with these matters in a short
article), I dare say that this attitude towards thought and feeling would be
as good an approach as any to the understanding of Mr Sparrow. Feeling
and thought are not separate objects; in one of their senses they are more
like an inside and an outside. At a moment you may be conscious of either
side in any proportion; you are more conscious of thought, for instance, if
the thing in hand is a novelty; more conscious of feeling if it is urgent and
not unusual. But if what you are conscious of as a feeling is badly thought,
that is part of what you feel; you wish then to be conscious of it as thought,
and put it right. Mr Sparrow, on the other hand, thinks that thought and
feeling are simple and different; he can see that beauty is not simple
thought, so he thinks it must be simple feeling, only different from other
feelings. And I suppose his idea of 'value' is another simple and separate
object; a sort of spotting the winner when you are valuing a thing you are
neither thinking nor feeling. Mr Sparrow's style is of a beautiful clarity: it
has the patient simplicity of Matthew Arnold; and it leaves him utterly at
the mercy of his vocabulary.

'Most of what he says is commonplace veiled in the language of psychology; old friends turn up disguised as "autogeneous emotions", ... "inhi-
bitions", and expect to be greeted as important strangers.' Now surely Mr
Sparrow must know better than I that the same subjects have always been
discussed in literary criticism; that the degree of delicacy, subtlety, and
profit with which it has been possible to discuss them has always depended
on the terms available; that a new word, even though (by miracle) it
referred to precisely the same things as an old one, must yet suggest different ideas, the same ideas in different proportions, a different way of dealing with the same things; that the substitution of one term for another, has
been the symbol and body of all advances in criticism. I cannot believe that
Mr Sparrow's attitude to this matter is as shallow as he pretends.

He then makes great play with a 'definition' of Beauty, which he finds in

an appendix on page 359. It is an amusing example of the barrister's attitude to criticism; the definition is given at the end of a list of possible definitions, heralded by 'we might say for this purpose', and used to illustrate a
point of language. If Mr Sparrow is really curious to know how Mr
Richards defines beauty, he might look at *The Meaning of Meaning* where
there are nineteen definitions shown in relation to one another. Not that the
advocate's method is doing much harm here, the definition is quite profound enough for Mr Sparrow's discussion.

What Mr Sparrow calls Mr Richards's definition of 'beautiful' and Mr
Richards does not, is 'having properties such that it arouses, under suitable
conditions, tendencies to self-completion in the mind.' I should myself say
against Mr Richards here that the word *self* seems inadequate; it obscures
the element of objectivity in criticism; it lets one forget that a reader, by a
valuable effort, can put himself into another century and another mind. But
Mr Sparrow is only concerned to say that beauty is a simple feeling. 'Certain qualities are such that to realise their presence in an object is to recognise that the object answers to a complex definition ... but beauty is quite
clearly not such a property; it is realised immediately, and the world has realised for thousands of years that certain things are beautiful without even
asking whether they arouse tendencies to self-completion.' Now if it were
true that the matter was so simple, if there was nothing more to be said, it
would be at least a linguistic convenience to treat beauty as a simple noun.
But as the view stultifies the intelligence, abolishes criticism, makes most of
the facts about beautiful things wholly unintelligible, and leaves us with a
sense that the whole thing is a necromancy to which any charlatan may
have the password, it is not found in practice to work as if it was true. It is
decently plausible about painting, because the modes of satisfaction are
there little understood, and are far removed from the verbal system on
which the discursive intelligence usually supports itself; but of poetry it
seems startlingly unlikely; any at all illuminating remark by a literary critic
(as to why a particular line is so effective) demonstrates that it is untrue. It is
made roughly plausible by what one must readily admit to be the extraordinary character of the arts; the way they convey *some* impression of their
value, to the trained critic, at the first glance of the eye. But I need only recommend to Mr Sparrow's attention what he has himself admitted, that
analysis is useful, and that it is possible to write literary criticism.

'Even if Mr Richards's "definition" is a true description of all beautiful
things, it must fail to be what it sets out to be, a definition.' Perhaps the inverted commas are the most obviously unfair detail in Mr Sparrow's
article; it is he who chose to treat the thing as a general definition, and he
now sneers at it for being called so. As for the rest of the sentence, he has
stolen it, if the reader will believe me, from the sentence by Mr Richards im-

mediately preceding the one he quotes. 'Lastly a perhaps still more sophisticated view reduces this formula to something so vague and general that it
ceases to be useful as a means for investigating differences between what is
said to be beautiful and what is not.' Though I am acquainted with Mr
Sparrow, I own I was a little surprised to find he had done this.

He comes back to the question as to whether beauty is a simple quality,
by way of the problems of communication. What creates a tendency to self-
completion in one mind has not therefore any reason to create it in another;
yet it usually does. Mr Richards says that beauty is an individual reaction;
yet he says that beauty is still objective. Mr Sparrow feels that this is a mere
disorder; that one or other must be true, not both. Now very little sense of
fact, very little sense of that rational modesty which realises it is dealing
with a complicated matter, would have suggested to Mr Sparrow that these
are in fact both true; that is precisely why people discuss these questions;
why there is a problem of aesthetic communication at all. It is obvious, it is
the necessary assumption for criticism, that a poem conveys very nearly the
same experience to extremely different people, if they are tolerably competent; certainly this is very extraordinary, and might make one think that
beauty was a simple magical essence. On the other hand, it is obvious that
there have been coherent, durable, and complete reactions to the same
work of art which were very different to each other; songs by Handel, for
instance, which Mr Sparrow would think charmingly funny roused Boswell
'to that pitch of resistance which he trusted he might never have to sustain'.
Beauty, in some difficult way, both is and is not objective; I am sorry if I am
puzzling Mr Sparrow.

Mr Richards said that for verbal convenience, and for the gratification of
the sense that poetry is an inexplicable power, it is very proper, after realising that beauty is not an inherent quality, to talk of it (on such occasions) as
though it were. 'From a writer who is attacking self-deception and exalting
sincerity this admission seems particularly strange,' says poor Mr Sparrow.
It is pathetic and at the same time a little embarrassing, like hearing death
called strange by a child. Surely everybody who talks about these matters
nowadays has heard of the problems about verbal fictions, and the philosophy of As if? The prime intellectual difficulty of our age is that true beliefs
may make it impossible to act rightly; that we cannot think without verbal
fictions; that they must not be taken for true beliefs, and yet must be taken
seriously; that it is essential to analyse beauty; essential to accept it unanalysed; essential to believe that the universe is deterministic; essential to
act as if it was not. None of these abysses, however, opened under Mr Sparrow's feet; he simply used the word 'strange' because he could not but
notice that he was making two contradictory accusations.

The same helplessness appears about Mr Richards's advice to those 'whose response to a poem is uncertain.' 'Mr Richards is continually forced to express himself in this way because he dare not say frankly either "those who are not sure whether a poem is good or not" or "those who are not sure whether or not they like a poem".' What is this question of daring? Why is it brave to use these forms of words? How far one's response to a poem is the complete one, how far it is the right one, how far it is the one intended by the author – these are mysteries, and if they could be answered would be answered differently in different cases. Since it is not necessary to bring in these matters, since Mr Richards was only *talking* about the business of arriving at a single coherent response, he did not drag in difficulties by a careless use of language. What Mr Sparrow is complaining about here is that the language did not allow him to misconstrue it.

Finally we come to Mr Sparrow's peroration. 'It is easy to see where this sort of criticism will lead ... finally Mr Richards will read poems, good, bad, or indifferent, to cats and dogs, and then present us with a volume faithfully recording their responses.' It must indeed have been easy.

In his reply to Empson (Oxford Outlook X, 1930, pp. 598–607), Sparrow expostulated firstly that

until a poem is understood it cannot be fully enjoyed ... Further, in order to understand a poem one must, usually, know something of the author – indeed it is, properly speaking, he and not the poem that one understands.

Empson shows confusion of mind, Sparrow alleged,

when he classes together, and then fails to distinguish between, analysis of the poet and of the reader, of the poem and its 'mode of action'. (In this last phrase there lurks a further confusion: what is a poem's 'mode of action'? ...) ...

True, the protocols gave me no pleasure; but this was not because I felt a need to 'protect a private sensibility' (whatever that may mean ...) not because I was 'embarrassed' by them ...

But I do understand Mr Empson when he says that 'if you are a poet the poetical public is what you are writing for', and I profoundly disagree with him ...

Mr Empson proceeds to manufacture another opinion for me: 'it is alarming to hear Mr Sparrow say that one cannot afford to sit by the fire and think about death before reading' Pope, and then to accuse me of 'starting at the mere shadow of virtue' ... the word which he so carefully italicises did not appear in my article ... I said that Mr Richards introduced worse considerations where they were irrelevant, and that he was a prig, and I am afraid that I can find no other word to describe one who, like Mr Empson, prefers 'The Rape of the Lock' to Shelley because Pope is 'brave' and Shelley 'hysterical'. I prefer 'The Rape of the Lock' to the hysterical parts of Shelley because it seems to me that it is well written, and that Shelley when he is hysterical writes badly ...

Mr Richards wrote in his book (p. 289) that 'to be sincere is to act, feel and think in accordance with one's true nature.' Before criticising this definition I corrected it

*so that it expressed what I believed (and still believe) Mr Richards to have meant.
As they stand, the words mean that you cannot be sincere unless you are thinking,
feeling, and acting simultaneously. No sane man believes this ...*

Beauty 'cannot be defined', Sparrow concluded:

*I do not see how any intelligent person could think that the beauty of a work of art
is an individual reaction to it, and when someone having said this goes on to say
that it is 'still objective' my doubts about his sanity are doubled ... and so it comes
about that we have a volume of psychology called a volume of 'criticism'. ... Mr
Richards and his followers are conducting a campaign against the intelligence; victims of yet another form of inverted snobbery, they will not admit that literature
has indefinable qualities, and that some people are able to detect and appreciate
those qualities and others are not, and that the 'reactions' of the latter are valueless
to the literary critic; they shrink from ... leaving the inexplicable unexplained.*

Empson's response to Sparrow's reply appeared as a letter to the editor in
Oxford Outlook XI (March 1931):

There is little use in continuing this controversy; Mr Sparrow and I have
made our points, and are never going to convince each other. But he makes
two specific accusations which I must answer if the case is not to go by de-
fault, and it seems reasonable that a few of the remarks he calls unintelligible should be said in a different way. It will be a labour of patience.

He says I misrepresented him, because I said that his objection to Mr
Richards's recipe for sincerity was that it produced 'a nineteenth-century
mode of judgement'. He did not say this, and he now says that he does not
know what it means. It is odd that Mr Sparrow should claim to have no historical sense, but I can assure him that he is not seriously misrepresented by
the phrase. He quoted Mr Richards's recipe, and then said, 'Old-fashioned
critics have often been derided for introducing moral considerations where
they were irrelevant, but we doubt whether any old-fashioned critic was
ever quite such a prig as this. We recommend the advice to those who are
not quite sure what they feel about "The Rape of the Lock" ...' 'Priggish,
old-fashioned, and unlikely to appreciate "The Rape of the Lock"'; I hope
every reader will substitute these words for 'nineteenth-century' in my
article, if he thinks them likely to help Mr Sparrow in any degree.

He says I misrepresented him, because he did not 'say that one cannot
afford to think about death before reading "The Rape of the Lock"'. Certainly my phrase confused statement with implication; if anyone, after
reading my whole passage as an argument, thought that Mr Sparrow had
said this in so many words, I am sorry to have misled him. What I meant,
obviously, was that Mr Sparrow implied it; and I am now even more convinced that I was right in my judgement of what he was implying, because
even now, in the act of denying it, he implies it still more plainly.

'Either [following Mr Richards's recipe for watching football] might put you into a suitable frame of mind for enjoying certain sorts of poetry, but either would as *certainly incapacitate* you (my italics) for enjoying others.' Now he certainly implied that Mr Richards's recipe could not reasonably be used before reading Pope, and I suppose he means by this that to do so would 'incapacitate' him. If so, I certainly think that he reads Pope in one of the less valuable ways.

There is a general point of some interest here. Controversy demands imagination; you must try to understand your opponent's position, so that you can select the things worth talking about; so that you can find the root of his errors, or of your disagreement with him. If I read too much into Mr Sparrow's article it was from a wish to understand him, and I should be better instructed by his reply if he had thought me worthy of the same treatment.

For instance, he gets in a good hit about the 'poetical public'; a clumsy phrase of mine; the matter is much more complex than either of us implied. Of course a poet must not pander to a public, but he must be intelligible, and so much of poetry is a matter of tone towards an imagined public (of good critics, but good critics of a certain sort) that a poet who does not expect ever to find such a public does not in fact write well, if at all. The matter is a topical one nowadays because much of the best modern poetry is so difficult to read, and so hopeless of finding fit readers. It is for this reason, I said, that it would be useful nowadays, both for the poet and the public, if the 'poetical public' had some process of interpretation for the verbal subtleties involved in poetry. And I used that clumsy phrase (assuming it would not be misunderstood) because I wanted to say this briefly, without tedium to the reader; it seems to me rather a pity that Mr Sparrow could only understand that one phrase.

'To be sincere is to act, feel and think in accordance with one's true nature.' I said that *and* might mean several things here; Mr Sparrow in effect challenges me to produce them. In part it separates the three verbs and so means the same as Mr Sparrow's *or*; 'To be sincere is to act in accordance with one's true nature, and to feel in accordance with one's true nature, and to think in accordance with one's true nature.' In part it suggests that you are not being sincere unless you are acting, feeling, and thinking simultaneously; Mr Sparrow took this as the only possible meaning; but I consider the sentence gains from the fact that it is suggested, so as to imply that when you know your own mind completely thought and feeling are peculiarly connected, and allow you to act directly. Also it may mean 'to be sincere in your attitude to a particular topic is, within the period that you adopt that attitude, to do all three things and relate them together.' The total impression given by an intelligent reading of the sentence combines these three more exact statements so as to convey something more general; and it is unprofitable for a reader to invent a special interpretation which makes nonsense. Of course I know that Mr Sparrow will not be satisfied by this, and will say that it is the wrong way to use language; I can only assure him that I think it a right, and in difficult matters the only possible, way to use language.

Mr Sparrow says that analysis of the poet and of the poem are legitimate criticism; and that analysis of the reader is legitimate, but only psychology. He then asks what the 'mode of action' of a poem can be, and how it can be analysed, and how its analysis can be different from the analysis of the reader. Certainly it would be valuable to know this. I think that people mean by the phrase (I assure Mr Sparrow that they use it) both the devices which a poet has employed to convey what he does convey, and the way those devices come to convey to the reader what they do. Evidently you cannot know this without knowing some part of what happens in the mind of the reader, and some part of what happens in the mind of the author; and some 'analysis of the poem', so far as it is different from this, will also be necessary to it. I suggested these different sorts of analysis, not as different objects, but as different elements of one act. And the reason I did not discuss them separately (a point he complains about) is that I think you cannot know, *a priori*, how much you need to know about any one of them before you can know about the others. That is why I think he is wrong in trying to separate them.

The essential objection of Mr Sparrow to Mr Richards, if I may attempt to sum up, seems to reside in this: Mr Richards considers that there is no one certainly 'right' way of reading a given piece of poetry; that poetry is important because of the way it acts on people; that it does not only act valuably on the best critics; that it would be useful both for the critic and the educator to know how it acts on people; and that this can be found out (in a sufficient degree to be useful) by a process of inquiry. Mr Sparrow and I may be content, so far as I can see, to differ on this series of issues, because only time and experiment can decide them.

I must thank you for your courtesy in allowing us to lay bare this difference at such length in your paper.

'Coleridge on Imagination'

Criterion, XIV: 56, June 1935

I. A. Richards, *Coleridge on Imagination*

There was a review of this extremely good book which gave much space to complaints about its arrogance, chiefly because it claims to be right because of psychology and does not give the evidence. It is hard to tell arrogance from humility, and the question is one of public convenience. Certainly experts should be made to put their cards on the table, and it would be better if Dr Richards had put in bits of evidence that would seem to him obvious and scrappy; the common reader, like myself, knows dimly what is hinted at but not how far there are reputable schools of psychology that disagree, and would like to be told of a nice book to read about the matter. Thus the remark (p. 34) that the distinction between Imagination and Fancy 'is of use in many branches of psychology' ought at least to give many references in a footnote. The main point is made clearly enough in the rest of the chapter; most of the ideas which Coleridge reached after a revolt against the scientific psychology of his day have come gradually to be accepted by that same dynasty of psychologists. Examples are the ideas that 'data are facta', that the belief in the existence of things without us is unconsciously involved in the belief in our existence (children develop the two together), and that the mind works not only by Hartley's Associations but by gestalts and a unique process of 'reference'. But it is not clear how far Pavlov, for instance, would agree.

At this stage of the book there is a clear distinction; Coleridge's philosophy is muddled or untrue but read as psychology is true and valuable. Coleridge would say that his philosophy was implicit in his psychology unless he was saying at the moment that to achieve his philosophy was to reach a state not of knowledge but of being, but Dr Richards makes a good case for his right to be as eclectic as Coleridge. By the end of the book Coleridge's philosophy is as true as any other; they are all 'myths' and so are the sciences. It is no fault of Dr Richards that the human mind has to jump this gap, but he seems weighted towards a negative position even in denying that it has any more sense than a positive one. I can suggest no better word

than 'myth', and Coleridge used it as he does (p. 167), but it is misleading
when it implies a creed outworn. A good 'myth' (p. 180) is widely 'supported' by Nature in sense 1, and is not true about her only because she is
beyond knowledge; there is less stretching of a word in calling it true than
false. And however Coleridge brought off his poetical achievement it is
only so far as the theory admits this heartily that it can claim to interpret his
intention.

The main argument about Nature-poetry is exciting and should be fruitful; such poetry works by continual shifts from Nature as 'the influences, of
whatever kind, to which the mind is subject from whatever is without and
independent of itself' to Nature as 'those "images" ... or "realities",
which, through the perceptive and imaginative activities of the mind (in
response to 1), we take to be the world in which we live'. The first sense
includes other people and the unconscious parts of the mind so far as they
are not interpreted, as they are in this sentence; neither poet nor critic can
do more than go through the motions of talking about it. The second sense
is at any rate part of *our* Nature, and 'both what we half-create and what
perceive' are treated as Nature in 'Tintern Abbey'. Certainly it is mere
justice to insist that the Nature of these poets was the nature of man as well
as the scenery of the lakes. But one needs also to say that the man who
obtains harmony by this process is somehow in harmony with the Nature
that supports him, and I see no reason why this ancient magical belief
should not be taken seriously. There seems no great need to be more sceptical than [David] Hume, who decided that 'the cause or causes of order in the
universe probably have some remote analogy to human intelligence' (in his
sense of cause language won't *say* this, but not to talk so is to take the negative position); and Wordsworth steps back from the chief mystical statement of 'Tintern Abbey' to say that 'if this be but a vain belief' still Nature
has some good effect undefined.

Dr Richards believes it is inherently impossible to say anything about
Nature in sense 1, but both this and the idealistic position are only straightforward so long as one forgets the existence of other people. It is easy to feel
that Nature is both outside us and in some larger sense inside us, or that
none of our interpretations of her are more than myths, but there is a jolt if
you remember that this must apply to your landlady. We are convinced that
there are feelings outside us in other people, and that we can know them in
degree; I should say that to take such Nature-poetry seriously one must
accept this conviction both about Nature in general (pantheist) and the
character of a locality (pagan; you can say you are sympathising with the
feelings of the vegetation). There is also a feeling that 'this could only be
known in a divine state, which the poet is not really in; but he is in a state
from which he can guess at the divine state.' The phrase 'we receive but

what we give', Dr Richards would agree, can be used in a very serious sense about our relations with other people, and this makes the doubts about poor old Nature less impressive. The linguistic approach has a dangerous tendency to say 'this question is merely linguistic' while getting support from an idea that the problem cannot be solved by language (it is at least certain then that the answer would not be linguistic). Dr Richards is very free from this in most of the book because of his sympathy with Coleridge's metaphysics, but there is a whiff of it when we are given the senses of Nature; they are really only a stage towards understanding Coleridge's position. Indeed, one of the great merits of Dr Richards is that he shows that even on the most rigidly materialist view the universe is as strange as it was before.

In the examples of Fancy and Imagination it is obvious that there is a difference, not to be evaded by talk about 'matters of degree'; but then poetry can differ in many ways; it is not clear how much Fancy can do, and why it is important, especially when Coleridge claims 'the sense of musical delight' in poetry for Imagination. (Dr Richards's chapter on that gives very soundly some conditions for receiving such delight, but what happens then, and whether 'music' here is a metaphor, is merely not known.) T. E. Hulme seems to have thought that the main advantage of Fancy was exact description, which is certainly among its powers;[1] it gives an air of detachment and so a truth-feeling. The example of Fancy from 'Venus and Adonis' seems to me to work another way.

> Full gently now she takes him by the hand,
> A lily prison'd in a gaol of snow,
> Or ivory in an alabaster band;
> So white a friend engirts so white a foe.

Dr Richards's points are that a lily is not trying to escape, nor snow to hold, Venus's hand is neither cold nor chaste, and we are not to think of her sweat as snow melting; so this is Fancy. But the pun on 'fair' is at the back of it; all beautiful women were white like Elizabeth, and this made their beauty display their virtue (sensuous idealism); 'fair' is light-coloured, beautiful, and calmly good without the effort of imposed standards (cf. 'fair play'). The suggestion that the rowdy and lustful Venus keeps all these qualities makes her a goddess because she resolves the contradictions of normal life; it puts her into a fairy-story world as cool as the metaphors. It is no use making out that the machinery of Fancy is simple here, or that its complexity is late in acting on the reader. But there is a real distinction from Imagination; the implications of whiteness are taken conventionally, as a matter of course, as an accepted myth, and do their work under cover of this solid 'form'. One could give a similar argument for the examples from

Dryden and Butler, and Dr Richards would agree (p. 75) that a fanciful style needs imaginative implications behind it. It would have been safe for Coleridge to say that only Imagination had *any* value in poetry (as he never quite did) if he had added that it may have great value when almost completely hidden behind Fancy. The distinction is certainly real enough to back up his theory, but probably he thought it more useful in practical criticism than it was because of his literary party politics.

Notes

1 'Fancy is not mere decoration added on to plain speech. Plain speech is essentially inaccurate. It is only by new metaphors, that is, by fancy, that it can be made precise.

'When the analogy has not enough connection with the thing described to be quite parallel with it, where it overlays the thing it described and there is a certain excess, there you have the play of fancy – that I grant is inferior to imagination.

'But where the analogy is every bit of it necessary for accurate description in the sense of the word accurate I have previously described, and your only objection to this kind of fancy is that it is not serious in the effect it produces, then I think the objection to be entirely invalid' (T. E. Hulme, *Speculations*, London: Kegan Paul, 1924, pp. 137–38).

'The Philosophy of Rhetoric'

Criterion, XVII: 66, October 1937

I. A. Richards, *The Philosophy of Rhetoric*

Probably the best way to review this good book is to quarrel with it on points of detail; that is often the best way of showing that a thing is interesting. Indeed there ought to have been more examples to quarrel over; the book is from a series of lectures in America, and the necessity of brevity has brought out one of the striking and baffling qualities of Dr Richards's mind. He likes to pose a small definite problem and then bound high into the air, and from then on you only see him leaping round the horizon. Of course, it makes stimulating university lectures, but, after all, he only regards his fundamental theories as useful in practice and detail, so you want to see them in use.

The first two lectures are a restatement of the context theory of meaning, and its chief interest is that he insists more than elsewhere on how little the theory is meant to say. It is not to be tied down as an Associationist or Conditioned Reflex view of the mind, and it does not pretend to explain the central mystery of how a mind can do whatever it does. It is a police theory, like his theory of value; it helps you to stop the narrower theories from obstructing your practice. Now I think this a just claim, but surely it is a bold metaphor. The police belong to the state, and it is not clear how the robber band of Dr Richards can have a similar authority. And it is not all countries that have just and peace-loving policemen. Certainly the claim is not mere assertion, indeed it shows one of the puzzling things about his theoretical work. You cannot be sure how much it is saying, whether it is giving a particular theory, as a rival to others, or the conditions which all theories must satisfy. The more reason for wanting to tie him down to detail.

But part of the breadth is to deny even settled details, and refuse to risk any theory on prophesying the next slate to crack on the roof. I thought that words like *struggle* and *glare*, that seem somehow fitted to their meaning, had been quite comfortably explained. Granting that we use a good deal of sound-analogy I should comfortably extend the Morpheme theory to give 'struggle' *muddle* and *trouble* as well as *strong* and *strike*, rough sound connections as well as exact ones. The business of exact ones is anyway very pretty (the reason the English want to say *skee* not *shee* is that they say *skid* and *skate*). But Dr Richards can jump through successive generalisations of this point until 'as the movement of my hand uses nearly the whole skeletal system of the muscles and is supported by them,' so to explain the effect of one word may 'drag in almost the whole of the rest of the language'. (You don't know what a word sounds like in a foreign language till you know *all* its words.) It is a great flash of poetry. The trouble is, if you take it seriously, there is no longer much hope of talking about a particular case.

The later part of the book is a survey of metaphor, and seems in close touch with detail. He points out how curious it is that we should be entirely without terms for the parts of a metaphor, and takes the valuable step of giving Tenor for the thing to be discussed, Vehicle for the thing to which it is compared or as which it is named. Then T. E. Hulme's essay on 'Romanticism and Classicism' [*Speculations*] depends on a confusion between the relation of tenor and vehicle and the relation of thing-meant and thing-said. The thing-said will often be a metaphor (tenor plus vehicle), and the vehicle alone is also called the metaphor. By means of rhetoric from this confusion you arrive at Imagism – 'Language ought to say just what it tries to say, therefore poetry aims at exact description, therefore poetry aims at finding vehicles exactly like their tenors.' The only point to criticise here, I think, is the suggestion that the confusion produced the doctrine. It allowed of argufying for the doctrine, but surely Hulme formed his personal tastes before he invented phrases to support them. An obscure sense of power, the hint of magic normal in the poets, has continual reverberations in Dr Richards's books, and you need to decide whether it is just in a given case – how much people were really influenced by the confusions he points out, how far he could change men's opinions who made them conscious about language.

This part of the work is close and tidy. But the first approach to metaphor is so lordly that the whole of language is treated as metaphorical: 'a word is normally a substitute for (or means) not one discrete past impression but a combination of general aspects. Now that is itself a summary account of the general principle of metaphor. . . . ' Now of course it is quite fair to extend the term 'metaphor' so as to bring in the whole field of problems within which those of strict metaphor must be set. But the device can make confusions of its own. One result of Dr Richards's approach is that it seems absurd to limit metaphor to assertions of similarity; all kinds of connections may be used, and in fact Disparity Action is as normal a basis for metaphor as likeness. The surrealists are brought in as wanting to 'put remote objects together in a sudden and striking manner'; this is praiseworthy as showing the real nature of metaphor, though they are 'too heroic' in wanting to put you through continual strain. Anyway, the idea of Identification or Fusion between the two parts of a metaphor could only have arisen from a narrow view of the term.

Personally I want to use the idea of Identification, and anyway I should want to keep the term Metaphor narrow. Metaphor as I want the word both works by likeness and proceeds from vehicle to tenor (the tenor is what is 'really meant'). It is always the queer but necessary machine of controversy to put up a case for a definition. Of course, there are various tropes such as synecdoche and transferred epithet, and if these are metaphor they are cases of metaphor not working through likeness. But transferred epithet ('the giddy brink') seems to work less through the business of choosing a word (when talking straight ahead) than the business of choosing grammar to fit the relevant words *into*. Surely these are quite different jobs. Dr Richards makes out a case for saying that the brink is really giddy (because the brink totters when the giddy man looks at it), but if so that is only Personification. His real case for metaphor not by likeness is Disparity Action. But I claim this on my side; one reason for giving a special name to tropes by likeness is that they alone can use Disparity Action. It never occurs to you that the living rock of the brink is peculiarly ungiddy. Whereas in his example of Disparity Action from *Hamlet*, 'such fellows as I crawling between earth and heaven', where (as he says) the point of the implied comparison to insects is that 'men should not so crawl' – there you get a Disparity Action, because you have first made a Parity. In fact this trick with the word *crawl* is normally used by pictures, so that the poor old Image theory is at home with it; you are made to look at men from a great height, as at insects – in this case from heaven, in Swift from Brobdingnag – before you are told that they crawl. An actual picture of insects is wanted to make the Disparity Action come into play. His other case of Disparity Action is when Othello says:

Steep me in poverty to the very lips,

and the notion of overfilling seems opposite to that of poverty. But he provides an excellent answer. The idea of a supply of water is continually imposed throughout the speech as an overriding metaphor, because Othello is losing his fountain or being swept away in a storm; and the clash of the general and particular metaphors here shows us that he is now particularly disordered. No doubt this is a rich and curious use of metaphor, well worth pointing out, but still both metaphors work by similarities.

Dr Richards rightly points out that in what he calls metaphor you sometimes get the main stress on the Tenor, sometimes on the Vehicle, sometimes on the whole combination. The 'without o'erflowing, full' lines, by

Denham on the Thames, give him a diagrammatic though rather unexciting case of the third. Some of the adjectives apply more naturally to a calm river, some to a balanced mind, and as they alternate you are held swaying between the two equally important topics until they seem magically connected, each able to interpret and sustain the other. Dr Richards is good on this case, and I hope I do not seem pedantic in denying that it is Metaphor at all. It is Mutual Comparison, a thing that works in a quite different way from metaphor; if it went on for longer everybody would recognise it as Allegory. So is the 'putting together of unexpected topics', which he quotes from André Breton; Breton himself in the same sentence cuts this device off from metaphor. All normal metaphors belong to Dr Richards's first type, which has the stress on the tenor. Here is a case of stress on the vehicle; when I was skiing recently I found myself reciting that Love is of the valleys:

> nor cares to walk
> With Death and Morning on the silver horns,

and suddenly realised that that grand lyric comes from 'The Princess'. It means that the girls won't get husbands if they go to college, and if you start from there all the description fits in. There seems no standard name for this kind of contortion (the thing must have fallen apart from the poem even when it was first published); but really you are stretching a term if you simply call it Metaphor.

I feel there are larger issues about this difference of definition. It might be a residue of behaviourism in the Doctor, an assumption that the behaviour of the mind is blank and goes by unknown rules so that the scientist must classify by result. Or it might be a metaphysical-poetry trick of my own mind, so that I jump to a likeness in any metaphor and feel happy with unlikenesses only on a strained basis from that. If I were to say that Disparity Action *ought* only to work on people through a previous parity this, of course, could only be an important moral truth if some people broke the rule, and this in itself would disprove my law of linguistics. And then if I said that all Disparity Actions proceed from *unconscious* parities (and people ought to be more conscious) – at once all those appalling Unconsciousnesses would fall together on my hands. Of course, a poem has to work on you before you have worked it out – or who would take the trouble – but that is another thing. Still, trying to collect the levels of argument possible, I think he is wrong about metaphor one way or another, and I admire his book very heartily.

A Doctrine of Aesthetics

Hudson Review, II, Spring 1949

I. A. Richards, C. K. Ogden, James Wood,
The Foundations of Aesthetics

It is an excellent thing to have a reprint of this exciting standard work, with all the pictures; and we are given the original page with all its variety of type, which by this time has a certain period charm.[1] The photographic process works well; even the small print of the long footnotes is clear, and this is an important point because so much of the positive doctrine is coyly reserved for them. The reprint gives one an interesting opportunity to reconsider the doctrine.

The impact of the Ogden–Richards line of criticism, a quarter of a century ago, was on literature much more than on the visual arts; and the interest of this book was that it was a determined effort to keep the whole variety of possible aesthetic experience clearly in view. The theoretical talk, while of the most relentlessly high abstraction, was to be kept ruthlessly short; even so, most of this short text was to be concerned with showing why other theorists were misleading. Meanwhile the reader was continually exposed to the shock of unintroduced quotations (often in translation) showing what a lot of good literary styles there are. Music could only be handled by short references. But the reader had sixteen illustrations, from Negro and Egyptian and Indian and Chinese and (rather impressively) Victorian visual art, and so on; and the selection was an impressive proof that the authors could really swallow the whole variety of the aesthetic world and still pick out the best. The contrast between the laboured dryness of the text and the astonishment of the illustrations made it a new kind of book, which it still is.

The main argument of the text is that people have meant a great variety of things by Beauty – sixteen meanings of the word are tabulated – and that though a unifying concept can be adumbrated in a general way at the end one need not expect people to stick to that. So far from sticking to it, they had better go on meaning by the word whatever they want to talk about within its ambiance; but then if they choose to write systems of aesthetics they had better not spend their time jumping from one of these ideas to another in an unconscious manner. 'It is easy for anyone who is not clear as to the question he is trying to answer to hover between several views, according to the interest or context with which he is momentarily concerned' says one of the footnotes (p. 47).

I have nothing to say against any of this; I think it is very fine. But there is an inherent tug between the tentative solution of the problem, offered in the last chapter, and the theory of Multiple Definition presented before. This is inherently concerned to say that in such cases one should tabulate the sixteen or more meanings of the term in question and expect nothing further. What you have gained by your tabulation is that you can no longer be deceived – never again will an argument by an aesthetician prevent you from appreciating something unusual but good, or force you into admiring a narrow type of mysticism. But if the last chapter gives the answer, the proper meaning for the word, and furthermore if all the deluded aestheticians were actually fumbling after this solution, so that they would be convinced once they had been given it, then the whole position is quite different. All their sentences are simply wrong even from their own point of view, and they could be made to see it, had we but world enough and time. This fundamental ambivalence of course makes the book more interesting. But after the lapse of a generation one ought to be able to form some kind of view about which side holds the field, whether the Multiple Definition theory or the Synaesthesis theory has survived. If they both survive for ever they are only another of those tedious pairs of frustrated Kilkenny cats, like Aristotle and Plato.

The extreme brevity and caution, not to say timidity, of the final chapter puts the weight in favour of the Multiple Definition technique. But I have long been inclined to believe that the Ogden–Richards programme really did say what Beauty is, though of course only in a rough, tentative manner. If so it is rather embarrassing for them; they are left with an Absolute Beauty on their hands, a baby which they never expected to have the trouble of bringing up. For that matter when Professor Richards wrote *The Principles of Literary Criticism*, not long after, he felt he needed to put in a chapter which in effect saddled him with an Absolute Goodness, an even more unwelcome baby. It is a familiar paradox; any serious attempt at establishing a relativity turns out to establish an absolute; in the case of Einstein the velocity of light, and I understand a good deal more by this time.

It seems to me that twenty years ago we were too frightened of absolutes, because of a confusion with politics which even the most abstract mind can hardly escape. To believe in an absolute goodness or beauty does no political harm, so long as you don't believe that you yourself have got a secret ticket into its bedroom which you can put up for sale. As soon as a body of priests or commissars or what not is organised (as has been done so often) on the specific basis of claiming that each such official has been issued with the secret key – there you have got something to worry about. Once these two ideas are separated there is no reason, I think, to be shocked by the idea of an absolute Goodness or Beauty, which mankind can in varying degrees approach but must not claim to have attained. Indeed a theorist on Beauty who tries to approach it is merely doing his job. Suppose the authors of this book had not put in any constructive reflections of their own, but had merely shown that all other theorists were muddle-headed; surely one would have felt that the book was sterile and even small-minded. It was only because one felt they had something to say that they could put across impressively their alternative to saying anything, their theory of Multiple Definition. But to put forward any theory, however modestly, is to suggest that it is true and therefore presumably 'absolute'. No doubt it is good manners and good tactics to keep your claims moderate, and then you can also set out to give a survey of what everyone else has said, and even claim that this gives a basis on which any later attempt to reach an Absolute must build. But you could not well combine this with a claim that you had refuted all Absolutist theories.

The main question of detail about the book, it seems to me, is the treatment of Emotions. In this intellectualist atmosphere they seem to be given a rather forced welcome, as distinguished foreign visitors. In questions of literature I feel I know what the pioneer Ogden–Richards work was doing; what they say about the Emotive Functions of Language is true and important, but was expressed in such an over-simplified way as to be liable to mislead literary critics. But that is a very simple case; after all we know a good deal about our own language. It is much harder to know your way about Emotion in the visual arts, for instance in some fascinating African fetish, where you pretty certainly don't feel what the sculptor and his original public felt, and yet the emotional force of the thing is pretty certainly what makes it good. At least this is the natural way to phrase the matter, but I am not sure that talking about Emotions is any help. What seems clear is that the internal goings-on when you appreciate the fetish are much less in reach of argument than the goings-on when you appreciate an English poem. This is what makes it plausible to talk about Pure or Significant Form. The kind of thing the book says is this: 'If the emotion is refined and developed, and general participation is made possible, it gains additional value' (p. 55). *Refining* seems a very unfortunate word; in fact you could argue that the real job of the artist is to learn how to refine the treatment without refining the original emotion at all. The main thing the book has to say on the topic is to agree with Tolstoy in his 'most original tenet' (p. 61), that the test of

Emotion in art is its universality, or at least its width of appeal. This is right, I think, but as soon as you try to estimate width of possible appeal you are let in for endless problems about what the public would accept if they had the opportunity to. I find my students in Peiping are very strong on Tolstoy, and when I agree with their judgements this line of talk seems to me simply bad tactics. For instance they tend to justify their interest in Chinese folk-songs, and modern music based on them, by saying that however vulgar these tunes may be they are universally enjoyed. But I think the sensible thing to say is that however ancient and deeply rooted they may be they are still fresh and beautiful. The only effect of the Tolstoyan principle is that they disparage the thing which they rightly want to praise. Perhaps the real test of an aesthetic theory, at any rate while so little is known about the matter, is how far it frees the individual to use his own taste and judgement; it must be judged in terms of practice rather than abstract truth. But then again, one could reply, the Ogden–Richards intellectualist approach is the safest for this purpose too; because after you have been faced with the variety of aesthetic theories you are less likely to have your judgement distorted by any one of them.

The final chapter is concerned to give a psychological account of the experience of beauty, in terms of how the work of art affects the structure of impulses in the individual. Here again, it is not clear what test of the theory could be applied; the usefulness of the thing is chiefly to show that the scientific picture of the world is not *necessarily* at loggerheads with the aesthetic one. If you felt that it was, that would be another factor likely to bemuse your judgement. The chief puzzle of the treatment by impulses is that you need to distinguish between a Balance and a Deadlock of impulses, and the only obvious difference is that one is called good and the other bad. However, 'We might describe balance as a conflict of impulses solving itself in the arousal of the other impulses of the personality' (p. 77). It seems very doubtful how this formula would apply to a Buddhist mystic, for example; he would consider that the process of meditation was excluding 'other impulses of his personality', but you could argue that the other impulses do get absorbed in some passive but unharmful way, so that he has a genuine 'balance' under the terms of the definition. Here again, the trouble with the theory is not that it appears wrong on fuller examination but that it turns out to say extremely little. One feels in reading the book that it is just on the verge of answering all sorts of important questions; this feeling I suspect comes more from its aesthetic side than from its theoretical one, but may still be true.

Looking back after nearly thirty years, in a more disastrous period, I find I wish that the authors had been more opinionated, though at the time no doubt they felt that would be greedy and impure – to have chatted about their own preferences would have kept the book from being universal. The book had better have ended quite positively, even if we would now be saying it ended wrongly. I am haunted by a feeling that they had something else to say which did not get said. To be sure, the three authors are all still alive, but they are sure to have forgotten what it was – that is always the punishment for not speaking out. Of course I also feel this gives a certain miraculous quality to the text; I am never sure that I have not missed a divine revelation lying about somewhere in very tiny print. It is a valuable book.

Note

1 One wishes, however, that the publishers had not been averse to indicating on the fly-leaf that this book *is* a reprint, of a work first published in England over twenty-five years ago. [Empson]

The Hammer's Ring

First published in
Reuben Brower, Helen Vendler, John Hollander (eds.),
I. A. Richards: Essays in his honor, New York: OUP, 1973

A splendid career, long and various, which has brought help and enlighten-
ment wherever it has turned. Surely one might say: 'Nothing is here for
tears ... no weakness, no contempt, Dispraise or blame; nothing but well
and fair'; but even in Samson's case, if you remember, there was a detail
which they might at least regret. Richards himself would feel impatient, I
am sure, if his career were praised in this way – as if he had aimed no
higher. He would feel it from the refusal of the world Departments of Education to adopt Basic English, to which he has devoted almost all his
powers, with unshakeable devotion (though with readiness to improve the
plan in detail), for so long a time. The same may be felt about his position in
literary criticism, and even in linguistics; his views have had much recognition, with good results, but have also been widely rejected.

When I was a student at Cambridge, more people would at times come to
his lectures than the hall would hold, and he would then lecture in the street
outside; somebody said that this had not happened since the Middle Ages,
and at any rate he was regarded as a man with a message. There were those
who called him a spellbinder, implying that there must be something wrong
with a lecture if it produced this effect; and I was glad of the opportunity to
hear him lecture again in London shortly before writing this piece (1972) –
as it has turned out, we have spent almost all our lives in different continents. I found him as spellbinding as ever, and many of the large audience
seemed to be feeling the same, but as we were most of us in our sixties it
didn't much matter whether we were spellbound or not. The spell had been
useful, as an incitement to action in young people who were just going to
choose a field of work; it held open a glimmering entry to a royal garden, or
an escape route which would entirely transform common experience, or at
least ordinary theoretical problems. In his moderate rueful way, Richards
has gone on being fertile in proposing steps forward, but he has never lost
the feeling that they are minor ones, because an immense opportunity lies
unrecognised just beyond our grasp. This indeed is what is so plainly lack-

ing from our present leaders in linguistics, and Richards demonstrated it in Chapter IV ['Some Glances at Current Linguistics'] of *So Much Nearer* – where the moderation of style and manner make an exhilarating contrast to the knockdown content. One cannot see (before I read this chapter, I had been feeling guilty because I could not see) how the theories of these writers could make any difference if true, or what they could be wanted for, let alone how they could be tested. Absence of vision is not inherently scientific; and in the lecturing technique of Richards the vision itself is the spell he casts. But the dazzle of it has evidently caused delay even to himself, and a disciple would often feel that his response to it had been inadequate. One can understand a growing appetite, in Cambridge around 1930, for some casting of the idol down.

It came in a series of articles by Dr Leavis in *Scrutiny*, largely devoted to denouncing the Benthamite Theory of Value. Till then Leavis had been adulating Richards, practically as the only known guide. It might seem odd to denounce a literary theorist for holding a philosophical belief more than a century old, and widely accepted at least in the university where he operated; but the inherent paradoxes of the doctrine allow of much chop-logic, and it was here I think that Leavis began to take his high moral tone. He was right in treating the matter as important, I cannot deny, because his own moral judgements about literature, and those of his disciples, have been wrong-headed ever since. Indeed, the whole of 'Eng. Lit.' as a university subject badly needs to return to the Benthamite position. Many of my colleagues, I think, reject it out of loyalty to T. S. Eliot, feeling sure that he would demand some higher criterion; and here I can offer a piece of gossip which for once might be really useful. I had gone to his office at Faber's to ask for a book to review for the *Criterion*, and he was looking at the current *Scrutiny* while talking about it to someone else; how *disgusting* the behaviour of Leavis was, what mob oratory his arguments were, couldn't something be done to stop him? – and then, with cold indignation, 'Of course, I know it's going to be me next.' At that time, Leavis was adulating Eliot with all the breath he had to spare from denouncing Richards. I was not an intimate friend, as the anecdote may seem to claim, but neither was I eavesdropping; he just accepted anyone who was in the office as an honorary member of the conversation. Being a disciple of Richards, I was already sure of the truth of what Eliot was saying, but I was surprised to hear him say it, and thought it did him great credit, as I still do. That is, one would expect him to think that Scientism needed putting down, but the character of the attack won all his attention.

The idea of making a calculation to secure the greatest happiness for the greatest number is perhaps inherently absurd, but it seems the only picture we can offer. Sensible people have long been accustomed to consider what would be 'for the best', bearing in mind the whole situation, and have often emerged from this effort with sensible answers. To claim that God has told you to act for the general harm would surely become blasphemous if made quite specific. Short of that, the only alternatives to Bentham are arty and smarty moralising; giving unreasoned importance either to a whim of one's own or to the whim of a social clique. Leavis appeared not to be doing this because he was taking a democratic position, in defence of the underprivileged students who were then beginning to arrive at Cambridge. Oscar Wilde had a rather nasty epigram to the effect: 'If a man is a gentleman he already knows enough; and, if he isn't, anything he gets to know is bad for him.' Leavis adopted this, merely changing 'gentleman' to 'lad from a decent working-class home' or thereabouts, and when I was a student I thought this was fun as well as useful; but all too soon the decent home was being saddled with highly specialised views.

This bit of local history is not important; I was much struck in 1948 to find that Eric Bentley, who was then publishing *The Importance of Scrutiny*, regarded Leavis as a violet by a mossy stone, half hidden from the eye – he deserved praise because he had echoed without knowing it the recent developments in American criticism. They do I think have a similar fault. The main purpose of reading imaginative literature is to grasp a wide variety of experience, imagining people with codes and customs very unlike our own; and it cannot be done except in a Benthamite manner, that is, by thinking 'how would such a code or custom work out?' In both countries, this whole conception seems to have been dropped; and I should think it was done, again and again, as if in solitude, by university teachers wanting to retain good relations with school teachers – who naturally want to tell the children that all decent people agree with Teacher. The influence of Eliot would be a great help.

Two examples may help to show the wide range of the issue. *The White Devil*, if you remember, has a good old mother, Cornelia, who begins the play by protesting against the adultery of her daughter, and towards the end of the play her wicked son, who has become generally exasperated, kills her only good son in her presence. Though she goes mad almost immediately, she retains the wit to give a pathetically confused account of the quarrel, such as might almost have saved the life of her remaining son – if there had been no other witnesses, and if legal procedures had been operating at the time. Probably this has always been thought a rather crude bit of tear-jerking, and yet somehow impressive, too real to be laughed off; at least, no one has voiced any moral puzzle about it before our own confused day. But a student at Sheffield wrote down for me: 'The corruption becomes total here. Cornelia has been presented as a good character, but now she tries to deceive the police in a murder case.' I suspected that my pupil had adopted the ideology of her headmistress, and yet the same puzzle-headed narrowness might be found now in any academic literary magazine. And then, I had a term at Legon University, in Ghana, just before the deposition of Nkrumah. He was becoming generally suspicious, and rather a problem for our Vice-Chancellor, Conor Cruise O'Brien, but I thought one of his complaints had a considerable ring of truth. The expensively imported teachers of 'Eng. Lit.', he said, were inciting the students to revive human sacrifice and other savage customs, and in every way were resisting scientific progress in Ghana. With what astonishment my colleagues would have denied this (I do not think it was reported to them); and yet how else could a vigorous-minded student in Ghana interpret their standard phraseology? Obviously Ghana, like other places, needs a Benthamite judgement of what is likely to be for the best in a rapidly changing world; and so does literature. In fact, the chapter on the Theory of Value is fundamental to the *Principles of Literary Criticism*.

I do not think he was much disturbed by the Leavis attack; when it came he was in the Far East, recommending the adoption of Basic by government schools for teaching the first few years of English. His feelings were much more deeply involved in the success of this project; after all, he had taken part in the invention of Basic, whereas Benthamism has always appeared to him merely a formulation of traditional common sense. The successive failures to get Basic adopted, over more than forty years, have continued to astonish him, and one may fairly say that he deserves credit for always keeping his temper. Often in such cases one has a lurking suspicion that an explosion might have done the trick, but here a decisive control experiment is given by the career of C. K. Ogden. There have been two major reasons for the failure. The first is that supplying the required school texts for a whole country is quite large money; not very big, but big enough to confront Ogden and Richards with methods of slander and shouting-down which they were hardly prepared for. Secondly, and as a much slower growth, there were the effects of the new English idealism, or as some would call it the retreat from empire; to use English as the international language (so their bones told them at once) opened an endless vista of whining and back-biting, creating hatred on all sides, and probably destroying the language for good and all. Clearly there has been a similar swing-back in America. Hence it was a fatal mistake for Ogden to keep on boosting the scheme as an international language; that was only a possible late incidental result of the main intention, and far more likely to grow if allowed to stay in the dark.

One needs first to realise what was already in being, and how badly it worked. Most civilised countries teach English in the schools, and nearly all the victims forget it all, except the few who go on to university and learn enough to be usable. If they were given a generally agreed word-list, without quirks of grammar, and provided with a fair amount of reading matter which was within their powers, the government expenditure would be less likely to be a total waste. As it is, or was then, the teachers realised the hopelessness of their assignment, being themselves badly paid, educated, and equipped, and would often invent some line of evasive action. A Chinese teacher was found who took a scholarly interest in distinguishing between nouns which took the plural with S (cats) or took it with Z (dogs), and his students, year by year as their turn came, learned the contrasting lists by heart for a sheer year. Richards, being Welsh, used the S for both, or could for purposes of effect, and would insist that the Welsh are very well-thought-of in England, look you, a good example to follow. But I must not treat the subject as mild classroom fun. Two of my Chinese students, who spoke excellent English, at different times startled me by saying how much they hated their first teachers of the language, and one said that if ever confronted with the man again he would throw a bucket of night-soil in at his study window; and this was very outside their style – they would never talk so about political opponents, though they had strong political opinions. They felt that an almost unsurmountable obstacle had been piled before them at the outset of their careers. And yet the wicked teachers would have behaved normally enough if they had been given a specific task, capable of execution. In all this, please observe, there is no question of an international language.

Any reasonable word-list would have been better than none, for both teachers and students, but Basic has several merits as a first landing-stage in the learning of English. For the student who is not going further, it allows a confident movement within what he has got, because he can rely on analogy without bumping into 'irregular' grammatical forms. To be sure, the eighteen fundamental verbs, called operators, are all irregular (except *seem*), as the English language requires, but after learning them you only meet nouns which can act as verbs, taking *-ing* and *-ed*, as *seem* does. Ogden insisted that they were not to be explained as verbs, to safeguard the interests of pupils with no verbs in their native languages; hence one might say 'I am pricing the goods' but not 'I have priced the goods' (the genders adopted by past participles in French, as they agreed with subject or object, gave a convenient marker to the dividing line). This seemed to me a quaint intrusion of theory into practice, but after all there would be no way of preventing the students from taking the further step, which is never wrong. Such quirks, I felt sure, would get cleared up once the system was operating – or might even turn out to have been justified.

So I was glad to do a little campaigning for Basic in the Far East, too little I feel now; it was nearly all a matter of writing to local papers and exposing the lies told by the opponents. Such letters were hardly ever answered; the opponents just told the same lie again later on. I translated some of the essays of J. B. S. Haldane into Basic [*The Outlook of Science* (1935); *Science and Well-Being* (1935)], though I am afraid a good deal of correcting my verbal usages had to be done in the office. Still, this gave me a certain fluency in the dialect, and while refugeeing in China (1938) I once lectured for an hour in Basic, meanwhile writing everything I said on the blackboard, which gave time for a second look at the grammar. This was to a teachers' training college who were well disposed to the plan, and of course I was lecturing *about* Basic, so no aspect of the affair can have had much novelty for them, except that of a dog walking on its hind legs. They seemed mildly content. I boast of the experience because I want to support a claim often made by Richards himself. Many literary people positively fear that English would be ruined by the use of Basic as an international language, becoming a 'dead jargon'; I suppose this is one of the things George Orwell feared in *1984*, though he never said it outright. But the language has already shown great powers of resilience. Also, much more than French or German, maybe because it has accepted so many foreign influences, it positively likes to purge itself and act simple. If you heard Charles II talking to a Bishop, you felt not merely that he showed the man up as a fool and a pedant but that this was the right man to be King, because he spoke in such an absolutely plain-man way. If you felt so you were deluded, and I do not say that the political effects were good, only that the effects on the language were. Very few of our recent writers, in either country, seem to me to appreciate the need for this plain-man basis under an English style, readily left without losing the power to return. Practice in turning their own stuff into Basic really would be the kindest education in style you could give them, even if it made them realise how often they are talking nonsense. To pretend that it could possibly make them use the language worse than they do already sounds to me farce.

Be this as it may, the remarkable thing about the early reception of Basic abroad was the dishonesty of its opponents. The exasperating thing for us was that they kept on denouncing the whole Basic system as theoretically wrong and then, when their next year's textbooks came out, taking over whole chunks of it. The effect was of course to raise the standard of the teaching a great deal. But every change made by a firm to pretend it was not adopting Basic had to be a change for the worse, and there could be no confidence in communication between two students who had been cheated by two different firms. In the learned world, a man loses his standing if he refuses to answer a plain refutation, but not in the commercial world. We were operating on the borders between them, and I do not pretend that the situation was easy to grasp. I remember two friends of one of our major

opponents, in a foreign country, describing to me how he had been sum-
moned by one of the native experts on the subject, for a dressing down; his
long succession of cheats about the matter were recited to him, patiently,
and then he was permitted to go. His friends said he probably went home
and drank himself silly; of course, they had no idea of ceasing to be friends.
At the time I doubted what they said; I knew he had been in the wrong all
along, but thought he had been able to deceive himself. Most unexpectedly,
I learned better long after; this conversation happened in 1934, and I
learned better in 1954. It was from an old friend describing his experiences
as a pilot during the Battle of Britain; he had had a mental collapse, and was
sent to a public hospital (of course there were many *ad hoc* arrangements at
the time); and on return, as I remember, was put on patrol duties but no
longer on raids. He had enjoyed meeting outsiders in hospital, and had
positively chummed up with a dusty old teacher, returned empty from
somewhere, so much so that they made a pact they would tell each other
their sins. My friend probably thought this would be an excuse for boasting
about his sexual triumphs, which he would earn by doing his quota of sympathetic listening; though he did also feel guilty – involuntary cowardice
was very guilty. But he was quite dismayed, he said, by what the old brute
told him; though he cheered up after reflection, because it showed he was
really in a very innocent way of life, making war. The man's confession was
about how he had destroyed Basic English; of course he was boasting in a
way, but not much, because his sin had preyed fatally on his mind. 'O do
tell what' I kept crying out, but no, my friend had resolutely expunged this
disgusting stuff, though he had kept to his bond and listened to the end.
Somehow, he felt, this procedure had turned a nasty incident into a positively health-giving one. Maybe under hypnosis he might yet give up his
dead, like the sea on the Last Day; but it could hardly be of much use.

   I wish I had something to tell about the negotiations of Richards with
high Chinese education committeemen, but I was never deep in his counsels, and anyhow I only reached China in 1937, on a Japanese troop-train.
The Japanese conquerors had of course no interest in allowing English to be
taught, and a lasting collapse of the previous broad knowledge of the
language set in at once. Richards had come much nearer to success in convincing China about Basic than any other country, and had very wide contacts there; I was allowed to travel with him in 1937 from Changsha to
Indochina, and was a bit startled to find him so well known and esteemed in
places which seemed to me remote (all through Chinese history, I suppose,
most of the really influential people have been in the provincial capitals).
Actually, the disaster was an occasion that cried out for a rapid and simplified method of teaching, but there was no hope of getting the organisation
for it; the east coast universities were refugeeing into the interior, and to get

that organised was as much as the authorities could do. There were some schools already using the method, and help must be arranged for them as far as possible; but that was about all. Richards, I have no idea of denying, fought his rearguard action with all the expected pluck, grit and panache, but he is not one to go on banging his head against a brick wall. The day came, or rather the dawn, when I walked across a few hills in the west of Hong Kong to his hotel, meaning to urge him to give it a few days longer, and was distressed to find he had already left for the airport. I feel sure now that he was right.

The kiss of death was the support of Sir Winston Churchill, which began in 1943; during a grand speech in America, he recommended Basic as the way to make English the international language, and later a government committee was set up to implement his intention. I remember Miss Lockhart, the very able secretary or manager of the Basic organisation, attempting comfort after the speech and saying that all might yet be well, so it was recognised as harmful from the start. Churchill was well able to understand that other governments, not the British and American ones, would in the end decide the question; and if he had been serious about it he would have acted differently. It gave just what he wanted for his speech, breadth of post-war vision and cooperation between our two countries, and if it annoyed De Gaulle that was fun. So it was not surprising that foreign governments were left in need of reassurance; what could not have been foreseen was the behaviour of the British committee. Maybe they felt that the behaviour of the prime minister had been unconstitutional, in not going through the proper channels; but surely a good negotiator could have cleared that point. Ogden had had reason to be exasperated, and by this time had settled into the habit of refusing to make any alterations or concessions. There must be a rapid early stage, in the file of documents, which will be interesting if made available, during which he and his committee become mortally offended with one another; after that an Ice Age was entered until his very unforeseen death from cancer in 1957. This should have been an opportunity for Richards, who has always been a much more adaptable negotiator, and indeed keen to find out the actual requirements of a given teaching problem. He devoted to it another fifteen years of intense activity, but somehow the terrible powers of nonsense had already had too long a run.

However, they may be defeated yet by some random turn of the wheel. In the poem by Richards which I take to describe this kind of process there is no actual denial that it may succeed. The princes of Abyssinia, in the poem, are trying to escape from the mountain valley which keeps them unspotted from the world; and we need hardly doubt that they often did escape from it:

Sleek slabs that lean and tilt
    And rear,
    On which to balance fear
And pride and guilt,

And learn there's no way through,
    No out,
    Whatever a stubborn doubt
May set us to

Up here with peg and sling.
    Who try
    The spider's way rely
On the hammer's ring;

Listen themselves secure,
    Until
    Will, over-reaching skill,
Its end endure.

I. A. Richards responded to this essay in a letter of 5 November 1973:

Dear William,

So grateful for your very gallant side-swipe on behalf of Basic English.... Your handling of F. R. L[eavis] amused me greatly: what a grimly comic figure he has been! To be as fully candid as I may, I do not think anything he ever did could much disturb me – though I have been sorry for people he did things against.

Thanks for quoting my verses at the end of your piece. It had never occurred to me that they might have any relation whatever to what had happened with Basic. I have had so many other utter failures that concerned me more and seemed, alas, far more explicable.

What I liked most was your word about the 'knock down content' of Chap. IV of So Much Nearer. No one else, that I know of, has touched on what, I felt, was a necessary bit of pest-extermination in an important field of our joint endeavours. That book So Much Nearer, so far, has had nothing but derision and abuse.

Thanks – beyond phrases – for your quote of 'The Hammer's Ring'. That is quite a thing to listen to when your party's lives depend upon it....

D[orothea] joins me in salutes to you both

                    I. A. R.

                                        [Empson Papers]

Remembering I. A. Richards

First published as 'William Empson remembers I. A. Richards':
London Review of Books, 5–18 June 1980

The death of I. A. Richards has at least endangered an opportunity which he had accepted with eager energy. In 1937, the Chinese Ministry of Education had decided to use Basic English in the schools, for the first years of English there, but just as the details were being fixed up the Japanese launched an all-out attack and captured Peking. One might argue that this was the right time to introduce a far more economical method: but it would require a great deal of organising from the centre, and to organise the refugeeing of the west-coast universities to the interior was already imposing an almost unbearable strain. There were some local centres where the method was already in use, and contact had to be maintained with them as far as possible; I was able to go with Richards to Kweilin and meet a distinguished headmaster. This seems worth recalling, as Richards returned to Kweilin on the final tour, 42 years later, and was soon afterward struck down. Touring the schools in provincial cities, and speaking in each of them, would be the most exhausting part of the work. He had been warned by a friend that the visit would probably kill him, but after all he had for years been risking his life on mountains, and this occasion might make all the difference (for him) between dying in triumph and dying as a failure.

There had been another exasperating bit of bad luck in Ghana, where Richards had made all the arrangements, touring the schools and so on, and was just going contented to his aeroplane when he was tapped on the shoulder and told it was all off: the dictator Nkrumah had been angered by a careless word from the sponsor (not from Richards) and had used this rejection for a punishment. 'It is a new way to fail,' said Richards, from his wide experience: but it would not be so painful, as the Chinese had understood the principles and taken an interest. Meanwhile there was always a barrage of vilification from the rival firms. It seemed when he retired from Harvard that he must admit that he had failed to launch Basic; and he took up other interests, continuing to be very good company; but his face when alone had come to look very grim, even soured. Interview and article, however, remained stubbornly optimistic, assuming that the cause could not have been lost; and indeed the Chinese invited him back as soon as they settled down after the departure of the Japanese, the defeat of Chiang Kai-Shek, and the death of Mao. Let us hope they had already made up their minds, so that the heroic death of Richards in their service will merely help to make welcome the agreed procedure. They could have given him no death that would make him happier.

Mrs Richards allowed me to visit him in hospital and he seemed so full of life that I felt sure he would recover: but he was delirious, and not much could be understood. Two recurring sentences were clear: 'It's time for me to go' and 'I ought to come back,' meaning he was ready for death except that the work was incomplete. I said, 'Of course you must come back; you are urgently needed,' and he looked at me quizzically, entirely himself for a moment. He was doubting my competence to pronounce upon the question. This of course was charming, but also, taken with some other phrases, suggested that he had done as much on this visit to China as he could usefully do. A too sustained pressure becomes irritating, he had long understood; they must now have time to think it over. He was struggling for life, with the tireless support of Mrs Richards, but he did not feel an immediate exasperating regret.

This fighting aspect of him is not what is most admired in his books, but it lay near the root of his achievement, and I had been eager for anything he let drop about his life in the mountains. He was firmly unboastful, but felt it all right to praise a technique; there was a flavour of H. G. Wells. Asked whether he had slept in an igloo, he said: 'Of course; those were the only comfortable nights we spent in Alaska.' It was only to explain how easy the thing is, once you know the trick, that he recalled what can surely not be a standard bit of life-saving. A fellow climber had broken his leg, and could not be carried down the cliff; one of the party went to get help, and Richards and another stayed with him. The important thing was to find a rock of the right size, which even the crippled man, after being planted out of the wind, could receive and pass on. They handed it round all night, 'and did not even catch cold'.

Professor Basil Willey, in a *festschrift* for the eightieth birthday of Richards (1973), said that he not only founded modern literary criticism but supplied it with a vocabulary which has become accepted currency for so long that its origin is often forgotten. I now think this is true, but it was not clear to me when he was my supervisor. Willey was present at the first lectures by Richards at Cambridge, which became the *Principles* (1924) whereas I (then a math student) attended one or two of the lectures which became *Practical Criticism* (1929). His position had become familiar. My literary faction (Bronowski, for instance) accepted Richards as a great liberator who had made our work possible: but he kept telling us that each of his doctrines was only common sense, and that somebody had said it in the eighteenth century. Like the Mona Lisa of Pater, we imagined ourselves to be older than the rock on which we sat. Also he was then expecting an intellectual revolution from psychology. While I was having a weekly supervision from Richards, in my final year, I was listening to the James Smith group, who favoured T. S. Eliot and Original Sin. After each of his supervisions, as I remember, though I had enjoyed and learned from them enormously, I would goad the enemy by reporting some theologically absurd remark, typical of an expert on Scientism. Within a year, I was defending him in some periodical against a particularly gross attack, so I was not actively disloyal: but it would be a mistake to suppose that Cambridge ever agreed on a monolithic acceptance of the views of Richards. He found himself warmly accepted by audiences but fiercely attacked in magazines, and there was the same contrast after he had moved over from literary theory to teaching procedures. He was by nature a negotiator, and on principle did not expect any doctrine to be more than an approximation to the truth; but his analytic power always made people regard him as an extremist.

This must partly explain his immense success as a lecturer: in my time, no lecture hall was big enough for him, and he enjoyed making *ad hoc* arrangements. And yet most of what he was saying was negative, and it was said rather dryly. He never played the fashionable game of 'revaluation', switching round the price ticket, upping Donne and downing Milton, for example. He was concerned with a bafflement about what happens when people read, or about the aesthetic experience in general; it is important to realise that they are usually reading wrong, but apart from that, when is the effect a good one? The difference between a deadlock and a balance of the impulses must be crucial, but what can it be? Some satisfaction of other impulses perhaps, or a general readiness; but we must hope for psychology to cast some light. Before trying to taste a literary work, he advised in *Practical Criticism*, it would be a good thing to clean the palate from previous assumptions by reflecting on the 'enormity' of time and space, and the 'oddity' of human birth and death. This advice was met with fierce ridicule by the professional literary critics, who seem to me now even more absurd than they did then. No wonder the audiences liked him for taking the guff out of the experts, and his dry manner was suited to it. But the only definite part of the programme, it seems fair to say, was the removal of obstacles.

Such was the appearance, but I have to add that he was a spellbinder, not at all shy about being Welsh. In his later writings he depends upon Plato rather than science yet unborn, but even there a reader could hardly guess that he had this extra power. Nor was he above calculating his effects.

When he visited Peking after the Communist victory, he required among other props a folding card-table at the side of the stage, not an easy thing for the British Council to find, and he used it by leaning upon it, as he went out from his lecture, to say: 'In my end is my beginning.' He would not have done this in either of the Cambridges, but the Chinese students would find hearing English a serious effort, and would need a bit of action; it went over very well. He was expounding something about Plato, as I remember, but he literally did mean to return to Peking.

The point is not at all that he would weaken or coarsen a doctrine to placate his audience; audiences had always been his friends, to whom he would tell things he dared not say in print. Only a few years ago, I heard him lecture on 'Complementarities' in London, and I was spellbound. When the book of that name came out, it reported only a slighter lecture elsewhere on the same topic. I wrote and begged him to restore what had been omitted, and received no reply. The big lecture, as I remember, had made no rash attempt at a solution, but merely quoted a much wider range of startling examples (of such findings as that light consists at once both of waves and of particles). He had written an introduction to the milder lecture, for the book, and here for once he sounds exasperated by the silliness of his opponents. It had always been central to his mind that an apparent intellectual conflict need not be a practical obstacle. He had not felt ready to print more at the time, but probably he would have gone further with this extremely uneasy topic if he had survived his call to China.

Basic English

The Spectator, 14 June 1935

I. A. Richards, *Basic Rules of Reason*
I. A. Richards, *Basic in Teaching*

Basic Rules of Reason was a paper to the Aristotelian Society done in Basic because that was the clearest way to put the argument; it is not so much on 'philosophy' as on the behaviour of language that makes philosophy necessary, with a list of numbered senses for key words at the end. One might get an idea that Basic was a 'pidgin', good for common use but not for thought; the fact is if anything the opposite; it comes from the Cambridge school of philosophy, and is most in comfort when talking of those ideas. So the purpose of the paper, to give some of the mixed senses at the back of *any* philosophy, takes on a further interest as to the range of Basic; the language seems to give the argument some support, but there is room enough for an attack on the argument in the same words, or at any rate a man on the other side in philosophy would say so. As a test of Basic in this field it is as good as possible; it seems the normal way of writing philosophy, but more natural. *Basic in Teaching* is a discussion about the uses of Basic for giving the learner a clear sense of English and some power over the tricks of language in general, and about the special need for Basic among English-learners in the Far East.

I had best give a rough account of the system. There are 'no "verbs" and only 850 words', and the 'prepositions' are all taken off one map from their root senses of place or direction. That is, there are eighteen simple verbs into which complex verbs are broken up (*disembark* becomes 'get off a ship'), while some 300 words such as *price* may be used with '–ing' and '–ed', which only makes the thing shorter, if the learner is certain that the word is so used in English. There are in fact some more words: numbers, measures, names of sciences, about ten joined words (*become* for 'come to be') that have to be got by heart, and some words now widely international; in all about 150, making 1000. The rules in using the words are very simple. What has by now become certain about the system is that some learners get it quickly and simply, and that some good English writing has been done by its rules (probably best *The Basic St Mark*).

I myself became seriously interested in the system when teaching English letters in Japan with no knowledge of Japanese; it was sometimes the only thing that gave me a feeling that I was of any use. In talking to a man with little English, the great need is for *any* agreement about what is simple, which words come first; one keeps away from long words and they may be the chief thing he was given at school. But my business was with young men of good powers and long knowledge of English, and for them the use of Basic was simply as a clearing in the mass of undergrowth of this great language; when their writing went out of sight in the undergrowth the only thing to do was to put down in Basic two or three of the possible senses. In China and Japan they say that English is their second tongue, and it is true enough that their chance of using French has gone. Learning French is some trouble, but after that you have a clear and beautiful language; in English the undergrowth is part of the language and listed in the NED. But in the East one only gets the point put sharply; the same thing goes on in all English schools. One chief reason for the specially English and American words 'highbrow' and 'lowbrow' is that the language is full of secret tricks, very good tricks that make the fullest of languages, and so hard that most men get tired of them. But it is now in need of a fixed regular form for special uses, such as was given to French more completely and much earlier, and the reason it still has a chance to do this well is that it has the clearest root forms of any language and has kept on going back to them.

There are three chief reasons why Basic is important: as an 'auxiliary' international language (this is clearly needed, and a special sort of English is backed by the present wide use of bad full English), secondly as a first step in the direction of full English which gives the right feeling about the words, even about words that come later (*disembark* is a word for 'get off a ship' taken as an important event, and only in English are these broken-up forms the normal ones; it is a great step to get a learner to see this in general), thirdly as a test of a bit of writing for the Englishman himself, a way of separating statement from form and feeling (it may then be used at school for 'paraphrases' and will be taken as the normal sort of English for international use). For myself at least it has become a fixed process on reading something deeply true to see if it is still good sense in Basic.

The first copy of *Basic English* was printed in 1930, and there is a general agreement on the principle of using a limited list of words while the learner gets a feeling for the language. Naturally other teachers of teachers, an important body, have produced other lists and are now fighting over part of the field. There is much to be said for Natural Selection; such is the mind of man that men do their best over small things; and if there was a fight over making the system better in detail I might be looking for my way in. But the system needed, though it may have to be less simple than Mr Ogden's, will have to be good in all three ways, and so far no other attempt has come near to covering them. But for a word or two in 'quotes', this bit of writing is in Basic, and the better for its limits.

Basic English and Wordsworth

A RADIO TALK

Kenyon Review, II: 4, Autumn 1940

Naturally no one says that keeping within the Basic words all the time would be a good way of writing poetry. The use of Basic with poetry is, in a sense, for the education of the reader of poetry. But happily not all our education goes on at school, and some knowledge of the ideas of the Basic system, of the *sort* of way in which Basic gets a complex idea broken up into its parts, may be a help even to a good reader. It lets him get more grip on what he is reading. That at least is the belief which I am putting forward today, and if it seems to you very foolish and unprobable at first, it would be kind of you, in place of judging against this talk at the start, to keep in mind that the test is in the examples, which come later.

But first, why did I say that keeping within the Basic words would not make good poetry? Chiefly because the great trick of poetry, the reason, you might say, for writing in verse at all, is that it lets the writer get his thought crushed into a small space. Then it is like gunpowder, if the trick is done well; the thought comes bursting into the reader's mind. But this is not the only way of writing poetry, or if it is, then the trick may be done with very simple words. We will take an example of Wordsworth doing that. Probably Wordsworth would be pleased with this bit of the argument. Because it was his chief opinion that poetry had better be made out of 'the simple language of men', though he made good poetry out of hard words as well.

> The sea was laughing at a distance; all
> The solid mountains were as bright as clouds.

That is Wordsworth, and in Basic, and good poetry; we will come back to it later on. You might get the idea that the Basic words are dead and uninteresting, because they are so simple; that all the bright and living English words are outside the list. This is clearly not true in the two lines from Wordsworth; they may be simple, but there is nothing 'dead' about them.

Or you might say that it is not possible to have poetry without verbs.

I. A. RICHARDS AND BASIC ENGLISH

233That is, complex verbs, not like the Basic *put* and *take* and so on. Because full verbs give force, and colour, and song, and the taste of the living minute, and all that sort of thing. Well, it is true that the thought is less crushed together in Basic, and being crushed together is a help for poetry, so no doubt it is true that poetry has a need for complex verbs. What is not true is that there is anything feeble or dead about *put* and *take*. Here is Swinburne writing about the place where dead men go to, and about Persephone, the great woman, or being, under whose authority they go. She is Death, and she is the daughter of the earth, because though the summer is fertile (and the earth is fertile) still the winter comes after it (and the winter is death). I will give the rough sense in Basic first.

She is waiting for everyone. She is waiting for every man from his birth on. She has let out of her memory the earth who was her mother, and the way of living when fruit and grain are coming to their growth. And the spring, and the seeds, and the birds who go away in winter, all take wing for her, and go one after another to this place where the sound of the songs that were made in summer becomes hollow, and the flowers are laughed at because they were beautiful.

> She waits for each and other,
> She waits for all men born,
> Forgets the earth her mother,
> The life of fruits and corn,
> And spring and seeds and swallow
> *Take wing* for her and follow,
> Where summer song rings hollow
> And flowers are *put to* scorn
>
> ['The Garden of Proserpine', ll. 57–64]

Now one thing is quite clear. It is no use your saying that *take wing for her* and *put to scorn*, in this verse, have only got the feeble little verbs *put* and *take*, so they are feeble. They are very strong, they come out of the lines like the right arm. In fact, they are kept back for the places where most force is needed. It is they who make the smash at the end. That does not say that the Basic verbs are the best ones for poetry *all the time*. But it is sometimes said that there is necessarily a dead feeling about the verbs in Basic, and it seems a good thing to give an answer.

Still, our use of Basic here is not for writing poetry, but for getting the effect of normal poetry clear. So let us take a look at the effect of putting the lines into Basic. There are two points of interest. *Life* seems quite clear at first – 'the life of fruits and corn' – but putting this into Basic has a strange effect. The word is not in the Basic list, and you have to say to yourself, What life? What *sort* of life of a fruit is in question here? And then it becomes clear that Swinburne has in mind summer, as the time of growth of the fruit, and the feelings that we have in summer as the opposite to winter and death. In fact, without this connection the lines have no sense. The swallow is not going to its death when it goes south from England at the start of the winter. It only comes into the verse as one of the signs that winter is coming, and because winter is used in the verse as a sign of death. The swallow goes with desire and hope to a warmer country. But men in the end, so the later verses say, get a desire for death and go to it quickly, as the swallow goes south away from winter. Now this is a simple enough bit of poetry, as poetry goes. But it is quite possible for a reader not to get all this system of comparisons that are working at the back of it. And then turning the poetry into Basic is a help, because it makes you put the right questions.

The other point is maybe of more interest to writers in Basic than to poetry readers. *Scorn* is not in the list, and to give the sense of this verse in Basic you have to get round 'put to scorn'. But it is not possible to give the 'sense' without giving the right suggestion, because the connections of thought, in this sort of poetry, are in the suggestions, and seem to be only feelings. It is no good saying that the flowers are made to seem feeble and unwise, though that is the simplest answer. Or even that they are laughed at cruelly, though that is much better, because it puts our attention onto Persephone, who is cruel. The idea, or so it seems to me, is that the flowers are laughed at *wrongly*. The more beautiful they were the more pain there would be in death. So the way Persephone is judging them is the opposite to the way they were judged in the summer, by living men and by the fertile earth. What is better up here on earth seems worse to her. So the best way to say 'put to scorn', it seems to me, was to put 'laughed at because they were beautiful'. Well, this may be wrong, but you see the line of thought that is needed. When you make this attempt at turning the sense of a bit of poetry into Basic you will get a feeling that your answer is wrong, at some points. This feeling is a sort of pointer. It is only through our taste about the effects of language that we get our knowledge about its working. In looking for the reason why your first answer was wrong, you are sent on to the important questions about poetry. So this process makes the structure of the poetry much clearer.

Let us go back now to the lines by Wordsworth. They are about the morning when Wordsworth first was certain that he had to give himself to writing poetry. It is early in the morning, and Wordsworth is up on the top of a mountain. There is an interesting point here, because Wordsworth made changes in the lines when he was older. So in our Basic account we have another thing to do. This is the first way of writing the lines.

> Magnificent
> The morning was, a memorable pomp,

> More glorious than I ever had beheld.
> The sea was laughing at a distance; all
> The solid mountains were as bright as clouds.[1]

Now an attempt at the sense in Basic.

> The morning seemed strong and beautiful. I had a respect for it, as if it was a King, a ruler, coming out before the eyes of his nation, and with a train of servants round him. It seemed that this would never go out of my memory. The morning was more brightly and clearly beautiful than I had ever seen it before. The sea was laughing at a distance; all the solid mountains were as bright as clouds.

Well, that took a great number of words. And one trouble is, in giving all those words for *pomp* we get a detailed picture, not a general idea. *Magnificent* and *glorious* seem all right; we are able to say why they are different; one is strong, the other bright. But there is another trouble here. We have made these three words seem much more different than they were in the poetry. In them all the morning (or the sun) is *making itself seem* great, like the ruler. When we see this we see why they are in that order. First the morning seems strong, maybe like a ruler who is doing great things (magnificent); then this gives the idea of the ruler coming out on view (pomp). But you are not to have any protest in your mind against rulers and the way they make themselves important. So the morning was truly bright in itself (glorious), and the sea was not self-important, it was laughing. There is a sort of pull here between two ideas, that of the authority of the good ruler and the natural good of being free. And the effect is that this beautiful morning is like a sign of some good secret at the back of all experience. As so frequently in Wordsworth, in fact, there is an idea of religion not clearly in view. It seems to me that putting the lines into Basic makes this turn of thought much clearer, for the very reason that Basic is so short of words like *magnificent*. The effect is like taking the cover off a machine.

But the last two lines are not simple, though they are in Basic. You get a strange feeling that *solid* and *bright* are two opposites coming together.

> The solid mountains were as bright as clouds.

The mountains are solid because they are heavy, hard, causes of danger; commonly they are dark; they have a cruel authority; they have a connection with the sad experience down here on earth. But now they have given up all that, and they are bright, like the clouds in the air. So all the parts of this morning view are working together; they are all a sign of the good secret, that is true about everything. And there is the same pull here as before between the ideas of authority and of being free.

But there is another point here. This surprising connection of ideas, *solid* and *bright*, was there waiting for us before, inside the complex words *mag-*

nificent, *pomp*, and *glorious*. The ruler makes us see his force when he comes out on view; he is solid. But he is a good ruler, and will make us happy; or at any rate his purpose in coming out on view is to give us that feeling. One of the effects of his force, in fact, is that we are now looking at something beautiful, as he goes by in his ornaments, and he does that as a sign that he will make us happy. So he is bright. And all this group of ideas, which may seem very complex, is not one person's invention but the normal feeling in words like *pomp* and *magnificent*. But Wordsworth was taking this idea in the words more seriously. It was his serious belief that the beautiful view was a sign of some greater good thing. And the way he gives us that feeling is by taking the complex idea in *magnificent* to bits. That is why he is able to give us this shock with the simple Basic words *solid* and *bright*. Because it is not only the reader who has to be able to take an idea to bits. We see here the writer having to do it as well. After starting with an old comparison, of the sun to a ruler, which would have no great effect, he gets a feeling, 'Why is that interesting to me? What is this suggestion that it has, of some more important idea?' and so he takes it to bits. The surprise which is so important for poetry comes in his further thought about the comparison, and there he is using simpler ideas. So it is not quite by chance that the last two lines here are only using words that are in the Basic list.

But when Wordsworth was older it seemed to him that there was not enough weight in these lines for such an important poet as the older Wordsworth. And he made changes, that take it much further away from Basic. One good judge has said that he made it much better, and maybe you will say the same. These are the new lines:

>   magnificent
> The morning rose, in memorable pomp,
> Glorious as e'er I had beheld – in front,
> The sea lay laughing at a distance; near,
> The solid mountains shone, bright as the clouds.[2]

The chief changes are in the morning *rose* for the morning *was*; the sea *lay* laughing for the sea *was* laughing; the mountains *shone* for the mountains *were*, and the new words *in front* and *near*. Now certainly this seems tighter verse. There are more facts in it. One writer says that this makes it clearer. For example, it is now clear that the sea was in the middle of the view, in front, and that the mountains were nearer to Wordsworth than the sea was. But here it is time to make a protest against something I was saying before. I said that it was important for poetry to get ideas crushed together. But *what* ideas? Why, after all, is it important for us to get the right picture here? Maybe some readers of the old lines had got the right feeling, though they took the sea to be nearer than the mountains. But now Wordsworth says to them 'You are making a foolish error. In *fact*, at the time when I had this important feeling, the sea was *not* nearer than the mountains.' That is, in the new lines Wordsworth is painting a picture. This is as good a morning as even he, William Wordsworth, has ever seen, and he is giving a clear account of it. You see how cold this makes him; he is an expert on views of mountains. But in the old lines it was his *feelings* about the sea and the mountains and the morning that were important, and the forces working in his heart. And that is what is interesting in the lines, if anything is interesting. The idea that pushing in more facts *about the view* makes the lines more interesting is simply an error.

The other changes are all changes in verbs; he takes out the simple Basic ones and puts in complex verbs. Then it will be better because more ideas will have been pushed in – that is his feeling. The morning *rose*, he says, came up, as if the sun sometimes went down in the morning. This detail seems very little indeed. But it makes clear that the time was very early in the morning, and maybe this touch has an effect. What *came up* was the sun, and the change puts your attention onto the sun. Possibly it was only the sun, not the morning in general, who was a ruler and *magnificent*. At any rate the sea *lay* laughing; it was flat on its back. It had no authority against the sun; it was in a feeble position. Taken by itself, the change to *lay* might be a beautiful one, but it has a connection with the others. And then the mountains *shone*; they gave out light. So it is clear that they gave back light from the first rays of the sun, which was then first coming up in the morning. They were not bright in themselves. They were only giving back light from the sun. So the old shock of surprise in *solid* and *bright* has quite gone. There is no secret about the morning. It was the *sun* that was making things bright. This is quite clear now that Wordsworth has given us all the details.

In fact there are only two important persons now, the sun and Wordsworth. Every one of the changes has been working in this direction. Wordsworth is important because the reader has to get clear the details of what Wordsworth saw. And the sun is important because it is the *cause* as it is from the point of view of science, of all the details in the picture. But the old effect was a pull between two feelings, between saying that authority is good and saying it is good to be free and open to experience. The weight now has all come down on the side of authority. When Wordsworth was young and in trouble he came back to the mountains and took them as teachers. The poor mountains are nobody now, but it is pleasing to see a smile from a mountain when Wordsworth or the sun goes past. A good mountain, at such a time, will take its hat off. It is a strange and sad thing, but it probably seemed to Wordsworth, when he made these changes, that he was

only giving the lines a bit of polish. What he was doing was more like turning the guns round from firing at the Germans and pointing them against
the French.

Well, you may say that this account is all false, and that the later lines are
better. That may be so, but it seems to me clear that the ideas we are using
are the right ones. If you gave a full answer to this account, you would have
to make use of the same ideas. Because the nerve of the poetry is in this complex group of ideas, which are inside words like *magnificent* and *pomp*,
ideas which we take in reading simply as feelings. We do not commonly get
the ideas opened up, and see the reasons for the feelings. So all this argument about the effect of the lines has come straight out of our attempt at
putting the sense into Basic. Without that start we would probably not see
what was important, in the structure of the thought.

Notes

1 *The Prelude* (1805 text) IV, ll. 330–34.
2 *The Prelude* (1850 text) IV, ll. 323–27.

III
Poetry (1): Medieval to Victorian

Love and the Middle Ages

The Spectator, 4 September 1936

C. S. Lewis, The Allegory of Love

The title is not a description of the book but of the excellent medieval works which it expounds and places in their long historical background; curious how one's heart sinks on supposing a modern specimen; what the Romantics could read as wild and fascinating needs now to be praised as exact and important. The book is learned, witty, and sensible, and makes one ashamed of not having read its material; in the first flush of renewed admiration for the Romaunt of the Rose I tried to read the Chaucerian version. But it is intolerable. Far better to read Mr Lewis and his admirable quotations, and recognise that these works were developing a method which is still normal and living, and frankly admit that there are great pleasures not our own.

The book starts with vast and vague claims for its theme. There have been 'three or four real changes of human sentiment' in history, and one was the discovery of 'courtly love' in eleventh-century Provence; compared to this the Renaissance was 'a mere ripple'; only because of this, the American film is now a surprise to the oriental. Certainly something important happened, and Mr Lewis might have found a narrow enough definition to make the troubadours unique. But he had only to open The Tale of Genji to find the practice of courtly love in full blast in tenth-century Japan; it came, and it soon went, with the conditions for it; and it comes rather when women are mutilated and imprisoned than when they are free. The main troubadour theory, the comparison of a noble successful love to the vision of God, could not well be pushed further into Buddhism than by the mutual suicides who still expect a Buddhist heaven; in Islamic poetry it could and did appear fully, and earlier than the troubadours. One does not need to claim Moslem influence (never adequately disproved) to refute this idea that love was discovered like matches, only once, which Mr Lewis has to support by calling Catullus an exhibitionist and hiding the Song of Solomon. Mr Lewis is rather bitter about 'the modern reader', that vulgar fool looking for excitement, and it seems fair to point out the journalism of his first pages.

Indeed he oversimplifies the allegories, too, but that is to our gain if it makes them readable. Before expounding the *Romaunt of the Rose* he produces various butts to make it seem easy, readers for instance 'who had never noticed that the fountain of Narcissus represented the heroine's eyes'. The fifteenth-century scholiast Molinet is then called crude, and he too had not noticed this point, preferring to combine in the Well the fountain of Wisdom, with Truth at the bottom, and that of Love, either divine or 'vain' enough to destroy Narcissus, and again, by stressing the overhanging pine-tree as the Cross, that of grace and piety in the water from the side of Christ. But Mr Lewis is making a real point, and no doubt Molinet could have produced a literal and a Freudian meaning if he chose. You have only to hold both the image itself and its most sensible interpretation, then read slowly and let fancy play. You then read the only known love-story (as Mr Lewis shows very well) which understands its heroine profoundly and never mentions her. But I cannot do this; the whole excitement of the slow poem was in gradual partial discovery; and even a simple-minded modern reader will start discovering from some wrong place. It is the rare case of a thing that one can see was very good and yet cannot enjoy.

This point about the Well seems important, because Molinet states what Mr Lewis leaves out; the Well is wisdom and the crystal in it that reflects the whole garden is the just person who includes everything in himself. The idea that love is a means to *knowledge* is already clear in the poem of Bernart of Ventadorn, from which Mr Lewis quotes a verse to prove that the well only meant eyes – the lady has 'stolen the whole world' into her 'mirror full of power'. Cavalcanti is perhaps the first to theorise in verse about this, but it is one of the few Provençal ideas that Europe still plays with, and incidentally just what might have been learned from the Arabs. (The *Koran* explicitly states, after providing houris in Heaven as a powerful allegory [Surahs 37 and 56], that they will be neglected because men will prefer the vision of God; this is exactly the position of Aquinas about the pleasures of Heaven, except that love is given the highest place among things neglected.) The other side of the Provençal position, the lady actually in control of the drawing-room, was alive enough among the Byzantines; what one would like to know is how far the Provençal mixture was a crucial cause of later sentiment. Were Heloïse and Abelard busily modelling themselves on troubadours? And I suspect another hole in his account around the allegory of triumph. We are told that Hawes, one of the last figures in the book, 'did a most surprising thing'; after the death of his Lover he describes successive triumphs of Fame, Time and Eternity, and Mr Lewis has an interested footnote about Sir Thomas More's father's pictures. Of course, this is simply Petrarch's *Trionfi* in order, and for that matter the stuff of many medieval pageants; when Mr Lewis feels an obscure triumph in the apparently depressing close of many allegories he is noting a variant of this stock form.

Such complaints as I can make are only an agreement about the interest of the topic. Mr Lewis is excellent on the essential point of allegory, and on its growth in Silver Latin, as against the gods, because of a new consciousness of an inner world of moral struggle, so that it was the basis of psychology and gave St Augustine tropes that no one has dared called unreal. But the real use of the book for a general reader I think lies elsewhere; it gives an effective account of works whose beauty and reality for us we need to recognise, and yet which, in all willingness, nobody who simply likes a good book can read.

Edmund Spenser:
Is he the 'Poet's Poet'?

A radio talk in a series *New Judgement on Edmund Spenser*,
broadcast on the Third Programme, 4 December 1952

I have the honour of being the final speaker in the celebrations by the Third
Programme of the 400th birthday of Edmund Spenser, which have like
their subject been fairly prolonged; and the final question, naturally, is to
be about the poetry itself, whether he really is 'The Poet's Poet', or at any
rate why he has been called so. The term 'Poet's Poet' is sometimes taken
like 'Holy of Holies', to mean that he gives a sort of concentrated essence,
much more poetical than most poetry, or nothing else but Pure poetry. But
this need not be praise, and might make him a sort of caricature; there is
some truth in it, but one needs also another meaning, that all kinds of later
poets have gone to him as a teacher. And yet it might occur, I think, to the
patient listener that most poets nowadays are at any rate brief; obscure and
disagreeable they may be, but the desire to be concentrated does at least
keep them from prattling endlessly. On this count, however rightly we may
revere Spenser, he seems about the last man a modern poet would study to
learn technique, or should be advised to. Most Elizabethan poets are diffuse, but Spenser stands out as an extreme example of it. We need to recognise that there is a considerable resistance to Spenser, which I partly feel
myself; or at any rate a resistance to the process of soaking oneself in Spenser at great length, which is the only effective way to read him. He is a
separate world, and the first question is whether you are willing to enter it
at all; if you are, you are willing to wander about in it indefinitely. So I want
to make some historical points, though previous speakers have already
made a lot of important ones; to the effect that he at any rate used to be the
Poet's Poet; before coming back to the question how far he still is now.

In his time, I think, he decisively *was*; he was a kind of basic engineer for
the English language in poetry; he got it to go. We all know nowadays that
Chaucer had done it 200 years before, but the grammar had changed so
that the Elizabethans thought Chaucer didn't scan. In between there had
been various kinds of disaster, and the effective but gradual methods of Elizabeth did not make her Elizabethan Age possible till she had been about

thirty years on the throne. Hardly anything important gets written till after the destruction of the Armada in 1588; the flowering seems to follow that great release, and the most obvious model for the new writers was Spenser, who had brought out the *Shepheardes Calender* about ten years before. Of course the development is more complicated than that, but Spenser positively undertook to be a model; he was prominent in deciding whether to use classical metres or not, for instance; the *Shepheardes Calender* has a mass of technical notes, as well as introducing thirteen metrical forms never before used in English, of which ten have been used ever since. If that is being a Poet's Poet, he did it in a very thorough and straightforward way, one might even think rather prosily. It is quite a different question from whether his later influence was a good one, on the eighteenth century for instance.

And it is clear that long-windedness was one of the requirements for his purpose; because what was needed was a regular idiom, so that you could go straight ahead and say anything in poetry, without getting flustered if some of it wasn't poetical. This is particularly needed for the drama, where the language for the ordinary or build-up parts has to be quiet enough to seem tolerably real and yet has to admit of modulation without too much jerk into the heightened language of the dramatic crises. This is very unlike what we think of as Spenser, the Poet's Poet, always dreamy and mellifluous, not to say elfin, but it is really what he does; and, of course, it was what he had to do if his epic was to survey all human experience. We need an example here, though I don't want to quote much as there have been full readings from him already. This verse which is just coming, is the end of Book II, Canto xii; the hero destroys what amounts to the Palace of Circe, on an island he has reached by ship, and turns back into men the people this sorcerer has turned into animals; but one of them, Grill, whom she had made into a pig, complains at this and upbraids Guyon.

> Said Guyon, See the mind of beastly man,
> That hath so soon forgot the excellence
> Of his creation, when he life began,
> That now he chooseth, with vile difference,
> To be a beast, and lack intelligence.
> To whom the Palmer thus, The dunghill kind
> Delights in filth and foul incontinence:
> Let Grill be Grill, and have his hoggish mind,
> But let us hence depart, whilst weather serves and wind.

He could not be cooler and more practical. By the way, for the engineering of this long stanza, the crucial point is regularly the fifth line. It goes abab – bcbc – long c, and the ear rather expects it to stop at the quatrain, at abab, so the decision to continue acts as a sort of elbow-joint. You can do many different things with it, granting in the first place that you can turn out these stanzas with sufficient ease. You can make the fifth line start, *after* a pause, on a second quatrain, for example to balance the first one in an argument, or you can leave *no* pause so that the fifth line acts as a little kick into the air and the stanza rises with unbroken rhythm to a lyrical climax, or you can have a stop at both ends of the fifth line, so that bits of information are being given, and the set form seems only to be retained by accident. In the verse I have just read a certain amount of flatness is wanted, but not so much, so there is a stop *after* the fifth line, where Guyon stops talking with an air of having merely rubbed in his opinion again, with an extra rhyme; then the Palmer starts talking independently, with his own rhyme-word, and bangs his point home with it.

> he chooseth, with vile difference
> To be a beast, and lack intelligence.
> To whom the Palmer thus, The dunghill kind
> Delights in filth and foul incontinence:
> Let Grill be Grill, and have his hoggish mind...

It is clear that the stanza would become intolerable during a long narrative if it did not allow of a great deal of variety of this sort. Spenser can afford in *The Faerie Queene* to be coarse or practical or stubbornly argumentative; the reason why we hardly notice it is that everything is framed by the tremendous stanza, the clock of fairyland, as someone called it, regularly pausing at its close, whose timing seems to hold us in another world.

Part of our feeling of remoteness is that Spenser is all the time imitating the sweetness of Italian, copying Ariosto but leaving out his jokes; and yet he was regarding that as a simple patriotic duty. English as he knew it was a barbarous mongrel language, with no rhythms and hardly any vowels, and it obviously needed training to make it able to show its face beside the civilised languages. The pretence of pastoral in the *Shepheardes Calender,* that the learned young Spenser from Cambridge, with all his languages behind him, and his grand friends like Sir Philip Sidney, were all coarse rustics, only on the fringe of the civilised world, meant to him something very real; because they were committed to using the barbarous language English and learning how to make it sing. And he did not want to make English *too* 'nice'; he gives a lot of experiment with dialect words and broken rhythms and so forth. The English language had its own merits, which should be sought out; as when he at last exploded to Harvey at Cambridge, who had induced him to try out classical metres, 'In God's name, let us have the kingdom of our own language.' And in the same way, in his politics, I think that this worship of the Queen, which earlier speakers in the series have rightly pointed out as a strange thing which needs to be historically understood, was in his mind a matter of applying the great ideas of European culture to an English patriotic purpose. It did not make him personally at all slavish; in fact, what got him exiled to Ireland seems to have been an early satire on the Queen, in 'Mother Hubbard's Tale'. It is unjust to think of him as always poetical to an almost sickening degree. He is a very practical type of poet, as they go.

This also appears in his dealings with love, as Professor C. S. Lewis showed very strikingly in his historical survey called *The Allegory of Love*. We tend to think of Spenser as copying out again the old themes of chivalry, the knight errant looking for a dragon, though they were completely out of date. But the main theme of the medieval romances had been the chivalrous idea of love, the love of an apparently unattainable lady which makes the knight good and brave. This was a most important invention, which would have been quite strange for the classical civilisation and is still prominent in our own. But it was taken for granted that this love was adultery, the marriages would already have been arranged for money or position. (There is – for that matter – a classical tradition about love making one good, which came to its flower in Plato, but that took for granted that love was between men.) The idea that the good kind of love had best be between married people, or people intending to get married, was not a platitude at all when Spenser made it the whole theme of his allegory in the third and fourth books. The House of Malecasta, from which Britomart rescues Amoret, is meant to show the actual misery produced by the glittering programme of chivalric love. To be sure, the change of thought had been creeping in for about 200 years, but Spenser made the first big attempt to take it seriously. Here again, when we realise what he was getting at, we are liable to think him prosy rather than too poetical; and our chief difficulty is to realise that it was new and worth doing.

I want now to come back to the question whether he is *still* the Poet's Poet; and the main objection to thinking so was that he is very diffuse and uses words flatly, whereas good poetry, at any rate nowadays, makes its language concentrated. Mr Herbert Read, some while ago, said, what seems obviously true as far as it goes, that Spenser 'kept to the visual significance of words; each word distinct and separate, pebbles in the stream. But now [in Shakespeare] words were to flash with interverbal meanings' [*Phases of English Poetry*, London: Hogarth Press, 1928, p. 56]. But by the time Spenser has finished building up one of his key words, for example Courtesy, which he is concerned to insist isn't learned at Court, a great deal of meaning has been put into it; though the effect doesn't feel like a pun, or other verbal surprise. We critics, I think, tend to make the contrast too sharp because we like to be able to quote a short bit and then discuss it. We should rather take the attitude of what is called *analysis situs* in geometry, where it doesn't matter whether the strings are pulled tight to make a knot; the interesting thing is whether their relations are such that they *would* make a knot, *if* they were put under strain. Spenser is not much interested in summing a point up, and this does I think sometimes make him irritating; he makes himself seem a prattling fool. Especially in what is called his Sensuous Idealism, which makes him say first that all beautiful women are good, that is how you tell a good woman, because our bodily nature, itself, expresses divine truths; and, yet, he will always go on, after saying this about twenty times, some beautiful women are very wicked, very bad indeed, and this will be said about ten times; and then he will placidly sum up:

> Natheless the soul is fair and beauteous still
> However flesh's fault it filthy make,
> For things immortal no corruption take.

To be sure, this is from the early 'Hymn in Honour of Beautie', which he published, long after writing it, saying he was afraid it could have a bad influence, so he had written another Hymn in honour of Heavenly Beauty and would print that with it to keep the balance. But the idea that, instead of being naughty, it was just a long flat contradiction of himself somehow couldn't enter his mind. And indeed, by the time you have absorbed the long procession of good and bad beautiful women in *The Faerie Queene*, you are likely to feel that he had some way of telling them apart in practice; even perhaps that *you* could say what it was; the fact that *he* couldn't, or not in an epigram, doesn't seem very important. Our modern verbal criticism finds this kind of case rather hard to deal with. And yet it is still a dramatic one; it might be suggested that Spenser's methods, again at a certain remove, could be useful to modern verse drama as they were to the Elizabethan. A recent American critic, Mr Watkins, was saying recently, rightly I thought, that Spenser 'seldom achieves the tension of Shakespeare's dramatic compression, [but] sets up a kind of vibration of interrelated meanings among various simple, direct statements'. (You notice how these metaphors from science have to come in nowadays before we can feel we are explaining anything), and for this process of waves rather than atoms, Mr Watkins goes on, 'The centres of radiation in the broadest sense are usually the allegorical cores of the books.'[1] But after all it is clear, even in saying this, that the effect is really very unlike a dramatic one, because it depends so much on long rhythms, beginning with the rhythm of the great stanza itself. I want to end by repeating something I wrote more than twenty years ago, after I had been soaking myself in it, reading the whole of *The Faerie Queene*, as I am afraid I have not done for this occasion:

The size, the possible variety, and the fixity of this unit give something of the blankness that comes from fixing your eyes on a bright spot; you have to yield yourself to it very completely to take in the variety of its movement, and, at the same time, there is no need to concentrate the elements of the situation into a judgement as if for action. As a result of this, when there are ambiguities of idea, it is whole civilisations rather than details of the moment which are their elements; he can pour into the even dreamwork of his fairyland Christian, classical and chivalrous materials with an air, not of ignoring their differences, but of holding all the systems of value floating as if at a distance, so as not to interfere with one another, in the prolonged and diffused energies of his mind. [*Seven Types of Ambiguity* (1930), 3rd edition, revised, London: Chatto & Windus, p. 34]

Note

1 W. B. C. Watkins, 'The Kingdom of our Language', *Hudson Review*, II (344–76), p. 367.

George Herbert and Miss Tuve

Kenyon Review, Autumn 1950

As the last of his examples of the seventh type of ambiguity – where 'the total effect is to show a fundamental ambiguity in the writer's mind' – Empson analysed George Herbert's 'The Sacrifice' (Seven Types of Ambiguity, pp. 226–33), in which 'the various sets of conflicts in the Christian doctrine of the Sacrifice are stated with an assured and easy simplicity, a reliable and unassuming grandeur, extraordinary in any material, but unique as achieved by successive fireworks of contradiction, and a mind jumping like a flea.' His interpretation reaches its climax in discussing this stanza:

> Oh all ye who pass by, behold and see:
> Man stole the fruit, but I must climb the tree.
> The tree of life, to all but only me,
>   Was ever grief like mine?

'[Christ] climbs the tree to repay what was stolen, as if he was putting the apple back; but the phrase in itself implies rather that he was doing the stealing, that so far from sinless he is Prometheus and the criminal,' Empson observed.

The phrase has an odd humility which makes us see him as the son of the house; possibly Herbert is drawing on the medieval tradition that the Cross was made of the wood of the forbidden tree. Jesus seems a child in this metaphor ... This gives a pathetic humour and innocence ... on the other hand, the son stealing from his father's orchard is a symbol of incest; in the person of Christ the supreme act of sin is combined with the supreme act of virtue. Thus in two ways, one behind the other, the Christ becomes guilty; and we reach the final contradiction:

> Lo here I hang, charged with a world of sin
> The greater world of the two ...

as the complete Christ; scapegoat and tragic hero; loved because hated; hated because godlike; freeing from torture because tortured; torturing his torturers because all-merciful; source of all strength to men because by accepting he exaggerates their weakness; and, because outcast, creating the possibility of society. ... Herbert deals in this poem, on the scale and by the methods necessary to it, with the most complicated and deeply rooted notion of the human mind.

Twenty years on, Rosemond Tuve, in 'On Herbert's "Sacrifice"' (Kenyon Review, XII: 1, Winter 1950, pp. 51–75), *complained that 'a reader familiar with the traditions out of which this poem sprang will find Empson's reading inadequate':*

its basic invention or structural situation, the sequence of ironies upon which it is built, the occurrence, setting and application of the refrain which binds it together, the very collocation of antitheses which make up the poem, are none of them Herbert's.

The conventions of 'The Sacrifice' derive from the liturgical offices of Holy Week, especially the Improperia or Reproaches of Good Friday. Accordingly, where Empson had perceived in the poem 'contradictory impulses ... held in equilibrium by the doctrine of the atonement', Tuve protested against the very notion of its uniqueness: 'the use of sharp antitheses ironically paralleling the tree of death with the tree of life is no novelty of a latter-day Metaphysical poet, and ... a considerable naiveté is required of us as readers if we are to think that Herbert's particular phrasing of the convention makes us see Jesus as the son of the house, climbing in the orchard.'

Tuve ended by admonishing Empson and other readers: 'whereas it is legitimate to look for and enjoy similarities between the meanings an earlier author opens up, with his instruments, in his myths, and the meanings our new psychological instruments open up for us, it is illegitimate to look willy-nilly for our instruments, and for all else they open to us, in what he wrote.'

Empson replied with this letter to the editors:

Miss Rosemond Tuve's article 'On Herbert's Sacrifice' in the *Kenyon Review* for Winter 1950 makes some good points against the way I wrote about it in *Seven Types of Ambiguity*, and raises important questions for critical theory. I am sorry not to have been able to see the article till now at the end of June, and hope I may make some belated comments.

My first feeling was that her complaints were quite right. It was rather absurd of me to call so traditional a poem 'unique', and to use as the climax of the analysis a faint bit of evidence for the presence of much more primitive ideas than the poet was consciously concerned with. I wrote the passage as an undergraduate over twenty years ago, and do not feel bound to defend it; though of course I may have been a better judge then than I am now.

At the same time, I cannot feel that the mass of erudition she brings down like a steam hammer really cracks any nuts. Generation after generation of poets and liturgists had handled this theme, no doubt, but she does not actually quote even one of them who clashes in plain words, as Herbert does, the idea of the mercy and yearning love of Christ against the idea of his terrible and inevitable revenge. I think she can be found hedging about this on p. 64:

> ... the secret of the power of this poem lies in the density of the serried layers of suggested concepts and emotions, in the frequently almost shocking juxtaposition of these emotions, and in the resulting variety and constant movement of the tone, from pitying to condemnatory....

I fully agree; but then she claims that all this (which as she says, makes it seem especially 'Metaphysical') is

> either explicit in the tradition, or implicit in the deliberate juxtaposition of concepts and images in the liturgy

(of Holy Week). Surely the act of making 'explicit' these very remarkable parts of a tradition is worth notice; it might even be worth calling a new style. And I cannot feel, as Miss Tuve seems to do, that you need to be soaked in the whole mass of a tradition before you can understand even the most explicit expression of it (a doctrine which would lay a remarkably heavy burden on us); still less that you ought to assume this ultimately explicit expression of it can *only* mean what you can trace in earlier ones.

There seem to be only two verses where she has detailed objections to my reading. The first is:

> Why, Caesar is their only King, not I:
> He clave the stonie rock, when they were drie:
> But surely not their hearts, as I well trie:
> Was ever grief like mine?

I said that the Christ here ironically identifies Caesar with Moses because 'both the earthly power of the conqueror and the legal rationalism of the Pharisees are opposed both to the profounder mercy of the Christ and to the profounder searchings of heart which he causes.' She says this is wrong because the tradition invariably took Moses as a type of Christ. Her objection may well be right, but I am uneasy about the mode of proof which seems to be offered. Surely it is also traditional to regard the Old Testament dispensation as different from the New; it would be quite orthodox, as well as natural from the text, to leave Moses as a middle term and reflect that though a more real and spiritual leader than Caesar he did not like Jesus try to cleave the heart. There is a progression, and Miss Tuve seems to argue that it could not be recognised as one, because it is not present (for example) in the liturgy of the Good Friday Reproaches. But surely Herbert did not feel himself shackled by tradition to this extreme degree; and if the

scholar is allowed to cut down the meaning of every poem to that of a previous poem there will be a considerable change in the literary scene. I am reminded of an emperor of China, who returned a poem to its author with a
somewhat embarrassed air and said 'But surely there is no such poem?',
meaning that he could not recall the classical poem which it must be presumed to imitate. However, to be fair, I didn't say clearly that there is
meant to be an ironical *contrast* between Caesar and Moses, a thing which
seemed to me the obvious basis for the secondary point, and maybe Miss
Tuve assumed from the flippancy of the style that I had failed to see this
primary one. The reason why I wanted the extra meaning, or thought it
wanted by Herbert, is that it makes the love of Christ more painful than the
law of Moses to which Christ tried to give a more merciful interpretation;
Milton, at any rate, found this paradox a very real one.

In her other example she seems to me on much firmer ground:

> *O all ye who pass by, behold and see*:
> Man stole the fruit, but I must climb the tree.
> The tree of life to all, but onely me:
> Was ever grief like mine?
>
> Lo, here I hang, charged with a world of sin ...

Interested in Freud and Frazer, in traces of the primitive and all that, I
jumped at an idea that the one who has to climb for the apple seems to be a
child, presumably the son of the house, and the son stealing from his
father's orchard is a symbol of incest; the Christ as scapegoat (or Prometheus) is thus unconsciously related to the most primeval of sins which
Freud had made the foundation of human society. There were other pretty
little fancies as that he is 'putting the apple back' or 'climbing upwards like
Jack on the Beanstalk and taking his people with him back to Heaven'.
Miss Tuve finds this sort of stuff completely irrelevant to the poem. I too
feel that is rather bad writing, or rather out of place, or something. One is
irritated at having the focus or level of interpretation changed so violently
at the last moment without adequate reward. But after granting these complaints about style I am still not sure that what I said is wrong.

Miss Tuve says,

... it is not meanings (they were already plainly visible) but *the precise images* of
modern analysis that we are asked to pursue – even at the cost of thinking that a
sensitive poet could write 'Man stole the fruit, but I must climb and steal it for him,'
or the equally vapid 'Man stole the fruit, but *I* must *climb* to steal it.'

Some theory connected with Imagism, which I can never plumb, keeps
cropping up in Miss Tuve's work; she says here that 'symbolical writing is

confusing only when we read symbol as picture, when we allow the concrete particulars of garden and tree to carry us, by connotation, into alien
contexts dependent on our individual fancies,' and yet that all symbols are
'capable of almost infinite variations'. I am sure I did not form any mental
picture or precise image here, but I can't see that it would have made any
difference if I had. As to the intonation required in reading the line, I entirely agree that neither of these queer antitheses should be brought out, but
I think they can rise in the mind without emphasis. Actually, it seems to me
very *like* Herbert to drop in a homely domestic analogy, though on so
solemn an occasion he would handle it with reserve. And, curiously
enough, after throwing scorn on my unhistorical fancies, Miss Tuve cannot
resist (or is generous enough not to resist) dragging out from the treasure
house of her learning a lot of cases where the child Christ *does* appear in the
Forbidden Tree, and other cases where the Christ *is* put back on the tree as
the apple. After that, she has not left herself much to scold me for. The
primal incest, I do agree, has come to seem a bit of a bore, and is anyway
very remote from the text of Herbert; but still the Apple which taught
shame and the need for fig-leaves, and that is the primal sin with which
Christ charges himself here, is undoubtedly mixed up with sex somehow;
and I think this verse does something to remind us of that. Why does the
'tree of life' come in, a quite different thing from the Tree of Knowledge
(and also growing in Eden; Miss Tuve appears to assume it is merely the
Cross), except to underline the dim suggestion of the sources of renewal?
Quite detachedly, tasting these wonderful lines with as clean a palate as I
can, I find I cannot now clear away a feeling that the Christ in torment is
made to appear, with ghastly pathos, as an adventurous boy. And come
now, if the whole thing is traditional, what previous author has said that
Christ must *climb* a tree which is not only the Cross and the Tree of Knowledge but also the Tree of Life? I may be excused for suspecting that, if there
was any such reference, Miss Tuve would have known it and quoted it. As
to the general problems which Miss Tuve raises, I can say definitely enough
what line I would take. I don't want to take any advantage of her offer, that
a critic may properly create an entirely new poem out of an old one by re-
interpreting it. This was done with the *Song of Solomon*, for instance, so
the idea is not merely farcical, but I think that a present-day critic has much
more rewarding things to do. He should entirely concentrate on how the
poem was meant to take effect by its author and did take effect on its first
readers. But this formula includes the way in which it took effect on them
without their knowing it, and that opens an Aladdin's Cave of a positively
limestone extent and complexity. What he does need to do is to make clear
how deep he is going, and not toss the reader unexpectedly to the bottom of
some remote internal crevasse. How to survey the thing tolerably smoothly

without doing it at intolerable length I did not know when I wrote this bit of analysis, and I rather fear that, if I have learned at all how to make a better appearance now, it is only at the cost of omitting the profounder parts of the survey.

Herbert's Quaintness

New Statesman, 4 January 1963

T. S. Eliot, *George Herbert*

Mr Eliot's pamphlet in the British Council series was clearly a labour of love, and has been carried out with cool charm. Thoughts of striking originality would be rather out of place, as the intention is to introduce the poet to foreign readers; yet some of Mr Eliot's disciples might be startled to hear him say (quoting 'Prayer I' as illustration) that Herbert's characteristic effects are not witty like Donne but magical like the fairy casements of Keats. He calls *The Temple* 'a more important document than all of Donne's *religious* poems taken together' (no one I think need complain about that), and finds in it 'a kind of gaiety of spirit, a joy in composition which engages our delighted sympathy'. The examples are so various and so well chosen as to make a kind of thumbnail anthology.

Among his quotations from the remarks of the critics, looking forward to the short reading list for further study, and perhaps to lighten the pamphlet a bit, Mr Eliot mentions a rebuttal by Rosemond Tuve (in *A Reading of George Herbert*, 1952) of some paragraphs by me (in *Ambiguity*, 1930) about a monologue called 'The Sacrifice'. Without having anything to grumble about, I want to take this opportunity to say what I think about the poem now, as I have recently had to mull over it again. Elsewhere Herbert speaks in his own person, conveying an entire sincerity and good feeling, and sometimes also an intriguing reserve; but this poem is written as said by Jesus during his trial and crucifixion, and the usual technique is inherently hard to apply. The line recalled in the pamphlet is:

> Man stole the fruit, but I must climb the Tree;

and Mr Eliot finds 'too ludicrous' a thought of Empson that Jesus might be putting the apple back. Here he thinks he is agreeing with Miss Tuve; but she listed a number of medieval epigrams and pictures treating the Christ as an apple on the Tree (her pages 57, 86–89), and as a child in the Tree (83,

89), and she claimed that the idea of his *climbing* the Tree was also familiar, though she gave no actual quotation. Her main complaint was against my ignorance, which had made me treat all this traditional material as a new 'metaphysical' style. The book was full of interesting news, at any rate for most of us; and, certainly, to know that much of a poem is traditional affects your judgement of the author's intention. All the same, the admirers of Herbert have called him homely and quaint for three centuries – in this pamphlet, Mr Eliot quotes Coleridge saying that he used to read Herbert 'to amuse myself with his quaintness' but now (1818) finds the homely language sincere and real. It does not seem likely that such various readers all made the same mistake, and Miss Tuve tacitly admitted that Herbert in this line made his own combination of the stock ideas. I still think it suggests a boy stealing apples, which makes it agonisingly pathetic, and though very strange yet 'homely' in Herbert's manner; also, if you try to make logical deductions from it, your mind can only produce comical ones, because it is another example of what Mr Eliot rightly called magic.

But this is not the central issue. I put 'The Sacrifice' last of the examples in my book, to stand for the most extreme kind of ambiguity, because it presents Jesus as at the same time forgiving his torturers and condemning them to eternal torture. It strikes me now that my attitude was what I have come to call 'neo-Christian'; happy to find such an extravagant specimen, I slapped the author on the back and egged him on to be even nastier. Also I found some puns most of which I would now agree to be impossible, and it was probably a mistake to drag in Freud. Rather to my surprise, Miss Tuve agreed that the poem carries the major ambiguity, which was traditional and noble; after rejecting most of my illustrations, she seemed disposed to treat me as a pagan stumbling towards the light. Clearer now about what the light illuminates, I am keen to stumble away from it. But we seem now to agree on a distinction between the traditional paradoxes, which feel noble, and the 'metaphysical' ones which, whether I invented them or Herbert, feel in bad taste.

The doctrine of the Trinity is necessary, or the Father appears too evil in his 'satisfaction' at the crucifixion of his Son. But to present Jesus as one with the Father only turns him into a hypocrite; when he prays for his enemies to be forgiven, he knows that under his other title he will take his revenge. Herbert avoids the full logic of it, but the wit of his Jesus is sometimes boyishly spiteful, as in verse 37: 'If they go on shouting for my death like that they will choke themselves before it happens.' We need not suppose that this had been sung in Latin every Good Friday for a thousand years. I gave a case where Herbert in revision altered the word-order to fit in an ambiguity:

> I left my crown
> And Father's smile *for you to feel* his frown.

No opponent has yet explained what other purpose he could have. Even this might be an accident, taken alone, but the poem has five or six of them, and the final verse allows of an elegant twist to the meaning of the refrain:

> Only let others say, when I am dead,
> 'Never was grief like mine.'

I should be glad now to have these ambiguities disproved, because I think they spoil the poem (and Keats's 'Ode on Melancholy' would be enough to show that a good poem can be radically ambiguous); but I think they are historically probable. It was in the air of Herbert's time that the paradoxes of Christianity were a moral embarrassment, whereas the medieval liturgists had somehow felt content with their harsh echoing splendour. The basic need for Metaphysical Wit, though seldom its conscious purpose, was to keep these new qualms at bay.

Mr Eliot remarks that Herbert retained a warm regard for his elder brother, a Deist, and was on affectionate terms with the saintly bishop Lancelot Andrews. In 1612 the consistory which handed over Bartholomew Legate to be burnt was 'strengthened by the presence' of the saintly bishop. Legate was a cloth merchant, which involved business relations with freethinking Holland, and maintained that Jesus was termed God in Scripture 'not from his essence but from his office', though he had been 'born free from sin' (DNB). This was more than Herbert's brother would allow to Jesus, and it seems that Legate was so surprised by English law that he threatened an action for false imprisonment. The burning of Wightman at Lichfield later in the year, where the crowd got scorched removing the faggots when he recanted as the fire reached him (but a few weeks later he endured to the end), was the last in England. The executions 'outraged public opinion' (*Development of Toleration*, W. K. Jordan); it couldn't stand any more, whereas the saintly bishop could. George Herbert took his BA that year, and we need not suppose that he attended these representations of Hell on earth. But surely we could understand his taking a rather uneasy tone about this aspect of the Christ; to suppose that his style was exactly like a medieval one does not seem to me even plausible.

Mr Eliot writes for once with a touch of asperity when he rebuts the sentimental preface to an old edition, in case it came into the hands of a foreign student: country parsonages were not peaceful then, he rightly insists. On the other hand, while showing how much the poet has been admired by non-Christian critics, he seems to report with sympathy an idea that the poet was 'driven to shelter' by an ingrained self-distrust. No doubt Herbert would be expected to expose his Puritan and Catholic parishioners to heavy fines; but he might have creditable reasons for thinking a country parsonage at least comparatively peaceful.

An Early Romantic: Henry Vaughan

Cambridge Review 50, 31 May 1929

Vaughan is a continual and close imitator of Herbert, both as to images (bees, shooting stars, and so forth, which are not particularly suited to his own mind), actual conceits, subjects and forms of poems as a whole. An example at random is

> 'Arise, arise, they come.' Look how they run.
> Alas, what haste they make to be undone.
> How with their lanterns do they seek the sun.[1]

(said by the Christ in Gethsemane – Herbert; and Vaughan, of the angels running between Heaven and earth on Ascension Day)

> They pass as at the last great day, and run
> In their white robes to seek the Risen Sun.[2]

A typical borrowing, where the point of the pun is left out. It is interesting to see how far Herbert's individual style could be used by so different a mind.

Different, in that his most effective passages are not metaphysical at all; it is often an apprehension of Nature, not an intellectual activity, which is at the focus of his consciousness. Wordsworth possessed an edition of his poems; the accident is historically an important one. From the poem on Joy:

> He weighs not your forced accents, who can have
> A lesson played him by a wind or wave.   ['Joy']

The point is not that this shows interest in Nature; Herbert often had such lessons played him, but he was interested in working out the particular lesson, not in the experience that extracted it from Nature; at any rate he would not have thought a generalisation about it had enough point or colour to be poetical. Nor does Vaughan seem anxious to remember what the lessons were, he is thinking merely of a state of melancholy peace experienced when he was out walking, and implying that it did him good, without conscious effort of his own.

> I have owed to them ('these forms of beauty')
> – feelings too
> Of unremembered pleasure; such perhaps
> As may have had no trivial influence
> On that blest portion of a good man's life;
> His little, nameless, unremembered acts
> Of kindness and of love.
>
> (Wordsworth)

Once you are interested mainly in such influences the whole seventeenth-century emphasis on conscious will and the discursive intellect becomes un-necessary and unwise. Vaughan's poem goes on

> Thou hast
> Another mirth, a mirth, though overcast
> With clouds and rain, yet full as calm and free
> As those clear heights which above tempests shine. ['Joy']

(I remember some critic producing 'It is a beauteous evening, calm and *free*' as a noble adjective, typical of its author, which was invented to suit the rhyme.)

I suppose it was in Wales that he sniffed the wide air of the mountains, and watched the thunder-clouds advancing into the valleys. It is perfectly good Wordsworth. Amusing, incidentally, to compare

> So in sighs and unseen tears
> Pass thy solitary years,
> And, going hence, leave written on some tree
> 'Sighs make joy sure, and shaking fosters thee.' ['Joy']

with Wordsworth's 'Lines left upon a seat in a yew tree which stands near the lake of Esthwaite', etc.; they seem, while adopting this suggestion, to reprove the extravagance of its tone.

> This is the heart he craves; and whose will
> But give it him and grudge not, he shall feel
> That God is true, as herbs unseen
> Put on their youth and green.

> Dear stream, dear bank, where often I
> Have sate, and pleased my pensive eye...[3]

(He recited flatly a flat emotion, and expects the reader's indulgence because it is about Nature)

> What sublime truths and wholesome themes
> Lodge in thy mystical, deep streams.

Sublimity mentioned but not expressed, 'wholesome', the streams of a stream (or of a bank) introduced for the sake of rhyme, and this entirely debased use of 'mystical' – it is surprising to find it all outside the nineteenth century.

As a bridge between this and Herbert, Vaughan's dramatic use of Nature –

> So hills and valleys into singing break,
> And though poor stones have neither speech nor tongue,
> While active winds and streams both run and speak,
> Yet stones are deep in admiration.   ['The Bird']

In part it is a conceit about stones in general, as one of the four elements; in part, from the setting, it seems to be the boulders on the hill side, struck dumb in the presence of the precipices, and in a giant silence waiting for their fall. For Palm Sunday

> Put on, put on your best array,
> Let the joyed road make holiday,
> And flowers, that into fields do stray,
> Or secret groves, keep the highway.[4]

Parts of Nature outcast and retiring, like Jesus, are to be brought, on this day of his showing forth, into the agora; there is both a conceit on the connection of Nature and the tribe through the cult-hero and an implied description of the solitary wanderings, the communing with Nature, of the Christ.

> Such was the bright world, on the first seventh day,
> Before man brought forth sin, or sin decay.
> When, like a virgin, clad in flowers and green,
> The pure earth sat; and the fair woods had seen
> No frost, but flourished in their youthful vest
> With which the great Creator had them dressed.
> When Heaven above them shined like molten glass
> While all the planets did unclouded pass,
> And springs, like dissolved pearls, their streams did pour,
> Ne'r marred with floods, nor angered with a shower.[2]

The last four lines do something very impressive with the manner of Dryden; his gong-like note, coming into this exalted and sensuous view of Nature, suggests that before the Fall the whole mechanism of the spheres, an enormous orrery, a circumterrestrial clockwork, could be seen going in the sky. It is these evanescent but powerful suggestions (like Milton's two-handed engine) that Vaughan gains by blurring the outline and losing the energy of the true Herbert conceit.

> God's saints are shining lights; who stays
>   Here long must pass
> O'er dark hills, swift streams, and steep ways
>   As smooth as glass.

One does not separate them in one's mind; it is the Romantic movement's effect; dark hair, tidal water, landscape at dusk, are dissolved in your mind, as often in dreams, into an apparently direct sensory image which cannot be attached to any one of the senses. This dreamlike or hypnotic intensity is never far out of sight in Vaughan's work (hence, like the Romantics, and unlike Herbert, the ruck of his work is merely bad); when it can be combined with the self-respect of conceits he is very impressive.

(Of Cain)   If single thou
> – Though single voices are but low –
> Couldst such a shrill and long cry rear,
> As speaks still in thy Maker's ear,
> What thunders shall those men arraign
> Who cannot count those they have slain;

(Sir Walter Scott)
> Who bathe not in a shallow flood,
> But in a wide, deep sea of blood?
> A sea, whose loud waves cannot sleep
> But deep still calleth unto deep;
> Whose urgent sound, like unto that
> Of many waters, beateth at
> The everlasting doors above
> Where souls behind the altar move
> And with one strong incessant cry
> Enquire How Long of the Most High.   ['Abel's Blood']

Notes

1 Herbert, 'The Sacrifice'.
2 Vaughan, 'Ascension-Day'.
3 Vaughan, 'The Water-fall'.
4 Vaughan, 'Palm-Sunday'.

The Love of Definition

Cambridge Review, C, 25 May 1979

E. S. Donno (ed.), *Andrew Marvell: The Critical Heritage*

C. A. Patrides (ed.), *Approaches to Marvell: The York Tercentenary Lectures*

This number of the Heritage series was inherently hard to edit, as there is so little early comment on the poetry. The preface says that the book will 'trace the development of Marvell's reputation,' so it gives Milton's letter to Bradshaw recommending him as an assistant Latin Secretary. A good idea, but then we need more of such documents. Just before Marvell was made MP for Hull he was made freeman of the city, and the citation says that he had done good work for Hull already. What does this mean? I was hoping for a text of it. We are given much secondhand biography, of a soothing character. It is nice to know that A. C. Benson (1892) felt Marvell when MP 'had his expenses paid by the Corporation,' but there had better be a footnote saying it is not in the accounts. Cooke's preface to his edition of 1726 gives the earliest version I know of the story of the flaunting courtier visiting his garret to offer a bribe when he was penniless, but the *Heritage* allows us hardly more than a page from Cooke, leaving this out. Many people must have reflected that Popple, Thompson, etc. would not be in the habit of exposing a fulltime agent to so much temptation, and this book should have examined the myth more directly. It does not drop one hint of the accusations of sodomy and impotence, in the replies to the 'Rehearsal', and yet surely this is part of his 'reputation'? Besides, the lack of evidence for casual relations with women is part of the evidence for his secret marriage.[1]

Still, the book has a continual mild gossip-interest; and it does at least show that the poetry was not ignored for two centuries; it was merely found dull. Mason's 'Ode to Independency' (1756) is only concerned to praise the Satires, but first praises the earlier poems as if he had read them:

and in the next age even the severe Jeffrey praised them for their tenderness. There is a graceful picture of Hazlitt denouncing the poem about Holland as not funny, but laughed down by Lamb and Leigh Hunt. None of them could endure the 'conceits', or not if they were 'forced', but then, no more could T. S. Eliot. He deserves much credit for appreciating a style so unlike his own, and of course wrote a famous essay for the tercentenary of the birth (1921). Two years later, he happened to write that Bishop King was the greater poet; and the *Heritage*, though it stops at 1921, allows a footnote to include this titbit. The main point seems to be that the reputation of Marvell only came to the boil after his centenary in the twenties. By the way, the dust-cover here presents him as an immensely complacent lady-killer, or professional cad, with no pretence of reference to actual portraits; pictures on dust-covers have been getting steadily worse, but this one could not even help to sell the book.

The York Lectures are a mixed bag in themselves, and some of them survey the various interpretations of Marvell since the twenties. Thus my old friend B. Rajan (everybody named here is a Professor) has a firm background when he calls his lecture 'The aesthetics of inconclusiveness' and takes for granted that 'a controlled uncertainty is the objective' in all the major poems of Marvell. He recalls an edition by J. H. Summers which gave three incompatible readings for each case examined. Rajan lets drop that this has given rise to exasperation, and it is also a good occasion for blasphemy; I think it proves that the grand American theory is all wrong. Marvell becomes a test case. The point where Rajan became incredible, I thought, was when he said that Marvell himself might be 'not displeased' at finding that his poems caused exasperation, or even, apparently, at hearing them called 'treacherous'. He would have become violently offended at that word.

Most of the critics I blame here are foreigners, so I had better bring in an Englishman early. The English have not the American theoretical drive, but this does not keep them pure. A comment on 'The Definition of Love' gives a typical example:

> And therefore her Decrees of Steel
> Us at the distant Poles have plac'd,
> (Though Loves whole World on us doth wheel)
> Not by themselves to be embrac'd.

A. J. Smith said in his lecture: 'That parenthesis so nicely takes off the Donne mode as to be almost tongue in cheek.' The reservation *almost* makes no difference to the insinuation, merely insisting that the judgement of the critic is exquisite. He is sure that any knowing man at the time found the trope deliciously ridiculous, the silliest of all the metaphysical pedantries, just as he does. But it was used by Carew, a smooth courtier if ever there was one, with splendid easiness, to introduce his best poem ('Those flowers, as in their causes, sleep'). Would Marvell still be jeering if he was imitating Carew? The cosy chortle of the snob is out of place here, because it assumes more knowledge than we have got. This pair of lovers has become the platonic ideal of such a thing, laid up in Heaven, from which all the standard properties of it, found in ordinary cases, derive; and the elevation is deserved because in this case the inherent readiness for self-sacrifice is forced to an extreme. Marvell does not use the trope elsewhere, but for once it was entirely suited. Surely it would be very *booksy* of Marvell, at this high moment, to distract attention onto a jeer at the style of Donne, who was not even a living rival? I grant that there is a touch of humour all along, because of the neatness of these wild assertions, but the persons in view to be laughed at are *we*, the lovers themselves, one of whom makes this cosmic claim. It is assumed that the situation is a familiar one. I take it that Marvell could not get married in the ordinary way because (although he had assisted Hull during the Civil War) he had refused to sign up with Popple's firm, so as to get a salary, reserving himself for higher things; but one does not need all that. Such obstacles were very frequent in life, though not described by love-poetry, so a reader at the time would not feel mystified. There had been at least one time when Marvell felt them keenly frustrating, though perhaps not just when he wrote the poem, and had consoled himself by reflecting that the situation was majestically familiar, a standard feature of human affairs.

These critics are often right in pointing out some nuance, but wrong when they yield to the craving to make it spicy. This is a bit hard to feel about C. A. Patrides, when he tells us that Marvell intended, at the end of 'Appleton House', to jeer at the young pupil of Marvell, who becomes a kind of goddess of the estate. As a Christian, explains the critic, he ought to despise her for being fallen like all the rest of us; and sure enough he 'associates her' with a comet, and the baneful parasite mistletoe, and (very indirectly) with a traitor-worm in an oak; so she is 'at least a threat'. Come now, Marvell was a susceptible young man much impressed by the estate, and had already written poems to girl children; there is no reason to doubt that he was bowled over by the stolid well-meaning heiress. No doubt he did not expect even her father to believe him when he described her magical power, though her father was willing to toy with such ideas; but Marvell was in no mood to jeer. Every detail that Patrides can find to prove she was a witch is real, and there were real Christians too, bright with craving to kill witches. Marvell was brave enough to ignore this powerful trend of thought, which Patrides apparently endorses. All the same, I think he does discover a slight undercurrent in the verse about her eventual marriage; but he has got it upside-down; Marvell expected her to be the victim not the wrong-doer:

> And, like a *sprig of Mistleto,*
> On the *Fairfacian Oak* does grow;
> Whence, for some universal good,
> The *Priest* shall cut the sacred Bud;
> While her *glad Parents* most rejoice,
> And make their *Destiny* their *Choice.*   [st. 93]

When the time came, Fairfax saved his estates by marrying her to the rake Buckingham, who neglected her shamefully. Her parents 'make their destiny their choice' merely in the sense that they excused the deed 'with necessity, the tyrant's plea'. I am glad to learn that Marvell wrote this rather bold hint into his poem of flattery; but presumably at the time the prophecy would seem very remote, and Marvell says it very tactfully. So maybe the parents never noticed.

Two other moves to belittle Marvell call for an answer. R. Ellrodt, speaking from France, describes an honest difficulty in getting an impression of Marvell, or even seeing the point of his poems, and decides that it is 'tempting ... to consider Marvell as a poet mainly interested in the craft of poetry'. He was so cool and detached that he could be at once a poet and a politician, so here too he was purely aesthetic. The picture is very unlike Marvell, but I hoped that this severe critic would at least admire 'The Coronet'. He grants that the poem shows a 'keen awareness of impure motives', but adds:

The discovery is not surprising and the poem derives its power from the mastery of form, not from any subtlety of psychological analysis.

The lack of any sense of reality here is majestic. But what other religious poet, writing at the time in English, had any conception of this unsurprising thing? Who did afterwards, except Dr Johnson, and is he not enough to keep the minority vote from seeming trivial? It is an explosive poem, and perhaps Marvell was wise never to print it. To say that the power is in the form seemed to me a howler, even if meant as a compliment; if the technique is not used to say something, it is not used at all; but I am glad to have been made to realise that the poem does have an adequate form. It is a sonnet with an extra quatrain in the first part, leading in to the shock of the sestet, *Alas I find the serpent old,* and after the sestet an eight-line coda combines two other forms of sestet; it begins *But thou who only,* and continues line after line each with a sustained astonishment, as in the madrigals. A powerful form; but it was hammered out to carry a firm and passionate mental operation: it meant the end of his religious poetry. There seems to be a general unwillingness among critics to let Marvell mean what he said; B. K. Lewalski, who lectured on the religious poetry, thinks that the last line, 'May crown thy feet ...' implies a permission for some types of religious poetry, just a few types, enough to permit everything that comes afterwards in the book. But before the fierce paradox of crowning the feet *these* must first *wither*, and their *frame* must be *shattered* too; it might have been argued that 'these' were not the simple flowers, only the towers perhaps, but the poem says both have to go. The order of poems in the book thus becomes a problem, and it has been pointed out that the publisher might see a slight precaution in putting the best religious poems first. The volume begins with three startlingly good ones, and continues with minor ones till the eighth, where the 'Nymph Complaining' presents a child who discovers the truths of religion independently. There are no further specifically religious poems. I suggest that Marvell did begin by writing religious poems, in considerable turmoil of mind, and we know that one of them was twice set to music; he was doing quite well at it, and when he said he was stopping he really stopped. After all, some are certainly out of order; no one believes that 'Tom May's Death' was written soon after 'Appleton House'. 'The Coronet' takes the Puritan suspicion of religious art to its final extremity, and you may find this crazy or perverse; but if you want the poem at all you do not want it castrated.

I was sorry to see that Christopher Hill, in his excellent survey of the political acts and contacts of Marvell, accepts the theory that 'Tom May's Death' was written or at least altered after the Restoration, when the corpse of May was thrown out of Westminster Abbey. He thinks that this 'makes it a less unpleasant poem ... and opens up the possibility of all sorts of ironical overtones'. It would become a disgusting poem, and the cowardice and the meanness of the turncoat would be thrust upon the public attention; the action could not even make him safer, because it would give many people an itch to reply. But if one accepts the obvious time-sequence the poem is not unpleasant at all. While still in his twenties, he arrives home romantically backing the side which had already lost the war; he comes to see faults on both sides (the 'Horatian Ode') and wishes not to make use of either side – at this stage he could feel violent irritation at a colleague who had cashed in by writing for the winners. He is then abruptly won over by admiration for General Fairfax, but the General himself has just resigned in protest against part of the government policy, so Marvell is still allowed a balance of judgement. Even so, he has made a decisive swing, so far from continuing to teeter among ambiguities. Also, it is only assumed that he could not have prophesied the later casting out of the bones; well, I grant he was a bad hand at prophecy, but any Cavalier would have said as much. May died in September 1649, and by that time all the copies of the King's

Book on sale were carrying the letter from Prince Charles promising his father to carry on with his policy. And the details about the carcass, how it will be eaten by birds, dogs and worms, and its bones will be broken, would apply equally to the body of Cromwell – if written in 1661. In December 1660 Marvell wrote to the mayor of Hull that the body of Cromwell and three others, by a vote of the House, were to be 'drawn with all expedition possible, upon a hurdle to Tyburn, there to be hanged for a while and then buried under the gallows'.

> Thee *Cerberus* with all his Jawes shall gnash,
> *Megaera* thee with all her Serpents lash.
> Though rivited unto *Ixion's* wheel
> Shalt break, and the perpetual Vulture feel.
> 'Tis just what Torments Poets ere did feign;
> Though first Historically shouldst sustain.

Jolly enough in itself; he seems not to believe in any Hell at all. But if the lines were written after September 1661, when the bones of May were extruded, May would have lost his priority. Marvell had written about Cromwell with personal affection, and he was not at this time in a state of abject terror; he seems more concerned to preserve his dignity than his skin.

There are two magnificent lectures in the series, standing quite apart, by Ricks and Carey; and both these authors evidently find Marvell transparent – they are not puzzled by him, let alone betrayed. The poetry does say, as they both explain, that the human creature in the world is inherently puzzled or betrayed; but a reader of the poetry is granted, for the time, a more lofty viewpoint. The essays themselves made me feel I was reading two new poems by Marvell. Presumably the authors would not be able to answer many of the questions raised in the other essays, but such questions no longer seem important, and all those accusations as to character just melt away. Such a critic inherently claims to know what the author finds interesting, what he would be wanting to say; and this is justified (though of course it might need further justification) by giving an immediate satisfaction. The two lectures are much alike, but Ricks is concerned with the idea of being self-inwoven, as when the dew-drop 'round in itself encloses' or in the conceit 'mine own precipice I go'. I feared that the sad cult of solipsism was going to crop up; 'A poem should not mean, but be' has so often turned out to mean 'the ideal poem is about poetical techniques and jealous quarrels with other poets'; so it was a refreshing surprise when Ricks found the trope typical of civil war, and produced a group of recent Ulster poets who also make great use of it. I doubt whether the Civil War was a crucial influence on Marvell, because he can apply his method to such a variety of themes; but one can't deny that it fits in. Also this account of his mind allows him to be an excitable poet, usually writing from impulse and sometimes foolishly; he does not need to work out his standard effects, arranging a special point of view (this I think is what has made so many people recently find him a pig), because he finds them inherent in the world all the time.

Carey, in his Inaugural Lecture on becoming a Professor, announced a rigorous policy; there must be no more paraphrase, no reading in or spelling out, because all such tampering with a text was the work of Vandals. I came in for some of the rough stuff myself, and thought he could have found stronger examples in what I wrote fifty years ago, though I would never have intentionally gone beyond the intention of an author, either in his consciousness or his unconsciousness. But it struck me that the programme as he announced it was actually incompatible with teaching, let alone his own style of written criticism; it became a question whether he would achieve a Houdini-like reappearance. But here he is beside Ricks, both of them galumphing like the new dinosaurs, each of them the weight of ten elephants and yet as agile as a kitten. He takes the general theme that Marvell's poetry is about 'restriction — the condition of being thwarted, confined and enmeshed' (or perhaps this need not be more general than Ricks's theme; the drop of dew is not confined, only self-absorbed); but he is not himself confined to his theme. I quote a description of the forest birds in 'Appleton House':

> The arching Boughs unite between
> The Columnes of the Temple green;
> And underneath the winged Quires
> Echo about their tuned Fires.   [ll. 509–12]

The poem says no more about them. Carey says:

The clamorous and bewildering bird-filled grove is conveyed through the syntax. The birds do not sing, but echo, as if in the pulsating air echo extinguished song. And they 'echo' about themselves, flashing like fire through the grove, seemingly substanceless, with their noise not issuing from them but quivering in the atmosphere.

The syntax does seem deliberately blurred, so it is reasonable to expect that Marvell would be pleased to hear that it had conveyed so much. I think this a splendid reading-in, and can even agree that the birds flash across, though the nightingale in the next verse sits still, and there is no mention of flashing anywhere near. But such a reading may sometimes be wrong about the author's intention, or, even if the author did feel optimistic when he blurred the syntax, his hopes may sometimes fail. What you can say is that Ricks and Carey are deeply in sympathy with the author, knowing what he often wants to do, so that they can get a remarkable amount into their interpretation; it is a welcome advance on Carey's Inaugural.

One of the lectures is so malignant that it calls for a detailed rebuttal. This is by J. A. Wittreich, on Marvell's poem in defence of *Paradise Lost*, which was printed in its second edition (1674), the year of Milton's death. Parker had attacked Milton as Marvell's friend while answering (1673) the first part of the 'Rehearsal,' and anything drawing attention to Milton might encourage attacks upon him at that excited time. Wondering why Milton accepted such a faulty tribute, Wittreich admits that Milton would realise that 'history demanded of Marvell the kind of defence he provided'; this proves, I submit, that Wittreich has no reason for his view except the presumption that Marvell is treacherous. Marvell says he approached *Paradise Lost* with alarm, but found as he read on that it omits everything improper and includes all that is fit; as to the style, as usual it is majestic and soars above human reach. He had feared that Milton would be like blind Samson, groping the Temple posts in spite. Wittreich objects that Milton had denied that Samson was actuated by spite: but spite was what the royalists would call it. Marvell seems bold to admit alarm, but it makes him a more reassuring spokesman; and what a lot there had been to fear he does not tell. Presumably he knew that Milton was an Arian. Most readers would expect Milton to rebuke God for having failed to support the Commonwealth, and make a few cracks in favour of polygamy, but nothing worse; so Marvell's treatment is adroit. Wittreich then makes a graver attack; Marvell is belittling a rival. He 'invites a retrospective glance at his own poetry' because 'Milton took the flight for which Marvell spent a lifetime preparing.' Marvell invites no glance, and had positively renounced religious poetry. Wittreich says that Marvell presents himself as leader of a rival school because he goes on rhyming, when Milton's preface on the next page of the 1674 edition tells him to stop. But Milton says 'in longer works especially', such as 'our best English tragedies'; of course one would continue rhyming in a brief verse compliment – not to do that would be pretentious. Indeed, Marvell does not present himself as a poet at all:

> Their Fancies like our bushy Points appear,
> The Poets tag them; we for fashion wear.
> I too transported by the *Mode* offend,
> And while I meant to *Praise* thee, must Commend.

'We' are the men-about-town, who of course can turn out a compliment, but have to follow the fashion, obeying the poets. Wittreich has already objected that 'commendation is the ultimate form of praise,' and claimed the support of the OED; a commender 'places the person commended under his own protection'. A reader 'misses the wit of the couplet', says Wittreich,

unless he realises that Marvell, regretting that he has to give excessive
praise, insinuates that rhyme 'may sometimes be an advantage'. This
example proves that the hold of Wittreich on the English language is an extremely shaky one, as might be expected. *Commend* is cold and dignified
and usually describes a grading by a superior; Marvell says he has to use it
for a rhyme, in place of a word that sounds warm and humble. There would
be no wit in the nastiness invented by Wittreich.

So it is still going on; this case is on a par with the theory that the shepherdess in 'The Coronet' was a 'recherché bawd' (thus proving that the
critic has no ear), and that the 'Nymph Complaining' is troubled by a slight
exhaustion after enjoying all the wanton troopers. Carey was right to call
such writers Vandals, but it is hard to say where the line should be drawn:
we certainly do not want a rule that critics must always whitewash authors.
Perhaps it would be enough to ask that, when they make or imply a judgement about an author's character, they should supply evidence from his biography. Wittreich does that, but he invents it; still, his procedure is more
humane than the refusal to admit help from biography, or any intention in
the author.

Note

1 For the full development of Empson's research behind this casual remark, see 'The
Marriage of Marvell', *Using Biography* (London: Chatto & Windus, 1984), pp. 43–95.

Rochester[1]

New Statesman and Nation, 28 November 1953

V. de S. Pinto (ed.), *Poems by John Wilmot, Earl of Rochester*

Professor Pinto's handy edition of Rochester is very welcome; it has been rather hard to get hold of a text. Apparently only two poems, of those considered genuine, were considered unprintable; to put a few of the more pointed and crucial verses in the notes, on the ground that they were cut from the Tonson edition, is not really distracting to the student.

Rochester became a legend in his own lifetime, and still more after his early repentant death, as the Type Case of the wicked lord of Charles II's court, roistering, sceptical and cynical, exquisite and depraved. Any obscene poem would be ascribed to him, like a proverb to Solomon; and even those who most reprobated his wickedness spoke of him with a certain awe and admiration. As Professor Pinto remarks, he was felt to be an explorer into human experience, with a kind of scientific interest (one must think of the newly formed Royal Society); he had gone into one of the possible ways of life as far as it was conceivable to go. 'His sins were like his parts,' says a pious biographer, meaning his intellectual brilliance; 'for from them corrupted they sprang, all of them high and extraordinary. He seemed to affect something singular and paradoxical in his impieties, as well as in his writings, above the Reach and Thought of other men.' His sins turn into his impieties; the point is not that they were pleasant but that they seemed a kind of blasphemy against normal life. They are connected both with religious disbelief and with the desire to be almost impossibly aristocratic; he was the last word in being a lord.

He fitted in with a fashion, but it is hard to know what the real impulses were. The Restoration turned so strongly against the Rule of the Saints that quite odd behaviour seemed justified merely because it didn't interfere with other people's enjoyment (a reaction which parts of the modern world might see again); there was a positive though vague feeling that the pleasure-loving man who satisfies his own nature thereby becomes kind to others, and a certain amount of cheating as well as self-indulgence could be included in this picture. A lot of upper-class persons, it seems obvious, were pretending to be reckless about the life of pleasure while really they were looking after their health and their money with decent care (indeed the gambler, one of the central types for this display of courage, could almost boast of this twist). But Rochester simply rode himself to death, with cries of despair and a sort of grim determination, and died at the age of thirty-three. One might think he died of a mistaken idea that his habits were required by fashion, which only makes him seem a fool. But nobody in his time thought of him so cheaply, though they complained at his getting other people into trouble; he seemed a man driven on by some unexplained force to torment himself like a saint; and that is what he says himself in his greatest poetry.

It seems to be assumed he died of syphilis, drink, and premature exhaustion, but one must always be a bit suspicious about the medicine of earlier times. Anyhow, it is clear that if he had survived his last illness he would have come out an entirely different man; Professor Pinto well points out that what little is known of his final religious discussions is not anything like a frightened betrayal of his intelligence. One might even feel that he died before he had stopped being a very clever spoiled child. But nothing later could have affected the inherent appeal of the few great lyrics, in which his feelings revolt against the life of pleasure, and he tries to understand why he has a kind of duty to stick to it, even though there is obviously no pleasure in it.

Not that he was sour about pleasure; his attitude to it has a heart-warming generosity. Humanly speaking, his obscenity is the most moral thing about him, indeed the chief thing that appears obscene is that he will have no nonsense about jealousy at all. The excuse for leaving his mistress (number xix in this edition) is that it is her mission to go to bed with all mankind; it might have been a 'banter' expected to annoy her, but even so it rises out of this possible bad temper into a splendidly gay picture of universal kindness, which really does treat her as a goddess. He was not at all the type of lady-killer who boasts of his powers; my impression had been that he often laughed at himself in verse for being impotent on some important occasion, but apparently Professor Pinto considers those poems spurious (wrongly, I suspect, without knowing the evidence); in any case, the tone of the accepted ones is the same. He does of course boast of his extreme indifference to scandal, as in the occasional claims to have enjoyed sodomy, but that is another thing. (By the way, the modern idea that it is an 'incurable disease', cutting him off from pleasure with women, would have seemed as absurd to him as to, say, Ovid or Genghis Khan.) He praises pleasure as a philosopher, whose serious opinion is that it makes people kind to each other. There is enough truth in this, especially after wars of religion, to have a startling moral weight.[2]

Inherent in the delightful ease of his style there is also a puzzle about class. The reason why he could talk in this absolutely plain-man way was that he was a great lord and a favourite of the king; a person of lower class, such as a university professor or a Puritan preacher, would obviously have to talk in a more affected manner. The trouble with the style of Donne had been that it stank of the professional classes; only in real high life could a man learn to talk so that anybody could understand him at once. This obscure claim has somehow stuck to the English language; and it does not much matter whether the 'easiness' of Rochester, in a particular case, was in effect harshly insolent at the time. I think the moral to be drawn is that class differences are less important than they appear but get used, like the American Parties, to carry any controversy that is going forward. It sounds a rosy view, but probably one could find other cases where a frightfully superior young lord had the effect of publicising a democratic way of talking.

This absolute duty to display 'ease' (for example, after being challenged to a duel, or gambling away the property due to your son) has to be remembered before it seems sensible to call the lyrics of Rochester very deep. As so often in criticism, one isn't sure whether this curious effect has been thought too obvious to be worth mentioning. Take even the poem, 'All my past life is mine no more', which ends

> Then talk not of Inconstancy,
>   False Hearts, and broken Vows;
> If I, by Miracle, can be
> This live-long Minute true to thee
> 'Tis all that Heav'n allows.

The violence of the meaning, the intensity of the idea of love presumed, the rigid logic of the philosophical argument – all that belongs to the style of Donne, but what was admired in Rochester was to do it so gracefully that it now appears conventional. Or take

> Absent from thee I languish still,
>   Then ask me not when I return;
> The straying Fool t'will plainly kill,
>   To wish all Day, all Night to Mourn.

> Dear, from thine Arms then let me flie,
>   That my Fantastick Mind may prove
> The Torments it deserves to try,
>   That tears my fixt Heart from my Love.

It goes on to say he wishes he may die as soon as he gets to bed with the only woman he likes (almost certainly his wife; his marriage was not as you might think arranged but involved a passionate struggle, including getting himself into jail) because it is the only way to avoid being stolen away from her by one of the appalling women he meets elsewhere. I think the first verse means 'Don't ask me to come back, because if I feel not only my own pain but also remorse at yours it will kill me,' but the effort to write smoothly has made him blur the point of the antithesis. One might think it all rather too weepy, from a man who seems to have so little to worry about; and to end with 'everlasting rest' seems rather a trick from a man who boasted he did not believe in Heaven. What saves the poem is the wild claim that his 'fantastic mind' somehow needs 'the torments it deserves to try'. One is prepared to believe it of him. He is a test case, I think, against some recent critics who have said that one ought to ignore biography because a poem ought to stand by itself – if one didn't believe Rochester, his poems couldn't come off properly.

I noticed a recent critic writing on one of the great anthology pieces, 'An age in her embraces past Would seem a winter's day,' who said that there is only one good or deep verse,

> Fantastick Fancies fondly move,
> And in frail Joys believe,
> Taking false Pleasure for true Love,
> But Pain can ne'er deceive.

and that it is merely tacked on to an otherwise conventional poem. But this is only so if you read the rest of the poem conventionally, as a polite excuse for being unfaithful, perhaps; the whole puzzle about Rochester is that he makes the smooth convention of the Restoration love-poem seem so serious. Indeed, the excellent change of tone in the middle, when he jeers at his supposed critics:

> You wiser Men, despise me not,
>   Whose Love-sick Fancy raves,
> On Shades of Souls, and Heav'n knows what;
>   Short Ages live in Graves.
>
> When e'er those wounding Eyes, so full
>   Of Sweetness, you did see,
> Had you not been profoundly dull
>   You had gone made like me –

would apply to this critic well. I am not sure what the line about graves need be made to mean, but it keeps up the pressure very adequately. In any case, the whole claim of the argument is that he needed to torment himself; he couldn't be sure his love was true unless he tried the alternatives and found they really hurt him.

The 'Satire on Man' is, I understand, partly imitated from the French, and no doubt would not be tidy even if properly finished; one cannot help regarding it less as a general truth than as a source of evidence about the deep dissatisfaction or resentment with the world which drove him to his death. The most powerful section is an argument as with hammer-blows that all human actions proceed from fear:

> Wronged shall he live, insulted o'er, oppressed,
> Who dares be less a villain than the rest –   [ll. 166–67]

so that the only question is, 'Who's a knave of the first rate?' All this is grand, but one might also wish the fanatics were *more* timid; and it doesn't explain why he himself had to fight so killingly hard to become a knave of the first rate – that seems clearly not done out of fear. (By the way, Professor Pinto refutes a story about his shirking a duel, but that wouldn't have been done out of fear either.) What made him do it one can't know, though guesses can be made; but anyhow he had a great influence. It took a number of pretty wild characters to create the placid and apparently unbreakable world of the eighteenth century.

Notes

1 Untitled in original.

2 Compare Empson's later remarks in a letter responding to a review by Anne Barton, 'That Night at Farnham' (*London Review of Books*, vol. 5, no. 15, pp. 18–19):

'"That Night at Farnham" remarks, speaking of James I: "The king and the labouring man both seem to have made the same extraordinary psychological separation between sodomy and what they themselves felt and did." Sodomy has been defined, not long before, as "sexual relations between man and man (or man and beast)", and we are told that it was "officially" regarded as so unnatural that it shocked even the devil, who was therefore not its patron. I think that the solution of the puzzle is obvious, though to explain how the confusion became so general might take a bit of psychology, or politics.

'Anal penetration was what shocked even the devil, and many homosexuals can satisfy one another without it. Consider the "labourer" (so-called) who was shocked and indignant at being accused of sodomy with his apprentice, who slept in the same bed, for want of another no doubt. If each of them was masturbating himself it would seem rude not to "give a hand" to the other, a process undoubtedly not so unnatural as to shock the Devil. Of course there are stages between that and the accursed thing, but it is hard to get evidence about them. As to Shakespeare saying "to my purpose nothing", he was always careful to avoid possible legal trouble, and seems at that age to have been rather prone to boast of success with the girls, and might well feel it would be bad taste to express hope for success with an earl. The phrase is comical rather than sanctimonious. In general, a theatre with boys acting as girls must be expected to extract fun from the charm of boys; this was regarded as innocent, so long as it was remote from anal penetration.

'I agree, however, that so widespread a confusion was not likely to survive against the intention of a Tudor or Stuart government, or even without its active support. The trick seems rather a healthy one. Young people are to grow up believing that there is one really dreadful thing about love between men, but if you keep right away from that it is good, as we are told by Christ and Plato. The penalty for the dreadful thing is death, but it never has to be inflicted in London, whatever the JPs in Somerset may get up to. One must expect so appalling a thing to be rare. In this way a decent moral tone may be preserved, without running into a great deal of public indecency, let alone the reprisals from important people which might be expected.

'It was a civilised arrangement, and ought not to be regarded with blank astonishment, merely emphasised by an appeal to "psychology", which presumes that they were all mad' (*London Review of Books*, vol. 5, no. 16, 1983, p. 4).

Gray's Cat[1]

'Ode on the Death of a Favourite Cat, Drowned in a Tub of Gold Fishes', 1747

The puzzle as between metaphor and allegory comes out well in Gray's 'Cat', a large poem, I think, though almost blatantly charming, so that people think it a small one. I wrote about it in *Ambiguity* [3rd edition, revised, 1953, pp. 121–22] and think what I said is all right except for some final remarks about Dr Johnson, but am not asking the reader to look them up. There are almost two ways of reading it according as you stress the cat or the 'beauties' (upperclass young women) to whom it is compared; I mean it seems either small and charming (sad about the cat) or large and allegorical ('ghastly truths about human life thrust themselves upon us even in trivial incidents' – nobody cares a rap for the cat). The two were connected for Gray because he very likely cared more for Walpole's cat than for most people he knew; they are badly connected for us because of Poetic Diction. At last Poetic Diction is being used on something it fits; that is nice but not much reason for praising Gray; it seems likely that he would have used the same grinding assumption of superiority (from knowing a special line of tricks) about King Lear or the Spartans at Thermopylae. And one must remember, even at the time, not merely the cat (Persian) but the tub (Chinese) and the fish (Pacific) were all painfully expensive and high life. Well might the Tyrian purple be called upon, and the gods of the learned; it is a very snob little poem. And the last verse, though all about girls not about the cat, is so very eighteenth-century in its tone about them (we only know women of the highest breeding, and even those are ignorant little bitches – older ones aren't thought of) that it fits into the picture. Even the chief surprise of the poem, the line 'A favourite has no friend,' appeals chiefly to the idea of the mistress of a prince. If allegory is continual comparison, then the sign of it here (because it comes early) is that the cat first looked into the tub to see her own reflection – 'She saw: and purred applause,' granted that the vanity of cats is not gratified by mirrors, this is a joke about women: the same, the too modish, joke about women.

But in spite of all these reasons the poem does not stay where it could be

279

classified. The whole charm of the thing, to be sure, is that it somehow puts into the cat and the fish the wonder of the conventionally applied gods, and so far they are more real than the ridiculed and ridiculous 'beauties'; but the first evident lift is in the last verse but one. (The cat has nine lives.)

> Eight times emerging from the flood
> She mewed to every watery god,
>   Some speedy aid to send.
> No Dolphin came, no Nereid stirred:
> Nor cruel Tom, nor Susan heard.
>   A favourite has no friend!

The come-down from the dolphin that saved Arion even to the hated Tom who would at last have been helpful now is a joke outside the narrow drawing-room of the modish jokes on the Fair; and then this breath of reality is met by the surprise of the last line. If a favourite (of the prince) is one whom rival courtiers will refuse to help, then the moral tag is absurd; Johnson could much more plausibly have objected to it. Even Tom, no kind of friend, would have saved this very expensive cat. But even a favourite of *everybody* has no friend; the body is an island; she is alone, whoever wants to help her. It is by *not* applying to the very limited type whom the cat is so far 'like', up to now 'like', to the girl already in society and on the make there, that the tag becomes large. As we advance on the last verse and the tidy moral the very 'beauties' themselves, at first merely the vehicle of the metaphor, then the real topic of the allegory, have already become only another example of some more serious truth about all mortal affairs.

> From hence, ye beauties, undeceived,
> Know, one false step is ne'er retrieved,
>   And be with caution bold.
> Not all that tempts your wandering eyes
> And heedless hearts is lawful prize;
>   Nor all that glisters gold.

Gold here is 'of genuine value'; somebody is in view who wants that; in 'What female heart can gold despise?' it meant simply money. The line that rhymes with it has an echo of this changed attitude; they are not asked not to be bold; that is necessary, and there is some risk in gaining anything valuable.

Note

1 Untitled in typescript.

Thy Darling in an Urn

Sewanee Review, LV, October 1947

Cleanth Brooks, *The Well Wrought Urn*

I have been reading Mr Cleanth Brooks's *The Well Wrought Urn* with
enjoyment and admiration, and want to write down the points at which I
disagree with it. The minds of critics often work in this disagreeable way,
and I hope I am right in taking for granted that the book as a whole does not
need summarising or defence. Indeed I agree so fully with his general position that if I were attacking him I should be attacking myself.

Obviously some of the poems suit his method better than others, but I
think they are the better poems. 'L'Allegro' and 'Il Penseroso' seem to me
ponderous trifles with a few good lines in them, so that they are a bad place
to look for profound symbols. What Mr Brooks finds to say about the light
symbolism – the way both poems move in halftones – is true but not surprising, and to claim 'a dim religious light' as a metaphysical paradox, reca-
pitulating 'the entire symbolism of the two poems', seems to me plucky of
Mr Brooks rather than anything else. Maybe the Victorians' acceptance of
this idea literally, their refusal to clean the stained-glass windows and
efforts to make ivy grow over them, have given me a wrong slant on this
phrase.

In the Tennyson 'Tears, idle tears', which really is a good poem, Mr
Brooks's approach has something to bite on and fully brings off, I think, its
effect of truth and surprise. I should only question his solemnity about the
first two lines; the paradox of 'idle' tears drawn from the 'depths' is pointed
out as if only the metaphysical approach could have recognised it. Surely
Tennyson thought of this obvious irony as good manners more than anything else; he describes his crying as it would appear to the world before he
says what it means to him. The later part of the analysis is certainly not trivial like this, indeed the detail is so good that one wants it to be generalised:
how far is Mr Brooks's account of the 'transferred epithet' of *wild* the only
real justification for any transferred epithet? *Wild with all regret* must be
said of the speaker, not of the days he remembers; but he is the sum of his
memories, and the old days themselves are *now* wild because they are

breaking out into his mind. I think this kind of identification must be the regular function of the trope.

In the chapter on Gray's 'Elegy' Mr Brooks gives me a mild rebuke. I had claimed to find reactionary political ideas in the verse beginning 'Full many a gem,' because it can be taken to imply that the poor are better off without opportunities [See *Some Versions of Pastoral* (1935), p. 4]. Mr Brooks says that I ignored the rest of the poem, which 'brings the proud and humble together in a common humanity'; the choice of the speaker to be buried in the churchyard himself was 'a kind of vindication of the lot forced on the rustics'. It is quite true that I did not think about the latter part of the poem, but on reading Mr Brooks's analysis of it I feel that it was even smugger than I had supposed. If the rustics are so much better off without opportunities that the speaker will leave the wicked world to join them, surely that is very near to saying that they *ought* not to have opportunities. What is more important, the paradox in the final epitaph of the speaker: 'Large was his bounty. . . . He gave to Mis'ry all he had, a tear,' seems to me more disagreeable than Mr Brooks allows. Presumably he was poor by the standard of the great world but still rich compared to the rustics. After all, he is a different order of being from the rustics; the poem takes for granted that he does not have to work. No doubt he really did give them a little money. But they ought to be much more grateful because he gave them a tear; that is what counts on the epitaph; the sympathy of a gentleman is enough, and ought to make them contented. All this seems to me much worse than, not any kind of justification for, the verse about the flower born to blush unseen. The verse taken alone conveys a permanent truth, whether or not it hints that you should regard this truth in a reactionary way. I am quite prepared to agree with Mr Brooks that Gray set out to express good feeling about the matter; I only claim that he failed to. Probably the reason was that he wanted to get a certain modish polish into the end of the poem, and did not realise what a disagreeable implication the smart tone would carry. All the same, I think, he ought to have realised; there is a failure of sincerity. The general criticism I want to make of Mr Brooks's approach is that he is too content to find the intellectual machinery of a fine and full statement in the poem; there is enough irony and paradox and so on, he feels, for the meaning to be made profound; this is true, but you still need to ask whether the machine worked the right way.

The discussion of the Wordsworth 'Ode on Intimations' is extremely good, I think, but the limitations of Mr Brooks's approach come out in his dislike for the stanza about the six-years' darling who is occupied in endless imitation. 'In some respects, it is a pity that Wordsworth was not content to rely on [the previous] imagery to make his point and that he felt it necessary to include the weak stanza VII.' But surely it is essential to have a bit of realism about the six-year-old before the apotheosis of the baby in the next stanza; otherwise Wordsworth is likely to seem simply ignorant about children. Mr Brooks feels that the only good parts of the poem are those which can be presented as profound paradoxes; but this conflicts with his own parallel between a poem and a drama. We need a build-up, and the flatness of the verse in the 'imitation' stanza is itself a dramatic contrast. This I think is the important point, but anyway the stanza *is* a paradox, if you need one; because the child may be in a golden age of imagination or may be struggling to get out of it into the light of common day, by copying the grown-ups. What he does is simple but includes both.

The chapter I chiefly want to examine is the one on the Keats 'Grecian Urn'. I agree with Mr Brooks (against so many critics) in finding that I can enjoy the 'Beauty is Truth' passage, at the end of the poem. But I find his explanation of it rather fuzzy writing, and I suspect the weakness here is due to a certain anti-emotionalism in his own whole mode of approach. He dislikes biography as a means of explaining a poem, since a poem ought to be complete in itself, and he is not very patient with personal expressions of feeling from a writer who is engaged in building one of these complicated structures. The whole of the third stanza of the Ode, he feels, is a falling-off; 'there is a tendency to linger over the scene sentimentally.' This is the stanza that begins 'Ah happy, happy boughs' and ends by saying that human passion leaves 'a burning forehead and a parching tongue.' If we are to try to defend it, says Mr Brooks, 'we shall come nearest success by emphasising the paradoxical implications of the repeated items. . . . Though the poet has developed and extended his metaphors furthest in this third stanza, the ironic counterpoise is developed furthest too.' He often uses 'irony' in a very extended sense, and this example shows that the practice can be a confusing one; because in the ordinary sense of the term the effect is more like dropping an irony; this stanza is concerned to tell us directly about the feelings of Keats. He is extremely *un*happy, we find, especially about his love affair, but also from the tedium of the pursuit of beauty or pleasure and from the expectation of death. I do not get this from 'biography' but from taking the opposites of the three things the stanza calls 'happy', and it seems to me that this prominent expression of feeling is bound to affect our interpretation of the poem as a whole.

Also there is a very dramatic effect, ignored by Mr Brooks, from the juxtaposition of this stanza with the next.

> . . . A burning forehead, and a parching tongue.

> Who are these coming to the sacrifice?

It is a cry of awe from the parching tongue, as the poet sees new victims approach, and the stanza goes on to say that none of them will ever go home again, so that their town will be mysteriously desolate. Mr Brooks has more than a page trying to rationalise this idea, and save it from being thought 'an indulgence ... which is gratuitous and finally silly'. The town cannot really be left desolate merely because these people are carved on a pot. 'The poet' says Mr Brooks 'by pretending to take the town as empty ... has suggested in the most powerful way possible its reality for him – and for us. It is a case of the doctor's taking his own medicine; the poet is prepared to stand by the illusion of his own making.' If this were all, I think it would still be pretty gratuitous. But the poet has just told us he is desolate too (if the critic will condescend to notice anything so sentimental); there is a comparison. The idea that the pursuit of beauty eats up the pursuer, who therefore sacrifices himself to it, is surely not a remote one for a Romantic poet. These people's homes will be left desolate because they have gone to make a piece of artwork, and so will Keats's home because he is spending his life on his art. Beauty is both a cause of and an escape from suffering, and in either way suffering is deeply involved in its production. Here in fact is the crisis of the poem – in the sudden exertion of muscle by which Keats skids round the corner from self-pity to an imaginative view of the world. None of these people can get anything permanent out of the world except beauty, and at once we turn back to the pot with a painful ecstasy in the final stanza; there is nothing else left. This is the force behind the cry 'Beauty is Truth' (obviously, I think) however the terms of it are to be interpreted.

And, by the way, if I in my turn may pick out the line which I think is the 'real' blemish on the poem, I have to report that I plump for 'Oh Attic shape! Fair Attitude! With brede'. The bad pun suggesting a false Greek derivation and jammed against an arty bit of old English is absurdly affected and ugly; it is the kind of thing that the rude and snobbish critics, in Keats's own time, called him a Cockney for. And the idea of a pot striking an attitude is I think ridiculous enough in itself. But on this point maybe my judgement is warped by finding so much weight laid on 'attitudes' in the theoretical writing of Mr Brooks and similar good critics; what Keats meant by it is really very close to what they mean, and I can never feel in either case that an attitude makes a comfortable permanent object. The complaint about the line of course has no bearing on Mr Brooks's exegesis.

We now approach the puzzling climax of the poem, and I feel there is more to be said than Mr Brooks has found to say, though I hardly know what, about

Thou, silent form, doth tease us out of thought
As doth Eternity. Cold Pastoral!

'It is enigmatic as eternity is, for like eternity its history is outside time, beyond time, and for this very reason bewilders our time-ridden minds. It teases us.' It teases us *out of thought*; it stops us thinking; the idea is more suited to a mystical ecstasy than to a metaphysical puzzle. And while we are in this peculiar condition is clearly the time for the pot to identity truth and beauty. (Mr Brooks does not point out that the usual function of an Urn is to hold the ashes of the dead.) What is puzzling about 'Beauty is Truth,' I think, is that one feels the poem has raised no questions about truth before; the reconciliation may be all right in itself, but it has got hold of the wrong couple. This, I take it, was why Middleton Murry defended the philosophy of the last three lines but doubted their value in the poem.[1] Such an objection would not occur to Mr Brooks, who takes it as doctrine that a lyrical poet is concerned with philosophical truth. Already in the first verse, he points out, the pot is called a historian, so it is expected to tell truth; but its history has 'no footnotes' and is merely an imaginative insight, hence the paradox. 'If we have followed the development of the metaphors ... we shall be prepared for the enigmatic final paradox,' in which the urn speaks as a character in the drama and 'makes a commentary on its own nature'. This is sufficient for an answer to Murry, I think.

But we cannot suppose that the aphorism is merely dramatic, in the sense of being a suitable remark for a silent pot (suitable because of its complacence, perhaps). If we were sure that Keats did not agree with the pot the thing would become trivial. However little we are to use biography, it is fair to quell this doubt by remembering that Keats had wrestled with the idea in prose. 'The excellence of every art is in its intensity, capable of making all disagreeables evaporate from their being in close relation to Beauty and Truth. What the imagination seizes as Beauty must be Truth.' That is, his mind was working on the ideas of Coleridge. But there is remarkably little agony in Coleridge's theory of Imagination (remarkably, I mean, for so unhappy a man); whereas Keats was trying to work the 'disagreeables' into the theory. It seemed to him therefore that the aphorism was *somehow* relevant to the parching tongue, the desolate streets, and the other woes of the generations not yet wasted. He like his readers, I think, was puzzled by the remarks of the pot, and yet felt that they were very *nearly* intelligible and relevant. The words *sacrifice* and *eternity* have made us expect a divine sort of truth, a revelation, and revelations are expected to be puzzling. In short, if we recognise the stress of feeling in the rest of the poem, I do not think a reasonable man should withhold his sympathy from the end of it.

Also I think there is another interpretation of the aphorism, philosophically a less ambitious one than what Keats had been feeling after, but one that makes the end of the poem positively satisfying. The essential dramatic process is that by feeling the beauty of the pot Keats is led to make reflections on human life. Its beauty can be said to be 'true' as a sound guide to human life, able to tell the artist how to digest his sufferings and turn them into beauty. He feels that he has already shown the identity in the poem, by going through the process it is meant to describe; he has therefore earned the right to assert the identity at the end. He wanted us to feel, I think, that the wise pot means a good deal more by its aphorism, but as far as he, the poet, is concerned there is at least enough meaning to make the poem coherent.

This account, more elaborate than Mr Brooks's, is I think needed if you are to show that the poem *might* be a good one. (His account, I think, only makes it seem a rather bad attempt at philosophising.) But of course a critic is still free to say that Keats's good intentions don't come off, that the machine may have been built but still doesn't work. You may well decide that the effect is still 'Cockney', like 'Oh Attic shape! Fair Attitude! With brede'; that this brash attempt to end with a smart bit of philosophy had not got enough knowledge behind it to justify its claims. I do not feel that myself, but I do not see how to argue about the matter, and much as I dislike a *non possumus* theory in general I am tempted to think that there aren't any arguments. Supposing that I had completely explained how the machine is meant to work (of course no doubt I haven't), the question whether it does work is surely a matter of 'taste'; it can only be left to the reader to try for himself.

All the other examples taken by Mr Brooks (Shakespeare, Donne, Herrick, Pope and Yeats) seemed to me excellent and full of surprising truths in the detail. If I have been playing Devil's Advocate here it is only because the success seems so great that one begins to fear a new orthodoxy. It would be an athletic creature, and I hope that the new history of literature which Mr Brooks suggests will be undertaken. But it would have a tendency, like all orthodoxies, to reject what it could not transform. The anti-emotional bias, which is so often obscurely present, could make it very arid. One of the important facts about poetry, after all, is that it can work on you before you know how it is working; and I suspect a tendency in Mr Brooks to enjoy only the lines in which he feels he does know how it is working.[2]

Cleanth Brooks, in a 'Postscript' to Empson's essay, registered his 'entire agreement' with most of the points Empson raised but felt it necessary to clarify what he called 'the general intention' of his book:

I deliberately chose to treat certain poems ... because I intended to try to bridge the gap between metaphysical poetry and the other poetries. I felt that I was committed to search for principles of structure common to all poetry; and this meant that I had to treat, not merely the big poems, but the lesser ones too; not merely the intense passages, but the more relaxed passages as well. . . . A temptingly simple solution would have been to throw out all poems that did not suit my 'method', but this procedure . . . would have brought down — with a vengeance — charges of an intolerant neo-orthodoxy. . . .

For I cannot quite accept the most handsome compliment that Mr Empson bestows upon me, namely that 'the success seems so great that one begins to fear a new orthodoxy.' I see little signs of that in our American universities or in our popular reviews and book pages. This fact may account for the 'anti-emotional bias' which Mr Empson feels in my writing and for what is perhaps an overstringent insistence upon the distinction between the poem as an object and as a personal document, between what has been put into the poem by the artist and what is smuggled into it from the poet's diary or correspondence, etc., etc.

Finally — and ironically (in view of the evidence of the review itself) — Brooks expressed the hope that Empson would aid the cause by producing another Seven Types of Ambiguity or Some Versions of Pastoral: 'If the new criticism is ever to become the orthodox criticism as well, the impact of more books like these will be required.'

Notes

1 See John Middleton Murry, 'Beauty is Truth', *Studies in Keats*, London: Cape, 1930, pp. 71–92.

2 For Empson's further discussion of 'Ode on a Grecian Urn' see 'A is B', *The Structure of Complex Words*, pp. 368–74.

Reading a Poem:
Cowper's 'The Castaway'

BBC broadcast, 8 October 1955

The idea behind this series, as I understand, is to get critics to talk directly about a poem, not work up a written text. And there is some hope that this will drag them away from being poky, or from what is called verbal analysis. And as I've had a lot to do with verbal analysis myself, it's only proper for me to be willing to play. I have chosen 'The Castaway' both because it's a very fine poem, and because it doesn't allow of much verbal analysis anyway. But even there, I think, a critic had much better take the text in detail. The first plan was to have the poem read out both before and after the critical remarks, but I don't think it need be read at the start too, here, because I shall be reading it verse by verse looking at the text. And I want to start doing that at once, and not make more general comments till afterwards – that seems clearly the right order. The poem was written by William Cowper in 1798, a year before his death, at the age of sixty-nine.

> Obscurest night involv'd the sky,
>   The Atlantic billows roar'd,
> When such a destin'd wretch as I,
>   Wash'd headlong from on board,
> Of friends, of hope, of all bereft,
> His floating home for ever left.

Well, you notice the language is plain, though formal, because of poetical inversions and so on, and the last two lines of this six-line verse – that is, the couplet after the quatrain – has a rather flattening effect; not for the meaning, of course, that's very strong, but from the rhythm and phrasing and so on. You might think it was meant to give the punch – the bang at the end – but it doesn't. In fact, to call the ship 'The floating home' is rather like Pope calling the fish 'the finny herd'. This often happens in the poem, but once you realise what's going on, somehow it gives a truth feeling, which is very much needed; it feels like a sober understatement. And when I say, what is going on, there is one quite simple thing which is very definite: there was a surprise brewing for the first readers, because they weren't as much accustomed as we are to the Romantic habit of talking about yourself under cover of talking about somebody else, and anyway they didn't expect it from Cowper. It really is rather surprising to have Cowper adapting himself so completely to the new style so late in life, and so unconsciously really, because if you'd said this to him, he'd have thought it a great nonsense. What he means, of course, is to compare the drowning of the sailor to his own life of despair and intermittent madness. And he says so at the end. But the first readers, when they had only got as far as this, must have thought he was just writing dramatically when he said 'I' – that is, making the sailor talk as in a play. The whole point of the poem is already there in the words 'Such a destin'd wretch as I', but you needn't realise it till near the end.

> No braver chief could Albion boast
>   Than he with whom he went;
> Nor ever ship left Albion's coast
>   With warmer wishes sent.
> He lov'd them both, but both in vain,
> Nor him beheld, nor her again.

There, of course, the couplet does feel warm, whereas the quatrain might be out of the formal patriotic ode. But it's a bit riddling, because 'she' has to be the ship. Of course, ships are called feminine, and are loved, but you don't expect it to come out so very strong. There's a slight riddling quality there which I think is meant, because Cowper himself is thinking about one of his own failures to marry, presumably.

> Not long beneath the whelming brine,
>   Expert to swim, he lay;
> Nor soon he felt his strength decline,
>   Or courage die away;
> But wag'd with death a lasting strife,
> Supported by despair of life.

That last phrase is very riddling. We say, a man fights hard when he is desperate, but what we commonly mean by that is that he won't recognise that there is no hope, he refuses to believe it against the evidence; so he still does hope. But Cowper did really think he was damned, that was his mental disease. So he might well mean not only that all men must die sometime; oh, it could come 'in despair of life', but anyhow life itself has no value, despair of the value of life, except so far as it leads you to heaven, which it won't for Cowper. 'Supported by despair of life' – it really is hard for us to understand why Cowper went on struggling when he was certain that the end would be the worst possible, and even more how he could go on writing his playful, cultivated little poems. I think that just at this point in the poem, it was seeming strange to Cowper, as it does to us, and there I think he did want the reader to realise that he was talking about himself too. But not at all because it's self-centred; more to the point is what he wants you to feel, that somehow in the nature of things this is true about everybody, we are all in the same boat – and there I stumble upon an epigram: we are all in the same boat as the man who has gone overboard. That is the central feeling, really, of the poem.

> He shouted: nor his friends had fail'd
>   To check the vessel's course,
> But so the furious blast prevail'd,
>   That, pitiless perforce,
> They left their outcast mate behind,
> And scudded still before the wind.

The chief thing here, I think, is that this stiff, rather Latinised English grammar lets him run straight across the metre in one sentence for the whole verse. It gives great energy. The story is now to be told in a masculine, economical way, and this corresponds to something important in his own story. One of the most trying things about mental cases, as many people have found, is that they are always complaining you have wronged them, or at least that you have neglected them. It's very reassuring here to have the mad Cowper tell us, as he goes on doing for several verses, that he realises people couldn't help neglecting him. And anyhow, he feels, they had their own troubles.

> Some succour yet they could afford,
>   And such as storms allow,
> The cask, the coop, the floated cord,
>   Delayed not to bestow,
> But he (they knew) nor ship, nor shore,
> Whate'er they gave, should visit more.

I suppose they didn't need that hen coop because they had eaten those particular hens already. It was very good of them to take so much trouble, even so, when they knew that nothing they did to the mad Cowper would be any use. This goes on, even in the climax of the last verse, when he's still remembering to say that help was given, but it was not effectual. Another point there I think is this curious visiting of his home, or visiting his ship. The idea of the soul visiting the world is somehow theological, but I'm not sure what it's meant to suggest.

> Nor, cruel as it seem'd, could he
>   Their haste himself condemn,
> Aware that flight, in such a sea,
>   Alone could rescue them;
> Yet bitter felt it still to die,
> Deserted, and his friends so nigh.

Now there we get the whole weight of the pathos of that feeling, which is so usual, that the mental case can't help feeling neglected, and it's expressed very strongly; but it's been so well prepared for that we also feel somehow, here, that it's true in a way after all about everybody. In any case, Cowper is trying to think about everybody. Without this logical build-up, you see, it would easily seem disagreeable. But here it seems very manly is all you could say.

> He long survives, who lives an hour
>   In ocean, self-upheld;
> And so long he, with unspent power,
>   His destiny repelled,
> And ever, as the minutes flew,
> Entreated help nor cried — Adieu!

Now here, in this emphasis on one hour, you might think that there's a collapse of the comparison, because Cowper is writing in the last year of a long life, and his first attacks of madness had been when he was quite young. I think the answer is something which doesn't get said in the poem. He had quite clearly in his mind that he was now just short of seventy years, and that's given as the days of a man's life in the Psalms; and it's been a regular poetical paradox, that this three score years and ten is in one way very long to suffer in, but in another way very short to enjoy. That, I think, is meant to be the sort of quite clear point of the comparison. You notice, Cowper is still feeling a sombre pride all along, he feels it took great power in Cowper to uphold himself, without any support that is, because he had no feeling for the future, except to uphold himself for the whole hour allotted to him.

> At length, his transient respite past,
>   His comrades, who before
> Had heard his voice in every blast,
>   Could catch the sound no more.
> For then, by toil subdued, he drank
> The stifling wave, and then he sank.

I said before that the couplet often feels flat at the ends of the verses unless you realise that it's meant to be deliberately sober. Now, as a matter of fact, I tried to read that couplet solemnly, but it might easily come in a joke poem by Hilaire Belloc; it might come in Ruthless Rhymes or something like that. You might find another case of that slight puzzle, because what it meant to Cowper was something dreadful. And you read something like that in the word 'respite' – 'His transient respite past'. Why did he call this hour a respite when it only meant hopeless and useless suffering? Well, it isn't angling; you might well say we'd all rather be alive than dead, but what it meant to Cowper was something more. He meant that however painful this hour was, it was a respite from the much greater pains of Hell. That, I think, is what he means to bring out, it was merely a suggestion.

> No poet wept him; but the page
>   Of narrative sincere,
> That tells his name, his worth, his age,
>   Is wet with Anson's tear,
> And tears by bards or heroes shed
> Alike immortalize the dead.

You might think it a bit odd to say that the sailor hasn't been put in a poem, when in fact he is being put in a poem, but of course what Cowper means is that the poetry is unimportant beside the courage. Well, if so, this must be true of Cowper's life as well as anywhere else, so what he's getting very near saying is that Cowper is a hero too. But he'd rightly have been very annoyed if you'd said that to him, because what he feels he's doing is being very self-effacing about the poetry.

> I therefore purpose not, or dream,
>   Descanting on his fate,
> To give the melancholy theme
>   A more enduring date:
> But misery still delights to trace
> Its semblance in another's face.

Now right up to here, you see, the main point of the poem might well have remained doubtful to the first readers, but now at last it's driven home. The reason why the poem is unimportant, says Cowper, is that the suffering of both poet and sailor make it a trivial thing to worry about by comparison. But I think we're liable to be misled there; this word dream simply meant occupying your fancy with unreal matters or bothering about the decoration. We have there a modern idiom 'I wouldn't dream of doing that,' meaning I'm not so wicked, and I think that's a later one, it certainly isn't wanted here. Cowper doesn't mean that he wants to prevent the sailor from being remembered, or he doesn't at all mind having for himself what's called immortal fame, he's quite willing for that. The only thing he does feel

is that they're trivial by comparison with these real things, they can't hold
the attention when put beside the actual sufferings and the actual sympathies which were felt at that time; and, for that matter, when they're put
beside the prospect of eternity.

And so we come to the last verse:

> No voice divine the storm allay'd,
>   No light propitious shone,
> When, snatch'd from all effectual aid,
>   We perished, each alone:
> But I beneath a rougher sea,
> And whelm'd in deeper gulphs than he.

Well, it's hard to say anything about that which is either needed to
explain it, or sufficiently in tone to feel a proper thing to say. I take it the
idea that everybody dies alone was a fairly reliable commonplace, so that
Cowper felt in suggesting [it] that he was still being moderate and reasonable; what he's suggesting or expressing is true in some degree about all
human life, or at least many human lives, even though most people do not
die as much alone as those two did. This generalising process, you see, is
what the eighteenth century thought a poet ought to do. I don't mean that
Cowper thought that everybody was predestined to damnation like himself, certainly not. Indeed, the last line presumably means that the sailor
didn't go to Hell: 'Whelm'd in deeper gulphs than he'. And there's a slight
puzzle there in 'We perished, each alone' – Cowper apparently says he's
dead already. I think what that means – in a way it doesn't fit, he must have
meant this struggle in the sea is his life; but I think that he's thinking just
here, the point where Cowper perished was the point – whatever it was, it's
a complete mystery, it was a most innocent life of course – was the point
where he committed the unforgivable sin. It was then that he perished, and
– nothing else was any more hope. Or it might be simply some occasion
when he went mad. It's a little hard to explain that past tense – 'We
perished, each alone' – unless you say he's writing as from his tombstone,
assuming he is already nearly dead, there is nothing more that can happen
to him.

No doubt at the time a reader would hardly notice more than the overwhelming pathos of the poem; that's what he was usually praised for, and
it's intellectually simple enough no doubt, but it is very four-square, and the
thought of it is steady and solid, I feel.

I daresay many people first got to know the poem as I did, from finding
mysterious bits of it boomed out by the father in Virginia Woolf's novel *To
the Lighthouse*. It's very impressive there – she couldn't have found a better
way to suggest the idea she wanted, and that is, the high claim to solitary

adventure made by the thinker or the artist; and this idea – it seems very familiar to us in a way, it's just being claimed by the father thinking about himself, but it's very familiar – was rather an invention of the Romantic period. Sir Herbert Read in a recent book called *The True Voice of Feeling* – I disagreed with a great deal of it, but I thought he was quite right in emphasising this side of the Romantics, and bringing out a basic assumption of them: assumption not in the sense that they all argued about it, but they were all acting on it. Now this assumption is a paradox, it can't help being rather a confusing thing to operate, and in a way it's the opposite of the Christian paradox that 'He that loseth his life shall save it'. It says that the artist has a duty to express his whole society, or the historical period which his society is just getting into, and that this process does good to the society; not to him, it's altruistic, and indeed it does good to later societies, and yet he can only do this – he can only discover what he has to express – by being ruthlessly sincere, which in effect means self-centred. You might say it is only by being selfish that he can do good to others; that's why he talks about himself so much, which is always the most obvious change when the Romantics come in. And according to Sir Herbert, the Germans first analysed the theory, but the English were doing it already. Of course, Sir Herbert thinks it's a permanent truth about artists, about art; the only point about the Romantics was that they were the first to know what they were doing. I think this is true and important, but when you call it knowing, there is rather a puzzle, because they seem just to act at the same time, they do the same things at the same time, like a flock of starlings.

It seems clear Cowper had no idea of being in the fashion, when he wrote this dreadful but splendid poem at the end of his life, he was past being interested in fashion. But he is somehow in period so much, it's odd for one thing that he feels quite sure he's as manly as the sailor. On the face of it, his mental disease had made him run away from everything; for instance, as a young man he tried to kill himself three times, because he was so frightened of going to an oral examination for what was more or less a sinecure job, being Clerk to the Journals of the House of Lords. And after that he had to live in complete retirement, on money which was given him, and nursed by a series of devoted ladies; and he always went mad again if there was any question of having to marry one of them. But he has no doubt at all when he looks at the tittering world of the successful job holders, the worldly men who can do these things, that he and the sailor are masculine and that they are not. We can agree that he endured great suffering very bravely, in a way we think he's manly – but it's surprising that he does, you can't help feeling. Of course you might say it's simply the old Christian point of view, what he was afraid of was Hell, and the private religious struggle had long been thought of as being quite as real as the struggle for worldly goods.

But then again, Cowper expresses this idea by going back to the Captains' narratives of the great voyages, just as Coleridge had done a year or two before, in the 'Ancient Mariner'. That of course is where Anson comes in – who he is. The poet W. H. Auden, in a recent critical book *The Enchafèd Flood* [London: Faber & Faber, 1951], was pointing out, very well I thought, how all the English Romantics harked back to this subject of the great voyages, because it fitted so well their own picture of themselves. You find the French Romantics do it quite a bit, but the Germans don't do it, as I understand, they just hadn't got it to talk about somehow.

The Romantics liked the idea of this subject because they too, you see, were lawless adventurers discovering new worlds, which others would afterwards use safely. It fitted very well into their own picture of themselves. But we needn't say that they're so very self-important; in any case they were quite right, I think, in having enough imagination to see that the subject was a big one. In fact, this expansion of the white races by sea, as an Asiatic will always feel as more obvious than we do, was the chief historical event of the last 400 years; when the Romantics were writing, they might very sensibly take an interest in it. But it was mixed up with their idea of discovering new worlds – something quite new might happen, do you see?

Now I think the mind of Coleridge was very clear about all this. He knew exactly what he was doing. But it seems quite clear that Cowper didn't, and yet there you get Cowper doing the same thing. Right at the end of his life he doesn't feel at all likely, as I say, to be inventive. There I think you do come up against the mystery of the Arts, or one might say the mystery of the fashions, or something like that. It's hard to see how Cowper knew that this theme was much the best way to express what he wanted: the best way to express not only his own life and its long suffering but in some way also to express the whole society which had driven him mad.

'The Ancient Mariner'

Critical Quarterly, 6:4, Winter 1964

I

Most people receive the impact of the poem when young, and to that extent it is not at the mercy of critics; but critics have done a good deal to spoil it for them when older, usually while claiming to point out its merits (as I am doing myself, I must remember). There is often a question whether you should read into a poem the beliefs and interests of the author when he wrote or instead allow it the traditional meanings imposed by his society; and I think wrong answers have been given here both ways round. The 'Mariner' appeals to a proud national tradition and evokes a major historical event, the maritime expansion of the Western Europeans; but a number of recent critics have expressed relief that the fanciful reverie is so free from politics. On the other hand, most of them take for granted that it is an allegory in favour of redemption by torment, the central tradition of Christianity; not liking perhaps to say in front of the children that Coleridge was a Unitarian at the time, that is, had cut himself off from most white-collar employment because he disapproved of this plan for redemption. To make the poem Christian one must argue that the Mariner committed a real crime, and this has afforded many critics a steep but direct path to the wild heights of Pecksniffery which are their spiritual home. Even Humphrey House, who wrote well (*Coleridge*, 1953) about what Coleridge meant in saying that the poem had too much of the moral, and should have been like an anecdote which he recalled from the *Arabian Nights* – even he went on to call shooting the Albatross 'a ghastly violation of a great sanctity, at least as bad as a murder'. A student at Sheffield wrote in an essay for me that she would have hanged the Mariner from the yard-arm with her own hands; I had to warn her that the External Examiner would consider this to be in the wrong tone of voice, but she was expressing the orthodox modern view. I think it does the poem a lot of harm.

II

Coleridge at this time called himself a Christian, meaning that he revered the moral teaching of Jesus; he was also fond of saying that ordinary Christians were materialists, because they believed that matter could exist without a soul (as a tea-kettle for example); but this is polemical or witty language. Most of the people he met would not have said he was a Christian till he was beaten down into agreeing that the crucifixion was the means of redemption. In 1798, the year after writing the poem, he was offered a post as a Unitarian minister, but said that the congregation must be free to reject him after he had explained why he could not administer the Lord's Supper (the rite most intimately connected with human sacrifice). He came of a clerical family and the unction was natural to him, also he thought it a duty not to encourage atheism, so that his objections to Christianity were left obscure; but they were binding upon himself. Whether absurdly or not, he was determined not to be seduced into supporting beliefs which he disapproved; he would not have done it even in a ballad. As to politics, his group of friends in Devonshire had told him to shut up; there was a real police terror, though it so happened that nobody we have heard of was among those hanged, and a spy had reported to the Home Office 'a set of violent Democrats' in Devonshire. Maybe Coleridge felt contentedly that he was still helping the cause, because he might be read by the censor, when he said in his letters, 'I have snapped my baby trumpet of sedition.' In a letter of August 1797, not long before starting the poem, he is trying to induce one of the set to seclude from the police the agitator Thelwall:

If the day of darkness and tempest should come, it is most probable that the influence of T. would be very great on the lower classes. It may therefore prove of no mean utility to the cause of Truth and Humanity, that he had spent some years in a society where his natural impetuosity had been disciplined into patience, and the slow energies of a calculating spirit.

No wonder he despised the government for suspecting him, as he made these statesmanlike plans; but the duty of discretion was not at all likely to exclude politics from his mind.

He wanted a theme of guilt and remorse and had been writing on Cain before Wordsworth gave him the brief anecdote about an albatross in Shelvocke's *Voyages*; this suited him as he had been reading earlier travellers' reports, chiefly for a series of Odes on the four elements. Also he positively wanted to write on superstition. A basic impulse of the Romantics was to escape from the eighteenth century, their enlightened parents in fact, so as to experience if only through history and travel-books the variety of the world. Superstitions were found everywhere on these journeys, and a Romantic would often adopt one; but Coleridge (as is obvious in the first draft of the 'Mariner') was quite ready to laugh at olde-worlde sensationalism. He needed superstition in poems for a philosophical purpose; to examine the psychological function which gave it this universal appeal. Wordsworth was himself writing poetry about his immediate experience, but agreed that Coleridge should contribute poems with:

[the] persons and characters supernatural, or at least romantic; yet so as to transfer from our inward nature a human interest and a semblance of truth sufficient to procure for these shadows of imagination that willing suspension of disbelief for the moment which constitutes poetic faith. [*Biographia Literaria*, xiv]

The famous phrase was thus coined to deal with a special effort of historical imagination; he was to show

the dramatic truth of such emotions as would naturally accompany such situations, supposing them real. And real in *this* sense they have been to every human being who, from whatever source of delusion, has at any time believed himself under supernatural agency. [Ibid.]

But we are not to suppose that Coleridge liked superstitions, or wanted to encourage them; in a letter of July 1802, which can be unusually frank as it is to a brother Unitarian, he says of possession by spirits:

not only did it imply frightful corruption in the great article of all religion, the moral attributes of God; but it must needs have had a bad effect and an anti-social influence on the intercourse between man and man ... Yet so far are these Exorcists from being condemned by Christ that their innocence is cited by him to prove his own. St Paul directly asserts the existence of wicked spirits swarming in the air.

Such beliefs in fact are rather like madness; the reality behind a superstition of fourteenth-century sailors may well be the same 'fact of mind' as the private neurosis of Coleridge himself. The works of the Romantics, I think, are merely tiresome unless one recognises that they are based upon assumptions of this sort; the authors were courageous and generous-minded, and right in thinking they had a new world to describe.

The great merit of John Livingston Lowes's *The Road to Xanadu: A Study in the Ways of the Imagination* [London: Constable, 1927] was in showing that Coleridge had read widely in the ships' captains' reports, and that whole verses of the poem were word-for-word quotations from their prose; no wonder it is so much better than what he had written before – the naked strength of the language is behind the 'Mariner', as if English had been evolved solely to write this one poem. Regarded as a summing-up of the maritime expansion, to make it turn on a superstition was no more than just; the sailors had dared their great journeys while notoriously fearing still greater perils than the real ones. We are told that this crew is the first to enter the Pacific and we see them invent a superstition about an albatross; probably they were the first to see an albatross, but as often in legends the name of the creature is taken for granted. The weather had become less unhelpful when it appeared, so the crew at first blame the Mariner for shooting it, but as soon as the sun comes out they say he was right – they are only sure that the incident was numinous enough to have a magical effect. (In a splendid illustration by Gustav Doré the sailors huddle, white with rime among burgeoning shapeless icicles, all gaping at a bird which estimates them quizzically like the Dodo in *Alice*.) The Mariner seems to imply a mild criticism of the crew for this rapid change of mind, and the author cannot have expected it to recommend the superstition to his readers. The Mariner, however, is struck down by guilt as by the Furies, and I have no wish to weaken the obvious violence of the effect; I only say that we are intended to balance it with an equally obvious reflection: 'How free from guilt he is, according to our own beliefs.' It took a sad lack of sturdiness in the modern world, I think, to obscure this point altogether.

The Mariner says nothing about why he shot the bird, partly because he now regards the action as beyond palliation, and the author wants a feeling of mystery. But we can get some indications from the first text. The storm had prevented revictualling:

For days and weeks it played us freaks:

and by the time the Albatross came what victual was left had become nauseating:

The Mariners gave it biscuit-worms.

Nobody who had been reading travellers' reports in bulk could doubt the motive of the Mariner after that; he shot it for food. All good explorers try out new sources of food; it is part of their scientific aspect, which gives them the dignity of Faust; and the darker Albatross mentioned in the anecdote of Shelvock, which is just small enough to be hung round a man's neck, does, I am told, make a tolerable soup which would help to keep off scurvy. Probably this soup was made and drunk, so that only the externals of the Albatross were hung round the Mariner's neck later on; it would be easier to do. The Polar Spirit has then some excuse for killing the whole crew, and the text when carefully examined does not say that they invented the superstition against killing it as soon as it was killed. (I do not believe that there were two hundred of them; Coleridge or the Mariner invents this number to heighten the drama of their all dying at once.) Coleridge did not disapprove of eating flesh, though he ate little of it unless invited to dinner; he revered all life, including vegetables. (Advanced thought had simplified and hardened by the next generation, when Shelley was a vegetarian.) He would thus have no temptation to suppress the thought of food. Take the philanthropist Nansen; all teams such as his team had a schedule for eating the husky dogs who pulled the sledges, so that each time a sledge became empty, as the men and dogs ate the food on the sledges, there were no husky dogs to pull this useless sledge. I bet all those dogs loved Nansen like crazy. Anyhow, even granting that the Mariner deserved to be killed for killing the Albatross, all the rest of the crew did not deserve to be killed even more.

I am not denying that Coleridge said the Mariner had committed a crime; he said it in the second edition, while removing a lot of archaisms. He had come to realise that the poem deserved more solemn treatment than he had thought at first (maybe they laughed heartily on that walking-tour, sharing in a parody of the fashion for archaic ballads); but there was a more pressing reason. Wordsworth was very sore at the reviews of *Lyrical Ballads*, which had jeered at his prosiness; he showed an unreasonable inclination to blame Coleridge, who as usual was far too ready to kiss the rod. He offered to suppress his poem, so Wordsworth claimed afterwards that his fatherly encouragement had induced Coleridge to make it presentable. Such was how he came to cut out the excellent technicality 'broad as a weft upon the left', which could have been explained at once in a footnote, and cut out some good though sensational bits of description; this caused some horrible discords in the sound as at ll. 372–3, 'a quiet tune. / Till noon we quietly sailed on,' wrecking the exquisite harmony which the sound has all through the first version. The facetious archaisms urgently needed removing, but we pay a heavy price for it. Well then, the *biscuit-worms* and the internal rhyme *freaks–weeks* (evidence of a long period without revictualling) were cut out for being ridiculous, not because the author had decided to hush up the food shortage. He also altered the brief 'Argument' introducing the poem. Instead of 'How a Ship ... was driven by storms' (reaching the Antarctic and the Pacific) 'and of the strange things that befell; and in what manner the Ancyent Marinere came back to his own country' (1798), it says 'how the Ancient Mariner cruelly and in contempt of the laws of hospitality killed a Seabird and how he was followed by many and strange judgements; and in what manner...' (1800). This was omitted altogether in 1802 and the frequent subsequent editions, chiefly no doubt because having an Argument at all came to seem tiresomely olde-worlde, but also perhaps because Coleridge did not care to explain his fable. However, the marginal glosses, added at any time before 1817, give the same explanation; 'And lo! the Albatross proveth a bird of good omen'... 'The Ancient Mariner inhospitably killeth the pious bird of good omen.' To call it a 'pious bird' must be intended as a mild parsonical joke, an aside to relieve the boredom of the parents who overhear the children being taught not to pull poor pussy's tail. The Antarctic is notoriously inhospitable, and its Spirit causes all the trouble; in most houses a guest would be allowed to eat the available meat rather than starve to death. Coleridge was trying to make his poem more acceptable by plugging the moral archly. Still, he was not altering the story, and would not think he was altering the interpretation. The poem itself says, or the Mariner before recovering from a fit hears a voice in the air say:

> The spirit that bideth by himself
> In the land of mist and snow,
> He loved the bird that loved the man
> Who shot him with his bow.

From the first, this was intended as a powerful kick at prosy-minded readers such as myself; and yet the rotund music depends on a distinction between the man and the animal so basic that one takes *who*, the other *that*. The Spirit is not inherently either good or bad, merely wilful, and a reader is free to decide that it treated the men wrongly.

The young Coleridge who wrote the poem, I don't deny, had strong impulses to agree with the Spirit; probably if he had heard about the extermination of the Dodo he too would have recommended the yard-arm. The orthodox Coleridge who made comments long after was inclined to laugh off this flouting of the rights of man over animals. But they both thought the childishness of the moral was an actual recommendation, since children unlike ourselves have not been corrupted by the world – they are 'blest seers'. In any case, the Mariner at the stage of his life when we meet him is being helped by magic to express a revelation – he can tell it in any language, recognising at a sight a man who needs to be told it, and the Wedding Guest was sadder for knowing it, as well as wiser. What else can it have been but that killing the albatross was a crime?

III

The poems that Coleridge had been writing just before make rather clearer how his mind had been moving. The terrors of Nature, he explains in 'Religious Musings' (1794), were planned by God to awake the spirit of primitive man:

> What mists dim-floating of idolatry
> Split and misshaped the omnipresent Sire;
> And first by Terror, Mercy's startling prelude,
> Uncharmed the spirit spell-bound with earthly lusts.
> Till of its nobler nature it 'gan feel
> Dim recollections, and thence soared to hope...

The typical 'idol' was Moloch; 'idolatry' means thinking God more malignant than he is, so the argument lets Coleridge believe that God is acting on
a good plan though he sends earthquakes. (If you believe in an omnipotent
God you have to admit that he sometimes chooses to act cruelly, however
much you deny that he was specially satisfied by the crucifixion.) But only
primitive man needed teaching by terror; Coleridge holds out against believing that we need it ourselves. Even so, it is clear from 'The Destiny of
Nations' (1796) that men were still primitive in the time of Joan of Arc. The
Mariner was also medieval, and I think we are expected to retain a certain
superiority to him. He has received an almost blinding revelation, but we
need not be sure that he knows how to interpret it. The author might indeed
modestly disclaim having had the revelation himself; but I think he felt intimately and confusingly involved. The wicked whisper that kept the Mariner from praying must I think be 'God is unjust to me'; it comes soon after
the line, later expunged, saying that Christ would take no pity on him; but
much of the poem is concerned to deny this idea energetically. Then again,
the question whether you can love the slimy creatures would be bound up
in his mind with the question whether you can love their Creator; and are
they perhaps in some metaphysical sense a nightmare of your own? Such
are the ideas that would be at the back of his mind when composing,
though I do not mean that he deliberately worked them in.

IV

What then did one find, reading in bulk the reports of the European maritime expansion, which made it suitable for the Mariner to be struck down
by guilt? Surely the answer is plain once the question is asked; they reek of
guilt. Indeed Columbus himself, returning to Europe in the first triumph of
discovery, when he sent a cutter racing ahead with the good news to Ferdin-
and and Isabella, lamented that the Caribbeans were so innocent, unsus-
picious, and doomed. It may fairly be answered that this is unusual in a
ship's captain; as a rule, what is startling in his narrative is the absence of
any sense of guilt. A bit translated from the Portuguese struck me as good
prose owing to its earnest piety;

Then might you see mothers forsaking their children and husbands their wives,
each striving to escape as best he could. Some drowned themselves in the water;
others sought to escape by hiding under their huts; others stowed their children
among the seaweed, where our men found them afterwards, hoping they would
escape notice. And at last our Lord God, who giveth a reward to every good deed,
willed that for the toil they had undergone in his service they should that day obtain
victory over their enemies, as well as payment for all their labour and expense; for

they took captive of those Negroes, what with men, women, and children, 165, besides those that perished and were killed.

(*The Colonial Era*, H. Aptheker, 1960)

'What *use* was their religion if it did not tell them that this was wrong?' –
such was the way it would appear to Coleridge, who boasted to correspondents around this time that he did not examine religious doctrines as a mere
arguer, but always in the light of their practical effects. Also he had been
considering what useful steps an anti-slavery man could take; boycotting
sugar appeared to be ineffective. Charles James Fox took advantage of a
brief interval of power to abolish the slave trade in 1805, not long after the
poem was written, and common opinion seems to have thought this
overdue. The only actual superstition about albatrosses, it has turned out,
was that they were ships' captains who had been drowned passing the Cape
of Good Hope; perhaps then the story means 'The explorers did not realise
that the natives were human.' One still meets this legend in print, and Coleridge might come across it; but I have not found any case of it in the
reports. The Tierra del Fuegans were thought to be devils, not animals; and
anyway to be classed as human gave a creature no protection. Thus it
would not be right to say that the Albatross was a 'symbol' of the ill-treated
natives, but the terrible cry 'I didn't know it was wrong when I did it' belongs somehow naturally to the whole set-up of the exploring ship.

I became conscious of this around 1951 in communist Peking. Sardar
Pannikar, the Indian Ambassador, needed books; if you had been sent a
book, not to hand it on would be cruelty, so I proffered *The Enchafèd
Flood* by W. H. Auden. Next time we met (I should explain that my wife
and I were fortunate in being among the few residents the non-communist
diplomats might still invite) he growled out that it was all spoof. I said
Auden had proved his case, because the English, French and Spanish
Romantics all treated the sea in the way he described, but the Germans,
having still no empire, didn't; the force of the argument lay in the negative
control test. He reeled off quotations from the epics of three Indian
languages to show that the sea is always the great sweet mother, to the
poets. But that was Auden's point, I said, only the poets of the maritime
empires did it. 'Then they weren't really poets,' he said, leaving me convinced that Auden had made an important discovery about the 'Ancient
Mariner'. Probably he reflected, though I did not, that India in the time of
the poets he had quoted enjoyed a maritime empire extending to Bali and
Indochina. Still, I can't really think it vulgar of the Europeans to be Fau-
stian. The effect on literature of their maritime empires was to make the
explorer a symbol of scientific discovery, upon which the ships themselves
had depended, thence of intellectual adventure in general, and at last for the

highest event in ethics, the moral discovery, which gets a man called a traitor by his own society. The Victorians continued to give a good deal of rope to a serious traveller; the *Art of Travel* by Sir Francis Galton (1855) says in its opening sentence that every traveller must be prepared to take the law into his own hands. Auden says:

The Ancient mariner and his ship represent the small but persisting class of mental adventurers... From the social point of view, these spirited adventurers are criminals; they disturb the social order and they imply a criticism of the accepted round of life; they are self-appointed outcasts... The Mariner escapes from his isolation by the enlargement of his sympathies in the manner least expected and he is allowed to return to common life... But he is still the marked man, the outcast, the Wandering Jew, the victim of his own thought. Further, although he has been judged by society, he has the reward of the courage that propels the mental adventurer; that of arresting and disturbing and teaching those who have had no such experiences.

Rather too cosy perhaps, but very central. This is what the poem is traditionally about; as it would still be if Coleridge did not discover the meaning till after he had written and then ratted on it as fast as he could.

v

But the poem was from the start more anchored to the poet than that, and none of the changes he made are really alien to it. He was himself a martyr to Neurotic Guilt, feeling guilty without believing he had good reason for it; the 'Ancient Mariner' is the first and best study of that mental condition. Such is the reason why he couldn't finish any of his books; 'My sickness has left me' he wrote to Longmans (1801):

in a state of mind, which is scarcely possible for me to explain to you – one feature of it is an extreme disgust which I feel at every perusal of my own productions, and which makes it exceedingly painful to me not only to revise them, but I may truly add, even to look on the paper on which they were written.

Many authors have felt like this, but to explain it to one's publisher is a heroic exercise of the Romantics' principle of self-expression. Coleridge usually just says he feels fear, and then shows by the example that he is afraid of being told that he has done wrong, or more usually that he has neglected a duty. He used laudanum to quiet this condition, and no doubt made it worse, but the condition was there beforehand. 'The Pains of Sleep' (1803) gives a splendid description of his nightmares:

> But yesternight I prayed aloud
> In anguish and in agony,
> Upstarting from the feverish crowd
> Of shapes and thoughts that tortured me;

A lurid light, a trampling throng,
Sense of intolerable wrong,
And whom I scorned, those only strong!

... Deeds to be hid which were not hid,
Which all confused I could not know
Whether I suffered, or I did;
For all seemed guilt, remorse, or woe,
My own or others still the same,
Life-stifling fear, soul-stifling shame.

... Such punishments, I said, were due
To natures deepliest stained with sin,
For aye entempesting anew
The unfathomable hell within,
The horror of their deeds to view,
To know and loathe, yet wish and do!

Such griefs with such men well agree,
But wherefore, wherefore fall on me?
To be beloved is all I need,
And whom I love, I love indeed.

In January 1805, he wrote in a notebook (*Inquiring Spirit*, Kathleen Coburn, p. 54):

It is a most instructive part of my life, the fact, that I have always been preyed on by some Dread, and perhaps all my faulty actions have been the consequence of some Dread or other on my mind, from fear of Pain, or Shame, not from prospect of Pleasure. So in my childhood and Boyhood the horror of being detected with a Sore head ... then a shortlived Fit of Fears from sex, then horror of *Duns*, and a state of struggling with madness from an incapability of hoping that I should be able to marry Mary Evans ... Then ... my marriage, constant dread in my mind respecting Mrs Coleridge's temper, &c ... since then every error I have committed has been the immediate effect of the Dread of those most shocking bad dreams – anything to prevent them.

This mental state, in which the sufferer from guilt does not admit he has sinned, was what Coleridge was likely to want to express in the poem, because it was so familiar and such a burden to him; and such is what his fable does express – in the mind of an unsophisticated reader, now as then, the Mariner does not deserve his sufferings. Modern critics must therefore be evading the real point of the poem when they so eagerly invent proofs that he did deserve them. You may answer that the author himself was too ready with pathetic excuses, though really he deserved the punishment he got, so probably he is trying to delude us about the Mariner. But his views on Nature make him prone to blame the Mariner more than the expected reader would, and this saves the author from suspicion; the ambiguity of judgement heightens the effect. It was a splendid invention to kill all the Mariner's comrades and leave him alive with their dead eyes still cursing him, because he is then forced to blame himself more than we feel he deserves. They have died because he shot the Albatross, though he could not have guessed that the Spirit would use them as weapons to torment him. Also they have died because he called a ship to help them, biting his arm to be able to do it; this was a phantom ship containing Death, but he could not have known. After the gods had done him this injustice, he would not show good feeling or good taste if he did not overblame himself to an almost lunatic degree. Such, I think, is the evident point of this main part of the story.

Mr D. W. Harding, in an article for *Scrutiny* during 1941, now available in his *Experience into Words*, described the psychological background of the 'Ancient Mariner'.[1] I wasn't seeing the magazine then, and did not find a reference to the article till after drafting this piece; but he and W. H. Auden hold the priorities for the 'inside' and the 'outside' of the poem.

Coleridge found that walks in hilly scenery could do a good deal to palliate neurotic guilt; and this was the main basis in experience for the doctrine of the healing power of Nature through Imagination. Wordsworth in *The Prelude* describes his nightmares about revolutionary Paris in a fine passage very near to 'The Pains of Sleep'; they had the experience independently, I expect, and then told one another about it. Coleridge's idea of a walk was a good deal: thirty miles over rough country he seems to have thought normal, as a young man, whatever he was saying about his bowels. There is an aside in one of his letters, perhaps the only time when he made an excuse which was more impressive than he realised. He could not have done what he has promised, he is saying as usual, because he has had a complication of illness, owing to crossing a pass in Westmorland during a storm; and perhaps, it occurs to him, he may be told that he should have turned back; but this would be impossible to him, as it is not his habit: 'I never once in my whole life turned back in fear of the weather' (*Letters*, p. 484, 1802). We have long been told he was self-indulgent and weak-willed, and I now hear him called fubsy, but the trouble was that he was a compulsive character, who stuck to a line once adopted with appalling persistency. The reason why he had read everything was that he was a compulsive reader, who dared not stop; rather than open a letter from his wife, he would read straight on all through *Purchas's Pilgrims*. Schoolmasters are familiar with the type, which either does well or fails badly.

He thus expected Nature to be a bit rough; his everyday approach to her was rather like that of the explorer. The fundamental revelation granted to the Mariner, somewhat obscured by his compulsive technique of total recall, was granted to Coleridge himself about five years later and described in a letter to Sara Hutchinson:

I began to suspect that I ought not to go on; but then unfortunately though I could with ease drop down a smooth Rock of 7 foot high, I could not *climb* it, so go on I must; and on I went. The next 3 drops were not half a foot, at least not a foot, more than my own height, but every drop increased the Palsy of my limbs. I shook all over, Heaven knows without the least influence of Fear. And now I had only two more to drop down – to return was impossible – but of these two the first was tremendous, it was twice my own height, and the Ledge at the bottom was exceedingly narrow (so) that if I dropt down upon it I must of necessity have fallen backwards and of course killed myself. My limbs were all in a tremble. I lay upon my Back to rest myself, and was beginning according to my custom to laugh at myself for a Madman, when the sight of the crags above me on each side, and the impetuous Clouds just over them, posting so luridly and so rapidly to northward, overawed me. I lay in a state of almost prophetic Trance and Delight and blessed God aloud for the powers of Reason and the Will, which remaining no Danger can overpower us! O God, I exclaimed aloud, how calm, how blessed I am now. I know not how to proceed, how to return, but I am calm and fearless and confident. If this reality were a Dream, if I were asleep, what agonies had I suffered! What screams! When the Reason and the Will are away, what remains to us but Darkness and Dimness and a bewildering Shame, and a Pain that is utterly Lord over us, or fantastic Pleasure that draws the Soul along swimming through the air in many shapes, even as a flight of Starlings in a Wind. – I arose, and looking down saw at the bottom a heap of Stones which had fallen abroad and rendered the narrow Ledge on which they had been piled doubly dangerous. At the bottom of the third Rock that I dropt from, I met a dead Sheep quite rotten. This heap of stones, I guessed, and have since found that I guessed aright, had been piled up by the Shepherd to enable him to climb up and free the poor Creature, whom he had observed to be crag-fast, but seeing nothing but rock over rock, he had desisted and gone for help and meanwhile the poor Creature had fallen down and killed itself. As I was looking at these I glanced my eye to the left, and observed that the Rock was rent from top to bottom. I measured the breadth of the Rent, and found that there was no danger of my being wedged in, so I put my knapsack round to my side, and slipped down as between walls, without any danger or difficulty.

There is a briefer record in his Notebook (August 1802):

... pass along Scafell precipices; and came to one place where I thought I could descend, and get upon the low ridge that was between Scafell and Bowfell, and look down upon the wild *savage, savage* head of Eskdale. Good Heavens! What a climb! dropping from precipices and at last should have been crag-fast but for the chasm.

– also a less attractive reference in a letter of 9th August: 'Hartley is almost ill with transport at my Scafell expedition.' Poor little Hartley was not then quite six years old, and far too much a wind-harp for Father to blow upon; one can see how hard Father had puffed. But he might well be pleased; he had just written 'Dejection' and a series of letters about the pain of losing his poetic genius, and now the thing had actually happened. There is no sign of the vanity of an author – it does not occur to him that he has enacted the Mariner; what has happened is far more important – the theory about Nature has been proved true.

In his dealings with other people, Coleridge was too inclined to kiss the rod and then shuffle out of reach of it: he deeply distrusted open conflict or resistance. His passiveness before Nature here ('I bear pain with a woman's fortitude' he writes often) is rather the same, but it feels unaffectedly grand (the style is like Defoe), and a modern climber would readily believe that it saved his life. When in a tight place one should collect oneself and not get rattled; otherwise he would have died like the sheep. Many climbers would also recommend appreciation of the scenery, as a help in keeping one's nerve at such a time; and this almost amounts to saying, 'Delight in Nature when terrible gives one strength to control it.' Coleridge of course went further, believing that such delight marked an intuitive sympathy with the natural objects by an act of Imagination (very remote from making up a poem), and therefore restored the individual to a proper relation to the universe.

The Active Universe by H. W. Piper (1962) [see Empson's review below] shows that the view of Nature held by the earlier Romantics, however strange, was in line with 'the current scientific orthodoxy'. Contemporary reviews of poems by Wordsworth and Coleridge regularly explained what was new in their philosophy; pantheism was familiar enough, even in Pope, but the new poets combined it with animism, the belief in various kinds of Spirits which had been formative for Renaissance science. Thus they believed

that the world-soul would be found in each material object and that, through the imagination, a real communication was possible between man and the forms of nature.

Coleridge and Shelley both believed this, but Coleridge (thinks Mr Piper) was dependent as a poet on a personal relation with Nature in some way that Shelley was not. It is clear at any rate that the Mariner did not need to be a criminal before he could acquire a revelation of this kind.

VI

We should now be equipped to reconsider the 'moral' of the poem, 'He prayeth best, that loveth best/All things both great and small.' I would do wrong to belittle the moral 'Don't pull poor pussy's tail,' which needs to be taught to children; but Coleridge came to feel, like many of his readers, that it forms an inadequate conclusion to so much lightning and despair. What the Mariner had achieved was love of almost intolerable creatures, products of Nature when particularly inhospitable. I said in my *Some Versions of Pastoral* that Coleridge 'insisted in the margin by giving the same name to both' that the creatures by which he was at first most disgusted were the same as those which he eventually blessed unawares for their beauty, so that they became his salvation. I still think this a fair point, but the engineering of the poet is more radical and complex. To call both of them 'creatures of the calm' does not prove them identical, but helps to suggest it; when Coleridge wrote these marginal notes he continued to encourage a suggestion already made in the text. When the ship reaches the equator in the Pacific 'the Albatross begins to be avenged'; the sailors are dumb with drought, and

> The very deeps did rot; O Christ;
> That ever this should be!
> Yea, slimy things did crawl with legs
> Upon the slimy sea. (l. 125)

The water looked like petrol spilt on a motor road (next verse). More than a hundred lines packed with incident follow before these details are recalled, so we do not easily notice that the legs are omitted. The crew deduce from a dream that a Spirit is avenging the Albatross, so they hang the remains of it round the Mariner's neck. Delirium is probable by the time the skeleton ship appears to him – nothing definitely supernatural has occurred before. The unreasonable quality of supernatural justice is plugged home by the game of dice. Death wins the others, but Life-in-Death the Mariner; his condition when we meet him is a life in death, and Coleridge made play with the term again to describe his own life in his 'Epitaph'. That sailors are often victims of women when they strike land is a standard reflection, and the grand description of the prostitute White Goddess is entirely fitting for the 'outside', though for the 'inside' all it can mean is that the innocent Coleridge had been badgered by Southey into marrying a scold. An incurable syphilitic, unable to seek honourable love because he would give the beloved the disease which yet allows him to linger on, would strike Coleridge as an eminent case of life in death, not unusual among retired sailors; and the disease had actually been brought by Columbus from America. The skin of the goddess is white as leprosy, which poets have often made a sort of literary alternative to syphilis. Mr Christopher Ricks has pointed out to me that Coleridge in one of his letters (quoted by House, p. 152), mentions fearing in a dream that the breath of a spectral prostitute would give him the disease, and one can see that a terror then so eminent would have to be present in his nest of secret terrors, though his morality and his passivity would alike make him fairly safe from it. So the White Goddess is needed both for the inside and the outside of the poem, but I think he uses her mainly as a conjuring device, to distract our minds while all those legs drop off. The spectral ship goes, the sailors all die, and now for the first time the marginal gloss says *creatures*. 'He despiseth the creatures of the calm' (the term of course reminds you that God created them) is put against:

> The many men so beautiful
> And they all dead did lie;
> And a thousand thousand slimy things
> Lived on, and so did I.
>
> I looked upon the rotting sea
> And drew my eyes away;
> I looked upon the rotting deck
> And there the dead men lay. (l. 240)

Their eyes continue to curse him. (It is not only wonderfully good, but wonderfully like a real ballad.) The healing Moon comes up, making possible his act of atonement by showing the creatures in a better light, and they are now 'water-snakes' (l. 275); the words insist upon, and the rhythm makes vivid, a beauty of movement very unlike the movement of things that crawl with legs. The spilt-petrol colours recur but now seem hallucinatingly beautiful. These colours and the words *rot* and *slimy* all recall the things with legs, and the confident rotund gloss 'By the light of the Moon he beholdeth God's creatures of the great calm' feels to me like a pious refusal to recognise a well-known unpleasantness: maybe they still had legs when he 'drew his eyes away', and maybe their legs just dropped off quickly when the Moon got up; this would have been a magical bit of luck for the Mariner, because obviously he couldn't have loved them if they were still crawly. But the matter is handled with great tact, as it needed to be, because in theory he had to be able to love any degree of crawliness whatever.

One might expect Coleridge, with his Ommjective and Summjective, to make the Mariner recognise the snakes as part of his own nature; but he keeps very clear of that. The snakes are absolutely other to him, like beings of another planet, and it is an alien part of his own mind which blesses them; he is astonished that the saving act has been performed. I do not think there is any traditional Christian parallel to this; the process is entirely unlike, though it may easily recall, the repentant saint punishing himself by kissing the leper's sores. The process indeed is exactly the other way up. The Mariner is astonished to find his inside admiring what his outside had thought disgusting, but at once feels happy and thankful about it, so that his outside joins forces with his inside; naturally his life can now be saved, and as the readers have been made to share his nausea for the creatures they can grasp the heroic character of his spontaneous reversal. This also deals with an objection, first raised by Wordsworth, that the Mariner does not do enough to make him the hero of a poem. The motives of Wordsworth in this complaint are obscure, but I am afraid that whatever they were they must have been bad. He was just as much involved as Coleridge was, or H. G. Wells later on, in a middle-class anti-heroic propaganda, justified up to a point – a feeling that aristocrats had patented the honour of a soldier so that ratting on it was a class duty for literary men. Though the Mariner does every possible action for the survival of himself and his fellows, he could never appear as a fighting man; in the same way, because the rest of the crew are always united in decision, this is the only eminent sea story which never uses the thrilling words *captain* and *mate*. As a Pantisocrat, Coleridge felt that a ship ought to be imagined as a democracy (and Kinglake in *Eothen* reports that a small enough Greek ship really was); but a kind of artisan courage, from one of the crew, he felt allowed to praise; and the Mariner is a striking case of it. We assume he is demanding water for all his comrades when he hails the skeleton ship, because, if he had been dying alone, he could not have raised the strength to bite his arm and suck the blood so as to soften his mouth enough to shout. I think Coleridge ought to have told Wordsworth to try doing this himself before calling the Mariner insufficiently heroic.

VII

Psychologists tell me that they do not recognise the term 'neurotic guilt', which I have long heard used as of a familiar reality. For example, Dylan Thomas, with the dead earnestness which so often came as a surprise, told me it was curious he was such a martyr to attacks of neurotic guilt, as he led such an innocent life, but he found the only way to handle them was to hide in the country for a week or two, stopping drinking altogether, speaking to nobody, and so on. His meaning in using this term was clear; he felt struck down by guilt though by his own principles he had done no wrong; and it was easy to reflect that he had done wrong by the principles of the hostess of Fern Hill, his peasant aunt. A psychologist (as I understand) finds this trivial because it does not involve the mechanisms of the deep Unconscious, and indeed it is more like 'split personality' – one moral code goes on dragging against another. But it is the most prominent cause of mental upset among present-day educated people, and I think psychologists belittle it because they dislike admitting that there can be genuine rational disagreement about a moral question. There was nothing mad about Coleridge except a peculiarly severe conflict of this kind; he could not bear to rebuff the fundamental sympathies of his society and yet found that accepting the theology in which they were expressed, when he was beaten down to it, was a kind of suicide.

The schoolboy Coleridge would enjoy being praised for his cleverness, however pathetic the elder man made him appear; but decided that there was no future for him in scholarship, since all the white-collar jobs which it dangled before him required a profession of belief in what Voltaire had shown to be infamous. In his charity blue-coat gown, he explored London and found a shoemaker willing not only to take him as apprentice but also to come and tell the headmaster. The headmaster threw out the man and beat the child (for being an infidel), and Coleridge in later life amused himself by saying that this was the only just beating of all his beatings at school. He was right, I expect, to remember it as important; it had made him unable to emerge from his childish terrors. This boy sounds a great deal more vigorous and enterprising than the grown-up Coleridge. There were two or three further cases of 'I didn't know it was wrong when I did it,' but the pattern had been established. He ran into debt at college, so he later said, because when a man came and asked how to decorate his rooms he said 'As you please, sir,' supposing the cunning tradesman to be a college official; so he ran away and enlisted to save his family the money, but this only gave them the extra expense of buying him out. His disastrous marriage followed the pattern; Southey had told him it was the right thing to do. We have two descriptions, by himself and by a student friend, of his behaviour at Cambridge in a week before he failed an exam, and it is an effort to believe that both are true. The brilliant gaiety was achieved by 'acting a part' with iron resolution; but perhaps the suicidal despair was a bit playboy as well. This Romantic style of behaviour has become tiresomely familiar, but we should remember I think that Coleridge had a genuine reason for it; he did not believe the religion which was technically required of him, so there must eventually have been a showdown when he refused to take the oath for his degree.

He made a principle of not publicising his basic religious objection, and I have only found one place where it becomes clear. On 27 September 1796, Charles Lamb, who had been a younger but intimate schoolfellow of Coleridge, wrote that his sister Mary Lamb in a fit of madness had killed their mother. 'Thank God, I am very calm and composed, and able to do the best that remains to do. Write as religious a letter as possible...' Coleridge was unable to resist writing letters which were too religious (he was twenty-three; Lamb was twenty-one). The first reply of Lamb (3 October) begins with the words, 'Your letter was an inestimable treasure to me,' but the next one grieves that Coleridge is not settling down to a serious course of life, and the third (24 October) questions the doctrines that Coleridge has preached:

... Again, in your first fine consolatory epistle, you say, 'you are a temporary sharer in human misery, that you may be an eternal partaker of the Divine Nature'. What more than this do those men say who are for exalting the man Christ Jesus into the second person of an unknown Trinity? — men, whom you or I scruple not to call idolaters.

Presumably an idol, a Moloch, is a God who demands human sacrifices. Lamb is objecting to the idea that suffering makes us better because God enjoys it; also, he finds it bad taste for Coleridge to talk as if God has been kind to arrange a disaster so as to make Lamb better. He is deeply concerned to comfort his sister, so he finds it morally disgusting to be told to reflect that he himself is being polished for Heaven; has her murder polished *her* for Heaven? Indeed, I think the case is one which makes the unpleasantness of Christian consolation especially prominent. But I must not claim that it was obvious to Lamb; his letters here express deep submission to the arbitrary will of God, as when he says, near the start of his first reply to Coleridge:

My poor dear, dearest sister, the unhappy and unconscious instrument of the Almighty's judgements on our house, is restored to her senses — to a dreadful sense and recollection...

He is in no mood to isolate himself from the religious sentiments of his society. Only just of age, he has already had a period in an asylum, and now the senile father, the mulish aunt, the greedy brother, and the sister who, whatever her merits, was liable to turn back into a tiger at any moment, all depend for their bread upon his earnings as a clerk; he is taking care to preserve his sanity, and rather surprised at his success. They are impressive letters, especially as they are so far from the usual line of endeavour of a Romantic; and I think they suggest that both the friends had been more logical and definite in their revolt against Christian doctrine while still at school. Lamb's other objections in this letter seem to be against Coleridge's pantheism, not his backsliding into orthodox Christian torture-worship. But the sentence he quotes is not pantheist; for example, the Athanasian Creed speaks of 'the taking of the manhood into God'. Coleridge presumably accepted the rebuke, as he remained a Unitarian for about six more years.

We can see how hard it was to surrender to Moloch in a letter to his parson brother George (July 1802); he thinks he has invented a way to make terms with the Establishment without actually conniving at its basic infamy. He has come to believe, he says, in an

original corruption of our nature, from which and from the consequences of which we may be redeemed by Christ, not as the Socinians say by his pure morals or excellent example merely, but in a mysterious manner as an effect of his Crucifixion; and this I believe, not because I *understand* it, but because I *feel* that it is not only suitable to but needful for my nature and because I find it clearly revealed.

What he still cannot endure to say here is that the Father was satisfied by the crucifixion; he would have called that, surely, as already quoted, 'frightful corruption in the great article of all religions, the moral attributes of God' (the quotation at least shows that he was not too innocent to regard a theological question in that light). The process he was going through here was a frequent one, summarised with ghastly exactitude at the end of *1984*, in the pathetic delay of Winston Smith before gulping down last of all a somewhat disguised form of the doctrine 'God loves torture.' A later stage of the same struggle is recorded in what Coleridge called his 'happiest effort in prose composition', the 'Preface to Fire, Famine etc.' (Appendix III in the Oxford text of the *Poems*), first printed in 1817 but claiming to report a conversation probably held in 1803; it is a laboured piece of sophistry to the effect that seventeenth-century theologians did not really believe in Hell. When he returned from Malta (1806) he had become keen on arguing for the doctrine of the Trinity, and for ever after treated himself as an interesting moral invalid.

I may well be told that, as the defences of Coleridge against the religion were so inadequate, he could let it creep into the 'Ancient Mariner'. There are indeed plenty of expressions of straightforward piety by the Mariner, as is historically correct. But Coleridge just then was enjoying his brief period of triumph, especially the triumph of finding a friend he could revere; he expects the religion to be easy enough to handle – technical difficulties will melt away when confronted with real vision, and the certainty of offering a real vision is the very tone of his voice and gleam of his eye. A recent book *The Enchanted Forest* (W. W. Beyer, 1962) gives an interesting sidelight. It shows that many of the details of the 'Mariner' came from Wieland's verse romance *Oberon*, which Coleridge was translating from the German at the time (so he claimed in a letter). It might seem that this discovery refutes the Auden generalisation, but I do not think so; the only sea travel is in the Mediterranean. The hero, a vassal of Charlemagne, kills a son of Charlemagne in self-defence when ambushed treacherously on his way to Court; he can only be pardoned if he carries off and marries the caliph's daughter. So far he is trying to recover his due status; but halfway through the poem he commits a sin. The daemon Oberon has blessed his union with the Saracen princess but added that it must not be consummated till blessed by the Pope; while they are sailing to Rome this rule is broken (the lady seeing no need for it) and they are thrown overboard in a tempest for prolonged trials and sufferings. Mr Beyer several times calls the temptation 'provocative', evidently as a term of praise; I think he means that the lust of the reader is excited by the needless exasperation imposed on the characters. If so he justifies, without meaning to, the behaviour of Coleridge, who never admitted his debt to *Oberon* but said in later life that 'Wieland's subject was bad, and his thought often impure' (*Table Talk*, May 1811). This reaction must have come early, because Wordsworth in 1798, evidently relying on Coleridge's judgement, snubbed Klopstock by saying it was 'unworthy of genius to make the interest of a long poem turn entirely upon animal gratification'. A snuffy thing to say, but Coleridge really did find the theme somehow in bad taste. The Romantics often anticipate the Victorians, who felt that a gentleman should know how to avoid the indecent struggles for virginity recorded of the saints. Wieland had his free-thinking side but was prepared to screw as much drama as possible out of Christian chastity; and this is already vulgar because insincere. The Victorians were right, I think, so far as they were tacitly recommending evasive action, with only as much hypocrisy as the case required; and Coleridge was right not to want to praise a God who made vast punishments the sanction for unnatural and useless regulations. One might answer, indeed, that he did worse; he turned the crime into something which hardly any of his readers could accept as a crime, deliberately writing a kind of parody of the traditional struggle for atonement. Just before the 'Mariner' he was writing another study of remorse, 'The Wanderings of Cain,' and the surviving fragments show the same twist in his attitude. Cain out of remorse plans to sacrifice his son, but the ghost of Abel solemnly warns him against it. The initial fault of Cain had been 'neglecting to make a proper use of his senses'. A spirit advises Cain to blind himself as a means of expiation, but he decides that this would make him morally worse, still further from proper use of his senses. The Spirit turns into a flame and flees down athwart the jagged peaks of the mountain range, so we know its advice was wrong – an insinuating asceticsm has been defeated. Evidently, what Coleridge wanted to write about was uncaused guilt, even though the story he was using made the idea particularly hard to convey; no wonder he gave up 'Cain' when he found a more suitable story.

VIII

I need to fit 'Christabel' and 'Kubla Khan' into this account, which may be done fairly briefly. Coleridge soon realised that the 'Mariner' was a grander poem than he had expected, and tried to repeat the formula; that is, a large historical period or event was to be illuminated by the reader's intuitive knowledge of the psychology of superstition. To do a Gothic narrative poem was an obvious test; all along, the great buildings of the Middle Ages had been hard for the Augustans to ignore, so the Romantics in trying to escape from the Augustans made immediate use of them. But the sensational Gothic tradition derived largely from anti-Catholic propaganda, too sectarian for Coleridge, and after rejecting that (I think) he just could not see any point in his medieval witch. The end as it stands, the conclusion to Part II, does find a psychological truth in a superstition; it compares witchcraft to an affectionate pretence of cruelty; but this is painfully thin and laboured. It is much to the credit of Coleridge if he refused to finish 'Christabel' merely because he found it was a silly superstition, with no philosophical meaning (and Scott just cashed in on the new invention regardless); or he may, as he said, have been inspired by Crashaw's 'Hymn to St Teresa', and then found the combination of sexuality and desire for martyrdom too nauseating. Though so good in detail, the poem hardly reaches a point where my account can be tested.

'Kubla Khan', however, comes out well. Like House, I find it a completely achieved poem; probably Coleridge was lying when he told the story about the person from Porlock, nearly twenty years later, after Byron had succeeded in overcoming his deep shyness about printing it at all. When you realise what it means, you are not surprised that he felt shy. It is a grand though brief statement of the claims of the Romantic artist, and no wonder Coleridge when a failure could not face that. Sir Herbert Read in *The True Voice of Feeling* (1953) gave I think the best account of the Romantic position, which he thinks was first formulated by Schelling but widely acted upon beforehand. A society is always in development, and an artist has a function in it like that of the designer of fashions; the ladies know they want something, but only after seeing the new models can they say, 'I know what I was wanting; it was that.' The paradox of the artist is thus·the opposite of the Christian one; he must say ruthlessly what he himself likes or wants, and only by this selfishness can he help his fellows. It is assumed that they all have the same unconscious desires, since they belong to the same developing society and are subject to its pressures; otherwise the self-expression of one could not help the others. The theory had always been true, but the Romantics were the first artists to discover it and act upon it; if they appear ridiculously self-centred, we must remember they considered it a duty. It is in this sense, of course, that the poet is the unacknowledged legislator of the world. By the comparison to the dress-designer I do not mean to make the belief ridiculous but to convey how literally it was held, and how rapid the effects were expected to be; also the French Revolution introduced a new pace for the changes of fashion in female dress, and we are still living by it. Every girl must grow up thinking 'Poor Mum looked a frump at my age' – there has to be a radical change every generation; before 1789 the process took several generations, and mercifully it has not been getting quicker than the pace then established. Coleridge thus lived in a world which literally did have a heightened sense of changes of fashion. But the original creative genius for which society craved usually emerged from poverty or remote solitude; in music he actually did often come from some unexpected part of Europe, drawing upon its folk-songs. He would then be said to 'conquer Paris' and so forth; comparing him to Genghis Khan was practically a cliché, though when expanded into a poem it somehow became 'obscure'.

After writing a very good poem about the European maritime expansion, it was natural for Coleridge to think of the immediately previous world conquest, of the land mass by Mongols. The story was a familiar one to his mind, and ought to be to ours; it is important for us to understand that the Mongol ponies were cantering up to destroy our society root and branch, in the neighbourhood of Vienna, when another pony galloped up from behind with the news that Mangu Khan had died in Karakorum; so the ponies all turned round and cantered back, to a family share-out of the world conquest; and in the next generation, when they came westwards again, it was known that the rich loot was all in the south, so the Hounds of God destroyed the great civilisation of the Moslems. This caused the Arab inferiority to ourselves which we take for granted; but the reason we were spared was that we were notoriously inferior to them. I thus feel irritated when students placidly call 'Kubla' 'exotic', meaning, 'I won't be bothered with anything outside Europe.' Besides, the stories about the Khans are terrible; if you know them, you realise that it is a startling thing to say, 'That, at bottom, is what an artist is like.' The revolution which he brings may do good in the end, but at the time, if it is any good, it will be considered wicked as well as terrible. Coleridge was by no means a hard man, and maybe the grimness of the meaning of the poem, rather than its pathetic contrast with his actual failure, was what made him twenty years later pretend that he had composed it while asleep.

In all three poems an Inside needed to be related to an Outside, a psychology to a history; and I think that only cases like these allow a useful sense to Mr Eliot's term 'objective correlative' – one does not say over the telephone, 'Do come to dinner on Thursday; and look, I'd be awfully pleased if you could bring your *stomach* with you this time,' because it is not expected to be detachable. The phrase was first used about *Hamlet*, and there I do not see the application.[2] But it genuinely is I think a source of the magical power of the 'Ancient Mariner' that the inside can be felt to be far from the outside (rather as the children, who have been its greatest admirers, are not really explorers) and yet somehow they keep fitting one another perfectly.

Notes

1 D. W. Harding, 'The Theme of "The Ancient Mariner"', *Scrutiny*, IX (1941), pp. 334–42; a modified version of the essay figures in *Experience into Words*, London: Chatto & Windus, 1963, pp. 53–71.

2 T. S. Eliot, 'Hamlet', *Selected Essays* (third edition), London: Faber & Faber, 1951, p. 145.

'The Active Universe'

Critical Quarterly, V: 3, Autumn 1963

H. W. Piper, *The Active Universe*

In the twenties, when I was a student, it was usual to despise Romantics for expressing insincerely optimistic views about the universe. Perhaps the views were also merely aesthetic – the author, it was supposed, hardly expected his earnest pronouncements to be believed; but that would only afford a further self-indulgence. A number of books have been written since then to oppose this blasting misinterpretation, but Mr Piper makes points which I think are new. He brings out of obscurity as far as possible the characters who struck the Romantic poets as scientific authorities, especially the English-speaking community open to Wordsworth in revolutionary Paris. Scientists did not carry quite as much prestige then as now, but they were naturally your main authority about the cosmos once you had rejected the Church, and any self-respecting young thinker of the period (even Charles Lamb, for instance) considered wicked the God who could be bought off by the crucifixion. Mr Piper sometimes admits that a use of words by a Romantic is bad, but even so he considers it bad in a different way from what we think:

> In the poetry of Shelley and Keats the use of such words as 'eternity' and 'immortality' is not an appeal to vague associations. The words are used in an exact, if peculiar, sense to mean the possession of the Wordsworthian *summum bonum* in this life.
> The arbitrary use of emotive words was perhaps a natural part of the war against religion, just as attempts to capture such words as 'democracy' are part of the modern political struggle. (p. 184)

This *summum bonum* was 'participation in divinity'. We fail to grasp the position partly because we haven't read the scientific authors that they had, but also because we despise *The Excursion*, which was the main source available to them for the philosophy of Wordsworth; they found in it evolutionary progress as well as this ecstatic participation.

Perhaps our resistance to the Romantics dates not so much from the twenties as from Matthew Arnold, who said they were no good because they were provincial instead of being abreast of the new ideas of the Continent. It is satisfactory to find that this was just impudent bluff on the part of Arnold; the Romantics were stuffed with recent continental ideas which Arnold didn't know. The presumption that a classical education teaches you how to think is particularly startling when Arnold doubts whether conduct is three-fourths of life or seven-eighths of life; what can be supposed to happen in Arnold's mind while he attempts this numerical estimate, and where, short of the central African rainforest, would one find a more uninstructed mental operation? The conviction of Matt that he is superior to the Romantic movement needs to be recognised as pathetic.[1]

After doing justice in this way, however, a reader may still find the basic ideas of the poetry unattractive. 'The belief that inanimate matter is in a literal sense alive came nearest to establishing itself as scientific orthodoxy during the years of Wordsworth's most active poetic life' (p. 115). Some inanimate systems, for example the causes deciding the temperature of this planet as a whole, are self-balancing like an organism; that seems to be the main argument, and various parts of the doctrine have survived into modern science. But when bold Walking Stewart, who almost certainly influenced Wordsworth, laid down that man must 'do no violence to any part of animate matter', in which he included 'minerals and other organic and inorganic masses' (p. 71), he was making things difficult. It is uncomfortable, as Wyndham Lewis pointed out, to have to worry about the feelings of the chair you sit in, or the water you boil for tea; and the worry is likely to distract your attention from organisms who do have feelings. The letters of Coleridge show that he was not a vegetarian, though he seems to have eaten very little meat except when dining out, so he could not really have blamed the Mariner for wanting to eat the Albatross. Mr Piper, I am sorry to say, asserts that 'the Mariner had shown contempt for a living thing when he shot the albatross in mere sport' (p. 103). Mere sport is his own armchair fancy. The narrator is so horrified by his act that he remembers no motive for it, and the author wants a mystery; the critics hunt for any motive which will let them scold. But the first version of the poem says that the storm-wind had isolated the crew for 'weeks' and that they had maggots in the hard tack, so presumably the Mariner shot it, as any capable explorer would do, in the hope that it would share out as a soup protective against scurvy (apparently the crew were too superstitious to try). On the system Coleridge then believed, sin had already been committed when the crew sacrificed all those innocent biscuit-worms to feed one hulking great albatross. It is hard to catch him thinking about the doctrine practically, but he came to recognise as dangerous the refusal of hierarchy which had been its democratic charm; the horror in his later references to pantheism is obscurely connected with the carelessness of human life shown in Paris under the Terror. Shelley, in the next generation, was simply a vegetarian, and the high scruples about the feelings of plants do not seem to have returned till the far end of the century, producing an article by Chesterton named 'Why should Salt suffer?' (Salt being the name of a leading ultra-vegetarian.)

These moral deductions were never the main thing. The doctrine that Nature is a spirit peopled by spirits was a return to the science of the Renaissance, which made real discoveries by using it (and has therefore sometimes been called more superstitious than the Middle Ages). The mysterious beings who crowd the 'Ancient Mariner' are the same as the elegant personifications of Electricity and suchlike in Erasmus Darwin, whom the young Coleridge considered 'the first literary character in Europe'; but this did not make the belief in them playful, and Mr Piper thinks Coleridge could not write major poetry unless it was serious: 'When he could speak of the "real or imagined life" of natural objects, then the theme of the 'Ancient Mariner' was lost to him' (p. 136). On the next page: 'for Coleridge, the soul created the One Life in nature, but in doing so it acted in imitation of the Creator'; however, this was the merely intellectual solution, not strong enough to carry a major poem, which he adopted at about the time when he 'lost his faith in Unitarianism' (a polite way of saying that he was beaten down into accepting the Trinity, and ever afterwards regarded himself as a moral invalid). I expect this is the personal truth about the matter, and in a way it refutes Coleridge on Imagination by I. A. Richards, who expects the intellectual solution to do Coleridge good. It might do good to another man, but Coleridge hardly even wanted any more to have good done to him. One may deduce that the real forces behind the movement are not to be found in the self-excusing Biographia Literaria.

Both Keats and Byron sometimes express in their verse the belief that after death they will be able to meet directly the Spirit of a locality, an experience which during life can only be indirect and partial, however exhilarating. Byron only says it in the third canto of Childe Harold, after Shelley had been dosing him with Wordsworth, he said, and he assured his publisher when the fourth canto was ready that there weren't any metaphysics in it. Here we have a man who was ridden by a Wordsworthian belief for a time and then bucked it off. I used to suspect that Emily Brontë was the only one of them who really believed in a Spirit of the moor, and that the poets who had fed her imagination would have thought her very superstitious if they had met her; but, even so, what appears as a pagan fancy in Emily was a literal acceptance of beliefs which they had taken seriously.

Maybe the book does not give enough weight to politics, though it shows that at least some of the authors only 'took seriously' the philosophical or cosmological doctrines as part of a political programme. Also, we readers tend to make too much of one author influencing another, whereas at the time Romantic sentiment was an obvious force, pervading Western European society, and often giving people decisive instructions though they could not have told us why. The reasons why in such a case are likely to be political. This was clearer to us in the twenties than it is now; I find that modern students are incredulous when I say that Shelley meant by *If Winter comes, can Spring be far behind?*: 'Though the Bourbons have got back their thrones, which is bad, the resulting exasperation will bring world revolution all the sooner, which is good.' Modern students, having been told that Shelley was 'self-regarding', find it obvious that he was worrying about whether his poems were good enough to make him famous, whereas he would indignantly call this an intolerably sordid thing to write a poem about. (It is interesting to reflect that they could not find out that they were misreading the poem, their minds being too low to grasp the mind of the poet, by any Practical-Critical expertise in judging his 'style'.) He was touchingly modest about his poems, except that they might help to spread the right atmosphere for world revolution, which would justify them because that was all that really mattered. Nature did seem to have moods or periods of creative change, and it would be great luck to be able to co-operate with one. But he would probably agree, though he did not say, that their importance to the imagination must be chiefly as analogues of what is hardly less mysterious, the shifts of public opinion which introduce a major political change – or indeed, not to forget the baffling achievement of Wordsworth, which balance a society and prevent change from coming too fast.

The assertions about Nature were thus always partly an allegory about human affairs, but they become trivial if viewed as that only. We are nowadays inclined to resist them as being too rosy, not realising that the rosy side of them was intended as a defiance to the torture-worship inherent in Christianity. Shelley, says Mr Piper, 'continued to believe that the cause of mind is utterly unlike mind, a point of view which some of Wordsworth's terms in *The Excursion* fitted very well' (p. 168); and this hard-headed position did not prevent him from writing *Prometheus Unbound*: 'with *The Prelude*, the greatest poetic celebration of the active universe and its dealings with man' (p. 178). There is no inconsistency in saying that Shelley could do this though Coleridge could not. It looks as though the race of man needs a feeling of being accepted by the universe, such as is immensely conveyed by Shelley, if it is to live with mental health or perhaps survive at all in the world presented by modern science. Communists used to be expected to manage without, but not after the Russians had rejected modern genetics on the ground that 'God is not a gambler'; they seem if anything too theocratic. The assertion long ago of Mr T. S. Eliot that Shelley was too silly for him to read feels to me now like a boomerang, though I still sympathise with his distaste for the bad writing.[2] However, a simple answer seems available; Shelley's first rush of inspiration was usually bad, and the good poems are the ones he got round to correcting ... In any case, the major Romantics are the last authors who grappled with the problem directly and with adequate equipment; a book which makes one reconsider them is bound to be important.

Notes

1 See Matthew Arnold, 'The Function of Criticism at the Present Time'.
2 See T. S. Eliot, 'Shelley and Keats', *The Use of Poetry and the Use of Criticism*, London: Faber & Faber, 1933.

'So, We'll Go No More A-Roving'

c. 1931

I

So, we'll go no more a roving
So late into the night,
Though the heart be still as loving,
And the moon be still as bright.

II

For the sword outwears its sheath,
And the soul wears out the breast,
And the heart must pause to breathe,
And love itself have rest.

III

Though the night was made for loving,
And the day returns too soon,
Yet we'll go no more a roving
By the light of the moon.

It is dated 1817, only a year before 'Beppo' and the beginning of *Don Juan*: a more mature work than one might think from its fire, its looseness of form, and its freedom from Byron's mannerisms: the same revived energy that enabled him to throw off Byronism and write *Don Juan* and 'Beppo' seems to have allowed him this, his best lyric.

The idea may be then that we (Byron) are growing old: we must give up active affairs though we still feel vividly about them. But in so far as he felt old he felt 'cynical' – never more on me the softness of the heart will fall like dew, and so forth. It was the soul rather than the breast, from that point of view, that was worn out in his own case. (Anyway he wasn't as old as all that [Byron was 29], and they are not a settled couple who have grown old

325

together, these people gratified by the moon.) There is a suggestion of old age but rather as a metaphor: it is their love (seated in the breast, not the soul) which has worn out, and must have rest. They have as much desire for romantic love, put as much weight on it as the most interesting matter, as ever, but in this case we find it inadequate to sustain the weight of value we put upon it, and just do it no more. But *we* may mean 'we two as a couple', we must separate and find other loves (though this is tacit) or 'neither of us will roam with anyone any more': we are sated with the achievement of love and yet burning with a sense that something more, which should have been in it, is unsatisfied: and 'though the heart is still as loving' may mean that our emotional life is as vivid (sympathy for people in general and desire for the ideal), though we have lost the first flush of passion, or may mean that we feel the same towards each other, except that for some mysterious reason we have discovered that the feelings cannot be satisfied. 'So' is in a way the crucial word of the poem: it means 'these things being so' and we do not know how they were: though we know the poem would be beautiful for a great variety of them. It has a curious air of being accidentally crystallised into what has turned out to be a wide generalisation.

The *sword* may be an unconscious genital symbol of love, or it may be a symbol of sterner activities than love; it may symbolise love, while the sheath is the body; or it may symbolise the energy of the soul which burns through, craves to lose interest in, any one form of activity (such as love) or even any one woman. And it may outwear the sheath by being taken out continually or by being left in it, eating its head off. 'Though the day returns too soon' must be a metaphor from death (we have little time, we must start roaming, or lovemaking, or roaming with hands over the rich country of one another's body, as soon as possible, before the beauty of night is over, or before the servants see us or her husband wakes up) but daylight is an odd symbol for death: it suggests rather falling out of love again.

As for the heart pausing to breathe, one does not know whether this is just careless writing (Byron did not care much about English as such) or means a great deal. The heart does not pause; if it does you die, or at least faint with all the sensibility of the period. The actual *pausing of the heart* may be taken to correspond with the period while a particular drop of blood is breathing in the lungs, but in that case the pauses the heart requires are brief ones – 'you must leave me alone for a bit, we must feel as if we were parting forever' – with a wilful insistence on the drama of the situation – 'and we will, as a matter of fact, go roaming again later on'. (It is reasonable to take the heart as some definite image, like the sword, and as opposed to the parallel *soul* and *love* in even lines.) Or there may then be a sort of melancholy in the claim of pausing to breathe, as if this claim is only made when old age is coming on, when as a matter of fact it is no use pausing for new strength, and all breathing will soon be over. Or if the *heart* means the affections, not a part of the body, there is a touch of paradox about the way it is phrased – 'because the heart is not the physical object, therefore it is liable to exhaustion', though one would have expected (and have just been told) that the soul was less easily exhausted than the body.

'Everything, soul, body, and all pleasures and purposes, require rest' is a resultant of this: 'and yet it is not safe to rest, because the heart dies if it rests: there is as much courage, somehow even as much generosity, in pausing like this than in going on with the life of romance.' The whole variety of human activity and sense of value is concentrated into romantic love, and yet conscious that there are other activities outside.

I wonder what Mrs Wilson[1] would think of the change from 'so' to 'though' in the last verse? It may be a property of the sound only that the thing has become darker and more solemn.

It is the scale of the thing that is so striking: it has the movement of the tide up a great river in the calm of the moonlight with which it is concerned. I think one must put this down in part to the way such a variety of conceptions of love, or situations as subject of the poem, of judgements about them, are left loosely combined in the same movement of generosity and (so far as one can see) renunciation. It is not only or mainly in love affairs, after all, that the soul wears out the heart (outlasts, or actually breaks up the fury of its activity?).

Note

1 Katherine M. Wilson, *Sound and Meaning in English Poetry* (1931): see Empson's review of the book, essay 3 above.

Reflections before reading
Coventry Patmore

c. 1930

The Angel in the House, 1854–62

A sordid spectacle, I think. The man sets out to praise an idealised domestic life on the basis of leaving out the rude parts and saying it is Heaven. The puzzles are (1) he may not know whether it is true and (2) it may not be his turn to say it. We must add the falsity in supposing that it is material to write down for the printer 'I went to the lavatory today', but spiritual to write down for the printer 'I am in Heaven'. The error here is prior to any philosophical discussion. On any view of the events, they are both cases of what would commonly be called a spiritual or mental creature performing a physical action; both factors are involved. Without knowing the context we only know that the second writer is telling a lie; but either writer may have had excellent spiritual intentions. Apart from this obvious point, there is the perhaps subtle point of spiritual life, known to every decent man, that handing yourself a bouquet, even if done on every page for hundreds and hundreds of pages, is inherently different from being given a bouquet by another person. In fact a man who could get a bouquet handed him would hardly want to hand one to himself hundreds and hundreds of times. The effect of Patmore is to make one think that the three wives must each in turn have had a heavy tedious job.

He has been called the metaphysical poet of married life, and the interesting point is I think that he shows no capacity whatever to understand the real metaphysical puzzle in writing about married life. It is that the better the marriage the less you can write about it. Attention to this puzzle might I think produce a few decent lines of verse, but they would have to be real metaphysical ones in the Donne tradition. It is clear that any unsatisfied partner can easily write his or her account of what went wrong in an unsuccessful marriage. The assumption of Patmore that he can say what went right in his successful marriages only appears puzzling if you take the relationship seriously, as he was pretending to do. When taken seriously marriage becomes the same kind of centre for a more general puzzle in human relations that the eye does in the problems of knowledge of the physical world. The married couple is presumed to be combined *against* the world (to which the poet publishes his verses); they share information for combined action, on a day-to-day basis, and they are so far a spiritual unity that they cannot give evidence against one another in the courts. But to make this plan work well requires a great deal of bodily and mental accommodation; each party to this fundamental unit is trying to make it a unit. The better it is being done the less the strains appear; but it would always be false and even unjust to both parties to suppose that on that account the strains had vanished. A happily married person cannot say, 'I know if I do this there'll be a divorce, and if I do that there won't,' whereas some unsuccessfully married persons can. It is often said that a happy marriage gives a deep knowledge and mutual intimacy, and this is often true; the question is what you want to know; if you want to know what would break the marriage you are likely to know that less and less as the marriage becomes more and more successful. And even if you still know it under head (1) you would have less and less right to tell it under head (2). In speaking of divorce I am only trying to take a definite enough example to be considered; the point I really want to make is much more general. Precisely because a happy marriage gives a gain of knowledge and general seaworthiness, it requires a loss of knowledge properly so-called about the other party. The wife's face is too close to be seen; her faults are well known but they cannot be judged in proportion, because the getting over them or making use of them is involved in all plans for dealing with the outside world; the wife's irritations and satisfactions with you (I speak from one side of the fence) are inherently absorbed into what you can do about her. The human animal is always buffeted by sense-data, and its whole claim to knowledge, which is its glory, presumes that one such animal has got somehow onto a hill from which the 'eye' can survey the scene. This condition is inherently not satisfied by a successful marriage, and less satisfied in proportion to its success. Such is the elementary material for a metaphysical poem about a happy marriage; a thing that neither Patmore nor any metaphysical poet (I believe) has ever seriously attempted.

Hopkins's 'The Windhover':
a controversy
1954–55

I caught this morning morning's minion, kingdom
  of daylight's dauphin, dapple-dawn-drawn Falcon, in his riding
  Of the rolling level underneath him steady air, and striding
High there, how he rung upon the rein of a wimpling wing
In his ecstasy! then off, off forth on swing,
  As a skate's heel sweeps smooth on a bow-bend: the hurl and gliding
  Rebuffed the big wind. My heart in hiding
Stirred for a bird, – the achieve of, the mastery of the thing!

Brute beauty and valour and act, oh, air, pride, plume, here
  Buckle! AND the fire that breaks from thee then, a billion
Times told lovelier, more dangerous. O my chevalier!

    No wonder of it: shéer plód makes plough down sillion
Shine, and blue-bleak embers, ah my dear,
  Fall, gall themselves, and gash gold-vermillion.

In Seven Types of Ambiguity *(1930) Empson cited the 'proud but helpless
suffering' of Hopkins's 'The Windhover' as an example of the seventh type
of ambiguity, which 'occurs when the two meanings of the word, the two
values of the ambiguity, are the two opposite meanings defined by the context, so that the total effect is to show a fundamental division in the writer's
mind'. Hopkins sacrificed his early poems on becoming a Jesuit, Empson
wrote, and this poem conveys 'an indecision, and its reverberation in the
mind'; his full analysis included these observations:*

Confronted suddenly with the active physical beauty of the bird, [Hopkins]
conceives it as the opposite of his patient spiritual renunciation; the statements of the poem appear to insist that his own life is superior, but he
cannot decisively judge between them, and holds both with agony in his

mind. 'My heart in hiding' would seem to imply that the 'more dangerous' life is that of the Windhover, but the last three lines insist it is 'no wonder' that the life of renunciation should be the more 'lovely'. 'Buckle' admits of two tenses and two meanings: 'they do buckle here', or 'come, and buckle yourself here'; 'buckle' like a military belt, for the discipline of heroic action, and buckle like a bicycle wheel, 'make useless, distorted, and incapable of its natural motion.' . . .

Thus in the first three lines of the sestet we seem to have a clear case of the Freudian use of opposites, where two things thought of an incompatible, but desired intensely by different systems of judgements, are spoken of simultaneously by words applying to both; both desires are thus given a transient and exhausting satisfaction, and the two systems of judgement are forced into open conflict before the reader [3rd edition reprinted, Hogarth Press, 1984, pp. 225–26].

In a footnote added to the second edition (1947) Empson had insisted:

the test is 'buckle'. What would Hopkins have said if he could have been shown this analysis? It is, perhaps, the only really disagreeable case in the book. If I am right, I am afraid he would have denied with anger that he had meant 'like a bicycle wheel', and then after much conscientious self-torture would have suppressed the whole poem.

In a letter to the Times Literary Supplement *(3 September 1954), F. N. Lees contended that Empson's negative paraphrase – his 'effectively contradictory development' – of the word 'buckle' could not be supported. After 'diagrammatically' supplying his own paraphrases, with the suggestion that they mean 'a fusion of the senses . . . not an invitation to use each in turn', Lees proceeded: 'But why not the bicycle wheel sense? Because "the fire that breaks from thee" is yet another subject for this verb, and it is as difficult to accept its buckling in [Empson's] "crumpling" sense as it is easy to accept its sudden addition to the "brute beauty and valour, &c.," its "joining in".' While conceding that there seemed to be a 'less contradictory hint of internal struggle and clash latent' in his own interpretative approximations, Lees asserted in conclusion that Empson (and I. A. Richards) attached 'the feeling of conflict . . . to the wrong places in the poem, which has thereby been deformed'.*

Empson replied with the following letter to the TLS on 1 October 1954:

I am not certain about the double meaning for 'buckle' which I proposed long ago in Hopkins's 'Windhover'; anyway, the main conflict of the poem is there without it; but I see no force in Mr Lees's argument against it. What I meant, and said more clearly in the second edition, was that Hopkins set out with the idea 'like a belt' and would have been shocked to realise that (in his extreme tension of feeling) he was also using, at the back of his mind, the idea 'like a bicycle wheel'. I believed this for the human reason that it was how his mind was likely to work, not for an aesthetic reason, that it made the poem better; though it does give an appallingly direct impression of his mental conflict. Mr Lees, in his first paragraph, flatly asserts that this may be 'attractive' but cannot be true; and his only argument is the offer of a joke case with no inherent plausibility.[1] The Hopkins case seems to me painful rather than attractive, but directly relevant to the central impulse of the poem. Merely to assert that the half-conscious pun is impossible is to ignore well-known facts about what strange things the mind can do.

I cannot see why Mr Lees makes 'the fire that breaks from thee then' another subject for the verb 'buckle'; buckling a fire is very strained, and the phrase need only be an exclamation – 'how much fire breaks from thee then' (after extreme self-discipline). And surely the newly ploughed furrows are what 'shine', not the plough; at least they do in the heavy wheat land that I come from – they look greasy. The idea is that the ploughman makes a beautiful shape though he is simply trying to plough as well as he can.

Then Mr Lees rejects the ideal of '*internal* struggle and clash', though he admits it to be 'latent' even in his own paraphrases; and his reason is only that this idea 'does not lead suitably to "no wonder of it"'. But the poem says it does, because all forms of worldly training have a likeness to the poet's terrible spiritual training; the trouble is that they give strength and beauty, whereas his, he says in another of these appalling sonnets, has made him impotent. Such is his recurring doubt; his training does not seem to have had good effects, at least in the world. Mr Lees thinks, apparently, that if you allow the meaning 'buckle like a bicycle wheel' it has to apply to the bird as well as the poet, and this would be absurd; but the whole topic of the poem is the contrast between them. The beauty of movement in the bird comes from the skill it has gained by laborious practice, a form of self-discipline which does have plainly good effects. For that matter, I think Mr Lees had probably do some more ploughing before he tells us that there is no 'struggle' in learning to do it well.

What does clearly fit in, I think, with the idea of the buckled bicycle wheel, the broken Old Adam, is the final frightful image of the ash falling into the almost exhausted fire, as the last movement possible to it, and creating a new diffused glow of torture; such is what happens when the bird stirs the poet's hidden heart, and 'gold-vermilion' is meant to recall paintings of martyrdoms. I cannot feel that a critic is being sober or well-balanced or any of those good things if he merely refuses to realise what the poem is about.

The following year, again in a letter to the TLS (6 May 1955), J. G. Ritz offered an interpretation of the poem which 'answers all the difficulties of the sonnet, while rejecting far-fetched explanations': 'The whole poem is at once one of Hopkins's splendid meditations on Christ's glory and sacrifice as God and Man-God, and one of his deep ponderings' over the necessity of imitating Christ. His account opens by observing that the poet:

watches [the bird of prey] as he glides and hovers in the air, and admires his mastery. He then sees the bird swoop down (or he imagines it) and 'buckle' or 'gather together' his beauty, valour, pride ... for his sudden fall upon a prey that he will snatch away from the ground. He drops like lightning ... and this 'fell swoop' is for the poet, who is eagerly watching it, even more lovely than the bird's masterly gliding in the air; and it is 'more dangerous', since it is a sheer fall and there is a victim. The second tercet justifies the 'fire' image. One should not wonder at it. The share and mould-board, as they sink into the soil and tear it open, shine – are on fire, one might say – and grey embers, when some poker stirs them, fall and reveal fire burning under the 'rind' of blue ashes.

The Windhover, Ritz proceeds, is symbolical of Christ who 'swooped down like a bird of prey': 'Christ's incarnation, his lowly life in Galilee, are "lovelier" and "more dangerous" since they imply the redemption of men and their salvation. To be Christ's prey is no small matter for Hopkins...' Any Christian can imitate the Windhover and Christ: 'By gathering together and humbling his own gifts, his spiritual life will become far lovelier and more dangerous than the mere enjoyment of his mortal gifts.'

'Too many critics seem to vie with one another in their quest of subtle niceties,' he concludes:

why should Mr Empson construe so strangely 'plough down sillion shine'? True, sillion may shine, but it is the shine of the plough that the poet is considering ...

Finally, the conflict between artist and ascetic ... is simply not there. The bird's 'achieve' and mastery are admired as those of a creature of God and as a great symbol of Christ. And 'buckling' beauty and valour and act ... is not self-destruction but self-dedication. It must be remembered that 'The Windhover' belongs to Hopkins's 'Welsh salad days', not to the terrible years of 'No worst, there is none'.

Empson answered with this letter to the TLS on 20 May 1955:

The letter of Mr Ritz on Hopkins's 'Windhover', in your number of 6 May, deserves respect for giving a consistent interpretation of the whole poem; and an interesting one, though I am not convinced by it. Some weeks ago you, Sir, were mentioning in an editorial [18 March 1955, p. 165] the recent letters about the poem, and said that I seemed to have become doubtful. That is not what I meant; I was so sure of the general purport of the poem that I thought it was little affected if one left out, say, the pun on 'buckle'. But Mr Ritz makes the purport quite different, and his argument from the date is rather strong.

I think the poem is about training and about the doubt in Hopkins's mind, expressed with painful force in later sonnets, as to whether the severe Jesuit training had only crippled him. The flight of the bird and the lines made by the ploughman are beautiful with the unconscious grace of an acquired skill; but all that Hopkins has got from his discipline, as far as he can see, is what the Americans call a 'slow burn'. He none the less exults in the sacrifice. I confess I had not realised that the poem was done in '77, the year of his ordination, whereas all the 'terrible sonnets' seem to belong either to '85, when he was sent to Ireland and felt overworked, or '89, the year of his death. However we need not assume that the suspicion was remote in '77; he had been under the training for nine years, burning his youthful poems in '68; and 'my heart in hiding' is bound to mean something like it. I can agree that the effect is meant to be less tragic than in the later sonnets.

Mr Ritz, on the other hand, takes the poem as about gloating over torture. Hopkins must have been 'stirred' by the hawk because he saw it, or imagined it, swoop and catch its prey, just as Christ has swooped and mangled Hopkins. The swoop, the act of violence, is what is 'lovelier' and 'more dangerous' than the masterly gliding (whereas I had assumed that the parallel spiritual achievement was more so than the animal one). The plough has now to be envisaged as both ripping up and searing the flesh of the earth, and what 'shines' is this hot weapon. Mr Ritz expresses surprise at my wanting the new furrows to be what shine, but our two views there merely follow from our basic assumptions. To take 'plough down sillion' as a whole scene in movement is not too strained, as grammar, for Hopkins if he wanted it; the trouble is that this mood of contemplation is not wanted by Mr Ritz, who even has to take a poker, in the last line, to the exhausted fire. I am not sure why he thinks this savage interpretation more suited to the happy 'salad days' of Hopkins, but he is well supported by the 'Deutschland' of '75 – e.g., 'the swoon of a heart that the sweep and the hurl of thee trod'.

Hopkins must have known, I agree, that the 'valour and act' of the bird, the source of its beauty of movement, was killing other creatures; and the idea of the fierceness of God was not strange to him; but if this is the point of the poem why is he so far from saying it? The need for a suggestion of conquest in the bird he does feel, and says merely that it 'rebuffed the big wind'. The swoop can only be deduced from 'Brute beauty and valour and act, oh, air, pride, plume, here/Buckle'; and if we insert this sudden crisis we have next to compare it to rather un-sudden things, the plod of the ploughman and the occasional fall of the embers as the coals that support them burn away. I agree and shall remember that the power to swoop was part of why he felt the bird made a good symbol for Christ; but I do not think it was in the centre of his mind here, where he is considering the gradual effects of a given course of life. At least, I was sure he was considering that till I was confronted with the date; but then again, it is not an odd theme for the year of his ordination.

The question, I think, has a larger bearing. Christian apologists nowadays, I seem to notice, have become rather defiantly keen on recalling the stark roots of primitive human sacrifice and their place in Christianity, even boasting in print (one is to suppose with a laugh) that the religion provides a more efficient sadistic drug than the forbidden Horror Comics. Hopkins like other mystics was very capable of scolding his God for cruelty, but I don't think this idea rode his mind all the time; a more impersonal cruelty in the nature of things is what he sighs over in 'no wonder of it'. I am not sure that he wouldn't have considered Mr Ritz's interpretation blasphemous, unlike the pun which I proposed on *buckle*.

Empson finally followed up the published exchanges with the following personal letter to Mr Ritz on 27 November 1955:

I have been trying to think again about Hopkins's 'Windhover' and your letter on it, having a quiet weekend; and wrote down some points; but then I found my old letter to the *Times Literary Supplement* and felt I was only making the same points again. I hope you too have the cuttings of the old controversy so that we can try to go forward from it.

As to the poker, I certainly did not mean as you suggest that it is too 'unpoetical' to be present; indeed it is you, not I, who now seem to think poking a fire a peculiarly humble activity. I thought it spoilt the *logic* of the poem (not an objection which only the French would make) because the beauty produced by the bird and the plough are both incidental results of an activity; they are not produced by a direct intention, whereas the renewed glow of the fire after poking *is*. Also the beauty of the image of the falling embers, applied to the suffering of the poet, is so great that I could only invent a somehow contorted impulse as your reason for rejecting it. I now understand that you wanted the poem to give a series of humble but steady and practical activities; but even so, a man does not have to poke a fire continuously, as he has to plough.

When you say that the falcon swooping on to its prey is by that act a symbol of Christ humbling himself to our manhood I still cannot help feeling that there is a frightful distortion of natural sentiment; it is like the slogans of the world of George Orwell's *1984*, such as War is Peace (and by the way that book attacks any system of power through inquisition, Christian quite as much as communist). When you say 'Christians have long accepted the image as depicting God's power over souls' I have to recall that they have accepted many different things in their long career, some of which would have appeared very bad to Hopkins as well as to me; and I really do think it alarming that modern Christians are so inclined to boast about the crueller aspects of the religion. The effect of the quarrel between communists and Christians seems to be that they egg each other on to the same grave faults. I realise that this accusation seems very unjust to you personally, but I was not trying to find an easy way to win an argument; I still do think that your mind at this point must have been slightly affected by this bad influence. The falcon when it swoops is more proud than at any other time (I believe there is a falconer's technical term about the bird's 'pride' as its going up, which could explain Hopkins's use of the word in this sonnet before it goes down, but I still think the feeling would be all wrong); the swoop may represent the power of God over the soul, traditionally as you say, but it cannot also represent Christ when humbling himself by becoming man; at least it evidently can because it does to you, but I still think that Hopkins would have found the idea very unpleasant and shocking.

You say that 'my heart in hiding' means that he blames himself for being merely contemplative, not at all that he has had to suppress part of his impulses in order to school himself to become a priest. I suppose you feel that you are defending him against an accusation; but surely he confesses no more than normal humanity, and your unnecessary defence, as so often happens, only imputes something worse. What would it mean if he blamed himself for being merely contemplative, in the year of his ordination? Surely the only natural meaning is that his heart is hiding from temptation towards the kinds of experience he has renounced, and the sight of the fierce beauty of the falcon brings them back to him. He then recalls, I don't at all deny, that it is itself an old symbol for Christ; but the bird, the ploughman, and the martyred saint (symbolised by the fire with the colours for the paintings of martyrdoms) are kept in their sequence; the blood-lust of the bird would not be what he wanted to emphasise at the start, let alone all through the poem.

What does emerge, I am afraid, is that the poem is rather a failure. Hopkins was writing more telegraphically than he realised; there is a failure of communication, as becomes very clear when we all struggle with one another's interpretations. The poem would be good if the various meanings could be resolved into a larger unity, and I could not object to having both the plough and the ploughland made beautiful; but I don't see how a reader's mind can both take a poker to the fire and not, and I quite see the poker follows from your belief that the triumphant bone-smashing act of the falcon is an illustration of how Christ humbled himself to become man. The alternative interpretations, it seems to me, cannot be experienced together to make a good poem, and I still think that Hopkins would have suppressed the poem if he had realised that it would be interpreted as you do.

Looking back at your letter, I see you say 'What other basic assumptions are mine than the *strictest* adherence to Hopkins's own words and images?' Perhaps the word 'image' is the confusion here, because in your exegesis you start with the symbol of the falcon as an already ancient and many-sided Christian tradition. But the poem does not do this; it evidently begins by describing a real accidental event, and then says what the poet thought after being moved by its beauty. When you say that the falcon swooped there is really no 'adherence' to the words of the poem, whether 'strict' or not; you could only claim an 'adherence to the image'. It seems clear to me that if Hopkins, who was a rather excessively sensitive man, had actually seen the bird catching prey he would only have been moved in the way he would have been moved by seeing a stoat catching a rabbit; and I hope I need not explain that I mean he would have felt disgust.

There seems little hope of our reaching a friendly agreement on this matter, because I really do fear that it raises large issues; but I certainly think that it is worth taking time to try to get the point of disagreement clear.

Yours respectfully
W. Empson

[Empson Papers]

Note

1 Lees mocked Empson's 'attractive' notion of 'a transient and exhausting satisfaction' in 'the Freudian use of opposites' with this analogy:

'William Cowper, in 'The Task', tells how, "as a truant boy ... I fed on scarlet hips"; yet while an appropriate erotic fantasy would not be hard to imagine, I think I shall not be reproved if I dismiss it to what Americans call the "pulp" magazines and confine my attention to the more innocent satisfactions of the hedgerows. Similarly, though it is clearly a trickier case, with "buckle": we must decide *which* it means; and I suggest that it has the *not* like a bicycle wheel meaning' [sic].

IV
Poetry (2): Moderns and Contemporaries

A Masterly Synthesis

Poetry, LV, 1939

Cleanth Brooks, *Modern Poetry and the Tradition*

Mr Brooks offers this as the consolidation of a critical position that many writers in recent years have been building up, what I suppose would be called the intellectualist position, and it is a masterly piece of work. The modest claim does not mean any lack of originality in the detailed interpretations of poems. The analysis of *The Waste Land* is much the best I have seen, and there is some striking material about Yeats. Perhaps the best single crack is the remark that it is not the obscure poet but the unwilling public who escapes into an Ivory Tower. A short review of such a book had best look round for the points of disagreement, but the main body of it seems to me true and convincingly argued.

But whom is it meant to convince? I suppose people who already read poetry, but bad poetry. They might be told more about the degrees of badness. It seems clear that Propaganda poetry ('I want you to feel like I do about this,' or what Collingwood recently called the magical use of art, more of a social function) is not in itself Sentimental poetry (keeping to a limited range of feelings, to let them run riot), and Uplift poetry is different again. Assuming they are all bad, there is a question what poetry is used for – what kind of threshold ought to be crossed before you spill over into it from normal life? Is it better to have second-rate poetry in your life than none? And what sort of effort is required to produce or enjoy the virtues Mr Brooks praises? Do you want to be cool or nearly crazy? Oddly enough, you seem to want one extreme or the other.

The demand that the imaginative act must keep a balance of judgement can come down to hardly more than writing with good sense. For instance Mr Ransom's poem about the little girl whose pet hen died ['Janet Waking'] deserves all that Mr Brooks says about it – it keeps just the right tone, it is good taste, it lets the general comment on life and death be there without fuss. It is a particularly good piece of Communication. And this sort of virtue is almost necessary to good poetry, and the Romantics tended to lose it. But surely it has not even a technical likeness to the frozen agony of *The Waste Land*. There the symbols may mean alternately life or death, as Mr Brooks well shows, and a frightful tension requires a frightful concentration of style. He denies that there is any 'despair' in the poem, and thinks critics who said there was have misunderstood it. To be sure, it does not say people can never be happy, but the poetry of flat contradiction is almost a clinical thing; it can only be done well as a way of treating yourself for a terrible state of mind. We had a lot of people in England trying to do that after Eliot; I don't know that it happened much in America, except for Hart Crane. It is perhaps an odd thing to try to do. But it seems to me that Mr Brooks's approach tends to treat the concentration of horror as no more than the balanced tone of good sense.

Rather the same thing happens in his account of Auden. He praises with great discrimination some poems from the first volume and expresses doubt whether Auden will go much further. But one of the impressive things about Auden is that after starting in the Eliot tradition of horrified concentration he refused to get stuck there; he is now able to use the same intellectual and technical power on normal and easily communicated states of feeling. The later poetry joins on easily to his ordinary life, and for that reason (paradoxically if you like) does not have to be a private poetry which only a few insiders understand.

It is in this kind of way, I think, that the things Mr Brooks's theory excludes cannot be excluded in practice. I suspect he would call the new attitude to communication in Auden's later work a desire to write Propaganda, which he disapproves. Indeed any poet who tells his readers what he thinks about the world is getting mixed up with Truth, which Mr Brooks wants to keep out of poetry. I agree that the case of Yeats is very odd, writing so earnestly about a magical scheme he can't really have believed in. But I should say he firmly believed in part of it, the Spengleresque historical forecast for instance – thought that part of it, for instance the classification of types of men by lunar phases, gave a handy system for a real set of differences, and felt that the particularly unscientific parts were a decent weapon against the harm done by scientists getting off their beat. Then the different parts fitted together and suggested each other to him. To call the whole thing a pseudo-statement seems to me to blanket the way a man's mind actually works. But Mr Brooks is careful not to talk psychology – about how a poet's mind gets into these contortions, or whether different kinds of people get good results from different kinds of poetry – even in his account of 'metaphysical' wit (where repressions come in naturally). That would be toying with Science, which he wants to keep out of Literature. Or maybe he doesn't want all this, and just outlined the critical programme. It is a cast-iron programme, and it makes for a healthy toughness in critics, but I can't see that it goes all the way.

A Time of Troubles

New Statesman, 23 July 1965

A. N. Jeffares (ed.), *In Excited Reverie*
Thomas Parkinson, *W. B. Yeats: The Later Poetry*
Edward Malins, *Yeats and the Easter Rising*

The Yeats centenary comes the year after the Shakespeare one, granting no break in the struggle to provide human touches. One of the reveries here says that Yeats happened to notice he had never been in a pub, so he asked a Higgins to take him, and when this Higgins had led him in he said: 'Please lead me out again at once.' What then becomes of the line: 'Companions of the Cheshire Cheese'? The poverty of Yeats for much of his life is to his honour. Gossip is a help, on the other hand, when you are uncertain whether a detail in a poem is ironical. The poem 'Among School Children' says that the children were being taught by nuns 'in the best modern way' and another reverie explains that this describes a school in Waterford using the Montessori method, recommended by Gentile, the Fascist Minister of Education, as developing a child's initiative and freedom: that was one of Yeats's ideals, and he urged upon his fellow senators that he had himself observed the method actually succeeding. To know this perhaps makes the poem sadder, but makes it better, I think.

The most interesting part of the book is the chapter on Yeats's politics by Conor Cruise O'Brien. He writes as a hereditary opponent of the Protestant Ascendancy, but an outsider can share his surprise: how could Yeats expect that a minority would receive consideration, after the victory of the revolution he had worked for? He even seems to have believed that he could eventually induce the priests to countenance his Theosophy. Compared to that, hoping for a political accommodation (not destroying the country houses) was almost modest. I think he was so confident about his religion that he expected it to become generally recognised, even where not accepted.

In 1925 Yeats made a speech in the Senate objecting to a new set of Catholic laws: the one before the house forbade divorce, but the next imposed in full form the clerical censorship against which he had fought all his life as a writer. He said that this was unfair to the Protestant minority, and Mr O'Brien says that the tactless Yeats, so far from being liberal, was 'the spokesman of a superior caste, denying the right of an inferior caste to make laws for it'. He did indeed urge that this minority had deserved well of the state, as an additional reason why it should be allowed to live by its own convictions. You may call him an ass for it, but while working for Irish freedom he had assumed he was not working for tyranny; and if the cause was hopeless, he need not be thought a petty intriguer.

I do not know whether Mr O'Brien would say that a majority vote in Cyprus would justify removing all land from Turkish farmers and giving it to Greeks; or that a Cypriot Turk, who was rather badly thought of by other Turks because he had become a Parsee, was a Moslem because he was a snob. You often find a hangover in the minds of liberated persons: if you say, for example, 'You ought not to engineer the water of the Punjab away from the Pakistanis,' they look at you with astonishment and say: 'But don't you know? I'm a sacred cow.' There is one hopeful side to this: a sacred cow can often behave with the needed brotherly gruffness towards other sacred cows remote from it.

Mr O'Brien considers that the young poet was cunning in self-advancement when he got a poem about the death of Parnell into the pro-Parnell Dublin paper on the day of the funeral:

There can have been few – and hardly any on the Parnellite side – who were not more moved by 'Mourn and then Onward' than Yeats was.

But Yeats was prone to love a stern, aloof leader, and savoured the theatricality of Parnell; and surely even a poet is allowed to be efficient about a funeral. Two or three times, as the essay goes on, Mr O'Brien laughs at Yeats for not going to this funeral; but if he *had* gone, with his poem in that morning's paper, how readily Mr O'Brien would have told us that he had tried to steal the limelight from the corpse.

These are minor points; the weight of the charge is that Yeats was a fascist. Surely the first point to get clear is: 'So were all the great writers in English in the first half of this century, except Joyce.' Yeats was accustomed to boast in later life that his poem 'The Second Coming' had been a prophecy, but the political substance of it had appeared in George Moore's *Confessions* almost thirty years before, arousing little alarm since it merely reported the gossip of the Paris studios. The popular novels of Belloc, around 1910, relied on a general indignation at the ease with which a voting system can be rigged so as to let capitalists control an ignorant population; and Chesterton, an acute as well as saintly character, believed that Mussolini stood for three acres and a cow (to each farmer). Mr O'Brien comes near to sneering at the Cosgrave party for accepting the majority vote in 1932 (which meant the final downfall of the Protestant Ascendancy), so that the reader can hardly feel great moral outrage at Yeats for taking an interest in a more virile reaction. Yeats of course would have said that he ought to consider the broad interests of the country, and was not morally bound by the votes of a people who had been told how to vote by their parish priests. Such was the context in which he wrote letters with glee about the prospect of a bit of rough stuff, assuming that it would be short, and that one need not hold the population down afterwards. He was not being sensible, as Mr O'Brien well shows, but we need not regard him as part of a world line-up with Hitler.

An outsider, trying to make sense of the words of these very vocal opponents, needs to consider the opinion of James Joyce. He was what is considered racially Irish and brought up as Roman Catholic, and he said that his country would get nothing by throwing off servitude to London except total servitude to Rome. Yeats did show an occasional realisation of this, as he had to do since he was intensely concerned in a literary and dramatic movement supposed to be based on the Irish peasantry, though using the Protestants as a help against the priests. James Joyce believed to the end, surely, that the final victory of the political revolution Yeats had supported meant a complete clamp-down on the literary movement he had supported. It is silly to answer that you can go to Belfast if you want a condom. But I grant that the Irish can now laugh the English off. When they say to me: 'Why need we plough through your appallingly boring filth, please?' I have to answer: 'Well, I never do myself unless it becomes a professional duty.' Maybe the Irish literary movement had spent itself already. Hardly any very good writing is going on now anywhere in the world, probably as an effect of the atom bomb; but Ireland stopped twenty years earlier than the rest, though great men continued writing in exile.

As for what Yeats wrote in letters towards the end, waiting for the second war, it wouldn't be much of a shock for the British public. He couldn't quite hope for a Hitler victory but hoped the British would have to liberate India – this was a very familiar position. The decision of Eire to neutralise her ports in 1939, which cost the lives of many English sailors, was strongly supported by the poem of Yeats on Casement, for example; but that decision would have been made anyhow; even Yeats did not imagine he had swung the vote of a government there. What he felt in his last two years, so far from trying to make a political comeback as Mr O'Brien assumes, was that *since* he had no longer any political duty to be tactful and could therefore at last say what he really believed, a helpless old man dying in a kind of exile, he could tell Ireland, for instance, that it would never be any good without a century or two of scientific breeding. It is gratuitous to suppose that this was a step towards taking office in a Quisling Irish government; so far as one can tell, Yeats was as fatuous as most other Irishmen in assuming that Hitler would respect Irish neutrality.

The queer thing about this collection, and the other centenary writings too, I thought, is that they manage to suppress almost entirely the central belief of Yeats, which was reincarnation. He hoped for some tactical advantage in talking as if he only toyed with his deepest beliefs, and his commentators have thankfully followed the lead; but there is no mistaking the venom in his letters when someone turns out to reject reincarnation, and we have few happier pictures of him than his reflecting that his infant daughter hated being a baby almost as much as he hated being an old man (but they would both get out of it). When the doctrine cannot be ignored, critics present it as pokey and lower-middle-class. But it is less unjust and narrow than Christian immortality, and more ancient, and still believed by the majority of the inhabitants of the Eurasian land mass. The refusal to recognise it in Yeats's poems often makes nonsense or gives a bad meaning.

He sacrificed a beautiful cover-design by naming a volume of his poems *The Winding Stair* instead of *Byzantium*. He had proposed that name to Sturge Moore, who would have been splendid with the dome, and a dolphin or two in the Bosphorus; but Yeats decided that the volume had to insist instead on the idea of gradual spiritual development through successive lives. None of the critics will touch this; they prattle about his Religious Values and his Religious Symbolism without ever once letting on what he actually believed. Towards the end of the reveries, on the other hand, Mr Bushrui of Abadan gives a chapter on 'Yeats's Arab interests', and quotes the final version of 'A Vision' (1937) as saying that he meant by the East, 'not India or China, but the East that has affected European civilisation'. Yeats explains in a footnote that Europe and the Semitic East are almost the same, and indeed they do jointly believe that an individual cannot be reborn as someone quite different. And yet, three pages later, he is remarking that only the later *Upanishads* were 'aware' of the soul's rebirth, so he still believed in it, in his last years; if not, he would have been in despair. Perhaps the queer assertion about the Arabs was what Mr O'Brien calls 'calculated'; Yeats at last dimly realised that he couldn't get the Irish priests to swallow reincarnation, but the *Arabian Nights* practically came from their home ground, and after all it would be better to have them believe that than nothing. Maud Gonne, says a biography, was converted because a priest told her the Church would let her go on believing in reincarnation, so here there actually was a bit of 'calculation' such as Yeats always expected from the other side.

An especially interesting part of Mr O'Brien's chapter comes at the end, where he is speculative and not polemic; he quotes a passage from 'A General Introduction for My Work' (1937) about the undirected hatred which sprouts in the modern world:

> in four or five or less generations this hatred will have issued in violence and imposed some kind of rule of kindred. I cannot know the nature of that rule, for its opposite fills the light; all I can do to bring it nearer is to intensify my hatred.

Mr O'Brien remarks that fascist power and the 'rule of kindred' were already in full swing, so the idea of having to wait for five generations was 'perhaps calculated'. Plainly the O'Brien riposte had not occurred to Yeats, who often expresses distaste for Hitler in the later letters, and would not spontaneously translate 'rule of kindred' into death-chambers for Jews. He had long forecast a Time of Troubles, not at all as a thing he desired, and he was merely consistent in saying that we would need a few generations to get back from it to normal life.

In a final footnote Mr O'Brien says, 'I think that the mysterious and beautiful poem "Cuchulain Comforted" may contain the fall of Fascism,' and proposes a detailed political treatment elsewhere. Yeats was concerned in 1937 about what would happen after his own approaching death, though ready to blurt out general political advice to the wind. The hero after death, as always in Yeats, meets a selection of people, four or five twittering ghosts who at last explain that they are all convicted cowards; they were frightened of him at first, they say, but maybe the group can all be comfortable again if he will sew shrouds, as they do; and then their throats change into the throats of singing birds. This kind of thing follows naturally if you believe in rebirth: a man has to accept after death an apparently deathly amount of remoulding, so as to purge himself from his victories as well as his sins; only if he can accept this opposite can he achieve a better return to this world. The dying lion had never said it so wonderfully before, but he had been saying it plainly for more than half a century. How cross he would have been if told he meant that perhaps the British would beat the Germans.

Mr O'Brien implies that Yeats did not publish the poem 'Reprisals' for fear of British reprisals. One would like a bit of evidence for this, as there is a much more likely explanation. The 'Irish Airman' says firmly that Major Gregory meant nothing by sacrificing his life in the First World War; but 'Reprisals' (in the Variorum edition) asks the ghost to come back and think again

> upon the cause you served, that we
> Imagined such a fine affair,

and see what the British are doing now in your village – you are among the cheated dead. It is much more respectful to the dead man to admit that he

thought he was fighting in a good cause, and much better propaganda –
more likely to affect English opinion. But Yeats could not bear to give up
the silly poem which said, 'Paddy loves a scrap.' J. B. S. Haldane wrote that
the First World War had done his psychology a lot of good, and he had particularly enjoyed smashing a man's face in with a spanner, which probably
cleared such impulses out of his system. He could not have said this unless
he had risked his life as a duty. To say he had only fought for fun would disgust him, and his listeners too; the 'Irish Airman' is a typical piece of the
stay-at-home bad taste of the period.

Mr Parkinson's book is written in a very foreign language, the high guff
of US Eng. Lit. which can only be breathed by angels, but he has an interesting quotation from Thomas Macdonagh (1913), showing that the claim of
the Americans to be superior to English scansion (as in William Carlos Williams) came first from the Irish, where it makes rather more sense. There
are still more ways to pronounce English in England than abroad, and the
point of battlement about scansion is overcome, I think – though of course
there is much more to consider – if you recognise that English poetry regularly uses the 'jammed stress', two syllables which count as one stress
together, and actually look like one jagged peak of sound on a recording.
The Irish accent is less jerky than standard English and uses this device
more often, but it is open to all. *Yeats and the Easter Rising* is a firm, brief
statement of the facts available, and contains the only photograph of Maud
Gonne which has ever made me understand how she could have been considered beautiful. On the reverse is a photograph of Constance Gore Booth,
also rippingly thrilling and like a rat-trap. The basic fact about Yeats, it
does emerge, is that he had terrific pluck.

Conor Cruise O'Brien, in a letter to the New Statesman *(27 August 1965),
took Empson to task for his apparent ignorance of Irish political history.
For one crucial matter, 'Yeats could not have said that the majority vote of
1932 could be disregarded as being "the votes of a people who had been
told how to vote by their parish priests". The party which won that election
was the party of those who had been excommunicated for their Civil War
activities; its leaders, and principally De Valera, were then regarded with
suspicion and some aversion by the Catholic hierarchy generally and by
most of the clergy.' Though obviously not a Tory, Empson sustains the old
Tory assumption that 'Irish votes had no moral authority because they
were cast on the instructions of the priests,' O'Brien argued: when in truth
the clergy does not exercise such a direct political influence as 'many
English writers would suggest'. Being uninterested in democracy, Yeats believed that 'the mob' should be ruled by their betters:*

a contradiction existed between Yeats's anticlericalism and his reactionary politics: reaction tended to draw him into alliance with the very politicians who sought with varying success to govern through clerical support ... But 'the priests' and 'the mob' were often on different sides and Yeats was often, though not always, on the same side as most of the priests, much as he disliked the situation.

Not surprisingly Mr Empson made some important and illuminating critical points, notably about Yeats and reincarnation – a theme which I hope he will one day develop more fully.[1]

Empson replied with this letter to the New Statesman *on 10 September 1965:*

I am sure Mr O'Brien is right in saying that the Catholic Church supported the Cosgrave government against De Valera, and this makes the picture less clear-cut than I had gathered from his article, but it does not settle the broad point I was trying to raise. The Indian Moslems, the Turkish Cypriots and the Anglo-Irish are each a minority, mainly descended from conquerors who arrived about 400 years ago, with an inherited tradition and a religion as part of it. It is generally agreed that the first two are entitled to live according to the beliefs which they accept, and may even fight for the privilege, but that the Anglo-Irish have no such right; indeed, an attempt to get it for them seems to be what both Yeats and Mr O'Brien call fascist. No doubt some minorities are too small or otherwise contemptible for special treatment by the law; therefore, a senator demanding such treatment for his own group will naturally urge, as Yeats did, that this group has deserved well of the state. I can well believe that the demand wasn't practical politics, nor even what Yeats himself wanted in the case of censorship, but it needn't be treated as shy-makingly caddish – how could a good poet be so fascist? One would be glad to learn of some general principles behind these sentiments.

Note

1 See 'The Variants for the Byzantium Poems' (1965) in *Using Biography* (London: Chatto & Windus, 1984), and 'Yeats and the Spirits' (1973) below.

Yeats and the Spirits

New York Review of Books, 13 December 1973

Kathleen Raine, *Yeats, the Tarot and the Golden Dawn*

W. B. Yeats, *Memoirs, Autobiography (First Draft) and Journal* edited by Denis Donoghue

A selection from the picture cards of the Tarot pack, especially the pictures on Yeats's own pack, compared to versions designed by his intimates, with quotations about symbols from Yeats and others which seem to derive from the cards (apparently, no direct discussion of them was encouraged in Yeats's circle) – the theme has a tantalising charm; and Kathleen Raine makes points which I suppose are still not adequately recognised:

For Yeats magic was not so much a kind of poetry as poetry a kind of magic, and the object of both alike was the evocation of energies and knowledge from beyond normal consciousness.

In fact, both were justified because they make us better, and results such as we coarse outsiders call magical are not of the essence. All the same, such results are firmly expected, sometimes with moral worry (as when 'I have often wondered if I did great evil' is deleted from the draft Autobiography [*Memoirs*, p. 481]).

Rationalist critics, who could not bear to have a great poet who believed in tosh, used to argue that Yeats only meant Symbolism when he used such language; and I used to suspect that his air of certainty was put on merely as part of his duty to encourage his disciples; but he expresses it even more when he writes for himself alone. The interest of the Autobiography and the Journal, I should have explained, is that they are the original material from which the versions now well-known were derived.

The layout was not oppressively moral. Though a very high-minded man, always striving to become better, Yeats found that the colleagues of his two major lines of secret public-spirited activity took a good deal of keeping out of jail. Maud Gonne with her casual gun-running, and the un-savoury magicians who are so hard to tell apart in Jeffares's *Life*, cost him a lot of his time, because he was the only one of them who could be relied upon to turn up (at the police station, maybe) and put a decent face on things. The doctrine of Masks has made him unpopular with anyone who expected to judge his character by his behaviour at an interview, and in almost all walks of life, I do think, it has to be called a silly theory, being so immediately self-defeating (as people are not such fools as you think, or not interested enough to make the assumption you have presumed); but for a man in Yeats's position, vowed to silence in two directions while neck-deep in the public quarrels of running a theatre, the unattractive procedure is merely imposed. He deserves admiration for getting through.

Kathleen Raine is evidently right in saying that he would dislike the in-sistently mucky mysticism of Aleister Crowley, and work against it on his secret committee, and yet that, in old age, when no longer responsible for keeping the Golden Dawn on an even keel, he wrote poems very close to the position of Crowley. In fact, he takes for granted a Benthamite ethic, altered by circumstances, and Kathleen Raine seems to recognise that. It gives all the more shock value to her *acte gratuit* for this occasion.

Number XIV of the cards from Yeats's pack has a winged girl pouring a liquid from one jug to another, and under this 'L'INTEMPERANZA' is printed. Kathleen Raine lists it at the bottom of the page, without comment, as 'Temperance'. I found a quite lavish Italian dictionary going back to the fourteenth century, which made clear that Italians have long meant by intemperance just what we do. Besides, in the two modern drawings given for comparison, the earth is splitting open beneath the girl's feet, and a vol-cano smokes behind her, or she stands in a cauldron with flames under it, and animals are grouped around. These artists seem to have expected that something would happen, even if in the old picture she is only mixing her drinks.

But then again, on p. 23 we are given a rather pietistic interpretation by Mathers (one of the founders of Yeats's Order of the Golden Dawn) for the twenty-two picture cards, and it says that a wise Combination (Tem-perance) will enable the magician to defy Fate (the Devil). No doubt this clears the point up; the devisers of the pack did not mean by temperance what we are prone to do, that is, total abstinence sustained by a vow, but drinking the proper amount for a given occasion. A magical occasion might demand quite a lot, but one should remember to use the resulting condition for its purpose. Still, even if the reading 'temperance' can be defended, the defence had better have been given in the book.

There is a similar puzzle about Number XI ('LA FORZA'); Kathleen Raine remarks (p. 44) that this 'shows a woman closing the mouth of a lion', but she has already quoted another expert, Mr Ussher (p. 27), saying that the woman is 'tearing open a brute's jaws'. In the picture, one of her hands is inside its mouth, not a good plan if the mouth is being closed; perhaps she is a Maenad, with 'a part to tear a cat in, to make all split'. The powerful though sickening design by Crowley makes a human-headed lion simply her ally, while she struggles by means of earthly desire to drag down passion from Heaven – Kathleen Raine's note positively remarks here that the figure has been turned from Chastity into Lust. Even in the old version once owned by Yeats, I think the woman looks frightened, furtive, and agog, so that one is not at all sure what she will do with the lion next. Of course, the main idea to be illustrated is that she has suddenly acquired power, and to make her hesitate over what to do with it does nothing to weaken that impression.

It might seem that the emblem, regarded as a means of edification or fortune-telling, has merely vanished in such cases, and yet one might claim that these uses of it show racial memory or intuitive grasp of ancient wisdom. I fell into a very similar doubt over some photographs of an early Sumerian icon, which the learned commentator regarded as the sacrifice of a human female to a lion – it was eating her. Three or four examples of this type survived, not at all uniform, and it seemed to me quite plain that the biting was of the sexy type prominent in the earlier verse of Swinburne; whether or not these reliefs were a bowdlerisation of some actively horrible ritual, they showed a goddess or priestess enjoying the embraces of a lion; and the lion enjoying those of the goddess or priestess. As I understand her, Kathleen Raine claims the Tarot as 'a full and effective formulation' of the basic reality especially because it has this riddling quality:

The archetypes – if we encounter them at all – are likely to appear as figures mysterious and nameless, belonging to no pantheon, no theological system. The Tarot symbols gave to the members of the Golden Dawn the freedom to evoke, in their living essence, those personifying spirits which by different nations have been variously named. To the poet especially this freedom is essential.

This presumes, I take it (the whole position is close to that of Jung), that the use of archetypes itself is essential for good poetry, though they must be used with freedom. We are next told that 'the incantatory style of the Magus' is liable to become absurd, and poets should not take it for granted. She is thinking about the technical needs of young poets, having used the method in her own poetry, as well as about their obvious need to be uplifted.

All this seems to me much better than the prattle about 'imagery' now standard in academic criticism, both because not liable to become trivial and because not based on a psychological belief actually known to be wrong. I should confess to a prejudice here, in that I am a nonvisualiser, never getting a row of pictures when I read a line of verse; though I can see visions as well as the next man, especially after an eye operation. But anyway the mere existence of nonvisualisers is enough to refute most of the cluster of Imagist beliefs. Yeats heard about them from Pound, and made use of them to emerge from the Celtic Twilight, but refused to let them get in his way; he went on to write some very piercing and minatory lines in very 'abstract' language. But I am not sure that he was hampered by these archetypes either, or that a coming poet should be advised to be. If you allow your mind to stray over a few examples of poets in the past – Donne, Pope, Wordsworth – all plainly and admittedly trying to do different things, surely it is very hard to maintain that they only wrote well so far as they embodied an archetype? The tethered theory was always bleating for its consummation, which turned out to be the rule of Mr Robert Graves, that the only archetype is the White Goddess.

Yeats when young was keen on magic and spiritualism because they refuted 'scientific materialism', and having convinced himself that that had been done (*Memoirs*, p. 266), did not demand anything very specific from the spirits he encountered. They are far too much like people. His movement, as I think he came to realise, harked back to a grand Renaissance philosophical turmoil which had produced the physical sciences, so that the Spirits of Nature were its practical side; but the poetry of Yeats can never recover contact with that. Quite often, it really is in the vast smoky hall of world politics, but never at the top of a mountain, seldom in the open air. He was a man of splendid energy, intelligence, and public spirit, fortunate in having a small country where affairs were almost of manageable size; it would have been beneath him not to take on the spirits too, and he was not defeated there, but one cannot feel they were among his major successes.

How much he really believed in his system is a question one cannot help returning to, though in a Christian of known affiliation one would take the periods of doubt for granted. I had thought that he remained confident of reincarnation after meeting a Hindu sage at the age of twenty, and some remarks in his later letters are indignant against anyone who doubts that belief, but here in youth (*Memoirs*, p. 48) we find him blaming himself because he ought to have warned Maud Gonne that it was after all only a hypothesis (she was very firm about it, and was afterward allowed to enter the Roman Church still believing in it, thus crashing a fundamental opposition between Europe and the wisdom of the East). Yet he goes straight on from expressing doubt here to expressing an astonishing confidence, talking about his handling of the spirits as a doctor would talk of the bold use of a drug – this is where he wrote 'I have often wondered if I did great evil' and then crossed it out.

Maud Gonne said she used to see a ghost when she was a child, and Yeats decided that this was an evil spirit troubling her life unseen, creating for example a desire for political power.

Perhaps when one loves one is not quite sane, or perhaps one can pierce – in sudden intuition – behind the veil. I decided to make this woman visible at will.

Because that would make it put its temptation into words, and then Maud Gonne would face it with her intellect. 'I made a symbol according to the rules of my Order ... and almost at once it became visible.' It turned out to be a past personality of hers, seeking to be reunited, which had split off when she was a priestess in ancient Egypt and 'under the influence of a certain priest who was her lover gave false oracles for money'. Yeats had been taught when admitted to the Esoteric Section of the Theosophical Society that all such requests for reunion should be refused. Nothing more is said about whether his treatment helped her to renounce the craving for political power.

The book edited by Professor Donoghue is in two parts, an Autobiography begun by Yeats in 1915, which became the first draft of his final Autobiography, also a Journal begun in 1908 and carried on fairly regularly until 1910, with a few later additions. The Autobiography ascribes these magical successes to his youth, hardly going beyond 1901, and it is plainly in rather an artificial style, but is quite frank in explaining firmly that a man may have a duty to tell lies for propaganda. Swift told lies in his campaign against Wood's halfpence (p. 84), but ('I ... had argued')

because no sane man is permitted to lie knowing[ly], God made certain men mad, and that it was these men – daimon-possessed as I said – who, possessing truths of passion that were intellectual falsehoods, had created nations.

This does not encourage belief, nor perhaps does the recovery of his uncle from delirium (p. 75), though his magic was obviously a comfort to his uncle. But I do have to find impressive an incident reported in Kathleen Raine's book, where the lad Yeats despises the scepticism of the master (Mathers) with whom he is staying in Paris:

He, like all others I have known who have given themselves up to images, and to the speech of images, thought that when he had proved that an image could act independently of his mind, he had proved also that neither it, nor what it had spoken, had originated there. Yet had I need of proof to the contrary, I had it while under his roof. I was eager for news of the Spanish–American War, and went to the Rue Mozart before breakfast to buy a New York Herald. As I went out past the young Normandy servant who was laying breakfast, I was telling myself some schoolboy romance, and had just reached the place where I carried my arm in a sling after some remarkable escape. I bought my paper and returned, to find Mathers on the doorstep: 'Why, you are all right,' he said. 'What did the *bonne* mean by telling me that you had hurt your arm and carried it in a sling?'

Here he is a logician, fit to deal through Sturge Moore with his brother G. E. Moore; and he probably had some influence on the general acceptance among scientists of the possibility of telepathy, though this would hardly be what he was aiming at. The Journal has practically nothing about magic (except for pleasure in recording a proof, p. 266) because he was neck-deep in the labours of being chairman, having a peculiar skill in dealing with committees, alarmingly beyond what he could do when left alone with one opponent. This also seemed to him a magical power, though he tried to analyse it; and at the time of writing he regrets bitterly that he must use it, out of loyalty to his own side, since he is found to have it:

I thought myself free, loving neither vice nor virtue; but virtue has come upon me and given me a nation instead of a home. Has it left me any lyric faculty? Whatever happens I must go on that there may be a man behind the lines already written. I should have avoided the thing – but being in it!

Whether men could be reborn no longer made much difference; the main fact was, he found himself alone with mankind.

Eliot Distilled

From 'Recent Poetry', *Nation and Athenaeum*,
21 February 1931

Poetry nowadays is no longer in the luxuriant condition of its nineteenth-century prosperity, when young ladies all over the country drank in the sentiments of the Laureate; a great part of the reading public for novels and biographies will not stand for poetry at all. As a result of this fact, or perhaps as another effect of its causes, the poets are now writing concentrated and distilled things, such as could only be said in poetry; they assume a small public interested in poetry as such. This tendency may have a good or a bad influence on poetry, but a poet can hardly ignore it. 'Enoch Arden' itself, for instance, if anyone is writing it now, had much better be done as a novel. . . .

'Marina' seems to me one of Mr Eliot's very good poems; better than anything in 'Ash-Wednesday'. The dramatic power of his symbolism is here in full strength, and the ideas involved have almost the range of interest, the full orchestra, of *The Waste Land*. One main reason for this is the balance maintained between otherworldliness and humanism; the essence of the poem is the vision of an order, a spiritual state, which he can conceive and cannot enter, but it is not made clear whether he conceives an order in this world to be known by a later generation (like Moses on Pisgah) or the life in heaven which is to be obtained after death (like Dante). One might at first think the second only was meant, but Marina, after all, was a real daughter; is now at sea, like himself, rather than already in the Promised Land; and is to live 'in a world of time beyond me', which can scarcely be a description of Heaven. At any rate, the humanist meaning is used at every point as a symbol of the otherworldly one; this seems the main point to insist on in a brief notice because it is the main cause of the richness of the total effect. In either case the theme is the peril and brevity of such vision.

'Marina'

c. 1931

One crux about the Eliot poem is how far it is religious: how far it is a conception of the birth into this world of a new order which he can conceive, like Moses, without entering: how far it is the life of heaven which is to be obtained after death. After shipwreck on the granite islands he may cast up among the wood and the thrushes (crux about *half* consciousness: you hear and smell what you cannot see or feel): after death find contentment or ecstasy. But it is his daughter, born in the uncertainty of the sea, he is half knowing: to live in a world of *time* does not firmly suggest heaven: and the ecstasy is not merely that she is in the 'sacred wood' but that she is to have hope and new ships. There is a crux, connected with this, about 'this grace dissolved in place'. Is it dissolved in *this* place, where I can hear and smell the wood, though befogged and in danger: or in *any* place, in space as a whole (*dissolved* suggests that it is immanent everywhere, or possibly that it is spreading everywhere from some one place where it is dissolving)? If it is everywhere, this bliss conceived is outside the world: if it is only here, the bliss conceived is that of a particular terrestrial order.

The root conception perhaps is that the heavenly bliss must be known precariously on earth: the daughter too is on sea; and one can come near with danger, for a brief space perhaps before necessary disaster, to the heavenly vision which it is death to reach fully. From this position you can conceive, not really the bliss of heaven itself, but new ships, a new order for those who also are confined to the flux of the real world. In a sense this implies, not a belief in heaven, but a belief in the value of belief in heaven.

He is himself his daughter because he can conceive her sufficiently to father her: because he can imagine and promulgate a state of mind in which he cannot himself find equilibrium.

Certainly the second verse opposes sharply the life of the flesh to the life he is now living, of the spirit: but that is in part also the language of the uncomfortable attainment of any valuable condition: he seems to be making the two ideas illuminate one another.

Return may mean only that this state of vision occurs at intervals; in that he is recognising it again he is more certain of its value. There may too be some conception of returning to the womb or the first chaos: all the waters are meeting in the sleep of death. This gives another meaning to the ambiguity of *place*: this place is all places, it is where all waters meet, and we (all in the same boat) can know only those places which are water, which are part of the flux of the world. 'Images' implies visual ideas, and it is precisely seeing (then face to face) which the fog makes impossible: he must draw therefore on past experience to conceive what would be seen: to make it intelligible to himself and so to others, and find the images of symbol and metaphor that make his poetry. The word also suggests 'idols': things visible put instead of the invisible divinity, which may degrade but make it more intelligible and controllable.

As there is no full stop after *place, by this grace* may go forwards and be an imprecation, so as to suggest that the face is an *image* of the grace, or backwards to say that the sensual world has been made unsubstantial by the grace. But looking at *reduced*, which may be verb or participle, so that one is uncertain how much weight to give it, how far its lead should be followed in interpreting the grammar of the next phrases, we see that the sensual persons may by this grace have become dissolved in place: or that the breath of pine and the fog may have been dissolved in place (they must, alternatively, either have *reduced* the sensual persons or been themselves reduced by a wind).

A *wind* is of course, as a historical pun, the spirit: one effect of the contraction *woodsong fog* is that it makes all the elements of the impression into a part, as we say, of the 'atmosphere', like the heath of pine. This is strong evidence that *wind, heath* and *fog* are grammatically parallel; a spirit, the atmosphere of the place (one does not think of it as very windy) has made the sensual world unimportant and unreal. But the word *reduced* is complex: the main meaning 'made smaller and weaker' jostles with the idea of reducing a garrison (making it give up), the derivation 'led back' (since they too, like the images, have *returned* here to become unsubstantial – and indeed those who live in ships must be led by winds, the sensual persons must yield in some degree to the spirit) and the classical derived sense 'having been deprived of their oxygen', or purified: as if the wind was hydrogen that took the rust from the surface of the ship, when *heated* in the fire of trial. This last faint influence contradicts the idea of *becoming unsubstantial*, because the most obvious forms of reduction (like that of a metal) makes a thing more solid. But indeed one might feel that difficulty in any case: *reduced to a wind*, since they have become *unsubstantial*, is a tempting misreading, and there is a touch of paradox in the idea that though unsubstantial they are not spiritual, which is repeated by the doubt as to the subject of *dissolved*. We are not sure whether they have been vanquished or converted, or whether they have merely found a *death* which includes both.

The story of Marina was that she was lost at sea and found again, like bread upon the waters, in the old age of her father; this fits in with the idea of *return* (of the vision of the young man as the dream of the old, of the excitement of conceiving success as at the end of a prolonged endeavour and the more exhausted, less pleasurable, but more solid exaltation of having reached the end), with the doubt as to whether she is indeed alive, whether this is a dream of a discovery, given or lent, and with the sense that though so distant for so long she is part of himself, and though *unknown, his own*. This aspect of the matter does not favour the more Christian, more otherworldly and despairing, interpretation. The daughter in the story at any rate was really alive and in the world, and he was glad to find her precisely because his stock would now *live beyond* him *in a world of time*.

There may be some doubt as to whether *less clear and clearer* is said of the *face* (than what, in that case: than itself, so that the vision wavers and seems unreal; than the *grace*, so that it is only a metaphor of the unseen glory and yet somehow strengthens it; or than the sensual persons, the normal world, so that it is affirmed to be more real than they, though a vision) or of the *pulse in the arm*, which is at once more and less *clear* and *strong* than the *face*; in this case it is the vision of the *face* which causes an exhilaration, a sense of renewed youth, which is more certain than the reality of the vision, though dependent on its reality; and though certain is yet a sort of mirage in that it is not he who is made young and strong, it is the daughter with whom he is in such sympathy as to share her youth, in the discovery of her by which she seems as it were to be reborn.

June and *September* have a rather pre-Raphaelite slickness; the point seems to be that the spiritual journey, lasting not for a full year but (such is his exhaustion or humility) for a brief summer beside the possible year of human activity, yet has also lasted, in the imaginative experience or strain of conflict compacted into it, for many such years; or since in *returning* to birth via death the natural order is being inverted (and he is taking strength from his daughter, as her son) we may suppose the voyage starting in September and ending next June: it has now extended through winter, yet included some of the heat of summer, and has lasted as long as a pregnancy, so that he is now giving birth to the daughter who will live in a summer he shall not see.

In the last line the *woodthrush, calling* to him, seems to call him its *daughter*: this final echoing of his own language in exhaustion seems to go finally over to the more Christian of the two versions: he is the daughter and has not produced one, and the mother he would return to is on the island where she cannot be reached except by the shipwreck of death. Even here that is not the only meaning, and he may only be asking the daughter to explain to him the *place* which she understands, but whose ecstasy is strange to him.

Kauffer's design [for the 'Ariel' edition, London: Faber & Faber, 1930], in which elements are displaced flatly, and it is not easy to see whose hand is which, uses just this conscious, wilful, and spare ambiguity of form.

This verbose stuff is made absurd by not knowing the point of the motto: it is Hercules' first words in Seneca when he is recovering from the madness in which he has killed his children: a madness sent from heaven, through no fault of his own, after a successful descent into hell and a successful killing of his enemies. (As a result in some versions he went to Eurystheus and performed the labours.)

So heaven, which is desirable but dangerous to arrive at, is a place where you have been tricked into disaster – Eliot becoming a Christian, which doesn't work? Or it might mean you are now waking up and finding yourself a Christian.

Rather ambiguity by vagueness, anyway.

The Style of the Master

Richard March and Tambimuttu (eds.), *T. S. Eliot: A Symposium*, London: PL Editions Poetry London, 1948

I do not propose here to try to judge or define the achievement of Eliot; indeed I feel, like most other verse writers of my generation, that I do not know for certain how much of my own mind he invented, let alone how much of it is a reaction against him or indeed a consequence of misreading him. He has a very penetrating influence, perhaps not unlike an east wind. All I can do here is to put down a few reminiscences of him, from meetings much rarer than I should have wished; stories greatly in his favour, I should have thought, but you never know how people will take things. And when I have tried out my Eliot anecdotes on an anti-Eliot man he has generally taken them as confirming his worst impressions. So they are not designed to flatter (and, by the way, I could not have invented them) but they are a sort of witness to the Eliot legend, and it deserves to be recorded.

My most impressive memory is of walking up Kingsway with him after some lunch, probably about 1930, when finding myself alone with the great man I felt it opportune to raise a practical question which had been giving me a little anxiety. 'Do you really think it necessary, Mr Eliot,' I broke out, 'as you said in the preface to the Pound anthology,[1] for a poet to write verse at least every week?' He was preparing to cross into Russell Square, eyeing the traffic both ways, and we were dodging it as his slow reply proceeded. 'I had in mind Pound when I wrote that passage,' began the deep sad voice, and there was a considerable pause. 'Taking the question in general, I should say, in the case of many poets, that the most important thing for them to do ... is to write as little as possible.' The gravity of the last phrase was so pure as to give it an almost lyrical quality. A reader may be tempted to suppose that this was a snub or at least a joke, but I still do not believe it was; and at the time it seemed to me not only very wise but a very satisfactory answer. He had taken quite a weight off my mind.

In this kind of case, indeed, the Johnsonian pessimism was quite practical and helpful; one felt more doubtful about it in generalisations. There was a party (I forget everybody else in the room) where Eliot broke into some chatter about a letter being misunderstood. 'Ah, letters,' he said, rather as if they were some rare kind of bird, 'I had to look into the question of letters at one time. I found that the mistake ... that most people make ... about letters, is that after writing their letters, carefully, they go out, and look for a pillar-box. I found that it is very much better, after giving one's attention to composing the letter, to ... pop it into the fire.' This kind of thing was a little unnerving, because one did not know how tragically it ought to be taken; it was clearly not to be regarded as a flippancy. There was some dinner including a very charming diplomat's wife, who remarked to Eliot that she too was very fond of reading. She didn't get much time, but she was always reading in bed, biographies and things. 'With pen in hand?' inquired Mr Eliot, in a voice which contrived to form a question without leaving its lowest note of gloom. There was a rather fluttered disclaimer, and he went on, 'It is the chief penalty of becoming a professional literary man that one can no longer read anything with pleasure.' This went down very well, but it struck me that the Johnsonian manner requires more gusto as a contrast to the pessimism; perhaps after all, looking back, a mistaken complaint, because if untruth is all that is required to justify this sort of quip it was surely quite untrue that he no longer read anything with pleasure.

My earliest memory of Eliot, speaking of untruth, was when he came to Cambridge to give the Clark lectures and was prepared to receive under-graduates after breakfast on Thursdays; this was in the middle 1920s. At the first of these very awed gatherings someone asked him what he thought of Proust. 'I have not read Proust,' was the deliberate reply. How the con-versation was picked up again is beyond conjecture, but no one cared to plumb into the motives of his abstinence. It was felt to be a rather impress-ive trait in this powerful character. Next week a new member of the group asked what he thought of the translation of Proust by Scott Moncrieff, and Eliot delivered a very weighty, and rather long, tribute to that work. It was not enough, he said, to say that it was better than the original in many single passages; it was his impression that the translation was at no point inferior to the original (which, to be sure, was often careless French), either in accuracy of detail or in the general impression of the whole. We were startled by so much loquacity from the silent master rather than by any dis-agreement with what he had said before; in fact it seemed quite clear to me what Eliot meant – he did not consider he had 'read' a book unless he had written copious notes about it and so on. I no longer feel sure that this was what he meant, but I am still quite sure that he was not merely lying to impress the children; maybe at the earlier meeting he hadn't bothered to listen to what they were saying.

Perhaps the most charming case of his peculiar note, which however wilful in its sadness is always at the opposite pole to malice, occurred when a younger poet (long ago now) published a diary [Stephen Spender]. I should explain that Eliot takes cheese rather seriously; as witness the pronouncement, 'I find I can no longer travel except where there is a native cheese. I am therefore bounded, northwards by Yorkshire ...' and the rest of the points of the compass were all tidy (I think he had a fair run to the south) but I no longer know what they were. The younger poet had recorded a lunch with 'Tom', at which he had told Tom that simplicity and deep feeling were what made good poetry, and Tom had agreed. This was what gave his own poetry its lasting qualities ('Yes,' Tom had said) and on the other hand gave good reason to prophesy that the poetry of Tom would only prove a passing fashion. Tom had seemed much struck by this. Meeting Eliot not long after I made bold to mention the diary, and he said, 'Very interesting. He did me the kindness ... to send me the proofs ... of the parts ... concerning myself.' I said I hoped he had found them all right. His manner became a trifle severe, though not noticeably sadder. 'I found it necessary,' he said, 'in the interests of truth, to correct the name of the cheese.'

Note

1 Eliot wrote in his introduction to Ezra Pound, *Selected Poems* (London: Faber & Faber, 1928; reprinted 1959), 'The poet who wishes to continue to write poetry must keep in training; and must do this, not by forcing his inspiration, but by good workmanship on a level possible for some hours' work every week of his life' (p. 16).

Eliot and Politics

T. S. Eliot Review, 2:2, Fall 1975

I was asked to reflect about the politics of Eliot, and after making the attempt felt rather surprised to conclude that he hadn't got any. He was not (so to speak) brought up to have any, because an aesthete rather boasted of having none; he inherited a healthy crop of family prejudices, but did not feel committed to them. His loyalty to old friends, a very attractive trait, was carried almost to the point of indifference to their opinions. When he became eminent he was expected to have world views, and showed himself willing and conscientious there; but it all feels overshadowed by a placid remark, which he once let drop by way of apology, that poetry has an urgent need to deal with reality, but in prose a man may allow himself to entertain ideals. When he wrote that a truly cultured society would only have a reasonable proportion of free-thinking Jews in it, he had no idea of planning how to bring this situation about.[1] He would try at times to keep some particular thing from being destroyed, but that is as near to politics as he got. I think indeed one can find cases where the blind spot about politics entailed a minor weakness of judgement.

Anyhow, recent critics who look for a plan are liable to be misled by a certain impishness, not far from a taste for practical jokes. It sounds like blasphemy now, but the first admirers of his work were chiefly captivated by this quality of nerve. He once remarked that every man of his generation had a taint of Original H. G. Wells; this he kept at bay, but he retained well into middle age a heartening flavour of Aboriginal Dylan Thomas (who was also, by the way, quite ready to hand out high moral blame). It may be found in the French sentence given quotation marks at the end of his essay on Andrew Marvell; at least, I wish TSER's scholarly contributors would enable us to be quite certain that this is a bogus quotation, invented by Eliot himself, for a tease. The great Legouis was asked about it, and naturally felt unwilling to pronounce that no Frenchman had ever said it; but only a few French writers would be likely to, he could say, and he was pretty sure none of them had. Besides, it was in bad French (I do not understand why). This is pretty decisive, but one of your research men may come upon a moderately parallel sentence in a French author.[2]

Eliot wrote this while establishing his position in the *Times Literary Supplement*, which was then wholly anonymous and chillingly learned. The article needed a closing chord, and the scholars would never admit that they had failed to spot a quotation; clearly, they deserved to have their legs pulled. I am confident that this was his attitude because I happened to hear him boast of a somewhat parallel case. Towards the end of his life he gave a poetry reading at Sheffield, which I was set to introduce, and I mentioned that, soon after he had published 'Marina', a Swedish Professor had written to me (I had just published my *Ambiguity*) asking where the Latin quotation came from. I did not know, but asked a brother poet Ronald Bottrall, who had done well at classics, and he paused, rolling the eight words over his tongue to taste the rhythms. He said, 'If it's poetry it's very unclassical poetry. It might be Seneca, for instance. In fact, it actually is from *Hercules Furens*,' and he raised his eyes from the paper, 'My God what a thing.' He had grasped at once that the words nail the reader to a dramatic moment, eternally refusing to tell whether the traveller will reach his daughter on the island paradise or be broken on the coastal rocks – the name 'Marina', recalling the happy ending in Shakespeare, is balanced or contradicted by the first words of Hercules emerging from the madness in which he had killed his children. So I wrote happily back to Sweden, saying that the quotation was from the *Hercules* and that was why the poem was so good. One could not grumble at the technique after seeing it achieve a success, though I think a modern edition should print '*Hercules Furens*' at the end of the Latin. This was the only bit of my lead-in that won a comment from Eliot after the show (of course nearly all of it was praise, on which he would not comment). He said: 'I didn't know Bottrall was a scholar. Seneca isn't in the school syllabus, so all the classical men were caught out.' The poem is splendid, and all the more so for being designed as a Faber Christmas card; but it is odd to reflect that this little tease was part of its basic planning. Of course he may have been wronging himself.

The bogus quotation about Marvell was a much bolder operation, perhaps more so than he realised. It says that Marvell had a fine spirit, such as are no longer found in London. But surely, no Frenchman would think that they ever had been found in London (at least, not in this assured elegiac tone). Well-born characters in Boston, on the other hand, habitually felt that England had been spiritually okay when it produced ancestors, but since then had gone sadly downhill. The young Eliot, as he revered the poets of France, felt sure he could use them as an authority for his own sentiments. But this one would still be bizarre whatever authority it had. Marvell, when he came to live in London as MP for Hull, so far from marking the end of an old line of virtue, was inventing a new type of Londoner who has since then almost always been present; the next well-known example was Defoe. The type is a generally left-wing politician, considered rather shifty, with strong literary interests kept on the leash, keen to have a finger in any important pie but preferring to stay in the background. He usually rents several small lodgings, most of them undisclosed like his sources of income. It was good luck for Marvell to die before the deception of Titus Oates had unfolded; he would have felt he had to back his own party, even after he had found it was in the wrong. The political side of Marvell was very remote from Eliot's mind, and I think remained so.

I feel sure that further useful research might be done on the lady, merely glimpsed at the start of *The Waste Land,* who said: 'I read, much of the night, and go south in the winter.' She is the only person in the poem for whom the author expresses outright contempt, and surely we need to know what qualities he is despising.

> What are the roots that clutch, what branches grow
> Out of this stony rubbish?

A good deal is known. Eliot accepted the discovery that she was Countess Marie Larisch, who published *My Past* in 1913, and said he had met her. My scraps of information about her come from *A Substantial Ghost* by Lady Violet Powell, a valuable book, but like Eliot himself it is too easily contemptuous of her. Her father was a cousin of the reigning Hapsburgs but had married an actress, partly Jewish the indignant family said, so it was 'unconventional' of the Empress to make his daughter her favourite, though it did not really mean taking a step outside her conventions. Excellent horsemanship was required of the niece who won her intimacy; and the sophisticated elegance of the Empress was well set off by the bouncing innocence of the confidante – however, this comment was probably written into *My Past* by the ghost, an English lady journalist who specialised in making the memoirs of grandees publishable. The suicide of the only son of the Empress, for reasons yet unknown, was the cause of the dismissal of Countess Larisch, but not till long after did she publish her memoirs, for a defence against accusations that she had been among the causes of it. As part of this clearing of her name, no doubt, she would face the world at a few grand receptions, perhaps in Paris or Berlin. On such an occasion Eliot would be introduced to her, during his first visit to Europe, studying at the Sorbonne perhaps; she would be about twice his age, and her career had been ended about the year he was born.

The poem uses her as a standard Establishment figure, empty-headed and self-important; but the reason why she talked to Eliot was that she had been wronged by her Establishment, and wanted some young writer to take up her cause. It is a mistake to deduce that she was inept at writing because she accepted the ghost. She opened negotiations by insisting that nothing she had written might be changed; she needed money, but she would sacrifice part of the money to be revenged upon the dead Empress. Considerable additions were made by the ghost, after questioning the author, but they were mainly gossip about how the Empress kept her figure and suchlike; the mysterious stuff about palace intrigue in the background, however wrong, did not disturb the London publisher and was left intact. As an author, the Countess is not contemptible. It is likely that Eliot met her more than once, because in reporting her he catches a speaking accent vividly, a thing he can only otherwise do, in the poem, for his first wife and their servant. He required habituation, as becomes clear in the parts cut out by Pound. He certainly did not get it from reading her book; no phrase in the poem is echoed from the book. It gives a welcome assurance of reality to have her say she has never been so happy as when tobogganing, in childhood. After one glance at the young Eliot she would think: 'Well, I suppose even he must have tobogganed when he was tiny,' so she embarked upon her pathetic description. Eliot could reply that he had never been so happy as when boating off Boston as a college boy, and indeed must have said this, or he would not have received her further confidences. But of course she herself had had much greater happiness among horses, when just grown up. After the 1914–18 war she was ruined and the ghost tracked her down in Berlin, where she was working as general servant to a Jewish family. The ghost at once took her out to a lunch with champagne, to recover her nerve, and sure enough she was soon married to an American millionaire. (This would be about six years after Eliot had known her.) At the moment of decision she sent a cable to the ghost, asking for advice, and received the stern brief answer MARRY. This detail I think saves her from showing an excessive amount of nerve; and she had shown nerve of another sort in refusing to beg. In fact, she turns out to be rather an impressive character, extremely unlike what Eliot had contrived to suggest.

The Variorum edition of *The Waste Land*[3] gives prominence to an assurance by Eliot that the poem was 'a personal and wholly insignificant grouse against life'; he seems to have said this kind of thing when irritated by some particularly sanctimonious interpretation of it. His feelings do him credit, but his words need not be treated as gospel; surely he didn't have a private grouse against the Countess. The inventors of Symbolism (Mallarmé for instance) did not use it for scolding the world at large; but the Variorum makes clear that Eliot had also been imitating Dickens – a kind of survey had been piling up. Obviously, Dickens would have had no mercy on a Hapsburg courtier. But then, he would have had a plot, so that we could distinguish between the characters, and know what to blame them for. The poem seems to blame the lady for the triviality of her life and her interests, or the footling character of her grumbles, whereas the grumbling of the actual Countess attained a fair level of melodrama. It already did in her book, and we know another thing that would crop up while she was hissing into Eliot's ear. One of her sons had killed himself because he had been told, falsely, that he was a bastard of the Crown Prince; this is probably what had at last driven her to write her apologia. Anyway, she was insistent that there was something the *matter* with the Hapsburgs, though not with herself, and this seems to have made Eliot regard her as a typical Hapsburg. The mind of an Imagist, and of Henry James too, is inclined that way; they are very good at conveying the 'atmosphere' of a roomful of people, and they assume that each of these people is not only producing the atmosphere but compelled to act in accordance with it. So there can't be any drama, or politics either, hardly even a palace intrigue.

It took a long time for the literary critics to discover the Countess, but surely there must have been somebody with a foot in both camps? The lady would presumably be in circulation again, once she had married her millionaire. Would not Nancy Cunard have known about it? There is a large field for inquiry.

Notes

1 Eliot once asked in a lecture (1933) how we might foster a desirable society with a genuine tradition and stability – 'the best life for us not as a political abstraction, but as a particular people in a particular place'. His prescription included these remarks: 'What is still more important is unity of religious background; and reasons of race and religion combine to make any large number of free-thinking Jews undesirable' (*After Strange Gods*, London: Faber & Faber, 1934, pp. 19–20).

2 Eliot's quotation at the end of his 'Andrew Marvell' (1921) – '*C'était une belle âme, comme on ne fait plus a Londres*' – introduces a grammatical solecism in alluding to the last stanza of Jules Laforgue's 'Complainte du pauvre jeune homme':

> Quand les croq'morts vinrent chez lui,
> Quand les croq'morts vinrent chez lui;
> Ils virent qu'c'était un'belle âme,
> Comme on n'en fait plus aujourd'hui!
> Ame,
> Dors, belle ame!
> Quand on est mort c'est pour de bon...

3 Valerie Eliot (ed.), *The Waste Land: a facsimile and transcript*, London: Faber & Faber, 1971.

A Note on W. H. Auden's
Paid on Both Sides

Experiment, 7, Spring 1931

I must first try to outline the plot, as it is not obvious on one's first reading. There is a blood feud, apparently in the north of England, between two mill-owning families who are tribal leaders of their workmen; it is at the present day, but there are no class distinctions and no police. John, the hero of the play, is born prematurely from shock, after the death by ambush of his father; so as to be peculiarly a child of the feud. As a young man he carries it on, though he encourages a brother who loses faith in it to emigrate. Then he falls in love with a daughter (apparently the heiress) of the enemy house; to marry her would involve ending the feud, spoiling the plans of his friends, breaking away from the world his mother takes for granted, and hurting her by refusing to revenge his father. Just before he decides about it, a spy, son of the enemy house (but apparently only her half-brother) is captured, it is the crisis of the play; he orders him to be taken out and shot. He then marries Anne; she tries to make him emigrate, but he insists on accepting his responsibility and trying to stop the feud; and is shot on the wedding day, at another mother's instigation, by a brother of the spy.

This much, though very compressed, and sometimes in obscure verse, is a straightforward play. But at the crisis, when John has just ordered the spy to be shot, a sort of surrealist technique is used to convey his motives. They could only, I think, have been conveyed in this way, and only when you have accepted them can the play be recognised as a sensible and properly motivated tragedy.

The reason for plunging below the rational world at this point is precisely that the decision to end the feud is a fundamental one; it involves so much foreknowledge of what he will feel under circumstances not yet realisable that it has to be carried through on motives (or by choosing to give himself strength from apparent motives) which do not belong to what is then the sensible world he lives in. For the point of the tragedy is that he could not know his own mind till too late, because it was just that process of making contact with reality, necessary to him before he could know his own mind, which in the event destroyed him. So that the play is 'about' the antinomies of the will, about the problems involved in the attempt to change radically a working system.

He has the spy shot partly to tie his own hands, since he will evade the decision if he can make peace impossible, partly (the other way round) because it will make peace difficult, so that the attempt, if he chooses to make it, will expose him to more risk (for this seems to make it more generous), partly from a self-contempt which, in search of relief, turns outwards, and lights on the man who seems likest to himself, for he too is half a spy in his own camp; partly because he must kill part of himself in coming to either decision about the marriage, so that it seems a first step, or a revenge, to kill by an irrelevant decision the man likest him (for whom he must at the moment, from a point of view which still excites horror in him, feel most sympathy), partly because only by making a decision on some associated matter can he string himself up to know his own mind on the matter in question, partly because what is in his mind makes him feel ashamed and guilty among his supporters, so that he mistakenly thinks it necessary for his own safety to prove to them he is wholeheartedly on their side.

In this way the spy becomes a symbol to him, both of the feud itself, of which he is part, so as to make it seem contemptible, and of his own attempt to escape from the feud, which makes him seem contemptible to his own camp; and in either case the spy is both himself and his chief enemy. And having united himself with the man he despises, he must feel some remorse and self-contempt about killing him for these accidental and neurotic reasons; at any rate it puts him in the wrong, and in part makes him deserve the consequences.

And yet it is precisely the painfulness and dangerousness of these expulsive forces that make it possible for him to give birth to a decision.

Hence we sink down, in this crucial and solvent instant of decision, into a childish scheme of judgement, centring round desire for, and fear of, the mother; jealousy of, and identity with, the brother, who is also the spy; away from the immediate situation, so that younger incidental reminiscences of the author become relevant; below the distinction between murderer and victim, so that the hero escapes from feeling his responsibility; below intelligible sexuality; and in the speech of the Man–Woman (a 'prisoner of war behind barbed wire, in the snow') we are plunged into a general exposition of the self-contempt of indecision. Then the spy is shot, and we return with circus farce like the panting of recovery, into the real world of the play; from then on he knows his own mind, and is fated to destruction.

One reason the scheme is so impressive is that it puts psychoanalysis and surrealism and all that, all the irrationalist tendencies which are so essential a part of the machinery of present-day thought, into their proper place; they are made part of the normal and rational tragic form, and indeed what constitutes the tragic situation. One feels as if at the crisis of many, perhaps better, tragedies, it is just this machinery which has been covertly employed. Within its scale (twenty-seven pages) there is the gamut of all the ways we have of thinking about the matter; it has the sort of completeness that makes a work seem to define the attitude of a generation.

'Another Time'[1]

Life & Letters Today, August 1940

W. H. Auden, *Another Time*

He is a wonderful poet, and I cannot see this falling off that people talk about. Wyndham Lewis has a phrase 'the surge and roar that greets a reader approaching one of the great Shakespearean tragedies'; that is, I take it, a whole cycle of ideas and feelings has been connected to the main theme so that even the casual phrases of the play seem to hint at a great deal. Certainly if you compare Auden with almost all his contemporaries it is clear that they have hardly anything to say. You often find that he has taped firmly what you had been dumbly feeling; for instance, I have found myself saying weakly in the recent disasters, 'I don't know why, but I feel it's somehow all my fault,' and I had forgotten how Auden can always say this with a bang:

> Out of the mirror they stare,
> Imperialism's face
> And the international wrong.
>
> ['September 1, 1939']

The sheer ability of the thing (for instance in the Housman sonnet) is enormously cheerful for a critic; he is free to talk about the opinions, fully expressed, instead of some failure to express them.

At the same time you are afraid on every page that a horrid false note of infantilism will poke up its head. The poems here about famous men give striking cases of it. Voltaire, we are told, 'cleverest of them all, He'd led the other children in a holy war Against the infamous grown-ups' ['Voltaire at Ferney']. About Freud, on the other hand, and the voice of the poet breaks at the thought, we are told, 'He wasn't clever at all' ['In Memory of Sigmund Freud'] (he was just such a *good* boy, your heart aches to think of it). No doubt Freud himself is largely reponsible for this idea that people are best understood by seeing them as children; and yet this curious line of sentiment about the word 'clever' would, I suppose, be as hard to translate into German as into French. It is something to do with the English system of education; it throws absolutely no light on Voltaire. At the end of 'Spain' the poet describes an ideal state, with the rather puzzled-headed introduction 'To-morrow, perhaps, the future', and it is a boys' school; there would be no room for Auden himself except as one of the masters. I see that some of the verses have been cut out; 'The eager election of chairmen/By the sudden forest of hands' is no longer put forward as a scene that Auden would take part in gleefully. He has also, very oddly, cut out the best and most characteristic verses, the comparison of aspects of suburban fretfulness with the instruments of war which they are supposed to have engendered. And 'The conscious acceptance of guilt in the necessary murder' has become 'in the fact of murder'.[2] We are still though to have 'all the fun under Liberty's masterful shadow'; it is a very fascist picture. I can't myself feel that the race of man is like this at all. What is heartening about people is their appalling stubbornness and the strong roots of their various cultures, rather than the ease with which you can convert them and make them happy and good. Probably a whole political outlook can turn on this. The poem 'Schoolchildren' is fine because there Auden finds it natural to admit that men are a bit different from schoolchildren. Maybe you could connect the utopian note of the politics with a remark in one of the love-poems:

> I believed for years that
> Love was the conjunction
> Of two oppositions;
>   That was all untrue...

['Heavy Date']

You can overdo it, to be sure, but things can't be all kiss and make friends either. Auden's later poetry, I think, gains by simplifying its machinery, but wouldn't gain if it came to simplify the ideas in the background.

The text, by the way, is bad. I am not at all opposed to honest farce on the part of a printer:

> all our whiteness shrinks
> From the hairy and clumsy bridge-room

['They']

seems to me a pretty line, if you see what has gone wrong with it. But take the last verse on the death of Freud:

> One rational voice is dumb. Over his grave
>   the household of Impulse mourns one dearly loved:
>   sad is Eros, builder of cities,
>   and weeping anarchic Aphrodite.

In the Faber text the entrancing rhythm of the last line has been murdered by the insertion of the word 'of'.

Notes

1 Untitled in original.

2 In a draft essay dating from about 1940 Empson observed: 'Voigt was saying in a political book that the poets are all warmongers now, and illustrated this by a line from Auden's "Spain": "The conscious acceptance of guilt in the necessary murder". Of course a paradox can always be read several ways: "murder" says this act of killing is wicked, and "necessary" (for the ends considered) says it is good, so you don't know what sorts of killing the poet has in view. But surely it comes from a conscience sensitive about war rather than brutalised. Cf. the song of Deborah, for real warmongering. But maybe there is a kind of German-philosophical quality in the line, which Voigt might feel more of a Nazi weapon than Auden did. The more striking thing about Auden is the horror of Power, e.g. "The Ascent of F6". All power corrupts ... It is remarkable to me that nobody has yet turned the epigram of Lord Acton backwards. All impotence corrupts; absolute impotence corrupts absolutely. This is quite as true as the other, but maybe they only recommend the same thing, a wide spreading of power through the country. It is always hard to translate the wisdom of the literary into political plans' (Empson Papers).

Early Auden

A TRANSCRIPT OF A CONTRIBUTION TO A
BBC TV *BOOKSTAND* PROGRAMME ON AUDEN

The Review, 5 February 1963

I very greatly admire the poet Auden: I think that he and Dylan Thomas, of the poets my age and younger, are the only ones you could call poets of genius. I think he's a wonderful poet. But when I feel that, I'm merely thinking about the early poetry. And I should say that what seems so astonishing, in the poetry he wrote in the thirties, you know, was the way he can bring in a disease caused by mental stress, and a political confusion or harmful arrangement, and then the threatening world wars, and make them all seem the same kind of thing; using these very startling comparisons – usually very strained really, but always shocking and striking – between one and the other.

They were what one thought was so wonderful; and there is always this curious curl of the tongue in his voice, which I think many people later disliked very much. But it seemed wonderful then. It is very hard, you see, to write what years later people called pylon poetry – to write about how you ought to have the socialist state and how you'd like it – without sounding phoney. And Auden somehow made it sound perfectly sincere by making it sound as if he was jeering at you for not being more sensible, but you didn't quite know what he was laughing at, but you could hear this, this mysterious tone of fun going on. It seemed to be immensely impressive. That was what was so striking about him. And he has moved away from it and so have all the pylon poets, who by the way were all at Oxford when I was at Cambridge. That's why as a poet myself I was never able to imitate it properly. You had to be in on the movement from the start.

But I have sometimes known later critics say, 'Oh, well, Empson wasn't so much of a mug as to be a pylon poet; he may have very little to say, but at least he didn't say that.' Well, of course, I agreed with the pylon poets entirely. I've always felt I ought to make that point plain whenever I had the opportunity: I think they were quite right, I just didn't know how to do this kind of poetry. And it does rather depend on the curl of the tongue.

You see, the pylon poets, beginning with the great slump of 1929 – you had tremendous numbers of people out of work, and the economic system was clearly badly out of order, and then you got Mussolini and Hitler coming up – what they were saying was that you ought to have more social-ism at home, you want the Welfare State, and you ought to have the popu-lar front against Hitler abroad, the line-up of the Allies. They went on saying that through the thirties, and by 1942 the whole country agreed with them. Well, it's a very lucky thing for a poet. I'm very sorry I wasn't in on it. So we needn't all try to laugh it off now, I think, as they rather tend to do. Some of it's wonderful writing, and it's very lucky for a poet to have some-thing to say which sounds very shocking at the time and everybody's going to think is right ten years later. Of course, you may say it turned out the Russians weren't angels and many hopes failed and so on. But, still, what they were saying was the right advice: you can't get away from that, even if they feel they did it rather excessively. But Auden, you see, has cut out so much of what he wrote then. This poem written during the – he went to China after Spain in '37 and this sonnet is about being bombed in Canton, I think. But the point I wanted to bring out is this – it is magnificent, good gracious – but it's slightly funny. He's saying whenever you hear bombing going on you hope all the people you hate will get killed, you feel it's an op-portunity, and your only impulse is a release, even though you're the victim.

> Yes, we are going to suffer, now; the sky
> Throbs like a feverish forehead; pain is real;
> The groping searchlights suddenly reveal
> The little natures that will make us cry.
>
> Who never quite believed they could exist,
> Not where we were. They take us by surprise
> Like ugly long-forgotten memories,
> And like a conscience all the guns resist.
>
> Behind each sociable home-loving eye
> The private massacres are taking place;
> All Women, Jews, the Rich, the Human Race.
>
> The mountains cannot judge us when we lie:
> We dwell upon the earth; the earth obeys
> The intelligent and evil till they die.

Very fine indeed. I think he ought to print that again soon.[1] But the change in his interest doesn't mean that he's no longer a great poet. The world scene now – and he was always writing about the current scene – really is rather gloomy. It may well be that he'll find interesting things to write about again; and, besides, a middle-aged poet often isn't very good: he often gets good again when he's old. I even hope it may happen to me. But in the case of the great Auden, I think he will write again magnificently before he dies.

Note

1 This poem is in the Collected Edition, so what I am made to say about it is nonsense, but merely as a result of cutting. I said it about the sonnet on A. E. Housman, beginning 'No one, not even Cambridge, was to blame'; that really is rather hard to get hold of, and I had to recite it from memory. I also remembered some of the passages from the pamphlet version of *Spain, 1937* which were cut in the Collected Edition: but evidently they too got cut again. [Empson]

The Just Man Made Innocent

New Statesman, 19 April 1963

W. H. Auden, *The Dyer's Hand*

The previous critical prose book by Auden, *The Enchafèd Flood* (1951), examined the influence of the maritime empires on the literatures of Western Europe; it showed that the prestige of the explorer made him a symbol for intellectual adventure and especially for the highest event in ethics, the moral discovery, which gets a man called a traitor by his own society. I had the book in communist Peking and lent it to Sardar Panikkar, then Indian Ambassador, who was perhaps irritated by the prominent position given to 'The Hunting of the Snark'; he said it was all spoof, and reeled off quotations from the epics of three Indian languages to show that the sea is always the great sweet mother, for the poets. But that was Auden's point, I said; the sea is different in the poets of the maritime empires. 'Then they aren't really poets,' he said, leaving me convinced that Auden had made an important discovery about the 'Ancient Mariner'. He cannot be expected to do this every time, and the range and grasp of his mind is always evident in the present book; but it strikes me that his mind is increasingly hampered, and that the resulting thoughts are often wrong.

A man converted to Christianity twenty years ago must be very strong and good not to have become corrupted into any of that religion's usual forms of nastiness. Some kind of ill effect was inevitable, but he chose an innocent one. He is determined to expunge from his mind the wickedness of the Christian God, and not let it poison his view of the world by a perversion of human values, so he 'looks on the bright side': he twitters like a curate in W. S. Gilbert, emitting a steady rivulet of the opaque distinctions suited to a spiritual director. It must be rather baffling for the Americans, especially as it is so unlike his personal character.

To stretch one's mind all round Falstaff is hard, and to defend him against legalism is at least to take the right side; but Auden regards the old brute as a saint. It then strikes him as odd (p. 183) that the errant prince did not choose to meet 'daring, rather sinister juvenile delinquents' instead of the mystical old failure at the Boar's Head. But Falstaff is their gang-leader;

he has the same job as Fagin, except that in a less policed society he can use older boys ('O for a fine thief of the age of two and twenty or thereabouts; I am heinously ill-provided'); that is why he is always telling the young men he loves them, as Fagin does too. After the magic words, 'Why, I never saw such a clever *good* boy,' every 'daring, rather sinister' alumnus will hand over the gold watch to the father-figure and patter happily out to pinch another one.

Auden is right, I think, in saying we are not meant to be shocked when Falstaff takes bribes to conscript the worst available men for his troop, but the overall reason was that the audience (even though otherwise pro-Hal) disapproved of civil war in England, especially when caused by usurping Norman barons. Later, Falstaff boasts to the audience that he has led his hundred and fifty to a place where they are almost all killed, so that he can keep their pay; this is bad ruling-class behaviour, so it would shock the masses at the Globe, not only Auden and me. I have never read a commentator denying that the words mean what they seem to; they might perhaps be got round, but Auden simply ignores them.

He does recognise two places where the text does not fit his interpretation, and he is content to blame the author (p. 185). It is rather bad taste, he finds, to make Falstaff cheat over the corpse of Hotspur; and when Prince John orders Coleville's execution, with facetious comment by Falstaff – 'How is any actor to behave and speak his lines?' Coleville surrendered on hearing the name of his opponent, because it had become so terrible, and Falstaff is as gleeful as the audience are expected to be at this long-built-up absurdity. Pleading for the man's life with the invariably treacherous Prince John would not be the slightest use, so we need not feel that Falstaff misses a chance to behave generously. I grant that military fun is often bleak, but there can be no problem here unless you expect Falstaff to be an archangel. The real objection felt by a modern audience, I think, is a different one: 'If Falstaff and the Prince are both bad, why is it all supposed to be nice?' Well, there did not have to be an answer in those terms. Different characters in the audience would be making fiercely opposed judgements, but there was an official answer which made the play possible: 'The Norman prince who wiped out the shame of the Norman Conquest became, first by his condescension in the taverns and thence by his understanding of his people, a forerunner of our present national monarchy.'

The villain Iago, says Auden with a most likeable distaste for pulling a long face, was probably a practical joker – and then we are given some penetrating remarks about practical jokers. Or else a pure scientist, who is a practical joker too – this comes at the end, an impressive stroke in favour of the Church. In no other play, says Auden, is the villain so completely triumphant (Iago tells the audience early on that he aims 'to make the Moor thank me, love me and reward me,' and no other villain in Shakespeare ends by being tortured to death). There is no need for Roderigo in the plot, says Auden, so he is there because it amuses Iago to corrupt him (there would be no tragedy unless Iago had cheated Roderigo out of large sums – 'go sell thy land' – on the pretence that this will buy him Desdemona. The clamouring Roderigo is twice brought onto the stage to force Iago forward, each time realising that his plot is getting more dangerous than he wanted, and perhaps feeling embarrassed by the women's tears). Iago can't really suspect his wife of adultery, says Auden, because his wife 'openly refers' to his suspicion as already past (I think I know what had gone on, but I am sure anyhow that Auden's remark is too high-minded).

The Tempest he finds 'disquieting', and his feeling is probably right; but the reason he gives is that the play shows nature refusing the influence of the spirit, a Manichaean view and unworthy of Shakespeare at his close. It is fine to have him so alert for an evil use of religious ideas; but these high anxieties can only arise here if you assume that Prospero represents God. English propaganda had been claiming for a generation that the southern Europeans were ill-treating the natives in their colonies, which meant it wasn't stealing if you looted the treasure fleets; and suspicion of magicians was so severe that the Queen could not protect the house and property of her cousin and adviser Dr Dee. The coarse audience would respect one thing only about Prospero: his struggle to forgive the men who have wronged him. The reason why these men are made unresponsive, perhaps also the reason why Prospero is made self-centred and ill-tempered, is to heighten the struggle. A man with infinite power offers no other dramatic interest except whether he can control himself; the audience, however rough otherwise, had quite enough theological training to grasp that, and the text gives plenty of support.

Auden is best on The Merchant of Venice, because that play was de-signed to ask the audience to think of extra allegories, and he really does provide several new ones. But even here he is too high-minded for the author: he finds Bassanio worldly, whereas Shakespeare was fully prepared to admire a cool young gambler. With great firmness, he shows all along how his interpretations ought to affect a production. 'If the actor were to appear in one scene in Elizabethan costume and in the next in top hat and morning coat, no one would be bewildered' – so much for Falstaff. And the rule for Iago is that 'he must deliver the lines of his soliloquies in such a way that he makes nonsense of them ... He must pause where the verse calls for no pauses, accentuate unimportant words, etc.' Ariel had better be rep-resented only by a spotlight, marking the failure of the spirit to interact with matter. This feels laughably skimpy, but it is harmless compared to the other two.

The Shakespeare criticism is less than half the book. He is good on D. H. Lawrence, indeed good whenever he describes an initial distaste followed by later acceptance. Very understanding about Kafka, except that he offers some weak evidence to disprove that the officials of *The Castle* were meant as agents of Divine Grace. This is what everyone has felt to ring so deep about the story, even if Kafka would have said that he was satirising other people's religious opinions – Kierkegaard's, one would think, and surely Kafka did not feel a positive opponent. However much Auden admires the book, he also needs here to coax you into ignoring the point of it: because it has become his duty to save God's face. Hell itself he turns to favour and to prettiness; and a Christian can do much worse. But this process, preventing Auden from understanding much of what he reads, has gone on long enough; and I hope and expect that, before he dies, he will recover the use of his power.

To Understand a Modern Poem: 'A Refusal to Mourn the Death, by Fire, of a Child in London', by Dylan Thomas

Strand, March 1947

Never until the mankind making
Bird beast and flower
Fathering and all humbling darkness
Tells with silence the last light breaking
And the still hour
Is come of the sea tumbling in harness

And I must enter again the round
Zion of the water bead
And the synagogue of the ear of corn
Shall I let pray the shadow of a sound
Or sow my salt seed
In the least valley of sackcloth to mourn

The majesty and burning of the child's death.
I shall not murder
The mankind of her going with a grave truth
Nor blaspheme down the stations of the breath
With any further
Elegy of innocence and youth.

Deep with the first dead lies London's daughter,
Robed in the long friends,
The grains beyond age, the dark veins of her mother,
Secret by the unmourning water
Of the riding Thames.
After the first death, there is no other.

The critics agree with hardly a dissenting voice that Dylan Thomas is a splendid poet, but it is unusual for anyone to undertake to say what he means, as I am doing here.

He works by piling up many distant suggestions at once, and half the time is not 'saying anything' in the ordinary meaning of the term. You are not expected to take in the whole of this poem on a first reading as the eye goes down the page, which is what good prose ought to allow you to do; the thing is meant to grow in the mind, or at least echo about there. On the other hand, I think there is no reason to feel that 'modern' poetry is some obscure new trick. Poets have always worked by piling up suggestions. Dylan Thomas does it more than most; you may say too much, but there is no fundamental difference of technique from older poets, certainly not from Shakespeare.

The difficulty about trying to give the meaning in prose is that the critic seems to be reading an unreasonable amount 'into' the passage he has chosen, so that it comes to look harder to understand rather than easier. The extra meanings are in the detail all right, but they are being put in all the time, as part of the style, and a reader gets used to picking them up casually. The fundamental ideas which Dylan Thomas is expressing in his rich technique are, I think, rather few, and the same explanations would do again and again. So you can enjoy one of the poems and form an opinion about it without making up your mind on the meaning of all the details. Also, as a rule, there is not much development in his poems; what stick in your mind are single rich phrases rather than a connected argument –

> While the worm builds with the gold straws of venom
> My nest of mercies in the rude, red tree –
> ['Altarwise by Owl-light', no. x, ll. 13–14]

and even these seem to point all ways rather than sum anything up. His last book, *Deaths and Entrances*, does contain a higher proportion of poems which you would remember as units, though it is still using the same concentrated technique.

In the poem printed here the title gives you the subject, and what Dylan Thomas feels about it is evidently like what many other people would feel. But even so, taking it line by line, there is a good deal which I feel I haven't got to the bottom of. Also, though this is a different matter, obscurity in a writer may be due, not to concentration, but to a refusal to speak out. This poem tells us that Dylan Thomas *isn't* going to say something. I take it that the child was killed in an air raid, and that Dylan Thomas won't say so because he is refusing to be distracted by thoughts about the war from thoughts about the child herself or about death in general.

It is perhaps worth saying that the form is a repeated rhyming verse with the rhymes in the order 'abcabc', having three stresses (or emphasised syllables) in the 'b' lines and five in the others. Nearly all the poems in the book are in regular though sometimes complex stanzas. The bad rhymes, I think, satisfy the ear like ordinary rhymes, and are not meant, as in some poets' use of them, to suggest strain or horror.

The first two verses and the next line are one sentence, with the skeleton grammar 'Till doomsday (or my death) I will not mourn the child.' *Darkness* is described as *making* mankind, *fathering* birds, etc., and *humbling* all; the same form as 'bed-making'. This would be a less discouraging bit of grammar if hyphens were put in, but you would need six of them and it would look ugly. The poem starts with a great mouthful as for a cosmic occasion. I am not sure about the distinction between *making* and *fathering*; perhaps the construction of *mankind* is a special process, as in Genesis. The darkness, anyway, is the unknown, undeveloped Nature from which all life came and to which it returns, also the particular night before Doomsday or before the day of Thomas's death. At Doomsday the sea gives up its dead; we may be meant to think of the water *tumbling* off them, and the sea might be *harnessed* in that it is at last controlled. Waves are called white horses. But the phrase is much more beautiful than this explanation; it may have an idea of the sea invading the land to end the world, and yet it could be just an affectionate description of a quiet morning sea. Shakespearean lovers tumble each other, but the word is more likely to suggest puppies.

The hour, at any rate, is an apocalyptic one, and the second verse gives it more positively mysterious or religious language. Dylan Thomas, like the dead girl, is to return to a state like that before birth, the heaven of the womb; the *bead* is I think simply a drop of water regarded as self-completing, making a round unit which does not spread into the outside world; but it could suggest the amœba as the undeveloped primitive cell of living jelly. A suggestion of beads as used for counting prayers would fit the general religious background and the word *pray* two lines later; the qualifying word *water* then dissolves this prayer, because Dylan Thomas's religion is pantheistic and absorbs the Godhead into the world.

Here I am evidently wandering from the direct impact of the line, but Dylan Thomas does not fit things into compartments and likes to throw extra suggestions into any possible phrase which merely belongs to the whole theme. *Corn*, which he must also re-enter, was said by St Paul to die in the ground before it sprouts; and bread and water are, in any case, the fundamental life-givers. The *ear* is a group of grains, who may be seen as piously collected to pray in their *synagogue*; but I suppose all our group activities are thought of as first made possible by the development of the blind life of the single cell.

The general theme is that Dylan Thomas at death, no less than the burned girl, must be absorbed into the Nature from which further life may mysteriously be born. The terms perhaps seem Jewish rather than Christian, but I should think he is remembering the Welsh Nonconformist preachers he heard as a boy.

Not till then will he *let pray* (as it might be 'let drop') even the ghost of a sound, which might seem external to him and outside his control. Nor will he drop a tear, though it is described in terms that recall both the *water bead* and the *corn grain*, and these appeared separate from his conscious will. To wet the smallest fold of his clothes with tears is compared to sowing a valley, on the general rule that events in Dylan Thomas's body are related pantheistically to more massive ones outside. *Seed* implies that the tear would be fertile if he allowed it to fall, but perhaps *salt* denies this, or the idea is that to allow false sentiment would encourage the sprouting of large weeds.

The wave breaks at the beginning of the third verse as the poem turns from Dylan Thomas and the universe to the child. *Mankind* is now used again as the name of a quality of her death; she is not chiefly to be thought of as a girl child, because death and suffering are common to all, and because she deserves to be treated with dignity. *Grave* seems to be a pun on 'solemn' and 'burial-place'; the poet will not make her death seem trivial by uttering platitudes suited to funerals. But this seems an improbably weak interpretation for *murder mankind*, and I think one might take the whole line another way. The mankind of her going may be all the men who made the world situation in which she was killed; with an ironical reassurance the poet announces that he will not give these people their due. The Stations of the Cross are, of course, the series of incidents on the way to the crucifixion often painted round the Roman Catholic churches; those of the *breath* are the normal sufferings, different for each age-group but common to all mankind.

Dylan Thomas will not blaspheme his way down these stations, as by making a speech wherever the train stops, nor will he break down the partitions between them by some blasphemy, for example by talking about the child as if she were a grown-up. *Further*: someone has already done it. *Innocence* indeed; the child had the life suited to her age; for instance, her sexlessness or undeveloped kind of sex ought not to be talked about as a model of adult chastity. The reality behind all this, I believe, is that Dylan Thomas had been tempted to write war propaganda, both by indignation and by the opportunities of his profession, and then felt that this would be disgusting; it would be making use of the child, and what was said would have nothing to do with her actual experiences. The final poem therefore does not even admit that there was a war.

Instead the last verse practically ignores her, and deals with death in general. However, she has now a *long* gown like an angel or like a shroud; these clothes are *friends* because all matter has become her friend; she has returned to it. Or indeed *long* (when we get to *age* in the next line) means that these friends last for ever. And then again the clothes, since she was burned to ashes, are now *grains* of dust, recalling the earlier grains of corn which promised further life (so that both parts of the conventional angel picture are denied). They are *beyond age* because death is clearly beyond *old* age (the age of the child ought not to be considered) and because being particles like atoms they are unchanged at all the stages of development of the things they build up. *Veins* in Dylan Thomas are nearly always puns connecting the part of the body and the ore hidden in the earth, because of the pervading pantheism of his ideas and the hint of a magical belief that one person's body can affect everything. The dust of the child has gone underground into mother earth, and can be mined out again for new uses; and yet the earth, like the *friends*, is still treated as living. *Riding*: the Thames is cheerful and practical, both riding over the earth and being ridden by men; and if treated as alive no doubt Father Thames is riding the Thames.

The plain meaning of the last line is that the child has no more pain and is well rid of such a world; it suggests also that she lives for ever as part of Nature. But the overtone is a summing up of the real theme. We ought not to talk nonsense about her; we cannot make her repeat her agonies for our own purposes, though we would be likely to do so if we were able.

A Poem by Dylan Thomas

?1953

'The force that through the green fuse drives the flower'

I mean here to give an exegesis of one of the first Dylan Thomas poems, indeed the one that first hit the town (London); it was published about 1933 in a newspaper of the sporting masses, the *Sunday Referee*, which gave it a prize. Thus began the Dylan Thomas revolt against the political poetry of the thirties, with Auden as its most brilliant exponent, in favour of a poetry of the inner world of magic, religion and guilt, or a world of personal relations. Most young poets in England I suppose have now followed this lead, but not in general for Thomas's reasons. Thomas would not agree that he had no political opinions, but they were not at any rate the surface of what he wanted to say. What the political poets and the intelligentsia in general were demanding in the thirties were socialist measures at home and anti-Fascism abroad; these were both practically secured early in the war, and the theme therefore lost its immediate relevance. Of course there is still plenty to argue about in politics, but nothing that goes into verse with such a bang. Thus if Auden had stayed in England he would still have had to write differently, even if he had not been absorbed into some propaganda agency, as he almost certainly would have been.

I shall quote the whole poem verse by verse.

> The force that through the green fuse drives the flower
> Drives my green age; that blasts the roots of trees
> Is my destroyer.
> And I am dumb to tell the crooked rose
> My youth is bent by the same wintry fever.

The *fuse* seems to be the slow-burning one that gives you time to throw the bomb, but the other fuse that is a safety-valve for electric wiring is probably in sight, because lightning may be what blasts the trees. Also fusing metals together to make them stick is a relevant idea; the violence of the vegetable growth and decay is compared to heavy industry before it is compared to the forces of Thomas's own life or body. In general this kind of poetry throws about the possible meanings of a word in an opportunist manner; the focus is not held sharp, because the background of the mind is being let loose, and the thing is free to mean more than the poet realised; however it is not surrealist in principle, and one could placidly say that the new style was a matter of imitating Shakespeare rather than Donne. *Wintry fever* (fever itself making you go hot and cold) seems to imply that the forces of life making him a poet have caused a precocious development which has caught a late frost. The recurring *dumb* of course says that the affinity of his own body and mind with all Nature can be obscurely felt but not expressed logically, and that even if it could be this would not interest Nature or the rose.

> The force that drives the water through the rocks
> Drives my red blood; that dries the mouthing streams
> Turns mine to wax.
> And I am dumb to mouth unto my veins
> How at the mountain spring the same mouth sucks.

The analogy descends from vegetables to the inorganic systems that make life possible, such as the sea–cloud–river cycle, which fits both the blood circuit and the digestive tube. The miracle of Moses in striking water from the rock may be in sight; the natural is miraculous (Thomas has behind him the spellbinding of the Welsh Nonconformist preachers he heard as a child, and echoes it for a kind of pantheism). Hence it is also sinister and its help may fail mysteriously. The streams I suppose *mouth* because they both chatter and need a continual supply. *Mouthing* is taking sensual pleasure in boastful or rhetorical talking; the attempt to talk to Nature or even theorise about her would be like this.

> The hand that whirls the water in the pool
> Stirs the quicksand; that ropes the blowing wind
> Hauls my shroud sail.
> And I am dumb to tell the hanging man
> How of my clay is made the hangman's lime.

The analogy between Nature and the human body is now heightened to the point of confusing them. The hand may belong to a human being in play or to Nature forming a small whirlpool as the water runs out. The same forces (as a big whirlpool can suck you down) illustrate the quicksand which seems to suck you into it with deliberate malice; the unusual stress required on *sand* calls out the paradox of the word, which means living inorganic matter. The sinister, as well as the forces of life, is to be found everywhere. And the wind may be *roped* by sailors in the course of business or by the influence of mythological wind gods; either of them is analogous to the forces driving Thomas's life through storm to its final peace. The criminality of the quicksand then recalls the quicklime that may be made from men's bones and is used to destroy the corpse of the hanged man; the unnameable affinities with Nature have turned into those with society. Thomas cannot tell the suffering criminal either that he shared in the society which condemns him or that he thereby shared in his guilt; and the materials of this throttling interrelation are to be found everywhere in the tools of ordinary practical activity.

> The lips of time leech to the fountain head;
> Love drips and gathers, but the fallen blood
> Shall calm her sores.
> And I am dumb to tell a weather's wind
> How time has ticked a heaven round the stars.

The mountain spring comes back with a deeper allegory which rather contradicts the first one; all temporal things cling to, and draw the blood of life and healing from, an external source. Love appears a business of accumulating and expelling secretions; death or the loss of virginity will cure desire. At least these seem to be the obvious way to take *fallen blood*, but blood as impulse presumably 'fell' once for all with Adam, and on this view the processes of common life will quiet the craving of the disease. The love of the eternal, we are to suppose, will remain, but the human love is not clearly separated from the ideal one. The lines are a good example of a trick Dylan Thomas is very strong at; he manoeuvres himself on to a sort of water-shed from which the consequences may go either way, and thus ties together intensely contrasted feelings – in this case, for instance, of intense disgust (at the pus of the unhealing wound) and half-religious exultation. The metaphysical and clinical views of love here are I think definitely meant to be applied to the same object. I have sometimes also fancied a reference to the superstition that the rape of a virgin cures venereal disease, and he is quite capable of throwing this hideous image into his landscape of vision, but there is not much basis for supposing it. When Auden in 'Spain' said that 'tomorrow' there could again be time for the 'poets exploding like bombs' I imagine he was thinking of the new Dylan Thomas technique as much as anything. The *weather's wind* is blowing hard in one direction, and Thomas cannot tell it that all directions are possible and will presumably occur, as the hand goes round the clock; the interrelation of the ideal world and the actual is now heightened by the odd suggestion that the eternal has actually been built up by completing all possibilities in the vast reaches of past time.

And I am dumb to tell the lover's tomb
How at my sheet goes the same crooked worm.

The final blow is directly personal; Thomas cannot tell the suicide who died for love that the same forces are at work in his own bed, where the sheet has already been called a shroud. The worm is *crooked* like the rose, no doubt for the same reasons again; it could be a genital symbol, a hell-worm of remorse, or simply consciousness of the approach of death. But the major idea from its crookedness, I think, is that all impulses have been shown to be complex and indeed compounded of contradictory elements, and one thing is inherent in another on such a scale that only vision not action can expect to grasp them.

The Collected Dylan Thomas

New Statesman and Nation, 15 May 1954

Dylan Thomas, *Collected Poems* and *Under Milk Wood*

The most interesting question about the poetry of Dylan Thomas, it seems to me, is raised by Cyril Connolly on the back of the dust-cover of the Collected Edition. He says that Dylan Thomas 'distils an exquisite, mysterious, moving quality which defies analysis as supreme lyrical poetry always has and – let us hope – always will'. This assertion has a certain truth, because the arts are a great mystery, but we must remember that the logic of it applies equally to Wordsworth. The suggestion of it is something quite different, that you needn't worry if you can't make any sense of the early Dylan Thomas poetry; you had better just be pleased, because you know you are in the fashion if you say you like it, and if it makes no sense that only shows it is profound. But this theory is dispiriting to good readers and a positive encouragement to the practice of bad reading; one ought not to rest content with it. And yet a good deal of his poetry does give countenance to this lethal formula; perhaps more so than any other top-grade poetry in the language. During his lifetime he was frequently attacked for (in effect) tossing the juice around so smudgily, though this has been ignored in the very deserved acclaim immediately after his death.

In any case, he had been changing. (And, incidentally, the early verse turns on rather few fundamental ideas, so that once you know what to expect you can find them with less effort; this makes it unlike the obscurity of Shakespeare when tearing on the tripod, which it otherwise resembles.) There is a period of sag in his work, already just feelable perhaps in the second book of poetry, where the succession of thrilling magical lines, each practically a complete poem in itself, fails to add up. The sonnet sequence called 'Altarwise by Owl-light' in the collected edition is a fair example, because a lot of it is undoubtedly wonderful and yet one can't help feeling that the style has become a mannerism. Evidently he became conscious of this, and most of the poems written during the Second World War are concerned to develop a particular theme. He went on to descriptions of his childhood, as in the splendid 'Fern Hill', which is not obscure at all; and meanwhile he was writing plays and stories which are fully externalised, though of course steeped in his peculiar tone or vision. He was just getting ready to be a dramatist, and knew he needed to, though the superb but rather static survey of *Under Milk Wood* was (as it happened) all he had time for. For that matter, as I have mentioned Wordsworth just to give the contrast of an author wishing to be simple in style, it is as well to point out that Wordsworth felt the need of the same process; he talks a good deal about the loss of his first inspiration and the struggle to become a greater poet as a result of that. We need not think of Dylan as a deluded or self-indulgent author. But, all the same, it is the first inspiration, the poems the young man hit the town with (overwhelmingly good, though one resisted them because one couldn't see why), which are the permanent challenge to a critic and in a way the decisive part of his work. I was disinclined to review the *Collected Poems* when it came out during his lifetime, because I would have had to say I liked the early obscure ones best, and I was afraid this would distress him; so I now have one of those unavailing regrets about my timidity, because he knew all that kind of thing very well and could be distressed only by a refusal to say it.

Many people recently have described their personal contacts with this entrancing talker. What I chiefly remember is hearing him describe how he was going to do a film of the life of Dickens, showing how he was determined to escape from the blacking factory and determined to send his children to Eton and finally killed himself by insisting on doing public performances of readings of the Murder of Nancy and so forth (not needed for money, only needed to make his life dramatic enough) when his doctors had told him it would kill him. You can't exactly blame the top chaps in the films for not hiring Dylan at his own valuation then; it was a question of time and one would think there was time in hand; but still the film he wanted to make about Dickens was very profound and very box-office. If Dylan had lived a normal span of life it would have been likely to mean a considerable improvement of quality in the entertainment profession; he ought not to be regarded as the Marvellous Boy who could not grow up.

Let us go back then to the early poems and their obscurity. It is quite true that they hit you before you know how, but that is no reason for not wanting to know how. When Dr Johnson went to the Hebrides he took with him Cocker's *Arithmetic*, because (he said) you get tired of any work of literature, but a book of science is inexhaustible. When I was refugeeing across China (in 1937–39) I too had a little book of school Problems Papers, but it was worth carrying the poems of Dylan Thomas as well because they were equally inexhaustible. This was not in the least because I thought a smart critic only tastes them and knows better than ever to wonder what they mean; they would have been no use to me in such a case if I had taken up this silly attitude. All the same, there is still a lot of his poetry where I can feel it works and yet can't see why. I have no theory at all about the meaning of the line:

> The two-a-vein, the foreskin, and the cloud,

though I am sure there is a reason why it seems very good; and indeed I don't much like the poem (called 'Now') it's the last line of, so I don't bother about it, but I assume on principle there is something there which I feel and can't see, but could see. On the other hand, of course, there are cases where a footnote would make no difference. Since I got back to England recently I have been asking about Mnetha in the tremendous verse

> Before I knocked and flesh let enter,
> With liquid hands tapped on the womb,
> I who was shapeless as the water
> That shaped the Jordan near my home
> Was brother to Mnetha's daughter
> And sister to the fathering worm.
>
> ['Before I Knocked']

Miss Kathleen Raine has at last told me that Mnetha is a suitable character in one of Blake's Prophetic Books [*Tiriel*]; but this acts only as a reassurance that the line meant the kind of thing you wanted it to, not really as an explanation of it – 'That'll do very well,' as Alice said when she was told the meaning of a word in the 'Jabberwocky'; because she knew already what it ought to fit in with. I think an annotated edition of Dylan Thomas ought to be prepared as soon as possible, and that a detail like that ought to go in briefly, but it would be hard to decide what else ought to go in.

The political poets of the early 1930s had good luck for poets in being able to recommended something practical (more socialism at home, a Popular Front against Hitler abroad) on which almost the whole country had come to agree with them by 1940. The idea that they ought to be ashamed of it, which is now creeping about, seems to me farcical. If they changed their minds later they did so like other citizens; they were right at the time, as the country soon came to agree. It is untrue (and I gather that the mistake is liable to be made nowadays) to think that, when Dylan Thomas broke in, it meant a change of politics. He had much the same political opinions as Auden, and was very ready to say so; but he was not interested in writing verse about them. What hit the town of London was the child Dylan publishing 'The force that through the green fuse' as a prize poem in the *Sunday Referee*, and from that day he was a famous poet; I think the incident does some credit to the town, making it look less clumsy than you would think. The poem is more easily analysable than most early Dylan Thomas poems, and we need not doubt that the choosers knew broadly what it meant (I would not claim to know all myself); but it was very off the current fashion. It centres on comparing the bloodstream of the child Dylan to the sea–cloud–river cycle by which water moves round this planet, and he is united with the planet, also personally guilty of murder whenever a murderer is hanged, and so forth. The mining term *vein* for a line of ore was naturally a crucial pun for the early Dylan, because of his central desire to identify events inside his own skin with the two main things outside it, the entire physical world and also the relations with that of other men. Such was the main thing he was talking about, and the point of vision was set too high for him to let the current politics into the structure of metaphors. There was no other reason for not letting it in. He really was a 'mystic', as the term is used, but he would have been very cross with anybody who supposed that this meant right-wing politics.

I am trying to consider a reader who is doubtful whether to read this poetry, so I am thinking whether I could give any useful advice. You must realise that he was a very witty man, with a very keen though not at all poisoned recognition that the world contains horror as well as delight; his chief power as a stylist is to convey a sickened loathing which somehow at once (within the phrase) enforces a welcome for the eternal necessities of the world. It is particularly important to realise this at the end of the sequence 'Altarwise by Owl-light', which I mentioned earlier as bad, but when it is good it is ragingly good. It ends:

> Green as beginning, let the garden diving
> Soar, with its two bark towers, to that Day
> When the worm builds with the gold straws
>   of venom
> My nest of mercies in the rude, red tree.

I hope I do not annoy anyone by remarking[2] that the Cross of Jesus is also the male sexual organ; Dylan would only have thought that tiresomely obvious, a basis for his remarks. But when you get to the worms instead of the birds able to build something valuable in this tree, and the extraordinary shock of the voice of the poet in his reverence and release (at the end of the whole poem) when he gets to his nest, you do begin to wonder whether he meant something wiser than he knew.

Notes

1 Untitled in original.

2 In the first published version the word 'remarking' appeared as 'explaining'. Empson explained the alteration in a letter (15 May 1954) to Janet Adam Smith:

'I agree that in principle it was very wicked of the Editor to change a word, but I hadn't noticed it and do not now think it disastrous. As I remember I put "I hope I do not annoy anyone by remarking that the Cross of Christ is also the male sexual organ" and he made it "explaining". This makes me heavyhanded and rather suggests I hold some theory of the sort myself, but otherwise does no harm. I can't see that it removes any obscurity, either, though.

'There has been some other puzzling about the style of that piece. Dear old J. Isaacs, when I ran into him at some party, said it was the most childish thing on the subject he had yet seen, and he gathered all I meant was that the only good part was the final Milk Wood. How he came to think that I can't imagine: I suppose he thinks if a critic says something simply that proves he means to be ironical. Then he said, "How do you manage to get it as loose as that? Do you dictate it?" I explained I used beer, but that when I saw the stuff in print (I had to admit) it shocked my eye as much as it did his. He was very friendly, you understand. One thing is, I have to read so much Mandarin English Prose now, especially in literary criticism, and am so accustomed to being shocked by its emptiness, that I feel I must do otherwise at all costs' (Janet Adam Smith).

Dylan Thomas

Essays in Criticism, XIII: ii, April 1963

Reviewing David Holbrook's Llareggub Revisited: Dylan Thomas and the
state of modern poetry *(1962) in* Essays in Criticism *(XIII: i, January
1963), Ralph N.* Maud *(author of* Entrances to Dylan Thomas's Poetry,
*1963) lamented the fact that Holbrook found it necessary to complain
quite so much. 'I find forty-two of the ninety poems in Dylan Thomas's*
Collected Poems *meaningless,' Holbrook had written – to which Maud
(whose review was aptly titled 'Holbrook vs. Thomas') responded with
gentle irony: 'I should have thought that Thomas's obscurities were becoming increasingly easier to handle. Mr Holbrook's protracted attempts to
prove certain poems meaningless only go to confirm this optimistic view.'
Thomas's 'true voice', Maud insisted, remains 'in the big, difficult poems'.*

*For Mr Holbrook the trouble is not only the difficulty of these poems but also the
moral irresponsibility of what coherent outlook he can find in them. I think it is fair
to say that Mr Holbrook is interested in poetry which has a good chance of improv-
ing our lives, raising our moral tone, helping us towards virtuous behaviour – and
he particularly has young people in mind. He is rather horrified, therefore, when he
sees Thomas from time to time rush in the other direction, back to chaos, back to
childhood, back – as he puts it – 'to the breast'.*

Empson firmly agreed with that view:

The attack upon Dylan Thomas by Mr Holbrook was reviewed by Mr
Maud in your last number with adroitness and good humour; he pointed
out that, when Mr Holbrook complains that lines are meaningless, his
words often betray that they have an excellent meaning. All the same, as the
attack is so total and prolonged, I think the reader deserves a bit more help
towards rejection of it.

Mr Holbrook says that Thomas was incapable of generous love but
craved for escape to the breast, for mothering; this allows denunciation of
his later poems such as 'Fern Hill', which many people had thought a great
turn for the better. For myself, I am thankful to have got out of being

young; but it is absurd to denounce poets who find a mystical beauty in the child's delight and wonder at the new-made world. The child Dylan is always presented adventuring away from Mum, sitting on carthorses and suchlike. We are also told that a great poem written early, 'The force that through the green fuse', 'exists only by its suggestion of unwilling growth in the immature boy' – 'Time, of course, brings the threat of maturity which the poem is a desperate attempt by the poet to conceal.' This is not in the text, and it is wildly improbable. Dylan at seventeen or so was the Young Dog, determined to find sexual pleasure; like many other men, he did not revere his childhood till he was safely past it. He did fear, we gather, that the precocious sensuality of his powerful imagination would warp his growth ('And I am dumb to tell the crooked rose/My youth is bent with the same wintry fever'); but even this serves to deepen his intuitive sympathy with all life. 'Of my bones are made the hangman's lime' (in which the criminal is buried so that he leaves no relics); the poet shares the guilt of the legislator and the judge. Mr Holbrook is always telling poets to brisk up and show public spirit, but when he is given it in the grand Dostoevsky manner he cannot imagine it. The verse ending 'And I am dumb to mouth unto my veins/How at the mountain stream the same mouth sucks' works by comparing the circulation of the poet's blood to the water-cycle of the planet, from sea to cloud to river, and it calls their affinity ineffable; in fact, the poet is a microcosm. A teacher of English literature ought to be familiar with this idea, instead of making lengthy boasts that he can't understand it. The poem does, I grant, become mysterious in the verse beginning 'The lips of time leech to the fountainhead,' somehow combining horror, glory, and a sense of boyish fun; Mr Holbrook contrives to smear bad feelings into it, as he does with various similar cases of Dylan tearing upon the tripod. I can find noble meanings in it, but perhaps I try to because of the extreme beauty of sound throughout the poem, which still knocks me down as it did a quarter of a century ago. Mr Holbrook calls the chapter in which he denounces it 'The Death of Rhythm', and I can't help him there.

The thought that events inside the skin of Dylan are like geographical or cosmic events outside it is inherently far from common social life, but cannot prove he had bad intentions about that; and he tends to present himself as the representative of mankind, but merely because any man would do as a specimen. Donne does the same thing. Mr Holbrook works up his denunciations about this to the point (p. 102) of accusing the jealous Thomas of telling Jesus to get back into the womb because he wants to be the Messiah himself. The idea that any man can become Christ, who is a universal, was a major sixteenth-century heresy and has been kept up among the poets; it is prominent again in the splendid poem 'Before I Knocked'.

On the poem 'A Refusal to Mourn' Mr Holbrook grumbles that it is not clear why the poet says he won't say things. The poem is about the German bombing of London, and the poet erected not writing propaganda into a point of honour. There is no great credit in not understanding this. Not understanding 'In Memory of Ann Jones' is more heroic, because Thomas was showing respect for honest worth, a major plank in the programme of Mr Holbrook. The poet is blamed for egotism, because he uses standard rhetorical devices to express how he is swept out of himself in admiration for the terrible strength shown in the working life of his 'peasant aunt'. He is accused of failure to control his passions, of over-rating his peasant aunt, of praising her after admitting that she requires no praise. . . . 'Why not let her lie then?' Coarse as the rivalries of poets, in our rough island story, have often been, this must be about the coarsest cry yet voiced.

Still, one must accept it as an incidental result of the Chadband movement. A prominent Malvolio has a duty of consistency in suppressing cakes and ale; if a poem laughs at Malvolios, he must say it 'reinforces untenderness. It is a cruel work, inviting our cruel laughter.' This is *Under Milk Wood*, which I find beautifully tender but at times a bit sentimental (the audiences at the play are obviously not being spurred to cruel laughter). I agree that some of the speeches feel like propaganda for drunkenness; but many drinkers do boast like that, however much they pay for it later. They are not all neurotics who wake up moaning; and really the males are not always impotent the night before – when Mr Holbrook asserts this, he must be forming a very unreal picture of Thomas's domestic life. He says of the last song of Polly Garter: 'Note the special pleading in *She loves him back*: in the circumstances, he drunk, she dreaming of Willy Wee, would she be likely to?' The answer is: 'Yes; we love her for being so unlike Mr Holbrook.' I had never heard the phrase *love him back* before, and thought it wonderfully good; it spotlights the comradely good feeling of Polly, with the real loved one far away. As Mr Maud says, Mr Holbrook regularly attacks the best things.

So he must, because he aims to destroy in principle the poetry of Dylan Thomas, and one gathers that he would include any poetry of the Auden and Thomas generations which had the real fire. He wrote to the *Times Literary Supplement* explaining in defence of this attack on Thomas that he had to write it 'before I could take myself seriously as a poet at all'. As he is a poet whom no one else need take seriously this is rather a majestic enterprise, likeable in a way if not viewed too gravely.

The article above represents a condensed version of Empson's response to David Holbrook's Llareggub Revisited. *The following letter, written to Christopher Ricks (co-editor of* Essays in Criticism) *on 6 May 1962, con-*

tains his first and fuller thoughts; although parts of it anticipate and there-
fore seem to repeat passages in the published comment, it otherwise
usefully expands Empson's observations and insights into Thomas's
poetry. Editorial cuts are indicated by ellipses.

I feel sympathy with Holbrook's 'A Dissatisfaction with Poetry Today';
Kingsley Amis (p. 27) is in rather bad taste even if the last two verses draw
some moral which I miss (but then it may be lack of virility which makes me
uneasy in brothels), poor Edith [Sitwell] seems to deserve her scolding, Betjeman is not at his best here – but the central trick can be observed in his
case.[1] Betjeman offers us an obscure kind of superiority to the scene and the
characters from its very correctness – from the very wholeheartedness of
our sympathy with such a familiar scene (and readers to whom it isn't familiar may be flattered). English sentiment is hard to analyse but surely not
puzzling – it turns on feeling cosily within some ring. Holbrook argues that
the poem is 'essentially cruel' [p. 27], and this is just credible to a thoughtful
reader because he can feel that there is some kind of bite in it. But the bite is
merely in saying 'How standard we good-class people are!' with perhaps
just a touch of 'How is it credible that any man can love a sports-minded
English lady?' – 'but they really do' the warning voice adds insistently.
Without this saving amount of bite the sentimentality and the snobbery
would become nauseating, or rather those rude words would become deserved: as is well enough appreciated by the very large Betjeman audience.
They view him much as they do a stately home. For Holbrook to call this
'essentially cruel' is grossly false . . . The same cultivated recoil from life [p.
35] is then found in T. S. Eliot while recoiling from priests[2] – he could not
be caught at a more sympathetic moment. . . . Such is the build-up of the
chapter to a terrifying three lines from Dylan Thomas [ll. 4–6 of 'Altarwise
by Owl-light'], said to show the same love of horror as the other examples.
The critic [John] Bayley is blamed (p. 36) for saying [in *The Romantic Sur-*
vival, London: Constable, 1957] that this is 'Thomas's obsessional theme,
the telescoping of existence', which is refusing to see the handling of
language as a moral activity. Well, Dylan really was liable to get the horrors, and they seem to go with flashes of insight and acceptance at their
high points in his verse, as well as with a deep sense of fun or parody
without which they would be dislikeable. The end of the sonnet sequence
which this example begins is a more mysterious case (I agree, with Orwell
rather than Holbrook, that the surrealism of Dali is nasty and also a form
of salesmanship) because at last the confident acceptance of love has
become the main overtone of the horror:

> When the worm builds with the gold straws of venom

My nest of mercies in the rude, red tree.

I looked up in the index 'Before I knocked', as this is an overwhelmingly good poem though marred by a rather unexplained bitterness at the end; and sure enough it is denounced ... 'The force that though the green fuse' and the final song of Polly Garter in *Under Milk Wood*, also but less strikingly 'Fern Hill', are the main cases I think where Dylan is expressing rather unexpectedly good or generous feelings ... Of poets my age and younger, only two I think have the real fire: Auden and Dylan Thomas ...

By the way, it seems absurd to accuse Dylan (p. 102) of telling Jesus to get back into the womb because Dylan is jealous and wants to be Christ himself. Critics have regularly got confused in 'Before I knocked' over whether Christ or the author is speaking. The idea that any man can become Christ, who is a universal, is a sixteenth-century heresy which has gone on knocking about. When Dylan talks about events inside his skin he takes for granted he is talking about all mankind, and free to call himself Christ as soon as it illustrated a point. I do not like or claim to understand 'Vision and Prayer', but I see no reason to accept the claim of Holbrook [pp. 102–03] that he understands it and Dylan didn't ... I call him Dylan because I knew him, like most of the other people who call him so, not because he has established himself as a universal child.

In 'Fern Hill' (p. 155) 'the retrospect is not that of a man placing his childhood and his nostalgia for it', but 'of a man pitying himself for ever growing up'. This is so, and I don't feel the sentiment in my own life at all. ... if Thomas's development into manhood had gone wrong in some way, which is the chief thesis of Holbrook, why may not Thomas regret it himself? Why would it be better to write poetry as if his manhood were perfect? All the same, I feel there is some adult comment behind the tremendous end of the poem, and would not admire it so much otherwise, but I can't be sure what:

> Time held me green and dying
> Though I sang in my chains like the sea.

The obvious literary reference has at least something to do with it; whatever Dylan may be pitying himself for, he is comparing himself to a man of eighty, who had the authority in his countenance which men would fain call master:

> Alack! 'tis he: why, he was met even now
> As mad as the vexed sea; singing aloud;
> Crowned with rank fumiter ...   [*King Lear*, IV, iv. 1–4]

And here too there is a mysterious reassurance behind a good deal of what might seem wilful horror; the sea is dangerous all right, but when we think it is angry it is really only singing.

... the chapter-title 'The Death of Rhythm' need not detain us; though most of his discussion of 'The Force that through the green fuse' (p. 163) has that theme. The poem is pantheist; all kinds of forces in the outer world are compared to things inside the young Dylan's skin, and he is already complaining he is beginning to grow up wrong. The things outside him are splendid, and cheer him up, though the corresponding ones inside him are likely to be a bit off. The comparison of the forces that make the green shoot grow to forces of human industrialism, chemistry or electricity, are meant to show how strong it is: ... [Holbrook] wrongly says that the poetic argument is 'against growth' [p. 163]. The roots of trees are eventually blasted I suppose by lightning or a high wind; Nature will make young Dylan too first grow and then die. There is no 'posture against natural growth in Time, because the poet wishes to pity himself for belonging to natural processes' [p. 164] ... Dylan I grant is complaining a bit, but it is only the *crooked* rose which has been bent by the same wintry fever as himself: plainly this is not a complaint against all life. I think it means that a false spring brought out the rose too early and it was nipped by a frost; the poet also took fire too early for a healthy growth – he was about seventeen when he wrote this, and probably thought he had started masturbating dangerously early.

The poem then says that the cycle of water, evaporated from the sea and returning to it by the rivers, is like the circulation of his blood ... The idea itself ought to be a commonplace, but the treatment of it shows I think great beauty of feeling. The next verse is I grant more mysterious; as is standard in pantheism, the dangerous forces in Nature have to be included in the Godhead. But 'my shroud sail' is not an 'irresponsible pun' [p. 164] because the same Nature blows him through the stages of his life and wraps him up at the end of it. Holbrook sees no point in the final lines of the verse but 'a Tarot touch from Eliot' and 'a sensational way' of uttering some universal thoughts by Holbrook.[3] Well, Dylan has been claiming identity with the ground of all Nature, in a correct Hindu manner, as of course the well-educated child knew quite well, and now he identifies himself with human society like a Christian: the body of the hanged man is destroyed, leaving no relics, by burying it in quicklime; but this is made from the bones of Dylan, who thus receives the criminal back into himself like an Earth-Mother. ... [Holbrook] grumbles that the hanging man has nothing to do with the force which is also time: 'Time, of course, brings the threat of maturity which the poem is a desperate attempt by the poet to conceal' [p. 165]. Now, just consider the lad of seventeen or so, writing this astonishing thing, and grumbling at the end of every verse that something was going wrong about his growing up; how can he be trying to conceal *that*? ...

> The lips of time leech to the fountain head;

'Time sucks the blood of the fountain head (?by making us old and drying our faculties)' [p. 165]. Holbrook calls his chapter 'The Death of Rhythm', and I suppose I started finding good meanings in this poem because of its extreme beauty of sound. The end of the poem is slightly terrifying, another case of Dylan confronting the full horror of Nature while praising her ... Given the suggestions of the sound, the line has to be interpreted 'Creatures who live in time draw their strength from an eternal source'; indeed, they drag their way to it, and stick till they are cut off. This does a good deal to make tolerable the comparison of the accumulation of semen to that of pus; my trouble is that I feel the whole verse to be consistent and very beautiful but find it hard to say why. The great spaces of time in evolution, surely, have gradually amounted to our Heaven by developing all the details of the human type which we consider ideal (young Dylan of course would be very fresh from reading about evolution); 'a weather's wind', the merely local trouble of his own life, is not a thing he can improve by talking to it about the general good intention which had taken ten to the tenth years. Not able to scold his own body, he is even unable to make contact with any other suffering lover, supposing the man to have got himself buried already. Funny as it sounds when translated, this interpretation makes a consistent poem and as it seems to me one of overwhelming beauty ... [Holbrook's] central argument is that the poem exists 'only by its suggestion of unwilling growth in the immature boy' [p. 166], and I deny that this is present in the poem in any degree. Good God, the child Dylan was determined to hit London and have pleasure, at whatever cost ... Like many other men, he did not revere his childhood till he was safely past it.

I can't go into all the cases, but should observe that in 'A Refusal to Mourn' (p. 170) Holbrook appears to understand the whole poem, or as near as makes no matter, but still hates it; then he remarks 'why he shouldn't say anything is not clear' (p. 171), meaning why the poet says he won't say things. The answer is plain; Dylan in wartime thought it wrong to be a propagandist poet, favouring one side, and while saying 'I'll keep myself pure' he says to the dead child, 'I'll keep you pure, too.' I myself thought it a duty to do propaganda against Hitler, and much of this was fun, but I had sometimes to eat dirt from people who replied to my advances that I must do my own dirty work. The reason why the greater poet Auden clung to America was that to become Britain's wartime bard would have meant unbearable phoniness, and the poet Dylan though so much less political had to insist on his purity....

Going back to p. 99 'whoever Ann was' [in 'After the Funeral'] – why not find out, if he wants to know? And why blame the poet for egotism because he uses wholly standard rhetorical devices while being swept totally out of himself in admiration for the terrible strength shown in the working life of the old servant[?] ...

I agree with Holbrook (p. 228) that the loving drunks [in *Under Milk Wood*] are a rather tiresome bit of propaganda for drunkenness; but it isn't so that all drinkers are neurotics and wake up moaning. Many of them do boast like this, however much they may pay for it later. The frightful nonsense talked about Ben Jonson is having its effect, I see; authors who mention rude things must always show they are shocked by them, as Ben Jonson is misread to make him do (in fact, of course, he was militantly anti-Puritan). The evident fact that Shakespeare didn't can be ignored as long as Jonson did. Of course, if you are a prominent Malvolio yourself you are keen on making sure there isn't any more cakes and ale. Maybe you will say that any poem which laughs at Malvolio 'reinforces untenderness. It is a cruel work, inviting our cruel laughter' [p. 201]. On any other ground, this is a fatuous thing to say about *Under Milk Wood*, which is beautifully tender but sometimes rather too sentimental. (I have seen the play, and the audiences are plainly not being spurred to cruel laughter.) Holbrook sometimes comes near recognising this, as about the last song of Polly Garter: 'Note the special pleading in *"She loves him back"*: in the circumstances, he drunk, she dreaming of Willy Wee – would she be likely to?' [pp. 223–24]. The answer is, 'Of course Holbrook wouldn't be likely to, but we love Polly because she would.' Holbrook seems to think that all drunken men are impotent, which would make his complaint more sensible; or at any rate that Dylan was. ... I had never heard the phrase 'love him back' before, and thought it a wonderfully good one; it seems to imply exactly the comradely feeling of Polly, with the real loved one far away. ...

This tiresome stuff is just a try-out, but I send it to express my gratitude.

Notes

1 Holbrook's first chapter discusses the following poems among others: 'A Dream of Fair Women' by Kingsley Amis, 'Metamorphosis' by Edith Sitwell and 'Youth and Age on Beaulieu River, Hants', by John Betjeman.

2 Holbrook cites stanza seven of 'Mr Eliot's Sunday Morning Service'.

3 Holbrook's full comment is: 'I see no point in this, except that it is a sensational way of referring to the unity of all flesh in clay, both murderer's, poet's and Christ's, and the clay which consumes all is itself compounded of all' (p. 165).

Dylan Thomas in Maturity

New Statesman, 29 October 1965

Constantine FitzGibbon, *The Life of Dylan Thomas*

The good taste and sober truth of this biography having been rightly praised, one might expect it to debunk the legend of Dylan Thomas, but I think it makes the legend shine all the brighter. One had heard that his first two volumes of poetry were drawn, though with some changes, from note-books compiled before he was twenty; but it is news (to me at any rate) that he sold the talisman on reaching the age when Keats died ('It's lovely when you burn your boats. They burn so beautifully'), so that the poems written after 1941 proved to him he could do without it. Surely, it is tiresome to hear critics upbraid the 'infantilism' of a man who could do that? Some of the early poems I think are the best, but some of the later ones undoubtedly have his full power.

The story of the book is a sad one: it seems clear that a poet can no longer act the part of the defiantly privileged bard in the modern world, and indeed that poets are unlikely to attempt it again after the awful warning of Dylan Thomas. One of the surprises of the book is that towards the end he was not merely seeing light at the end of the tunnel but had almost emerged from it; it became touch and go whether our young people were to receive their salutary warning. I have long believed that he died a martyr to the Income Tax, and indeed that any noticeable amount of success was bound to be fatal to a man who refused to submit a statement. The Income Tax people, if you say you don't know the answers to their questions, make a high estimate of your earnings and demand payment on that or a refutation of it; myself when young once felt the wind of this fell sword. They did not get onto Dylan till 1948, and then demanded a large backlog; he could have been jailed, and for the remaining five years of his life 'he was never, for a single day, free of financial terror.' This is why the American tours were necessary, and he felt he had to give in full what a crowd expected from him, so the combination of worry and jolly-show produced nervous collapse. Even so, it appears from the reserved last pages of Mr FitzGibbon that a very unwise combination of medical drugs was what killed him. He did not leave his sick-bed to drink eighteen straight whiskies alone in a bar; this was a last pathetic boast – he had four or five, in an hour and a half. Combined with the drugs, this was a disastrous way to try to soothe his nerves, but it was not an act of desperation.

The Income Tax people were willing to take payments as available, and the huge success of the *Collected Poems*, the readings, and the first performances of *Under Milk Wood*, with the advance on the libretto for Stravinsky, were going to be enough. There was surely one day free from financial terror half a year before he died, when he wrote to his wife, after the meeting with Stravinsky: 'There'll be plenty of money. This time it's working.' He never expected to live long, but without medical bad luck in this crucial period of strain he might well have had a dozen years in calm water. I expect he would have developed a revulsion against making a show of himself, as soon as it became unnecessary; he would of course have stopped being lordly about his friends' money, shirts etc.; and he was always unabashed about being censorious, not a man to dislike becoming a pillar of the Establishment so long as his warm heart was not affronted. His mystical poetry had become too hard to write, but he had found how to write for the theatre. Probably we would be learning very different moral lessons from his career if the obituaries were appearing now.

There seems to be a growing irritation with his poetry, caused by a belief that it is a hoax, not really meaning anything. A great deal of it, I confess, I have never cracked, and when people make sense of it for me I feel: 'That is not enough.' But I find magnificent meanings in a number of complete poems, both early and late, and surely this earns permanent regard. The reason it is denied, I think, is that the kind of thing he meant is so out of fashion as to have become, for many critics, invisible. It is not part of T. S. Eliot's 'tradition'. Several reviewers of this book, I notice, have found it weak on literary criticism, but the author at least knows what the poems are about. The poet thought he had not long to live, but this preoccupation with death was in some ways transcended by his own sort of pantheism, by the identification of himself and his body with all nature. A letter written when he was nineteen gives more detail:

The old, fertile days are gone, and now a poem is the hardest and most thankless act of creation ... It gives me now a physical pain to write poetry. I feel all my muscles contract as I try to drag out, from the whirlpooling words around my everlasting ideas of the importance of death on the living, some connected words that will explain how the starry system of the dead is seen, ordered as in the grave's sky, along the orbit of a foot or a flower. But when the words do come, I pick them so thoroughly of their *live* associations that only the *death* in the words remains.

In another letter of the same year, he ascribes such thoughts to an earlier poet:

The greatest description I know of our own 'earthiness' is to be found in John Donne's *Devotions*, where he describes man as earth of the earth, his body earth, his hair a wild shrub growing out of the land.

When this was written, T. S. Eliot had just issued his ukase, 'Donne was, I insist, no sceptic,'[1] and by now, in Eng. Lit. circles, it seems mere ignorance to fancy that Donne could have meant anything pantheist. That would be 'provincial' no doubt, as Eliot called the beliefs of Yeats, so that they too became invisible. I do not mean to say that Dylan Thomas's philosophising, apart from its expression, is very recondite; he could have found most of it in Shelley, and probably did; but the indoctrinated modern reader is unwilling to find it anywhere.

To realise this clears the ground a bit, but I am puzzled by Dylan Thomas's relations with Christianity. Mr FitzGibbon writes sensibly about it, saying that he was an agnostic to the end but took the tone of the friend he was with; and he could fairly use Christian language for beliefs which were intimate and inexpressible. But the poem 'Death Shall have No Dominion' seems almost like cheating his public unless he believed in some kind of life after death; every sentence perhaps can be interpreted to mean that an individual rejoins the eternal Spirit as a raindrop returns to sea, and the parsons must not be allowed to monopolise the handsome offers, but this is hardly enough. Perhaps he meant that the return of the raindrop to the sea causes a lasting satisfaction, and yet that this can only be said paradoxically, because one cannot say who enjoys it. 'Though lovers shall be lost love shall not' was altered to 'Though lovers be lost love shall not', I suppose to avoid specific denial that true lovers will be together in Heaven, though he did not expect it. He continued to think very wicked any religious interference with their freedom.

Mr FitzGibbon is of course thoroughly at home in England; but the American point of view about politics must sometimes be irrelevant. In Prague in 1949 (it had become communist in 1948) Dylan Thomas

was heard to shout, 'I am a communist, but am I also a bloody fool?' If such pronouncements as these have any meaning at all, which is doubtful, it is surely that Dylan had no comprehension whatever for politics as that word is normally understood.

Normally in America, I suppose. A lot of communists in Eastern Europe (since the death of Stalin) seem to agree with Dylan on this point. He had for some years refused to believe anything written in periodicals against communism, so that he was out of step with his brother poets in England;

but he was quick in Prague to realise that he only liked the unofficial poets, and the honest reporting of Mr FitzGibbon shows him to have behaved kindly and adroitly. (It is an effort to remember that he was already in daily financial terror.) Similarly in 1940, during the 'phoney war', he followed the communist line by refusing to believe in the war; he proposed to be a conscientious objector, a Welsh Nationalist perhaps. But he took the precaution of attending a tribunal, and was sure at once that he could not be mixed up with the persons he saw pleading their cases. He volunteered for an anti-aircraft unit, expecting better company, and was much shocked when he was rejected for ill-health.

I remember his telling me how frightening it was always to have nothing to do next day: sometimes, he said, 'I buy a Mars Bar, and I think tomorrow I will eat that, so then I can go to sleep, because I have a plan.' I did not much like this highly polished bit of tear-jerking, but there is little doubt that unemployment would have driven me to drink too. Infantilism due to mother-fixation is what critics give as the cause, but he seems to have found his mother dull: though he insisted on having both helpless parents come and live with him permanently, just after the blow from the Income Tax, which not all his mature critics would have done. As it happened, I did not see him after I got back from China, in the last year of his life, so I can't pronounce about his 'increasing corruption'. He was prone to confess it by despairing epigrams and fits of intense depression, but on another side of his mind he would still believe he lived as a great poet ought to do, until he gets rich. He was so immensely entertaining that many people felt themselves adequately repaid. Drink was necessary to screw him up to the duty of entertainment, and because the whole party (however assembled) must be seduced into joining the feast of wit. Very unhealthy no doubt, but towards the end he was craving to get out of it, and was within sight of earning enough money to be quiet.

Note

1 'Donne in Our Time', in T. Spencer (ed.), *A Garland for John Donne*, Oxford: OUP, 1932, pp. 11–12.

Some More Dylan Thomas

Listener, 28 October 1971

Walford Davies (ed.), *Dylan Thomas: Early Prose Writings*
Daniel Jones (ed.), *Dylan Thomas: The Poems*

Even in the minor works of Dylan Thomas, a glittering or searching detail is always liable to crop up; besides, his major poems are hard to plumb, but the ideas get repeated, so that a weaker but simpler use of one of them may turn out a great help. There is nothing in these two books which did not need to be revived.

Most of the stories collected by Mr Davies are about Welsh characters in an exalted state of religious mania, and they are full of fun in their own way, but the author does not seem to share enough in their exaltation. Life, he felt, was magical and exhilarating as long as you kept the nerve for it, but ludicrous and horrible once you caved in; and most of his great poetical moments which feel mysteriously wise contrive somehow to combine the two visions. But in these stories, I think, he is uneasily trying to come to terms with life – not with being Welsh, as he simply thought better of Wales for producing such deep extravagant types – so the exhilarating and horrible merely jostle one another. Some of the stories have not been printed before, and those which appeared in long-defunct periodicals are now unknown. There are two excerpts from joke writings, which ought to be longer. Surely it is high time to publish the detective story 'The Death of the King's Canary' (the murder of the Poet Laureate), or at least to announce which elderly poet is threatening to sue for libel if it appears. From the bit given here, I suspect it is kept under wraps merely because it is so dull.

The second half of the book gives Thomas's early critical writing (how few articles from school magazines get reprinted forty years later), and his occasional reviews, apparently up to the end of his life. He was a surprisingly large-minded critic, able to see merit in a lot of different styles, though also readily made indignant; but most of this part has only the interest of old gossip. However, it includes the most beautiful passage in the book:

Scene Two of 'Spajma and Salnady', a joke posted to the future Lady Snow when he was nineteen, early in 1934. Scene One is general satire on the literary world, but in the last two pages the two friends (with the letters of their names disordered) adventure onto the Welsh mountains at night:

A GREAT VOICE: There is a hole in space. (*And all the time we see Salnady's darkness, we see the darkness of Spajma, climbing the sides of the rocks. We hear:*)
THIRD MOUNTAIN: I am a happy hill. (*We see a contented lightning light him up like a match. We hear:*) There is laughter in my green, there are sheep on my sides, there is piping in my shades. (*And all the hills echo. We see that the sky is an old man. We hear:*) You cannot help but climb me.
FOURTH MOUNTAIN: I am a strange, new hill, blacker and whiter than all the boys' bones under the sea, than all the girls' bones in their unhallowed acres. (*The old man has gone, and the sky is naked. She has unbuttoned her stars.*)

The book would be worth getting for these two pages alone.

I am not so sure about the new edition of the poems. Apart from two jokes and some fragments, it gives nothing not already available in Ralph Maud's *Notebooks of Dylan Thomas* (1968), or of course in the *Collected Poems*, with a few minor poems in the two volumes of *Letters*. It seems meant to be bought instead of the *Notebooks* and *Collected Poems*, but it only gives a smudged combination of them. In his boldly-phrased introduction, Mr Jones says: 'I have had to use my own judgement in recognising the moment when the essential poem has come into being,' and I foolishly hoped that he would have the nerve to print this essential poem, instead of allowing the author to spoil it by later refinements. But no, he only meant that he used the process to decide the order of the poems in his edition, which always gives the final version approved by the poet, but sometimes pretends that it had been arrived at earlier. Professor Maud prints the lines as they were first written in the notebook, and then lists the corrections written on them afterwards (not telling us, what seldom can be known, whether the corrections were made after five minutes or ten years); if the author never printed the poem, nor any version of it, Mr Jones just prints it with these corrections, as of the original date. (At least, I only once found him ignoring a correction.) His notes on the poems occasionally remark that he is doing this, as if it were an unusual step. It seems clear that most of the corrections were made during the first writing and were genuine improvements, so that Professor Maud had better have printed them in the text, though letting us know what the first draft was, in case the change had been made long after the first writing. Here Mr Jones does offer a convenience in his text. But in the cases where there was a lot of rewriting, and perhaps two different magazine publications before the final text appeared in a book, he tells us far less than the Maud edition, though that has a more limited aim.

These notebooks made a wonderful story. They were filled with poetry before he was twenty, and regularly used as a quarry for the poetry he published later, because further invention had become mysteriously hard, till he reached 'the age when Keats died' and thought it best to sell them to America: 'It's lovely when you burn your boats; they burn so beautifully.' Gradually he found that he could still write, and was coming to write more directly and intelligibly – not, I think, better, but obviously selling the talisman had been a good thing. And yet, maybe its importance had been largely a delusion of the poet (always humble before his art): many of its poems he rewrote, but I do not know of a case where his later poetry uses actual fragments from the others. And it is hard to see why a poem such as 'Being but men, we walked into the trees' could not be printed as it stood. It is graceful and resonant; nobody could call it empty-headed; and it is not a preparation for anything he was to write later. Considering his endless shortages of money, it was very high-minded of him to refuse to print such work merely because it was not in the style he had made his own.

There is one point where I think a modern edition should reject the variant which the author printed, though of course it should be acknowledged in the notes: the last line of 'Before I knocked and flesh let enter'.

> You who bow down at cross and altar,
> Remember me and pity Him
> Who took my flesh and bone for armour,
> And double-crossed my mother's womb.

In the notebook it is 'his' not 'my', without even a later correction, and I think the change for print was merely a bright idea to screw the poem up tighter, such as he always had a weakness for. Jesus by choosing virginity ended an immense series of births, betraying the purpose of the creator which his mother had obeyed; but he did not end it for Dylan Thomas. Only ten days later, the notebooks show him writing a poem, which he never published, saying that a labouring mother pays twofold, 'once for the Virgin's child, once for her own'. So his mind was then working on the idea that Christianity had been bad for everyone's sex life, and particularly hard on women. He would continue to think so, but he never again tried to express it by this confusing epigram. I must admit that there were also two verses cut out of the poem before publication, apparently because they need to be spoken by Christ himself: one says that false lips cursed him and gave him a kiss of death, and the other that

> A virgin was my sad-faced dam,
> My sire was of wind and water.

Even Dylan's very helpful parents might have raised their eyebrows at this.

So he took it out, but he would want to fit in the main idea somewhere else. The poet represents Man in the poem, as Jesus does within Christendom, so it is understandable for Dylan to speak as Christ, when describing a universal experience; but now he puts it immediately after distinguishing between 'me' and 'Him'. I think that the poet did not notice the change made him boast of being a martyr, in the style of D. H. Lawrence and Middleton Murry, and that he would have changed it back if he had done.

Some of the obscurity of the poems, though not all, comes from shortening the notebook version. Mr Brian Finney remarked on this when the Maud edition was new, taking as his example the poem 'I have longed to move away'. In the final version the scene is as usual menacing and vast, and he wants to escape (after various other things) 'the thunder of calls and notes'. It would feel like debunking the poem to guess that this meant letters and telephone calls from fussy poets, but the notebook draft actually says 'telephone calls'. And surely the 'hissing lie' must be a forecast of delayed-action bombs? But no, in the version written when he was eighteen, it is all unassuming and clear:

> Night, careful of topography,
> Climbs over the coal-tips where children play ...
> Some life, yet unspent, might explode
> Out of the lie hissing on the ground
> Like some sulphurous reminder of November,
> And, cracking into the air, leave me half blind.
> This must be avoided at all costs.

The tone of the old gentleman, in this last line, lets him recognise that he is complaining about very little: or perhaps he is one of the children, hanging about the pitiful waste ground where they let off their fireworks. The poem was far better before he concentrated it to make it 'boily'; and a modern edition ought to quote at least this much of the first draft in the notes. (A misprint in line eight of Mr Jones's text adds to the discomfiture of the reader.) One must admit that this kind of poem, personal, social and fretful, is unusual for Dylan, but '(O) Make me a mask' is another example, and this too is far less melodramatic in the first draft; the notes to the modern edition should at least quote the pathetic bit about the girl who, passing, 'smiles back confessing a treacherous heart'.

One might think that the purpose of the rewriting, always bringing a surface obscurity, was to give a more balanced account: for instance, an anti-Christian poem would regularly have the reverent language of his pantheism welded onto it. But this can hardly be argued of the splendid poem 'Incarnate devil in a talking snake', which had said from the start that good and evil had to grow together before the Fall, and that God and Satan were indistinguishable there. The language becomes more exalted and evocative at the expense of the convincing human details; but this need not make Mr Jones print the poem late in his book, as if it did not exist before its final revision. The only important phrase added is that God in Eden was a 'fiddling warden', and this is found in an intermediate version, somewhere between 1933 and 1936. Evidently Dylan had just learned the usage of 'fiddling' which became familiar in wartime, for black market activities and such-like: if possible, an edition should estimate where he learned it.

I disagree with Mr Jones on a matter of theory, made clear in his long note on the sonnet sequence 'Altarwise by Owl-light'. This is not only the most obscure of Dylan Thomas's poems but the most static: it is a succession of minatory gnomic lines, each of them almost complete in itself. Mr Jones, with the support of some remarks by the poet, says that this is 'absolute poetry ... a pattern of words and images. In other words, the poem, in spite of its length, sustains a single metaphor, and it would be vain to seek in it logic, narration or message in the usual sense of these words, though they are all present metaphorically. Comprehension here is irrelevant ...' and so on. Dylan had needed a way to fob off tiresome or embarrassing questions, especially after giving a reading, and evidently did sometimes use Symbolist patter: I even agree that in writing this sequence he was trying to act on it. There was some controversy about the poem in the magazines during 1936 and 1937, and though unrepentant he evidently recognised that the method had become a dead end. I feel sure of this, not only from his subsequent work, but from a quaint moment in the pub at Marshfield, when we were both visiting John Davenport during 1941. (Come to think of it, as Keats died when he was twenty-six, this would be the year after Dylan sold the notebooks.) George Barker had just brought out a slim volume, and Dylan was spluttering over it: he said, 'No man has the right to throw a bucket of sheer nonsense into the public's face,' and I would have been tempted not to believe my ears, except that Davenport, who was much deeper in his counsels than I, clearly regarded this outburst as a healthy symptom. None of his good work, early or late, was written in obedience to that lethal theory, even more harmful for critics and editors than for poets, and we must thank his wonderful powers of recovery for releasing him from it.

The Use of Poetry

New Statesman and Nation, 18 May 1935

George Barker, *Poems*

Poetry is so much less in demand than novels that the reader can assume considerable merit in verse which gets reviewed at all; not much can be said about it without prolonged quotation and probably unnecessary exegesis; to trace 'influences' is fairly fatuous; and the poet is perhaps of all artists the least helped by advice, so the large part of criticism which amounts to covert advice is more impertinent than usual. But as well as saying that Barker's verse is worth reading one can say roughly what it is 'about'.

Though up-to-date in ideas and technique it has no machines or politics (there is a surprise when 'political meetings' are classed with parties as the obvious places to meet people). Compared with poetry on such themes, indeed, it is egotistic, but all thoughtful egotists come to disbelieve in the individual. The event, not the person, is alone and unique and includes the universe in itself, and hence the eternal values must be expected to appear in flashes, between contradictions, and at random. The traditional 'spirit–flesh' antithesis makes a fine reappearance with the spirit as brief and subject to as many corruptions as the flesh, and fully parallel to it. It is masterful and by no means imitative poetry, but it seems moving though with unusual energy through a familiar and narrow field, and the themes are not such as to give much staying power. The plainest tricks (not made too much of) are the use of false rhymes for an effect of toughness, and a rapt repetition of words and assonances for lyrical effects which seems hypnotic and withdrawn. He sometimes throws the language about, inattentively thrashing it into large words as with his tail, and some of the points (certainly not all) lose by not being put more clearly. For instance, the idea at the end of 'Narcissus I' is surely that he could *only* see to drive, through the dazzled windscreen, within the shadow of his own head; this fine metaphysical illustration has largely to be guessed from:

> The reproduction on, the reality through
> I now no longer wander wondering who.

Indeed, the energy often seems wilfully slackened in the last line of a poem.

   Poets in these days come to the end of their inspiration, or at least firmly stop writing, more commonly than they used to do, and one looks for an assurance that Barker will go on. The last poem of the book, one of the best and most sustained, itself raises the question. After the poet has achieved his purpose:

> That height for which is strained, poising between
> World and the broad divine, now multiplies
> And, like an image under moving water
> Moves and shows many. At this the energies
> Of the slick man disperse from their mean
> Like flies dart all ways after. Later
> Also like flies, lie buried in his blue meat.

If sincerity in poetry is to write only when you must the thing becomes in a sense clinical, and once it has done its work of healing neurosis the poet will stop out of mere honesty. However hard to shake off in feeling this is clearly a misleading aesthetic even within its own limits; due partly to taking poetry too seriously and partly to feeling too sure it has no public. Must the poet then

> Loosen to lesser endeavour the limbs of daring
> After so arduous a defeating of
> My youth's mad ghoul?

The answer in theory is misleadingly simple – 'Only if you stick to this clinical view of poetry.' (And if madness is the essential, Heaven knows, the cured poet has only to look at his neighbours.) But the Zeitgeist now holding English poetry for all but a few writers within a narrow field seems curiously strong.

   One had best keep on the dust-cover, which is lively and sensible; the cover itself is rather Georgian. Also this will preserve the blurb, surely by Mr Eliot, which says that the book is published for people 'who have wanted to see more of George Barker's work, so that they might make up their minds about him. This volume gives them the opportunity of committing themselves to an opinion...' But the truth is they may sneak a little pleasure out of it as well.

A London Letter

Poetry (Chicago), XLIX, 1937

A question that obviously ought to be raised by a British number of *Poetry* is whether the distinction is real, whether the position and intention of the poets isn't much the same anyway under the two flags. Ignorance of America makes me unlikely to have anything of importance to say about this, but then it might make me a better specimen of our prejudices.

There was that remark by Ezra Pound, in some Outline or Short-Cut of his, that after a certain date the English gave up writing decent poetry and the Americans took over in a body. The sting of truth here comes from people like T. S. Eliot and Pound himself, who don't live in America, and say Marianne Moore, who might live anywhere. Hart Crane seems to me often first-rate, and distinctively American as he wanted to be, but he didn't feel he had a body to be a member of. Any discussion of this kind of body must go into politics and social conditions, and it seems worth putting down some obvious differences between the countries, which affect the verse written in them.

The first thing is that America has no enemies in reach and the necessary imports are trivial in quantity; if it could decide what it wanted to do and get the politicians in hand, it could do it. England is the only country (the Japanese claim to the same excuse is still fairly bogus) which depends for most of its food on people who send food from outside, and who do this only because they believe in an obscure and toppling credit system. You can argue against this assertion, but the country feels it so much that the least political poet comes to absorb it. The thing that struck me when I came back to England recently after three years was a queer kind of patience in every bus-driver; not fatalism or conviction of doom, but a feeling that we have to keep quiet and watch our feet because any hopeful large change might make everything very much worse. This is quite foreign to America; the panic feeling of the slump was a feeling that something rather undefined was urgent as a last hope and must be done. Much the same difference comes out in jokes about war; many people in England were puzzled like myself by the Mothers of the Unborn Veterans. It was a real strong joke if they thought the war was coming unless stopped; if they thought the other countries were going to have a war but not them it was nasty. A friend of mine [Julian Trevelyan] paints in an old wharf on the Thames; he said it was sure to be mistaken for the Houses of Parliament, so he was going to paint Bomb Me on the roof. One doesn't know whether the American jokes are like this charming plan or not. The difference comes out for instance in the comparatively large (and well deserved) sales in England of poems by Auden and Spender, who were viewed as young communist uplift. The bulk of that new public of buyers, which was mainly interested in the political feelings expressed, were not I think idealists in the sense of enjoying sentiments they did not mean to act on, nor yet definite sympathisers who wanted to get something like that done. In America they would have been one or the other; in England there was an obscure safety and bafflement in moving from the poem to consider what the country could possibly do.

You hear it said that in a real democracy the writer can tap the life of the whole country, whereas in a class-conscious country he is tied to his clique and the stuff is bound to be narrower in range. I doubt whether this applies much to verse, which has narrowed its range anyway because people feel you need special reasons for choosing the verse form at all. No doubt it has some effect on novel-writing, but even there the difficulty is much less in getting to know people than in getting the result across to the public. For instance, the point about dialects in England is that most villagers have a wide range between standard English and the dialect or indeed the several dialects, and put a great deal of weight on varying the talk with the person addressed and the feeling towards him. It is the same kind of thing as the elaborate syntax of polite forms in languages of the Far East. Nobody puts this into dialect novels except for the crude change to standard English (which is hardly used except for rudeness) because the novel-reading public would not understand it; I wouldn't myself. In fact if you are expected to talk standard English you are not allowed to learn this game; the old style squire still does it a bit, but it seems patronising. We have so little machinery for handling speech that if a novel admits its characters don't talk standard English they are assumed to talk a flat complete dialect. Here the American novelist is obviously better off, or simply more competent, partly because the variations of language in America are felt to be less touchy and important. But the difficulty is in the public (it would be a bore to keep on *explaining* the exact impact of some shade of local dialect), not in any isolation of the author through snobbery; the interesting uses of dialect would not appear if the talkers felt stuck in their classes.

I was shocked recently by a Welsh poet who turned up in Kleinfeldt's saying he needed money and had had an offer as checker-in at a Welsh mine; this was very absurd, and he had a much more cozy plan to become a grocer. What with the Welsh nationalism, the vague and balanced but strong political interests of this man, the taste for violence in his writing, and the way he was already obviously exhausting his vein of poetry about events which involved the universe but happened inside his skin, it seemed to me that being a checker-in was just what he wanted; and I shouted at him for some time, against two talkers I should otherwise have been eager to hear, to tell him that he was wasting his opportunities as a Welshman and ought to make full use of a country in which he could nip across the classes. I still think that something like that ought to happen to him, but no doubt he was right in saying that the plan was no good. The English no less than the Americans cling to a touching belief that social distinctions in modern England are more bitter than elsewhere.

However the difference in the *public* for poetry in England and America seems to me very real, though I know little about it. For instance MacLeish's *Conquistador* struck me as an able and agreeable verse book which would have no point without a fairly large public for verse books, a thing that you don't find in England. This is not the grousing of a verse-writer; publishers are generous to verse, apparently because it looks well in the catalogue, and it gets a good deal of space in reviews, apparently because people who don't read poetry still like talk about poetry, and there are always corners needing to be filled in the magazines. But of the people I come across and like, I doubt if anybody reads much modern verse who doesn't write it. You could pick out in *Conquistador* a series of authors who had been borrowed from and used, and I felt rather critical about this at first, but of course if you have a public to write for it is an excellent thing to use the existing tools (compare the Elizabethans). The English poet of any merit takes, I think, a much more clinical view of his own products. The first or only certain reason for writing verse is to clear your own mind and fix your own feelings, and for this purpose it would be stupid to borrow from people, and for this purpose you want to be as concentrated as possible. Mr Eliot said somewhere that a poet ought to practice his art at least once a week [see note on p. 363 above], and some years ago I was able to ask the oracle whether he thought this really necessary, a question on which much seemed to hang. After brooding and avoiding traffic for a while he answered with the full weight of his impressiveness, and I am sure without irony, that he had been thinking of someone else when he wrote that, and in such a case as my own the great effort of the poet must be to write as little as possible.

Foundations of Despair

Poetry, XLIX:4, January 1937

A. E. Housman, *More Poems*

It is long since I cut pages with more curiosity and expectation than I did these, and they are not disappointing. The editor says he will publish a chronology of the poems later; so far nothing has certainly been written after the preface to *Last Poems* except the hymn for Housman's own funeral. This curious document may have some bearing on a question one cannot help raising, as to how far the poet means what he says; but probably it only tells you that he took the same view of his church as Thomas Hardy and most Anglican atheists of that generation. The poems here were mostly rejected from the two earlier books, some for a flaw in the workmanship, some for making the stock situation of the poems too obviously a personal one, some for no clear reason. They have been kept back till the fashion that would have made them more obvious had gone.

It would be interesting to know why the stinging nettle one did not appear before. The lads are sowing, but it does not matter what they sow, because only one thing will grow:

> The stinging nettle only
> Will still be found to stand:
> The numberless, the lonely,
> The thronger of the land,
> The leaf that hurts the hand.

[*More Poems*, no. xxxii; *The Collected Poems*, London: Cape, 1967, p. 128]

It is first-rate Housman, both in the nostalgia and the power. It seems also to consist of remarkably untrue statements even for first-rate Housman. When I went to Japan as a teacher I chose *A Shropshire Lad* for detailed reading in my first term, and several of the class were drafted to Shanghai, where there was a row at the time. 'I think Housman is quite right,' one of them wrote in an essay before starting, 'I will do no good to anyone by dying for my country, but I will be admired, and we all want to be admired, and anyway we are better dead.' I thought Housman would have been as much shocked by this as I was; it is a fishy game, to play the amateur of tragedy. A thing like the stinging nettle poem is splendid verse, therefore not fishy, but you would have to talk for a long time to give an adequate account of why not.

An attack on Housman by Cyril Connolly appeared in the *New States-man* recently,[1] and needs to be faced by anyone who feels the strength of this poetry, though it was an unfair bit of work. A curious muddle about classical poetry became prominent. Connolly said that no classical poet wrote about the lower classes, but when a correspondent mentioned Theocritus, he said that no classical poet had serious personal feelings about the lower classes, though they might be pegs for verse. Whereas Housman among his lads was a scoutmaster. Very likely this complex insult will not seem blasting outside England. It is true I think that all Despair Poetry needs a good deal of 'distance' (of the poet from the theme); you can only call despair a profound general truth when you are looking beyond all the practical particulars, which might well have been hopeful if the man had been stronger; and in a personal story, even a half-told one, you cannot do this easily. In the same way, on the face of it, the poem in *More Poems* about how the speaker will not enter the Promised Land but other people will, is a contradiction of the general poems which say that nobody will, and its statement is much smaller than theirs even if less untrue.[2] But there seems no decent ground for calling all Despair Poetry about love sentimental, and then all tragedy sentimental, as Connolly is at the edge of doing. And granting the stuff can be good, it has a technical condition, whatever the personal background. It wants as its apparent theme a case of love with great practical obstacles, such as those of class and sex, because the despair has to seem sensible before this curious jump is made and it is called a universal truth. Of course the jump may be done badly, but Connolly found no argument to show it was done badly here, nor is it.

Housman himself gives this reason why this one of his stock themes can carry a large implication, in a poem that imitates Andrew Marvell, a pleasant thing to see in a man who despised the metaphysicals, even though he refused to publish it. 'All things may end, for all began':

> But this unlucky love should last
>   When answered passions thin to air;
> Eternal fate so deep has cast
>   Its sure foundations of despair.
>
> [*More Poems,* no. xii]

And indeed the foundations of all this narrow and haunting poetry seem to me very solid. But it is the only poetry I have yet seen having a pernicious effect on the young.

Note

1 'It must be remembered,' wrote Cyril Connolly, 'that classical poetry is essentially aristocratic; such writers as Gray or Horace address themselves to their own friends and would be incapable of using Maurice, Terence, and the other rustics as anything but the material for a few general images.' A number of correspondents disputed the point, among them F. L. Lucas (who pointed out that Theocritus 'took shepherds for his heroes and founded European pastoral') and John Sparrow. Connolly responded: 'Homer is detached from his swine-herd, the shepherds of Virgil and Theocritus are either genuine, or the poet and his friends are playing at being them, not both in the same poem. Now, in the case of Housman there is an uneasy and variable relationship; he is not quite sure whether he is a peasant himself; with some his relations are more than friendly, at other times he is a distant monitor – or are they all Cambridge professors?' (See Cyril Connolly, 'A. E. Housman: A Controversy', *The Condemned Playground*, London: Hogarth Press, 1985, pp. 47–62).

2 'When Israel out of Egypt came', *The Collected Poems*, London: Cape, 1967, p. 109.

'Selected Poems of Thomas Hardy'[1]

New Statesman, 14 September 1940

G. M. Young (ed.), *Selected Poems of Thomas Hardy*

Mr G. M. Young deserves a great deal of respect, and his introduction makes nearly all the points about Hardy with warmth and without over-praise. That the Romantic 'Titanism' had become 'simply disapproving' is an excellent phrase. He does not bring out the flat contradictions which are the most irritating feature of Hardy's philosophy; but then, some monism like Hardy's seems to me probably true, so what irritates me must be in the treatment not in the belief. Probably it is the complacence of the man, which saw no need to try to reconcile the contradictions; the same complacence which could be satisfied with a clumsy piece of padding to make a lyric out of a twaddling reflection. No doubt he needed this quality to win through as he did. Most people who are admired for 'unpretentious integrity' have it.

Plodding through the *Collected Poems* I marked about ten that really ought to be in any selection. Mr Young had let in two of them. He has left out 'After a Journey' ('Hither I come to view a voiceless ghost') and 'The Voice' (last line 'and the woman calling') and 'Who's in the next room?' and 'A Broken Appointment' and 'The Sleepwalker' (where the philosophy comes off for once). Instead we have several long ill-written anecdotes and a good deal from *The Dynasts*. It is a pity, because a working selection from Hardy's mass of bad poetry is much needed.

I suspect that Mr Young's views on rhythm in poetry, which I don't understand, are somewhere at the back of it. Some while ago he published an essay saying that the innovations of modern poetry were destroying the very basis of English verse rhythm, the root itself from which poetry might have flowered in the future, and the example he took of this final rotting was:

Down arterial roads riding in April.

You would think that this gay and clear line would suggest Horace to a classicist more than ultimate corruption.[2] Then he wrote an essay on Miltonic scansion, which he clearly felt might be a bit unadventurous but gave the normal sane view. The four or five lines which he scanned as examples seemed to me totally impossible. Maybe the scansion marks were misprinted. Very likely he has some special way of reading aloud.

Sure enough, in the introduction here, we are told that Hardy's choice of words is often clumsy, but his impeccable merit is his wonderful rhythm. Now there is a quality in Hardy easiest called good rhythm, though it might be called a certain clumsiness that fits his grim scenery. Or rather it is a closeness to the accent of spoken English won through indifference to the poetic conventions of his time. For instance the line:

And a pond edged with grayish leaves.

But the good poem ['Neutral Tones'] of which this is the last line only gets into Mr Young's introduction, as an example of Hardy as an imitator: 'any young man who had read Browning and Swinburne might have written it.' Swinburne my foot. In the poems selected it seems to me that Hardy often simply drops his rhythm, as a child drops its rattle and stares before it straight at the skyline, dribbling slightly. He can, to be sure, 'beat his music out':

None answered. That she'd done poor John
a cruel turn thought we.

['The Rash Bride']

Mr Young's claim for this bit of rhythm, and for many like it, seems to be that Hardy was deliberately imitating dialect ballads. In his enthusiasm for this 'ancient music', Mr Young harks back to the troubadours. They are quoted in comparison with the rhythm of *The Dynasts*, the greatest example of Hardy's 'singular purity of rhythm', in which 'every measure is handled with equal aptness and assurance.' Many of the selections from it deal with the World Will, which is actively malevolent whenever Hardy chooses to give us a good dig but otherwise wholly unconscious though described as half-conscious:

Heaving dumbly
As we deem
Moulding numbly
As in dream.

How the very hindquarters of the bewildered mammoths loom through the bog! The words echo in the mind, as we critics say, rumbling humbly in a team or stumbling tumbly to a gleam.

It is quite true, as Mr Young says, that you come back to the few good poems of Hardy as to a source; you want their honesty and find their beauty. And I am very sorry to have to be rude to Mr Young, one of our few valuable literary critics. But there it is, a man coming back to Hardy does want to find the good ones.

Notes

1 Untitled in original.

2 G. M. Young, in 'Forty Years of Verse', quotes C. Day Lewis's line 'Down arterial roads riding in April' – from *The Magnetic Mountain* (1933), part four, section 32 – as a typical example of modern verse which 'does not scan . . . Why does he write prose when he might write verse?

'I must define my terms. I say that a line scans when, without any straining of the words or melody, it can be sung to an easy and popular tune' (*Daylight and Champaign*, London: Jonathan Cape, 1937, p. 200).

Cauldron Bubble

New Statesman, 1 November 1952

Kathleen Raine, *The Year One*

There is some very good poetry here. It struck me as more exciting than
Kathleen Raine's previous books, and on pulling myself into a calculating
frame of mind I became puzzled to see how she had got so much breadth
into a mystical theme which seems inherently narrow. Mr Robert Graves
and his White Goddess have had an important effect, I think; not because
he invented this topic, which he would fervently deny, but because he
would sometimes express such vomiting loathing of the goddess he revered
and told us we so urgently needed to revere. In her previous book *The
Pythoness* Kathleen Raine made some attempts to appear in person as this
murderous bitch, sow and what not, patiently following out the formula;
but though the formula gives a certain range to the gentleman poets it is
hard to handle for a lady poet, in particular for a rather saintly character;
and Kathleen Raine seems now to have absorbed it by keeping to the narrower form of presenting herself as a disgusting sinister old witch, mutter-
ing spells. This may seem a flippant view of her very sincere verse, but it is
needed, I think, when you read 'Northumbrian Sequence IV' where the
main dramatic force comes from the variety of orchestration. The initial
lines

> Let in the wind
> Let in the rain
> Let in the moors tonight

and their varied repetitions need to be a wicked gabble, low but corresponding to oboes and tom-toms, to get the astonishment of the contrast of
the solo violin:

> Fearful is my virgin heart
> And frail my virgin form,
> And must I then take pity on
> The raging of the storm

> That rose up from the great abyss
> Before the world was made...

and so on. A lack of vanity about her role as magician, I suspect, has weakened the end of this splendid poem; the penultimate verse is right to start by pitying the lonely stars but ought to continue amid such grandeur, not merely be sorry for the local scenery, before the gabble comes back for the final blow:

> Let in the wound,
> Let in the pain,
> Let in your child tonight.

'Your' as apart from 'my' is (I take it) intentionally baffling, as a generalisation; the two women might be different persons or might not; just as the conception of a child might be expected, from the visit of an appalling lover, or simply the return of a prodigal child, or one might think of Emily Brontë standing at the open window to hasten her death.

Such a poem has the direct hitting power on the page which is one of the crucial tests; you are forced to feel how it reads aloud. I am less fond of the 'I am' form to which Mr Robert Graves's researches gave prominence: 'I am the shudder in the udder, I am the scramble in the bramble, I am the third lamp-post on your left.' The English language is so fond of this game that it lies on its back, as soon as you start, and asks to be tickled; one can't feel very solemn about that; and apparently the ancient riddles had very detailed pedantic answers. Kathleen Raine, as I understand, uses it to assert that each individual soul is at bottom identical with the Divine Ground (not that the prophet is here the mouthpiece of the god), and uses the surprise of her details only for incidental poetic pleasure; a different aim from her originals at both points. The effects are good, but it is a limited formula; whereas when she uses modern science she gets it right.

The technical merit of her free verse is something much harder to talk about, an exquisite ear. It is full of half rhymes which are much better for not being full rhymes, so much so that her occasional rhymes sometimes feel a mistake, a slight flatness rather than an emphasis. It comes off the page as a beautiful voice.

An American Poet

Listener, 26 March 1953

Wallace Stevens, *Selected Poems*

This selection made by Mr Wallace Stevens from his poetry ought certainly to be welcomed in England; he has been highly admired in America for thirty years, and it is time he was better known here. There is one unfortunate feature of his style which ought to be noticed, what he calls 'beau linguist' perhaps (p. 106), as in the line 'I call you by name, my green, my fluent mundo' (p. 128). Walt Whitman also liked throwing in foreign words, to the effect 'Comes the dawn, *camerados*; pre-sophisticate your *tief toilettes*', but Henry James, having more actual foreign contacts, said it was rather a pity Whitman knew all those bits of foreign languages. It is not offensive in Whitman once you realise that he is trying to be all-inclusively democratic; a reader is supposed to feel personally welcomed, in the new dawn, when he meets a bit of his quaint old mother-tongue, though it is out of date because American English is somehow taking over the whole world. But other writers, English as well as American of course, have taken a very different attitude to Europe and felt themselves raw by contrast to it; then the suggestion becomes 'Just look at our Wallace, bandying the flashing bon mot with the foreign lady of title; doesn't he seem at home?' It was also a fault of Oscar Wilde to be startlingly at home in high society, and Mr Wallace Stevens, very well-to-do it appears, and growing up in the heyday of Oscar Wilde, was perhaps more influenced by him than by Whitman. But then again, though one can pick on examples which seem definitely mistaken, it is obviously a good thing for a poet to be aware of foreign languages; maybe the English-speakers are no longer learning them enough.

Actually there isn't a great deal of this foreign-language trick in his poetry, but there is a lot of something rather like it; an idea that it is enough entertainment for the reader to see the poet trying on a new fancy dress. There is also a good deal of philosophising, which the reader dare not say he has quite understood, but the main point of it, and indeed the reason why it is hard to follow, seems to be an idea that a person like this doesn't really need to philosophise. One need not object to this attitude in principle, in fact it can make good poetry, but it comes to feel very airless. One can't help wishing he had found more to say, if only because he could evidently say it.

He is not however such a narrow poet as these remarks might suggest; the elegant pungency of the nature-descriptions (birds especially) is invigorating, and the fine poem 'Dry Loaf', with the line

> Regard the hovels of those that live in this land,

is after all more unself-centred than most poets nowadays care to be. He is also a master of what is perhaps needed most for poetry in English, a long delicate rhythm based on straight singing lines. The long poem 'Sunday Morning' has this all through, and ends with a splendid example of it:

> Deer walk upon our mountains, and the quail
> Whistle about us their spontaneous cries;
> Sweet berries ripen in the wilderness;
> And, in the isolation of the sky,
> At evening, casual flocks of pigeons make
> Ambiguous undulations as they sink,
> Downward to darkness, on extended wings.

Edgell Rickword

Alan Munton (ed.), 'Edgell Rickword: A Celebration'
(a *festschrift* for Rickword's eightieth birthday in October 1978),
PN Review 9 (VI: 1, 1979), supplement

There was a time, around 1929, when Edgell Rickword was the Sage of the Fitzroy Tavern in Charlotte Street; much jostled by other sages, and very unassertive, indeed he could hardly be got to speak, and then hardly above a whisper, but he was the real one, if you happened to know. John Davenport knew, and advised a few other Cambridge students, including myself; we felt that a visit to London had to include looking for him there. I remember straining my ears, and of course I often succeeded in hearing him, but I cannot remember anything he said. This is the less odd because what he said was remarkable for its studied moderation, and respected for that, even by us; to renounce poetry on becoming a communist, as we all supposed he had done, seemed such a vehement thing, almost like Rimbaud — after that, a man had the right to speak placidly about current quarrels.

He was with Betty May at the time, and this was recognised as greatly to his credit; if I could meet her again, I believe I would still regard her as an impressive and romantic figure, as well as a beauty. However, we thought of him as very old; actually he was only about ten years older than we were, and nobody mentioned the war, but he had known an earlier literary generation. Meeting him now, it seems to me that his appearance has hardly changed at all; he has even retained his seniority.

It seems absurd, but I don't think I had read his poems while these meetings were going on; certainly there was no occasion to mention them. But John Davenport gave me *Invocation to Angels* quite early, probably in 1931; and I admired them very much, as I do still. At that date an English poet struggled to emulate either the recent French or the English of 1590–1640 (and please do not tell me that a poet ought to admire no poetry but his own); Edgell was very strong on the French side, and drew attention to that influence, so I feel it is worth pointing out that he could also make great use of the then recently recovered Englishmen. Anyway, it gives an opportunity for quoting some of his poetry, which is the main thing to do.

'Don Juan Queasy' does not make him feel till the last verse that the girl has become too much for him; her awakening to love is carried through four quatrains with much sympathy and breadth of comparison. But the initial situation is what I want to pick out:

> She is a solitude in which arise
> no wings to break the tranquil eyes' repose,
> an arctic stillness where the traveller lies
> dazed with such silence in such perfect snows.

Surely the impact of this, the freedom of its muscular movement, is much more like the Elizabethans than any French poet that my ignorance could name. There is a splendid poem, 'Farewell to Fancy: the Suburb of Adolescence Re-visited', which is equally at home with both influences; the 'nubile daughters' of the suburb are still finding places to make contact:

> On building sites by tall stark poles
> sweetly their maiden languor droops.
> O dandelions and rusty hoops
> and low foundations in their souls!

The refusal to elaborate the tacit comparisons, which yet seem rich, is I suppose very like Rimbaud. The poem goes on to say that such a situation is the essential one:

> Let us abjure the stately creeds,
> love's plangent groves and choristers,
> with all that Eloquence confers
> upon our elemental needs.

> We will go with them by the tram
> beyond the city's lamps, and sit
> with such emotions as befit
> those born between the *Plough* and *Ram*.

It is magnificent, and surely the tacit symbolism of the names of the pubs calls up Donne rather than Baudelaire. But I do not know why these two things which I have just called 'tacit' give such a strong impression of different backgrounds.

The monumental side of him is what draws on Baudelaire, as in the last verse of 'Poet to Punk', which is to be inscribed on the tomb of both of them:

> 'They reaped the tedious harvest of the eye,
> not contumacious to the laws of dust;
> content to suffer and avoid the just,
> numb with the gradual ruin of the sky.'

It has become true. But this is because people expect disaster, from atom bombs and such like, not because the increasingly democratic society becomes increasingly vulgar, which the quotation from Baudelaire at the start seems likely to imply – as do some of the verses of the poem itself. It is of course quite possible to dislike the effects of commercialisation and regimentation without being anti-democratic: but this could hardly be worked out in the style that Edgell was using. One need not be surprised that he went on to write political satires instead. But this earlier stage was when he wrote really very good poetry.

V
Fiction and Narrative

Forster-Mother

Granta, 28 October 1927

E. M. Forster, *Aspects of the Novel*

In these charming and in some ways stimulating lectures Mr Forster clings very coherently to a particular view of the novel's methods, ingredients and purpose. Apart from the style, the little soft pat of butter that surely, on second thoughts, has been doped with brandy, they are chiefly noticeable for their defence of the crude formula-built minor character. He well insists that our attitudes to persons in novels and in real life, the things to be got out of them, and the ways of doing it, differ in kind; and shows in particular how Jane Austen, finding them elsewhere memorable and convenient, passes a ripple over her flattest characters, as a measure of the greatest turmoil. He even goes so far, in fact, to point out that flat leading characters as in Dickens can exist and produce effects in the grand manner, in terms which confess the inadequacy of his approach to deal with them.

After so much of interest and value, it is [in] his treatment of the more elaborate functions of the novel, under the mild heads of 'fantasy' and 'prophecy', that one feels least at home. He is found, to take examples at random, complacently saying Defoe 'shut the door on infinity'; one would think that sensible and stripped complexity, where Moll Flanders through bad conscience forces her lover to seduce her maid, involved very far reaches of our attention. He speaks highly again of *Zuleika Dobson*, all but in one place, that one place where the string of jokes seem to fuse together and climb up like a wave, to reach, by mere accumulation of absurdity, sweeping pathos and understanding; no, really, he decides the death of Noakes is a little horrid.

After this we need not be surprised to find him turning merely in horror from *Ulysses*, calling it 'an insult to the universe', in a strangely simple phrase. An attempt, successful or not, to include all possible attitudes, to turn upon a given situation every tool, however irrelevant or disconnected, of the contemporary mind, would be far too strenuous and metaphysical an exertion.

Within the clearly stated limitations of his treatment, and the common-sense limitations of his sympathy, his judgement is excellent and his critical criteria most handy; you feel you want to apply them to things at once.

Where the Body Is ...

Granta, 2 December 1927

Wyndham Lewis, *The Wild Body*
Jane Hillyer, *Reluctantly Told*

It is nice to be told what the point of a book of short stories is, it shows a worthy attempt at self-knowledge; but the fact is a good short story has a lot of points, and the two Mr Lewis wrote after he had decided what the main point was are both lamentably thin. He always throws in, too, a great deal of innocent self-revelation, about how he is a great ruthless he-man, and it may be taken for granted that, besides being rational, he has slept with the parlour-maid (why does he never call himself a Great Blond Beast, by the way? It would throw a rich sidelight on this very Teutonic humour). But his chatter is irrelevant, so is his bad grammar.

For these are good stories, neurotic egotist though he is, and painful though it is to read his accounts of himself as flaying in conversation some crippled mind. What he has is the humour Eliot claimed for Marlowe,[1] he exhilarates by describing people with strong, able, well-marked systems of habits, absurdly unlike one's own. It gives a sort of courage, and it makes you feel more competent, even to have imagined them. (He makes a great muddle (as in his essays) about the characters being mechanisms. In describing odd people you must show their main habits, in describing people the reader knows about you can get on at once to the more delicate variations. Odd characters, therefore, seem more predetermined. That is all.)

But it is a strange literary device, and in Miss Hillyer's case even stranger. She describes carefully, from experience, four years as a dangerous case in a rather brutal lunatic asylum; one reads with elaborate interest and pleasure. Now it is not better in real life, that the lady should bite her warders than help on her pupils, but there is no doubt, in the book one prefers a well-documented account of biting; and she writes so much better in the grimmer parts that we may take it she herself felt the same.

It does not please, I think, as exotic, as a relief to undigested neuroses, or simply as unexplained; given a fundamental knowledge of Freud it seems perfectly sensible, motivated, indeed, stage by stage, and there is no hint of fantasy in her carefulness. We must fall back on that magic word 'scientific' used by the doctor in his introduction; both these books, I think, gratify our strong and crucial curiosity about alien modes of feeling, our need for the flying buttress of sympathy with systems other than our own.

Note

1 T. S. Eliot wrote in 1919 that the last act of *The Jew of Malta* develops a 'most power-ful and mature tone' of farce – 'the farce of the old English humour, the terribly serious, even savage comic humour, the humour which spent its last breath in the decadent genius of Dick-ens' (*Selected Essays*, London: Faber & Faber (1932), 3rd edition, 1951, p. 123).

Roses Round the Door

Granta, 8 June 1928

Rose Macaulay, *Keeping up Appearances*

There is no doubt that this is superbly done; Miss Macaulay has never written with fewer loose ends, with more unity of structure; every character is not merely essential, but used to the full; almost every detail of the story is brought back into your mind, and adds its factor to the intolerable climax. Intolerable; I am almost tempted to say it [is] morbid, so I suppose it catches me on the raw for some quite private reason (it is more graceful, at any rate, to say that of oneself than of Miss Macaulay).

Antic Hay, to which this is comparable, both in wit and in the painful state of nervous tension disclosed, was less painful reading (and, in fact, a better novel) because there was more variety; the climax gave a bird's-eye view of the gay and variegated terrors of its people, but it did not narrow and tighten as if the ceiling was closing down on you. It was a public work, as Dryden would have made it a public work; *Appearances* (I will say it) is morbid because it fulfils the condition of madness; before the end the heroine is more than cut off from the world within her private suffering, the whole world seems subservient to her private suffering. Miss Macaulay continually says that most of the characters are practically as badly off; if she had made this part of the plot it would have been less distressing. Of course unity is very Aristotelian, but Aristotle said the tragic hero must have greatness of soul, and it is depressing to be locked up in Daisy's soul because it is impossible not to despise Daisy, whether we are all like her or not; after she has pretended her mother is the charwoman, anyway.

Baby Austin

Granta, 11 May 1928

Lady Murasaki, *Blue Trousers*, translated by Arthur Waley

This is the fourth volume of the series; Genji he is dead before the next one begins. It is, I think, the best so far, partly because the opportunities for those references to earlier parts, which form a large part of one's pleasure, are by now becoming very great; partly because in this book, as it is more concerned than the others with death and old age (blue trousers were worn in sign of mourning), Murasaki brings out as if in compensation her subtlest and richest comedy. And it is here, too, that the architectural qualities of the novel, the way in which the larger units have been fitted together, can be appreciated in its full grandeur.

The critic, in giving way to boundless superlatives, might seem to be led astray by accidental qualities; by the romantic fantasy gratification in a hero of matchless beauty, charm which (we are told) had never been seen in the world before, rich with imperial scents (the privilege of his house), master of palaces 400 yards square, of vast gardens adorned with forgotten cunning, and pathways of finely powdered jade, of numberless concubines, each of whom, when going on a journey as unostentatiously as possible, takes twenty coaches (and the number of outriders is extremely small), of uncounted mysterious and guilty secrets, such as the paternity of the Emperor, and of endless details of polite versifying; by the Wordsworthian air of simple truth, with which all this *Vathek* detail is carried off, and without which, even from so courtly an authoress, it would be too crude to please; by the curiosity continually excited as to what exactly the customs were, and how they worked, the shock of being reminded that these witty and cultivated women were entirely secluded, and the difficulty of finding out, for instance, Genji's methods of governing, or the nature of the labour troubles so often hinted at; by the mingled sense of our civilisation's inferiority in these extremes of delicacy, and of the practical Westerners' superiority to so 'quaint' and flower-chattering a people, from which we are startled back into fantasy identification with Genji when (filling an awkward pause) he embarks on a discourse about plum-blossom or novel-writing, or the limitations of their social love-poetry, making criticisms that seem so naturally one's own; indeed, by the modernity of the conversation of all the characters; one is continually thinking, 'Waley *must* have made that up,' and then finding it woven incidentally into the next paragraph.

It may be such factors as these, superimposed on the original novel, that make it such a continual delight to read, and so liable to be rated too highly. But there are in this volume three or four comedies of situation; between Genji, his new child wife, and his chief concubine (what gross farce it sounds); about Yugiri, the faithful lover, now in domestication; and about the marrying off of Tamakatsura, who was prevented by a sad accident from entering the Emperor's household; in each of these one is dizzy with the subtlety of the writing; with each clause, each placidly given detail, there is a new twist to the dialogue, a different construction is put upon the relations of these always charming people. There is nothing exotic about it, it is what the Western novel has done continually, but it is done supremely here.

Waley's Courtesy

New Statesman, 13 March 1964

Arthur Waley, *The Secret History of the Mongols*

This is a collection of translations, and of literary–historical articles in which much translation is embedded, mostly later than 1952; the translations are from 'Chinese, Japanese, Ainu, Mongol and Syriac', and the one that gives the title occupies about a quarter of the book. Mr Waley has always been confronted with a problem which is as much one of tact as of literary style. Rare and fascinating delicacies are liable to irritate or cloy, and even the most generous host has to consider how much the stomach of his crude guests will bear. At many points I have felt in the past that he should tell more, but undoubtedly part of his success has depended upon stopping short and leaving the rest to be imagined at choice. Thus here the 'Secret History', a traditional account of the early life of Genghis Khan (the only reason for hiding it from the Chinese was that they might call it barbaric), is given without footnotes or background for 'its quality as literature and hence its value to ordinary readers'. I expect the scholar does not realise how much interpretation he puts in when he savours it as literature: for instance, I kept getting baffled by the motives of the characters, whereas the first hearers would find them plain.

I fell back on the scenery in the narrative: wooded but open, hilly but seldom craggy, in fact just like an English park except that never, never for thousands of miles would one sight the Hall. The hero's mother is widowed when he is eight; he is the eldest, and she raises them all in total solitude on roots and fruits. Then the hero rides out to contact his cousins, contriving to escape alive, and contriving to find the new valley in which his family have hidden. When a reader's reaction is unaided in this way, deliberately thrown back upon his personal experience, he can feel that it is being narrowed; thus it never occurred to me that I would have got killed in the fighting, but I knew the country enough to feel with a real pang: 'I would never have got back to Mum.' Almost at once we find the hero in command of 10,000 men, and they are far too few; but the really interesting part of the story is how he emerged from solitude into command

440

of that much. It seems plain that the reciters of the legend did not know, whereas the translator knows a lot more than he will tell. However, this will probably stimulate a lot of readers into looking up the information elsewhere.

At the other extreme, Waley is plainly right to use this method when the author translated is using it too – as when 'a Chinese poet in central Asia' reports in verse that, while he is feasting with the General,

young ladies are straining the wine into jade cups and scattering here, there and everywhere a profusion of bronze bowls full of wild-camel cream.

In recent times a Chinese in Peking successfully pretended to be a visiting Mongol prince till an inevitable cup of milk made him vomit at the banquet. The English reader who has smelt camels at the zoo will wonder a little about their cream, but the intended Chinese audience would find it exotic to the point of horror. Even so, a bit more gossip would have been welcome to both audiences; tips on exactly how to milk a wild camel would surely be a help.

The courtesy of Waley is finely seen when he reports that the Ainu, in the northern island of Japan, are famous for their long beards. The Japanese say that they are covered with fur, and merrily showed them to a visiting Indian prince (within living memory, in the interests of Asiatic solidarity) as typical Aryans; they are Caucasians like ourselves, but so was the prince, so this was a sad gaffe. Their epic has fine spirit and vigorous action. The Owl of the Ainu legend, who arranged to inform mankind how to make ceremonies so that fish and deer would feel gratified at being killed, deserves mention as the most terrifying teacher on record. It is interesting that high beds are marks of Ainu aristocracy; the Buddha forbade them to his monks, regarding them as vanity, but probably this is an important case where vanity meant hygiene, and breathing in dust while asleep on the *tatami* is still making the Japanese far too liable to TB.

Long ago, when the first volumes of Waley's translation of *The Tale of Genji* were coming out, another English expert on Japanese told me that Waley was treating Lady Murasaki (who wrote in 1066 or so) chivalrously: that is, he was allowing her to say what she probably would have wished to say, if she had had at her command the full resources of the English language. I thought this was so grand that it almost ceased to be catty. Now Waley says it himself, but with the reservation that there were also great resources unknown to modern English at the command of Lady Murasaki. In the example he gives, the version of women's language used by trusted old servant to young aristocratic girl is full of hints which explain why the heroine reacts hysterically; therefore, the only way to translate the passage into English was to invent a corresponding Jane Austen set-up. He is convincing on the point, and it needed clearing up.

A large capacity to accept the assumptions of any world-view, without assuming any merit for our own, is the basic virtue of Waley's mind. The only modern Western man who gets a credit even by implication in the book is a psychiatrist to whom a patient, after a moral struggle, confessed that the dreams he had been reporting were all invented. 'That makes no difference,' was the stern reply, and back he went to the couch. What the translator brings out all the time is not the strangeness or the beauty of the persons described but their firm practical good sense; the bounce of this conviction is what makes the translation feel so lively; and though so aesthetic it amounts to a bracing moral atmosphere. After a victory:

those that would be any good as wives were made into wives and those that would be better as slaves were made into slaves.

Virginia Woolf

Scrutinies, 2, London: Wishart & Co., 1931

Shakespeare was like Nature; we have been saying it for three centuries. There were more echoes in his work than he knew; he wrote from his pre-consciousness; any work in hand formed a world he was living in, so that he could find his way about in it as if by habit; any of his stones may have been made bread, and repay turning. Novelists have seldom been called Nature in this sense; at any rate they have not been commented on in such detail; and by way of showing that the same claim might be made for Mrs Woolf I shall try to pick up, turn in my hand for the moment, two quite small stones from the road to the lighthouse, till they catch the light, and are seen to be, if not bread, at least jewels.

Mrs Ramsey feels tired at the beginning of her dinner party.

... the whole of the effort of merging and flowing and creating rested on her. Again she felt, as a fact without hostility, the sterility of men, for if she did not do it nobody would do it; and so, giving herself the little shake that one gives a watch that has stopped, the old familar pulse began beating, as the watch begins ticking – one, two, three, one, two, three. And so on and so on, she repeated, listening to it, sheltering and fostering the still feeble pulse as one might guard a weak flame with a newspaper.

Watches don't beat up to three, they beat up to two, or four in pairs. Before calling this a harmless small mistake, however, one must consider an earlier passage. James has just gone to bed; she feels at peace over her knitting.

Not as oneself did one rest ever, in her experience (she accomplished here something dexterous with her needles), but as a wedge of darkness. Losing personality one lost the fret, the hurry, the stir; and there rose to her lips always some exclamation of triumph over life when things came together in this peace, this rest, this eternity; and pausing there she looked out to meet that stroke of the Lighthouse – the long steady stroke, the last of the three – which was her stroke, for watching them in this mood always at this hour one could not help attaching oneself especially to one of the things one saw; and this thing, the long steady stroke, was her stroke.

443

The Lighthouse becomes a symbol of energies at the basis of human life, which support and exclude the understanding; Mrs Ramsey sets herself going like the Lighthouse to sustain her party, and it is for this reason that the pulse is like a flame. Or one may say that the Lighthouse has at times been the symbol of reason and male power of setting large-scale things in order (for it is in sight of the Lighthouse that Mr Bankes and Mr Tansley go and talk politics on the terrace after dinner, as if they had gone on to the bridge of the ship to take up their bearings), and it is then with a sort of feminist triumph that it becomes a symbol of Mrs Ramsey. The complex working of her symbols continually involves devious motivations of this kind; one must remember with some alarm (thinking of feminism) a moment in *Jacob's Room*, when Betty Flanders, that good and generous woman, remembers in passing how she did not like red hair in men, and how she had the cat castrated that was given by one of her admirers.

The other example is more controversial; it comes in the second part of the *Lighthouse*, when Mrs Ramsey is dead and time is passing in the empty house. (The War is mentioned two pages later.)

Nothing it seemed could break that image, corrupt that innocence, or disturb the swaying mantle of silence which, week after week in the empty room, wove into itself the falling cries of birds, ships hooting, the drone and hum of the fields, a dog's bark, a man's shout, and folded them round the house in silence. Only once a board sprang on the landing; once in the middle of the night with a roar, with a rupture, as after centuries of quiescence, a rock rends itself from the mountain and hurtles crashing into the valley, one fold of the shawl loosened and swung to and fro.

Some people, when you tell them that this patch is of rare excellence, say that it is not true; that a shawl, especially only one fold of it, does not roar; perhaps even that this is a neurotic cultivation of hyper-sensitivity for hyper-sensitivity's sake. The image in any case speaks very truly about such small domestic changes, startling both because apparently uncaused and because of the gulfs of time that surround them; but it is relevant to the shawl for a reason you have to remember; because of what Mrs Ramsey said when she put it there. Cam was frightened of the boar's skull in the night nursery, so Mrs Ramsey wound her shawl round it and said how lovely it looked now:

it was like a bird's nest; it was like a beautiful mountain such as she had seen abroad, with valleys and flowers and bells ringing and birds singing and little goats and antelopes ...

It is only if you have remembered this fancy that you realise with how terrible an irony it has come true. Mrs Ramsey is dead and the house empty; even her most domesticated and personal piece of matter has become monstrous and inhuman, like a mountain, like matter in astronomy. But you have had to remember the words for a long time, and it seems as if Mrs Woolf herself was not so much remembering them as finding her way about the book as if by habit; it is this sort of small correspondence, used so often, that makes up a full and as it were poetical attitude to language such as would gain by an annotated edition.

A more serious objection, I think, can be brought against the sentence about the mantle of silence weaving things into itself. Mrs Woolf can show very brilliantly how the details of her characters' surroundings are woven into their moods; this is an important part of a novel, and what I have just called her poetical use of language is the best way of doing it. But here the whole point of the situation is that *no* character is in the room; what is eerie about the sounds is precisely that they are *not* being woven into anybody's mood; and the sentence seems to have the falsity that comes from always using a single method. As long as this sort of method is being used dramatically, to show how a character felt, it is excellent if only because it is true; people's minds do work like that; it may really be the only way to deal adequately with motivation. But when it is being used to show merely how Mrs Woolf is feeling about what she describes the result is not always formal enough to be interesting. One thing reminds her of a lot of others, and the story is held up while they are mentioned; but one feels that the reasons why she thought of these things at the moment of writing are not part of the book.

When the shawl made her think of a rock it was, I believe, part of the book, for the reason I have given; but such a method makes extraordinary demands on the author's sincerity; he must be living in his work very completely if he can indulge in free association and be sure that it will be relevant. Of course you may say that an author must always attempt this condition, regardless of consequences; this, I take it, is the main doctrine of surrealism, but it has an air of putting the cart before the horse. A novelist's wit (of which Mrs Woolf has so much) is likely to carry its own setting and explanation, but his personal poetry is not reliable in the same way.

It is necessary in talking about Mrs Woolf to consider these problems of form, because her solution of them is so closely connected with her choice of subject; if in her later novels she treats them high-handedly it is not so much from indifference or undue concentration as from a change of emphasis. I shall look, for example, at the way she makes a novel stop.

Night and Day and *The Voyage Out*, if one thinks of the earlier ones, end respectively with marriage and death; these, of course, are the traditional, and might seem the only reliable methods. But for stopping *Mrs Dalloway* these ways would be no use, because of the particular sort of person whose functions and modes of thought are being described. For the person now in the centre of the stage is a sensible and highly sensitive married woman, not concerned to lead the life of independent intelligence, who is the sun of her world, who acts as clearing-house for the emotional needs of her household, who is always intensely aware of the mood of everybody in the room, and who frequently does not listen to the conversation. Such a person has, in a sense, renounced her private drama, so that one does not wish it to be brought to either of these climaxes. For one thing, we are only shown the day of Clarissa's party; the map is on too large a scale to include the coast as well as the central towns. *To the Lighthouse* is a story about Mrs Ramsey, but in a sense her death is a minor incident brought in to show how her influence lived after her; things centre round her in the third party just as continuously, with just as little natural climax, as they did in the first. You might indeed say that it is hopeless to look for an orderly plot about such a heroine, because the things that are interesting about her make a plot irrelevant. And yet it is a mistake to suppose that you can say even those things in a novel without a plot.

Mrs Woolf's later style is very beautifully adapted to the requirements of this subject; so much so as to attack very directly the problem of motivation. Indeed I think it is for this that she will chiefly be remembered; in this administrative but domestic setting, by the very structure of the sentences, we are made to know what it felt like for the heroine to make up her mind. Of course in itself this is not new; it is the main business of a novelist to show his reader, by slow accumulations, all the elements and proportions of a decision, so that the reader knows how the character felt about it; but Mrs Woolf, so as to be much more immediately illuminating, can show how they are at the back of a decision at the moment it is taken.

We arrive, for instance, with some phrase like 'and indeed' into a new sentence and a new specious present. Long, irrelevant, delicious clauses recollect the ramifications of the situation (this part corresponds to the blurring of consciousness while the heroine waits a moment to know her own mind; and it is here, by the way, that one is told most of the story); then by a twist of thought some vivid but distant detail, which she is actually conscious of, and might have been expected to finish the sentence, turns her mind towards the surface. From then on the clauses become shorter; we move towards action by a series of leaps, each, perhaps, showing what she would have done about something quite different, and just at the end, without effort, washed up by the last wave of this disturbance, like an obvious bit of grammar put in to round off the sentence, with a partly self-conscious, wholly charming humility in the heroine (how odd that the result of all this should be something so flat and domestic), we get the small useful thing she actually did do.

Most of the important things for a critic to say about Mrs Woolf have been said by herself in *A Room of One's Own*, and centre round a peculiar attitude to feminism. For instance, she says there that woman novelists must be expected to do something entirely new in describing the mental attitudes of women, and their relations with other women, which male novelists do not know about. This seems a large claim; surely Richardson knew how women talked when there wasn't a man in the room; and when you have said, as Mrs Woolf does say, that every complete author must be spiritually hermaphrodite, you seem to have quelled this aspect of the sex war as vehemently as you called it into being. But her best work is certainly illuminated by this notion; in particular, it has a sort of submissive sensitiveness to immediate circumstances (helpless sensitiveness, one might say, except that it is just this quality that improves them) which gives her work both the delicacy with which she can seize on a shade of domestic atmosphere and (so as to raise the formal questions I am talking about) the peculiar evanescence of her designs as a whole. One might also put down to this a concentration on domestic details as dramatic; Mrs Flanders, for instance, not knowing what to do with her dead son's boots; but again it is no use saying it could only be done by a woman novelist. Shakespeare is full of details of this sort, which would be humorous if they were not terrible.

Not, by the way, that he would have used the detail as a means of ending a long work; there is a sort of self-consciousness in the way it is thus thrust upon you as peculiarly good, and you have to decide it is peculiarly good if it is to make a satisfying ending at all. Still, there is no doubt about the finality of the situation; the end here is Jacob's death. The end of *To the Lighthouse*, though much more arbitrary, is as satisfying, and leaves one remembering the whole book, partly by the unifying and mystifying effect of the symbol, chiefly because there is nobody left at the end about whose future behaviour you feel immediately curious. On the other hand this is almost shockingly untrue of *Mrs Dalloway*: most of the book has been leading up to what happens just after the last page. Of course Clarissa did not allow the situation to become melodramatic; if you thought she would Mrs Woolf is snubbing you. But I do not know how she carried it off, or what effect it may not have had on Peter; and even if I ought to, I feel the snub is a harsh one. Certainly the book stops (like a dance tune) at one of the possible stopping places, at one of the minor apotheoses of Clarissa; but so far as one has any sense of finality it is for more or less arbitrary reasons. The party for which she has prepared all through the day of the book is over; the shell-shock case is dead; and he has been connected with the main story in some degree since she has heard of him from Sir William Bradshaw. None of these outweigh our curiosity about the meeting of Clarissa and Peter.

The influence of the Chekhov short story, I think, has been misleading in

England; Chekhov can afford to stop in the middle of a conversation because you know how it would go on. He is hopeless about his characters; they will never do any better; and one stops in the middle as with a final gesture of despair. But a novel in which the characters are capable of dealing with many different situations must stop either when they are dead or when they will from then on have to deal with different situations, and have brought to some order the ones they were dealing with before. So that once you abandon death and marriage the sea is uncharted. For instance, Proust's great novel, you might say, could not stop, because the descriptions of motive were too minute and the interconnections too many; it rolled on by its own weight to end in a rather cumbrous series of universal reconnecting generalisations. On the other hand, Mrs Woolf's early short stories – 'Kew Gardens', for instance – use what may be called the Vase of Flowers method; things seen in the same mood are described together, and there they are; two lovers and a slug; so you stop. This seems inadequate, whether derived from Chekhov or not; the range of interest (identifying oneself with all the characters and so forth) in the crudest melodramatic story is much greater than the range of interest (mainly contrast and correspondence) in a vase of flowers. Indeed the impressionist method, the attempt to convey directly your own attitude to things, how you connect one thing with another, is in a sense fallacious; it tries to substitute for telling a story, as the main centre of interest, what is in fact one of the by-products of telling a story; it tries to correlate sensations rather than the impulses that make the sensations interesting; even tries to define the impulse by an accumulation of the sensations it suggested to the author. Even those delicate interconnections on which the impressionist method depends (those two I considered at first, for instance) need a story to make them intelligible, and even if Shakespeare (since I have dragged him in) could afford to abandon himself to these delicious correspondences he had first to get a strong and obvious story which would be effective on the stage. I think myself, at any rate, that Mrs Woolf's most memorable successes come when she is sticking most closely to her plot.

Still, of course, the trouble about sticking closely to a plot is that in that case (for the most interesting plots) you can't deal adequately with motivation; Defoe's method only worked because his characters were undomestic people in dire need of money, so that their motives were fairly plain. All one can say against the wilful and jumping brilliance of Mrs Woolf's descriptive passages is that, as part of a design, they come to seem unsatisfying; however delicate and brightly coloured they seem cut in low relief upon the great block she has taken for her material, and even when you are sure that some patch is really part of the book you often cannot (as you can in my two examples) see why it should be. Of course her methods catch in-

FICTION AND NARRATIVE 449

tensely a sense of period, of setting, of the immediate person described; are very lifelike, in short; and I do not know how far it may be due to just this quality; to the fact that so many of her images, glittering and searching as they are, spreading out their wealth of feeling, as if spilt, in the mind, give one just that sense of waste that is given by life itself.

... the great revelation perhaps never did come. Instead, there were little daily miracles, illuminations, matches struck unexpectedly in the dark.

'How far that little candle sheds its beams'; but still it is the business of art to provide candelabra, to aggregate its matches into a lighthouse of many candlepower. If only (one finds oneself feeling in re-reading these novels), if only these dissolved units of understanding had been coordinated into a system; if only, perhaps, there was an index, showing what had been compared with what; if only these materials for the metaphysical conceit, poured out so lavishly, had been concentrated into crystals of poetry that could be remembered, how much safer one would feel.

Mrs Dalloway as a
Political Satire

Essays in English Language and Literature (Tokyo), 1, April
1933; first published as 'Mrs Dalloway', in Eigo Seinen (The
Rising Generation), LXVIII: 6, 15 December 1932

Mrs Dalloway, hot from her Prime Minister, told Lord Gayton and Nancy
Blow that it was angelic, it was delicious of them to have come to her party;
they never had much to say, she felt, but they looked so clean and so
interested in outdoor sports. Mrs Leavis in her excellent book has given a
sharp reproof to Mrs Woolf for adopting this fond tone. It is true that she
seems, for all her display of advanced political notions, to be not so much
admiring as cuddling the rulers and the empire builders, with a certain perverse air of petting them all the more for getting on her nerves. You may dislike this but the most effective satire is usually made out of such mixed
feelings. There are two main characters, Miss Kilman and Warren Smith,
presented as tragic and insane because outside the safe world of the people
at the party; Mrs Dalloway, safely inside it and delighted by it, but afraid of
thinking herself a snob, is always conscious, so that it is one of the refrains
of the book, that you might get outside her world, that that would be madness, that if you did the guardians of sanity would sweep down on you in all
their brutality, that in all profound calm, since you are then free from the
forces holding you to society, something terrible seems about to happen.
There is a tone of girlish petulance about her claims to safety which Mrs
Woolf seems not so much to satirise in the worldly as to view with distaste
in herself.

She cared much more for her roses than for the Armenians. Hunted out of existence, maimed, frozen, the victims of cruelty and injustice (she had heard Richard
say so over and over again) – no, she could feel nothing for the Albanians, or was it
the Armenians? but she loved her roses (didn't that help the Armenians?) – the only
flowers she could bear to see cut.

The snuffle and titter of this is Mrs Woolf's own voice, but she is not praising it in Mrs Dalloway. The whole structure of the book is based on an occasion where Mrs Dalloway does feel something about a man she has never
met; the shell-shock case Smith lives in a nightmare world wholly unlike

her own and yet that she understands on the faintest hint because she fears it; and the unity of style of the book is based on the fact that her wandering receptive mind and his crazed one work in the same way. (The root of the thing, one may take from a hint about Smith's educating himself on the advice of well-known authors consulted by letter, is Mrs Woolf's own feelings about a painful case in her fan mail.) The irony that clinches this, after pages of Mrs Dalloway's exquisite symbolical thinking, her play of judgement rather than fantasy, that so far from being neurotic is what attaches her so firmly and sensitively to the world she lives in, comes when Smith has been caught by the specialist.

'You served with great distinction in the War?'
The patient repeated the word 'war' interrogatively.
He was attaching meanings to words of a symbolical kind. A serious symptom to be noted on the card.
'The War?' the patient asked. The European War – that little shindy of schoolboys with gunpowder? Had he served with distinction? He really forgot. In the War itself he had failed.

At the end, at the triumph of her party, her assertion of the same order of her tribe, she hears of the suicide of the man who thought of himself as Christ and scapegoat and feels that her sense that she might have done the same is a sort of proof that she is genuine; she feels outside her snobbery because she can understand him; he becomes indeed to her for a moment what it was his madness to think he was to everybody; he is the sacrificial hero and his tragedy reconciles her to the world. The effect is to make Mrs Dalloway seem more real and deeply rooted, because less dependent on shelter, to show the gulfs across which she can reach her understanding, the uselessness of this power, even to herself, and its dignity, the falsity and the truth of Smith's belief that he is an outcast, the intimacy of the most distant human relationship, the dissolution of one of the most far-reaching of human beliefs into one of the flickering and random illuminations which go out immediately in her mind.

These more general issues tend to swamp the political ones: they make one feel that the empire builders' world is the only sane one because it is the only one Mrs Dalloway knows (this set of ideas has in fact generally been used to support the system existing at the time). The same sentiment, very tempting for the sort of Englishman the book aims at, animates Peter Walsh, Mrs Dalloway's socialistic but well-connected old admirer; he is feeling, on his first day or two back in London, after ten years' ruling in India for an empire he disapproves of, that 'after all' it is all wonderful, it is a civilisation; and the crashing ironies opposed to this sentiment only make such a reader feel that it can be enjoyed with decent honesty.

One of the triumphs of civilisation, Peter Walsh thought. It is one of the triumphs of civilisation, as the light high bell of the ambulance sounded. Swiftly, cleanly, the ambulance sped to the hospital, having picked up instantly, humanely, some poor devil ... It struck him coming back from the East – the efficiency, the organisation, the communal spirit of London.

It is taking away the corpse of Warren Smith, after the suicide he committed because of the effects of his patriotism in the war and the inhumanity of the common sense of the doctors, because of the things Peter is admiring.

And one never quite gets over the shock of finding that the reason Mrs Dalloway has not seen Sally for so long, Sally whom she loved as she has never loved a man, whom she has remembered all through the book with so much pathos at the ending of their love and pride at having once felt so deeply, is that she will not go and see her as Lady Rosseter, the wife of a manufacturer in Manchester; for which Sally, in spite of the egotism that Peter and Clarissa despise so much, has forgiven her.

And then all this. She waved her hand.

Hugh Whitbread it was, strolling past in his white waistcoat, dim, fat, blind, past everything he looked, except self-esteem and comfort.

'He's not going to recognise *us*,' said Sally, and really she hadn't the courage – so that was Hugh, the admirable Hugh!

'And what does he do?' she asked Peter.

He blacked the King's boots or counted bottles at Windsor, Peter told her.

. . .

How remorseless life is! A little job at Court!

The point is not that she loves her aristocrats too much but that the book, like most post-war good writing, makes a blank statement of conflict; she shows that she can feel on both sides, knows both how to love and to hate her aristocrats, and takes that for an achievement, which indeed it is, but not a fertile one.

Myth

Life and Letters, XVI:7, Spring 1937

Lord Raglan, *The Hero*

The trouble with this amusing book is that it is too busy lashing a sea of adversaries to expound a theory of its own, or even work towards getting one. For instance, the part about English pedigrees is only a good and well-informed joke; it adds to the general atmosphere of scepticism, but by the end of the book it is, if anything, a point against the main argument. There is no doubt that something like what the argument asserts is true, but you want to know when and how much; and this is not what the enthusiastic champion of it wants to tell you.

The story is that figures like Falstaff, Robin Hood, King Arthur, Achilles, etc., are essentially cult-heroes, and therefore derived from primitive ritual, not from history. Now there seems a fair case for saying that the *Iliad* and the Norwegian Eddas had religious rituals behind them; though even this gives no reason for saying that Achilles never existed, because it is admitted that a stock myth can be attached to a real person – e.g. Henry V in this book. And it is likely enough that very old conventions of storytelling, so old that they go back to primitive ritual, were used in building the stories of Falstaff and Robin Hood. But for Lord Raglan's case against the historicity of these people he needs a regular tidy religion with an established ritual, devoted to them by name, and falling out of use about when the stories were put together. This he makes no attempt to provide; but he is prepared to throw us a theory, for instance, that all Rip Van Winkle stories are derived from a yearly drama, in which 'Robin Hood, or whoever the hero was, might well come on and explain that while the audience were a year older than when he saw them last, he himself was older merely by the length of a night spent with his May Queen' (p.253). No doubt this would go down well enough if there was such a drama, and if he said it, but why should a medieval make a myth out of that? The rituals they took seriously were things like marriage and the mass, and in some cases a cult of Satan; but Robin Hood was a story, a thing on a different footing – whether there was some village jolly-making about him or not.

The reason Lord Raglan has to suppose that these dramas existed is that he wants to plunge over the horizon of history into the dawn of the human mind; the minds of really primitive people are half devoted to a practical magic and half blankly unimaginative; therefore, they will only get ideas for stories out of the magic ritual of their religion. Now it is quite possible that ancestral memories of sun-worship or Druids or whatnot are still dimly maintained in English villages. But if this is what he has to claim, it is grotesque to mix his thesis with the assertion that no tradition lasts longer than a century and a half; and it gives him no basis for saying that King Arthur or Robin Hood never existed, because there must, anyway, have been some reason for tying the much older ritual on to a myth about a special period. And whatever may have happened about Arthur, Lord Raglan clearly means the mistakes in family pedigrees as examples of the same kind of unhistorical myth; now he really cannot argue that the squires have been secretly maintaining a Golden Bough ritual, in which the head of the house must at set intervals be ceremonially disguised as the pretended ancestor, and appear to be slaughtered and reborn.

The difficult question about the Frazerian tradition of the hero seems to me to come in here, in the question how it was maintained among people who no longer took it seriously. It is easy to make the Golden Bough a stick to beat the historians, but there is a good deal of Frazer material in English literature, and you want to know how it got there. Lord Raglan tends to a diffusionist idea, that it all came from Egypt; one could more easily say that it is inherent in the human mind. Even so the Far East seems to produce Frazer material of a different type, the hero One with Nature, not the Dying God, so that different races would have to have different inherent ideas. Actually, a man like Herrick may well have known quite clearly what he was about; even the gossip about savages became popular as soon as they were discovered, and he knew his classics and his village – the whole range of sources that Frazer took in detail. But if there is anything in Lord Raglan's method of interpreting history, these ideas must be attached to us in some more serious way.

The main objection to explaining things by 'ritual dramas' is, of course, that nothing is explained – how did the ritual dramas come to be different? To be told that Rip Van Winkle and Robin Hood are two more of the same old hero is quite different from being told their stories. If the stories had to come in from outside they might just as well have been actual striking events, treated metaphorically or otherwise, which would refute Lord Raglan's view that myths never contain fragments of history. (Anyway, the main use of tradition for the historian is that it shows what people thought important.) If they were invented by founders of primitive religions, this would presumably refute his view that no illiterate ever invented a story; if they were learned from dreams this refutes his view that dreams cannot affect religion, a view already refuted in detail by fieldworkers on Red Indians. And so on. Even if the problem could be solved in this way, by making a mosaic of cases which fit one theory, still the real problem would lie behind. But certainly the detached cases here are well worth reading, and the question raised is important.

Jane Austen: a letter

1940

D. W. Harding, in 'Regulated Hatred: An Aspect of the Work of Jane Austen' (Scrutiny, VIII: 4 March 1940, pp. 346–62), argued that the common view of Jane Austen as a writer who aimed to entertain 'a posterity of urbane gentlemen' offered a lopsided estimate of her work, which is in fact – consciously or unconsciously – subversive: 'her books are, as she meant them to be, read and enjoyed by precisely the sort of people whom she disliked . . .' While she 'genuinely valued the achievements of the civilisation she lived within', Harding's essay went on, the flavour of her satire often represents a 'disintegrating attack' upon the social intercourse of her civilised acquaintances, an attack which can only be the expression of the author's own 'fear and hatred':

To speak of this aspect of her work as 'satire' is perhaps misleading. She has none of the underlying didactic intention ordinarily attributed to the satirist. Her object is not missionary; it is the more desperate one of merely finding some mode of existence for her critical attitudes. To her the first necessity was to keep on reasonably good terms with the associates of everyday life; she had a deep need of their affection and a genuine respect for the ordered, decent civilisation that they upheld. And yet she was sensitive to their crudenesses and complacencies and knew that her real existence depended on resisting many of the values they implied.

Empson responded with the following undated and unpublished letter to the editors of Scrutiny.

I have a point or two of objection to the article on Jane Austen in your last number, not very serious, but it seems a good thing to have a discussion about so good an article.

This left-wing-intellectual approach to the lady, the idea that Tories think she is praising the present system, but we pink boys know that her heart is with the rebels – it is equally grim whether Mr Harding is being absurd or the readers he considers normal are. Surely anybody ought not to need to *discover* through Unconscious Psychology that Jane Austen hated and feared her comic monsters or cruelty and stupidity; or that Dickens did either, for that matter. Mr Harding says it is 'unbelievable' that Henry Tilney [in *Northanger Abbey*] could have said that in polite society in the English counties every man is surrounded with a neighbourhood of voluntary spies. It is unbelievable (apparently) because he is not presented as an embittered or politically dangerous person; and because Jane Austen knew so well in her own life the nuisance of affectionate family observation, so that she could only have meant this to be said bitterly. What would really be surprising would be if Henry Tilney had got through one speech in the whole novel without dragging in his stock vein of humour. It seems very likely that Jane Austen found the attack on romantic novels, which she seemed to make through his mouth, was getting too solemn, so she put this phrase in as an afterthought to keep him 'in character'. The only 'paranoiac' part of the question is Mr Harding's idea that nobody could strike out a phrase like that without 'a touch of paranoia'.

Do not accuse me of taking a cosy view. Jane Austen undoubtedly felt the suffering of living in 'a neighbourhood of spies', and of what Mr Harding calls the thesis of another of her jokes, that 'the ruling standards of our social group leave a perfectly comfortable niche for detestable people and give them sufficient sanction to persist'. He is only wrong in saying that if she had said this she would have aroused 'the most violent opposition'. Because she did say it. He is only discovering the obvious. What is this revolution that he feels she might have sponsored? – that is the only political question. Nowadays no doubt she could have had a private revolution and gone to live somewhere where she would only meet other lady novelists, instead of a whole cross-section of the life of the country. She would certainly have thought that, personally, and in a small degree socially, harmful, as it is. As to any public revolt against Upperclass Politeness, the idea is faced very squarely in *Mansfield Park*. After many pages of growing horror at the evils of subsidised snobbery and stupidity the heroine is sent back to her mother, married to a decent highgrade worker in Portsmouth, and nobody there is unkind to her. Weighing the contrast slowly, the heroine decides that the evils of life at her grand aunt's house are *nothing* beside the pains of life in Portsmouth, and that these pains come chiefly from the (natural and inevitable) want of Politeness in Portsmouth. Now it was because Jane Austen was willing to work for general Politeness that she had to endure the evils against which Mr Harding represents her (if I am right) as unconsciously but feverishly revolting. And from what I remember of her life she had a good deal of experience of Portsmouth and what it stood for to make her decision with; there was a good deal of discussion, wasn't there, about whether she had better be sent to keep house for one of her cousins in a debtor's jail? And little jokes about bastards and so forth in her surviving letters which presume a less prim attitude in her intimates than we find in her books? And at the same time phrases like 'I think we all maybe ought to be Methodists', as you might say now 'Salvation Army lasses'? What I am trying to argue is that the things Mr Harding thinks he is discovering in her Unconsciousness or in her secret tricks with an unconscious public are quite simply in the sunlight of her writings, and in the experience (one would presume) of any reasonable critic who praises her.

It is wrong to assume (much more widely than in this case) that Jane Austen must *either* have had 'an ambition of entertaining a posterity of urbane gentlemen' *or* some dark psychological need to write something that would let her complexes creep out and yet pass off as normal. What any tolerable urbane gentleman enjoys in her writing is precisely her full illustration of the moral which she herself clearly drew. In any tolerable society, whatever its political arrangement, you will have a variety of people meeting each other, and therefore Politeness will be necessary, and to maintain Politeness is liable to involve serious sacrifices. Yet they are worth it; if only because Politeness is the outward sign of more serious values less often called on. That is what all the urbane jokes are made out of. It may be very offensive to a communist. But really it isn't buried in the unconsciousness of the author or the normal reader.

'D. H. Lawrence and Susan his Cow'

Horizon 2, December 1940

William York Tindall,
D. H. Lawrence and Susan his Cow

It is fair enough to laugh at Lawrence, who got into some absurd personal and intellectual positions, and no doubt for some people was a harmful leader. Hugh Kingsmill [*D. H. Lawrence,* London: Methuen, 1938] has done it recently very well, but he was funny with the human breadth that the subject requires. It is fair to say that Mr Tindall is often very funny, but this is a repulsive little book. Melancholy to have it come from an American university man; it is what the Americans very rightly hate most in the English. The style is a skimpy parody of Gibbon without his power to praise; it is designed to guy anything that it describes, and to give a continual obscure hint of the author's social or moral superiority. In time, it comes to affect you like a man who can't stop twitching. An immense air of the footnoted and final treatise is given to a discussion of the books that Lawrence borrowed and from whom he borrowed them, with neat hints that all his ideas were 'stolen'. Lawrence was a comic if you like, but he was a man of very wide and intelligent reading, in several languages, who did not choose to live near a public library: there's nothing more to say about that. With all the parade of learning we needn't, perhaps, get 'Lord Chatterley' and the solemn footnote, 'The cow is worshipped today by certain African tribes', as if there weren't any Hindus. There are innumerable coy but shocked jokes at Lawrence's *sexual* relations with his cow, as if Lawrence didn't have sexual relations with everything. It seems very little good being Smart Alec on this topic. I am not clear whether Mr Tindall means to insinuate police court matters or simply to jazz the book up; he doesn't give the effect of knowing what he is talking about. It can't be called indecent, surely, even on the staff of Columbia University, to say that you feel fond of an animal.

Then there is this great business about how Lawrence was a fascist and therefore all his ideas must have been wrong. I thought Hugh Kingsmill made rather too much of that, as well as Mr Tindall. Literary people often don't have much to do with personal power and leadership and teamwork, or it seems very separate from their business of writing. Surely at this time of day it is clear that the business of getting good leaders and being loyal to them, on this side of idolatry, is the chief problem of the democracies. It was a nightmare of Lawrence that a mean craving comes up among the herds of a machine society to pull the big man down, so that his only way out (if he wants it) is to make them worship him. There is a terrible range of examples of that. And it is no good quoting a page or two of *Apocalypse* to prove that Lawrence took a poisonous way out of the problem. In his way he was very well balanced, that is, he could swing over till he was sickeningly near coming off his balance and then swing up and pass it again. The whole subject of *Apocalypse* is that he feels the meanness and evil of the lust for power over men as strongly as he feels its necessity and beauty. To be sure the book comes to no conclusion, but it is an experience; it is a walk round an important subject. And in his evasive way he had a very political mind; the whole point of the mystical and anthropological and psychological background was to see how life can be lived well in the unique conditions of the modern world. Mr Tindall claims that alone among writers on Lawrence he 'accounts for him historically', that is, he finds some other writers who thought in rather the same way, about the same time. This is not as masterly as it appears. It is just as bad not to know what ten men are talking about as what one man is.

In an unpublished draft essay of about the same date Empson developed the observations he made in the last paragraph:

Hugh Kingsmill's book on D. H. Lawrence was very witty, and I think Kingsmill has been neglected, but it failed over Lawrence's last book *Apocalypse*. We are told that Love is the important thing, not Power, and that Lawrence was too weak a character to grasp this point. A good deal of rather pat stuff about Love (as opposed to Power) has been going on in the biography, and now we have the clinch at the end. Lawrence had such a craving for power that before he died he actually drew up a regular Nazi programme. It is a good attack, because it makes you see much more in the book when you re-read it, but Lawrence knew much more than Kingsmill about the way these two principles interact. I think he balances them like a great rock. The trouble is that the balance is worked entirely from the Temperament; he swings one way till he feels it is sickening, and then heaves up the other way, swearing. He is altogether too free from the capacity to draw up a political programme. But he gets all round his topic – the ugliness of the Power group of feelings when they go wrong and their poetry and effectiveness when they can be done right. And if the Nazis can cash in on that line of wisdom they are simply being effective; it is no use pretending that they invented it. For that matter the book also answers Mr Eliot's remarks about him (in a review of *Son of Woman*),[1] an attack on his Love. Mr Eliot said that it was absurd to suppose the love of two persons for one another was enough unless supplemented by the love of God, adding at this point a pawky footnote, that of course a common interest in e.g. tariff reform might appear a working substitute for God. Lawrence is saying here, and it seems obviously truer, that a complete life needs elements of all three types, none of them substitutes. He is an irritating and self-indulgent writer but keeps seeming larger than the attacks on him. . . .

Many of the literary, in fact, seem to be sweeping into pacificism and quietism and Nirvana, not of course simply to stave off the German bomber, but to show how much nobler we are, on our side, than the Nazis are. The Nazis have come to replace the Victorians as the people who invented all the more disagreeable facts of life; we may yet get to the extreme case where everything written in metre is called Nazi poetry, because things written in metre are not free. But this is not probable because the communists have also to be evaded. Really it seems to me foolish to attack Lawrence merely because he was ready to consider the psychology of power – bad thinking and bad politics. It is not a question of being on the Hun side of a simple alternative. People enjoy within limits the actual processes of ruling and of being ruled, and it is necessary that they should, or civilised societies couldn't happen. [Empson Papers]

Note

1 T. S. Eliot reviewed *Son of Woman: The Story of D. H. Lawrence*, by John Middleton Murry, in *Criterion*, X (July 1931), pp. 768–74.

Lady Chatterley Again

Essays in Criticism, XIII: i, January 1963

John Peter, in Essays in Criticism *(October 1962), took issue with two articles by John Sparrow in* Encounter *(February and June 1962) which argued that D. H. Lawrence had woven a panegyric of sodomy into* Lady Chatterley's Lover *(chapter 17). Peter rejected the imputation of unnatural intercourse, but Sparrow reiterated his argument in* Essays in Criticism *(XIII: iii, July 1963), where he explained his view that Lawrence's approval of anal intercourse 'was limited to cases where the parties were of opposite sexes, just as his hero sought by means of this act to "burn the shame" out of his mistress, so Lawrence was seeking to persuade his readers that it was not a thing to be ashamed of, but a proper element in a full sexual relationship between man and woman'. In this instance Empson supported his old contemporary and sparring partner (see 'I. A. Richards and Practical Criticism' above), who had become Warden of All Souls College, Oxford, in 1952; John Peter stuck to his case in* Essays in Criticism, *XIII: iii (July 1963).*

Mr Peter makes a gallant defence, but the Warden could still claim that no one had 'even attempted to pick a hole in the *nexus*' of his reasoning. After quoting a long description of the seventh amorous encounter of Connie and Mellors, he said in effect, 'What was she so ashamed of? What seemed to her new and frightening, after she had made so much progress in the six previous lessons? And why did she not get the usual pleasure, though she felt satisfied afterwards?' Then Mellors's wife turns up and accuses him of unnatural pleasures, and Connie reflects jealously that he had 'known all that sensuality' even with his wife. To deny that Lawrence intended the inference here only makes him look ignorant. During the second half of 1961 five critics printed a belief or suspicion that he did mean it, and judging from the conditions of publication they must have decided independently; except that (as I understand) the idea had come quite near the level of consciousness by the end of the trial itself.

Mr Peter replies: 'One does not need to practise them to know that there are dozens of sexual procedures which diminish the woman's pleasure'; but he does not explain why the one adopted satisfied the deepest longing of Connie by affronting her deepest shame, nor yet why Lawrence tacitly recommends it. I think he has only one argument that needs answering; Mellors in chapter 14 grumbles against women who love feeling and cuddling, every kind of going off except the natural one: 'They always want you to go off when you're *not* in the one place where you should be, when you go off.' But the grumble is that these women try to enjoy themselves, instead of letting the man master them. They are particularly well mastered if the man uses the anus instead of the adjacent vagina, as we are told of Connie – 'It cost her an effort to let him have his will and his way of her. She had to be a passive consenting thing, like a slave, a physical slave.' Mellors would only laugh at the pedantry of anyone who called him inconsistent there.

Professor Kermode, I thought, printed the best comment; that Lawrence thought Connie mentally very sick and only to be cured by drastic treatment, like the old-style lancing of a boil. She, like her whole civilisation, needed a 'gros baiser'. This is morally much beter than what Mr Peter imputes to Lawrence; but we still need to plumb into Kermode's French and ask why this particular kiss was expected to heal her. It is one of the few basic ideas of Lawrence that the emancipation of Western women is driving them mad, because a woman needs to be mastered, and therefore western civilisation will soon collapse. His disciples tend to ignore the doctrine, and maybe it is what Mr Peter is resisting here. I think it is all nonsense, myself; what would he have made of the emancipated women of communist China? Women do not require bullying; men can keep their mental health under a regime of bullying better then women can. To be sure, a woman likes to feel in the hands of a reliable man; and so does a reliable man. It is clear from the many reports of the Lawrence menage that Lawrence himself, to his credit, had no direct knowledge of what he was recommending; and I don't think he succeeds in imagining Connie as a patient who could only be cured by the treatment he describes. The story is thus rather like a daydream about a Limerick.

All the same, Lawrence was deeply informed and sympathetic, and likely to have got hold of some important idea.

She would have thought a woman would have died of shame. Instead of which, the shame died. Shame, which is fear; the deep organic shame, the old, old physical fear which crouches in the bodily roots of us, and can only be chased away by the sensual fire.

But how old? Not implanted by evolution into our 'bodily roots'. Ralph

Hodgson told me about 1932 that the human disgust for turds must have been acquired by natural selection at the start of the Neolithic, because all villages died of typhoid except those few which made a cult of shame; and that the civilised mind was still contorted by this initial struggle. The thought is so much of Lawrence's period that I expect he meant it by 'old, old', which is otherwise panting nonsense.

How she had really wanted it! She knew now. At the bottom of her soul, fundamentally, she had needed the phallic hunting out, and she had believed she would never get it.

But what was being hunted? It has been argued that Mellors entered the vagina from behind, which many peoples consider normal; to do so makes the cervix, the mouth of the womb, harder to reach, among Nordics at any rate, so that Mellors would be setting himself a handicap:

...it took some getting at, the core of the physical jungle, the last and deepest recess of organic shame. The phallus alone could explore it!

If the phallus is going up the end of the digestive tube, it is pathetically little able to explore that mystery – about as long as a cricket pitch, with the last eight inches or so usually empty. We need to find something other than the cervix for the 'core' to be, or Mr Peter's side wins after all.

A man has the prostate gland which can be stimulated through the anus, and it is liable to go frighteningly wrong even without. A woman has nothing so specific there, but she can get pleasure from the inside of the whole ring of bone through which a child is born; the chief cause of her birth-pangs is also one of her deepest areas of satisfaction. To awaken her all round in this way is not a sordid ambition, and the hands may well be working on it while the normal act is in progress. Probably this was Lawrence's basis in experience for the phrases about exploring the jungle, and probably he was drawing upon folklore for the belief that sodomy is the way to melt the frigidity of a lady. (Professor Wilson Knight in describing the row about Byron quoted a man making this charitable reflection – *Lord Byron's Marriage*, p. 252). We should remember that the earlier novels take a rather mysterious stand on telling men to refuse orgasms to women, or at least to refuse one kind of orgasm; and at one point the hero's penis is hurt by the beaklike cervix of an elderly admirer, who is denounced for doing it on purpose though unconsciously. The excitable areas around the cervix, I take it, were what a man should protect himself by refusing to satisfy, and the woman should accept a longer act of pleasure which gave her a more diffused kind of satisfaction. It sounds cuckoo and maybe it is, but it is not merely an excuse invented by Lawrence; for instance, what appears to be the same discipline for the harem crops up in Dr Needham's great treatise on Chinese science (Vol. II, pp. 146–52).[1] At any rate, in supposing that Lawrence thought sodomy would be good for Connie, one is not making him inconsistent with the beliefs he had published before.

Information in this field is hard to come by. I revere however the capacity of Professor Wilson Knight to stretch out his hand and say, without requiring to know the practical details, 'This means something noble'; before his colleagues have even got upset about them.

On an undated page among his notes Empson once wrote:

Now that the great battle for frankness has been won, or so people seem to think, now that A. Huxley the lost Leader is always telling people that they have the millennium already and oughtn't to like it, surely it is curious that so little of the Wisdom of the Ages has actually been printed. When I first got to Changsha [in 1937, during Empson's period of teaching with the Combined Universities in flight from the Japanese: see *The Royal Beasts and Other Works*, London: Chatto & Windus, 1986] the main thing to do was to help agree on a skeleton library for the English School, to be sent out when possible, and as we thought closely of names and got to D. H. Lawrence, George Yeh [then Professor of English] said to me, 'Yes, *Lady Chatterley*' and put that down alone. I kind of minced a bit at this, and he said, 'Well, that's the only one where he got anything said he wanted to say, isn't it?' – or I understood him to mean that, if he didn't say it. It is painfully true, and he only says one thing, as far as I remember, about how ageing women get a power to hurt the men who please them and enjoy it. Only one *physiological* thing, you understand; and maybe he only wanted to talk about the spirit. But granting he wanted to say things of this kind he made a poor list of them. Half the men you meet in a decent bar could say a good deal more; I could give one or two tips myself. [Empson Papers]

In a letter of 10 February 1957 Empson had written to compliment Graham Hough on his 'excellent book on D. H. Lawrence' (The Dark Sun: A Study of D. H. Lawrence, *London: Gerald Duckworth, 1956):*

I can't expect [Lawrence] to be wise because it seems (for instance) that after Lady Ottoline Morrell had helped him by asking him round to meet some people he published the profound thought (thinly disguised) that it was because of her murderous hatred for men that the mouth of her womb had hardened into a beak which scratched the cock of any man who poked her. Now, if this had been physically true, any man capable of blowing his own nose and fond of the woman could have handled it, I suggest by wearing plasticine under a French letter. But as she had never let him go to bed with her at all the invention seems to me just farcically caddish, a long way beyond the invention of Evelyn Waugh. The theory that a really manly man does not allow the woman he is enjoying to have an orgasm seems to me to have the same quality of pathetically ignorant nastiness. It was a Victorian middle-class theory about one's wife, often earnestly held (a class where men tend to marry late in life might intelligibly feel that to avoid awakening the wife's desire would avoid the dangers both of overstraining the old man and of making the wife want adultery); Lawrence no doubt heard it said and felt it was the kind of Puritanism he liked to boast of; but I bet it wasn't working-class, and I bet he only took it up because he wasn't adequate for Frieda. The picture of him surrounded by adoring unsatisfied women who say 'Isn't he original?' when he writes down 'The moon is a glowing core of phosphorus' and suchlike in the *Unconsciousness* books does not make one expect him to say anything wise. I cannot respect him either for being so interested in homosexuality and never daring to have any experience of it. I do not think him very outspoken about sex, because it seems to me he must have meant something quite simple in *Women in Love* about why one pair of lovers was bad and the other good in spite of 'exploring the dark depths of shame', something quite simple about what they did in bed, but he left the novel as an obscurantist tease because he didn't dare to say what it was. The best book about him, I still think, is poor old Hugh Kingsmill's which you do not allow into your bibliography. But still I think yours is a splendid book; it is a fine flower of the wilful refusal to attend to biography; it sticks to the text only till that process feels [like] Simon Stylites or the man who always faints after running a mile in four minutes (the science journals have been telling us that the trick is he doesn't breathe, but I may have got this slightly wrong).

However, looking over the pages I have dog-eared again, I think you do manage to get in a great deal of comment from a basis of human experience while maintaining the technical status of a judge who has only access to the text. It makes the book too impressive to be ignored. [Empson Papers]

Note

1 See 'The Wisdom of the East' below.

'Zuleika Dobson'

1944

Maybe it is not really outmoded a great deal, but what social changes there have been make it depend more on the structure and fundamental plot than it did thirty-five years ago; Beerbohm no doubt would have always wanted his smart book to be judged in this way at bottom.

However facetiously it can be dressed up the story is of course tragic; the conflict of two prides makes it impossible for the hero and heroine to be happy together though they seem designed for one another, and each can love the other only when unloved. This structure can carry any amount of comic decoration. The trouble is that the crisis of the plot is one of the comic details which can only be accepted as a joke, and this makes the story silly; the arch collapses not under the weight of ornament but because a bit of ornament is used as the keystone.

I think this is true, but a lot can be said on the other side. Dorset has decided to kill himself out of despairing love for Zuleika and on his last night finds that he doesn't love her and rejoices in his freedom. Early in the morning he receives a telegram from his butler saying that the ancestral tokens have been observed and his death is therefore foredoomed. Rather than confess the absurdity of the position (since he must die anyway) he dies in the pretence that the suicide is for love of Zuleika, and all the undergraduates of Oxford (whom he would prefer to save) die with him out of snobbery. Now of course Beerbohm is playing with literary models, but it would be silly to object that the belief in fate is itself only silly. The heroes of the *Iliad* do something very near to what Dorset does; they behave as they believe they should in spite of the foreknowledge of doom. But they think it would be their duty to fight (and recover the corpse of Patroclus and so forth) whatever was fated; their doom does not order them about because they ignore it as far as they can. The gods are impressive in Homer because they are only symbols of the necessity of the case; or rather, what is a more serious way of putting it from the point of view of readers who believed in the gods, they are worth reverence because even when they interfere in an unfair manner they are at any rate concerned with the human partisans. The gods in Beerbohm are not even enemies of Dorset; they only want an amusing bit of irony, just as the author does.

This is not Greek, but it might be Shakespearean. 'As flies to wanton boys, are we to the gods;/They kill us for their sport'; and the death of Cordelia at the end of *Lear* is in accordance with this comment because it is hardly more than bad luck. Shakespeare does not do this elsewhere, and I think he brings it off here because of the stress on lunacy in the play and the elaborate symbolism about 'fools' as clowns. Talk about 'the gods' was forced on him by the supposed date of the pre-Christian story and the Elizabethan censorship arrangements for the theatre, which forbade the name of God, and he used the pagan gods as symbols of the clumsiness and confusion of Nature. The gods become fools like the characters. They are endurable because we are not asked to respect them and because they symbolise something real; unendurable accidents do happen. It seems that Thomas Hardy was using this rather accidental tradition for his solemn 'pessimism' when he produced the 'Spirit Ironical' in the *Dynasts* and the remarks about the gods 'finishing their sport' with Tess of the D'Urbervilles. But nobody is allowed to call Hardy's Spirit Ironical a clown; it is a pompous upper-class entity in the clouds uttering part of the sentiments of Thomas Hardy. The belief that Nature is deliberately planning to make human efforts ridiculous seems to be a really nasty backwash of superstition, with no scientific evidence in its favour, bred among Victorian rationalists in their struggles to get away from God. Beerbohm was banking on the false solemnity of Hardy when he tried to palm off the crisis of his story as a profound piece of fun.

Though this is I think the historical set-up the crisis of *Zuleika Dobson* might escape on its own merits. It would really have been embarrassing for Dorset not to kill himself after he had tried to dissuade the other undergraduates by warning them of his own fate. The book makes the American Rhodes Scholar tell him he would be a skunk if he did not kill himself. It insists however that the pride of Dorset was quite enough to carry him through this petty embarrassment. The later ancestral warning which he at once accepts can be taken I suppose as a warning from the depths of his own nature that in some other way he could not stand the ignominy of the refusal; it was not a matter of personal pride but of his whole position in his society. All the other undergraduates were going to kill themselves whether he did or not, and if he failed he would be hounded down; the thing has become so public that the contrast between what his own pride can carry off and what his ducal house can carry off is a real and practical one. It is in this way I think that the book will be interpreted by readers and will continue to be read with pleasure.

But all the same I think that the blank acceptance of the telegram from the butler at the crisis of the story is a silly piece of facetiousness; the snob appeal of the joke is a slavish one, and indeed leaves the reader equally slavish whether he accepts aristocracy as a principle or rejects it. If he accepts it he must follow any ruling from accepted powers such as the butler however patently false; if he rejects it he must feel that all such crucial decisions are fatuous and withdraw to save his own skin while claiming that his skin is a spiritual one.

Then again you must admit that Beerbohm, with his cult derived from Baudelaire about what an English dandy ought to be, could not have written his story better; the symbol is exact; the dandy must be ready to accept very odd and entirely unintelligible rulings (to a dandy) about what his position requires. Even historically it is a just satire; four years after the book was published such people did go and die in Flanders with few reasons that they could have named outside those in the book. Yet from this background (regarding it, I mean, as a pre-1914 pacifist tract) it is I think seen all the more clearly as a silly satire. Whatever the French may have thought up about the English milord the real English class feelings have the merit of being peculiarly un-dandy; unlike most of Europe the English aristocracy was putting the younger sons into trade in the Middle Ages, and the practice was only partially and delusively interrupted by the increase of money available for corruption in the eighteenth century. However misguided and unformulated the feelings may have been, the whole historical picture hinted at by *Zuleika Dobson* is a delusion; the undergraduates did not die in imitation of the Duke (even if that was all they could say about it) and even he did not die because his butler told him to.

The body of doctrine about dandies deriving from Baudelaire really has some truth I should say about artists, one which an artist may often have to face with heroism. But the trick of the nineties (particularly of Oscar Wilde) was to tie this on to politics and claim that the dandy ruled the world; he was the unacknowledged legislator of Shelley's epigram, though not yet 'outcast' because he had not yet been found out. Dorset in *Zuleika Dobson* has got the Garter robes to die in because he played with politics carelessly at a crucial moment. Dear me, of course it would be nonsense to say that artists ought to be cut off from the work of government, but I think there is some real delusion about the political role of the dandy which makes the book petty. Maybe the reason for dissatisfaction can be brought down to no more than this: you feel that if Beerbohm had been able to see round his subject he could have made it an enormous one.

A Family Monster

Nation, 7 December 1946

Franz Kafka, *Metamorphosis*

This brief masterpiece is so direct, so like a punch on the jaw, that there should be little to say about it. But the introduction and the illustrations of the first American edition are so wrong-headed that they provide employment for a critic. The story is that a youngish man, who is supporting his parents and sister as a much-bullied commercial traveller, wakes up to find himself turned into a monstrous 'vermin' (the charlady says 'cockroach') of human size. The other three have to get jobs, and take in lodgers; the sufferer hides in his bedroom, and the sister in spite of her loathing makes efforts to keep him comfortable. His father is afraid of him and once injures him when driving him back to his room. The lodgers give notice when they discover him. But by then he has almost completed the process of starving himself to death, which he undertakes because he is so hopeless and such a drag on his family. At the end the sister is beginning to say that this is not her brother but only a monster which it is essential to kill, but we do not know whether they would act on it. All the family are trying to behave well. Once he is dead they find they are better off than when he was normal, because they have all got jobs, and having something to do the father has recovered his vigour. It is time the girl got married.

The introduction says that Kafka describes animals in all possible ways at once; as in a fable, where they are like men; as having qualities also interesting in men; as themselves, realistically; and as men acting as beasts. 'He makes an identification of man and beast. Kafka's animals are *totems*.' In accordance with this view, the pictures at the two ends of the book show dogs and pussycats in human poses, and the picture of the monster in the middle, swaggering in white tights, plumes, and a military carapace, might be a society portrait of Lord Byron fighting for the Greeks. Of course it is in a sort of Picasso style, but everyone knows that isn't meant to be horrid; it can be used to advertise ladies' underwear. Now I think that all this gives an entirely false idea of the story. The point which the story rams home is that the monster is unbearably nauseating, not in the least like a pussycat. The question of what the actual feelings of a man-sized woodlouse would be (he has more legs than a cockroach) is obviously not considered by the author, except perhaps in the one remark that his legs enjoy running. So far from being like *any* animal, for that matter, the sufferer is always human and nearly always high-minded. What he chiefly reminds me of is an elephant-iasis case described by a doctor ten or more years ago in a horrible book called *The Elephant Man*, who had an even more unbreakable sweetness of temperament in spite of the loathing which his body inspired. The whole story, indeed, might have been told about a real disease, and would only have lost (what is no doubt its chief value) the wild poetry and the sense of the appalling strangeness of the world.

If this is true, you may say, it is very unlike *The Castle* and *The Trial*. I don't deny that the book satisfied the neurotic side of Kafka as well as the mystical one. No doubt the preface is right in quoting the reproach which Kafka supposed his father to give him, that he fought his father like vermin which both sting and suck blood. But though the first idea was a justifi-cation of the vermin, that is, the young writer who refused to get a job, the story as it worked out rose entirely away from those foggy troubles and became clear-cut in the sunlight. I think there is a lurking bit of neurosis right at the end, when we are told that the sister looked healthy 'despite the make-up which made her cheeks look pale'. She was dressed before she knew her brother was dead, but she had no need to pretend to be pale. It is a typical piece of the puzzle-technique which is used so magnificently in other Kafka books; not really out of place, because she might easily have been dramatising the situation a bit, but quite trivial here; whereas in *The Trial* it would have carried some monstrous and enervating suspicion. It is also part of the Kafka atmosphere that the monster never tries to speak after the first day, though his mother certainly understood one thing he said through the door before she saw him ('he must be ill, even though he denied it this morning'), so that if he had had the courage to go on talking he would have been less completely cut off. Here, you may say, is the wilful defeatism of the usual Kafka; but you can also believe that the man would have acted so within the framework of the story. Indeed, the real Elephant Man, during the years he was with the travelling show, was never spoken to because everyone assumed he was imbecile. It is because the story is so real that the spangles tucked onto it by this edition look so tasteless.

However, there are several minor inconsistencies. For instance, his back is described as a hard carapace onto which this large animal can fall without getting hurt, but his father can throw a 'red' (therefore presumably soft) apple which cracks it and makes it fester; no doubt it is the apple of Adam, but one wants the details more convincing. And the statement of p. 59 that he had not heard his mother's voice 'for so long' is quite incompatible with the previous story, though here there seems to be no symbolical excuse. Considering how much he is supposed to stink, it is unlikely that they would take to leaving his door open in the evening so that he can watch them; but perhaps this shows how remorseful his father was for throwing the apple. After the apple incident there could surely be no question of 'cleaning himself several times a day by lying on his back and rubbing against the carpet' (p. 83). In the other major Kafka books one feels sure the contradictions are intentional, indeed the more baffling they are the more carefully they seem placed; but this is a different kind of story and does not need them. Maybe he could never bear to read over the manuscript.

'The Minister's Black Veil'
[Nathaniel Hawthorne]

c. 1950

This story, it seems to me, cannot properly be called ambiguous because the intended reader knows quite well what it all means but is too afraid and ashamed to let on; its appearance of being ambiguous is therefore an insinuating pretence. The young minister, brought up to attach unique importance to ideal love, and daydream about it, but never to have any sexual contact, is addicted to masturbation; this causes intense shame and depression, and he is especially afraid of being caught at it by a woman, since he believes that women are incapable of it. By the age of thirty, after a long engagement to an equally pious girl, he believes he would be incapable of normal sex with her; but similar feelings are excited by any likely sexual partner (he had not had any previous relations with the girl he sees dead).

The author regards all this as a usual result of the Puritan way of life, though heightened to an exasperating degree in a devoted minister; it is not a result of an unusual failure in the system, but a thing to be regularly expected; and he must realise that it is a very bad one. He pretends to think it good, maybe, so as to startle some of his readers into realising how bad it is; but meanwhile he uses his apparent approval to heighten his general dramatic tone of sickened and despairing secrecy. I am not clear about the moment when the young man tells his young woman that in Heaven there will be no darkness between their souls – surely a real Puritan of that time (it is assumed that the story happens at least a century before the writing of it) would believe he was going to Hell for it. Here he seems to take a 'modern' or 'advanced' view, regarding his shame as merely part of living in a body, not as a mortal sin; and perhaps this was necessary to make the reader Hawthorne aimed at able to accept his frame of mind. We are told that he preached gently, not (that is) trying to make the hearers realise the pains of Hell; perhaps the first readers were meant to deduce that he did not really believe in it, any more than they did, but that this relief did little to reduce the intensity of his neurotic condition.

The only positively dishonest bit, I should say, is when the author says that the hero's condition did a lot of good; especially when he preached the election sermon, and

wrought so deep an impression that the legislative measures of that year were characterised by all the gloom and piety of our earliest ancestral sway.

Much the most probable meaning of these carefully chosen words is that he induced them to burn witches again, however much against his intention; his artificially produced sexual disorder excites a public craving to gloat over tortures. It may be said that this sentence is intended as an irony, but if so not nearly enough is done to alert the intended reader; so far from that, gloating over the tortures of deluded old women seems to be recommended as part of the holy frame of mind, so earnestly revered throughout the story, a beautiful old-world virtue which we should all labour to retain, even if we have lost the theological beliefs upon which it was once supported. Not only tormenting young people about their sex, but also burning old women alive, are positively good activities, even if done without the beliefs which once partly excused them.

This, I submit, is propaganda work, very easily calculated; and as such very unlike a poetical ambiguity, which comes from thinking spontaneously about a complex situation. However, I don't deny of course that there may be poetical ambiguities in prose, as when we are told of Mr Hooper that the black veil 'enabled him to sympathise with all dark affections' (such as the affection of James II for the torture-chamber, I suppose; he could no more be kept away from it, when in Scotland to deal with the Covenanters, than the traditional boy from the jam cupboard). Hawthorne is an aesthetic writer, I don't deny, a premature decadent, in fact; but I think the result is shockingly nasty.

Humanism and Mr Bloom

New Statesman and Nation, 11 August 1956

Hugh Kenner, *Dublin's Joyce*

For a third of a century, critics have gone on assuming that the plot of *Ulysses* is positively intended to be nerve-wrackingly and needlingly pointless, except so far as it drives home that nothing and nobody in Dublin was good enough for Joyce. This of course makes them think the book frightful, whether they admire it or not. I think the whole idea is wrong; he meant it as a very gay book, about how he escaped from the appalling condition in which he describes himself. There really was an Ur-Molly, and when he looked back he felt she had saved him. She was the first woman not a prostitute he got to bed with, and she broke the dichotomy of thinking all women either sexless or vampirish; a few months after that, he was able to win the devoted Nora and induce her to run away with him; after that, he was a settled character, with no more autobiography that he had a duty to tell. It must have been a great relief when he decided that that brief affair with poor old Molly could truly be described as the turning-point; 'Thank God I needn't drag my wife in' would be the first reflection of the author famous for his shamelessness. Of course altering Molly out of all recognition was also a duty, but an entertaining and creative one.

A second happy ending is adumbrated in the book so long regarded as consecrated to frustration. The whole point of the correspondence to the *Odyssey* is that Bloom somehow gets back his wife and his son. Now both Bloom and his wife are described, with intense pathos, as aching to have a son; and Bloom is given a very special psychology such that the results of this day might enable him to do it. The death of his baby ten years before gave him such a horror of the whole process of having children that he hasn't copulated with his wife since; but if he could arrange a *ménage à trois* with Stephen, as he very frankly hints to Stephen that he wants to do, incidentally getting rid of her present lover whom he detests and launching Stephen as a concert-singer, then he might recover his nerve. The book refuses to tell us whether this happened, except indeed by the correspondence to the *Odyssey* and the almost incessant symbolism about paternity and childbirth; because it is constructed as an Ibsenite Eternal Problem, ending while the exhausted Stephen cannot yet decide – that of course is the point of the Question-and-Answer chapter. But I do not believe that Joyce could have invented such a story (that was his only weak point as a novelist); and one must remember that he made his friends treat Bloomsday as his private Christmas, an occasion for vaguely farcical rejoicing; I think the reason for this glee was that the Ur-Molly, later on, did have a son, by the Ur-Bloom. Also he enjoyed having something to hide which he had already told to posterity; indeed, the situation is one which novelists do not dare to treat.

I am less sure of the second happy ending; that is, less sure that it really happened – obviously, I think, the opportunity for it is the central drama of the novel. In any case, it seems to me extraordinary that all critics take for granted Stephen never returned to the Blooms. To be sure, he calls them his doom, but every time he has seen a doom so far he has run smack into it as fast as he could go. He has promised to come back ('ratified, reconfirmed' it) and he greatly despises people who break their promises. He has not yet seen Molly, and the Bloom Offer must at least excite curiosity; and his various quarrels have left him practically nothing else to do. He goes away because his pride forbids him to meet her first as a stray cat brought in by Bloom during the night; also, no doubt, to decide when sober. I think the critics have been too ready to swallow the melodrama of the starving idealist who rejects everybody and walks out by himself into the night.

Mr Hugh Kenner has produced a vigorous book of exegesis on Joyce, pointing out a variety of 'influences' and showing in detail how they work as correlations in the text (there has been much more of such work in America than in England); and he can't be called merely a 'verbalist', because he gives a massive historical background to his picture of total despair. Writing from California, he has a generous respect for the now extinct virtues of European philosophy and social life, and explains that a last gleam of them survived in Dublin at the date of the story of *Ulysses*, though not elsewhere. None had ever reached the Norway of Ibsen, and Joyce had to fight to get free from Ibsen – the reason why the play *Exiles* is so bad is that it is a kind of satire on Ibsen. (I find this very absurd.) In *Ulysses* he meant not only to describe this last gleam but to present it as the very end of a great historical period; whereas in *Finnegans Wake* all he had left to describe was the echo of it in the mind of his bedridden father, who lay in Dublin bursting with grand stories of his own past and of what the town had been like before Healy and De Valera. I think this human approach to *Finnegan* is extremely penetrating, and there seems no doubt that Joyce did mosaic a lot of grumbling about local politics, with supposed world background, into that text (surely it was very absurd for Joyce and

Pound to make political recommendations in a style which could not affect votes); but Mr Kenner gives no reason for supposing that the same is true of the earlier *Ulysses*. So far from having a human approach there, he denies that Stephen represents the young Joyce at all, even in the *Portrait of the Artist as a Young Man*. Stephen represents a type incapable of development (p. 112), the heir of Hume, Shelley, H. G. Wells and all *that* lot, for whom Joyce, we are to gather, felt the same unqualified contempt as Mr Kenner does. Joyce in fact was simply a Roman Catholic philosopher, devoted to Aquinas and occupied in bemoaning the whole of European thought since the Renaissance. Now, on the face of it, Joyce consistently said he had rejected violently the religion he had been brought up in; surely there is a tiny suggestion of special pleading if a critic takes for granted that every implication of that is only 'irony.'

The theology, of course, alters the literary effect; for example, the endings of all three novels have to be called 'ironical'. 'Some critics have oversentimentalised' the exultant last words of Molly in *Ulysses*; they only 'mark her authority over this animal kingdom of the dead' (p. 262). Mr Kenner regrets that Joyce 'for structural reasons' had to put the Anna Livia episode, in which for once 'writer and reader are being borne along,' at the end of *Finnegans Wake*; people like it best and think it representative of the book, whereas the really high-minded parts are the nasty-tempered ones (p. 298). The last forty pages of the *Portrait*, in which the liberated Stephen feels that life is opening before him, are described as 'painful reading'; but they are all right once you realise that the author despises 'life', as Mr Kenner does, and meant you to despise the whole triumphant end of his book (p. 121). There is a similar point about *Exiles* (p. 89).

This disgust for life, of course, explains why such critics never think it would be a happy ending for Bloom to get the son he wants; a 'spiritual' son is all a philosopher could want. To be a real father is quite shocking: 'The panther-theme exfoliates into an image of paternity *secundum carnem*, laying its curse on all the inhabitants of this animal hell' (p. 246); as for mother-love, it is 'rank nursery sentimentality' (p. 306). But Joyce was a family man himself, and not at all afraid of sentiment; also he was cross with priests and their claim to spiritual paternity; in his mind, only a real son for Bloom would count. The contrast is carried very far. Answering an old objection of Mr Wyndham Lewis, that there are no interesting ideas in the book,[1] Mr Kenner is triumphant: 'It is precisely the pathetic absurdity of Bloom's and Stephen's bits and pieces of speculation that is being exposed' (p. 209). He points out the happiness for a fit reader of watching this exposure; it is like the bliss which the blessed were said to extract, as he recalls with complacent approval, from their perpetual view of the tortures of the damned (p. 157). Now I think that to read Joyce like this, as solely concerned to jeer at all human affections, is to make him a very disgusting author; in fact, to make him exactly what the early critics supposed when they denounced him. To have a critic in sympathy with this frame of mind does not make it any more agreeable.

Perhaps to strengthen his position, Mr Kenner jeers at the *'transition'* group, who rallied round Joyce, and at Joyce's biographer, Stuart Gilbert, whom he helped with inside information; Joyce, he feels, must have been jeering at them in his heart (p. 360). I expect he thought his friends decent people enough, but I too need to maintain that he kept a secret from them. This is not unlikely, because it was the duty of a disciple of Ibsen who had written a Problem Novel; only if the public worked out the meaning for themselves, by a gradual process of debate and turmoil, would it enter deeply into their minds. He would endure a great deal of denigration for this high purpose. But, then again, he was a very self-important man, rightly enough; he was unlikely to think that nothing important had happened at the crisis of his autobiography, and he was very unlikely to present to the world, under the guise of himself when young, a character totally incapable of developing into a creative writer. If he had lived long enough to see his books made respectable for classrooms at the cost of this frightful distortion, there seems no doubt, he would have been driven to break his conscientious silence.

We didn't in England have such thorough controversy over 'humanism', twenty or thirty years ago, as the Americans did; though Dr Leavis has rather the same resonance. We do not therefore easily realise that the reason why Bloom, Stephen, Hume, Shelley and so forth are all treated as sub-human by Mr Kenner is that they are 'humanists'. It strikes me that the anti-humanists, now that they are a secure orthodoxy, are overplaying their hand.

Note

1 Wyndham Lewis alleged, for example, that the 'radical conventionality of outlook ... exhibited in the treatment of the characters' in *Ulysses* 'is invariably the sign of the simple craftsman – an absence of meaning, an emptiness of philosophic content, a poverty of new and disturbing observation' (*Time and Western Man*, London: Chatto & Windus, 1927, p. 119).

Laying Joyce Bare

New Statesman, 20 June 1959

E. Mason and R. Ellmann (eds.),
The Critical Writings of James Joyce

Some reviews have rather jeered at this collection, as a plainly empty labour of scholarly piety or mere book-making, and indeed the editors mildly remark almost at the end, while considering Joyce's refusal to write a preface in 1932, when he had every reason of friendship and conviction to do it, that 'he was not going to play the man of letters after avoiding the role all his life'. But he could not avoid it altogether, and you need to know what he put his name to if you care to check the interpretations of his work. Besides, considering how determined he was to do it only with his left foot, he doesn't come out at all badly.

There has been a tendency to argue that he never really quarrelled with the Church, and he certainly differed from his brother Stanislaus, who hated it as much as he did the drink, an upbringing which might have been expected to be disastrous. Joyce remarked to Padraic Colum in later years, speaking of his youthful revolt: 'It was not a question of belief. It was a question of celibacy. I knew I could not live the life of a celibate.' This might appear to settle the point, but on the evidence here (and of course elsewhere) his decision must be put back into his teens. Joyce, when he said it, no doubt felt that he was being generous and unself-important, and could have found grander terms for preferring normal life if he chose; but the joke presumes that he would have been accepted as a priest, which would probably not have been an unself-important thing to presume when he first took this line. We can none of us be sure how we first arrived at our opinions, and can only test whether we have adequate grounds for them now. Joyce is already in 1901 (when nineteen) determined to express his reverence for Bruno, whom the Catholics burned, and explains in 1903, writing in the notoriously pro-English Dublin *Daily Express*, that this was for Bruno's 'vindication of the freedom of intuition'; 'religion and all that is allied thereto can manifestly persuade men to great evil' comes in 1902, and a more sectarian reference to 'the horrible image of the Jansenist Christ' in 1903. There is a break in the record of his public expressions of opinion till 1907, when he lectures to 'a kind of adult education centre in Trieste', and writes his text merely because he doubts whether his Italian is good enough to lecture extempore. The first lecture, while bursting with the wrongs of Ireland, contains the fine sentence:

I confess that I do not see what good it does to fulminate against the English tyranny while the Roman tyranny occupies the palace of the soul.

For that matter, the piece in the style of *Finnegans Wake*, so rightly printed by the *New Statesman* in 1932, 'From a Banned Writer to a Banned Singer', passionately trying to get a job for the Irish opera tenor John Sullivan (and surely it is needlessly dismal for this chatty book to remark that the campaign 'was not altogether successful' but not let out why it wasn't altogether successful), manages to drag in an appalling series of rhymes about the Paris churches preparing for the Massacre of St Bartholomew.

Get ready, get ready, scream the bells of Our Lady. And make sure they're quite killed, adds the gentle Clothilde. Your attention, sirs, please, bawls big Brother Surplice.

Come to think of it, I suppose this was where George Orwell drew up Big Brother from, in the wells of his memory, when he wrote *1984*. So I think it is wrong to argue that this author was really half in favour of the Church that had schooled him. Following Ibsen and whatnot, he rather tiresomely treated it as a heroic duty never to tell us what he really did think, and also (as he lets leak out, so that the programme was not a sensible one) he felt it would not be sensible to remain permanently cross with a large part of the world, as brother Stanislaus did; but, all the same, his Irish tongue continued to be terrible against Catholicism whenever he let it loose.

Whether he ever weakened about that seemed to me the main interest of the book, and there is really not much else to look for. It seems he told the Italians that a Pope gave Ireland to the English and also to one of his bastards, and that Queen Victoria sent ten pounds to the Irish Famine Relief Fund but got it back by return of post, and that Blake's wife was so injured in one of his quarrels with her that she was unable to have the children which Blake longed for. Joyce was obviously very good as a retailer of legends; and I do not think we English need call this trait particularly Irish, now that we consider we have the Irish off our consciences, because it seems to go more generally with an intransigent or maverick frame of mind. The claim behind his legends would always be that they are the essential truth even if they don't fit the individual; a point of view expressed once for all by the boy Joyce while praising Ibsen:

The naked drama – either the perception of a great truth, or the opening up of a great question, or a great conflict which is almost independent of the conflicting actors, and has been and is of far-reaching importance – this is what primarily rivets our attention.

Evidently he intended to carry out this programme in both *Ulysses* and *Finnegans Wake*, but the sad truth is that we are still wrangling about what the removal of the veils disclosed.

The Joyce Saga: Before Bloomsday and After

New Statesman, 31 October 1959

Richard Ellmann, *James Joyce*

It is a grand biography, and must be the last of its kind about Joyce because Mr Ellmann, as well as summarising all previous reports, has interviewed a number of witnesses who are now dead. You want this ample detail because the picture is so interesting in itself, and besides, you no longer suspect that Joyce was mad when you realise how Irish the rest of them were. The picture of father trying to strangle mother, remarking 'in a drunken fit', 'Now, by God, is the time to finish it,' and prevented by the author at the age of twelve, is now adequately balanced by the last words gasped out by father: 'Tell Jim he was born at six in the morning.' The author had written asking about this because he wanted to have his horoscope calculated, so they realised afterwards that father had not been delirious. It helps one to realise why Joyce, at the age of eighteen, spent the money for his Ibsen article on taking father to London, saving him from fights about the Boer War all the way. Not that you have to be Irish to live in this style; the aged M. Dujardin achieved it, when he rushed across the room during a recital of 'Anna Livia' and slapped the face of an American editor, supposing that he was secretly despising the thick ankles of Madame Dujardin. Joyce was a prickly friend, but not very prickly compared to this; and Mr Ellmann is fond of saying that Joyce described everyday life, without needing drama to bring out its dramatic potential, but you need to realise what kind of life he considered everyday. Then again, you need to know what Joyce was feeling because otherwise it is often hard to tell whether a passage in the novels was meant to jeer. The speech at the party in 'The Dead', where the conventional hero in his dismal style praises the unique hospitality of the Irish with applause, has struck me as an undeserved bit of satire by Joyce on his homeland; but it turns out that, after finding how much he disliked working in Rome, a great change from Trieste, he decided that his picture in *Dubliners* had left out a real virtue of the place which justice required him to include.

He takes for granted that a thing is still real though he describes it as ridiculous, an admirable trait but one that has often baffled his readers; the most striking example is Bloom's vision of his dead son at the end of the brothel chapter.

May I, however, complain about the system, now becoming universal, by which using the notes and index is made like climbing a 10-foot wall with broken bottles on it. References to source are far too hard to look up, and ought to be put at the bottom of the page; the index should either be drastically reduced or at least use different type for the (say) five out of forty numbers which somebody might really want. The question here is not only one of convenience; as the immense machine is often reporting gossip, and Mr Ellmann wrongly remarks that 'Dubliners usually make the remarks which are attributed to them' (p. 105), one often needs the source on the page. For instance, when Nora is eloping with Joyce in 1904, and they reach London, we are flatly told (p. 185) that he 'left Nora in a park for two hours while he went to see Arthur Symons. She thought he would not return.[98]' After tracking down the secret number of the chapter and reaching its note 98 we find 'Interview with Eva Joyce, 1953'. I have not space to describe what happens if you follow the index under Eva Joyce, a pious sister of Joyce who was induced for his spiritual good to travel with him to Trieste in 1909, but she was then greatly upset by being left with his young son in a park in Paris while he succeeded in recovering a ring given him by Nora, with the help of an attendant, from the bottom of a lavatory drain. Surely it is obvious that, when Eva got to Trieste and burst out at once with this wrong, Nora said, 'Arra, I never believed he'd come back to the park either'; and Eva, who disliked her two years in Trieste, had brought the accusation to quite a high polish when it was recorded forty-four years later. This is not really a scientific way to write biography. It is a libel on Nora to believe so easily that she ran away with a man whom she was expecting to abandon her; and other sources merely report her as cross at the time about the parking system (p. 190).

The inherent eeriness of going on writing *Finnegans Wake* comes out very strongly when Ezra Pound refuses to read the samples, and Joyce refuses to read the *Cantos* either, but they remain friends; most of the experimental authors of the time felt like that (Virginia Woolf felt intense despair when the last two books she saw in print came); and Mr Ellmann is right to remark that the fascination of living in this effort for seventeen years was impossible to give up, so that the depression of having nobody to appreciate it was a merely external thing. All the same, I always feel from the examples that he made it worse every time he rewrote it.

Mr Ellmann is ready to laugh at Joyce's assertions, one is glad to find, usually by calling the motive behind them personal and selfish rather than general and public-spirited; one often feels that the biographer does this out of charity, to make the novelist appear less shocking. Thus the young man gets jeered at heartily for saying he is a socialist; 'he needed a redistribution of wealth if he was to be a spendthrift'; and as for writing to his brother:

> If you look back on my relations with friends and relatives you will see that it was a youthfully exaggerated feeling of this maldisposition of affairs which urged me to pounce upon the falsehood in their attitude towards me —

the comment is, 'Socialism has rarely been defended so tortuously.' But it often has; a better retort would be that Joyce (in 1905) was parroting these advanced views. However, even that would not be an impressive retort; he went on saying he was a socialist, and showed understanding of the theory in talking about it (there is a particularly absurd jeer from Mr Ellmann at his remarks on p. 248); he remained strikingly at home with working-class people and prone to take their opinions seriously; and towards the end we find him smilingly on top of the scene of intellectual confusion: 'I am afraid poor Mr Hitler will soon have few friends in Europe apart from my nephews, Masters W. Lewis and E. Pound' (in 1934).[1] He was 'not at all offended' by a rather fierce letter about his work from H. G. Wells in 1928, feeling politically on Wells's side, whereas: 'the more I hear of the political, philosophical, ethical zeal and labours of the brilliant members of Pound's big brass band the more I wonder why I was ever let into it' (p. 621). By this time, I was wondering why Mr Ellmann found Joyce's political record so ridiculous; then I realised that, to an American, a socialist is a commie, and it would hardly be more shocking if Joyce had said he was a cannibal, so the only thing for Mr Ellmann to do is to laugh it tenderly off.

The same process, I think, goes on about Joyce's treatment of the Eternal Triangle; extremely bad motives, indeed rather lunatic ones, are attributed to him, but this is done out of charity, to hide the truth that he was toying with an unacceptable ideal. The main position of Mr Ellmann, which came out more clearly in his article 'A Portrait of the Artist As Friend' (*Kenyon Review*, Winter 1956) than here in the self-effacing biography, is that Joyce enjoyed feeling betrayed by his nearest and dearest and kept on trying to trick them into the position of having done so. No doubt a novelist usually makes the most of a situation in real life which he has been meaning to write about, because he wants to learn about it; and the account of Joyce 'helping to produce' a flirtation with his wife by his admirer Prezioso in Trieste about 1912, ending with Joyce being seen upbraiding him in the street and 'tears running down Prezioso's humiliated face', does make him seem an alarming friend, though we are given no evidence that he 'produced' the situation. He was almost crazily possessive, largely from feeling isolated, so there were bound to be convulsions whenever the triangle was approached, whether we say that he arranged it himself ('unconsciously' perhaps) or not.

What Mr Ellmann will not recognise, it strikes me, is that he earnestly considered that disposition in himself a bad one, and believed that in a better world it would be overcome; and he was particularly prone to the idea that wives, when the world coarsely calls them adulterous, are often at bottom trying to give the husband a man friend. Mr Ellmann has some useful jokes about how Dubliners consider men friends more important than women, since they meet only men during the long hours in the pubs, and indeed that women are chiefly important to them as a means for men to betray one another; but this frame of mind often goes with a deep belief that women are nobler than men, as in the great cry of Joyce in a letter to Nora: '*How on God's earth* can you possibly love a thing like me?' We are shown Joyce collecting Nora's dreams here, in 1916, as part of his field-work, with his own confident interpretations; she dreams of Prezioso weeping, and he explains the details as 'a secret disappointment that for herself so far it is impossible to unite the friendship of two men through the gift of herself differently to both'. Whatever 'differently' may amount to, this proves that he assumed the impulses of his revered wife to be pretty near what the notes for *Exiles* ascribe to the heroine:

Bertha wishes for the spiritual union of Richard and Robert, and believes that union will only be effected ... carnally through the person and body of Bertha, as they cannot, without dissatisfaction and degradation, be united carnally man to man.

Surely it is plain that Joyce considered this as one of his advanced ideals, suited to Ibsen or Blake, and not at all as a sordid technique for putting his wife and his friends in the wrong; all his writing about adultery looks different if you recognise this in the background. Mr Ellmann had every right to say in the biography that he thinks the ideal harmful and ridiculous, but he is somehow committed to a duty of insinuating that Joyce hadn't really got any revolutionary ideals at all. Even in describing the story of *Ulysses*, where it is made farcically plain that Bloom schemes to get Stephen to bed with his wife, though maybe just to drive out the present incumbent, Mr Ellmann can only bring himself to say that 'Bloom is appropriately under the influence of his wife, whom he dissatisfies (to some extent intentionally), and wishes to bring Stephen under her influence too.' No wonder critics find the book sordid and gloomy, if the hopeful and high-minded side of it must at all cost be ignored.

Before reading this, I had been arguing that probably *Ulysses* really is a bit of autobiography, as it pretends to be; because Joyce was quite unable to invent a story, and must have got to bed with a motherly woman very unlike a prostitute before he managed to induce Nora to run away with him. I still think that he probably did; consider the 'accommodating widow' in whose house the book-title *Chamber Music* was found so funny – she would look about as out of place in *Dubliners* as the Dalai Lama. But I confess now, after reading the snatches from his letters to Nora at the time, and his stubborn determination to refuse her the word 'love', that most of the credit for saving him belongs only to her. The question turns largely on the date of Bloomsday, as Joyce was superstitiously literal; and I think Mr Ellmann has cleared it up. The 10th was the day he stopped her in the street and took her name and address, but after that letters had to pass, and the 16th was the first day the hotel servant voluntarily walked out with him; so the 16th really does eternalise their first official meeting. Even so, you are ignoring his intense conviction that he is a gentleman, let alone a judge giving a slightly appalling sentence to everybody he puts in the book, if you imagine he described his wife as Molly Bloom. After he was dead somebody asked her whether she was Molly, and she said with immense truth: 'She was much fatter.' When he decided at sight in a street that he must win Nora it was a genuinely magical moment, because he seems to have imagined before that he could only marry an intolerably aristocratic woman; the stubborn good sense and gaiety of Nora, it seems, were at once visible in the way she walked, and this would make it possible for him to continue life. A splendid moment, but all the same what the novel *Ulysses* is really about cannot be thought clear from the biography. Why, for example, did Joyce remark in later life that 'the nature of the legend chosen would be enough to upset anybody's mental balance'?

Note

1 See footnote 1 on p. 631.

The Symbolism of Dickens

John Gross and Gabriel Pearson (eds.), *Dickens and the Twentieth Century*, London: Routledge & Kegan Paul, 1962

A point about *Oliver Twist* seems to me where one needs to start in considering this topic. Oliver, though a gentleman by heredity and heir to a property, has been brought up from birth in an orphanage with no other contacts; it is a wicked place, but he is uncorrupted by it. This is very believable; but also, unlike the other orphans, who are represented as talking some kind of dialect, he talks the stilted grammar of a hero of Scott or a 'juvenile lead' in Victorian melodrama, which he has had no opportunity to learn. I suppose the readers never quite believed in that, but many would regard it, if they had it pointed out, as a convenient simplification carrying the essential truth; it could also be recognised as a fairy-story tradition, and like the immediately recognisable royalty of the shepherdess Perdita, but they would rightly feel that this kind of explanation was not what was needed. Dickens would impute a serious meaning even to this first example of his symbolism, though he probably took the method for granted; he meant that all the little boys in the orphanage were being robbed of their English heritage, and he thought the best way to make his readers feel so was to make them imagine one of their own boys in such a place. The farcical plot, in which the villain spends his whole time tracking Oliver to keep him out of his rights, is good enough theatre but can only be felt as sensible if it is given this symbolical meaning. But then again, the melodramas Dickens was imitating would regularly gain weight from social feelings which could only be fitted on to the plot through an unconscious use of this kind of symbolism; the method was all around him, and his great power of sympathy gave him an easy intimacy with it. He seems to have become interested in the theory later, when he found churning out plots more of an effort.

However, after recognising the naturalness and force of the symbolic process, we should also recognise that it is liable to have unintended side effects. The great protest of *Oliver Twist* is somehow less alarming than it sets out to be. After all, for a reader looking at it in a practical way, and wondering what to do about the sad cases which the new novel is exposing, the detail of the story is likely to offer a very soothing reflection. All you need do, really, is go through these workhouses and pick out the little gentlemen, because all the other little boys are just pigs. Dickens would have been indignant if anyone had told him that this was what the book meant, but the method is always liable to be caught out in some such way. It might be argued, indeed, that Dickens was deeply in tune with his audience, and himself scarred by the memory of the few months in the blacking factory, so that unconsciously he intended this effect, as part of the symbol which he found a satisfying whole. Perhaps this is true in a way, so far at least as he was determined to let no shadow fall on his young hero; but if he had been warned of this possible misreading he would (obviously, I think) have struggled to find a way of getting round it.[1]

Critics tend to invoke symbolism, by a very worthy impulse, when they know that something about the story has been found absurd but none the less feel that the effect as a whole is good. They are often right; but it is never a sufficient justification of one of these strained bits to prove from the rest of the novel that it is symbolic. I think, indeed, that the history of literary controversy, especially about Dickens, has led to a rather comical false distinction. Many people in his time, and even more people just after his time, said that the old vulgarian was theatrical; as for example in the fierce parody of Dickens by Trollope in The Warden. To be theatrical was part of being crude and popular, though the real accusation of Trollope was that it meant lying political propaganda. Scholarly critics at last spoke up in favour of Dickens, after such different authors as Ibsen and Mallarmé had been praised for some kind of symbolism; they felt, no doubt, that the great reputation of Dickens on the Continent must be a warning sign that previous English critics had been wrong in disagreeing with the English people about him; so they began finding he was full of symbolism. This technique was intellectual or aesthetically advanced, so it gave Dickens class. But really the devices which are called symbolic are precisely the same as those which were called theatrical; I agree that they are often good, but calling them by the new name does not give any help in deciding which of them is good.

It seems to me a misfortune that the literary theory about symbolism has developed so much without thought of the tradition of fair-minded public controversy. To take what is perhaps the most prominent case, I find the injustice altogether too tiresome when D. H. Lawrence expects us to believe Chatterley had always been psychologically impotent because he has got wounded in battle; but, for that matter, if I were a negro I would be very cross with the excellent work of Conrad, Heart of Darkness. After presenting the wickedness of the whites towards the blacks very firmly, he uses all his power of 'atmosphere' to suggest that the primitiveness of the blacks somehow seduced the whites into treating them wickedly, an idea which is quite undemonstrated even if he could have found some defence for it. The symbolism of Dickens, I think, is often fully justified as well as dramatically or poetically very impressive; but the bad bits in Dickens come where it isn't. I find the rhetoric over the death of Jo ('and dying thus around you every day') very good, chiefly because of the argument that epidemics are no respecters of class; this makes it quite different from the death of Little Nell, which is made worse by a falsity in the religious position. A literary critic who thinks he is forbidden by aesthetic theory to consider the beliefs of the author naturally cannot tell the difference between one bout of sentiment and another. Such at least is the position I would wish to take up, though I realise that it would take a great deal more work to offer a sustained argument about Dickens.

Note

1 I was so confident of this that I did not check it as I should have done; Dickens is an author we are prone to re-write in our own minds. Since then I have found he *did* 'take precautions', chiefly by using reported speech for all the charity-boys, the hero included. The only sentence from any child at the orphanage is the demand for More, which Oliver has been deputed to speak (however, a dying inmate of the baby-farm which he leaves at the age of nine has spoken with high poetry). Oliver and Noah are allowed direct speech after they have run away, when the contrast feels mainly one of character; even so, the characteristic rhetoric of Oliver is delayed till farther on in the novel. He is then very little older; and the arrangement, I submit, is a matter of precaution rather than of realism. [Empson]

'Wuthering Heights'

1965–66

In October 1964 the periodical Paunch *(Buffalo) ran an article entitled 'From* PMLA *to* Wuthering Heights', *by John Doheny, a professor in the Department of English at the University of British Columbia. Doheny took as his text an article by Wade Thompson, 'Infanticide and Sadism in* Wuthering Heights' *(*PMLA, *March 1963), which had argued for the 'importance' of the 'power' and 'significance' of Emily Brontë's preoccupation with sadism and infanticide; he protested that by itself such terminology afforded no help whatever to an evaluation of the novel, and proceeded to argue that other critics including Mark Schorer and Dorothy Van Ghent had all too often insisted on discussing the work as a poem and so had neglected the human motivations of the characters presented in preference for searching out 'large thematic patterns'. Nearly every critic since Charlotte Brontë, he wrote, 'has emphasised Emily's poetic power, her great untutored genius, and her non-human, mystic philosophy.' Readers should attend not to the putative 'spiritual ideals' Emily expressed but to 'the psychological reality and individuality of the characters' – the 'human passions' of the novel.*

The novel is about sadism, violence, and cruelty; but, more important, it's a novel which shows how the characters got the way they are, and why they do what they do; finally, it is a commentary on the society which made them that way.

The passion of Heathcliff and Cathy is not extra-human or sub-human passion; it is frustrated passion resulting from stunted, aborted emotional development. And since neither of them is aware of this halted development, they can find no outlet for their passion other than the one they do (not very unusual?). Their emotional development was stopped in a pre-puberty stage.

Wuthering Heights, *he concluded, gives us 'a vision of implacable unsatisfaction, implacable, that is, to everything but a full development of genital sexuality and love in the child-become-adult ... it shows that the reason Cathy and Heathcliff are unhappy is because their emotional, sexual devel-*

490

opment stopped at puberty and never arrived at a kind of perversity that includes genital sexuality. The novel's bearing on life derives from this central fact of its impact as a work of art . . .'

Empson's response to Doheny's article (written 17 January 1965) figured in a letter to the editor, Arthur Efron, published in Paunch, number 23 *(April 1965):*

I write to disagree with the piece by John Doheny on *Wuthering Heights.* As long as he is faulting neo-Christian critics he does needed work, but he decides at the end that 'the reason why Cathy and Heathcliff are unhappy is because their emotional, sexual development stopped at puberty . . .' Now, this may have been what was wrong with Emily herself, and maybe she demonstrates it unconsciously; the book certainly echoes all along with terrible schoolgirl nagging; but it isn't the *point* of the story, and to regard the book as propaganda for honest sex is remote from what the author would be likely to take on as her mission or chore. Your movement deserves to succeed, but won't if it opposes the neo-Christians all the time with 'the opposite', phoney in the same way.

Charlotte's preface to the posthumous first edition says that of course her sister never met these peasants, it was all her imagination; but both the farms seem to be enormous estates (the park of Thrushcross Grange is ten miles round, and that was tops; it was the size of the Duke of Devonshire's one at Chatsworth). Wuthering Heights would obviously need several hundred men to work it; what on earth old Joe can do when he goes out 'to work' at dawn is quite as much a mystery as how Heathcliff makes a fortune in two years' absence, or indeed why he has no sex. An admirer of Emily must admit that she had been kept short of experience. The chief shortage was company; the girls could have gone to a fair number of parties in the pony carriage, but their father had quarrelled with all the local gentry, a few miles away; and the girls weren't allowed to meet the local farmers, near by, for fear they married a farmer's son. The heir to a farm would be much richer than their father's curates, but after marrying him one was no longer a lady. (The girls would visit the labourers' cottages with Christian aid.) Now the girls were largely brought up on Romantic literature praising pirates and suchlike, and were convinced that pirates were real men, whereas curates were not. The forbidden sons of farmers were obviously real too; they killed sheep or something; and admiration for some such man, whom she would arrange to pass on her long walks but must never speak to, seems to have led her to believe that her bedroom was visited by the Spirit of the Moor. Heathcliff is found as a child in the world seaport of Liverpool, and is frequently said to be black; but there is a phrase 'a black Yorkshireman', meaning a particularly cross one, and he is described as that with loving particularity. She did not know what Byron's Corsair looked and behaved like, but she had a model under her view.

Thus the novel ignores class as she knew it in detail, but the essence or agony of it is what makes class. Heathcliff is the soulmate of Cathy, but he isn't given enough education for her to recognise it in time; he seems too coarse. He fights back at the world by acquiring both farms, which though high-class and low-class in decoration are equally rich. He can then get his revenge, trampling the son of his enemy into the same mud that engulfed him. Now the revenge story had a long history, and had always been considered a genuine moral dilemma. The remarkable thing about this novel is that it invents a new end for a revenge story, more suited to the Far East than Christianity perhaps though I don't know of a case there. After he has got full power to brutalise the second generation, and though he insists he has not been so weak as to forgive them, his interests have been decisively torn away; he can no longer keep his mind on his plot; he can no longer keep his mind on eating, so that his actual death comes from starvation. He keeps being distracted by thinking he has almost seen the ghost of Cathy; this is what she would want to do, if you can believe in ghosts (to save the second Cathy), but you may also believe that his Subconsciousness, influenced perhaps by the spirit of the moors, rose up and saved the lovers.

Anyhow something saved them, and what saved them is presented as a thrilling mystery. Such is the *point* of the story, and any account which ignores it is no good.

I expect we would think Emily a very superstitious girl if we met her.[1]

Doheny's reply in the same issue of Paunch *credited Empson with producing 'a short account of the girl, Emily, from common sense': but such an approach is insufficient 'simply because the common-sense view fails to take into account the creative imagination. To see* Wuthering Heights *as no more than the conscious expression of an extremely immature, uninformed, superstitious young girl fails to explain why it is a great novel...'*

I agree that the novel isn't propaganda for honest sex. It isn't propaganda for anything...

Though I don't find Empson's presentation of Emily incompatible with my view of the novel, I suspect the reverse is not true, and the whole thing seems to hinge on what Emily got into the novel as her 'mission or chore' and what she got into it unconsciously ... I've spent years arguing against the critical approach which agrees with Empson's description of poems as crossword puzzles (The Gathering Storm, 1940), so I'm not at all tempted to start filling in blanks in a novel now.... If it weren't that we know enough about Emily to know better, we might assume she made it confusing on purpose, just as Empson said he made his own poems con-

fusing on purpose to make his readers guess the right answer. (It's only fair, though, to point out that this assertion was made twenty-five years ago.)

Empson countered in Paunch, *number 25 (February 1966):*

Mr Doheny is right I think to argue, 'The book is obviously about something important, because one can feel it is good, as writing, so it can't be about anything so dull as you say.' But many people have found the problems of status and revenge oppressively interesting, and maybe what saves him from feeling the same is merely his happy innocence. I read the book after sending you my comments (the first time for years I suppose) and found it much more rawly and brutally about the degradation produced by the class system than I had remembered. Compared to what the book is really about, a psychological sex theory is a twittering ghost.

Americans would perhaps feel more at home with the book if they realised that it is practically the same situation as *Pudd'nhead Wilson* [by Mark Twain]. A son of the family is to be brought up as a slave, and this cannot simply be put right afterwards, because he is really the worse for it. Heathcliff is told he will never again meet the woman he loves, though he will be living in the same house, because he will be in the servants' quarters; this belongs to a larger and more efficiently organised house than the one in the story, but I wouldn't call it dull. When he overhears the girl saying, 'It would degrade me to marry Heathcliff now,' he escapes and becomes ruling-class in both cash and manners within three years but at the cost of becoming a criminal type, and that does seem the only way, in the time. We don't hear that he even invites her to leave her husband for him, but he only sees her alone once, when she is dying, after his return.

Most of the black–white miscegenation in the States happened under slavery, one is told, and I don't mean to say a word against the act of love – I expect it sweetened the institution of slavery very much; but it did nothing to weaken the institution. The man was the ruling-class partner in the approved cases there, but the historical works of Robert Graves have made very clear that the instincts of a lady allow her to conduct a satisfactory sexual relation with the third footman without ever ceasing to treat him as the third footman. Catherine of course assumes that this is impossible; but does Mr Doheny mean that she ought to have done it?

When she says she loves him like the eternal rocks beneath he has to be somehow a local man, as Emily herself had such extravagant local feelings, though he is also from all the wild parts of the world. It seems clear what Emily would have added to the plot if she had not wanted to avoid shocking the public. Old Earnshaw sets off to Liverpool on foot because a letter has told him that his younger brother's son, by a lady of mixed race in the Port of Liverpool, has been left destitute. He avoids scandal by not saying that this is his nephew, and leaves telling the secret until too late. This is all that is needed to explain the assumptions of the story.

Mr Doheny says I said I made my poetry confused to give the public a tease. What I was saying at the time was that poetry is insincere unless it is clinical, resolving conflicts in the author and thus preventing him from going mad; to do this it must satisfy himself as completely unconfused and indeed bare; and if the effects of doing this were trying for the reader, that was nothing to worry about – he could have the pleasure of doing a puzzle. Emily was not a patient girl, and would not have put up with the critical technique of misunderstanding nearly so quietly as I do.

Note

1 Cf. Empson's concluding observation to the essay 'Double Plots' (*Some Versions of Pastoral*, 1935) that '*Wuthering Heights* is a good case of double plot in the novel, both for covert deification and telling the same story twice with the two possible endings.'

Orwell at the BBC

Listener, 4 February 1971;
and in Miriam Gross (ed.), *The World of George Orwell*,
London: Weidenfeld & Nicolson, 1971

On the day when a stranger offered me his hand and said, 'I am George Orwell,' we were both students at the start of a six-week course in what was called the Liars' School of the BBC: my future wife was also a student there, and it seems to me now a time of great happiness. He must have been writing *Animal Farm* while employed by the Corporation, but he never discussed work in progress, and had resigned some time before it was published. We remained friends afterwards, and sometimes had dinner together; but practically speaking, as I went back to China soon after the war, the Indian Editor of the BBC Eastern Service was the only Orwell I knew.

It is interesting to consider why he was there, a question which would not occur to us at the time. My future wife and I, come to think of it, represented the two main types of student at the 1941 session (the School was a yearly event). I had served an apprenticeship, working for a year on the big daily Digest of foreign broadcasts, and towards the end writing earnest memos recommending myself as a propagandist to the Far East (the Digest staff acted as a kind of pool for the propaganda expansion); whereas Hetta, like many other high-minded people at the time, had been dubious about working directly for the government until Hitler attacked Russia, though it had been all right to drive lorries or ambulances through the London blitz. Orwell was the only student who jeered at those who expressed pleasure at having recently acquired the powerful ally. One might expect this to have annoyed people, and maybe it would have done but for another recent event, slightly earlier; the Battle of Britain had been won, so that we were no longer afraid, in a furtive and astonished manner, of losing the war, as we had been for a year, since the fall of France. (There was a night when the figures of German aircraft shot down over Britain, chalked up on a blackboard in the sub-editors' room of the Digest, rose so high that no one's bet was anywhere near, and the sweepstake had to be given to charity. Maybe the figures were wrong, but they were decisive for many people, and Hitler decided the same way.) During that year before I met him, Orwell, though quietly growing food in the country, had been to do with an official scheme planning resistance after a successful German invasion. Survivors of the Spanish War were being taken seriously, by some elements of the British Army, as advisers on how to organize a *maquis*. I did not ask about this, but realised that he would love teaching the British Army how ignorant it was. Still, he would not do even that for mere pleasure, and now the immediate occasion for it had stopped. He would have liked to be a war correspondent, but his health stood in the way. 'I hold what half the men in this country would give their balls to have,' he was accustomed to remark, 'a yellow ticket' (or whatever colour it was, meaning that he could not be conscripted), 'but I don't want it.' In writing this I paused and searched my memory, feeling that another bright phrase should come next; but no, he did not sustain his rhetoric, though he would use a phrase intending it to glitter. He was indignant at being told he was too ill to go abroad. 'The impudence of it, when they know perfectly well I'm too ill to stay here. Probably save my life to go to North Africa. But if it didn't, they might have to give the widow something, d'you see.' No doubt he would have enjoyed being a war correspondent. But radio propaganda to India might offer a more important role. If Hitler broke right through Russia to the Persian Gulf, and India joined Japan, the Axis might win after all. And then again, if Churchill won, he might prevent the liberation of India. As it happened, Orwell was Indian Editor at the time when these major questions became settled, though he could not have been sure they were settled when he resigned. He always regarded his work in a high manner, not to say a self-important one, as many of us were prone to do.

It was lucky for me that George thought I was all right, as I admired him and wanted his friendship, and he might easily have decided I was not. I had come back from China voluntarily for the war, and no doubt this made me sufficiently unlike the types he was denouncing. 'I don't know people like that,' he was soon remarking about Kingsley Martin, who (it seemed) had printed a picture in the *New Statesman* of how much gold would make a u s dollar, so as to help rats to rat. George, I thought, sounded a bit like what one had read of Lord Curzon, another isolated ailing and public-spirited Etonian who had cultivated a funny accent. I had returned feeling that the defeat of Hitler was of immense importance, to be sure, but also feeling reasonably confident that I would be allowed an interesting war by being let into the propaganda machine; and, then again, I was protected by my obscurity, unlike the poet Auden who, I still think, was right in refusing to become the laureate of Churchill. For that matter, my Chinese university had simply assumed that I would require indefinite wartime leave (the Chinese were already regarding our war as a part of their war); it would have been embarrassing to act otherwise. Having practically remained on my tram-lines, I felt it was a rather undeserved bonus to be approved by Orwell. But we never cleared this point up either; he was not a man who asked personal questions.

When the two editors were settled in, which took another year or so of the gradual expansion (I rather think we each had a brief period as Burmese Editor, but it was I who held the office during the fall of Burma), they worked among many others on the open space of a whole floor of an Oxford Street shop, in offices separated by partitions about nine feet high; one of these lay between us, so that I could hear parts of his interview with the Indian propagandists whom he was vetting or briefing – or rather I could hear the bits which he said in a special tone of voice, as a rule one standard sentence. At first the visitor would do most of the talking, with George increasing his proportion gradually; no doubt he had to lure the visitor into providing an entry for the tremendous remark which one learned to expect towards the end of the interview. 'The FACK that you're black,' he would say, in a leisurely but somehow exasperated manner, immensely carrying, and all the more officer-class for being souped up into his formalised Cockney, 'and that I'm white, has *nudding whatever to do wiv it.*' I never once heard an Indian say, 'But I'm not black,' though they must all have wanted to. This no doubt was a decisive part of the technique; if he had used the phrase to actual negroes, from an official position, they would be likely to object, and he would have to stop; but the Indians, who of course chatted to a variety of people in the basement canteen, were clearly in no mood to complain. They thought he was a holy saint, or at least that he must be very high-minded and remote from the world. Nobody ever mentioned, to my knowledge, that this dread sentence was being pronounced; I never even mentioned it privately to George. In his writing, of course, he often uses shock tactics, but I actually did feel a bit shocked to hear them put into practice. (Naturally the Chinese Department had an entirely different layout, having to handle so different a situation.)

One can see, however, that the tactics might have an important function. George was intensely devoted to the liberation of India (though the discovery that his number two was working for an independent Pakistan came as a great shock) – so much so that he felt Hitler's war would be worth while if it spelt the end of the British Raj, as it was likely to do if properly handled; but the 'advanced' Indians who imagined they would secure this result by helping Hitler to win were (he was convinced) disastrously deluded. Actually, most of the Englishmen you could have found for the job would have held these opinions (though Churchill insisted that he himself did not), but to political thinkers from the subject countries the English attitude was incredible; and it could only be made credible by someone who was plainly not mealy-mouthed. George would be uniquely good at this

rather odd line of work. However, for all his skill, he found himself having
to allow broadcasts to go out to India, from speakers too important to
offend, which he thought likely to do more harm than good; well then, the
great organisation should accept the advice of an Editor, and simply tell the
engineers to switch off the power. The man would be thanked and paid as
usual, and could be told later if necessary that there had been an unfortunate technical hitch. He seemed genuinely indignant when complaining
that the B B C had refused; surely we could not expect to defeat Goebbels, if
we were so luxuriously honest as all that. (The stories about Milton when
he was a propaganda chief amount to saying that he behaved as George
wanted to do, very charitably in a way, so I won't believe that they are
merely libels, as is always assumed by critics with no propaganda experience.) The Liars' School, I should perhaps explain, had only dealt with lies
in passing, and only under the form of warning us against the methods of
the enemy. I chiefly remember two young disc jockeys who put on a very
saucy turn with two gramophones and two copies of a record by Churchill;
the familiar voice was made to leave out all the negatives, ending with 'we
will (hic) surrender.' Towards the end of his time with the B B C, Orwell
brought out a volume of specimens of the political reflections by Indians
which he had provided for India, with part of a speech by Hitler as a contrast; and at this late hour he was really pleased to discover that Hitler too
was receiving his due royalties, forwarded to him by the Royalty Department through neutral Sweden. The modern world, it now occurs to me, is
liable not to realise how high-minded the whole affair was; George and the
Corporation were both leaning over backwards, though in rather different
directions.

'The working classes smell' was one of his famous debunking pronouncements, printed in italics if I remember; and this was a settled enough assumption in his mind to make him feel that only tramps and other
down-and-outs were genuinely working-class. It was a serious weakness in
his political judgement, otherwise very good, and it clearly resulted from
deep internal revulsions. I judged it to be connected with his firmly
expressed distaste for homosexuality: at that time, or when we were both a
bit younger, many young gentlemen who loved the Workers did it practically, and would explain to you that the ruling classes, owing to their vices
and their neuroses, were the ones who stank. You may think I should have
confronted George with someone who said this, but it would have been
worse than useless. For the truth is that he himself stank, and evidently
knew it – well, his (first) wife talked to mine about it quite frankly, and she
would be unlikely to treat her husband to a frozen silence on the matter. It
was the rotting lungs that you could smell, not at once but increasingly as
the evening wore on, in a confined room; a sweetish smell of decay. Maybe

I will be told that this does not happen, and indeed I have never met it in other TB patients. But then, Orwell told me more than once that he hadn't got TB; he had an allied lung disease; and as he made no bones about the threat of death I expect some doctor had really told him this. Most other doctors would call his disease merely a variety of TB, while agreeing that the condition of the lungs was unusual. Bodily disgust, or rather a fear that a good man may at any moment be driven into some evil action by an unbearable amount of it, is deeply embedded in his best writing; and at the time I thought all this was easy to explain – he just hated his own smell. But surely, he wouldn't be likely to live many years with his lungs in so extreme a condition. Much more likely, when he was putting himself through the experience of being down-and-out, or among down-and-outs, he smelt quite all right. It would be like what they say to children pulling faces, 'you'll grow like that'; and, in a way, it would suit his expectations, as the later writing became more and more confidently grim.

Whether because of this background of suffering or from his very active experience of life, he had a great power to make you feel ashamed of yourself, or, if your moral resistance held firm, to feel sorry that poor George felt ashamed of you. My wife and I ran into this at a quite unexpected point. At that time the government, or Churchill himself probably, had put into action a scheme for keeping up the birth-rate during the war by making it in various ways convenient to have babies, for mothers going out to work; government nurseries were available after the first month, I think, and there were extra eggs and other goodies on the rations, clearly a reward for Mum, or even Dad, since they could not be digested by baby. We took advantage of this plan to have two children; it seems rather athletic, looking back, as one or other parent had to retrieve them from the nursery as soon as the official worktime stopped, and the arrangements in case of illness were left to be improvised. I was saying to George one evening after dinner what a pleasure it was to cooperate with so enlightened a plan when, to my horror, I saw the familiar look of settled loathing come over his face. Rich swine boasting over our privileges, that was what we had become; 'but it's *true*, George,' I cried out piteously, already knowing that nothing would alter his mind. True, that is, that these arrangements had been designed for the whole population, and did apply to all factory workers. He did not refer to the subject again, but at the time his disapproval was absolute.

And yet, as so often when one brushes up an old anecdote, I am not sure now that I did not get him wrong. Not long after that his wife died, and he resigned his job. They had adopted a child, which needed attention during the day, and so did the two goats living in his garden to supply the child with proper milk. Writing articles for *Tribune* was all right, because he could do that at home, but he could no longer spend most of the day at an office. This looks as if he thought the government arrangements inadequate rather than too luxurious, but perhaps he was objecting to something else in what I had said altogether. Also it looks as if he was not quite so devoted to his high duties as I had presumed (in writing this, I felt so baffled to understand why he had resigned that I asked John Morris, who was our boss at the time; but now I feel sure that George had told us what he told John Morris). He can hardly have decided that the problems of India had been solved, but they had become less explosive, and I dare say these goats were partly a polite excuse; he might well feel, as well as wanting a change, that the post-war election would be decisively important and was beginning to loom up, so that writing internal propaganda for Labour in *Tribune* was the most important duty now before him. Also he had at last found a publisher for *Animal Farm*.

The experience of being Indian Editor continued to work on him, and the early parts of *1984* were evidently conceived as farce about it, so that one expects the book to be gay. Many people get the impression that the author merely chose, for some extraneous personal reason, to make the later parts as horrible as he could. But one cannot understand either book without realising that he considered having to write them as a torture for himself; it was horrible to think of the evil men, stinking Tories, who would *gain* by his telling the truth, let alone jeer about it triumphantly. But tell it he must, he could do no other. Awful, though, for instance, to think of Hetta reading *Animal Farm*; 'it is like cutting off the baby's arm', he said. (So far as I could tell, she did not feel any of the distress he feared, because she did not believe him.) 'Anyway *Animal farm* won't mean much in Burma,' he said to me one day with timid hope, 'because they won't know what it is about; they haven't got mixed farming there, like the English mixed farming.' A year or two later, when I passed that area on my way back to China, every detail of English mixed farming was being explained to the Burmese on a comic strip of a vernacular newspaper, solely in order that they might relish to the full the delicious anti-Russian propaganda of Orwell. And though he was rather anti-aesthetic, indeed one might sometimes think philistine on purpose, he was inclined to retreat into an aesthetic position when the book first came out. With all the reviews ablaze he stayed cross about the reception of the book, so that we said: 'What more do you want, George? It's knocked them all right back. They all say its terrific.' 'Grudging swine, they are', he muttered at last, when coaxed and stroked into saying what was the matter; 'not one of them said it's a beautiful book.'

In an unpublished 'Afterthought' (in a draft letter addressed to the volume editor Miriam Gross on 2 July 1971) Empson wrote:

I had not realised when I wrote this article that such full information is given in the notes to the posthumous *Essays, etc. of George Orwell* (1968). The only thing it lacks is a note on the medical set-up, preferably from the lung specialist Dr H. V. Morlock whom Orwell had consulted before the war, and returned to in his last illness (pp. 473, 487). It seems as hard now as it was at the time to know just how bad his condition was, and whether he knew it. I feel sure he had good motives for any lies he told, so I want to know when he was telling them. But at least I can correct my simple errors.

He resigned from the BBC in November '43, and had resigned from the Home Guard the day before 'on medical grounds'; now, those chaps he would feel ashamed to tell a lie to, whereas telling lies to John Morris and me he might consider somehow good manners. I remember urging him not to resign, because I feared he would starve (our boss John Morris reacted in the same way), and I still think he gave some family obligation as his ground. But his first wife died in 1945, so her death was not the ground. This came into my article because I wanted to illustrate his immense power to convey a shaming rebuke, and how he sometimes turned this power on in a baffling manner; the occasion in view now seems to me all the more baffling.

His letters describe his disease quite consistently; he had 'bronchiectasis' (p. 147) all his life, already when sent to his preparatory school, where he wheezed like a concertina, supposedly from overeating, and had a tummy-cough too, and 'running was a torment' (p. 346). He had 'defective bronchial tubes and a lesion in one lung', not discovered till long after. This condition made him very liable to develop TB, as he once did before the war, but in itself was not lethal. The tormented little boy, he wrote in 'Such, such were the joys', believed that he stank, because that was part of his acceptance of being treated as horrible; and indeed the whole propaganda effect depends upon our feeling sure that he didn't really stink. But Orwell's lungs, by the time he wrote this in 1947, really did stink, and it is impossible to believe that a man who was so oversensitive about the matter did not know it. In his prime he obviously had great stamina, as he came through rough experiences without getting ill; I expect that his lungs only began to stink shortly before we met, after his pre-war mild attack of TB. But surely, among the many voices, we ought to have a medical statement on whether the breath of the brave horrified child already stank (as the yelling children told him) when he was first confronted with the stenches of his appalling school. [Empson Papers]

Reading
The Epic of Gilgamesh

Journal of General Education (Pennsylvania State University Press), XXVII: 4, Winter 1976

I should perhaps begin by recalling what most readers will know. The recovery of this epic is one of the great achievements of modern archaeology and scholarship, as it was already forgotten in classical times, never achieving translation into an alphabetic script. It has been fitted together from broken slabs of baked mud inscribed with translations of it into five or six dead languages of the Near East; the scholarship required deserves a certain awe. But an ignorant member of the public may be allowed to consider the editions of it for general use, especially in universities.

It deserves a place in any broad literary training. Students tend to feel that they ought to be grappling with the modern world, whereas this epic gives a powerful means of coaxing them into the gulfs of time. Its hero reigned in Uruk about 2400 B C, well over a thousand years before those of the *Iliad*, and it feels much more contemporary. Legends about him were presumably being recited, in an incipient saga form which became part of our present text, within two centuries of his death, so that part of our text is almost twice as old as *Ecclesiastes* or the *Bhagavad-Gita*, and it retained an international eminence till shortly before their time. It is both heartwarming and (in a sufficiently grim way) edifying; it has considerable romantic appeal; and it has the great practical advantage that what survives is so short, only about 20,000 words in English.

There is an extremely good prose translation by N. K. Sandars in the Penguin Classics series (*The Epic of Gilgamesh*, 1964), with a thorough introduction and an appendix giving a brief account of the sources of the various episodes of the narrative. However, surely an American edition is overdue, and this would seem an opportunity for adding ten or twelve pages to a paperback which is rather shorter than usual. An 'Apparatus' is needed, in the old standard form, giving the source (Hittite or whatnot) for every variation from the 'copy text', presumably the late Assyrian one which claims to be already a collation. Two or three pages (beyond what we are given already) would be enough so far; but also notes with line-references to details of the text are much needed, even if they act only as soothers to our baffled questions by answering 'Nobody knows' – which one may be sure they would never need to do. The debate on these questions has gone on long enough for a standard opinion to be arrived at, though of course any strong minority opinion should also be mentioned.

Just lately I have been made to feel the need for a fuller apparatus with extra force by learning that an improved edition of the Sandars text came out in 1972, and that some at least of the changes have no comment or explanation attached to them at all. One of them, I think, is plainly wrong, and I am glad of this opportunity to defend my old Mumpsimus. The first sentence of the epic (after the prologue) now reads: 'Gilgamesh went abroad in the world, but he met with none who could withstand his arms till he came to Uruk.' It used to be '*returned* to Uruk', and surely the change makes nonsense (unless it is regarded as insignificant, i.e. he came *home*). Whether his mother is a goddess or a head priestess she clearly lives in Uruk, as did both his fathers; he makes himself too much at home in Uruk, and certainly no one defeats him there. Thus the change taken alone is merely misleading, as it implies that Uruk is not Gilgamesh's original home and that someone did withstand him there. But it may be that some translator a thousand miles away and a thousand years later felt that the hero needed to be made universal; and he might argue that Enkidu at least 'stood up to' Gilgamesh, and won him over in the end after conceding defeat in the wrestling. Can this be the reason for the alteration in our text?

There is one notable improvement in the new edition, in a passage admiring a gate. Gilgamesh is so active when he becomes king, commandeering the young men to build the city walls and demanding every bride upon her wedding night, that the people lament to the gods, who decide that another demigod is needed, and tell the goddess of creation:

create his equal; let it be as like him as his own reflection, his second self, stormy heart for stormy heart. Let them contend together and leave Uruk in peace.

Her new creation, Enkidu, might seem to be the opposite of Gilgamesh, being a totally wild man, with no parents, who eats grass with the deer; when at last he comes to Gilgamesh he plans to 'change the old order', which surely must imply some idea of political change. However, the only effect of their fight is that they become comrades. Enkidu knows that Gilgamesh is certain to die, and it looks as if a passage explaining how he came to this knowledge is missing; but he was first tamed by a priestess of Ishtar, goddess of Love, who apparently taught him to speak, so we may presume that all his wisdom has the same source, coming eventually from the hero's mother. The effect on Gilgamesh of knowing he will die is to make him determined to achieve lasting fame: 'I will set up my name in the place where the names of famous men are written.' Anyway, the newly-invented city has been found a depressing place to live, prone to breed disease:

> Here in the city man dies oppressed at heart, man perishes with despair at his heart. I have looked over the wall and I see the bodies floating on the river, and that will be my lot also. Therefore ... I will go to the land where the cedar is cut.

A heroic expedition is made to the wild country to bring raw material to the alluvial plain, though Gilgamesh weeps and upbraids his god for giving him such restless desires. Enkidu of course is equipped to help him there, though we chiefly hear him give awful warnings. In this way the prayers of the people are granted: the weight of a hero king is taken off their backs at least for a time. The chief obstacle to the expedition is that the cedars of Lebanon (we should be told how early this name is first used) are guarded by a monster, Humbaba. The two heroes wear armour weighing tons, and can walk in a day what an ordinary man can walk in a fortnight, and yet they can defeat Humbaba only by an enormously powerful magic, specially presented by the sun god. As they approach the ogre, after crossing seven mountains, they reach 'the gate of the forest', and admire its timber:

> ... the pivot and the ferrule and the jambs were perfect. Craftsmen had made it in Nippur, the holy city of Enlil.

The gate is so beautiful that Enkidu will not break it with his axe, but pushes it open. His hand becomes weak and trembles, but this passes off. When he lies dying (in the 1964 version) he curses the gate, saying that 'its splendour has cost him his life,' but still praises its beauty; and two sentences are repeated:

> ... the pivot and the ferrule and the jambs were perfect. Craftsmen had made you in Nippur, the holy city of Enlil.

This seems too absurd, whatever the inter-relations of man and Nature. The forest is ten thousand leagues in every direction; are we to think of it as walled? Probably the explorers are going up a ravine, to keep near a supply of water (on the next page, Gilgamesh dreams of being in a mountain gorge when an earthquake makes the sides fall on him); a gate blocking a ravine, on the path leading to the castle of the ogre, is quite credible, but it should not be made by particularly smart human craftsmen. In the new version, as Enkidu lies dying in Uruk, he looks out at one of the city gates made of the cedarwood which he wrested from the forest, and the beauty of that is what he curses. Experts had been imported from Nippur, one of the neighbour cities, less than a hundred miles to the north.

> Ah, if only some future king had brought you here, or some god had fashioned you. Let him obliterate my name and write his own, and the curse fall on him instead of on Enkidu.

This seems much better to us, but we need to be told more; especially, whether the other version was ever accepted as standard. *The Gilgamesh Epic and Old Testament Parallels* (New York: Alexander Heidel, 1946) gives the Assyrian collated text as the only source of this praise of a gate, which it translates with no mark of doubt as 'the gate of the forest'. It also explains that the passage comes on a broken-off patch of baked mud, and that there are gaps on the tablets where it might fit in either place, the entry into the forest or the city death-bed. Is it now believed that the modern translation of the Assyrian version had made a mistake, or that the version itself had?

The 1972 edition also alters the order of lines in the dirge of Gilgamesh over Enkidu, and even here one would like to know the history of the difference, in case it cast any light, because what is said is so remarkable. But probably it is only a copyist's error. The introduction lets drop that the original version, the Sumerian one, does not contain this dirge, which appears in the Akkadian one, the first translation into a Semitic language. In the 1972 English text Gilgamesh first complains that his friend and brother was his sword and shield; the loss of him is very bad luck for a hero, an evil fate. Next he thinks of the wild animals, long-tailed, all mourning for Enkidu, and then on inanimate Nature; in both versions the sorrowing warriors and the great ones of Uruk come later. The 1964 version leaps straight to the gazelles – a more graceful arrangement but perhaps too implausible. It says:

> All four-footed creatures who fed with you
> Weep for you,
> All the wild things of the plain and the pastures;
> The paths that you loved in the forest of cedars
> Night and day murmur.
> Let the great ones of strong-walled Uruk
> Weep for you,
> Let the fingers of blessing
> Be stretched out in mourning....
> Hark, there is an echo through all the country,
> Like a mother mourning.
> Weep, all the paths where we walked together,
> And the beasts we hunted, panther and tiger...
> The mountain we climbed where we slew the Watchman
> Weeps for you,
> The river along whose bank we used to walk
> Weeps for you...

You are lost in the dark and cannot hear me.

This is so like Shelley on Adonais that with a less scrupulous translator one would become suspicious, and even as it is one feels baffled to know whether the two poems are alike inside. Sandars appears to be aware of the parallel, and to derive from it a certain distaste for the passage she has translated so splendidly. It is more 'elaborately expressed', she says, than the Sumerian lament for Gilgamesh, at the end of the epic, which 'has a nobility and ritual force which the other lacks'. She goes on:

We have become so used to the more sophisticated literary versions of myth that we may be tempted to suspect a 'poetic' or 'literary' overtone where none exists, reading too much into symbols which chance to have caught the attention of later and more self-conscious writers. How far a deliberate poetic effect was aimed at we cannot now tell, nor at what point freedom from ancient ritual sanctions may have been achieved. Once a myth has crystallised into literary form it is already dead as belief or ceremonial, but it is possible that, at least in the earliest strata of our material, this change was not yet complete, and for that reason we must not be surprised to find embedded in such early poems fragments of belief which appear grotesque or banal; while at other times we are confronted by the *disjecta membra* of a poetry which never quite emerges.

These views, I think, belong to the naughty nineties and are entirely wrong, but we are probably fortunate that she held them, because they made her concentrate upon giving her translation good though accurate prose. The Gospel accounts of the Last Supper are plainly 'crystallised into literary form', and could not otherwise have come to life as belief and ceremonial. It is hard to think of any sensible origin for the conviction that all good writers are liars, though the idea has long had practical uses as a joke or an excuse.

But the question whether a writer himself sincerely holds a belief is quite separate from the question whether he regards it as clear-cut and held by some other people. What belief about Nature is presumed by this dirge? When Pope writes, 'Trees, where you sit, will crowd into a shade,' he does not believe it, but he expects you to remember pagan beliefs about Orpheus. He pretends to be a lover so enraptured that he might accept them for the moment, and expects the reader to share with the poet a graceful sadness that they are not true. The beliefs in themselves are both 'grotesque' and 'banal', and perhaps readers full of opinions about Pope are sometimes held up by the passage, but when it is sung nobody is puzzled or irritated, surely. With Shelley the question is harder, because he did earnestly believe something like that (e.g. believe that Keats 'is made one with Nature', and his voice is heard in all her music) but did not think it useful to attempt more accurate definition. It would not be enough for Shelley to say that

Keats had been reabsorbed into the Universe or the Absolute; a *local* Spirit of Nature was needed, so that the sunsets in north Italy were much better because Keats had decided to die there; but one cannot be sure that Shelley would have held to that. Still, everyone at the time believed that he was expressing a system of belief, separate from Christianity though not necessarily opposed to it: in fact, the system of Wordsworth. This is clear, I think, when Byron writes to his publisher assuring him that there isn't any metaphysics in the fourth Canto of *Childe Harold*, now on its way; when he wrote the third, Shelley had been dosing him with Wordsworth, but he has shaken it off. Evidently Sandars would regard what Byron called 'metaphysics' as a convention, or as 'elaborate expression', or in effect as mere decoration, but at the lowest it was an attempt to revive certain magical beliefs, and even they proceed from certain assumptions about the world. Surely it is a pantheist Nature who mourns at the death of Enkidu.

Gilgamesh himself would feel more at home with such thoughts than his public, early or late. Enkidu is a special creation of the gods, emerging in the wild country, with neither father nor mother, and eating grass with the gazelles; the hunters first interfere with him because he saves the animals from their traps. But Humbaba the ogre of the cedar forest had had just the same origin — or so he said while pleading for his life, and begging to become a servant of Gilgamesh, as Enkidu had done. Enkidu advised killing him, and then

there followed confusion; for this was the guardian of the forest whom they had struck to the ground; he at whose words Hermon and Lebanon were used to tremble. Now the mountains were moved, the ranges of the hills were moved, for the guardian of the cedar lay dead.

The forest had no such allegiance to Enkidu, who certainly could not order the hills about when he was alive; but Gilgamesh had seen Nature react spontaneously at the death of one nature-man, and his thought is not far-fetched if he expects a moderate reaction, not an actual 'confusion', at the death of another. Hence the public might come to expect such language, in a poem, from the dirge over any notable hero.

And the procedure has not required giving very distinct powers to Humbaba in his lifetime (the earthquake at his death is supernatural only in its timing). 'When the wild heifer stirs in the forest, though she is sixty leagues distant, he hears her'; so he guards the cedars well, and is a dangerous opponent: 'What man would willingly walk into that country and explore its depths?' But spirits can usually hear a prayer from any distance and arrive at the speed of light; it is not much of a jump to let a nature god hear a disturbance to his cedars. The poem lets us imagine that the hills used to shake because they were afraid of what he was saying, but perhaps they merely reverberated at the noise.

When we find a poetic strategy of this sort being used, we may deduce that the hearer or reader is to be tricked or coaxed into enjoying a half-belief in some doctrine which the more sober part of his mind would resist. To say that the paths in the forest that Enkidu loved continually murmur at his death seems to me an advanced form of this trick; surely it is meant to be obvious that the trees surrounding the hill path almost always get enough wind to murmur slightly but evocatively, whereas if you actually believe that 'the path' mourns the death of the hero you are ascribing conscious-ness to an entity with extremely indefinite boundaries. However, the ascrip-tion (in such a case) is not meant to be rejected; the point is rather that the familiar objections to it can for the time be ignored. No nameable god is supposed to be acting; the idea is that a part of Nature mourns; it is like transforming the mathematics of action-at-a-distance into field equations.

I conclude that the epic really is thoroughly like Shelley in this dirge, and which bits of poetry Sandars considered to be *disjecta membra* I have no idea. We gather that Gilgamesh became a hero because he put strong walls round one of the comparatively new master cities, and that Enkidu, though specially created to be his twin, is a totally-wild-nature man. The desire to find some kind of relation between civilised man and wild Nature ('The Country of the Living') lies at the root of the whole story, so that it is only consistent for the civilised man to invoke Nature at the nature-man's death. Also Gilgamesh may feel a desperate hope, though a mistaken one, about the 'finger of blessing': a man, we know, cannot call his brother from death by 'stretching it out', but in this case Nature might be able to. It is sensible to invoke her.

An obstinate determination may be observed among commentators on the epic to make the gods act on moral grounds, so that the sufferings of men are punishments for their sins. I have no wish to deny that its first hearers were moral too, and that some of them would expect their gods to be moral; that is why it is remarkable that the author refuses to satisfy them. In the face of the forthright denunciation of Ishtar by Gilgamesh, to say that the author could not have intended such a refusal would be absurd. But the scene might be a kind of ritual, with the hero speaking as Tammuz; obviously the Goddess of Love can survive being scolded. So to decide on the attitude of the poem to the gods one needs to look at other details of the narrative. Sandars remarks:

There is no explanation of the immediate cause of the gods' decision to destroy mankind. Probably it was much the same as in Genesis: 'The earth was corrupt before God, and the earth was full of violence'; for later there is talk of 'laying his sin upon the sinner'.

But she rightly puts into her text a sentence from another Akkadian flood narrative, which gives the only reason that happens to survive; 'the people multiplied, the world bellowed like a wild bull, and the great god was aroused by the clamour.' The noise irritated him. I find this an entirely convincing reason, as would any tetchy old man to whom the grasshopper has become a burden. And *who* talks about 'sin', later? Only a god, talking to gods. After the Flood, the dynamic god Enlil is indignant to find that Noah and his sons have escaped, but the wise and sober god Ea, who had betrayed the plot to Noah (he whispered outside the wall of his hut: 'Reed-house, reed-house! Wall, O wall! Hearken reed-house, wall reflect. O man ... build a boat') says in a coaxing way to Enlil:

> Lay upon the sinner his sin,
> Lay upon the transgressor his transgression,
> Punish him a little when he breaks loose,
> Do not drive him too hard or he perishes.

That is, 'Even if they did do something wrong, you need not wipe them *all* out'; and, to be sure, it would be a very silly god who did that, because the gods depend upon people for their food. Just before this speech we have been given the grimly convincing detail that Noah made a big sacrifice as soon as he got out of the ark, and the hungry gods gathered over it like flies. It is usual to say that the beliefs of early Mesopotamia made everyone hopeless, but I do not know that these gods are worse than the self-righteous Jehovah, who also appears to deal out blows at random. Ea and Shamash are both good gods, if you can manage to get them away from the others, and even Ishtar has points. It seems clear that the Mesopotamians (consider Hammurabi) were much better at doing justice on earth than the Egyptians, each of them scrambling to secure his own afterlife. Judging from these other parts of the Gilgamesh flood narrative, it would have kept in line with the Atrahasis narrative by giving the gods no excuse, or no adequate excuse, for sending the flood. Indeed, the whole epic gives no example of human evil; but then, we see very little of mankind.

Granting that Enkidu may count as a man, though a very peculiar one, I have next to defend him. Sandars comments:

It is through *hubris* that disaster comes. Enkidu refused the prayer of Humbaba for mercy, he broke the taboo of the gate, opening the enchanted barrier with his hand instead of breaking it by force, as no doubt he should have done, and he insulted Ishtar. Gilgamesh seems less guilty; he was moved by Humbaba's prayer, though when they had killed the bull and the young men and singing girls crowded round to admire him, he let them cry, 'Gilgamesh is most glorious among heroes, Gilgamesh is most eminent among men.' So retribution falls first upon Enkidu.

Gilgamesh died in his palace on the day originally decreed for him, full of achievement, and worn out with labour. Does Sandars think he would have lived forever if he had forbidden his people to praise him? Any such order would have been considered very queer and rude. *Hubris* does not mean letting other people say you have won some competition or otherwise done better than other men; it is a kind of blasphemy. This mean-minded line of moralising has run through the schools of English Literature like a plague, touching nothing which it does not poison; surely Gilgamesh and his twin need not be tainted too.

Whether the advice of Enkidu to kill Humbaba was wrong we cannot say – except that when Gilgamesh remarks, announcing his plan, 'We will go to the forest and destroy the evil,' his divine mother, praying to the sun god Shamash, blames him for making her son desire the exploit, and demands protection for him 'until he kills Humbaba and destroys the evil thing which you, Shamash, abhor'. After this, it is hard to say that Enkidu deserved death because he gave the impressionable Gilgamesh a bit of stiffening at the crucial moment, so that he carried out the divine intention. Sandars plainly does not know this 'taboo of the gate', which she presumes, having had no opportunity to learn it, and no more had Enkidu. As the trembling of his hand gets no further mention, it is fair to suppose that he was simply afraid. The frank terror and frequent changes of mind and appeals to one another of the two enormous heroes make them seem like small boys. As to insulting Ishtar, what Enkidu did and said, backing up his master, is nothing compared to what Gilgamesh himself had said: she offered him her body, and he spat at her for a page and a half. 'So retribution falls first upon Enkidu.'

Whenever I read these academic critics, pronouncing morals on established literary works, the thought of exam-time forces itself into my mind; they must be frightfully bad at giving marks. However, their kind of rule *might* be operating in the mind of the authors, and one should look at all sources of evidence. There is one, I think, when the exhausted Gilgamesh arrives (on advice from the magical barmaid) at the magical boat by which he may be taken to Noah to learn the secret of eternal life, but only (she warns him) if he can agree with the ferryman. 'When he heard this he was seized with anger,' and taking a sword and an axe in his two hands he ran down and smashed the gear (whether magical or practical is in some doubt) by which it was intended to sail. This is excessively upper-class behaviour, and might fairly be said to be like *hubris*. But the ferryman remains unrattled, placid, friendly, and at once invents a punting technique to use instead – Gilgamesh must cut 120 poles and paint them with tar so that his hands never touch the lethal water. There is no suggestion that anyone thinks the worse of him for his hysterical behaviour; they all tell him he looks dreadfully ill. The mission fails because a snake eats the herb of immortality while Gilgamesh is bathing, and this is taken as accidental, though one feel that something like it was bound to have happened. The whole atmosphere of the Tragic Flaw, I submit, is absent, and to read it in is much worse than reading in 'self-conscious poetry'.

In the debate among the gods, after the heroes have killed the Bull of Heaven which was sent against them, wise old Anu says: 'One of the two must die; let it be the one who stripped the mountains of the cedar.' And indeed, odd though it may seem, this really is the guilt of man in the poem – polluting the environment. It doesn't matter much about other things, but cutting down trees is awful. Gilgamesh has done the actual felling, but Enkidu had cleared their roots as far as the banks of Euphrates (of course, the trees were needed to make the city of Uruk splendid). So there is no distinction in guilt here, but the executive Enlil sees at once that Enkidu must die. The reason is that of the two he has the inferior status. Although a direct creation, he has no divine parentage, whereas Gilgamesh is by parentage two-thirds god and one-third man. At the actual killing of Humbaba, Gilgamesh struck the first blow, and Enkidu the second; the third blow killed him, and the text does not say which one of them struck that. But it is soon saying 'Enkidu has struck him' and assuming that Enkidu will take the blame. Probably this was meant to be recognised as a slight tease, preparing us to find that the one of inferior status is given the blame.

This then is a proper occasion to consider how Gilgamesh could be two-thirds god and one-third man, a bit of arithmetic which offends our own semi-sacred beliefs about genetics. His mother Ninsun is said to be a goddess, but plainly operates as head priestess of a temple of Uruk. Before her son went on his exploit to the forest, she put on her court dress and jewelry and 'went up to the altar of the sun, standing upon the roof of the palace'; there she addressed Shamash the sun god. She would have flown up to heaven if she could. But if we deny her divinity we receive a snub; Ishtar herself, undoubtedly a goddess, uses her own temple in Uruk (probably the same one) in much the same way when Gilgamesh and Enkidu kill the Bull of Heaven. 'They cut out its heart and gave it to Shamash.'

But Ishtar rose up and mounted the great wall of Uruk; she sprang onto the tower and uttered a curse: 'Woe to Gilgamesh, for he has scorned me in killing the Bull of Heaven.' When Enkidu heard these words he tore out the Bull's right thigh and tossed it in her face . . . Then Ishtar called together her people, the dancing and singing girls, the prostitutes of the temple, the courtesans. Over the thigh of the Bull of Heaven she set up lamentation.

As one of the incidental effects of this scene, the earlier behaviour of the

mother of Gilgamesh is shown to be like that of a goddess; and indeed the
gods call her a goddess at the start, to explain why he is too strong. Her husband Lugulbanda, who 'reigned in Uruk second before Gilgamesh and
third after the flood', is called a god; and Gilgamesh once claims him as
father. But if this were true Gilgamesh would be all god. Sandars reports:

His father in the king-list is rather mysteriously described as 'lilu', which may mean
a 'fool' or a demon of the vampire kind, as well as being high priest.

The human father sounds a good deal more supernatural than the old
priest-king, Lugulbanda, who may be supposed a god *ex officio* merely. Besides, Gilgamesh himself becomes king when the story begins, so at that
rate he too becomes a god *ex officio* without more ado. There is an answer
to this; we know from the king-list that Gilgamesh lived on the cloudy edge
of the plateau of divine royalty. During the recovery after the Flood, kingship was again 'let down from Heaven', and each of the first four kings
reigned a long time, Lugulbanda, the third, for 1200 years; but Gilgamesh,
the fifth, had only about 120 years, and his son only thirty. All the later
kings on the list are also said to have reigned for periods possible to man.
An efficient king might have produced this effect, without requiring any
great change in opinion about the past, merely by establishing thenceforth
the post of chronicler, a priest responsible for writing down the dates of
public events. But Gilgamesh lived about the time of the Royal Tombs of
Ur, where half the court would be sacrificed to accompany the dead king.
Rather bafflingly, the whole ethos of the epic feels immensely far from this
barbaric custom; but we need not be surprised if the ideas of Gilgamesh
about immortality are confused, and may readily accept King Lugulbanda
as his divine half-father (a plausible claim from his mother on this point
might be necessary to admit him to kingship, when he was already recognised as the best candidate), leaving the high priest of the temple of
Tammuz at Kullab to be his human half-father. Such an arrangement continued to be familiar for thousands of years: no eyebrows were raised when
Jesus was said to be both a direct descendant of David, father to father, and
also the Son of God.

It may be observed, however, that Lugulbanda is never mentioned again
in the epic after Gilgamesh has killed Humbaba – his very first exploit, after
which he feels he is standing on his own legs. Of course negative arguments
are especially weak in this case. His mother Ninsun also never mentions the
supposed father, but we know that a large patch of destruction on a tablet
carried her further advice to her son before he set out. The counsellors of
Uruk tell him not to forget Lugulbanda, his guardian god (maybe they just
think it politer not to touch upon his parenthood), but when he is terrified

at the approach of Humbaba he stiffens himself with the full claim:

By the life of Ninsun my mother who gave me birth, and by the life of my father divine Lugulbanda, until we have fought this man, if man he is, this god, if god he is, the way that I took to the Country of the Living will not turn back to the city.

After the death of Enkidu, when Gilgamesh scours the world for immortality, he has frequently to present his claims before mysterious beings, but he never falls back upon this one. And yet 'the mate of the Man-Scorpion', while the Scorpions are considering whether to allow him a complete use of the underground passage through which the sun returns to the dawn, contributes rather acidly the comment that he is only two-thirds of a god: one-third is man. Mere length of life would be nothing to his purpose, now that he has seen the worm emerge from the body of Enkidu, nor yet the claims of the old kings to an immortality elsewhere. He is committed to the life of man.

Returning now to the arithmetical question, it is clear that what everybody meant by saying he was two-thirds god was that the three parents all counted as equals: divine mother, divine father, human father. But whether his mother is a goddess or a priestess creates no problem for him; either way, she does the same helpful things. And he is soon addressing the sun god directly, secure in his appointment as king by the town council of Uruk; he no longer needs a divine half-father. He identifies himself with man, or at least with the men of Uruk; this becomes clear when he plans to make the old men of Uruk young again with the herb of immortality. It is not that he rejects gods, a thing he has no reason to do; but he regards the refusal of immortality to mankind as merely an unreasonable caprice of the gods, such as is usual in their behaviour, and the divine part of his nature is useful only for giving him an opportunity to negotiate with them. This is the most impressive part of his character, and it allows us to suppose him at peace in his last years, exasperating though his major experiences had been.

This particular translation never makes you drop through an unexpected trapdoor, and though sometimes rising to a sober magnificence always feels concentrated upon conveying as much of the original as possible. Verse translators are inherently tempted to be 'contemporary', and I suppose Ezra Pound made it practically a duty (though his best work in this line, for instance Canto XIII summarising or describing Confucius, is keenly observed and almost verbatim from the *Analects* – he is trying to prove the case for his view of Confucius). We ought to feel sickened when we are coaxed to eat pap already chewed for us, a 'modern interpretation'. The first interest of Gilgamesh is that he is very far away and long ago; anyone who can't endure that had better leave him alone. Here is a recent

version (Herbert Mason, *Gilgamesh: A Verse Narrative*, 1970) of the
wrestling-match between Gilgamesh and Enkidu, at their first meeting:

> The dry dust billowed in the marketplace
> And people shrieked. The dogs raced
> In and out between their legs.
> A child screamed at their feet
> That danced the dance of life
> Which hovers close to death.
> And quiet suddenly fell on them
> When Gilgamesh stood still
> Exhausted. He turned to Enkidu who leaned
> Against his shoulder and looked into his eyes
> And saw himself in the other, just as Enkidu saw
> Himself in Gilgamesh.
> In the silence of the people they began to laugh
> And clutched each other in their breathless exultation.

I do not say that that is bad poetry, but here is Sandars:

Mighty Gilgamesh came on and Enkidu met him at the gate. He put out his foot and
prevented Gilgamesh from entering the house, so they grappled, holding each other
like bulls. They broke the doorposts and the walls shook, they snorted like bulls
locked together. They shattered the doorposts and the walls shook. Gilgamesh bent
his knee with his foot planted on the ground and with a turn Enkidu was thrown.
Then immediately his fury died. When Enkidu was thrown he said to Gilgamesh,
'There is not another like you in the world. Ninsun, who is as strong as a wild ox in
the byre, she was the mother who bore you, and now you are raised above all men,
and Enlil has given you the kingship, for your strength surpasses the strength of
men.' So Enkidu and Gilgamesh embraced and their friendship was sealed.

The introduction lets drop that in the original Sumerian they do not kiss,
and that Enkidu is described as the servant of the hero, not his friend; the
more intimate version comes in the Akkadian, the first translation. In both,
of course, Gilgamesh becomes devoted to Enkidu, and reacts to his death
with an enormous challenge. But he probably needed time before he fully
appreciated his ally, and even if they did fall in love almost at first sight I
don't believe that they giggled. This reaction of laughter is winningly 'contemporary'; it is meant as a kind of reassurance that they aren't really
pansies. But both these beefy men were glutted with women (Gilgamesh has
come as usual to take a bride's virginity) and confident that they are the
manliest men you could find anywhere; why should they feel it polite to
giggle? Enkidu is concerned with something much more important to him:
he came expecting to overthrow Gilgamesh, but now he finds he is willing

to vow allegiance. So he says: 'Your mother is as strong as a bull.' Surely you want to know what he really said; it is better not to read translations at all than read doctored 'contemporised' ones.

Advanced Thought

London Review of Books, 24 January 1980

Frank Kermode, *The Genesis of Secrecy*

Frank Kermode's new book contains a great deal of graceful and dignified prose, especially in the last chapter, and many of the examples are of great interest. It seems to argue that no history or biography can be believed, but must be regarded as a kind of novel. Any narrative is necessarily incomplete, and the details left out may for some readers be the important ones – what is taken for granted may become the crucial question. Such is the justification for the title. The chief theme of the book, or source for its examples, is the Gospel of St Mark, and it attends to many recent works on this subject, mostly in French or German. A tone of yearning sorrow is often present, but Kermode's theory must be applied to his own work: this tone should be part of his novelistic technique.

He has long been keeping abreast of the latest ideas from the Continent, and I have certainly no business to jeer at him for that; I ought to feel ashamed of not having done the same. But I do not feel so in this case. We know that Oscar Wilde is much revered on the mainland, and it looks as if Kermode has merely been getting the aesthetic nineties echoed back at him. No doubt Imagism comes in too. He looks at a landscape with half-closed eyes through a mist, or in a Claude-glass, or upside down from between his legs; and this is not a good way to read a novel, which is usually better read as if it were a history. Also it is rather unfair to take the chief examples from the Gospels, because there many readers have an extra difficulty about the miracles. A brief paragraph about Sir Philip Sidney, thrown in as an extra, does more to make the position clear.

Lying wounded on a battlefield, the aristocratic young officer was brought a cup of water, but handed it on to a wounded trooper, saying: 'Thy need is greater than mine.' Kermode makes it 'thy necessity', quite spoiling the tone of the thing; he always wants to insert a long fussy word which is a bit off the point. He then says: 'The story was first told by Sidney's friend Fulke Greville, in a biography written twenty-five years after the poet's death, and first published forty years after that. We know from what he says of Sidney's own writings that Greville approved of characters in books only when their conduct might serve as an example to the reader ... There were no surviving eyewitnesses to his dying act, for which we have only Greville's word, and it has been pointed out that Greville seems to have been remembering a passage in Plutarch's *Life of Alexander*.'

I would agree that the story is a bit unpleasant, because it is aggressively holy: many a trooper would resent having gratitude and admiration dragged out of him at such a time. The okay thing would be to drink some of the cup himself and pass it on, leaving most of it to the other man if that seemed fit; then the noble sentiment might actually be pronounced, and not appear self-regarding. I do not mind the evident craving of Kermode to assault the story, only his conception of evidence. *When* were there no surviving eye-witnesses, pray? The man who brought the cup must have been one, at the time. As to Plutarch, surely Sidney had read him as much as Greville, and was more concerned to present himself as a hero. Kermode feels that the man making a document at a desk, by copying bits from previous documents – he is real, but any man on a battlefield is a kind of puppet. Even Sidney, though a writer himself, could not have done any copying on a battlefield, when he was a puppet. 'The story was first told' twenty-five years later – how on earth can Kermode claim to know this? Greville was a clumsy writer, prone to the labours of the file, but he was the same age as Sidney, and a close friend, and had been in the Low Countries, taking notes, just around the time when Sidney died there. Kermode would be credible if he said: 'The story was first written down...' But even this is very unlikely. Greville would write notes as soon as he got reports, and write them up at his leisure for a formal memoir. And what can we make of the phrase 'characters in books', implying that Sidney became a mere figment in a novel as soon as he stopped writing his novel?

Kermode used to be very decisive about 'genres', insisting that every writer around 1600 was always tied down to one convention or another. If true of anybody, this was true of Greville, who would be very indignant to hear that he thought it proper to invent lies in a memoir, merely because he liked a romance to be allegorical. As to the lateness of the publication, the one thing it does prove is that the story was not a cooked-up piece of propaganda, for use while the death was hot news. Of course, somebody else may have invented the story at the time, and told it to Greville, but none of the confident arguments of Kermode affect the probability.

Coming now to the Gospel, the first and most impressive example given by Kermode is Mark 4.11–12, which has long been recognised as a crux. The disciples ask Jesus why he uses parables, and he assures them that they will be told the mystery of the Kingdom, but outsiders will only get parables: 'That seeing they may see, and not perceive, and hearing they may hear, and not understand; lest haply they should turn again, and it should be forgiven them.' Kermode drives home that this means he is 'telling stories in order to ensure that they will miss the point'. The disciples ask about the parable of the sower, and Jesus indignantly explains: 'The Sower soweth the word.' But this is an unusually pointless allegory. Does it mean that the seeds which fell on stony ground are doomed to eternal torture? It suggests that God is a casual and wasteful type of farmer: not an intolerable view, but then he ought not to put the blame on us.

Kermode reports shock and bewilderment among certain commentators, and then describes the rescue operation of Matthew: 'The whole passage about seeing and hearing comes from Isaiah 9–10, though Mark, in paraphrasing it, does not say so. What Matthew does is to quote Isaiah directly and with acknowledgement, so that the lines retain a trace of their original tone of slightly disgusted irony.' This assumes that the sordid Mark, who of course was lying when he pretended to report the words of Jesus, was meanwhile stealing, though he also garbled, a passage from a long-dead author. But the disciples were pious Jews, quite certain to recognise one of the most famous passages in Isaiah, which Jesus again recalls in Mark 13. Matthew is merely explaining the reference for the benefit of Greeks, though he does make possible a softer view: that the hearers make themselves stupid, to avoid having to understand. But it is quite false to suggest that Isaiah was speaking with mild humour. He saw the Lord sitting on his throne, and the Lord said, 'Whom shall I send?' and Isaiah said, 'Send me'; and the Lord said: 'Make the heart of this people fat ... lest they see with their eyes ... and be healed.' The Jews are driving themselves pigheadedly into some disastrous international situation, and Isaiah warns them that they will no longer be God's chosen people unless they stop.

Jesus quotes him to show that it is all happening again: in all four Gospels he gives a warning that bad times will soon come. Modern commentators often assume that these bits can only have been written into the text after AD 70, but all sensible men were expecting the disaster beforehand. Jesus was not too unpolitical to care about that, because he weeps over Jerusalem, which had rejected his help. The saying becomes very bad if Jesus speaks as God, saying, 'I will harden their hearts,' as God had hardened the heart of Pharaoh (Exodus 7). But a quotation from an ancient vision does not give that effect – he is saying: 'I can't help it.' Here, and nowhere else, he says, 'From him that hath not shall be taken away even that which he hath,' and surely no one supposes that he boasts of arranging this himself, on purpose. He is saying: 'Life is hard.' Kermode here, just as with Philip Sidney, gets into nonsense because he refuses to read the passage as part of a novel; he will not imagine a 'character' who makes a literary quotation on purpose, and hearers who know he is doing it.

I agree that the passage gives a striking example of a painful mystery. How could he combine turning the other cheek with cursing the barren fig tree, though it was not the season for figs? Bertrand Russell, in *Why I am not a Christian*,[1] remarked:

> In the Gospels, Christ said: 'Ye serpents, ye generation of vipers, how can ye escape the damnation of hell?' That was said to people who did not like his preaching. It is not really to my mind quite the best tone.

Surely it must be agreed that Jesus miscalculated: it would be torture for him to have to watch what has been done in his name since his death. But if you grant that he was presenting himself as a Messiah, of a special kind but fulfilling the Scriptures, it was part of his programme to recall the prophets; and scolding had been their regular custom. You may feel that Jesus was all too human here, but not, like Kermode, that he is unintelligible.

There has been immense discussion about the 'testimonies', the points where the Gospels say Jesus did something the prophets had foretold. Kermode regards them as an unconscious confession: each detail recommended like this has plainly been cooked up by some deskworker. C. H. Dodd has been prominent in arguing that Jesus himself is much the most likely person to have invented this unique procedure, and Kermode mentions him quite often but never lets the reader know what he maintains, except on one point where he can fit in a retort. Dodd had said that you would expect many more, if all the writers were inventing them, and Kermode has fun with this argument, calling it 'desperate'. It was perhaps carelessly phrased: the point is that the doctrinal ones are all about the Suffering Servant, as described by various prophets, and not, for example, about the warlord Messiah who would have been more widely welcome. Of course there are some details, such as those about the crucifixion, which the writers claimed as fitting in. Robert Graves has made splendid use of this line of explanation in *The Nazarene Gospel Restored*, deducing an entirely credible character.

According to Mark and Matthew, the last words of Jesus were 'My God, why hast thou forsaken me?', though the other two Gospels give two different sayings, less likely to excite doubt. This is the start of Psalm 22, which goes on to express absolute personal despair and ends, by a considerable jump, with a nation in triumph. Thus Jesus might have said it to let off steam without any risk of betraying his cause, even if he did fall into doubt at the end. After saying it, he gave a loud cry and dies; he had been under torture for several hours. It may seem improbable that anyone would make a literary quotation at such a moment, but it is believable in so strange a case, whereas the Gospel-writers were very unlikely to invent it, as two of them found it embarrassing. Robert Graves thinks he felt a quite practical despair, having been sure that this procedure would force God to take immediate action, and after his recovery felt intensely guilty, realising that one must never force the hand of God: that was why he appeared seldom and briefly. If you compare him with Graves, Kermode shows a remarkable inability to appreciate the literary effect of these literary quotations.

His other main example is about the dance of Salome, which he considers an 'intercalation', an intrusion allowed by Mark into his narrative. He feels that, as it has no rational explanation, it probably has some aesthetic explanation, to be found by structural analysis perhaps; and probably a sexy one, as the story of Salome has always been found kinky. But all his long technical words are simply wrong: there is no break in the narrative.

The story of Jesus inherently involves a great early popular triumph which causes a gradual build-up of official hatred and suspicion, leading to an execution which he chooses not to escape. Matthew puts the Salome incident only three chapters later, when the story moves to Jerusalem, but there it seems a bit clumsy, a hark-back. In Mark, it comes immediately after Jesus has first sent out his disciples, in pairs, as trained men with detailed instructions and a delegated authority to cast out devils. This makes him an organised power, and of course the established government pay attention. We hear that the Herodians are working against Jesus, and from now on Jesus tries to avoid trouble until he is ready for his sacrifice. Herod has murdered John as a reward for Salome, and now believes Jesus to be a reincarnation of him: this makes Herod more dangerous. Surely, any dramatist would agree that an early report of how the previous prophet John has died helps to alert to the build-up. Mere competence of presentation does not give you any reason to disbelieve the story. The account of the Spanish Armada by Garrett Mattingley is a wonderful bit of writing because it deploys all the forces at work in the different capitals, with an entire change of scene each time, so that you are made to realise how the result was inevitable. I suppose an expert on the anti-novel would deduce that it was totally bogus.

There is another intercalation at this point. A great crowd has come to Jesus on the borders of the lake, and he preaches to them, and by miracle gives them all something to eat, but they must be induced to go away, so he takes a boat across the lake to a foreign country, and meets an immensely strong madman, living among the tombs. He expels the devil, who is a legion of devils (they lack distinction), and the devils beg him not to deport them: may they not go into the nearby pigs? Jesus kindly allows it, the pigs stampede into the lake, and the villagers beg him to go back again. Jesus forbids the man to come back with him, and tells him to tell everybody about his cure, and so far as I can find he never says this to anybody else.

Kermode glimpses a great mystery about secrecy and publicity and the clean and the unclean: Lévi-Strauss perhaps. But there are two very plain reasons.

This ex-lunatic must rapidly become accepted in his village as sane again, or he will be miserable and probably return to madness; also, he is out of Herod's jurisdiction and probably knowledge – he can say what he likes, so long as he does not cross the lake. When Jesus gets back, a leading man in the nearby synagogue wants him to save the life of his daughter, and on the way to his house, jostling through the crowd, he feels that virtue has been taken from him, and orders the person to speak up. The woman with an issue of blood confesses, and he gives his blessing, without which she might have felt guilty; he does not order her to be silent, which in the crowd would be absurd. He then goes on to the daughter, refusing to admit that she is already dead, and after raising her tells the family curtly to give her food. He does not want to be known as a miracle-worker, both because it may cost his life and because it isn't really his business. As to the 'intercalated' incident, the healing touch in the crowd, it makes the scene vivid, as it would in a film: why does it need to be talked about in language that vetoes any direct response? There is no need to insinuate that Jesus had a devil: one of his opponents said he did, but that all devils recognise him as the Son of God is not further evidence, because all angels do as well (Mark 1.13). Kermode says: 'One cure is from an excess of maleness, the other of related effects of femaleness. The lake divides the two like a slash, and the cured demoniac is forbidden to cross it.' But the lake is a frontier; and why must we ignore the story, while Kermode looks at it upside down? There is no problem about whether we may read St Mark as a novel, but there really is a problem about whether Kermode and the rest of his school are allowed to read a novel properly. However, I am sure that his last chapter about the mystery of the Gospel, its incessant glimmering of the unapprehensible, is a fine piece. This is the way Whistler contrived to look across the Thames.

Note

1 See Bertrand Russell, *Why I am not a Christian and other essays on religion and related subjects*, London: George Allen & Unwin, 1957 (and Empson's piece 'Bertrand Russell, God, and Immortality' below). 'There is one very serious defect to my mind in Christ's moral character,' Russell observed, 'and that is that He believed in Hell. I do not myself feel that any person who is really profoundly humane can believe in everlasting punishment' (p. 22).

VI
Cultural Perspectives:
Ethics and Aesthetics, East and West

Pontifical Death

Granta, 9 March 1928

Thornton Wilder, *The Bridge of San Luis Rey*

I have put off reviewing this book, partly because it is obviously very good indeed and deserves consideration, partly because I was hoping to find out what was the matter with it.

Mr Wilder writes such beautiful English that one feels he must be going to say something profound; the same thing happened with Mr Strachey. They both send delicate modulations of the speaking voice worming about one's head, 'of course you won't miss *this* point, need I mention *that* return of feeling?' and remembering how everyone else is slopping about in grammar and carpet slippers one feels 'obviously this man is keeping hundreds of balls in the air, if he has to be as subtle as that it must be a most elaborate poise of feeling.' So one usually reads a modern stylist for the second time with a certain sense of finding him out.

The point of the book is the conflict in the writer between the heartlessness of Nature and the loving care of God. Five people are killed when the bridge breaks, and the dust-cover tells me they all had a 'fitting end'; possibly Mr Wilder, in his whimsical way, really meant that; if so, he is trifling with our feelings. I suspect he did, because of Brother Juniper, an irrelevant mythological figure standing for the author (only with more faith) who is finally burnt alive, much too playfully, by the Inquisition, and 'leans upon a flame and dies'. Such false notes are struck often.

These objections have on the whole been captious, and I have not praised the book sufficiently highly. When Mr Wilder takes his subject seriously he is magnificent; but he is continually exploiting his style to make an escape from his subject into whimsicality.

Bertrand Russell, God, and Immortality[1]

Granta, 1 June 1928

H. G. Wood, *Why Mr Bertrand Russell is not a Christian*

It is an excellent thing that Mr Russell's statements should be taken up and complained of; he has a great power of producing arguments enough for the immediate effect, and going no further than seems convenient. He knows the latent fallacies as well as anyone, thinks himself capable of reconciling them with his position; often has already done so; but is subtle only where it seems interesting, and is not pained by crudity elsewhere. This is the English way of thinking which seems so unscrupulous to the Continental; it has great virtues; it gives great resilience to the thinker, never blurs a point by too wide a focus, is itself a confession of how much always must be left undealt with, and is beautifully free from verbiage. To an enemy it looks like sheer cheating.

Mr Wood, when he is not, to his own frankly expressed shame, indulging in casual and rather witty nagging, is often deceived by this, and will call a dilemma trivial when it has much in reserve. For instance, both in the First Cause argument for the existence of God, and in the crux about whether goodness is created by God, so that it is not for him absolute and he is not good, or independent of God, so that he is a subject of it, Mr Wood is betrayed by Mr Russell's chattiness into mixing up before in time with before in logic, and then complaining of superficiality. 'I see no difficulty in saying that such eternal truths form part of God's nature from all eternity' means merely 'At no particular time does the problem force itself upon my attention as a sort of picture.' In the same way, the argument against 'arguments in general for the immortality of the soul', they all prove equally that the soul must pervade all space. Mr Wood answers, not by taking any particular argument and showing it doesn't work for *that*, but partly by complaining of incidental carelessness of phrasing, partly by saying it has not been shown, point by point, to be true. But it is absurd to complain of Mr

Russell's elegance before you have shown that it has led him astray.

Note

1 Untitled in original.

'The Sceptical Biologist'

Nation and Athenaeum, 18 January 1930

Joseph Needham, *The Sceptical Biologist*

In the nineteenth century one was only a pile of billiard balls, jerking about according to mathematical rules; scientific determinism spelled horror and despair. It is a real and terrible ghost, one must remember, that Mr Needham is exorcising, and much depends on his success. One can forgive, then, a touch of the bedside manner, its complacence, its lack of imaginative unity with the patient, its wish to soothe him rather than to enlarge on his difficulties; even its trick of repeating itself, which is perhaps inevitable in collected papers. For he speaks comfortable words; I must pass them on.

Scientific research is an activity of the human spirit, and must be accepted like any other. If you are using the scientific method, you must assume that determinism can always be applied to the matter in hand; if however you are not using the scientific method (for instance, if you are deciding not to use it), then you must assume that determinism does not apply to the matter in hand. These actions are not conflicting but complementary, and the distinction between them is one of method, not of subject matter. From another point of view, if the organism shows purpose in fitting its environment, so does the environment show purpose in being such as can sustain an organism; the first form of purpose is no more within the field of science than the second. All things are alike determined, all things are alike free.

Science is a closed system of pointer-readings about what is measurable; it is built up by assuming that individuals can be regarded as members of classes, that conditions are repeatable, and that induction is valid. It is a product of the mind; a product, too, of the universe which allows it to yield results; and cannot make final statements about either. There should, then, be some mode of thinking other than the scientific one, but to mix the two will only confuse both. Thus vitalism, in so far as it denies necessity within the organism, must recede before a scientific advance such as it would desire; in so far as it introduces purpose among other causes, it has introduced something not conceived as measurable, and therefore incapable of fitting it into the scientific scheme. Mr Needham is indefinite about the other modes of thought; they include the apprehension of beauty, the acceptance of one's apparent power of choice, and the practice of a religion after rejecting its verifiable dogmas. He admits that true beliefs may destroy one's power to act rightly, and is concerned to show, in the case of determinism, that this might be avoided as a matter of philosophy, rather than can be avoided as a matter of psychology. On the face of it the belief 'science and religion are equally subjective' (p. 261) drains a lot of sap out of both of them.

Many scientific laws, in particular the one that energy is always diffusing itself towards a dead level, are laws of averages; not certain, but very probable for large numbers of molecules. Now in small living cells there are so few of the large molecules concerned that large variations in these laws are to be expected. Some writers have sought their freedom in this; Mr Needham points out that all the molecules are still obeying their individual laws. This attack has since the date of the essay been pushed further, and makes 'probability', once a device by which human ignorance dealt with large numbers, now an inherent property of each separate molecule; but this does not upset Mr Needham's position; the notion of an atom's probability is a mystery, and very *like* what one feels about people, but it is not its business to give freedom to the organism. But, speaking of recent developments, I was sorry not to find Schroedinger in the index; his latest theory says that the more exactly you know the position of an atom the less exactly you know its velocity, and vice versa. Now that complete scientific knowledge should be impossible, so that science, though it can be applied to anything, never tells you everything about it, is a valuable buttress for Mr Needham's building. And this building, leaky as it may be, is the only one which is still habitable.

'The Metaphysical Foundations of Modern Science'

Criterion, X, October 1930

E. A. Burtt, *The Metaphysical Foundations of Modern Science*

It is the ambitious purpose of this work to lay bare for criticism by a historical survey, and to correct with the aid of present knowledge, the subject of its title; to a great extent it achieves the first of these, and is therefore well worth reading. One need not complain if it does not achieve the second.

Mr Burtt hopes that the problems of materialism and determinism, that that Ice Age of the imagination which the sciences seemed to impose, will be resolved by a study of the adolescent fancies of Kepler. Certainly this may be one front of the war, but it can hardly be an important one; the stress in history is fallacious here, because just that 'present knowledge', in the light of which he interprets his history (but which he assumes almost without recognising) is the real parent of his conclusions.

If it was shown that the metaphysical ideas of the early scientists could, for their own objects, have been different and more agreeable, if it would have been possible for them, for instance, to locate feelings as objects in space, or to include human purpose in their casual scheme, then a study of their reasons for choosing the 'materialist' metaphysics might be fruitful. But Mr Burtt himself shows that they were forced into adopting the materialist scheme because it was the only one which would order adequately the facts they knew. He makes great play with some amusing evidence that Newton believed in absolute space because it was the sensorium of God, and Kepler believed in Copernicanism because he was a sunworshipper. But Mr Burtt's thesis is that the early scientists drained the real world of spirituality unnecessarily, because of unrecognised metaphysical assumptions. On this evidence, they were trying to be as 'spiritual' as they could.

This assumption, that the metaphysics of science might have been quite different, makes Mr Burtt tease Newton about absolute space as if it was a wild and unnecessary fancy; Newton ought to have been sensible, and believed in a sort of halfpenny-press relativity. But this (apart from being ungenerous) is untrue; something has to be thought of as settled; the point of that ill-named theory is not that everything became relative but that a new thing (not space but the velocity of light) was found which could be treated as absolute. Before (for instance) the Michelson–Morley experiments it was necessary to fix space, if not really for physics, then habitually for the imagination. The fact that Newton gives so much attention to the metaphysical idea of a fixed space does not show him as an inconsistent empiricist, but as a man with an extraordinary grasp of the assumptions of his own thought, an extraordinary foreknowledge of the lines on which it must be modified. Mr Burtt is unfair again (p. 266) about a passage where Newton says that 'the *variety* of motion is always decreasing' and therefore there must be some principle of conservation, perhaps something directly in the hands of God, to stop the universe from running down like a clock. Mr Burtt wrongly repeats this as 'motion was on the decay' and treats it as a theological misunderstanding of the principle of Conservation of Energy. Of course it is an extraordinary forecast of the second law of Thermodynamics; it is precisely where Newton's mind must be regarded with something hardly less than reverence that Mr Burtt accuses him of prescientific modes of thought.

It is part of Mr Burtt's thesis that the impulse behind the Copernican astronomers was not empiricism but mathematical convenience; he seems to feel that this is part of what was wrong about their metaphysical assumptions. But of course this double stress on order and truth, on the *simplest* rule that covers enough *facts*, is the essence of the scientific method. He makes it clear, indeed, that the desire to order facts simply was stronger in Copernicus than the desire to include extra facts, but then obviously, at that stage, it would have to be; Platonism and sunworship may be the historical but are not the logical causes of this. In so far as Mr Burtt is attacking (rather than describing) this early stress on mathematical convenience he is acting on a personal and arbitrary dislike of mathematics.

And it is unsafe to explain discovery in terms of a man's intellectual preconceptions, because the act of discovery is precisely that of stepping outside preconceptions. Thus Mr Burtt says that the Copernican theory was conceived as a charming piece of mathematical fitness, not scientifically, as a thing empirically true; he gives as evidence of this that people ignored the apparent absence of stellar parallaxes. He also says that Aristotle's view of space prevented him from conceiving the heavenly bodies as bodies, and as subject to geometry, so that astronomy had to wait for a revival of Platonism. Now Aristotle himself produced the argument about parallaxes, and Copernicus over-rode it; I find this a pleasing historical fact because it shows that both these great men were more intelligent (less at the mercy of their own notions) than Mr Burtt wishes to think them.

Two small points may suggest that Mr Burtt's attitude is not mathematical enough to repair the bases of physics. He says that when Pythagoras said the world was made of numbers he meant that it was made of geometrical units of space; that the early idea of number was geometrical. It was Pythagoras, on the contrary, who first showed that geometry involves incommensurables, so that it is impossible to reduce it to the natural numbers. (And anyway, the primitive idea of number is obviously not three inches but three pigs.) What Pythagoras meant I do not know, but it must have been something vaguer, more general and perhaps more profound.

I am in doubt, again, whether Mr Burtt fails or refuses to state clearly the mathematical objection to the Newtonian idea of time. The old physics conceives time as a dimension, as a ruler with the present moment like a spot of light moving along it. But this requires a second time dimension in or by which the present moment is moving along the first, and a third in or by which it is moving along the second. There is an unprofitable infinite regress, and time as experience must therefore be something more than time as a dimension. Mr Burtt knows there is something queer about time and on several occasions apparently tries to say what it is, but either he can never quite remember or he never chooses to phrase it in mathematical terms. And yet, while this is an important objection to the Newtonian assumptions, while it may be an important objection to the assumption that the universe is mathematical, yet it can only be stated in mathematical terms.

A non-mathematical analysis cannot tell one what the metaphysical foundations of physics ought to be, but it may tell one what irrelevant effects the existing foundations will have on their believers. One might go about this in various ways; I should myself like the irrelevant terms chosen to be psychoanalytical rather than religious. Kepler said not only that the sun was a god but also that it was the father; this might please Freud. Successors of Freud, such as Rank, would call Newton's desire for a self-regulating world-system a desire for return to the womb; his absolute, underlying, sustaining space an unconscious memory of the amniotic fluid. This sort of approach would maintain that the Newtonian system was the fantasy of a man who escaped dementia praecox only by a successful externalisation into mathematics; it would then have to consider in what way such a system is likely to be unsatisfying to normally sexed people; why, for instance, it is such an annoyance to Mr Burtt. It would be interesting, just as Mr Burtt's theological version (and collection of materials for it) is certainly interesting.

But such modes of approach are irrelevant to the serious claim made by the Newtonian system, and now made by relativity; it was accepted because it worked. If people nowadays will listen to a destructive analysis of the ideas of the Newtonian system (in particular, of absolute space) it is because there is another system which works better. Mr Burtt's dislike of mathematics makes him unreasonable at this point. He is claiming to attack the Newtonian idea that the world is fundamentally mathematical, and he gets his ammunition from the fact that there is now a more exclusively mathematical way of describing the world. It is likely, indeed, that the view of space taken by modern physics will eventually alter our notions of reality; but one would have to face that view more fairly than Mr Burtt is doing if one intended to discover its consequences.

Death and Its Desires

1933

The text of this unfinished talk is taken from Empson's untitled holograph draft. In substance it shows him working out a number of the ideas he would presently incorporate in Some Versions of Pastoral *(1935) – notably in chapter 1, 'Proletarian Literature'. Taken in conjunction with the appended letter to I. A. Richards (which was evidently written at the same time as this essay), it anticipates Empson's published views (see section II above) on the so-called 'Theory of Value' that Richards had promulgated in* The Foundations of Aesthetics *(1922), and then more fully in chapter 7 – 'A Psychological Theory of Value – of* Principles of Literary Criticism *(1924); crucially, it leads straight to Appendix I of* The Structure of Complex Words *(third edn, 1977, pp. 420–29), where Empson fully developed the critique of Richards's theory that he first advanced in this essay and the accompanying letter.*

The early Buddhist assertion that all existence is suffering, Empson observes in that dense Appendix to The Structure of Complex Words, *is nowadays interpreted as suggesting that the concept of Nirvana stands for 'a re-absorption into the Absolute':*

This brings it into line with a mystical strain within all the great religions, one which has usually been at loggerheads with the offer of Heaven; and there I think we find the great historical antagonist of anything like the Richards Theory of Value – that is, of any self-fulfilment theory. It is opposed to any such theory not because it is pessimistic but because it does not believe in the individual. I cannot pretend that I have any capacity to act as a go-between in this quarrel. It looks, however, as if there is one chink through which a Buddhist conclusion might creep into the arguments of Professor Richards: his rather mysterious distinction between a deadlock (which is bad) and a balance (which is good) ... if the Theory of Value merely recommends the satisfaction of the human creature, whatever makes it really satisfied, Professor Richards need not be as secure against the religions as he intended to be. What satisfied the most impulses might turn out to be the same as what was to the glory of God or even as what tended to Nirvana.... I suspect that the necessity of egotism, not the mere loss of a heavenly reward, was what made

534

[Richards] feel so horrified [as in Science and Poetry, *1925].... I do, on the other hand, think that believing more rosy things about the universe, on the specific ground that we will otherwise feel frustrated (and this is what the arguments that are proffered to us nowadays by nearly all religious leaders tend to make us do), is extremely harmful.... Certainly, by comparison with that kind of thing, the glumness of the theory of Professor Richards is its most attractive feature.... No doubt the position I am recommending is what the philosophers like to call naive realism, but I hope that need not be confused with religiosity. It seems to me that statements about value ... are capable of being true or false; and the ultimate criterion though likely to remain obscure is, I should think, very much on the lines of the Richards Theory of Value* (The Structure of Complex Words, *pp. 424–9).*

To prate about death and its desires is almost necessarily silly, if only because the mood of theorising is so far from the mood of experiencing, and the state of mind in which a great work of art is based on death wishes is not one to be hailed with delight because it caps a theory. I shall begin this paper by reciting the Fire Sermon of the Buddha, a work used by Mr Eliot in *The Waste Land* but not well known, I think only because its structure is not suited to the printed page. It is a supreme example of the beauty of at any rate one sort of death wish when in an almost pure form, and it will make discussion look very flimsy. Bhikkhus is the same word as beggars, disciples.[2]

Everything, Bhikkhus, is on fire. What everything, Bhikkhus, is on fire? The eye is on fire, the visible is on fire, the knowledge of the visible is on fire, the contact with the visible is on fire, the feeling which arises from the contact with the visible is on fire, be it pleasure, be it pain, be it neither pleasure nor pain. By what fire is it kindled? By the fire of lust, by the fire of hate, by the fire of delusion it is kindled, by birth age death pain lamentation sorrow grief despair it is kindled, thus I say. The ear ... say. The nose ... say. The tongue ... say. The body ... say. The mind ... say.

Knowing this, Bhikkhus, the wise man, following the Aryan path, learned in the law, becomes weary of the eye, he becomes weary of the visible, he becomes weary of the knowledge of the visible, he becomes weary of the contact of the visible, he becomes weary of the feeling which arises from the contact of the visible, be it pain, be it neither pleasure nor pain. He becomes weary of the ear ... pain. He becomes weary of the nose ... pain. He becomes weary of the tongue ... pain. He becomes weary of the body ... pain. He becomes weary of the mind ... pain.

When he is weary of these things, he becomes empty of desire. When he is empty of desire, he becomes free. When he is free he knows that he is free, that rebirth is at an end, that virtue is accomplished, that duty is done, and that there is no more returning to this world; thus he knows.

I called that an example of one sort of death wish in an almost pure form, and there are two qualifications; the state arrived at is Nirvana not annihilation and suicide is no use as a means of getting there. The suicide is merely popped back into life, probably in a worse condition but only because of his lack of patience; to accept the death wish of Buddhism is to plan for yourself a number of glorious and hopeful lives. (It is clear that a religion praising death has to provide some stoppage against suicide or it would be useless as a defence of the living, and Buddhism as a working system therefore hangs on the doctrine of reincarnation.) As to Nirvana, the Buddha himself and many saints were in that state for the rest of their lives after illumination, while still working and capable of pain; their state after death, free from rebirth, has the same name but cannot be described by language. 'It is wrong to say,' the Tathagata insisted, 'that the saint does exist after death . . .' It would also be wrong to say that the saint becomes one with the soul of the universe, as that was the Brahmin mystical position which it was so important to refute. When first setting out on his mission after illumination the Buddha said to a sceptic on the road, 'I go to Benares to set moving the wheels of righteousness. I will beat the drum of immortality in the darkness of the world,' and he was indignant afterwards when called an unbeliever who thought that after death the saints were annihilated. To a philosopher who maintained that happiness was the highest goal the Buddha replied that perfect happiness was only reached by renouncing the conscious pursuit of happiness and that absolute happiness when attained was not the highest goal: Nirvana was then described in terms of freedom and knowledge. On the other hand *arupa*, or desire for life in a formless world, is the seventh of the ten fetters all of which must be broken before *arhat*ship is attained; the fundamental source of evil is craving for life in any form.

Thus the main effect of the doctrine, however profound it may be, is to remove *all* doctrinal props about immortality and still claim that death is somehow of the highest value. This rationalising escape from the fear of death is carried so far that there is much less sense of tragedy and of the fascination of a sacrificial death than in Christianity with its certainly immortal individuals.

Did not Moses give you the law, and yet none of you keepeth the law? Why go ye about to kill me? The people answered and said, 'Thou hast a devil, who goeth about to kill thee.'

Christ appears here as the more set on death of the two. The nearest thing I know to a Buddhist tragedy is to be found in the Noh plays, where the theme is not a hero fated to death but the ghost of a hero who cannot enter Nirvana because he cannot forget the grandeur of his last battle. The same paradox appears in the Bodhisattvas of Mahayana Buddhism, who have refused to enter Nirvana till they have helped the last grain of sand thither before them; they I believe are admitted to have made a mistake, though a noble one for which they are worshipped. You have to learn to care about other people in order to achieve the merely personal aim of release from personality and the Bodhisattvas have made the slip of developing their altruism too far. Being still in the world they are necessarily tainted, though in the smallest degree possible, and their taint is to be busybodies. Merely to die for other people like Christ is of course a quite harmless exercise, often performed by the Buddha in previous lives. It will be observed that though the Bodhisattvas are similar to Christ, and appear soon after the Christian era along the caravan routes there is about them nothing of the Christian tragedy: they have sacrificed their deaths for the sake of man, not their lives.

These logical puzzles need I think to be stressed in praising Buddhism; the worship of death here goes both with a plan for a better life and a fundamental doubt about the nature of death when attained. One of the few clear points in the aesthetics of death wishes is that the lust for death to be beautiful must always be balanced by some kind of contradiction.

It may seem then to a psychologist that there are far less urgent death wishes in Buddhism than Christianity, but the special Buddhist version of a death wish I think needs isolating. It is that no sort of temporal life whatever can satisfy the human spirit, and therefore that we must work for an existence outside time on whatever terms. (The popular Christian heaven is of course merely unending.) There is no need to hunt about among the primitives for this conception. Primitive man is always liable to need things which he can hope to get, he has no room to be disillusioned with such things and the main business of his religion is to get them. To say this is not to under-rate the spirituality of the primitive thinkers but to praise their modesty: they were not in a position to decide whether life at its best was inherently unsatisfying. It must be remembered that to the Buddha it was a bad step in the game of life, and quite a possible one, to get yourself reborn as a deity: you would then remain for some millennia as it were in baulk, supremely happy but not able to get on with your death. As the son of a minor prince, a great landowner in a successful military clan, the Buddha could claim with some plausibility that the life he had given up was good enough for him to decide what life could possibly be. For that matter the life of a religious beggar that he chose, given the climate, the readiness of the people to feed holy men, and the fact that he was going to the equivalent of a number of universities, does not show any necessarily perverse taste for horrors; even though he gave asceticism a fair trial before he gave it up. The point I want to make about this version of a death wish is that I doubt whether any process of analysis could show it to be wrong.

It is an opinion that made D. H. Lawrence very angry, and he planned with Huxley to write a series of essays on the great perverts who thought that life was not good enough for them. Certainly it is easily perverted and difficult to display well. You must have done a great deal before you can appear disillusioned with any dignity; you must then remember that anyone else given the accident of your successes would also be disillusioned, otherwise you can be placed as a poor creature unhappy in his psychology; avoiding boastfulness you must not be plaintive, or you may be pitied for having lost your strength; and in either case you become fatuous once you expect people to admire you for making a to-do about a truth that, by hypothesis, they themselves are at bottom facing with fortitude. But it is at the back, I believe, of all the grand examples in the aesthetic of the death wishes. Shakespeare makes Lear hint at an odd and interesting reflection on this topic when faced with the despair of Gloucester. 'Thou must be patient. We came crying hither. Thou knowest, the first time that we smell the air, we waul and cry.' Along among the young of the mammals the human infant is subject to blind fits of fury at finding itself thrust into the world; it is nasty, he feels, to the point of mysticism, and I suppose Freud could hardly disagree.

Beyond the Pleasure Principle, which introduces Nirvana, is a splendid and awe-inspiring book: it gives the effect of involuntary poetry one finds in the archaic Greek philosophers, and also their effect of being only a quarry for thought, a collection of profundities. I shall not pretend to understand or to criticise it, and it has given up the medical standpoint so completely that [it] no longer carries a covert valuation of the things it might explain. It will be worth reading a few sentences from Sir Charles Eliot, whose valuation is not medical but rather that of an ambassador at the court of the Blessed One.

[No quotation provided in manuscript]

It seems clear to me that psychoanalysis has not the logical standing required to refute this sort of talk. A true and complete analysis of the Buddha, if his opinions are right, might only show *how* the distorted human creature can gain strength to recognise the truth. The psychoanalyst relies very much on a suggestion of blowing the gaff, very proper in a doctor confronted with insane fancies, but one that an aesthete who admires the fancies must be concerned to dispel.

When a Buddhist view of life is taken outright by a psychoanalyst, as in Money-Kyrle's *Development of the Sexual Impulses*, he is in a less strong position either as preacher or stylist. Money-Kyrle decides that only suicide could satisfy all impulses, but that one cannot psychoanalyse a man deeply enough to make him feel and act on the decision.[2] This would be a paltry reason for not acting on his principles; people have killed themselves before now, and on similar grounds. At bottom he is only confessing that he does not believe in his theory, and it is undignified to make the confession with so much pomp.

The solution of his logical puzzle, if I understand the matter at all, involves insight and consciousness. A mere collection of powers to react to stimuli could not want anything. It may of course be possible to make a useful new definition of the word so that one could speak of the wants of wholly unconscious organisms for things wholly unknown, but there is no reason to expect that something true about these wants is true about ours even when ours are repressed into the unconscious. When a creature has the sensation of a need, the sensation of a means, and the idea that the means will soon remove the need, it has a different kind of satisfaction from that of simply removing the need. If this common-sense idea is right it is enough I think to leave Money-Kyrle's conclusion unproven. Also he is probably wrong in calling it a Buddhist one, or anyway it would be the furthest from the Buddha of all the sects. When the Buddha says that life is on balance painful and that pleasures entail greater pains in the future he does not imply a proof and so does not suggest a refutation. But in any case his word *pleasure* is a rude word: he claimed that there are very great satisfactions in becoming an *arhat*, deserving a different name from pleasure, which do not entail further pains. The whole doctrine of course is a collection of fundamental paradoxes, and this one about pleasure is important to it.

I ought to try and fix the vague term 'death wishes', which I am not competent to do properly. The Freudian unconscious can form no idea of death, so one might either say that it has no death wishes or that its death wishes are a large mixed class. Freud uses the term for three clearly distinct ideas: the fact that all living things either die or split in half, which he treats as an instinct therefore an unconscious desire; the tendency of living things to react only when stimulated, which he treats as 'seeking' absence of stimulus; and an aggressive impulse sometimes directed against oneself. Probably the first is relevant only because we feel we have got to accept it, and the other two deserve the same name only because the human mind easily muddles them up. Two further desires more in reach of psychology are muddled up with these: the desire to return to the narcissistic state of being completely mothered in the womb and the obscure perversion of lusting after corpses, about which I know very little. Common sense agrees with Freud in connecting it with a regressive pleasure in dirt, and it may clearly be both sadistic and masochistic: corpses may be what you want to make of people or people who cannot stop you from ill-treating them; also you may want to hurt yourself by the unpleasantness of the pleasure or view yourself as similar to the corpses. Of these the desires for absence of stimulus and return to the womb are the obviously Buddhist death wishes, and are clearly a large element anyway in all but the most primitive religions. But one need not be a Freudian to agree that the others easily get mixed up with them; there is a pathetic tale in the casebooks about a religious young man who was 'deeply grieved' because he was excited by churchyards, a theme for the composer of limericks. The Buddha himself revolted against 'mortifying' oneself, becoming like a corpse, and left elaborate sanitary directions to his monasteries; at the same time dirt lust and corpse lust were things for him to guard against, and still of course prominent in Indian religion.

But if one agrees to this account of death wishes the question of aesthetics – which are bad and which good works of art based on death wishes – remains exactly where it was. Even when one is also sure about the relative merits of two works, it is not likely to be much use looking for a correlation between their merits and the character of their death wishes. The desire to return to the womb, conceived as a place of permanence and peace, is I believe much better in itself than the desire to rape corpses, and it is irritating to feel that when one is being humble before the first, in the poet Dante for example, one may if the truth were known only be being cheated by the second. It is reasonable to want to know which is which, and I think genuinely hard to find out. But it would be no use going on to say that all works of art based on corpse lusts are bad, either because this when frank is an unpleasing perversion or because no work of art is based on it frankly. There is a very nice postage-stamp collection of perversions in Romantic poetry by Mario Praz called *The Romantic Agony*, but it is prevented from being anything more important, I think, by its reproving tone. Of course he has every right as a critic to reprove the work of art, but what he reproves is the perversion. (The reproving is comically mixed up with the scientific tone: he has only to treat his authors as case histories and one feels that to touch them with anything but the scalpel would be defiling.)[3] Also he is convinced that the appearance of perversions in literature is something peculiar to nineteenth-century romanticism, an idea which seems to involve the evil influence of the philosophy of Croce, and is in any case certainly untrue. The critic who takes a Freudian point of view is in the opposite difficulty: there is so much perversion at the back of the normal, and so much oddity about the position of the artist in particular, that there seems no way of deciding what version of a perversion is to be admired. On this fundamental issue I can only hope to take a few clear examples and show the main process by which one comes to a provisional conclusion.

One rough principle can be invoked to avoid portentousness: work known to be good by the critics influenced by a fairly long series of changing fashions is not going to be spoilt by being explained. The combination of Freudian understanding and puritan sentiments is liable to be paralysing. I knew a young man who wrote that one of the most painful things about life was that any sentiment of affection, even for a cat, could be shown at bottom to be an impure one, thus calling up a fearful picture of the poor young man eyeing his cat and wondering if he might stroke it properly. To say that the 'Ode to a Nightingale' involves death wishes and the 'Ode on Melancholy' masochism, or that Shakespeare uses the language of love about the pleasures of fighting, is to point out what was always on the surface; a psychoanalysis of the authors would not show why generations of various readers have found these versions of these perversions noble and sensible, nor would it show that all these readers were wrong in their opinion.

With a contemporary author one cannot feel so sure of not being deceived, and I think the issue arises for instance about T. F. Powys. He is perpetually writing about and praising death, in a somewhat sniggering manner, and in one way of reading him you are faced very directly with a puzzle as to whether this is fine or offensive. The method is to make a demure use of the language of Christian consolation and put behind it only a vague Buddhist sense of the value of emptiness,[4] and there is a quite conscious game with necrophily when he makes his rustics feel that it is a fine thing to be a nice corpse treated in a tidy and loving manner. One has a dim feeling that a man who writes well about death ought to have something to say about it.

Taken away from an ironical game with death he seems to me merely to write badly; *The Soliloquy of a Hermit* [1916] is diffuse Anglican sentimentality. The book does however show him I think to be one of Nature's parsons, as he claims to be: this saves one from thinking the work merely ingenious, and by calling it a game I do not mean to deny that there is an emotional force behind it or that we can be seriously [?stirred] when the grotesquely distorted villagers talk noble Biblical prose. And it is not Romantic in a sense that makes one feel most nineteenth-century games with death wishes to be bogus: the artist himself is not covertly put forward as Christ or as uniquely submitted to these issues, uniquely strong enough to handle them. Nor for that matter is it genuinely clinical, with the personal stress that saves Poe from the effects of a bogus literary style: the effect is at once cosy and universal, and the style draws as much on Samuel Butler as on his flaunted Jane Austen. Llewellyn Powys in the course of one of the books about his tuberculosis tells an amusing story about Theodore coming to see him in the sanatorium: the expert on death said hardly anything and remained firmly by the window to make sure of not catching it. It would be arguable that he talks about death merely because loss of faith leaves him no other solid way to talk like a Christian: he has suggested this himself through the parson in *Mr Weston* who talked a great deal about Eternity because he no longer believed in God and had somehow to get the

right bass note into his sermons. (The analogy with the bass note is I believe
very old, though I could only think of seventeenth-century examples.) But
he shows I think very directly that this class of death wishes is not a random
collection, that you can move across from a craving for peace to a lust for
dirt and destruction without making the reader disbelieve in the character.
One of the best examples is the short story about John Pardy, an appalling
tramp who had spent his life trying to discover what was happiness, and
observing a miser who was happy in counting money gave this method a
fair trial by counting a considerable number of lice and rats. Passing on to
count the waves of the sea he was told by the waves that if he joined them he
could not only destroy himself but become one of the great elements of destruction and perhaps take part in a typhoon to destroy a city. The search
was then ended, and John Pardy walked into the sea. The main cultured
trick here is a historical one: you are forced to see the lunatic tramp as a
tropical ascetic who may at any moment start a religion. The thing is also at
least as funny as it is fearful, and no doubt one of the main and typical
places to deal with the literary death wish would be the joke. But the main
feeling resulting from this very direct use of a version of death wishes is at
the greatest distance from the feeling of perversion: the effect is single and
noble, and Pardy accepts his new career of destruction with the air of a Bodhisattva setting out to labour on behalf of the world.

Powys's weakness or perhaps his [?morality] comes out clearly I think in
the short story called 'The Only Penitent' [London: Chatto & Windus,
1931], though here the death wishes are not the main point. The parson
decides he ought to receive confessions, and the village taking a pagan view
of its sexual sins will not confess them: finally God comes in disguise and
confesses that it is he who has caused all the sin and cruelty of the world.
Lastly he confesses that he destroys man at death, and on hearing that the
vicar rises and gives him a complete absolution. This grand notion is
robbed of its force by the fact that no one in the book has committed what
Powys would consider a sin. He has a frightful power of describing characters of insane cruelty, and *if* one of them had been brought in here we
should feel the force of the Christian paradox about God taking on himself
the sins of the wicked: that would be too Christian: the sins in the book are
only little bawdy jokes. If one takes Powys simply as providing cultured
and tasteful entertainment his combination of sly corpse lusts with a tired
wish for peace is not annoying at all; it tells a minor truth about the human
mind in general and his village characters in particular. If he has tricked you
into feeling that he is telling some profound truth about life then I think you
need to become angry, as a next stage in your development, and discover
that on the contrary the stuff is nasty.

At the same time this suggestion of playing a joke on the reader is itself a grand and traditional part of the theme. The imbecility of death seems easily to connect itself with the imbecility of the clown, essentially a critic of the powerful whose function was to blow the gaff, and conceived as with an insane insight that leads him to throw off profound truths. Nor need the author be covertly deifying himself in the Romantic manner if he sets out to make the jokes of death; if the joke is to be made manifest it is he who has to do it anyway. It might be said that you have to believe in immortality before you can be macabre in good taste: the macabre seems in fact to begin in medieval and flower in late medieval times, when the Christian sense of the importance of death as the gateway to immortality was somehow strengthened by a sense of the death of a social order. And yet the Holbein dance of death engravings depend very little on a Christian Heaven or even Hell; the fact of physical death is the only thing clearly in sight however firmly the fear of hell was used as it were outside the picture to make the horror of death inescapable. Death here, a skeleton still skinny, is often an elegant and charming little figure whose small waist gives him a certain mixed-sex quality; and he is seen at his best when piping to an idiot clown and leading him on, presumably to some precipice; treating this great coy figure with so much gaiety and sympathetic admiration that the picture stays in one's mind chiefly as a love scene. Whether the Romans gave Death himself a grim humour as apart from making jokes about death I am too ignorant to know, but it would clearly have suited them. [   ] and people who believe wholeheartedly in immortality like the Egyptians or death like [   ] seem not to have invented the macabre. On the other hand the Indians have their version of it, and the sense in which the individual is immortal in Indian religion is very two-faced. I should [?say] then that this reason for disapproving of T. F. Powys, that he does not believe in the ideas he plays with, falls to the ground.

But it should be noticed that the process of critical apologetic when carried to this point becomes practically null; anything about death however silly and artificial might safely be argued to be very fine. I daresay the final criterion here is very little concerned with death and more nearly a political one; while pretending to talk about death the man is coming to some sort of balance between charity and a sense of social values. The fact that the books are about rustics is of course a central part of Powys's theme: death like the clown is a sort of perverse figure of pastoral. What you are to feel is that the simple people are in a way the best, the nearest to the truth about life, and yet that, if this is borne firmly in mind, a social structure can be rightly based upon them, with people in another way better at the top. The rustics include all the other virtues as it were in solution, and therefore they can accept their society without feeling it to be too unjust. This is the side of the books that Dr Leavis has praised very rightly in *Scrutiny*, though I seem to have given a ruling-class account of it of which he might disapprove. Probably the trouble about Emily Dickinson, an American poet and refined hermit who wrote a great number of striking metaphysical poems and became very ghoulish in later life, is that she does not get enough of this support from social ideas.

And I should say that one of the political faults of Buddhism is that it does little to make people feel in practical life the reality of the brotherhood of man: the great religions on that point probably go in the order: Islam Christianity Buddhism Hinduism.

But if that is what the books are about, this indefatigable game of talking about death must be a mere blind; the use of death wishes in such literature is only to protect something else. I said something about that in a book.

This I think is true is far as it goes, but it is a fairly superficial account of the thing: it can't stand up to the Fire Sermon. It only explains I think why one doesn't much mind whether Powys's remarks about death are in a degree bogus or not; he is already making a good use of them as it were on a lower level, and he could fairly claim, as the fundamental meaning of his clowning, that that level is not really a lower one.

If you read him like this his whole work is based on death wishes only so that the death wishes may be made trivial by comparison with the values which grow in their shadow.

I should say then that Powys's work, though liable to triviality and monotonousness, is very safe from attack: he occupies all the strong positions of the fort of the death wishes. The reason that the work is not very good indeed seems to be that one feels this too well. It has been arranged, you remember in reading, that one can feel about this in different ways, and the different ways do not add up. But it is a massive achievement in its way.

It is instructive to put against what Praz calls Romantic perversion in his examples the formula by which the thing could be idealised. The fascination for horrible or terrifying aspects of nature would no doubt be classed as masochistic, and that again could fairly be taken as pleasure in the idea that this aspect of nature could kill you. A romantic author will often compare it to the fascination of watching a passionate woman making a scene (e.g. Byron on the Jura). There is an idea at work here which I think goes back to the myth of Orpheus, and certainly does much to dignify or transform the theme of masochism; that by having courage to take delight in Nature when [it is] terrible man gains strength to control it.[5] The 'Ancient Mariner' is a good case of direct necrophile feeling transmuted in this way. The curse comes because the Mariner shoots the Albatross, symbol of the courage that can live among desolation which he has failed to enjoy, and he goes about carrying the corpse. Then in the tropics he despises the creatures of the calm.

The following sections are draft passages of the abandoned essay taken from a number of separate loose sheets.

I

and Powys will use what anybody has said. The Fables use an idea of the rudimentary and corpselike consciousness of all matter, again a Buddhist conception though not exclusively so, which allows the state of death to be treated as a humble but profound sort of life, the sort most pleasing to God, and a conscious satire on the triviality of the living. But he certainly uses in other stories both the ideas of death as merging back into the divine original and as a complete assurance of escape. 'I cast all men into the pit,' says Mr Jar at one point, 'they become nothing' [The Only Penitent', p. 57].

II

There are some theorists who would put all art on a basis one would have to call a version of death wishes, but I doubt whether this is of much importance. Elliott Smith appears to believe that art developed from mummification; a fantastic concentration on the deaths of divine heroes was necessary before the refinements of civilisation could be discovered. Clive Bell considers that a period of art starts with a spiritual discovery of some divine abstract forms and then gradually waters them down into naturalism. Otto Rank's book *Art and Artist,* so far as I understand it, takes a similar but vaguer and more fundamental view; all art is concerned with one or other version of immortality, personal or collective or whatnot, and these produce the various styles.[6] Some version of doubt about immortality would be a more plausible claim. He then has to regard Aurignacian man as a passionate individualist, which seems possible but unlikely to be proved; in fact the historical evidence rather goes against all these opinions. It is no doubt true that there is a strong desire for permanence at the back of the arts; the moment of value must be fixed and kept. This is no less true of naturalistic than abstract painting, and the dancer or bullfighter tries to perfect his technique so that the thing may be done again and again. But it is equally true of the scientist and the responsible politician; everybody tries to keep what they think valuable; there is nothing here peculiar to aesthetics or likely to be more obvious in the arts than in all human activity. The tidy and amusing view that all art is based on a contradiction with death wishes seems too sweeping to be fruitful.

The same might be said about the opinion I have tried to maintain, that all noble art, all art that suggests a better life, is based on some sort of contradiction. The immediate effect of this is to paralyse the critic, because it depends on the appreciator whether the contradiction leads him up or down. Or rather it leaves the critic in a particularly safe position especially against the encroaching scientist; the decision depends on taste, and only he can do it. The view is I believe nowhere maintained with such subtlety as by Swift in *A Tale of a Tub*. 'The highest things,' he is perpetually hinting, 'always have low and disgusting things, natural parodies, both in the arts and in religion, so like that no argument can make the distinction.' So as to help taste in making its distinction he occupies the book in providing a complete set of obscene puns; in every situation the refined reader is fortified with the indispensable irony. It is an obviously unpleasing position but one of much plausibility. It seems clear at any rate that no advance of science, for example of psychoanalysis, in aesthetics can conceivably replace the necessity for mere judgement; the knowledge at every stage is finite, and beyond that one must rely on the man who claims to feel his way. If the doctrine means no more than that indeed it is harmless. But it may mean more than it seems to mean; the great danger with Swift, who [was] always in hot water with his irony, was that he became more and more liable to class high things among low things. The idea that all life and all products of life are essentially inadequate I think hangs on the mind not as what one feels but as what it is decent to recognise *would* be felt, were one ever in a position to know; the art of death wishes, static as it may appear, essentially wishes to move you beyond itself; and I at least after poking [about] in this topic can only leave it with the drone of [the Fire Sermon] still sounding in my ears. He becomes weary of the [. . .]

III

Since a fascination with death and horror of the wrong sort must lie behind any version of this it is not clear why some types of art have so much more of the life-in-death quality than others. No doubt the habits of rich Egyptians after death were a great stimulus to artists and saved them from unemployment, but that is another thing. The earliest surviving works of art, paintings of animals by Cro-Magnon man, probably not more than 50,000 years old, whatever religious beliefs and artistic traditions may lie behind them, work as it were by drawing a line round a shadow, not by a process of abstraction. Still in Aurignacian times you get a very naturalistic bison licking its lips; an ivory head dated 'fairly early Aurignacian' shows a definitely pretty girl in a cap. The art suggests a fresh and lively interest in the subject, and seems as far from death wishes as any art one could name. Periods of abstract art seem to have arisen both in Aurignacian and later Magdalanean times (supposed to be by the same race) but never adopted completely:

they do not seem very deathly; and the stylised men shooting naturalistic animals in Spain are extremely gay. It seems unlikely that the earliest true men should have been some of Rank's fullblown individualists. The feeling in the drawings no doubt tells one very little; the sorcerer deep in the Trois Frères cave is clearly meant from his setting to be as macabre as he looks, and he is surrounded with naturalistic animals; the same people left traces of their mutilated hands. Still this is a later development. As to burial, Neanderthal man buried his chiefs with their valuables for hundreds of thousands of years, and produced no art of any kind. If Leakey[7] is right in saying that these apemen exchanged techniques of flintnapping with the ancestors of present-day man, shortly before the days of the earliest surviving art, and continued to use the improved technique for some time afterwards, one might hazard a guess that they were not interested in pictures of statues when they saw them. At any rate it is pretty clear that the artistic impulse is not always produced by the practice of burial. Coming back to the civilisations, elaborate royal funerals do not occur in the early Sumerian or Indus cultures, and the later Ur burials are supposed to have been imitated from Egypt, while the notion that all civilised habits came from Egypt has been widely blown upon. No doubt any early civilisation has to insist on permanence while suppressing many impulses of many of its members, so that one would expect it to produce an art of fixity and repression, but the tidy and amusing plan of basing all art on death wishes has not on the whole much support from the little we know of early man.

IV

Nor is a fully developed humanist art free from contradictions of the same kind; indeed I should say that in classifying any kind of heroic or exalted aesthetic formula the simplest thing is to give its root contradictions. This is not of course to say that a contradiction is valuable in itself or that an artist can safely repose on a statement of blank contradiction, but it needs to claim that given a contradiction the artist will be led to a certain class of notions and feelings. I remember saying something about Michelangelo in this connection to a lady who at once went off into a story about how she had made a scene in the Sistine Chapel and denounced all the frescoes; they were bogus; their version of the heroic was always based on shapes of exhaustion or fear. I was going to say that this was *how* the heroic was expressed, an interesting point of technique, and the puzzle about valuing the result was a complete surprise. The fact itself seems clear; he takes for example a pose of a homosexual young man deliciously shrinking back and covers it with enormous muscles; it then surges forward and looks nobly masculine. It is interesting to look at some well-considered praise in a recent book by an Italian expert. We hear of the 'primitive grandeur in the Herculean limbs, faces furrowed by intensity of will, and great muscles that seem to conquer the weight of the masses'. The muscles may well seem to conquer the masses; they are the spiritual part of the picture. The reason that this seems primitive is that it is like the simple conception of the idea of good in which a very strong man must be very good since he has a great deal of *mana*, but obviously its motives are not so simple. 'Still Christian and already pagan, he expresses no longer the religious content of but the pure humanity produced by Christianity.' The pure humanity here are not all comfortable; if that is the essential thing there is much to be said for the people who thought Raphael was doing it better. 'The muscles are fluid; they ripple in waves under the impulse of powerful breathing.' This is a helpful remark; there is an ambiguous quality even about the muscles themselves for which one needs the heroic interpretation. Without muscles many of these delicious mixed-sex creatures would be wallowing languorously about; covered with muscles they roll and bubble with divine afflatus.

V

[On the 'Ancient Mariner'] He then sees the beauty of the creatures of the calm, and the spell breaks. This conception I think really is of the greatest magnificence: the trouble with the poem is that Coleridge thought he could put his clash into a plain Christian moral at the end. In later life he used to say sometimes that he had put in too much of the moral, sometimes too little, and crossed out the verse about crawling with legs. It is clear that on this formula any perversion may have great value if it gives power to find delight in the macabre situation and therefore courage to face it; the central theme is that the man must have some power to stand up between the conflicting impulses of life and then he will make them valuable.

VI

In the same way the dignity of [Swinburne's] *Poems and Ballads* is essentially one of courage, both in the social conditions of the poetry and its themes. Nicolson's picture of the poet squeaking at recitation and working himself up as out of a morass with little hen-like movements of the elbows is surely the essential one;[8] the business of a singer, he said, was to sing: under the stress of the most fantastic contradictions life is still valuable if he can stand up between them. It is clear that on this formula *any* perversion may have great value if it gives power to find delight in the macabre situation and therefore courage to face it. A Victorian account, this may appear, searching for a formula to make the thing respectable, but no merely blow-the-gaff account seems to me not to explain the merits of the subject in hand. The advantage aimed at is of course not obtained if the artist puts in the moral at the start or holds to it as a lifebelt; to do that is to refuse to accept the conditions.

VII

The plainest case of this notion of control and its connection both with a scientific notion and a perverse one comes I think in Poe's story 'A Descent into the Maelstrom'. The sailor in the whirlpool falls into a half-imbecile condition of fascination at the spectacle of so great a death; he has as little will, and the same nerveless interest in the symptoms, as the typecase of necrophily in 'Eleanora'. Just because of this he watches the thing with the interest of a free mind; he sees that barrels sink more slowly than ships; he escapes by jumping on to a barrel. The perverse pleasure turns into the intellectual type of power. The theme here by the way is the opposite of the Faust theme, the tragic hubris of knowledge, with which it is generally combined. I should not call this a very great achievement in itself, only a very direct dramatisation of one of Poe's fundamental ideas, but it shows the dignity possible to a neurosis.

VIII

This is true as far as it goes, I feel sure, of the refined death cult of the Romantics, but that was a revival of stranger and more primitive affairs; one ought also to have something to say about the fourteenth-century 'Danse Macabre', the sexless rigid decorations of Egypt, Byzantium and the Aztecs in praise of death and eternity, the feverish wriggling sensuality of the cult of Durga the destroyer. It seems roughly true on these examples that a cult of death goes with lack of economic and social freedom – Byzantium returned to the caste system of Egypt, and the Indian death cults seem to become stronger as the caste system becomes more elaborately rigid. This says nothing about why the Indian was so far the most frankly concerned with sex. Rank says that sex appears in art when a people gives up matriarchy for patriarchy, but I don't understand what historical [...]

IX

This I think is true as far as it goes, but the refined death wishes of the Romantics are clearly not a simple case; mixed up with desires to use neuroses for what had once been done by religion, to protect the artist against the scientific outlook by giving him the freedom of lunacy, and to let him join the sciences as a profound psychologist. I claimed the Buddhist other-worldly feeling (not of course peculiar to Buddhism) as the only sort of death wish which can be wholly admired in itself; one might look then for a pure and direct art of death wishes in Byzantium and the art of Buddhism. The use of a fundamental contradiction between death and a completely satisfying life is I think in these cases particularly clear. There are three main types of Buddha, clashing the sage and the child, the court lady and the male ascetic, and in early work the bruiser and the flower. This last I believe is also the basis of the successful statues of the Pharaohs; it is not so fundamentally concerned either with death or spirituality. I myself find it the most moving of the three; it is perhaps quickest described as what everybody feels about carthorses, and has a strong element of pastoral or feeling of the brotherhood of man; it is the pathos of the strong man doing his best at the work of being a deity. The other two are clear cases of contradiction about the Buddhist type of death wish, and are best when the contradiction is felt most keenly and imposed most firmly on the forms. Byzantine work is quickest approached through its influence on the Cubists, about which T. E. Hulme wrote some interesting praise [*Speculations*, 1924]. He divided art into that based on mechanical, human and divine forms, these being rigidly distinct; negro forms were mechanical and based on fear of the material universe, Byzantine forms on the divine abstractions; both might be borrowed by Cubists for a new sort of divine abstraction useful in rendering the Machine Age, but when the frequently communist Cubists believed their work to be mechanical not divine they were acting more [. . .]

X

I ought now to try to face the whole business of tragedy more directly. The prime object of tragedy is to make you feel that the death of the hero with whom you identify yourself, and even in the least 'inevitable' cases, even in the clown's tumble of the surprise deaths of Lear and Cordelia, is aesthetically satisfying and therefore what you wanted. This seems the plainest case of the transmutation of a death wish. One might suppose the business was not death but immortality, but Christian tragedies are very little concerned with Christian ideas of the afterlife. That Macbeth went to Hell *is* I should say part of his tragedy, though not an essential part since he arrived at Hell on earth, but it means very little that angels should sing Hamlet to his rest. Indeed if you believe quite simply that Othello and Desdemona have been transferred together to Heaven their story is not tragic at all. It seems not to be denied that *Uncle Vanya* is a tragedy, and the introduction of eternal life at the end acts as a last irony; they build castles in Heaven only when it is grindingly hopeless to build them elsewhere. So far as immortality comes into tragedy, it is essentially contradicted.

XI

One main idea at the back of tragedy is that the hero arrives at knowledge of himself and the world by a process which destroys him: he would have been safe if he had known before, but this was the only way to get to know, and to reach the truth even by this route is felt to be worth the consequences. The same desire to try out the worst and know about it is clearly at work in making the spectator sit through the tragedy, and I should [think] that this very worthy impulse has always something of what Lawrence imputed to it with so much fury, a lust to become superior to life and to kill it by getting it fixed and known. The other main theme of tragedy is the acceptance of fate. The idea of 'necessity', a word employed by critics without much show of logic, also no doubt involves making the audience covertly desire what they no longer hope might be avoided. It is worth notice that the literary use of the philosophical argument about free will and necessity tends to involve very bad philosophical arguments. In this the literary men may be right; the question had occupied the European mind continually since Homer, and never occupied the Eastern mind at all, so the reason we are so much interested in it is probably less a matter of logic than of cultural bias.

XII

To explain away the death-wishes business like this is only to deal with the edges of it.

*

MS letter from Empson to I. A. Richards, written on a visit to Peking, 2 April 1933 (apparently not posted):

Dear Mr Richards,
  Peking very good in more ways than one, but no Buddhas of any merit. No train to the caves with Buddhas in a loop of the Wall till Tuesday.
  Buddhism is relevant to what I am trying to think about, in connection with the Value business (what a *stupid* writer Westermarck is).[9] The

question obviously rises on the Calculable Value theory whether optimism or pessimism, otherwise such dim terms, are true: whether the total satisfaction of all lives is negative (e.g.) Freud's dim but rich concept of death wishes comes in here: one sense of it is certainly that all impulses are reactions to a stimulus aiming at the removal of the stimulus: if this is all that the fuss is about, the way to remove all stimuli is suicide. And if we could be completely psychoanalysed we might accept and act on this conclusion – whether psychoanalysis is really a process of showing the subject the truth or of hypnotising him into agreeing with the analyst. Westermarck escapes this issue by taking what he calls emotions as reliable: if the psychoanalyst can change them, and really many people can change them, this is no longer true. (Clearly to do this the analyst would have to analyse down to the most primitive organic levels: the question whether 'bringing into consciousness' is possible, in the end, or can possibly have any effect, comes up sharply here.) The suggestion of 'satisfaction' as opposed to its derivation carries the puzzle neatly, and '*content*' has gone the other way – starting with the idea of still holding a satisfaction as a thing you can keep after its simpler part is over – as your *content* – turning to 'putting up with what you can get'. It seems clear that there is an issue in this about value, because it raises the question whether value other than avoidance of pain can be achieved.

You deal with this by the pregnant words 'balance – deadlock', which make an ingenious claim to be unemotional and scientific.[10] Certainly they bring in the value considerations which the analysts try to shirk. But the suggestion that a balance is a fertilising sort of flat conflict because it allows the energy to flow into other channels (thus at once giving a store of energy, a sort of battery, a storm that shakes things to a more reliable level – and a process that brings more of the whole organism into a single reaction) – which obviously goes a long way – still doesn't face the issue that this may be done badly: it is just this process that sends energy into perverse desires that give pain when unsatisfied and no pleasure when satisfied. Some such perverse desires give satisfaction when satisfied by sheer luck from an irrelevant source as a discovery, and no doubt those are kept up; this idea of development from perversions is exactly parallel to the idea of organic evolution from the very few mutations – accidents to the germiplasm – which happen to be useful. (So that the use of the origin of an idea as a test of its validity is fully refuted by the men who use it.) But there is nothing in your distinction to distinguish these from pathetic perversions.

What *balance* and *deadlock* suggest is respectively a man able to walk on a tightrope and two men fighting where both are unsatisfied and neither able to get further or escape. There is a subtle introduction of the Will here. The *balance* is between falling to left or right: there is no balance between walking forward or backward, or between falling or not falling. (The conception of will itself is such a balance, between random and fixed.) The Buddhist position as I understand it is that impulses within causation are essentially avoidances of pain, and that (apparent) satisfactions are harmful because they are creators of desire which eventually produce more pain. One might say that some satisfactions are obviously positive because the aged bewail the failure of their desires, but the Buddhist answer does for this. The Mahayana business then claims that there are positive satisfactions but they are essentially apart from causation and therefore 'impersonal': you get in Money-Kyrle's *Development of Sexual Impulses* e.g. an early-Buddhist pessimism which obviously excites this sort of escape. (By the way when D. H. Lawrence said that Buddhism was all pomp built round a vacuum, he was in Ceylon and talking only about Hinayana Buddhism, about which what he said may be true.) I certainly do not see what other means would introduce positive satisfaction: on the whole, you understand, since the pleasure is defined as the removal of an equal pain. A conceivable loophole is in his definitions of 'desire' – a sensation of a need together with the idea of the means of quieting it; 'appetite' – a sensation of a need together with the sensation of the means of quieting it. It is the intellectuality of the creature, the fact of its consciousness, which alone makes a state of want able to be a state of pleasure. This at least gives consciousness a legitimate importance: in his book there is no suggestion as to why it should occur or whether everything would be the same if it didn't. Counting the impulses satisfied in a creature with an appetite relieved without consciousness the total value is nil; counting in the consciousness the value is positive.

Consciousness of course (which people so cheerfully give to atoms 'in a dim form' to make everything 'continuous') is an alarming business because (supposing it to be consciousness of something) you must be conscious of that and of its alternative, of two things, of the number two – 'dimly' – of the rest of mathematics. Nothing is gained by saying that consciousness may be 'dim': if the rocks are conscious the universe is peculiar: I don't say it isn't. ('Insight' needs fitting in here just as 'will' did before.) It seems clear that consciousness is somehow involved in value, because if there was no consciousness we would at any rate feel there was no value. I am not sure that the 'consciousness' issue does not cover the 'will' one: the real puzzle about choosing is that you must be able to choose to choose to choose, as to know that you know that you know. Both regresses are only the reflections from two mirrors got by turning the mirror of consciousness back on itself.

A more literary point is the question why Money-Kyrle's pessimism is so annoying, why one feels he has no right to it. Just the same idea really is behind Powys (T. F.) who makes it seem Eternal Truth, as Buddhists do:

one is tempted to talk about 'experience behind it' but I don't believe in Powys's experience of country people – I was beaten by the village idiot as a child, come to think of it, which will do for an 'experience' – I am sure country people in Yorkshire aren't like that, though of very little else about them. His early books are obvious records of shock at finding himself unpopular in the village.

The point is that death wishes of that sort aren't even impressive unless they drag other things into them, and in the right way. 'The Only Penitent', I have been sorry to have to decide, is the wrong way, though only if you take it seriously. The whole point of the climax is that God takes on himself all sins: this pretends to be a striking and advanced blasphemy but is in fact God's forgiveness of sins. The objection here is that the issue is not made real because there is no real sin in the book. Powys is very capable of describing cruelty and some sort of death wishes (cruelty to oneself) which he *doesn't* consider valuable (this alone blows the gaff on his death cult) but though there are endless little jokes about sin in the book they are all bawdy jokes about things Powys himself doesn't think sinful. The sexual amusement of the village might easily be made to seem sinful by letting in an abortion or what not, but he is careful to make us feel that it is all 'pastoral'. It is disappointing to find him playing this trick because it is typical of the nineties. Wilde's 'Pen, Pencil and Poison' is trying to make you feel that Wilde too is an 'artistic' sinner – even to prophesying his own 'curious courage' in causing his own trial – but he only found this satisfying because he was really talking not about sin but about scandal – he didn't think his sexual habits (anyway) *as* wicked as poisoning a friend with arsenic to annoy an insurance company. The trick is slavish (that is the nineties' 'sense of sin') because it is intellectual dishonesty – he isn't trying to deal with what *he* thinks right but what is considered right in the drawing-rooms he is pet of, and with his relation to them as a 'wicked artist' from outside. Powys's 'naughty jokes' are a shockingly poor preparation for the enormous issue he tries to raise as a climax – if he put *his* idea of evil into the book it wouldn't stand the strain. (One can see he is cheating when he makes the parson's wife think of seducing a farmer so as to have a sin which she could confess – this is out of place because it involves the suggestion if not of real sin at least of real pain.)

What seems clear as a matter of taste is that this set of ideas, so far from being a straightforward statement about life, is a peculiarly tricky play with symbols. Money-Kyrle doesn't bring it off and the 'pessimism' he arrives at (apart from the nonsense of his last chapter) affects me as 'boyish'. It really seems clear that there are positive satisfactions, and that a majority of the people in this bar, like myself, are receiving them as I write. But I do not see how they can be accounted for if all action is attempt to escape immediate pain: and if there are no such satisfactions there is no complete thing, no whole individual, which you would call valuable.

Yours etc.

W. Empson.

Notes

1 The manuscript does not include a text of the Fire Sermon; the version given here is Empson's own translation from *Collected Poems* (1955).

2 Empson has in mind the following observations by Money-Kyrle: 'Our private purpose is to remove and avoid our needs and injuries as effectively as possible, but only if we do so in the same manner as our ancestors, shall we in turn perpetuate our race. There is thus the possibility of an opposition between the interest of the individual and that of the race. If, by intelligence, we discover more rapid methods of removing and avoiding our needs and injuries than the methods inherited as instincts, we shall presumably adopt them. But there is no guarantee that these methods will be of equal service to the race. It is possible that the most economic way of removing and avoiding injuries and needs is to seek death rather than life, and that nothing but an inherited false idea of death as a state of pain and want has prevented our race from exterminating itself' (R. E. Money-Kyrle, *The Development of the Sexual Impulses*, London: Kegan Paul, 1932, p. 61).

'The danger that knowledge will destroy instincts is of course remote. But it is just possible that the individualists of the future not only may be too lazy to propagate their species, but that they may even discover that the lethal chamber is an easier and more permanent means to the removal of their needs than the circuitous method of sowing, reaping, harvesting, eating, and copulating, which they now employ' (pp. 201–2).

3 Compare Empson's remarks in 'Feelings in Words': 'The art works which can be viewed as glorifying death wishes cover a large field; T. E. Hulme seemed to regard all Byzantine art as of this type, Otto Rank argued that the invention of portrait sculpture by the Egyptians derived from a sort of necrophily, Mario Praz in *The Romantic Agony* extended a solemn clinical disapproval over most of nineteenth-century literature. It seems to be a general rule, however, that if the effect is beautiful the lust for death is balanced by some impulse or interest which contradicts it. One might argue that the contradiction merely supplies the tension, and does not decide the note on which the string will vibrate – the resultant meaning may have very little to do with the apparent despair' (*The Structure of Complex Words*, p. 12).

4 Compare Empson's remarks in 'Proletarian Literature': 'nobody would take the pastoral of T. F. Powys for proletarian, though it really is about workers; his object in writing about country people is to get a simple enough material for his purpose, which one might sum up as a play with Christian imagery backed only by a Buddhist union of God and death. No doubt he would say that country people really feel this, and are wiser about it than the cultivated, and that he is their spokesman, but the characters are firmly artificial and kept at a great distance from the author' (*Some Versions of Pastoral*, London, 1935, p. 7).

5 Empson added in the margin of his manuscript: 'delight for any cause hence any such perversion may be valuable'.

Compare his observation in the essay 'Marvell's Garden' that 'the idea about Nature' of the 'Hymn to David' and the 'Ancient Mariner' is 'the Orpheus idea, that by delight in Nature when terrible man gains strength to control it. This grand theme ... has a root in magic; it is an important version of the idea of the man powerful because he has included everything in himself ...' (*Some Versions of Pastoral*, p. 120).

6 Sir Grafton Elliott Smith, *Culture: The Diffusion Controversy* (London: Kegan Paul, 1928) and *The Search for Man's Ancestors* (London: Watts & Co., 1931); Arthur Clive Bell,

Art (London: Chatto & Windus, 1914) and *Civilization: An Essay* (London: Chatto & Windus, 1928); Otto Rank, *Art and Artist: Creative Urge and Personality Development* (New York: Knopf, 1932).

7 Louis Leakey, *The Stone Age Cultures of Kenya Colony* (Cambridge: Cambridge University Press, 1931).

8 Harold Nicolson, *Swinburne* (English Men of Letters), London: Macmillan, 1926.

9 Edward A. Westermarck (1862–1939): Finnish sociologist, philosopher and anthropologist; author of *The Origin and Development of the Moral Ideas* (1906) and *Ethical Relativity* (1932), which argued that no moral truths or judgements could have an absolute validity – they were merely subjective and relative.

10 See, for example, Richards's observation that 'The equilibrium of opposed impulses, which we suspect to be the ground-plan of the most valuable aesthetic responses, brings into play far more of our personality than is possible in experiences of a more defined emotion.' Aesthetic experiences provide 'a balance of opposites' or 'states of composure', Richards argued: 'What happens is the exact opposite to a deadlock, for compared to the experience of great poetry every other state of mind is one of bafflement' (*Principles of Literary Criticism* (1924), London: Routledge & Kegan Paul, 1967, pp. 197–8).

The Ideal of the Good[1]

c. 1933

The theories to the effect that mankind is essentially a fighting creature, built up during the revolt against Christianity, have clearly done great harm during the last fifty years. The subject is very complex and must therefore be approached in an impressionistic way (however much consolidating could be done eventually), but it is one that everybody has to have an opinion about as a basis for his political stand or even his ordinary life, and the less muddled he is the better, so one should not be put off it merely by dislike for amateurishness. The points need to be made not in specialised scientific language.

Calvin's necessitarianism (or rather the use he made of that side of St Augustine) is probably the historical starting point, but I am ignorant about it. Its feeling of harshness and its connection with the growing business world seem to set a tone for quite different theoretical constructions formed later in northern Europe.

In a way the neatest and most attractive case of a 'heretical' theory of human nature is Rochefoucauld's. It is like a working model, both from the deceptive clarity of its form and from the feeling that it is charming because it is a toy. One feels that this proof that all human actions are and must be selfish is, in some fundamental and subtle way, securely wrong; or rather that it doesn't matter whether or not the theory is literally true, for some very subtle reason which cannot be stated. But meanwhile, one feels, the theory has a delightfully large field in which it gives true answers, and this is valuable because human pretensions need to be exposed; a great deal of cruelty is due to self-righteousness; a noble mind never wishes to make claims that its actions are truly generous, but is concerned to see all the possible sources of satisfaction in a given situation; and we under-rate our neighbours if we do not admit the painful complexity of their position. The triumph of the style is that he can say a very long list of mean things without your ever deciding that he himself is mean. In short, the *Maxims* would not even be good writing if they did not carry a hint of paradox and self-contradiction. There is a similar position about determinism; we know that (however hard it is to see why) we would be silly to be frightened by determinism, because we aren't tied up and gagged like a man who really isn't free.

A more scientific theory was provided by the Marquis de Sade, whose disciple Swinburne gives evidence about the effects of the theory when put into action as literature. This theory treats the lust to inflict pain on others as fundamental, as the idea in terms of which a complex affair should be analysed and understood. Swinburne cannot set out to describe passion felt between ordinary lovers (historical personages for instance) without dragging in the tortures that they inflicted on each other:

> By the lips intertwisted and bitten
> Till the foam has a savour of blood
>
> ['Dolores', ll. 115–16]

is the centre of his invocation of the Queen of Passion. Of course it is not the perversion as such which one cocks one's eye at. If they both like it (and many couples do like a reasonable amount of biting) they are only giving each other a nice time. The question is rather what they think radically nice; whatever the means, what is the end.

Then in the full-blown scientific theory of Darwinism the criterion of good becomes 'survival', not any selfish gratification but to keep your own stock in being and to make it even more fit to survive. The indignation of the clergy at the time does not now seem so foolish as it did to enlightened people in the later nineteenth century. When the theory became generally taken for granted it really was used as a justification for racial and nationalist wars of conquest and extermination, and indeed for the earlier private armies of the American capitalists. Considering that the exquisitely adapted tapeworm and the unadvancing amoeba have both proved themselves successful by this criterion of the good it seems an obviously unsatisfying one; and to have appeared satisfying it must I think have bolstered itself on the other reasons for thinking that struggle is good – because selfishness is inherently unescapable, or because pleasure is gained from mastery and from imposing pain.

To be sure, Darwin did not lay down survival as the only good, or claim any ethical theory as such. But the effect of his way of putting the theory was to suggest that a stock could only survive by harsh methods of struggle. One man can die for what he believes to be good; many men have done so; it is psychologically possible to carry the thing through. But a statesman has no business to be heroic; it is not his function to destroy the whole group he leads. Whatever may be said in absolute ethics, if a moral theory can be shown to cause the annihilation of any group that carries it out, then that theory will not long survive – it is patently not fit to. Even God in theology has to exist as well as to be good. Thus there might have been a fundamental argument over Darwin, but the dilemma was not seriously raised. What happened was rather that Darwin described the daisies and buttercups in the meadow as 'struggling' with one another, like tigers for instance, and the effect of this trope was to make people feel that men would do better to act like tigers rather than like buttercups. There was a preference for the language of struggle which Darwin himself admitted to be metaphorical. In the same way the counterattacking Lamarckists said that the daisy was like the patient giraffe, gradually willing its neck to be longer and that men ought to recognise that they are necessarily like this giraffe. Neither side admitted that man on the one hand can choose between the lines of effort of the tiger and the giraffe, whereas daisies on the other hand cannot take part in either. There is a large background of wilfulness, obviously, to the moral theories derived from the biology.

The theoretical structure raised by Freud was of course a deservedly great influence on the mental climate, but it is hard to see that it implies a new ideal of the good. Politically it is negative, because the difficulty of becoming sane is so great for the individual that he has little basis for saying he knows his rulers are wrong. The theoretical grounds for altruistic action are made even more dubious; a man is obviously likely to be deluded by his unconscious when he claims to have an ethical theory. And the actual aim of the healing work on which the Freudian world picture was based is simply release from torment. The Freudian disciple Money-Kyrle carried this to its logical conclusion when he argued [in *The Development of the Sexual Impulses*, London: Kegan Paul, 1932] that after a completely satisfactory psychoanalysis a man would be free to kill himself in peace.

This aim is also the ideal of the lofty religion of the Buddha, whose theology has a better reason for avoiding immediate suicide. Money-Kyrle I suppose could only say that though he knew what he ought to do he hadn't yet been analysed enough to do it. The Buddhist believes that if he kills himself directly he will only be reborn in a lower existence, so he must woo his real death by the more circuitous technique of good works. This makes the religion a practicable system for men who take their theories seriously enough to act upon them. Idealisation of death as the supreme good has of course been common enough outside Buddhism, and the Christian anathema on suicide was very necessary to make its programme practicable – in the same way Mrs Eddy decided to put a stop on childbirth by faith-healing (though heroines of the cult still sometimes break her rules) because it put too much strain on the faith of the rank and file. The straightforward argument for the ideal of death was best put by Pascal, who said that any man feels miserable if he shuts himself up alone for long enough, and that this proves that his ordinary occupations are only a device for hiding from himself his real and fundamental misery. It is logically on a par with saying that all men are really and fundamentally dying of famine, and that they only keep on eating in order to delude themselves into forgetting this truth. But the ideal of death is a protean and recurring element in our mental climate (the Nazis on their Wagnerian side seem to have used it as a queer sort of last justification) and it needs listing in any attempt to survey the ethical theories which active people take for granted.

I will now try to say what mankind really does want, regardless of platitude and of the narrowness of my own experience. They like affection and good humour on a basis of adequate mutual respect. Of course you do not want people too soft, but toughness is not an end in itself, only the basis for securing affection. We tend to under-rate the craving for company because we are seldom short of it; but after a few weeks of complete solitude most people will 'do anything' (as they say) for company; it is a much more imperious craving than sex. Our whole mental life is based on being social animals. Of course the man may quarrel with his company when he gets it, and feel pleased about that; but what he chiefly needed was the company. The test of Pascal, in short, is I think the decisive one, though he chose to draw exactly the wrong conclusion from it. Rather in the same way the idea that readiness for death is the final good can I think also be given a humble and practical application. It is interesting to consider what the protagonists of the grimmer theories of value thought about when they went to sleep. It is clear that by our evolutionary development we cannot abandon ourselves to sleep till we feel safe; also we cannot sleep if any unsatisfied craving demands activity. To get to sleep you must therefore in some moderate degree have reached a state of permanent satisfaction. The popular joke about counting sheep only describes a process of trying to exclude painful or lustful thoughts. The positive step is to fill your mind with some idea of placid affection, and I imagine that people only don't say this often because they protect their tenderness and their daydreams with what is called a natural shame. Mr Bloom in *Ulysses*, always a practical man, puts the point well when before going to bed he decides to think about the house he will build for himself and the errant Mrs Bloom when he is rich; he regards this course of reflection as a measure of hygiene.

I don't remember seeing references by any school of psychologists to the fact that a working psychological setup must allow you to get to sleep. The novelist Anthony Trollope however emphasises it among the effects of drink. The later stages of a drunkard, he brings out, are miserable because the man can neither eat with his drink nor sleep without it; he thus creates a bottleneck, because to carry on life a man must be able to do both. The point is relevant here because drink is much used to escape remorse or to carry through a supposed duty of cruelty, more so indeed than to give courage. Many men get to sleep on drink without reaching the bottleneck of failing to eat, so that the problem of getting to sleep is less hard than they seem to pretend. On the other hand the universal demand for narcotics throughout history does I think suggest that many people need help in getting to sleep; it is a weak point in the average day-to-day psychology.

How do Swinburne's biters get to sleep? No doubt if they both enjoyed it they can go to sleep not only satisfied but proud; feeling, 'My word, I've given this girl a good time – she's almost bitten to rags' and so forth. The fundamental pleasure to which they sink back, in such an arrangement, is a feeling of pride in their own generosity, however grotesque the path by which it was achieved. Much fuss has been made about the idea that the primitive instincts of sex are fundamentally brutal; Aldous Huxley for instance in *After Many a Summer* made the undying earl become a sadist as a logical part of his return to the ape. But it is usual among the mammals for the male to woo the female; on this argument it is a deeply rooted element in human sex that the man is vain about his power to please, and the desire to please is not a brutal thing. Pure sadism, in the sense of only wanting the partner to suffer, is not an outbreak of the primitive but a very specialised form of disease. It should not therefore, it seems to me, be regarded as a fundamental thing in terms of which you interpret a more complex situation (as selfishness, for example, can be used). And after Gilles de Rais had had a bout of his tortures it seems to me hard to imagine how he got to sleep; or rather, since it may have acted as a drug, how he got to sleep the night after. On the other hand, the idea that you can get love for force, that is, that you can break the woman's resistance and make her enjoy the act against her will, is reassuring to a man. So long as she admits enjoying it in the end he feels no immediate guilt to keep him from sleeping; and he is safe, because he has shown he can get his pleasure again when he wants it; on this ground too he can sleep. More generally, to feel strong is to feel safe, and to have a strong partner is to feel safe; nobody likes mere weakness. Even an element of revenge is often felt to be a reasonable impulse, and if it has satisfied itself that at least is over and we can sleep. In various ways you can get close to pure sadism without madness through the craving for extra stimulation and the sense of power; and of course I am not pretending that the mental disease of pure sadism does not occur; I am arguing that it needs to be analysed into other terms and not treated as fundamental.

Calvin must have gone to sleep by thinking about heaven; there at any rate, if nowhere on earth, he could conceive conditions of affection and good humour. The famous view of Tertullian and Aquinas that the saints in heaven enjoyed the tortures of the damned must I believe have been a theory of their waking hours. I may of course only be showing innocence in

writing down these conjectures, but I cannot stretch my mind round the
process of sending yourself to sleep by imagining the tortures of the
damned. Swinburne in the days of his good verse commonly drank himself
to sleep on whisky, and it occurs to me that the mysterious ailment of
Darwin, apparently a strong healthy man who yet suffered for all his later
life from a painful and crippling mental illness, may be due to the practical
difficulty which faced the inventor of Darwinism in finding anything nice to
think about before going to sleep.

The reader may feel that there is a contradiction here between the ideas
of the good in action and of the absolute good in peace. Pascal and the
mystics in general were waved aside, he may say, in favour of Aristotle's
view that value is in activity [see the *Politics*, VII. iii]. But then a triviality
about how people go to sleep was brought forward as a test of value in activity, though it could only buttress itself on the analogy of the absolute
good in peace. This is so; but the two pictures of the good are both necessary; we cannot finally choose one and not the other. It seems to me that they
have more practical connection than they appear to do, and that the ideal
which stands up to both criteria is the humble but not irreligious absolute
good of affection and good humour on a basis of adequate mutual respect.

Note

1 Untitled in manuscript.

T. E. Hulme's *Speculations*

Eigo Seinen (The Rising Generation),
69:1, 1 April 1933

I have been asked to say something about T. E. Hulme, which I can only do very imperfectly. His views had a great deal of influence on the Imagist group of poets, and were at any rate intended to support the Cubist painters. I doubt whether he has much influence now, though he certainly would have if he had not been killed in the war; the only cheerful thing about that is that he enjoyed the war very much, right on till September 1917. The corresponding man now is Wyndham Lewis, except that Hulme was still a disciple of Bergson when he wrote such of his papers as survive.

He claims that a notion of continuity, between nature, man, and the divine, was the central idea of the Renaissance; that this produced humanism and the sciences, and of its own nature degenerated into humanitarianism as in Rousseau, so producing democracy; and that this notion is not true in itself and can no longer be maintained even as an attitude. There is a real jump, a discontinuity, between matter and life (not apparently between animals and man) and another between life and the perfection which living men can conceive. The Christian doctrine of the Fall of Man is therefore a fundamental truth; it is the nature of man to conceive a perfection which he cannot attain. There are two main sorts of art, naturalist art, concerned with the triumph and sufficiency of man, which tries to imitate man and nature, and anti-human or divine art, which tries by static unnatural means to express perfection. Greek and Renaissance art are naturalist, and the new sorts of art then first influencing the painters were not; of these Byzantine and medieval art, and Buddhist sculpture, were based on an effort towards perfection, and negro sculpture was based on fear of life. (One of the difficulties of the theory is to keep these two distinct; he seems very unjust to the negroes.) The divine is fixed and orderly like the mechanical, while life is a disorderly affair in between them; so forms derived from religious paintings work very well for painting machinery; when the communists take this sort of painting to be materialist they know not what they do. (Here again, though the theory is very neat, it is hard for him to distinguish what he would admire from what he would despise.) Belief in the Fall involves Institutionalism and rejection of 'the bastard concept of personality'; since man is always contemptible by his own standards he must be supported always by chains. (The trouble is that the sciences and the arts, no less than democracy, depend on the free judgement of individuals.) And the whole set of ideas which Europe has worked on since the Renaissance are now for various reasons breaking up, so that these truths will again have to be recognised.

As for the 'fundamental change', which may of course be taking place, one must remember that both conceptions have always been held and made somehow to work together. It is not true that the Christian belief in the Fall was wiped out by the Renaissance. You get medieval monks doing very vivid and entirely naturalist animal-sketches. There is naturalism soon enough in the art inspired by Buddhism; the Far Eastern tradition of landscape painting, for instance, seems consciously to have depended on making the two conceptions fit. Certainly great changes have come, and may again, from stressing one rather than the other, but the theoretical argument goes neither way, nor does the historical one.

There seems to be a muddle about infinity in his 'perfection'. Man might be able to conceive a perfection he couldn't attain in the same sense as the numbers can't attain infinity; nobody is much hurt by this, because you can use infinity as a conception and you can take as big a number as you like. In the same way you can't make a test tube perfectly clean, but for a given purpose there will be a method of making it clean enough. In our own lives we are not so cheerfully placed; if Hulme meant no more than this Rousseau himself would think it too favourable. People who talk about human imperfection always seem to mean more than they say, except in their metaphors, which say more than they mean.

It is worth looking to see how much difference Hulme's views really make. It looks as if the attack on humanitarianism and Rousseau and the praise of institutionalism implied some sort of aristocracy. But he says that some attacks on democracy (p. 259)

are really vicious, in that they play with the idea of inequality. No theory that is not fully moved by the conception of justice asserting the equality of men, and which cannot offer something to all men, deserves or is likely to have any future.

It looks as if the attack on the whole set of ideas of the Renaissance implied some disapproval of its results. But (p. 58)

a new anti-humanist ideology could not be a mere revival of medievalism. The humanist period has developed an honesty in science, and a certain conception of freedom of thought and action which will remain.

It seems very unlikely that they would remain without the ideas behind them, but at any rate Hulme wanted them to remain.

It looks as if the assertion of free will and the values of religion implied some dislike of utilitarianism. But (p. 231)

> Disillusionment comes when it is recognised that all heroic actions can be reduced to the simple laws of egoism. But wonder can even then be found in the fact that there *are* such *different* and *clear-cut* laws and egoisms and that they have been created out of the chaos.

So he would have no reason to deny that Mr Richards's Theory of Value, say, tells you what is valuable, and how valuable it is; he would only deny that it told you what value is, which it doesn't claim to do. And to do this, one would think, he must be saying that the anti-vital sort of art involves a conception of absolute values; but so far as I can understand 'Cinders' he is trying to combine two things in them, to say that nothing can be known about the absolute and that he knows that no values are absolute (he seems puzzled about this on pages 218 and 243; of course they are only rough notes). Even the attack on the Romantic artists who keep dragging in infinity doesn't seem to follow from his root ideas; if man can conceive an infinity he can't reach why shouldn't he refer to it in his poetry?[1]

But this aesthetic part is much more convinced and solid than the philosophical, and has had much more influence. The metaphors are better than the arguments all through; I have done no justice to him in these nagging notes. The tone of the stuff is still very rousing; he was in a sense 'ahead of his time' because, unlike almost all other intellectuals, he had an attitude to life which was quite unaffected by the war. You may say he had always thought life was as bad as that.

Note

1 Even the best of the romantics, wrote T. E. Hulme, 'cannot see that accurate description is a legitimate object of verse. Verse to them always means a bringing in of some of the emotions that are grouped round the word infinite ... The great aim is accurate, precise and definite description.' The 'positive fundamental quality of verse,' he went on, 'has nothing to do with infinity, with mystery or emotions'; only with visual images as 'the very essence of an intuitive language' (*Speculations*, London: Kegan Paul, 1924, pp. 127, 132, 133, 135).

Mr Eliot and the East

Introduction to T. S. Eliot's *Selected Essays*, Tokyo: Kinseido,
1933

Mr Eliot's views have already been discussed very fully and need no introduction of mine, but this volume raises an interesting question; how far,
being so traditionalist, they apply to a quite separate tradition; whether
they are any use in Japan.

Of course his appreciations of particular writers, the most important
part of his prose work, are useful to anyone who wants to understand those
writers; not least useful when he is wrong, because to decide why such a
critic is wrong is to discover real issues. It is reasonable after saying that to
give examples where I myself think him wrong. His essay on *Hamlet* only
shows what desperate steps a critic must take if he is altogether to bar out a
psychoanalyst like Ernest Jones (anyway *Hamlet* is a good play; it was a
good play for two centuries before it was a problem. And yet the problem is
so much part of the plot that Mr Eliot seems clearly wrong in saying that
the emotions at work are not adequately symbolised, not carried by the
plot. The whole theme is a play within a play, and contains one as illustration; the chief actor is forced to 'act a part' so necessarily that he
cannot tell how far he is acting; of course he is 'theatrical', and knows it; he
warns even the players against being theatrical. It is simple to say that there
is too much 'unconsciousness' about the play; its whole theme, which is
made tediously clear, is the difficulty of self-knowledge. And it is true to
say, if we are to use these terms at all, that there is a 'personality' at work
not properly expressed in 'plot'. But to say that this necessarily makes a bad
play is to say that this crucial theme must not be treated, however well). His
essay on Marlowe is misleading in that it brings out what was inherent in
Marlowe, what Marlowe might have found himself doing later, rather than
what he wanted to do and did (anyway *The Jew of Malta* is a bad play, and
he was probably drunk when he wrote it). His use of the word 'sin' about
Baudelaire begs the question, even if it thereby raises it, for a non-Christian
reader. (Certainly Baudelaire hurt himself very much, but can the cosmos
be involved so readily? How far was it political or economic? Was it

'theatrical' of Baudelaire to take sin as he did, to be Byronic, to accept emotionally the social standards he was revolting against intellectually? Does not the same trick become obviously false in Oscar Wilde? And if he was merely a case for psychoanalysis why was he such a good poet?) Mr Eliot has a great power of raising such issues under a pretence of settling them. But I want to look not at details but at his general position.

Most of his later work has been a defence of the effects (not the truth) of Christian belief, by a series of demonstrations that particular Christian writers have been able to leave less out, been less *borné*, than the corresponding (European) heretics; that Christianity has been fitted for so long and with such a concentration of intellectual ability onto the emotional and mental needs of the West that there is nothing to put in its place; that nations that give it up (or give up any non-national creed) will fall into the surrogate-religion of nationalism, which will destroy them; that a single mind in a Christian environment cannot seriously give up Christianity, since a pragmatist or behaviourist, for example, cannot know how a society would 'work' (his own test of a belief) if his beliefs were adopted, or even how he himself would work in it; that the extremest individualist if his mind was formed in the West, will find Christianity the only real means of self-knowledge. Now all this about tradition is in a sense obviously true, but it is based on a recognition of the weakness of the individual which cuts both ways. The individual cannot even know whether what seems to him right is a right development of orthodoxy till he has worked it out as best he can on its own account; Mr Eliot makes clear that right orthodoxy must be acquired with great labour and is something quite different from the drift of society at the moment. Of course what seems right to the individual may become different if he wants his position to be orthodox in the end, but if he keeps this in mind too much he may keep himself from True Orthodoxy. Mr Eliot even says that the fundamental beliefs of a religious tradition (such as he believes to form the society that maintains it) may be changed; he expects Christianity to change, 'as it always has done,' so as to be still believable; but 'unconsciously'. This must mean gradually, through councils of professing believers; I think it actually an odder use of the word, though this is a bold saying, than any of the uses of it in the literature of psychoanalysis; but he means it to be (even here his use of language is half satiric); his whole claim against the psychoanalysts is that the perfect man they conceive would be a monster if he lived in an imperfect society. Nor is it necessary for those who want to make a right development of true orthodoxy, for instance in Christianity, to remain professing Christians; the believers, he remarks elsewhere, adding that he is not unorthodox in saying so, may be forced into true orthodoxy by unbelievers. It is from this background that he can make such piercing play with the different 'sorts of belief', and be half in sympathy with Mr Richards. The reason for Mr Eliot's immense standing, as a Christian writer, among some intellectual non-Christians, and for his intensely irritating effect on others (e.g. Max Eastman), is that his claim for Christian dogma is essentially no more than a snub for ignorant fools; and that very few honest thinkers can feel sure they have not been snubbed. But his views are a great deal less repressive than they look.

Now all that Mr Eliot says may well be true, and his stress on society and tradition rather than the individual is likely to be welcome in Japan, but in the Far East it is not an argument for Christianity but for Buddhism. Indeed the same conceptions have been so far developed in the two religions, originally so different, that I should think the Japanese reader will find a great deal of truth in these essays, provided that he reads Buddhism for Christianity throughout.

Mr Eliot's own references to Buddhism, though naturally the point is irrelevant to Tradition, show a sort of uneasiness ; as in the sad case of Mr Irving Babbitt, who cannot become a Christian, because hardly anybody in America knows more about early Buddhism than he does,[1] and as in Mr Eliot's review (*Dial*, March 1927) of Mr Richards's *Science and Poetry*. 'The Buddhists have another name for Equilibrium,' he replies grimly to Mr Richards's Theory of Value; with an air of invoking all Hell against this heresy (I take it the other name is no worse than Nirvana). And yet 'I am not so naive as to say that Mr Richards's theory is not true; it is probably quite true.' But he is also able to believe, he explains, that the prime good of man is to live to the glory of God. The essential claim here is that man can somehow escape the valuelessness of mechanism, though Mr Eliot chooses to put it in Christian language; he is right in saying that Mr Richards's theory is not essentially incompatible with such a claim; but the claim is inherent, of course, in the very evasive Buddhist concept of karma.[2]

I do not think I am seizing on a trivial point here. A central strategic element of Mr Eliot's war is the attack on 'personality' – the personality through which the artist claims to find 'self-expression' through 'freedom' – the random humanitarian claim that man would be free if he were not put in chains. Mr Eliot himself says in 'Tradition and the Individual Talent' that 'the point of view I am struggling to attack is perhaps related to the metaphysical view of the substantial unity of the soul' – I believe I am right in calling this the central issue between Christianity and Buddhism. It is a great issue, and I had best look a little aside from the personality of T. S. Eliot. T. E. Hulme was among the first leaders of the movement whose chief leader is not Mr Eliot, of the recent attack on the ideals of the Renaissance, and he at once adds to his attack (*Speculations*, p. 58):

a new anti-humanist ideology could not be a mere revival of medievalism. The humanist period [that is, the period that believed in personality] has developed an honesty in science, and a certain conception of freedom of thought and action which will remain.

That is, whether they will remain or not, and whether Eliot and the Buddhists are right about personality or not (I think they are certainly right), Eliot and Hulme and every sane contemporary thinker wants these ideals to remain. The fact is simply that while everybody is dependent on society, every advance of society depends on somebody doing what seems to him best; no human system can work without the free judgement of the individual. The dogma of the eternal unity of the soul is at bottom only a device for insisting on this fact; whether or not, in practice, there is no other means for making men recognise it adequately. Certainly in theory there is nothing against it in Buddhism.

If one was writing at the other side of the world this point might not seem of much importance. Of course both religions have degraded popularised forms, and the True Orthodoxy of both may only be found 'with great labour'. I would be sorry to hear of one of my friends becoming either a Buddhist or Christian monk, though I would expect him to be less hurt in bringing his mind to accept being a Buddhist one. But this is not really a question of applying Mr Eliot's views on tradition to the needs of a Japanese reader bound inevitably to the traditions of Japan; the race of man, largely because of an irrelevant improvement in machinery, is now pooling its traditions. Either Mr Eliot's support of Christianity from tradition is a claim that the truth is national or racial or otherwise accidental, or the True Orthodoxy must not limit itself to the traditions of Christianity. (Of course his main business is as a literary critic, but his claim is that aesthetics cannot eventually be kept separate from the fundamental beliefs inherent in the arts.) And if there is any sort of practical issue between the two, it is worth pointing out that Buddhism is the last of the great religions that can be conceived as changing itself in the future 'so as to be believable'.

Notes

1 Empson is alluding to Eliot's essay 'The Humanism of Irving Babbitt', in which Eliot acknowledged that Babbitt (in *Democracy and Leadership*) 'cannot accept any dogma or revelation', and that for Babbitt 'humanism is the *alternative* to religion':

'I should say that he regarded Confucius, Buddha, Socrates and Erasmus as humanists ... It may surprise some to see Confucius and Buddha, who are popularly regarded as founders of religions, in this list. But it is always the human reason, not the revelation of the supernatural, upon which Mr Babbitt insists. Confucius and Buddha are not in the same boat, to begin with. Mr Babbitt of course knows infinitely more about both of these men than I do; but even people who know even less about them than I do, know that ... Buddhism endured by becoming as distinctly a *religion* as Christianity – recognizing a dependence of the human upon the divine. ... the humanistic point of view is auxiliary to and dependent upon the religious point of view. For us, religion is Christianity; and Christianity implies, I think, the conception of the Church. It would be not only interesting but invaluable if Professor Babbitt, with his learning, his great ability, his influence, and his interest in the most important questions of the time, could reach this point' (*Selected Essays*, London: Faber & Faber, 1951 (pp. 471–80), pp. 472, 474, 480).

2 '[Richards's] goal is the avoidance of "conflict" and the attainment of "equilibrium",' wrote T. S. Eliot in his review of Richards's *Science and Poetry*. 'The Buddhists have a different name for "equilibrium".

'I am not so unsophisticated as to assert that Mr Richards's theory is *false*. It is probably quite true. Nevertheless it is only one aspect; it is a psychological theory of value, but we must also have a moral theory of value. The two are incompatible, but both must be held, and that is just the problem. If I believe, as I do believe, that the chief distinction of man is to glorify God and enjoy Him for ever, Mr Richards's theory of value is inadequate: my advantage is that I can believe my own and his too, whereas he is limited to his own. ... Poetry "is capable of saving us", he says; it is like saying that the wallpaper will save us when the walls have crumbled. It is a revised version of Literature and Dogma' ('Literature, Science, and Dogma', *Dial*, LXXXII, 3 March 1927 (pp. 239–43), pp. 241, 243).

Three Ethics

The Spectator, 29 November 1935

John Laird, *An Enquiry into Moral Notions*

There have been times when a new theory in ethics made a difference to men's actions; nor are they far off; the utilitarians had a real effect on opinion and law. It is clear that Professor Laird does not aim at this; not so clear what else he can be doing, in this learned and sensible book. As professor of ethics he is not a preacher, only a lover of knowledge; nor does he seek to know what men ought to do, a thing a professor in a Chair already knows, but how what is known about practical ethics can be fitted into a tidy theory. Yet we get hardly a hint of the army of workers who have given information about the fantastically varied practical ethics of the humane race; the enquiry is into the professor's own moral notions. He writes very well, I think, about Westermarck's opinion or phrase that moral judgements are 'merely emotive' [see 'Death and Its Desires' above], and decides that it only makes them 'relational'; this sets him free to use Westermarck's mass of results, but he does not.

The survey includes 'an Ethic of' Virtue, another of Duty, another of Benefit and Well-Being, and the system of each is supposed to be inadequate alone. Thus many claims of a utilitarian view ('open to reason' in the practical sense) are admitted, but it must sometimes yield to an ethic of virtue. One can think of cases where this might be a very important defence against a stupid utilitarianism, but that is off the point; it is assumed that all moral actors are at least as clever as Laird. He seems to decide that the three are fundamentally distinct, but in a case of conflict we are told that 'the question is almost indefinitely complicated.' The charm of having three ethics seems rather its unassailable simplicity; you ought to do three things in three different sense of 'ought', and there is no more to be said about the matter. Still, of course, this is a sensible position; such conflicts do occur, and are puzzling. How such a conflict would actually be carried on, in one of Professor Laird's friends, is not a question he considers. By contrast the Intuitionists, who get so much attention here, seem to me definitely to poison the wells. They claim direct moral knowledge of each rule that they

were in fact taught by their nurses; this would put whomever they controlled at the mercy of such nurses, or rather with less hope of mercy than
from the worthy bodies themselves. In a changing society, at any rate, a
complacent moral atomism is likely to do harm. Not that Professor Laird's
position gives much defence against such people; whenever their rules are
found to do mere harm they can say '*Here* we require an ethic of Virtue.'

The view that there are several distinct ethics has at least a practical
truth; whether or not the values open to us are measurable, we cannot
measure them, and it is of much value merely to stand up between the forces
to which we are exposed. The only puzzle is how a man who has reached
this conclusion can keep to so narrow a field as strict ethics, or rather why,
already giving examples, he should choose them almost entirely from his
own milieu. What sort of men adopt only one of the three ethics, after what
training, with what consequences? Are Margaret Mead's Arapesh or her
Tchambouli people, for instance, nearer to an ethic of well-being? Are there
any professors of ethics in Leningrad? Do you get more neurotics with an
ethic of virtue or of duty? Can Piaget's results be interpreted to mean that
children spontaneously have an ethic of well-being towards each other and
of duty towards grown-ups? Professor Laird no doubt would say that these
are irrelevant bypaths, but it is not clear how he knows it, if they are. He
does not argue *a priori* but from the evidence of his conscience, partly assisted by those of other philosophers. It seems fair to ask what steps are
taken to train these consciences before they grasp the whole gamut of
human experience. There can be few odder branches of specialised learning.

The Faces of Buddha

Listener, 5 February 1936

There is room for an amateur to say something about Buddha faces, because the experts tend rather to avoid so indefinite a topic, while there are two likely misunderstandings for a man in the street: that the Buddhas have no expression at all, an idea set on foot by Lafcadio Hearn, who had a genuine feeling for the East but was almost blind; or else that they all sneer, a thing G. K. Chesterton, for instance, often says, which is less easy to answer. Certainly in each Buddhist country, after a few centuries, the type becomes conventional and is liable to be complacent; also one thinks first of the Buddhas of China, and as soon as the Buddha arrived in China he was given something of the polite irony of a social superior. There was some real falsity when they came to treat the Goddess of Mercy as a fashion plate of the court lady. Yet before merely disliking that look it is only fair to see where it comes in the system. The Buddha has delivered himself from the world and may well look superior to it, but he is telling you that you can do the same; also he could not achieve this apparently selfish aim without first learning complete unselfishness. The Ajanta caves occasionally give him the face of a typical Italian Christ, but only in previous lives, while he was dealing with that aspect (giving his body to a hungry tiger and so on). As to the after-dinner look of many Buddhas, and the rings of fat on the neck, a puzzle of the translators seems to show the point; one expert gives a remark of the Buddha as 'While I live thus, after having felt the extreme sensations, I am pure,' and another as 'after having felt my last sensation.' An idea that you must be somehow satisfied as well as mortified before entering repose goes deep into the system, and perhaps into human life. However, what you are meant to feel in a Bodhisattva (which is roughly any 'Buddha' with a headdress, shown not as a monk but a king) has escaped these doctrinal puzzles and become clearly sacrificial. They are saints who have given up their Nirvana, their heaven, till they have helped their last fellow-creature into heaven before them, and the face is meant to show it. In a sense they have given up their deaths, not their lives, but the conception appeared in the first centuries after Christ and along the caravan routes to Europe; the two religions may very well be connected. The drooping eyelids of the great creatures are heavy with patience and suffering, and the subtle irony which offends us in their raised eyebrows (it is quite a common expression in Europeans, though curiously avoided in our portraits) is in effect an appeal to us to feel, as they do, that it is odd that we let our desires subject us to so much torment in the world. The first thing to say about the Buddha face, granted that many later ones are complacent, is that the smile of superiority can mean and be felt to mean simply the power to help.

The next thing, I think, about the stock type, is that it is the simplest conception of high divinity the human race has devised; people say it is monotonous, but there is a sort of democracy about its repetition. In a way Europe has agreed on the face of Christ, but you have to be a good artist to do it. Anyone who cares about the Lord Buddha can do his face in a few ignorant strokes on sand or blotting paper, and among all the crude versions I have walked past I do not remember one that failed to give him his effect of eternity. It is done by the high brow, soaring outwards; by the long slit eye, almost shut in meditation, with a suggestion of a squint, that would be a frighteningly large eye if opened; and by a suggestion of the calm of childhood in the smooth lines of the mature face – a certain puppy quality in the long ear helps to bring this out. If you get these they carry the main thought of the religion; for one thing the face is at once blind and all-seeing ('he knows no more than a Buddha,' they say of a deceived husband in the Far East), so at once sufficient to itself and of universal charity. This essential formula for the face allows of great variety and is hardly more than a blank cheque, but one on a strong bank, so to speak. To my feeling a quite unrealistic Buddha is far more ready than a European head of Christ to be conceived as a real person in the room; as you sink into it you seem to know what it would feel like to have those extraordinary hands.

It is a mistake to explain this type as merely racial, though it was exaggerated in the Far East and somehow fits in with their normal outlook. Greco-Roman artists in the northwest, about the first century A D, seem to have broken the Indian convention that the Buddha must not be portrayed, and the calm of their Apollo made a conflict with the human and muscular earth-god tradition of Mathura. Then by the Indian Gupta period (fifth century) the Buddha has settled down to a high brow and half-shut eye; they are not a Far Eastern invention. The eye had to follow the brow; a wide open eye under the high brow would be in great danger of the coy surprise of George Robey, or anyway of an unquiet sort of surprise, which is not meant. Of course a good enough artist can avoid the obvious; it is terrible when the Buddha in the Ajanta caves once fully opens his eyes, as he takes his last look at his wife – a picture, by the way, which has been destroyed by varnish, and can now be seen only in photographs. But this, I think, gave a main reason for closing it. The photograph here from the great Bodhisattva of Cave I will serve to show how the type was going, though not to show the Titian richness of the flesh-painting and the Tintoretto glitter of the crown. Not that the Far East was afraid of Robey; there is a further threat of him when the brows curl down again on the outside, and this was used mainly for the late Vairocana Bodhisattva, who stands for the energy behind the universe (or thereabouts). This strange conception tends to particularly puppy ears and a certain winning bounce in the raised finger; the type can aim at something near Robey and be still a god. For that matter both Kwannon and Maitreya have a version as a great fat laughing sprawler, which helps to show that this is not a misunderstanding. The merely racial difficulty in understanding the faces is indeed smaller than you would expect, and the artists at Angkor no less than Ajanta seem to have amused themselves by putting the same face on to all the races of mankind.

The formula leaves much of the face free. The nose can do what it likes, and is used for anything between childishness, sensuality, and administrative power. The mouth can do what it likes, and varies from a rich sensual repose to the strained tight-lipped alert smile seen on flying aces and archaic Greek sculpture. This of course is not borrowed from Greece; the Greek influence was not archaistic, and anyway the typical thing about an archaic Apollo is not simply the mouth but a peculiar half-baked look about the jowl. The point about the archaic fixed smile, on Buddhas or elsewhere, is that it would be made by a pull on the main zygomatic, the muscle most under conscious control, leaving the others at rest; thus it is an easy way to make a statue look socially conscious, wilful, alert. Many of the Chinese Buddhas from the Yun-kang caves, the earliest period, get a strong effect from using this quite flatly (e.g., the fine one that dominates Room 2 of the Chinese Exhibition). But you have only to sink the ends into the cheeks to give it an ironical or complacent character, and my example from Yun-kang, almost winking as it is, gets, I think, with these simple means, an extraordinary effect both of secure hold on strength and peace and of the humorous goodwill of complete understanding. The Koriuji example is traditionally a gift from Korea and can stand for the second main influence on early Japan; its very subtle mouth is not at all of this type, and the future Buddha has a plaintive and somewhat foxy elegance not yet developed as an active force in the world. In the Chuguji one, who will also when he is born bring a new revelation, it is rather the older convention for the mouth, toned down and with a couple of ripples in the smooth wood, that gives all that lightness and tenderness which will at any moment brush away the present universe as an unwise dream. The Horiuji Goddess of Mercy, though not very clearly on her copy in the British Museum, uses it for a rueful puggy puzzled expression, faintly suggesting the White Queen, that needs for its interpretation the great sweep of the flamelike draperies, stretching as far as earth, and the jerk of the extended arm, like a stalk, exhausted but still offering. Noble stupid creature; at least no one can say that she is sneering.

Ballet of the Far East

Listener, 7 July 1937

Ballet has become very popular in recent years, but people still know very little about the Far Eastern sort, because it is an expensive thing to make a ballet travel. Kikugoro, the best dancer in Japan, took a troupe to Moscow a few years ago, and it had a roaring success and stayed on and on, to the grave alarm of the Japanese government, but that is as far west as the first-rate dancers have been. I think it is important that we should realise what good ballet they have in the Far East, and how different it is from ours. If you get used to their methods the Russian ballet comes to seem a special and limited kind of thing, nowhere near the full range of the possibilities of dancing.

It is hard to describe either dancing or music in words, and I must attempt both here, as the Far East has its own music. But the important differences between our ballet and theirs go back to a fundamental thing which *can* be put into words. In the West, the supreme God is a person, in the East He is not; their ideas about man follow from that, and you come across examples of it all the time. It is much the most fundamental line of division between the civilisations of the world, and we need to understand the people on the other side. The Jews and Mohammedans and Christians all make the supreme God a person, and the line of division crosses the riots in India between Moslem and Hindu. Of course Europe has always known about pantheism (since Pythagoras), but the important thing is that people can get an idea into their bones, and when they agree, intellectually, to the other side they cannot see how it works out in practice. Almost the only kind of man who can tell you how it works in practice is the artist who has worked with it in his bones. So it is a good thing, if possible, to tie the points about the ballet on to the difference of theology, and I think that this explains the things that most need explaining. Also it keeps us from calling the difference a mysterious matter of race (slit eyes or whatnot). The man who made the supreme expression of the Far Eastern view of God and man was the Buddha, and he was an Aryan, the same race as ourselves; in fact it

577

was he, not Herr Hitler, who first used this adjective as a term of general praise, rather as we use 'noble'. And in fact there is no peculiar racial difficulty about understanding Far Eastern art once you see the ideas behind it.

I know more about Japanese theatre, and shall keep to that, but the Chinese theatre is the same kind of thing. The things I am calling ballet are actually plays, in some cases, but few Japanese know the ancient language that the plays use; when you know the plot you can see the performance as ballet. The Japanese have two main sorts of theatre, Noh and Kabuki, and Arthur Waley has done an admirable translation of a set of Noh plays. If you are actually going to the theatres you want to take it with you, or Mrs Stopes's book of translations [Marie C. Stopes, *Plays of Old Japan: the 'Nō'*, London: Heinemann, 1913] if none of Waley's plays are on. Anyway Waley's book is the first thing to get if you are interested in this kind of theatre.

The Noh theatre is fantastically slow. The performance goes on all afternoon and evening, though one play only takes an hour or two. But if you actually get there you will probably stay even if you say you are bored, because the music has a direct effect on the nerves. It is based on eight slow beats, taken separately by different percussive instruments. Now the scientists seem to agree that we feel differently about rhythm according as it is slower or faster than a heartbeat, and nearly all European music goes faster than a heartbeat. Our limit of slowness is the dead march, which goes about the pace of the heart. This music goes slower, and that is the real reason why it is no use imitating Far Eastern music on European instruments. All our instruments are meant to go bouncing along very frankly like a nice well-intentioned dog; in their music you sit still and strengthen yourself like a cat. There are long squalling noises that hold you up during the wait for the next beat, and at last the beat comes with a snap, as if you had stretched an elastic till it broke. There seems a touch of parody about this account, but you have to caricature things to describe them. I think it is true to say that European music is a much larger creature than Far Eastern music; it is the fresh air. But the fundamental difference in all these things goes back to the view taken of God and of the individual man. A rhythm quicker than the heartbeat is one that you seem to control, or that seems controlled by some person; the apparently vast field of our music is always the frankness of the West, always the individual speaking up. Music based on rhythms slower than the heartbeat can carry a great weight of emotion and even of introspection, and of course incidental runs will go quick, but it remains somehow impersonal. I only want to say here that you must take the music seriously as something that fits in with the whole story, and the story may well be the other half of the truth about the world.

The actual plays of Noh are at the opposite pole to realism, and generally act the dreams of ghosts. If you see no point in Buddhism at all I suppose they seem quite pointless. A good Buddhist wants to enter Nirvana and leave the individual passions of the world, but the typical ghost of the Noh stage is unable to forget his last battle because he is still loyal to his over-lord. There will be a traveller who discovers that he is a ghost, and then the ghost will dance an echo of his last battle, because he is still torn between the Absolute and the world. So that the play works up slowly to a tremen-dous dance at the end. This is strikingly different in theory from our idea of tragedy, because the tragic thing here is not being able to die enough. But the effect, once you have got this main point, is obvious high tragedy. By the way his dance is not what you might imagine from Waley's translation of the words, which makes the thing sound very subdued. Actually he crows like a cock and stamps like a buck rabbit; it is pretty near an honest South Sea island war dance. I do not mean that this is a fault of the trans-lation; it is the topic of the play. Violent forces of life in the action are opposed to the ideal of death which is in the words. There are other types of Noh hero, particularly the mother who has been sent mad by losing her sons, but she has the same story. She is quite unlike Shakespeare's mad people, for example. Their madness is at bottom an escape into sanity; they seem to be raving, but this lets them show the wisdom which is still at the back of their minds. Her madness is a state of passive power, good in itself because like Nirvana, and when this sinister woman becomes violent it means nothing; it only shows the weakness, and therefore the pathos, of her way of getting to Nirvana.

The other main type of theatre is the Kabuki. It is a more popular kind of theatre, with an enormously long stage and continual terrific changes of scenery. The music tends to be quicker than in Noh, and we feel more at home with it, though it keeps getting back to the slow beat. The perform-ance is made up of single scenes from enormous plays that everybody knows already; they do the same in China, and it is important to see that this means a quite different attitude to the stage from ours. It would be amusing to make up an evening from bits of *Hamlet*, *The Dynasts*, *School for Scandal*, *Oedipus* in Greek, and *Charley's Aunt*, but it would not go well. We would want to go on sympathising with particular characters; we would want to know the end of the story. The characters in a Far Eastern play are not even what we call 'types', far less individuals. It is the situation that is typical. The situation often happens in real life, and a play about it is therefore real, and may be very moving. But in real life the situation ends in all sorts of ways, and you are not much interested in the way *this* one ended. Why should you be, when the individuals who happen to be in it are not the important thing? If you put in a definite ending it would be unrealistic; it would look as if the thing always ended in that way. Of course a lot of people in the theatre know the ending, but they are happy without seeing it, and we would want to see it.

The best thing for us in the Kabuki performance is the dance act, which comes on about half past seven. 'Kasane and Yoyemon' seemed to me about the best of them. The hero in this dance is escaping with his young woman, and it turns out that, owing to the strain of the affair, she had become possessed with a devil. There is a long business about finding the skull of some other person she owed loyalty to, which brings on the attack. The first symptom is when she begins driving him away by twirling her parasol; towards the end he is running away like mad and the steps only bring him slowly backwards. She does not kill him on the stage because a Japanese dance never finishes a story. The thing depends a great deal on the interpretation, because it is so near to actual casual movement. Kikugoro makes the girl charming and sensible, and puts a terrible pathos into her feeling that she has begun to change, and then makes her simply a strong passive devil. But I saw Baiko do it, and he is a man of seventy now and takes care of his strength, so I was just in time. He has an entirely different dance; he makes the girl so insinuating and so powerful that you feel she is the same person at the end when she is a devil. It takes a man dancer to make a woman seem so terrifying.

If you have got used to the Far Eastern stage it is very hard to take the Russian ballet as seriously as all its audiences do. Beside dancing like this, the Russian ballet is a glorified form of romping. In dancing of serious power, the dancer can stand still for several minutes and make you watch the imperceptible movements of his breathing like a cat watching a mouse. Now Western music cannot stand still; it is not built to give a dancer these opportunities. If we ever get what there is so little hope of at present, that is, a reasonable attempt to take the world as one place and use the best things in it, then it will be obvious that Far Eastern music is the normal kind of music for serious dancing. Sensible people who love the European ballet will tell you that the permanent thing about it is its eternal youth. This is quite true, but it is a limited kind of pleasure. In all the other arts the Far East has one thing and we have another, and it is stupid to say that either is better. But in dramatic dancing the Far East makes us ridiculous.

Asia

Life and Letters To-Day, XXVII, October 1940

Michael Prawdin, *The Mongol Empire*

A thorough and suggestive book on an intensely interesting part of history; one which used to be neglected; but recently there has been a fashion for whitewashing the great nomad Tartars. It affected the idealist—communist Ralph Fox as well as Mr Prawdin, who writes like a patriotic German. The world conquests suit the school-story power-politics of today; the Golden Horde in Russia, especially, gives a Wellsian effect of Martians ruling men efficiently while wholly above contact with them. The great Khans had got so much more information about the world as a whole than either the Europeans or the Chinese, and came to it so free from preoccupations, that their comments on the civilisations they laid waste can give an effect of super-human intelligence. The whole claim for the Noble Savage (that important myth) was that he had a free mind, like Genghis between the four great religions (though the nomad sentiment was always closest to Islam). The book, I think, doesn't make enough of Friar William of Rubruck, the only recorder who was so intelligent that he saw the challenge of his visit to Karakorum. He learned there the theological difference between the West and the Far East, which Gibbon and Voltaire never did; and we can check Rubruck's account of the only world religious conference, and Mangu's piercing comments on it, by a Chinese one. And the merely administrative ability of the illiterate Khans was very high. By opening the trade routes to China they gave us printing, gunpowder, Italian painting, the urge to the discovery of America, Heaven knows what; it is a strong case. The Pax Tatarica, it can be claimed, was the first, the only, the only rational world government, and, if it failed early, it at least produced the sciences and the modern world. Mr Prawdin also feels that the Mongols, like the Germans, illustrate the importance of Central Land Power; sea power will no longer be important after the German victory, and so we are due for a world-constructive Mongol revival. The book starts with Genghis and ends with the confused Mongolian politics of the present day.

You can overdo this. Admittedly the only people who gained by the Pax

Tatarica were the Europeans who by chance were left outside it. And even for them the chief thing useful was not the long land route; it was safe passage overland to Baghdad for taking ship to India. If the Mongols had gone on beyond Austria to the Atlantic (and they would have done if Ogotai hadn't died of drink next door to China, so that there was an election to attend) we might still have our machine world today, but it would be a Mohammedan one. The fact that they went the other way has long given Europeans a sneaking fondness for Mongols. Marlowe himself liked Tamburlaine for being wicked with such a bang, but Marlowe's audience only endured this attitude because it was still practical politics to back the enemies of Islam (Tamburlaine was only about fifty years further off then than Napoleon is now). Nobody can understand the curious clinging horror of the heritage of Russia without the idea of Moscow building itself up for centuries by betraying the other Russians to the Golden Horde; and it is stupid to blame Russia if she still feels the effects of saving Europe from destruction. China stood the Mongol conquest better, but the Chinese themselves don't think, as Mr Prawdin does, that it did them good. The story cannot be made a cheerful one. Genghis was anyway of course gloriously able (the book does a good deal to explain his methods, but never clears up whether he was using maps, and how he got them). But the genuinely noble thing about him, and in a lesser degree about Mangu and Kublai, is that he did not know what to do with the world when he had got it, and said so, and died a profoundly puzzled old man; and nothing we could tell him today would enlighten him.

As for this coming revival of the great central Mongol block, I hope very much they won't simply die out, diseased and cheated and depopulated as they are. A pan-Islam movement in Sinkiang and West China is more likely, and more convenient for the Russians. It would cut off the surviving Mongolians from their co-religionists in Tibet. Islam is very strong, and the Japanese are probably out of the running if they get so far. It is a baffling business. You can't expect German romanticism to go all the way, even in a useful book.

'The Foundations of Empirical Knowledge'[1]

Criterion, III, March 1941

A. J. Ayer, *The Foundations of Empirical Knowledge*

An excellent book, much more sensible than the author's first, which was too blow-the-gaff. The liquid-flowing style might still have a bit more body in it. 'Philosophical problems are largely linguistic'; the term 'sense-datum' is 'convenient for his purposes' merely because it gives quick grammar for 'what we seem to perceive', so he will frustrate all attempts to treat a sense-datum as a 'thing'. But to a literary man his idea of the purposes that govern a choice of words seems naïve; there are generally several purposes at once, and even the chooser may not be clear about them till later.

Consider a man who looks at a picture and says, 'This isn't the original, it's a copy,' and suppose the reason can be said simply; two patches of red had different tones in the original but are alike in the copy. It is a characteristic of the human mind that this man can judge correctly about the difference of colour scheme before he has analysed it out. But in Mr Ayer's terminology his judgement is not based on any sense-datum, because he doesn't 'seem to perceive' anything but an unlocated feeling of difference. This might be called a sense-datum, though we are told (p. 135) that sense-data have to be located in space. But the word sense-datum, even when used by Mr Ayer, suggests 'given by the senses' and implies that we can only build up our knowledge out of what our senses give. It works by an appeal to scientific rationalism, and Mr Ayer feels that he is blowing away the nonsense of metaphysics. The whole development of rationalism since the sixteenth century has been playing round 'sense'. If Mr Ayer will not let us say that this man is 'sensing' the difference of colour, he makes the term actively misleading. Tennyson believed in immortality because his heart felt it, evidently sense-datum of visceral type. Sense-data become opinions rather than perceptions.

In this book other people and the past are let exist. Any statement is viewed as reducible to infinite groups of statements about sense-data (for different positions of the observer, etc.), and 'the matter of the earth came out of the sun', or 'Tom feels tired', are about the sense-data one would receive if in logically possible positions (being in a spaceship a long time ago or being Tom now). The plain man may remark that the universe has been sturdily indifferent for eons to the observers to whom its reality is reduced; Mr Ayer will reply that we only *can* be referring to logically possible observations. But he seems very anthropomorphic about observers. Bees see ultra-violet light; perhaps birds feel the points of the compass; some people say atoms have dim sensations – is it logically possible for me to be an atom? The objection to assertions about matter is that we can't conceivably observe it. How are we better off by reducing it to sense-data, which we can't conceive ourselves as having? Here again, we know less about the sense-data than we do about the things.

One impulse 'active in the phenomenalist' is a desire to push out of sight the immense queerness necessary in the universe before we can get any knowledge at all. There is nothing here about probability; why do we give a higher *a priori* probability to simpler scientific laws? Without that we could get nowhere. One might justify it simply because the universe is so big; though many different principles are likely to be at work, their effects are likely to be spread out into different orders of magnitude. But this brings in cause, over which Mr Ayer dances in some excellent pages of history and psychology. He feels free there because he believes that modern physics agrees with him. There is curiously little in the chapter about the experience of pushing. It becomes strikingly perverse in the argument against Professor Stout (p. 187), where, of course, it was the archer himself who could *feel* the tension in the bow, not an outside observer. And we get nothing at all about Eddington's monumental book, in which he claims to calculate all the absolute physical constants, to any degree of accuracy, starting merely from the fact that the universe is one which can be observed by the creatures it contains. (He tends to say that we make it ourselves, which isn't the point; there may be innumerable other universes, but ours is the only one that could produce a book describing itself.) This is so Kantian, and so many of its results are actually used by modern physics, that Mr Ayer can't get away with just ignoring it when he appeals to the physicists.

Note

1 Untitled in original.

The Nude

Tsinghua Tyro (Peking), II: 1, April 1948

This is a subject I am fairly ignorant about, but one I think of some importance for the mutual understanding of Europe and the Far East; and I write about it in the hope of knowing more.

The obvious point is that Europe has 'gone in for' the nude human figure in art since the earliest Greek sculpture, whereas the Far East has hardly used it at all apart from the torso of the Buddha, who was imported. Similarly in the Far East a landscape is an early and somehow obvious art form, whereas in Europe it was hardly recognised as an art form at all till the seventeenth century. Probably this is the most radical difference between the two broad aesthetic traditions, and its causes and effects are deep and wide. Incidentally it goes the other way round from two lines of difference often said to be important; first that the Far East believes that Man or the Complete Man is the norm, whereas Europe makes Nature the norm and thinks man ought to be back to it, second that the Far East takes sex naturalistically and placidly whereas Europe keeps dragging mental horrors and splendours into it. Both these seem to have some truth but can hardly go to the heart of the matter.

Some theorists in Europe have assumed and elaborated a view that the visual arts must necessarily depend on the pleasure in the proportions of the human body. Any satisfying proportions, in a cathedral or a landscape or a pattern in a blanket, must, they would say, have been unconsciously borrowed from the proportions of the body, either as the body really is or as the culture habitually distorts it when making a picture of it. The second idea, I thought, was quite a useful one to take round what is rather impudently called the Ethnological Section of the British Museum, which has the arts of primitive peoples in it; that is, you really did find the patterns on the blankets of a given tribe more interesting when you had seen how the tribe distorted the human body for the carvings of gods; the same kind of proportions would be used. But this of course is a very different thing from the idea that the human form is the standard of beauty, because the distortions get right away from it. Indeed I think one could say that no primitive art takes the actual human body as the norm or even admires it; the art is often sensual, in the way of exaggerating the buttocks etc., but does not feel that what excites lust is also something calmly graceful in itself.

I am very ignorant about who started the idea that the human body is the norm of all proportion. It was undoubtedly much talked about in Italy during the Renaissance, and coupled with the belief that the ancient Greeks had established the proportions. Partly from measuring the available Greek statues or Roman copies, as they were collected, the Renaissance Italians drew up a series of rules, dividing the body into eight equal parts and putting the navel exactly halfway between the breast and the genitals and so on. The fact that the theory is wrong, it seems to me, could only be proved by a knowledge of Far Eastern art; it could not be discovered from inside a culture whose proportions really were largely based on those of the human body. How far anyone took the theory quite seriously, for instance whether Renaissance architects were patiently copying proportions from the human body, is another thing; I take it this kind of theory generally remains at the back of the mind of a practising artist and is used unconsciously where it is convenient on other grounds. But the theory has never been abandoned; a European-style art school anywhere in the world will still assume that drawing from the nude is an essential part of the training of any artist, because that is where he learns the fundamental proportions. For that matter when Mrs Bloom in *Ulysses* reflects cosily, 'The woman *is* beauty, of course; that's admitted' she is drawing on the same highly metaphysical theory, and the reason why she can use it to express a vague resentment against men is that the nineteenth century, by a very peculiar twist of puritanism, decided that the female nude was pure art but the male nude somehow shocking. However the theory (in the vague form which gets practically applied) has been very much weakened in recent years by being generalised, in the sense that even academic art now admits the existence of different racial types. An art school will feel that you are being trained to paint landscapes all right if you do pencil drawings of a nude Chinese; you no longer need to have a specially selected model who can just be imagined as an ancient Greek. Indeed the effect of romanticism has been to make (I suppose) the majority of the ordinary European visitors to picture galleries feel that an alien nude is more picturesque and even more 'exciting' (in some vaguely sexual way) than a European one.

There is a rather charming consequence of this, and it should be pointed out because hardly anything is charming in the field of racial differences; a cultivated European nowadays will often feel that the Chinese have the more beautiful bodies, whereas a cultivated Chinese will often feel the opposite. I have myself sometimes heard, both from Chinese and Japanese, this idea that the European body is more beautiful than their own, apparently because it was some kind of standard, like a patent taken out long ago by the Greeks; and I never felt able to explain to them that their theory was out of date. What the European tends to feel is that the Chinese body is less raw, coarse, unfinished than his own, rather than that one set of proportions is better than another; but he may well like the proportions too and certainly does not feel there is an aesthetic rule against them. My dear friend Norman France, who died in the siege of Hong Kong, was rather conscious of having a red spotty face and the lumpy body of a taipan, and was greatly comforted one day by a remark he overheard about himself while he was sitting reading in a Japanese gown, outside a temple where he was staying. A party of American-born Chinese were viewing the temple and said (as he reported them), 'My, look at that old Chink; he's not going to worry.' This made poor France feel that he must look all right after all. The Chinese, on the other hand, do not seem to have any anxieties of this sort; and perhaps the reason why they are prepared to say politely that the European body is better is that they do not much care what a body looks like. The real surprise, I think, for a European comes when he looks at Chinese or Japanese pornographic paintings, which provide almost the only traditional Far Eastern type of nude. The body of both sexes is there found to be like a sack of potatoes with knobs on it, rather slimy in texture, and he is astonished that anything so frankly ugly could conceivably be meant to excite desire. Of course most pornographic art is extremely bad, but the Far Eastern painters have not even an ideal 'attractive' body which they are failing to draw. Even the combination of meanings in the word 'attractive', the idea that desire would normally be excited by a body with good proportions, has not occurred to them. Indeed, even in the human face, it seems to me that the Chinese (and Japanese) are very unconscious of their own beauty, apart from the beauty of old people's faces, which is a different thing; one sees this particularly well in the displays outside photographers' shops. And the Chinese artists who work in European styles never seem to realise whether the nude they have drawn is in effect half pornographic or not; that is, the whole idea of a nude is so alien to their tradition, quite apart from any question of mastering a technique, that they do not recognise the case where the 'attractive' effect is predominantly sexual, and aesthetically too simple, as against the case where it is predominantly aesthetic. I have no ideas at all about how one could explain where this very practical line of distinction comes, and yet in a given case it feels obvious. Of course many European artists have shown bad taste in the matter, and are available to copy; they form a trap. This confusion seems to me far the greatest difficulty in achieving any synthesis between the Eastern and Western styles of painting, which would be a tremendous thing if it could be achieved; and I should fancy that the solution of it needs to go a long way back into everyday experience.

I want now to put down a few ignorant reflections about the history of the nude, which perhaps throw some light on it though not much. The Greeks did not invent it, though they boasted about their superiority to barbarians in not being afraid of total nakedness in real life, especially during athletics. They took their main sculptural tradition of the nude body from the Egyptians, where it goes back to at least 3000 BC. The custom no doubt is largely a matter of living in a hot country, and therefore frequently seeing at any rate the naked torso. One might connect the Chinese rejection of the nude with the fact that Chinese culture was developed in more northerly areas. But I don't think there is much in this; there are plenty of torsos about in the summer in Peiping, and the peoples of Mesopotamia, which is very hot, always represented themselves and apparently lived (like the modern Arabs) wrapped up in blankets. The Egyptian and Mesopotamian civilisations were equally important for the early Greeks, and only the Egyptians gave a precedent for the nude. To be sure, the Greeks introduced total nakedness, an important mark of Naturalism, but the Egyptian loincloth had done nothing to obscure the proportions. Now the function of the naked torso in the statue of the Pharaoh (which we must take as the origin of the European nude) is to excite rather complex feelings about the divine king, certainly not just to make him 'attractive'. He is much formalised and the general effect is extremely rigid; partly indeed with the rigidity of the dead, for his claims are supernatural, but also with the inhumanity of supreme earthly power. But in contrast to these harsh lines the chest is tender, not with any weakness or femininity but with the sort of tenderness that you get in a carthorse; the curves are calm and strong and yet somehow comforting – in short, *not* harsh. The point is that you are to accept the supreme power of the divine king and yet also to love him and trust him; and this feeling could only be put in by showing part of his naked body. This I think continued to be the idea that the Greek sculptors were working on, though they applied it in the first place to the naturalistic gods instead of the divine king, and if so the origin of the nude has nothing to do with sex at all (except in a remote Freudian way, where one could say that the trick was to transfer to the strong man the feelings due to the mother).

One would not expect that the Egyptians were the only patentees of this idea, which seems a natural one for any society worshipping divine kings and not positively shocked by torsos. There is just one statue dug up in the Punjab, of the early Indian civilisation around 2500 BC, which seemed to me in a photograph to be relying on the same sentiment (though there is none of it in the intervening cultures of Mesopotamia). In any case it is present in the Indian earth-god statues (Yakshas) surviving from a few centuries before Christ, earlier than Buddhist sculpture, and no doubt Professor Cooma-raswamy was right in claiming that this Indian tradition was at least as important for the earliest Buddhist sculpture as the Greco-Roman influence along the land route to Europe. The torso of the Buddha, I think, even in China, has the same kind of function as the torso of the Pharaoh, but it did not get to the Chinese Buddha from the Greeks but from an independent de-velopment in India. (The Greek influence got into the Buddha type in other ways, but the debased Greek styles available through Afghanistan had hardly any of the divine carthorse sentiment left.) In Europe this line of sen-timent was revived in the Renaissance, particularly by Michelangelo, who liked to get a quality of almost pathetic nobility into the strong male body; and it is still in frequent use.

But, all the same, this seems a long way off from the later developments of the nude, especially the idea that the female nude was a standard orna-ment even for a puritanical home, where a male nude would be considered rather shocking. I do not understand what kind of balance between the sexual and the formal kinds of interest in the ornament was taken for gran-ted: maybe there was simply an idea that it proved you were very pure if you could assume that one would regard the thing entirely purely. For that matter, when Victorian morality was most rigid the girls were showing more of their breasts in an evening dress than they commonly do now, though of course hiding their legs altogether. The whole subject seems to me to need examining sociologically rather than aesthetically, and I do not know where any of it has been done.

Classical Theatre of China

BBC broadcast, 3 November 1955

Well, it's a very exhilarating show, and it's also exhilarating to have the audience take to it so strongly at once. I understand the show very nearly didn't get here, because the organisers thought it would be so exotic, so highbrow, so slow, such an ugly noise; and then what arrived was a spanking vaudeville or circus entertainment. On the first night, I confess, I rather joined the minority of grumblers, the people who had been to Peking. We grumbled not at the choice of items, though one or two short ones did seem unnecessarily Europeanised, but because the band wasn't deafening enough, and the ear-splitting effect of that caterwauling falsetto voice was hardly allowed to be painful at all. The Japanese company did the same thing, when they were here a few weeks ago; both of them had evidently been warned that Europeans can't stand noise. I don't think this is true; Europeans make a great deal of noise, and so do their operas. But I went another night, as anybody would want to do, to see the next half of the Monkey King, and I began to realise the show had been well calculated. There is enough of the noise to take effect on the audience all right, and if they had much more they might get distracted by it. All the same, I think one ought to have more, especially of the percussion, which the Far Eastern orchestra has such a variety of; it is needed to pick out the sharpness of the timing in the dance movements, sometimes for a very slight movement which needs underlining, or indeed to work up the excitement when the dancer is waiting. Now that the Chinese opera has really got its audience, we may hope that it will come again another year; and I think we ought to ask them, next [time] they come, to put us through a bit more strain in the way of noise.

You may think it sounds contemptuous to say that the show would go all right in a circus, because then, you may think, it can't be art. But that, I think, only shows how narrow the opera, and ballet, and even miming, have become in Europe. The chief reason I think is that our music, though it is much the most wonderful and fully developed system of music in the world, has become so exacting and in a way separate that it is not adaptable enough. It doesn't occur to us to try and make acrobats move beautifully to music. To make ballet out of two armies fighting in a lake, and really make the audience feel the clumsiness and slowness and hampering quality of this process, and yet do it by very quick incessant somersaults and tumbles from the whole corps-de-ballet, is a thing that European ballet can't do. This comes at the end of the show except that it is followed by the capture of a hill fort beside the lake, and one feels this fast bit is certain to be an anti-climax; but then, after a fair amount of massive swordplay by titanically dressed rival generals, the army just does double somersaults over the walls. You feel that nothing more could be required.

The most charming thing on the list, as everyone has felt, is the Monkey King; what perhaps needs pointing out is that it really is also very beautiful dancing. He is theologically the same 'Monkey' as the hero of the wild and profound novel of that name mainly about Buddhism, of the sixteenth century, translated by Mr Arthur Waley; he is meant to mean something. It is a wonderful conception, because there is so much accurate observation of monkeys in it, which makes it funny, and also touching; the god is always in a way less than human, and yet he always excites a sort of eerie reverence. Perhaps Man as the Scientist is the best way for us to regard him; he is man being clever. One of the main sentiments is 'What next?' It requires very great perfection of movement and timing, and here again it seems a kind of thing that the European ballet simply couldn't do.

This dance *is* a classic of the Peking theatres, but not all of them are; there are various short items derived from local peasant dances. That always went on in some regions, but the present government has done a great deal to encourage and develop it. It could be very adroit, as its developed form here undoubtedly is, but it never aimed at the high strained formality of the professional stage. If you say that this show isn't real Peking theatre, because it is so much adapted for foreigners, one could answer that it is also adapted to the way that modern China is going. However, one shouldn't think of the traditional theatre as being aimed only at the ruling class; almost any rickshaw man in Peking would know bits of the operas, and I remember, soon after the communists had taken over in Peking, how you would continually hear, sitting in your courtyard, from far or near, both someone in the streets singing one of these falsetto bits and one of the little bands from which the young people were now practising peasant dances.

The only bit of high strained opera in the show, as Miles Malleson points out (I think he does the work of introduction very tactfully and clearly) is the suicide of the Concubine of the Defeated General. She insists on making a last dance to please him, but if she lived after that she might impede his escape; therefore, when she has ended, she steals his sword from him and kills herself. As what she dances is a sword dance, she presumably means to encourage him to make a last desperate attempt, which we are told he does. By the way, the dance itself isn't so very old; it was composed by the most famous living Chinese actor, Mei Lan Fang, who personally trained for many years the dancer who takes the part in London; indeed part of her name is taken from his. You don't get told this in the programme because a determined drive against the Star System is going on, but it seems a pity not to be told, if you are actually getting stars. The only real difficulty about viewing this performance is that you are expected to know the story already; during the dance itself, the real situation can only be shown by very tiny movements, because both people are supposed to be so heroic that they don't show it. But if you know the answer, I think, you can feel at once that it is a high dramatic effect.

Waiting for Godot: a letter

Times Literary Supplement, 30 March 1956

An anonymous review of Waiting for Godot *('They Also Serve', TLS, 10 February 1956) construed the play as a Christian allegory conveying a message of religious consolation. The following weeks brought a flood of letters offering different interpretations; Philip H. Bagby (23 March 1956) thus felt moved to write:*

Surely Mr Beckett must be chuckling away somewhere in France at the attempts of your reviewer and correspondents to extract some clear message from the manifold ambiguities of the play. Its strength clearly lies in its uncertainties, in the fact that it gives no final answer, no decisive reason to prefer either hope or despair . . .

At the end the playgoer leaves the theatre puzzled, disturbed, forced to worry about the uncertainty of the human situation, but what choice he makes or whether he makes a choice at all is up to him.

Empson came in on cue:

Mr Bagby was quite right, I think, to point out the radical ambiguity of *Waiting for Godot*, but not all ambiguity is good. Here it expresses the sentiment: We cannot believe in Christianity and yet without that everything we do is hopelessly bad. Such an attitude seems to be more frequent in Irish than either English or French writers, perhaps because in Ireland the religious training of children is particularly fierce. A child is brought up to believe that he would be wicked and miserable without God; then he stops believing in God; then he behaves like a dog with its back broken by a car, screaming and thrashing on the public road, so that a passer-by can only wish for it to be put out of its misery. Surely we need not admire this result; the obvious reflection is that it was a very unfairly risky treatment to give to a child.

To be sure, we all ought to feel the mystery of the world, and there is bound to be a kind of literary merit in any play which makes us feel it so strongly; but we need not ourselves feel only exacerbated impotence about the world, and if we did we would be certain to behave badly. 'Oh, how I wish I could go to Hell! Why can't I go to Hell? It does seem a shame I can't go to Hell.' In itself this peculiar attitude deserves only a rather disgusted curiosity. But I would hate to suggest a moral censorship against the play; it is so well done that it is an enlarging experience, very different for different members of the audience. It would only be dangerous if it was liable to suck a member into the entire background to be presumed for the author, and that it cannot do.

On 7 December 1971 Empson wrote to Francis Doherty (author of Samuel Beckett, *London: Hutchinson, 1971):*

I liked (in a way) and certainly admired the London production of *Waiting for Godot*. It was said to be much more cosy and human than the Paris one, but Beckett is a very intelligent man and probably allowed nature to take its course. Your letter speaks of a vague memory of something I had said about disliking Beckett. I have a specific memory of you here, but these things are always liable to be wrong. I had written to the *TLS* saying that the play was about the effects of the fierce religious education still prevalent in Ireland, which tells the children that life becomes worthless if they stop believing in God, and they have nothing to keep them from crime, so when they grow up and discover that the Christian God is the wickedest devil ever invented they behave like a dog on the road with its back broken by a motor-car; and I said that this is a very unfair way to treat a child. I was very surprised when you came up and told me (having read my letter) that you agreed that this was an unfair method of education. It struck me that no other Roman Catholic would have made this generous admission; but later on I found that Beckett was brought up as a Protestant (which of course would make no difference to the Irish insistence on the most evil features of the religion), and then I am afraid I presumed you must have known he was a Protestant when you spoke to me. I am rather sorry now to hear you have forgotten all about it. Your report of his remarks about his childhood religious teaching and reactions does not really alter the position: he had religious feelings at his first communion, and it stuck in his head that his 'brother and mother got no value from their religion when they died'. God had cheated the family somehow, and it was an excuse for him – this emerges even when he tries to debunk the idea. . . . what you want to tell the children is that everybody feels absolutely miserable unless they worship the God

who could be bought by the offer of having his son tortured to death to let off mankind from Hell in exchange; but he ratted on the bargain so completely that the vast majority of mankind will go to eternal torture all the same; and the tiny remnant who escape to Heaven are condemned to spend their whole time in gloating over the tortures in Hell of those they loved on earth, meanwhile incessantly praising God for his mercy.

I indent it hoping to win your attention. This is the most evil God yet invented, which means that his worshippers are under great temptation to imitate his evil. And the present Pope is demanding the destruction of all mankind, by forcing them to breed to the point of famine – offering no reason whatever (as he cannot offer any religious one) except the snobbish one that 'human dignity' demands it. [Empson Papers]

The Wisdom of the East

Observer, 19 August 1956

Joseph Needham,
Science and Civilisation in China, vol. 2:
History of Scientific Thought

Here is the second volume of this extremely magnificent project, and I am conscious of the inadequacy of the reviewer; he ought to be someone with a range of knowledge hardly less astounding than the author's. However, the subject of this volume is, in effect, the history of the philosophical background with which the Chinese approached the sciences, and here a literary man feels more at home. A scientist might object against the title that the Chinese didn't really ever get to 'scientific thought'; but, as a matter of linguistics, the verbal analysis here of the concepts with which they were approaching it seems to me splendid.

The first volume was a survey including much detail about the gradual and prolonged introduction of mechanical knowhow from China to Europe and I often didn't know the words; a general glossary of technical terms in the English language, let alone a reference summary of the Chinese terms which have so rightly been left untranslated, ought to be supplied in the final volume, which I think is the seventh. I deduce from a section-reference that the third will include the story of the mariner's compass – a strange story, because they invented it and we used it for the maritime empires.

The impulse behind this vast survey is the first thing to consider. A recurrent question in it is *why* the Chinese didn't develop scientific thought, whereas Europe did; and the answer on the whole is that their bureaucracy was too strong. It was not really because of any weakness in their fundamental ideas, as has often been maintained, except that their 'organicism' made it hard for them to get through the necessary mechanist phase. But this in itself would be too slight, not to say dismal, a theme for such major treatment; a hierarchy of questions erects itself, like a pagoda, and they are always present in the great book.

596

It is important to realise that, until Europe exploded with its new knowl-edge about four centuries ago and more or less conquered the world from ships, China had been comfortably ahead; an obscure realisation of this by the Chinese (fifty years ago it was simply called their conceit) made them determined to catch up once they had been forced to realise they were behind. More important again, perhaps, is that they were not *much* ahead; the baffling thing about the history of China, India and the Mediterranean basin is that they developed in parallel, stage after stage, for 3000 years; again and again you have to ask whether it is harder to believe that they somehow communicated or that they just developed alike.

Dr Needham goes into the evidence very informatively each time, but surely, anyhow, a good many contacts, or rather chains of gossip, were always going on at a level too low to get reported. On top of all this, what is of chief importance in the mind of Dr Needham, as I understand him, is that the Chinese were *right*, so far as they were different from the other civilisa-tions of the land mass; even though it put them at a temporary dis-advantage, because it let Europe get the first hold on the sciences. They insisted on an organic approach to Nature, and this (whether or not 'scien-tific humanism' is a suitable term) will be found the only philosophy toler-able to man in the world he is discovering.

To this extent, one should realise, there is a propagandist intention in this vast collection of knowledge; it delights Dr Needham to prove (always with that stubborn curiosity and sense of fact which makes a historian reliable) that the apparently contemptible approach of the Chinese to science kept on giving important practical results to Europe, and sometimes also gave important ideas.

His comments on his Chinese philosophers often remind me of a joke in Boswell, who boasted that, when he introduced his Corsican patriot, Gen-eral Paoli, to Dr Johnson, Johnson admired the man so much that, after every brief reply, he would interrupt with 'The General says well. He says ...' and the remark would at once be turned into some elaborate pro-fundity. This needs pointing out, because the book might look absurd unless you realised how deep the mind of Dr Needham is always going. The European mind has kept on getting itself increasingly hag-ridden by philo-sophical dilemmas (whether or not this was *why* it got the terrible strength needed to take the jump into the sciences), and the chief dilemma is this: either the universe is merely a fortuitous concourse of atoms, or else the atoms (even within the brain) only do what was ordered by a man-like law-giver, who is God; in either case, our minds cannot be expected to do what we want of them.

Now a biochemist such as Dr Needham takes for granted that this di-lemma is nonsense, because what he has to study, deep within some organism, is a rather puzzling balance between hierarchy and democratic check; like a human committee, the process is very liable to be stupid, but if it works out well it does something which no outsider could have arranged. What fascinates Dr Needham is that the Chinese mind seems always to have realised this. Now the first reaction of both the scientist and the theologian, when you read such a doctrine, is liable to be that they can refute it by their ancestral chop-logic, a thing which in practice has so often meant 'Heads I win and tails I burn you alive.' It feels wonderful to Dr Needham (instead of invincibly stupid) to see how the Chinese mind habitually winced away from this type of chop-logic; and especially from the belief that there had to be a personal lawgiver before the laws of Nature, at all their levels, could exist, with at their summit the Natural Law of man.

That is the philosophical purport underlying the book, but it is such a mine of information and analysis that many who disagree with its purport will have to read it. I feel myself that the line of thought which it suggests is the only one offering a future to mankind.

Everything, Beggars,
Is On Fire

Arrows (University of Sheffield),
New Year edition, 1957

The fact that Empson prefaced his Collected Poems *(London: Chatto &
Windus, 1955) with his own version of the so-called Fire Sermon (preached
by the Buddha at Mount Gaya) caused a number of reviewers to put forward the idea that he had actually espoused Buddhism. In 'A Style from a
Despair: William Empson'* (The Twentieth Century, CLXI, April 1957),
*for example, A. Alvarez observed that 'the later poems seem to be less per-
sonal discoveries than expansions of the passage from the Fire Sermon
which Empson has put at the front of* Collected Poems.' *Empson publicly
disavowed the notion that he was advocating the Buddhist faith – as in 'Mr
Empson and the Fire Sermon'* (Essays in Criticism, VI: iv, October 1956),
*and in this splendid response to a Sheffield periodical which certainly
merits wider attention.*

Arrows of last year carried a generous review of my *Collected Poems*,
which, however, said I had 'taken as my text' the Fire Sermon of the
Buddha. I feel I ought to try to clear this up, as I am also having to do in the
Oxford *Essays in Criticism*. I realise now that it was rather asking for misunderstanding to put the thing first, as authors generally mean that
seriously, but I meant hardly more than that I admired the famous object
and thought I had made, by picking words from various learned translations, an English version suitable for reciting in full – a rather unnerving
experience if you do all the repetitions.

It is said to be one of the earliest sermons of the Buddha, and carries the
unearthliness of his system as far as is conceivable. One should realise that
it denounces not only all existence on earth but all existence recognisable as
such, even in the highest heaven. A man may naturally pause before agreeing that he believes all that. To be sure, the coolness of Buddhism towards
Heaven, and towards the supernatural in general, is one of its most attractive features. On one occasion when the Buddha was preaching, the magic

of his words became too much for him and he rose forty feet into the air, but he shouted down to the audience begging them to pay no attention; it would be over in a moment, and wasn't of the smallest interest compared to what he was saying. Any lecturer can sympathise with this point of view. Also we are told there was a minor god who became interested in philosophy, and one of his questions was so difficult that he was referred up and up in the hierarchy (it is always thought of as like a government department) till he was asking it of the Supreme God, who was rather embarrassed but quite plucky about this, so he waved his hand and the clouds gradually rolled back till at last, infinitely far below, the divine eyes could pick out the Buddha, crosslegged under a bo-tree. 'I can tell you who knows the answer,' said the Supreme God; 'it's That Man, down there.' The basic position, of course, is that Buddhists believe in abandoning selfhood, sometimes interpreted as merging oneself into the Absolute or the impersonal Godhead. If you are good but rather a busybody you are liable to be reborn as a god yourself, which may hold up getting to Nirvana indefinitely; just as over here a too virtuous scholar is liable to be made to do administration.

When I was first confronted with the idea that I had advertised myself as a Buddhist I said that, if a son of mine wanted to become a Buddhist monk, I would beg him not to; this is so, but I would not want to speak of the condition with great horror. When I was refugeeing with the Peking universities at Kunming (on the Burma Road) in 1939 there was an English Buddhist in an entirely genuine and severe monastery across the lake, who could sometimes be induced to boat over for a vegetarian dinner. He was keen to get a monk's passport, but I believe he left that monastery before the yearly three weeks of marathon, or almost incessant, meditation, with bangs on the head if you were found dozing at the squatting-post. He turned up at the War Office a few years later as an intelligence officer; I forget whether we sat on committees together about the Far East, with me representing the BBC Far Eastern division, but I remember him in his uniform very well; I heard he was considered the only man they had had there who continued throughout his military career to think it wicked to kill even the lice on his body. Not that it was very surprising; a number of people felt they disapproved of Hitler enough to allow of stretching one or two points.

Buddhism obviously deserves respect; for one thing, though not only, as an extreme; it needs to be remembered when one tries to survey what the human mind could think about a subject. But I naturally would not want to present myself as a believer by mistake.

Christianity and *1984*

1959

Richard Gerber, in an essay entitled 'The English Island Myth: remarks on the Englishness of Utopian fiction' (Critical Quarterly I: 1, Spring 1959, pp. 36–43) argued that although the main theme of 1984 is 'utopian satire' – 'the breakdown of the liberal insularity of the individual' – it is yet 'a curiously ambiguous book'. 'On the surface it is doubtlessly a savage political satire in which the individual is opposed to the party collective,' Gerber wrote; but an important level of its meaning is surely carried by religious metaphor – 'Winston Smith ... is tracked down by some irrational, illiberal, binding (which is the meaning of religious) otherness, which does not take the form of the fierce Hound of Heaven, but the less usual metaphorical form of the political machinery of utopian prose fiction.'

Empson felt incited (in a letter to Critical Quarterly, *I: 2, Summer 1959) to take issue with Gerber's implication that Orwell may not have been fully aware of such an anti-religious tenor in his work.*

May I send my congratulations on your first number. I also want to send some comments on Mr Gerber's remarks about the novel *1984*. There, he says,

the individualistic, rational, liberal and humanist conception of man is opposed, not only to party collectives, but also to the complete unconditional surrender to the transcendental, paradoxical nature of God. It almost seems as if Orwell, being gradually broken down bodily and on the point of death, had filled his political satire with unconscious or halfconscious meanings of another kind.

He gives a series of details to show that the satire

has the age-old symbolic structure, and even phraseology, of resistant man's breakdown and conversion to some power which we generally call by the name of God.

The trouble about modern criticism, a wonderfully powerful instrument, is that it is always liable to be applied totally upside-down. Every point Mr

Gerber makes (I think) is true and piercing, except the presumption that the author could not have been 'conscious'. Orwell considered that the ultimate Betrayal of the Left, the worst thing about the way communism had developed, was that it had nearly got back to being as bad as Christianity. For a few centuries the enlightened sceptics had managed to prevent that loathsome system of torture-worship from burning people alive, but it would spring like a tiger again at any opportunity to revive its standard techniques; and in the increasingly crazy modern world, with whole continents regarding Christianity as the only alternative to communism, the opportunity was almost sure to come. Communism had no inherent ideological need to be as torturing as Christianity, but had so far shown itself very ready to learn from its opponent. In the world of Orwell's book, it would be fatuous for the author to mention whether the capital in view is the post-communist or the post-Christian one, because they have become indistinguishable, and maintain a permanent half-hearted state of war merely to secure for both sets of rulers the pleasures of police terror. Surely Orwell made very clear that he considered it the ultimate shame for a man to hand over his conscience either to Stalin the Big Brother or to the incessantly gloating monster God the Father, so that he took pains in his writing to confuse them. Surely the conception of a Ministry of Love, whose towering office hag-rides the city because each citizen believes it has calculated for him the torture he would find most unbearable, corresponds to nothing in communism and a great deal in the history of Christianity. It is not even known in the story whether Big Brother is a living human ruler, a dead one presented as still alive, or a god imposed by the ruling group. That is presented as unimportant; because a man who has yielded up his conscience to an authority which craves to torture him and can only be restrained by the observance of taboos has in any case lost all real morality, both the sense of personal honour and of the public good. A reasonable criticism, I think, would be that the story becomes tiresomely incredible, owing to the determination of the author to make his allegory apply to both political groups at once. The bland presumption that he must have been unconscious at the time seems to me almost too absurd to discuss; though he himself, to be fair, regarded the certainty that his work would be used for evil as one of his inevitable torments.

I think literary criticism has got into a very corrupt frame of mind when it can regard a sustained denunciation of the Christian God as an unwitting testimonial for him; and indeed when it assumes that not even an eccentric like Orwell could still believe his own conscience must ultimately tell him the difference between right and wrong.

Two correspondents in the next issue of Critical Quarterly *(I: 3, Autumn*

1959) responded to Empson's letter. Empson's hatred of Christianity limits his judgement, wrote G. S. Fraser, 'as any really obsessive hatred limits any critic of literature or society. The notion of Christianity as essentially and always a "loathsome system of torture-worship" shows that lack of feeling for history which is Professor Empson's great limitation as a critic'. In any event, he concluded, 'violently obsessive stock-responses do not make for ranging and fruitful criticism.' Likewise, John Blackie described Empson's definition of Christianity as 'the language of vituperation', and cautioned him that 'Vituperation is very well but to be effective it must be just.'

Empson returned to the subject in Critical Quarterly I: 4 (Winter 1959):

Two letters in your last number consider me blinded by hatred in using some phrases about Christianity when discussing 1984. I tried hard to make my letter clear though short, and I see that its grammar does make these phrases describe the attitude to Christianity of the author in the book; the letter was an answer to a critic who had found Christian tendencies in it. What can be said to literary critics who must not be told what the book means, because that hurts their feelings, but must be allowed to cosset one another with explanations that it has a morally low meaning which would have hurt the author's feelings intensely? The cult described in the novel *ought* to be called 'a loathsome system of torture-worship', and literary critics who have so accustomed themselves to conniving at anything which can be called a Christian Paradox that they smile with tender broad-mindedness even at that, I again submit, have done moral harm to their judgement by their religious revival.

George Fraser tells me to correct my ignorance of history, and assumes I can only have a mathematical reason for thinking Christianity liable to persecute; we can be sure at least that this was not why George Orwell expected it to start persecuting again. I well know that many very saintly characters have been and are Christians; one is not tempted to deny this in thinking it a tragedy that Europe got saddled with a religion so very predisposed to enter phases of great evil. Well may Fraser appeal to the last two centuries, but the relevant question is how the Christians managed to stop burning people alive just before. A hundred years ago, Buckle's *History of Civilisation* gave a lot of evidence to prove that the growth of scepticism was what had made the change possible; during his recent centenary the reviewers all jeered at him, confident that he was out of fashion, and betrayed no idea even of what he had been discussing, let alone of why the question had ever seemed important. They had been affected by the revival too.

The forecast of Orwell, in this horrible novel written while he was dying, is that Christianity and communism will soon wear each other down till both have lost their original ideals, and become the worship of a monster. I first read the book in communist Peking, and thought its forecast absurd. But now when I find literary critics praising the final moral collapse of the hero of the novel, because it is so Christian somehow, thus exactly fulfilling Orwell's forecast of how their minds will work, without having the faintest idea that the book itself makes the forecast, I think I am justified in letting out a small cry of horror. An opponent cannot much better the position by scratching up sordid bits of evidence purporting to prove that Orwell was a sadist, or by saying that I myself am blinded by hate, unless he can support an argument that the forecast was something different. The immediate imputation of bad character is not enough; many people would not consider it actual proof of sadism to have a man regret the prospect of a revival of the Christian use of rack, boot, thumbscrew, and slow fire.

A Full-Blown Lily

New Statesman, 6 January 1961

Arthur Koestler, *The Lotus and the Robot*

It has immense impact; the arrival at Bombay which starts the book must be the most gripping space landing in science fiction; and the chapter 'Yoga Unexpurgated' is far too horrible for me to read. In between comes an acount of 'Four Contemporary Saints', and one is bound to feel the splendid breadth with which Hinduism is being scrutinised, novelistically, mystically, scientifically, at every level and through every chink. It's a rash fakir that looks gruff at Koestler, let alone makes him stand in a queue; a sharp test of sanctity there's going to be for that revered pagan, in the next batch of press cuttings for him or her. The spirituality of the East and the materialism of the West, one should readily agree, have become harmful clichés which deserve attack; indeed the book would be justified if the chapter on Yoga Research induced even one young Indian on the verge of those practices to believe that their promise of magical power is false. Even so, it is hard to believe that Indians, owing to their neurotic fear of sex, are peculiarly unable to eat curry.

The chief moral of the book is that Koestler is now proud to be a Western European, as he is disillusioned with Zen and Yoga. But India and Hinduism are not all Yoga, nor Buddhism and Japan all Zen. After his renunciation of politics, one is interested to know what he will recommend. He is indignant because Nehru planned a Pink Utopia, suited to the Fabianism of the twenties, or perhaps because the Indians were too father-ridden to stop him. We are given no reason to think that Nehru's plans were mistaken, and to call them pink feels to me suited to Mosleyites in 1939. He conveys powerfully the horror of the over-population of India, and then we find him 'depressed' because the Japanese have halved their birthrate, or perhaps because they have legalised abortion. The book keeps on implying that he is less materialist than the Asians are, whereas it ought to be exposing the bogusness of that term.

In Japan the main thing he attacks is a certain silliness, already well known from previous tourists, and one might fear that this would be an anti-climax after the monstrosities of Ancient Night. But no, he manages to get the real Sunday-newspaper panting horror into his description of the deportment of the young ladies; they are wired within, like the flowers. It is eked out with claims to intense sensibility: 'I have lived through the London blitz and was bombed out by a V2, but this quite insignificant tremor is something different.' He has rather bad luck ('I felt, for instance, a curious affinity ...') in his explanation of how footling the Noh plays are: 'All violent emotions, like uncouth nature, have become ... daintified.' If he had waited to the end of the play, which only takes about an hour and a half, he would probably have found the ghost of the warrior doing a good old South Sea island war dance, stamping like a buck rabbit, to a terrific chorus of yowling. The forces of the world are strong at the climax in the music and dance, as they need to be since loyalty to them keeps the ghost from his peace; but, as they are not in the words, we tend to assume that the whole performance is just Celtic Twilight. Koestler would have had to blame the play for something different if he had sat it through. (By the way, I can't believe that Japanese madmen are never violent.) As to Zen, a mystical school which denies the value of explanation would be inconsistent if it gave a reporter sensible answers; but much of Japanese Buddhism is very like the Church of England, both in its weaknesses and virtues.

The thesis of the book requires 'Europe' to be a single though growing entity; Christianity and science have always been one, and the only astronomers mentioned are Jesuits. A mention of 'Judeo-Christian monotheism' is as much credit as the Semites can expect, especially as the Arabs only copied the Greeks. It all brings comfort because it proves that the whites are genuinely superior. I think that this belief, even if true (it is grotesquely untrue about Christianity), is not likely to do us good, and the mind strays from the doctrine to its preacher. Soon after the war, Koestler felt he hadn't enough petrol, and wrote to the *Partisan Review*, 'The Labour Party is betraying its trust. I have to bicycle a mile and a half for my groceries. We old-established country squires are being wronged' (or words politically leaving that impression). I had managed to get back to China and had taken on more bicycling than Koestler, so I laughed at this; but no doubt he was reporting a widespread sentiment.[1] Yet again the press shakes with the throbbing bellow of Koestler being wronged: 'It's a shame. With all the publicity Zen and Yoga are having, we Christian saints can hardly get on the telly at all.' Still, the exposure of Yoga was needed, and there the claim to speak with authority seems justified; and maybe the support for Christianity won't do much harm.

Note

1 Arthur Koestler wrote to the *New Statesman* on 20 January 1961 to 'pin a lie' – 'a forged quotation' – in Empson's review; his protest included these remarks:

'After obliquely hinting that my attitude is that of a sympathiser with Hitler (suited to Mosleyites in 1939) and similar smears, Empson proceeds: "Soon after the war, Koestler felt he hadn't enough petrol and wrote to the *Partisan Review*, 'The Labour Party is betraying its trust. I have to bicycle a mile and a half for my groceries. We old-established country squires are being wronged' (or words leaving that impression)."

'The alleged quotation, from beginning to end, was invented by Empson, and the qualifying phrase in brackets does not diminish the effect of this slanderous fabrication. The article to which he refers appeared in *Partisan Review* in November 1947. It discussed the Labour government's decision to abolish the petrol allowance for private motoring, and pointed out that it compelled the little man to lay up his family car or motor bike, whereas – "the squire has his farming allowance and will be seen driving about the countryside as before, by using the simple dodge of putting a sack of potatoes or pig-food into the dicky to prove that he is on some farming errand. In industrial areas the directors, managers, executives, etc, will have their business allowance ... From the point of view of the working man-in-the-street it is still 'they' who flit past him in their cars" ...

'I expect your reviewer to apologise in unambiguous terms for imputing to me words which I never wrote and opinions which I never held or expressed.'

Empson was obliged to put his signature to the following apology:

'The sentences in quotation marks were meant to be a parody of the article in *Partisan Review*, which I had not seen since it was new. I thought I had made this clear and I am sorry if they were taken as a quotation, and for suggesting that Koestler used words "politically leaving that impression". I agree that unchecked reminiscing is a bad thing, since one's memory is likely to play one false, as it has admittedly done in this case.'

The Age of the Telly

Universities Quarterly, XVII, March 1963

Marshall McLuhan, *The Gutenberg Galaxy*

The blurb says that the style glitters like a galaxy itself, and I do find vision rather obstructed, but the Prologue suggests that the intention is to express the future. The inventions of alphabets and of printing involved two decisive changes in human consciousness, and 'we are today as far into the electric age as the Elizabethans had advanced into the typographical and mechanical age'; we are already more deeply involved than we realise in a third change. Hence the book had to be written in an imagistic manner, not following up an idea and relating it to other ideas, but letting it splash onto a page and then poke up on later pages at random. It strikes me that many of the ideas deserve kinder treatment. There really does seem a likeness between Imagism as a theory of poetry and the way discussions on the telly tend to break down into displays of rapid shooting-a-line. No reason is ever given for thinking that the Telly Age will be pleasanter, more interesting or better in any way than the one we are to lose; pretty strong reasons would be required, but Mr McLuhan seems to feel no need to recommend the future, which he eyes with an invariable spry brassy readiness.

I read for some time with glum submission to this crushingly depressing prospect, and then it occurred to me that the people envisaged were only viewers of the telly, not the mechanics who make it work, let alone the scientists of varied capacity and inventiveness who are essential in any society which keeps it going. If they all become submen, the machine which incapacitates them still stop.

It is curious that a man of such very wide reading and sympathy can give with panting unquestioning approval a picture of the coming age which Wyndham Lewis for one, but with full sympathy from many of his generation, had given long before with vomiting horror. Everyone who wishes to be sensible, I suppose, has been telling himself that these rebel aesthetes were wrong, and that some tolerable or even agreeable way round their dilemma will eventually be worked out; but I can't feel I've been helped at all when I read a man who is tremendously abreast of all the puzzles, except what made them puzzling to start with.

Beardsley's Mother

Listener, 28 November 1968

Brigid Brophy, *Black and White: A Study of Aubrey Beardsley*

Brigid Brophy's book on Aubrey Beardsley is a very nice thing to have, with forty-four reproductions and plenty of information. I was disappointed in the pictures at first, expecting them to have more charm; but after reading the text I realised that, while about a third have charm, the others illustrate interesting points.

The text is very strong on psychology. Beardsley was the polyperverse infant later described by Freud, which involves being afflicted with horror and terror at the discovery that Mum lacks the male organ. The death wish and the craving to inflict torture are still more prominent among the impulses of this draughtsman; it is all documented unflinchingly, and he is not supposed to be blamed for it a bit. Sensible remarks occur about the public reaction to his work, then and now; but it strikes me that they are too incidental. Beardsley invented a mode; the mere line of his drawings came to be felt by a quite large public as like a signature tune, so that a magazine editor was glad to have any drawing by Beardsley that would not make too much trouble. The drawings didn't *need* the characteristics defined in Brigid Brophy's essay. This is what needs explaining: why did the quality of his line suddenly get under people's skin, a thing which hasn't happened since to any major artist – though it has to one or two political cartoonists, none of whom survive now?

The admired effect does not come out more plainly when the drawings are directly obscene. We should of course rejoice in the freedom so bravely fought for which allows the point to be illustrated in this book; and almost anyone would enjoy the first look at the three men with monstrous erections in the chosen drawing from the *Lysistrata* series, which was done by Beardsley, in the last year of his brief doomed life, for a private edition by Smithers. But many people will feel at the second look that this is hardly a Beardsley: it is a vigorous observant drawing, but the peculiar grace of his line has almost vanished. Brigid Brophy says that it 'aches with frustration', and that he was presumably 'exiled from sexual intercourse' in that last year because it made his lungs bleed. Well, the story of the *Lysistrata* is that the women refuse the men sex until they stop their beastly war, so the men in the drawing ought to show frustration; but they only look to me cross and embarrassed. However, so they do in the Japanese prints which Beardsley was copying. I am told he used (in earlier years) to go to the London docks and buy these as yet unvalued treasures, whether obscene or not, from simple sailormen just back from Yokohama; and it struck me as a remarkable thing, when I was in Japan, long ago, that the Japanese print-masters, too, lose their distinctive line when they turn aside and create Porners. One might expect that this only happened to Englishmen, or Europeans, or Christians, but no doubt the slender antennae of a line-draughtsman are easily disturbed. Maybe not if he is Chinese, but the few examples I happened to see in China were not very good, and anyhow Beardsley could not collect them. And then again, surely Beardsley was doing this work because the enterprising Smithers would pay him for it. He knew he was dying; the reason why he so determinedly earned the biggest money he could in his last months was to provide for his mother and sister, who were going to be left in difficulties, and were wasting money on useless care for him. One way and another, the 'psychological' comment of Brigid Brophy, though very sympathetic here for once, seems likely to be irrelevant.

The pleasure in looking at impossibly large male erections does not count as unnatural, very rightly, I think, though it would be hard to say why. In another case, Brigid Brophy writes some thrilling prose about a revealing unnaturalness, and thus falls into a trap deliberately set for her by the artist. This is an illustration of the initial M (for Mum) in the posthumous edition of *Volpone*. She knows from her theory that the child in the artist Beardsley was in agony about its Mum. In the picture a naked child toddles up simply adoring its naked Mum; behind, at the sides, two rather disgusting statues have the many breasts yet visible on the mother-goddess of Ephesus. Brigid Brophy says: 'A bitter sensual sadness surrounds them. The child's wings are bedraggled, and he reaches towards his mother in desperation. Even Venus's breasts cannot satisfy this hunger.' And so firmly on, rather like Pater doing a set-piece. We need not deny that she is expressing the reactions of part of the intended audience. But it is one of the jokes against censors that they struggle earnestly to hide representations of women's breasts from children who have only recently been weaned. The little boy here, aged about two, is in excellent health and temper except that he is rather too fat; he will take no harm at all from being allowed to love his mother. The drawing has an unusual depth of feeling; Beardsley could allow himself to be tender for once because all the asses would be sure he was being terrifically shocking. None of this makes his point of view an infantile one; as so often, he is just playing the rude lad or mocking urchin. It is interesting to read of a particularly obscene gesture, from which he could only be restrained by weighty advisers, among them Bernard Shaw. The first cover of the *Savoy* was to include a small cherub pissing on a copy of the *Yellow Book*: not a sensible mode of advertisement perhaps, but not one that betrays great depth of corruption. On the other hand, when Salome kisses the severed head of Jokanaan, I don't deny that we are in funny country. The original drawing reproduced here is immensely better than the simplified one printed with the play; it is all furry and tousled, and the faces are convincing. But to say that this triumph of imagination proves that the author was a sadist would throw all good tragedians under suspicion, and Oscar as well. As the chief virtue of Wilde was his golden good humour, and his chief idea of fun was to flatter the hired young men exactly as he had just been flattering the duchesses (having come on in a cab), it was absurd, as well as asking for trouble, that he should drop hints at the great dinner party about his monstrous sins, so that the thrilled ladies really imagined he was going off to do something dreadfully cruel. The flavour of the Naughty Nineties still manages to cling to most discussions of its heroes, and rather needs to be debunked, but the solemn language of Psychologism is a positive nutrient for it.

We need then to distinguish between the inner nature of Beardsley and his impact on his public. As Brigid Brophy well remarks, although it was the need for speed, knowing he was dying, that made him stick to black-and-white drawings intended for reproduction, the effect was the fortunate one of showing he worked for a young uncommitted public, who did not need large oil-paintings to cover the walls of the dining-room; also this insinuated that they could be fashionable without being ruling-class. She adds later that he is having at present a kind of Pop revival; his 'kinkiness' has become prized: his kingdom now is 'the transvestitely dandified realm of Carnaby Street'. Yes, but I think what these chaps like about him was always his main and best feature. He needed to be shocking for immediate impact, and brought a powerful intelligence to that line of effort, using especially the mode for Satanism which poor old Eng. Lit. still finds so absorbing; and his actual situation was macabre; but what his line immediately conveys is something else. The stern rigidity and implicit puritanism of the evening dress of the time, with its harsh lines, and the same qualities anywhere else in the modern scene, even an ordinary sash-window, are presented as a comic affectation, adopted merely for fun by the people who use them. The mixed-sex quality of most of the characters is (and was) reassuringly cosy, implying 'you needn't bother' about being particularly virile or womanly; 'Well, you can't be surprised, dear, can you?' is the expected comment on his grotesques. This is the likable side of him, and surely it must be very close to the tone of a love-in among flower persons. It is made almost invisible by the hell-fire treatment of Brigid Brophy, and even by her choice of illustrations. But she is often illuminating in other ways, I don't deny.

Resurrection

1964

John Wren-Lewis, in an article headed 'The Passing of Puritanism' (Critical Quarterly, V: 4, Winter 1963), took issue with the validity of the time-worn polarity between 'the positive, world-affirming outlook of the great classical and Catholic tradition' and the Romantic tendency to deny the world by affirming 'individual creativeness' and personal values: 'affirmation of the values of personal life must sooner or later lead to a denial of the claims of organic life, and vice versa.' *What we need to recognise, he argued, is that the classical and Romantic traditions in the West are 'both other-worldly', both escapist. The answer is to overcome the apparently neurotic conflict between personal values and organic life by embracing the scientific and technological revolution which can 'provide a genuine answer to romantic despair, a real alternative to puritanism': it can* change 'the workings of nature so as to make the physical world subserve personal values instead of overriding them'. *The original Hebrew background to the concept of bodily resurrection 'meant nothing less than the faith that the whole physical order of nature could be changed so as to subserve the values of love, beauty and justice which are involved in the original religious impulse' – the faith in our 'human power to transform nature' as first asserted by 'the Hebrew–Christian doctrine of creation* ex nihilo'. *But that doctrine has been falsely used, he went on*

to sanctify the ordinary order of nature as the reflection of the Will of God – a view which in my judgement fully justifies Mr Empson's stricture, in his book on Milton, that 'the Christian God the Father is the most wicked idea that ever entered into the heart of man.' But this view of the doctrine of creation also makes no sense, and must have arisen originally by distortion of a radically different idea, which I would express by saying that there is no substantial system in the natural world at all, except insofar as human action, based on the service of the personal values of creativity and love, puts it there.

Empson responded to Wren-Lewis's plea for a 'revolution in ethics' in a letter to the editors (Critical Quarterly, VI: 1, Spring 1964):

Mr Wren-Lewis, in your number for Winter 1963, says that for most of Christian history the doctrine of creation *ex nihilo* has been used

to sanctify the ordinary order of nature as the reflection of the Will of God – a view which in my judgement fully justifies Mr Empson's stricture, in his book on Milton, that 'the Christian God the Father is the most wicked idea that ever entered the heart of man.'

This does not say why I said it, but a reader might easily think that I said it for the same reason as Mr Wren-Lewis, and I am anxious to be allowed to clear myself of that.

I said the Father was bad because he could be bought off by the crucifixion, which gave him 'satisfaction', so that he will spare a tiny remnant of mankind from Hell, but they must eternally watch from Heaven the torments in Hell of those they have loved on earth, praising him for his mercy. I did not say he was bad because he created the world, and I think that idea a disgusting one. It is petulant snootiness to say, 'The world is not good enough for me'; the world is glorious beyond all telling, and far too good for any of us. The world includes, of course, what Mr Wren-Lewis calls 'personal values', and I do not see how he can get them into his eternity with a resurrection of the body, which would be like a toy-shop full of working models. An eternity of contemplating God is conceivable, that is, our fancy does not bump at once against a contradiction, but the function of a body is to go through processes in time. The world is equally good whether made by a personal God or not; but I agree that the God is bad if he is using its accidents to trip us up, sending earthquakes to punish us for example. I thought that this extremity of superstition had become quite rare, but even so Mr Wren-Lewis does well to reject it.

A resistance to the style may be making me stupid; it always makes me echo the Negro Spiritual and think, 'Everybody talks about "values" aint got any.' What could possibly be meant, for example, by saying:

in all previous ages it would have seemed self-evident ... that the affirmation of *personal* life-values such as beauty, peace and love, is ... almost certainly antagonistic to the affirmation of *organic* life, in the sense of the general principle of growth and vitality operating throughout nature.

A monk oughtn't to have a baby, but somebody else has to have babies, if only to keep up the supply of monks. C. S. Lewis in *The Allegory of Love* quoted any amount of medieval praise for Nature in this sense. What *happens* when an affirmation is antagonistic? And why would it stop being antagonistic if we made 'a tremendous act of faith' in the resurrection of the body? This would bring 'a revolution in ethics', 'a belief that in general bodily pleasure is positively good'. People had much better think so, I agree; but if something is good on earth, even if it only lasts for half an hour, it is still just as good whether or not it lasts for eternity in Heaven. The idea that its 'value' is different if it happens in Heaven as well as on earth strikes me as like selling a packet of tea by saying 'The Queen drinks it'; though of course not nearly so sensible. By the time Aquinas has finished with Heaven it is not a recommendation but a smear.

P.S. I have got round rather belatedly to reading *Objections to Christian Belief*, and find that the Dean of St John's, in its last pages, agrees with me. What is most needed for religion is a natural theology, which the sciences may yet supply, and meanwhile nothing can justify condemning the universe, he says, and so on [see 'The Cult of Unnaturalism', essay 117 below]. Probably Mr Wren-Lewis thinks that this is on *his* side, which again shows how tricky these matters are to discuss.

'Surely Professor Empson is being naive?' Wren-Lewis queried in the same issue. 'The image of a wrathful God who permits extreme cruelty is no more than a reflection of our common experience that nature deals out pain and death without regard for individuals ... it is not only an extremely superstitious notion of God which one must reject if one regards this sort of thing as an abomination: it is any sort of God who could be responsible for the creation of the natural world as we see it.' Empson's observation that 'the world is glorious beyond all telling' Wren-Lewis presumed to be 'a poet's statement, made because, in the poet's vision, the transformation of the world is something which has already begun. May I not invite Professor Empson the poet to join hands here with technologists like myself, so as to translate this vision into reality as best we can? ... will not our joint effort be precisely in the direction which was implied by the original Jewish notion of resurrection?'

Empson replied in the next number (Critical Quarterly, VI: 2 Summer *1964):*

Mr Wren-Lewis is right to insist that Christians are in a dilemma about their God, but to an outsider it merely looks like a penalty for self-indulgence. Mrs Eddy found comfort in the belief that bodily pain and disease do not exist and in later life she built one house outside another for protection against distant enemies willing mental poison into her. In the same way, Christians find comfort in the belief that a well-intentioned creator will reward the good, until they are faced by the problems of Job. The most energetic statement of this dilemma in a novel is the description of the ten-day death of a child from meningitis in Aldous Huxley's *Point Counter*

Point; he seems to have been smeared somehow – I find it discreditable that these modern discussions never mention his *Perennial Philosophy*. His answer is that one should stop believing in this all-executive Father, but accept an impersonal 'Divine Ground', as in Hinduism and in the mystics of all other religions; thus becoming morally free to recognise that the world contains wonderful things as well as horrible things.

Mr Wren-Lewis, as I understand, believes that the only nice things in the world are constructed by technologists, perhaps under the leadership of an emergent deity. His article approves of belief in the resurrection of the body as 'a tremendous act of faith' which is 'required for a confident technology'; it seems to be a real case of *hubris*. His letter answering mine repeats that 'personal values' are not 'irrelevant to God', and takes this to prove that they exist in Heaven – eternal existence is somehow what validates these values. I must again ask what difference it could make to their value in time on earth. I realise that the doctrine gives authority to the preacher who says: 'If you don't do what I tell you I won't let you live for ever'; but this is not in itself a proof that we will live for ever.

When Mr Wren-Lewis accuses me of 'primitive technology' he is surely sporting with the impatience of your readers. Moslem theologians, we have long been told, decided that an orgasm with a houri could last a thousand years, but that even the most heroic of the blessed would then pause for contemplation. Can there be some recent biological experiment which has proved that it may continue for all eternity?

The Abominable Fancy

New Statesman, 21 August 1964

D. P. Walker, *The Decline of Hell*

This is a scholarly and elegant documentation of an important change of feeling. In the later seventeenth century, the doctrine that nearly all mankind, including all the babies who die unbaptised, are to receive for ever tortures more severe than any earthly expert can contrive to inflict, with the corollary that (as this is right) to watch the tortures eternally is one of the delights of the blessed, became unwelcome. It was still thought socially necessary: a man whose children were starving would be sure to steal food if only threatened with torture for eons, not for eternity. Hence, apart from fanatics who expected an early end of the world, the theologians who printed doubts on the subject were nearly all exiles, a shifty crew in Holland. Among these the dishonesty of Bayle (1647–1706) was the most splendid; pretending to defend the Calvinists, as their God was considered the worst of all, he 'copiously showed' that 'all actual and possible Christian Gods are morally repulsive.' He thus invented the irony of Gibbon, but Mr Walker, a sensitive judge, thinks he was not ironical when he wrote: '*il y a même je ne sais quoi qui choque*' in the belief that the blessed gloat over Hell. The change of taste was no confident result of argument; it somehow drifted into the study with the air. To us it is bound to seem important; people who held the older religious view, surely, could hardly pass themselves off now as sane.

Mr Walker says little about why it happened, and does not mention, even to deny, the conclusion of the Victorian Buckle: that it was a result of widespread scepticism, which was a result of the sectarian persecutions and wars. As soon as each church was being called wicked by some other church, with obvious truth, the human conscience could begin to work again, and people felt as if they were coming round from a drug. The reaction was a good deal earlier than most of the books considered here, though we are given a Dutch poet from the start of the century. By 1612 in England King James became frightened at the public reaction to his burning a couple of Arians; bishops continued to recommend further tortures and boast how effective these ones had been till Charles lost his head, but the monstrosity was not done again in front of an English crowd. But a kind mayor of the medieval Low Countries bought a criminal for his town, so that the people could have the pleasure of torturing him to death. There seem to be no such records from the parallel civilisations of India and China; great cruelties were practised, but not as an admitted pleasure for a crowd. It happened in Europe because the Christian Father, though satisfied by the crucifixion of his Son, arranged infinitely greater tortures for almost everyone else; the moral effect of worshipping him was sure to be disgustingly bad. When secular resistance to the religion became strong enough to stop its public tortures, its whole character seemed to change; but there is no reason why it should not change back again, in our excitable time, if it regains sufficient power.

Such is the main point, but there is great variety of interest. Did anyone tell Yeats, I wonder, that his Theosophy (eternal recurrence, with everyone reborn into each new age but given a chance to improve, after a purgative interval outside the flesh) was the theology of Origen, not pronounced heretical till more than a century after his death? It was much admired by Erasmus and the texts were fully edited in the sixteenth century; the authors of Mr Walker keep recurring to it. Geoffrey Gorer deduced from a questionnaire that a third of the modern English still believe they will be reborn on earth,[1] though few of them know of an organisation that teaches so. The merit of the belief is that it saves God from being unjust.

'The abominable fancy' was what Dean Farrar, in the pulpit of Westminster Abbey about a century ago, called the belief that the blessed will enjoy the tortures of the damned; he was also convinced that syphilis was a punishment sent by God for sexual pleasure. It seems very odd that the religion was imposed on the state schools after the Second World War.

Note

1 Empson corrected himself in a letter to the *New Statesman* on 28 August 1964:
'Geoffrey Gorer found that half of the 5000 English people answering a questionnaire believed in an afterlife, but a quarter of those, an eighth of the whole, did not "appear to believe that this afterlife would be eternal", and one in twenty expressed specific belief in reincarnation. I am sorry I got the figure wrong; I could not get hold of the book in time to correct my memory.'

Heaven and Hell

Listener, 30 November 1967

S. G. F. Brandon, *The Judgment of the Dead*

A splendid work of scholarship, and full of interesting detail, but such works often leave one doubtful about the basic intention. The doubt here is resolved on the last page, where Professor Brandon laments the recent slackening of fear of Hell even among the faithful: 'Because belief in judgement after death, with its eternal consequences of Heaven or Hell, constitutes the "teeth" or ultimate authentication of the Christian ethic, that belief has now become practically even more necessary than it was before. However, the secularisation of Western society has coincided with a growing uncertainty among Christians, of most denominations, about the traditional eschatology.' A footnote, actually the last words of the book, adds: 'Ideally, of course, the Christian moral code should be practised for love of God, and not for the hope of gaining Heaven or escaping Hell. Nevertheless, the validity of that code depends logically upon an ultimate distinction, made by God, between the just and the unjust.' 'Validity' and 'authentication' and above all 'logically' are words grossly misused here: the problem does not only arise 'ideally'. Now that the arguments from prophecy and suchlike have been so thoroughly refuted, the only argument for Christianity is that it appeals to the convert's sense of right and wrong, which he must therefore have enjoyed before he accepted the doctrines of the religion. The difference between right and wrong does not depend upon an arbitrary decision by a divine tyrant, and Professor Brandon could have learned this from the other half of Christian theology, let alone the other half of the Old World – India and China and their satellites. Fancy saying 'logically'.

He does not say why he omits the Incas and the Aztecs, who are essential test cases; maybe not enough survives about their beliefs for a conscientious scholar to include them, but he could at least have said that much. As he begins with Neolithic man, who was an efficient globetrotter, and gives a charming though dubious picture of Neolithic corpses who even though beheaded have succeeded in becoming ghosts, he can have no ground for excluding the Americans, who are generally agreed to have had a remote basic contact with the original Neolithic breakthrough; a bit of theology as well as pottery must be envisaged as being carried across the ice of the Bering Straits, or the tropical Pacific. The Spaniards who conquered central America were shocked and astonished to find these people worshippers of Moloch exactly like themselves, and Professor Brandon ought to have told us so.

And why, even in his limited field, does he never discuss the actual moral consequences of the different beliefs of the Egyptians and the people of the Fertile Crescent, around Mesopotamia, who started town civilisation earlier? Why does Hammurabi, the first known lawgiver, not appear in the index? The Mesopotamians held a dismal view of the afterlife, but they were better at doing justice in this world. At least, there is some evidence for believing so, and it is what a reasonable man would expect, but Professor Brandon simply praises the Egyptians for the 'moral achievement' of inventing their farcically horrible nonsense-technique for achieving immortality. Early Egyptians had also while dying to recite a ritual saying that they had been good, but one can hear the mental reservations, almost as loud as the words: 'I have not caused weeping' (except as part of my sworn duty as a magistrate); 'I have not had sexual relations with a boy' (he was fully 14 – a lad, plainly). Why is it taken for granted that the belief in life after death (always a very strained thing) actually produced better behaviour? The most notable effect of belief in the Christian Hell has been to induce good men to burn one another alive.

The Butler Act, it seems to me, did a desperate amount of harm to the schools by making the teaching of Christianity a state requirement. Children are very sensitive to insincerity in a teacher; they hear it at once in the tone of voice; and many of the boys who would have made good scientists stopped learning and became gangsters instead when they heard this horrible sound being forced out of poor teacher in the classroom. That is why we are so short of scientists.

The Satisfaction of the Father

c. 1972

When the New Testament was written, the later doctrine of Redemption already existed but there were rivals to it. The authors seem to have felt that the details of that part of the story could be worked out later on. The later doctrine seems to be present in (for example): 'give his life a ransom for many' (Matt 20.28), 'gave himself up for us' (Eph 5.2), 'him who knew no sin he made to be sin on our behalf' (2 Cor 5.21). I take these examples from the entry 'Sacrifice (Christian)' in the *Catholic Encyclopedia*, which also says that the belief was not invented by the Apostle Paul, because it is also found in 1 Peter 18–20: 'ye were redeemed ... with the blood of Christ' – apparently assuming that Peter would not have accepted an idea from Paul. The belief seems to have been first officially promulgated by the Synod of Ephesus (431), rather late: it says that the incarnate Logos 'offered himself to God the Father for us', and the Encyclopedia does not report any earlier statement that the offering was made to the Father. Rather quaintly, the article ends by saying that 'a comprehensive theory' of the subject 'is still a desideratum in speculative theology'.

The term 'satisfaction', for the reaction of the Father to the offering, is first used by Tertullian, an author chiefly famous for the enthusiasm with which he described the tortures in Hell of those who had enjoyed life on earth. To the credit of the theologians, much later exegesis of the doctrine has been concerned to remove or mitigate the suggestion that the Father took a sadistic pleasure in watching the crucifixion, but Tertullian is very unguarded in writing up his own gloats, and would probably see no need to deny such pleasures to the Father. Irenaeus (second century) answered that the ransom was paid to the Devil, not to God, and gives the most definite statement of this view; but there is general agreement, if one turns to the *Encyclopaedia of Religion and Ethics*, that the first centuries regarded the crucifixion as releasing man from the Devil somehow, never mind how the trick was done. The term *redemption* was introduced in the presumption that man is a slave with a bad owner, so that he needs buying out by a good owner; and the decision that God himself was the bad owner must surely be thought a notable change.

Nor was it soon complete. Peter Abelard, in the early twelfth century, thought of some refined ethical reason for the Father's satisfaction at the crucifixion, as a high-minded intellectual theologian always did; but this excited keen suspicion in Bernard of Clairvaux, who thought that such men regularly produced heresy, and he answered that the ransom was simply paid to the Devil. This was nearly a thousand years after Irenaeus had said it, and Bernard was made a saint later on; so the theory cannot be called remote from the main Christian tradition. Aquinas in the thirteenth century settles it with immense coolness, saying that this metaphorical ransom was paid to God in one sense and to the Devil in another; he seems to feel that only barbarians or children could interpret the story so crudely. But then, in Aquinas, the realities of the doctrine have been tidied almost out of sight. He also deals with a position that Anselm had taken in the later eleventh century: that the *honour* of God was what demanded satisfaction, so that God reacted like a duelling lord (in the Renaissance this became a separate use of the term 'satisfaction', but Anselm would not need to feel it so). Aquinas merely answered that 'satisfaction' was not essential here; God might have adopted other ways of redeeming mankind, but this one was the most fitting. His treatment of the whole tender area feels deliberately soothing.

The English version of the Latin word 'satisfaction' often conveys a body-feeling, indeed with a suitable context the word can mean an act of sex. The Latin word is much the same, but of course these theological uses are very legal in tone, and expect us to remember the derivation. Legally, the word meant 'the discharge of an obligation by some other means than its strict fulfilment, which is yet agreeable to the creditor' (*Summa. Theo.* Part III, q. 48, art 2). Thus it has to be something the creditor is 'able to agree to' – something he likes enough for it to do instead. 'He properly atones for an offence who offers something which the offended one loves equally, even more than he detested the offence.' So far we have got hardly any nearer to the important question – what is it that God finds so satisfying or agreeable? Perhaps from an impulse of caution, feeling safer if he need not depend on one argument, Aquinas insists that there were a number of causes, yielding a superabundance for the Father (pursued for several Questions after the one just cited). For example, Christ's grief at the sins of man was very great, and this added to the Father's satisfaction. Besides, Christ felt more bodily pain at the time than an ordinary man would have done:

His body was endowed with a most perfect constitution, since it was fashioned miraculously by the operation of the Holy Ghost ... and consequently Christ's sense of touch, the sensitiveness of which is the reason for our feeling pain, was most acute.

This of course made the crucifixion a particularly great pleasure for God. How glad one feels that he was able to enjoy himself so much! And what a condescension it is too, when he allows us almost to share in his pleasures! I may be told that Aquinas could not possibly have intended this; but he was listing the possible considerations, likely to be accepted by his readers, and would feel no duty to differ from common opinion here. A mayor of a town in the lowlands during the Middle Ages was much praised for buying a criminal from a neighbouring town, so that his people could enjoy seeing the man tortured in the marketplace; it showed he was a jolly, earthy kind of mayor, who knew what everybody would enjoy. This degree of perversion does not seem to be recorded from India or China, and it is plainly likely to be a result of implementing, in a high-powered way, the basic doctrines of Christianity. Of course, to enjoy the torture of a man who is held to deserve it is different from enjoying the crucifixion – it is less shameless; but the distinction is not likely to stand up to any strain, once the pleasure in cruelty itself has been established.

These remarks do nothing to prove that the Father *must* have had bad motives in being satisfied by the crucifixion; some of the motives listed by Aquinas are clearly good ones. But are they sufficiently compelling motives, after he has assured us that the Father could have saved mankind in other ways, and merely chose this one as the most 'fitting'? The whole sequence, which is a powerful bit of literature, comes to feel more than merely soothing. The catlike tread, as of a man only just able to carry out the acrobatic feat which has cost him many years of strict training, the coolness and decorum with which the fantastic and outrageous unnaturalness is sustained – what it calls to mind, surely, is the handing over of a heretic to the secular arm, with a strict recommendation for the merciful avoidance of bloodshed (meaning that they will have Hell to pay if they don't burn him alive). Aquinas plainly knew that the most intimate place of the religion is a horrible one. So did Milton, who writes in a very similar though more self-betraying way at the corresponding place of his *Christian Doctrine*, positively nagging at us to agree that the crucifixion must have been a *terrific* satisfaction for the good Father:

[No *quotation figures in the manuscript, but presumably Empson had it in mind to quote from Book I, chapter* XVI, *of* De Doctrina Christiana – '*De redemptione administratione*' (*'On the ministry of redemption'*): *see* The Works of John Milton, *vol.* XV, *New York: Columbia University Press, 1933, pp. 302–41.]

I had expected that they would use the word with stern legalism, glumly avoiding its more human associations; but no, they feel they have to insist that the Father was satisfied all round. Milton, of course, had rejected the 'identity' of the Son and the Father, which for C. S. Lewis was the heart of the mystery, making the scene awe-inspiring and astounding: the Creator was torturing *himself* to rescue mankind. No wonder Milton is a bit out of touch here, I thought. But so is Aquinas, just as completely; the identity of the Son and the Father is never mentioned in his account at all. Surely Aquinas would know that the doctrine was relevant here, if anybody did. And without that shaft of light the doctrine is merely impudent sadism, like the determination of the present Pope to destroy mankind by forcing it to breed to the famine level.

The converts who joined Christianity during the first two centuries, who of course were found in great numbers, were not affronted by this nasty and corrupting picture. Man had somehow fallen into the power of a set of devils, each of them using one of the planets as his palace (S. G. F. Brandon, *Man and his Destiny in the Great Religions* [Manchester: Manchester University Press, 1962]); and these devils naturally enjoyed having Jesus tortured to death for them, as he was a particularly good and effective man. But it turned out that he was a God; they had been tricked into thinking he was only a man, with the connivance of the Father apparently, and this put them in the wrong; somehow it allowed us to get out of their clutches. St Paul makes incidental references to this belief quite often, but he uses abstract nouns as titles for the devils (Thrones, Dominations, Princedoms, Powers), with the effect that translators could avoid being worried by them; and the *Catholic Encyclopedia* can assert that the whole story was 'erroneously derived' from such uses of language. Interesting examples come at 1 Cor 2.8 ('Which none of the rulers of this world knoweth; for had they known it, they would not have crucified the Lord of glory'), 2 Cor 4.4, Col 1.13, 16; 2.15 ('Having put off from himself the principalities and the powers, he made a show of himself openly, triumphing over them in it'), Gal 4.8 ('Ye were in bondage to them which by nature are no gods'). St Paul, though he made the most use of this myth, is not for certain the inventor of it; consider 2 Peter 2.19:

Promising them liberty, while they themselves are bondservants of corruption; for of whom a man is overcome, of the same also is he brought into bondage.

'They', the subject of the sentence, are apparently human preachers of a gospel of sexual liberty (like Cromwell's Ranters); but they are slaves of something more than human, and would need buying out. It is hard to say at what point the metaphors crystallise into a myth.

One might think then that the early Church had no fear of the Creator, and did not need the Messiah as a protection from him; but this is plainly unlikely, considering the God of the Old Testament, and the Gospels can be found saying that Jesus will mediate with the Father, and be a propitiation for our sins. It would be a familiar scene at court, and very naturally imagined as one of his functions. Making this relation the all-important one, so that in effect the Father became the villain of the story, seems to have been done to aggrandise him; the devils must not have powers of the same order as those of God, and therefore the Saviour must buy us back from the Father. [? Incomplete]

The Cult of Unnaturalism

First published as the Preface to John R. Harrison,
The Reactionaries, London: Gollancz, 1966

'Oh, it's a wild life in the Near West, between one revelation and another,'
said Wyndham Lewis, describing the intellectual scene around him as a fun
fair; that was in *Time and Western Man* (1928), and I felt the exhilaration
of it, even then. Now that everything is so dismal we should look back with
reverence on that great age of poets and fundamental thinkers, who were so
ready to consider heroic remedies. Perhaps their gloomy prophecies have
simply come true. But may it not be that their curses are still operating, or
their confusions adding to the fog, in some preventable way? Mr Harrison
feels that the political scandal of their weakness for fascism is what most
needs to be faced; and the great merit of his book is to present the evidence
about that aspect of them coolly, with justice and understanding.

It is well worth doing, but one may doubt whether that question is the
central one; and Mr Harrison himself judges in terms of breadth of sympathy rather than political technique. An early stage in the revolt against
parliamentary democracy can be seen in the comic novels of Belloc, written
around 1910, largely inspired by the Marconi scandal. Anti-Semitism is
already prominent, perhaps mainly as a device for smearing capitalists. Parliament is attacked as a pretence behind which an oligarchy of capital rules
as it chooses; being a distributist, Belloc is putting forward a mild form of
anarchism. His objections to the existing system are practically those of a
communist, and the split between communism and anarchism strikes him
as fairly recent. His own sentiments are presented as vigorously democratic; the joke of the story is regularly that the voting system is used to
cheat the voter. One needs to realise that these squibs sold very widely, and
were a welcome expression of what honest men felt needed saying. Looking
back, the line of talk seems plainly dangerous; a modern type of state needs
a secret ballot and a broad electorate more than a previous one did, instead
of having grown out of the need as Belloc somehow suggests; precisely
because it is otherwise too strong, too convenient for a vested interest or a
mad dictator. But that the electorate are liable to be deluded we ought not

to deny; nor even that a patriot (whether under a fossilised old constitution or a rawly new one) may sometimes rightly thrust aside a technicality to meet an urgent need. At any rate, for a poet to think so is not proof of a bad heart. I cannot help feeling that Lewis was tiresomely silly to be taken in by Hitler, but by the end of the war he was almost willing to say that himself; and maybe if Yeats had lived another ten years we would be thinking of him as rather like Smuts.

The cult of unnaturalism, I think, is the real trouble with the whole school, and it is still very much with us, at any rate in academic literary criticism. Almost anyone who writes in literary journals about these great reactionaries would agree that they have had a good intellectual effect, for example, in making people deny that man is the measure of all things, or deny that he should aim at the greatest happiness of the greatest number. There are logical fallacies here, and one of them may be observed in the Sammael of Wyndham Lewis [in *Malign Fiesta*, Book Three of *The Human Age*, London: Methuen, 1955]. It is pleasant to find the author expressing tender admiration, for the first time, in his old age, even though he knows it is for a devil. He assumes that his mind can realise that Sammael is greater than mankind, and that the minds of his readers can too; apparently he also meant them to realise that Sammael's policy was wrong. But at both stages they are to 'measure' him. Very likely there are states of being too high for us to conceive, but then we had better not pretend to talk about them. The result of pretending, as one can see in T. E. Hulme as well as Lewis, is to imply: 'Because all men are infinitely below God, some men ought to be free to bully others – the ones who are on God's side, like I am.' As to Bentham, the idea of a false claim to calculate is no doubt offensive, but I have never found an opponent giving a telling example to prove that a man ought not to attempt the estimate which Bentham recommends. No doubt he should look after his immediate dependants unless prevented by a clear public duty; but a citizen must be ready to act on such a duty, or democracy becomes impossible. Most people who deny the Benthamite position do not realise, I think, how far a preference for transcendental modes of judgement can go: 'I shot the President because God told me to, in a dream; it was not for me to calculate, after God had spoken.' No state can carry on if it produces many of these citizens, whatever voting technique it has. The same line of talk sounds harmless about our preferences in literature and the arts, where sensibility needs to act ahead of theory; but to put a premium on being capricious encourages bluff, and we have had plenty of that.

James Joyce is the test case here, proving that an original and rigorous author of the time could avoid these political and religiose fashions. He remarked in a letter of 1934: 'I am afraid poor Mr Hitler will soon have few friends in Europe apart from my nephews, Masters W. Lewis and E.

Pound,'[1] and in a more fretful mood wondered why he was thought a member of their clique. He was untempted, no doubt, because he had actually escaped from a theocracy such as many of the authors examined in this book were recommending. Lewis is the most theoretical and fanatical, at least on this quasi religious side; and I share Mr Harrison's disgust for his descriptions of the fiery tortures imposed on mankind by Sammael. The books which ought to be banned for obscenity are those which pander to sadism, but what can you expect from a state religion whose symbol is a torture? These descriptions in Lewis are no worse than the sermon which made the young Joyce vomit in the *Portrait of the Artist*. Joyce meant to satirise his teachers there; he expected life to be normal, and found this abnormal; but he treated it as so usual that Mr Hugh Kenner could regard him as in favour of priests and intending only some merry paradox. Lewis on the other hand, judging from his *Letters* (1963), held a heretical view but did not know it. He explains that 'Sammael's idea was to combine the best of the Human spirit with his Angel's nature,' and on 29 August 1955, Mr Hugh Kenner, who had written a book on Lewis and was writing a further article, received a fuller statement:

In the last book of all, the hero, Pullman, is at last in Divine Society. He favours the Divine. I favour the Divine. There is a gigantic debate, in which Sammael's purpose to combine the Human and the Angelic is discussed, the Celestial spokesman naturally attacking Sammael's big idea ... Pullman is, of course, an adherent of the Divine, not of the Diabolic.

Naturally the spokesman of God had to attack the idea, because T. E. Hulme had said that one must keep the divine and the human absolutely separate, boasting about seducing shopgirls and then boasting about revelation. But the Athanasian Creed calls the Incarnation 'the taking of the manhood into God'. Lewis evidently felt he needed to hustle Mr Kenner into accepting the orthodoxy of his layout, but I don't believe he realised that his theology was completely upside-down. He did not live to write this final debate.

There is some hope of a lifting of this fog. The Cambridge theologians who took part in the symposium *Objections to Christian Belief* (1963), at any rate, reject the entire position of the aesthetes discussed by Mr Harrison. The Dean of King's says that an ethic of sacrifice leads to a great deal of cruelty, and 'we need fresh air blown upon these discussions by a sane ethic of utility' – thus recalling the utilitarianism of Bentham.[2] The Dean of St John's says that:

nothing can be true *for any mind* except as that mind can be brought to perceive its reasonableness ... alleged revelation is of no use except as it enables man to attain his own insights.[3]

So he rejects any dichotomy such as that of Hulme. I am afraid that nothing can purge Christianity of the Father who was satisfied by the crucifixion; an impersonal Divine Ground, as in Aldous Huxley's *Perennial Philosophy*, is the only Supreme Being that can be worshipped without moral shame. But it is comforting to find the Divinity School at Cambridge nowadays talking with the clearheadedness and generosity of H. G. Wells, however much the English Literature School still regards the basic Christian tradition as enshrined in the textbooks of unnaturalism, *Les Fleurs du Mal*, *A Rebours*, and *The Portrait of Dorian Gray*. I notice too that Mr Harrison cannot help looking at his authors with a kind of social surprise, all the more because he is trying to be charitable. They have come to seem rather odd, in the eyes of the young, whether it is the fault of the modern world or not.

*

Anthony Burgess wrote in his review of The Reactionaries *that 'it is perhaps silly and pointless to look for a nexus between misguided political beliefs and supreme works of literature ... The alleged pro-fascism of these dead writers [specifically Yeats, Wyndham Lewis, Pound, Eliot and Lawrence] touches their art at no vital point' ('Fleurs du Mal', The Spectator, 9 September 1966). With respect to Empson's introductory argument that the writers' political positions are less damaging than their 'religiose fashions' – from which Joyce happily escaped – Burgess observed, 'Alas, not so ... the penultimate episode of* Finnegans Wake *presents the modern world in terms of sexual impotence; a thunderclap is needed to recall a theocratic age.... Empson, after another slam at Milton's "sacrifical theology", finds comfort in the neo-Wellsianism of the Cambridge School of Divinity. I don't think any such ethos is likely to produce a new Hopkins or Eliot, but one never knows. Literature is disconcertingly autonomous.'*

Empson responded with the following letter to The Spectator, *16 September 1966:*

What Mr Burgess says about 'the penultimate episode of *Finnegans Wake*' is very interesting and one day if I am spared I will try to decide what the episode means. Joyce might (just) be saying that the world needed God, but not that it needed the Roman Catholic Church. Surely, the story that he was secretly in favour of that was exploded by the Ellmann biography. However, it is a side-issue here.

The main point of my little preface to John Harrison's *Reactionaries* was to say that one of their main tenets was not standard Christian doctrine, as they supposed. It is the idea, mostly explicitly supported by T. E. Hulme[4] and Wyndham Lewis, that the human should be kept rigidly distinct from the divine, whereas the Athanasian Creed, a work not usually thought to be worm-eaten with liberalism, recommends 'the taking of the manhood into God'. This (I think) is why they can fairly be called unnaturalists. Mr Burgess might well have answered that, instead of telling us he despises the Cambridge School of Theology.

Notes

1 Empson slightly misquotes Joyce's letter to Harriet Shaw Weaver, which should read: 'I am afraid poor Mr Hitler-Missler will soon have few admirers in Europe apart from your nieces and my nephews, Masters W. Lewis and E. Pound' (quoted in Richard Ellmann, *James Joyce* (1959), new and revised edn., Oxford: OUP, 1982, p. 675).

2 Empson is actually quoting D. M. Mackinnon of Corpus Christi College (Norris–Hulse Professor of Divinity): 'The ethic of sacrifice indeed provides a symbolism under which all sorts of cruelties may be perpetrated, not so much upon the weak as upon those who have been deceived by a false image of goodness. We need fresh air blown upon these discussions by a sane ethic of utility, properly designing the most humanly prudent course ... seeking to liberate human energies not to confine them' (D. M. Mackinnon *et al.*, *Objections to Christian Belief*, London: Constable, 1963, p. 25).

3 Ibid., p. 108. J. S. Bezzant goes on: 'If there be Divine revelation it may transcend but it cannot contradict what we have reasonable grounds for regarding as knowledge or reasonably grounded belief, because otherwise it implies an overriding of the proper dignity of the moral or ethical personality which God has created; and if He does *this*, God at the same time removes all possibility of human judgment as to whether it is Divine revelation or not' (p. 109).

4 See Empson's review of T. E. Hulme's *Speculations* above.

Literary Criticism and
the Christian Revival

Rationalist Annual, London:
Pemberton Publishing Co., 1966

One might expect that bringing into a literary work the ideals of the Religion of Love would at least have fairly mild results, and so it used to do. Henry James seems to me too prone to regard any renunciation or self-crucifixion as a happy ending, but his point was that this was not done on principle (he does not admit principles) but out of some delicate aesthetic squeamishness. It answered the claim of the dogmatists that men cannot be noble without religious belief; probably it supported what Matthew Arnold had said, that morality is to be taught by a nurture of the feelings. Thus one might argue that the effect is positively anti-Christian or pro-humanist, even if sickly and factitious. W. H. Auden, on the other hand, specifically became a Christian, I think from deciding that the communists were wicked at the time of the Russo-German pact; and his later poetry has hardly any of the penetrating thrusts (especially from comparing politics and morbid psychology) which had been so exhilarating. He twitters and 'looks on the bright side'; he really has become (in print, not in person) like the stage curate of fifty years ago. His tone of feeling, at any rate, is very different from that of the modern Neo-Christian Movement.

Authors in that movement realise (I suppose from reading Comparative Religion and the earlier history of Christianity, but much else in modern thought would be relevant) that it is horrible to worship a Father who was satisfied by the crucifixion of his Son but would still release only a tiny minority of us from Hell for it, and still causes all the evil and suffering of the world, as punishments for whatever the sacrifice was meant to excuse; let alone making the saved join him in gloating for ever over the tortures of the damned, who must include almost all those they loved on earth, while incessantly praising him for his mercy. Realising that this is Belsen, they still answer: 'Then it is like life. Your objections make me love Big Brother more than ever.' I used to think that this tendency was in some way 'unconscious', but some mild controversy after I had written about it convinced me that many of them understand it well. Such a religion must be bad for them morally, as well as aesthetically; and they tend to boast how dismal it is. Naturally, they bring out the shocking side of Christianity, which the apologists of the last century or two had tended to omit or evade; and the same with a work of literature – the interpretation of the metaphors of the author, or the motives of the characters, has to make them nastier than the author would have intended. This constitutes a victory for the doctrine of Original Sin. Mercifully the more hysterical examples are self-defeating; I have tried to concentrate here on examples moderate enough to be fairly seductive.

One should take care not to let an explanation become a formula, repeated every time, and quite a few modern interpreters adopt this grisly tone without having any religious commitment. It seems unlikely, for instance, that Professor Kott is a Christian, from what we are told in the preface to his *Shakespeare Our Contemporary* (he works in Poland and writes with boyish enthusiasm); but he praises Shakespeare for being sufficiently horrible and nihilistic for the modern world, or the modern stage. He is good on *King Lear*, which often really is like *Waiting for Godot*, but he labours to show that the history plays mean 'all politicians behave like these ones; all human life is like a bucketful of scorpions'. This was at least not what the licensing authority thought the plays meant; they were Awful Warnings against civil war, to make you obey the Tudors; and a warning inherently says, 'So long as you don't do this, things won't be so bad.' The greatest height of absurdity is reached over *A Midsummer Night's Dream*; the fairy courtiers of Titania should be acted as filthy drivelling old men and repulsive hags, all exploding with delight at getting her to bed with a stinking hairy Worker. The entire horror of the Night, both its cravings and revulsions, is thus thrust upon the audience.

This might make a successful production, but it has no support from the words. Bottom, when loved by the Queen of the Fairies, feels deeply gratified in the vanity which is his ruling passion; but he behaves as if she is a girl of six who has taken a fancy to him on the sands at Margate; he doesn't mind jollying her along; the parents will turn up soon enough. Kott says he wakes up afterwards in an agony of shame, and so he probably would if he had enjoyed her and then been rejected with disgust. But we see him wake up, and he begins at once on what will evidently be a career of boasting about the mystical dream. The dignity of the working man, in fact, is protected with surprising care, and it is odd that a communist theatre should insist upon dragging him down. But one can see that this fits the general tone of the modern theatre, and the Christians can hardly be blamed if they use the fashion for their own ends.

As I spent some time teaching in the Far East, and left England in 1931, the literary tastes of the twenties are still encapsulated within me; and I was startled on coming home in the fifties to find what was being taught as a routine. A man so placed is liable to gratify himself with an over-simple explanation. But the interpretations made by critics who claim to be taking a high-minded Christian view are very various; I could not make the same complaint every time, and the religious bias gives the only connection. Thus in the twenties we used to think that the love-poetry of the young Donne, around 1600, was defiant, though evasively so, against the authorities of both Church and State. Maybe the reason was not given clearly enough. The pair of lovers at odds with their own society are presented as living on a new planet, like Adam and Eve; thus they are outside the jurisdiction of both the Pope and Queen Elizabeth. Melanchthon, as soon as Copernicus published, had denounced him for implying an argument against Christianity: 'Does Jesus Christ get crucified on each of the planets in turn? Or is the Father totally unjust to the Martians?' Donne, as a professional theologian, would have to know about this, and I suppose it was what F. W. Payne meant by saying in a book on Donne (1926): 'His correct interpretation of the dark beginnings of modern science places him on a level with H. G. Wells for piercing insight.' Everyone in the Eng. Lit. business under forty is deliciously outraged on hearing this sentence, but I still think they both did have piercing insight. This view of Donne was rejected by a determined campaign, beginning with *A Garland for John Donne* (1932); I just missed seeing the crown of thorns, having left for Japan. T. S. Eliot said, 'Donne was, I insist, no sceptic; it is only that he is interested in and amused by ideas in themselves'[1] – in short, he was a tiresome fribble, and meant nothing. Professor Marjorie Nicolson was still saying in 1935 (*Studies in Philology*), 'The idea of a plurality of worlds, which Donne had suggested in his earlier poetry, was indeed for a churchman a dangerous tenet, even, as it came to be called, the "new heresy" ...', but the sentence does not appear in the recent paperback which collects her articles. I have not been able to find that any serious evidence was offered at any time for this general change of front.[2]

Webster, on the other hand, was not thought much of as a theologian in the twenties, but good at describing Italian villains. We are now regularly told that, since Webster found London full of free-thinkers, he wrote plays showing that a man becomes miserable and harmful unless he is a Christian. In the Neo-Christian 'tradition', I should explain, there are not wars of religion; everybody was always an Anglo-Catholic. This was why the main point became invisible: that Webster described, to the ready delight of his Protestant audience, how a man becomes miserable and harmful if he is a Spanish or Italian Roman Catholic. The audience would have been astonished to hear that the characters were Londoners.

This misunderstanding of *The White Devil* does no harm in production, but a harmful one was developed for *The Duchess of Malfi*, who married her major-domo. We are told that the first audiences were eager to see her killed because of her carnal lust and irresponsibility in not marrying a rich lord, as her brother wanted; also because of her flippant remarks about religion. But these are all Protestant remarks against Roman Catholic beliefs, as when she says it is superstitious to worry about pilgrimages. The legal crux of the play is that the Council of Trent, around 1550, had made clandestine marriage by a promise before a witness illegal for Catholics, whereas it was till open to Protestants. The audience is to take the Duchess and her husband as 'like us', naturally Protestant souls who make a stand against tyranny and keep down the taxes. An artisan audience is not likely to have hated her for this marriage, whatever pedantic scholars like Belleforest had said; indeed, only one character in that theatre does take the Neo-Christian attitude to a romantic marriage. It is Iago, and the author does not assume that the audience will agree with him. Very like Iago, the critics invent conflicting dirty accusations against the Duchess, thinking that this proves how high-minded they are; whereas the first audiences obviously took the play as an attack on aristocratic family pride, driven home as with the sledgehammer of Dickens.

If now you compare these two cases, you might think the critics merely inconsistent; why should one author of the period be said to mean nothing about theology, though he seems to, and the other a great deal, though he seems not? Because Donne was using in his love-poetry a real argument against Christianity, still unanswered, but the plays of Webster could be strained round, if the critic wrote vaguely enough, into a warning in favour of it.

T. S. Eliot wrote in an early number of the *Criterion*, but I think did not reprint, that the last chapter of *Gulliver's Travels* is one of the greatest productions of the human mind. The degree of contempt for the world expressed by Eliot here would in Swift's time be called Manichaean or Calvinist, and he was uneasy when he tried to explain the chapter himself. Gulliver tells the horses that in England, where he comes from, a judge will decide in favour of the cheat even after he has been bribed by the honest party; and after a doctor has said you will die he will poison you if you start to get better. I didn't mind about princes, but when it got down to a professional man like myself I didn't believe a word of it. A doctor can always say that his medicine has been even better than he expected; the situation does not tempt him to kill you. And surely a corrupt judge works for the larger bribe with decent care; he does not act from this monkeyish preference for wickedness. The chapter is very good as a description of persecution mania, and Swift no doubt arrived at it by an immense release of personal spite, mixed with some public spirit. In America, on the other hand, about ten literary dons have produced arguments that Swift meant to satirise the horses too, because they were eighteenth-century rationalists. This is the real Buddhist contempt for all existence, even in the highest heaven, as found in the Fire Sermon; but I believe the theory has now been quietly dropped. We should remember that American literary dons are Neo-Christian more frequently and more extravagantly than the English ones; partly because they are not restrained by even a folk-memory of what these authors really meant, but also because they take the latent politics of the movement more seriously. The English don just feels that he is helping to keep the Ad-Mass at bay; the American one feels that he is keeping communism at bay, and that all human life will become worthless if he fails. I do not know whether he always tells the truth to the enemy while locked in so terrible a struggle.

But on the whole the critics in these examples felt that they were interpreting an accepted author in accordance with their principles, and that the results were creditable to both principles and author. I doubt whether they feel so about the poet Yeats, who is found to need a great deal of explanation. The trouble is that few of them will even 'let on' that he believed in reincarnation: we hear plenty about his Religious Values and his Religious Symbolism, but not what the belief was. The motive I take it is simply to keep the children from wrong ideas. And yet the belief is less cruel and unjust than the Christian one (since it gives further chances, whereas the conditions of one life often make it almost impossible for a man to develop a good character), more ancient, still believed by more than half the inhabitants of Eurasia, and even, I think, rather less incredible. To leave it out often makes the religious poetry of Yeats feel greasy and self-righteous. Thus we are told that the poem 'Byzantium' takes place in Heaven, and its Emperor 'symbolises' God; though we find at night there 'drunken soldiery', and in earlier drafts 'that roaring rout of rascals', 'the thieves' last benighted traveller dead', 'the drunken harlot's song'. Yeats is thus made to say that after death he will insist on living in the highest Heaven, as a mechanical toy whose function is to keep God awake; and this God when awake causes some spirits to be in an agony of flame. But there is no such Christian nastiness in the poem. The Ghost of the Japanese Noh play, from which Yeats took one verse of 'Byzantium' was assured by the Buddhist priests that she need only cease to believe she had done wrong, but she said she could not yet, and continued her dance of flame. Yeats assumes that spirits can do all kinds of things while preparing for their next incarnation. The poem takes place in tenth-century Byzantium, to which spirits come from centuries before and after (the spirit of Yeats among them) so as to purge themselves, as Victorian gentlemen went to Baden-Baden after the excesses of the season. Read like this, it makes a good science fiction short story, and we learn from 'A Vision' that Yeats believed all the details to be possible. Surely, if you read it as the Christians do, Yeats appears as a very unpleasant character.

Thus I think that the Neo-Christian method of literary criticism leads frequently to large and unpleasant misinterpretations; but also I am inclined to believe, as well as hope, that it is on its way out. I have taken so long to get my attack ready that perhaps it is no longer much needed; one tends to forget that the young people, as they grow up, have usually a cold eye for the follies of their parents. But I am afraid that the alliance with Professor Kott makes the monster still vigorous enough to do harm.

Notes

1 T. S. Eliot, 'Donne in Our Time', in T. Spencer (ed.). *A Garland for John Donne*, Oxford: OUP, 1932, pp. 11–12.

2 In 1956 the sentence appeared in the following form: 'The idea of a plurality of worlds, for a churchman, was indeed a dangerous tenet, even, as it came to be called, the "new heresy"' (Marjorie Nicolson, 'The "New Astronomy" and English Imagination', *Science and Imagination*, Ithaca: Great Seal Books (Cornell University Press), 1956, p. 55). In response to a personal enquiry from Empson, Marjorie Nicolson wrote to him on 12 May 1966 that she had been unaware that she had dropped the sentence quoted; her early work may have come to seem 'superficial' in the light of more recent researches by Professor Grant McColley, she surmised, but she saw no reason at all to change her mind on the subject (Empson Papers).

Envoi

Professor Empson's Reply on behalf of the Honorary Graduates

University of Sheffield Gazette, number 54, November 1974

Empson received an Honorary Litt.D. at the Degree Congregations on 20 July 1974. Professor B. R. Morris, who succeeded him in the Chair of English Literature, remarked in his presentation that in literary criticism two names stand out from Cambridge in the 1920s: 'F. R. Leavis and William Empson, two mighty opposites perhaps best likened to Cavalier and Puritan in the Civil War. As Cromwell was to Prince Rupert, as John Pym was to King Charles, so was Leavis to Empson. The imperfect analogy serves to distinguish the rigour and the uncompromising dogmatism of Leavis on the one hand, and the graceful, seemingly careless, aristocratic intellectualism of Empson on the other. I am not sure that the two men have ever greatly loved one another, but the intellectual world has been richer for their mutual disdain.... It is above all this quality of mind, this impeccable civility of thought, which we honour today.'

I am to give thanks, on behalf of my colleagues and myself, for the honour done to us by the University, and to express our consciousness of it.

But I am too ignorant to say more about them, so I have to talk about me. That is bad, but I was a Professor of this University till I retired, for nearly twenty years, and perhaps I can say something about that. Indeed, listening to that splendid praise given me by the Orator, it struck me that the University also deserved some praise for making the appointment. It was what is called bold; when I was made Professor here, I had actually never done any teaching in England at all. When I was leaving Sheffield, about three years ago, I was given a farewell party, very friendly and generous, and when it was over I went to the bar, where I found one of my colleagues. I said, 'I'm glad they feel it has worked out all right, because at the time I was considered a bold appointment.' 'I know you were,' he said, 'I was a bold appointment too. They were making them then, but they don't now. That's what's the matter with the place.' I do not know whether this is true, but I thought it ought to be reported to you. I expect it is true; one can think of so many reasons why it might seem inevitable.

I did not arrive feeling any conscientious need to make radical changes. The danger of a bold appointment, of course, is that the man may want to destroy what has been built up before. The first thing to realise, I said to myself, is that you have here a working system, and it should not be tampered with except for strong reason. Actually there was a good deal of change in my time, and I seldom regretted it; but that basic attitude has become stronger in my mind now than it was at first. I think that Sheffield and the other universities of about the same age are in effect holding the fort; the very old universities and the very new ones have both given up, on this issue. We still, by and large, try to cover the field in the three years to the BA degree, without breaking it up into options.

This would seem important when the basic planning was being done for new universities during the nineties of the last century. The students themselves wanted three years rather than four, and wanted a skilfully planned bit of packing to give them enough during those three years; in the fourth year, if all went well, they would be earning a salary, and they would get married on it. Almost every detail of this picture has become remote from the modern scene; no wonder that the pressure of the package deal has been so much moderated. And yet you really do want a student to have at least an impression of the whole field after three years. I can only speak for the subject of English Literature, but much the same problem crops up in other departments. You may meet a graduate (from some universities) who has deservedly been given a high class in his degree, and you say, 'What do you think of Alexander Pope?', and his jaw drops, and he says, 'Never heard of him.' So you try saying, 'How about W. H. Auden?', and his jaw drops; it becomes quite a familiar sight if you persevere; and he says, 'Never heard of him.' At some point he will explain himself, defiantly or proudly, by saying, 'I majored in Beowulf and Jane Austen.' Now, this is plainly not what you want, probably not even what the people who made his regulations wanted. Here, I think, is where Sheffield and the other universities of the same vintage have a claim; stodgy we may be, but we do still try to cover the field.

I was asked also to say something for those now taking their first degree, so as to encourage them in the life of learning. Something that applies very widely is needed here. I became interested in *Ecclesiastes* when we had it on the syllabus; the book has of course been enormously discussed, and it seemed clear that King James's translators understood it much better than later scholars. The preacher is a moody disgruntled old man, living in Alexandria (they say) when it was new and a centre for advanced thought, and very much a don; white-collar in class though not rich or notably successful; but he keeps coming back to the merits of 'labour', and you might think he is praising the worker, the labouring man. And yet all the time he is pretending to be Solomon, the ancient glorious king who had a thousand con-cubines; so that he is holding in mind all three conditions of life. The effect is certainly not cynical. I think he is saying: 'A man needs to be proud of his skill, and he is fortunate if it is one which he can still exercise when he is fairly old. Of course being a learned writer is rather a bore; not like a dic-tator or a jobbing plumber, who leads such a masterful life, and has so many people pleading with him; but it does give a man enough to go on with. You should keep that in mind' (such is the point of the tremendous last chapter) 'while you are still young.' He tries about five times to say what is good for a man, and I think his best shot at it is the first attempt in Chapter Two:

There is nothing better for a man, than that he should eat and drink, and make his soul enjoy good in his labour.

A strange phrase, and I should think very true about the human condition in general.

Acknowledgements

The editor and publishers, and the Estate of Sir William Empson, are grateful to the following for permission to reprint material within their copyright or other control.

Associated Book Publishers (U.K.) Ltd.: number 86, 'The Symbolism of Dickens', first published in *Dickens and the Twentieth Century*, edited by John Gross and Gabriel Pearson (London: Routledge & Kegan Paul, 1962). Basil Blackwell Ltd.: number 111, printed from *Universities Quarterly*. The British Broadcasting Corporation: numbers 31, 39 and 105. *The British Journal of Aesthetics*: number 17. *The Cambridge Review*: numbers 34 and 35. *The Critical Quarterly*: numbers 40, 41, 109 and 113. The Editors of *Essays in Criticism*: numbers 59 and 79. Victor Gollancz Ltd: number 117, first published as the 'Preface' to *The Reactionaries*, by John R. Harrison (Gollancz, 1966). David Higham Associates Ltd., for permission to reproduce 'The force that through the green fuse' and 'A Refusal to Mourn the Death, by Fire, of a Child in London', from *The Poems*, by Dylan Thomas (London: Dent). *The Hudson Review*: number 25, 'A Doctrine of Aesthetics'. Reprinted by permission from *The Hudson Review*, Vol. II, No. 1 (Spring 1949). Copyright © 1949 by The Hudson Review, Inc. *The Kenyon Review*: numbers 7, 29 and 32. *The Listener*: numbers 18, 61, 67, 100, 101, 112 and 115. *London Review of Books*: numbers 27 and 90. *The Nation*: number 81. *New Statesman*: numbers 8, 9, 10, 13, 15, 19, 33, 36, 46, 55, 58, 60, 62, 65, 66, 73, 83, 84, 85, 110 and 114. *The New York Review of Books*: numbers 21, 'Compacted Doctrines', and 47, 'Yeats and the Spirits'. Reprinted with permission from *The New York Review of Books*. Copyright © 1973 & 1977 Nyrev, Inc. *The Observer*: number 107. *Oxford University Press*: number 26, 'The Hammer's Ring', from *I. A. Richards: Essays In His Honor*, edited by Reuben Brower, Helen Vendler and John Hollander. Copyright © 1973 by Oxford University Press, Inc. Reprinted by permission. *Paunch*: number 87. Pennsylvania State University Press: numbers 20, 'The Voice of the Underdog', reprinted from *Journal of General Education*, XXVI: 4, Winter

1975; and 89, 'Reading the Epic of Gilgamesh', from *Journal of General Education*, Winter 1975; The Pennsylvania State University Press, University Park, PA. *PN Review*: number 68. *Poetry*: numbers 45, 'A Masterly Synthesis', 63, 'A London Letter', and 64, 'Foundations of Despair'. Copyright © 1939 & 1937 by The Modern Poetry Association. Reprinted by permission of the Editor of *Poetry*. The Rationalist Press Association Ltd.: number 118, 'Literary Criticism and the Christian Revival', first published in *The Rationalist Annual* 1966 (Barrie & Rockliff with Pemberton Publishing), reprinted by permission of the Rationalist Press Association. *The Spectator*: numbers 28, 30 and 99. The *Times Literary Supplement*: number 16, and the letters reproduced in numbers 44 and 106. George Weidenfeld & Nicolson Ltd.: number 88, 'Orwell at the BBC', reprinted from *The World of George Orwell*, edited by Miriam Gross (London: Weidenfeld & Nicolson, 1971). *Yeats Eliot Review*: number 51, 'Eliot and Politics', first published in *T. S. Eliot Review* in 1975; reprinted with the permission of Shyamal Bagchee, Editor. Previously unpublished writings by the late I. A. Richards are printed by kind permission of Dr Richard Luckett, literary executor of the Estate of I. A. Richards.

All possible care has been taken to trace the ownership of the essays and other writings included and to make acknowledgement for their use.

Index